Play of the Hand with Blackwood

BY EASLEY BLACKWOOD

Winning Bridge with Blackwood

PLAY OF THE HAND WITH BLACKWOOD

EASLEY BLACKWOOD

A Corwin Books Paperback

PINNACLE BOOKS LOS ANGELES

First Edition

10 9 8 7 6 5 4 3 2 1

Blackwood, Easley, 1903–
Play of the hand with Blackwood.

1. Contract bridge. I. Title.
GV1282.3.B536 798.4'153 78-6537
ISBN: 0-89474-017-2

Designed by Jerry Tillett

A Corwin Books paperback
Published by
CORWIN BOOKS, a division of
PINNACLE BOOKS, INC.
2029 Century Park East
Los Angeles, California 90067

Contents

THE SQUEEZE

CHAPTER 9 PAGE 300

COUNTING

CHAPTER 10 PAGE 352

THE LOSER-ON-LOSER PLAY: THE FAITHFUL SERVANT

CHAPTER 11 PAGE 360

SAFETY PLAYS

CHAPTER 12 PAGE 371

HOLD-UP PLAYS

CHAPTER 13 PAGE 390

AVOIDANCE PLAYS

CHAPTER 14 PAGE 410

DECEPTION

CHAPTER 15 PAGE 419

EIGHT EVER, NINE—WELL SOMETIMES

APPENDIX A PAGE 439

SAFETY PLAYS

APPENDIX B PAGE 455

Preface

IN the last forty years, the majority of bridge books written have been on bidding, not on play of the hand. There have been some excellent books on play at the advanced level, but only a few on basics. Louis H. Watson's classic, *Play of the Hand at Bridge,* was published in 1934. Since then, the few books published on basic play have simply quoted Watson—many using hands identical to his for illustration. Some claim that, while there is much to learn about bidding and bidding systems, there is nothing ot learn about play—everything is known. Personally, I doubt whether anyone knows all there is to know about the play of the cards, but I am sure that whether it is known or not, there is a great deal which has never been published, especially at the basic level. Somehow the word "basic" has been confused with the word "simple." I use basic in the sense of being fundamental. There are basic techniques in most performances—playing a musical instrument, participating in sports games, being a mechanic, running a business, playing bridge, you name it. Some techniques may be easy; some others may not. Knowing them may not be enough to make you a good performer, but you will never be a good performer unless you do know them thoroughly.

In this book you will find the things that the experts may have known, but which are published here for the first time.

Acknowledgments

I want to thank Tannah Hirsch, who first suggested that I write this book and then did some editing in its early stages. My thanks are also due to Steve Becker, Beatrice Blackwood, Ira Corn, Joe Musumeci, Tom Smith, Richard Oshlag, and Bobby Wolff, all of whom have gone over parts of this manuscript, straightening out some of my prose and correcting errors in analysis. Especially, thanks go to Sue Emery, who edited a large portion of the book, and to Carol King, who typed the entire manuscript.

The errors that remain are my very own.

Play of the Hand with Blackwood

WHIST, a game of English origin dating back several centuries, is the granddaddy of contract bridge. Many of the features of contract are taken from whist, including the principles of trump, partnership, "book," tricks, games and rubber, and honor bonuses. But there is one essential difference between the two games that makes them as different as night and day—in whist there is no bidding. Instead, the dealer turns over his last card to set the trump suit, and the scoring is based on the number of tricks taken by each side. Play is initiated by the player to the left of the dealer making the opening lead, as in contract bridge, but there is no dummy.

It is obvious from this that at the beginning of a deal, neither partnership knows which side holds the majority of the trumps. Therefore, it is vital to the ensuing play that the side with the bulk of the trumps learn of their good fortune as quickly as possible. To this end, whist players of yore began almost immediately to devise signals in the play to inform partner of the length of their trump holding so that whichever side held the master suit could take command of the deal. Eventually, signals were developed to indicate distributions of the side suits as well.

After a period of time, the methods of signalling became more or less standardized, and the first maxims of the play of the cards began to appear. The oldest known were published by the Crown Coffee House in London in 1728. Today, whist is still widely played in England, and it is far from unknown in this hemisphere. Those who have tried it claim it is an excellent game, in some ways more fascinating and more difficult than contract.

I never played whist. My introduction to bridge came in 1914, when the auction version of the game was in vogue, having come into popularity in the last decade of the nineteenth century. Nevertheless, the maxims developed at whist over the centuries had been retained, and new ones had been added. So deeply were they ingrained in the fabric of the play at auction bridge that people actually referred to them as "rules." Indeed, when I first took up auction, I was given a list of twelve "rules" to memorize and told that if I followed them religiously I would be well on my way to becoming a champion player. Here is the list I was required to commit to memory:

1. Lead an ace so you can look at the dummy.
2. Lead the fourth best card of your longest and strongest suit.
3. Do not underlead tenaces.
4. Lead the highest card of the suit bid by your partner.
5. When in doubt, lead trump.
6. Lead through strength.
7. Lead up to weakness.
8. Always return your partner's lead.
9. Second hand low.
10. Third hand high.
11. Cover an honor with an honor.
12. Do not finesse partner.

After applying these "rules" faithfully for a while, I began to become aware that some of them seemed to work out badly more often than not, and that even with those that did usually work out, there were some exceptions. Furthermore, sometimes I could spot the exceptions right off simply by reviewing the bidding or studying the dummy. As I gained more experience, I concentrated more on looking for exceptions to the "Twelve Commandments" and I discovered that as I became proficient in spotting these exceptions, my scores improved. Finally I developed for my own edification what I choose to call privately Blackwood's Thirteenth Rule.

I found that this new rule superceded all twelve of the others, but I also found it more difficult to apply. However, as I improved in its use, my scores continued to improve. So at the very beginning of this series, allow me to let you in on my secret weapon: Theenk.

I might add that I was never considered a very good speller, but that through the judicious application of Rule 13, I did get to where I could play an acceptable game of bridge.

I will examine the twelve "maxims" presented to me over a half century ago but which, for the most part, are still commonly practiced today. I will try to show you how you can find exceptions to them by applying Rule 13, taking into account the bidding you have heard, the dummy you have seen, and the cards that have been played. I must warn you, however, that deciding whether a particular situation does or does not call for an exception to one of the old "commandments" is not always easy and sometimes requires considerable mental effort on your part.

Let me give you a typical example. Suppose you hold:

♠ K J 9 6 ♡ 7 4 2 ◊ 9 4 ♣ Q J 10 6

You are on lead, and your opponents are playing in four hearts. What card would you lead?

First of all, you should tell me that you are playing contract bridge and not whist and that you refuse to answer because you have to know what the bidding has been. Accordingly, I put you in the West seat and tell you that the bidding has gone as follows:

SOUTH	WEST	NORTH	EAST
1 ♠	Pass	1 NT	Pass
2 ♡	Pass	3 ♡	Pass
4 ♡	Pass	Pass	Pass

Now, before doing anything, let us see what we can deduce about the probable makeup of the other three hands at the table. I say probable because there are very few sure things in bridge. Nevertheless, the likelihood is that the other three hands look something like this:

For his bidding, South is a near certainty to hold at least nine cards in the major suits, most probably five spades and four hearts. Of course, he could hold just four spades and four hearts, but this is the least likely of all distributions. With this many cards in the majors, he has to be short in the minors, and it would not be surprising to find him holding a singleton in either clubs or diamonds.

Now let's think about North. He is probably short in spades and should be expected to have either a singleton or a doubleton in that suit. He could hold as many as five hearts, but his most likely holding is four. This means that about half his hand consists of cards in the minor suits.

In addition, neither of our opponents seems to have any great surplus of high cards. South's first rebid was not three hearts but two. North's initial bid of one no-trump indicated he held somewhere between 6 and 10 high-card points and his second bid would seem to mark him with somewhere near the middle of this range. It is a pretty good guess, then, that some of the values the opponents hold are distributional and that altogether they are likely to have fewer than 26 high-card points.

This brings us to the values held by the defense. We, as West, hold 7 high-card points. If, as we presume, declarer is in game on 23–24 high-card points, then our partner holds 9–10 points in high cards. And, while we cannot define his distribution precisely, we can be sure that partner has no more than two hearts and holds fewer spades than we do.

Putting all of this information together, what is our best chance to defeat the contract or at least limit declarer to the minimum number of tricks? We can see from our own hand that declarer is not going to get rich in clubs, nor will he have much success in attempting to establish his spade suit. Furthermore, if he has to take any finesses through dummy's diamonds, he is going to find the missing honors in our partner's hand. What then will be declarer's most probable course of action, either from the very beginning or after he finds out how some of the suits are distributed?

The answer is quite obvious. Since he is short on high cards, his most likely plan will be to play a crossruff, trumping spades in the dummy and minor suits in his hand. And, if the dummy has only one spade (giving our partner three), declarer's plan will undoubtedly succeed. Therefore, we should begin to attack his source of tricks by leading a trump immediately, and at every opportunity thereafter.

Now suppose you held exactly the same hand, but the auction went this way:

SOUTH	WEST	NORTH	EAST
1 ♡	Pass	2 ◇	Pass
2 ♡	Pass	3 ♡	Pass
4 ♡	Pass	Pass	Pass

This is an entirely different situation, and you should come to the following conclusions before making your lead:

North-South are likely to have more high cards than in the first example, since North's initial response showed a hand worth 10 points or more. (The most probable alignment on the auction is 11 points for North and 14–15 for South.) South is also known to have at least a five-card heart suit, while North should have a minimum of three. In addition, South is not marked with a long side suit he wants to ruff in dummy.

Your decision should be that you had better get your high cards established as quickly as possible before declarer sets up dummy's diamond suit for discards. You could consider leading a small spade, but since neither black suit has been bid, why take a risk when you have a ready-made safe lead in the queen of clubs? Hopefully, you will be able to establish a club trick or two while your partner still has some sort of diamond control. Failing this, there may still be time for your partner to shift to spades.

While this is a book on declarer's play of the hand, we are going to start off talking about opening leads. You can't fight a good battle unless you know what the enemy is likely to be up to. In the case of bridge, the declarer is opposing two armies, each with a general, and they will doubtless be sending code messages back and forth. The opening lead is the first message sent, and we are privy to the code. Knowing that code will help us plan our own campaign, where we have also two armies, but only one general.

After discussing opening leads, we are going to take up a quick summary of the problems facing each of the three players. (There are only three players, since declarer's partner has become the dummy.) While the dummy plays the second card to the opening trick, the second play is in reality played by the declarer, so we are going to take a quick survey of the twelve techniques available to him to develop the tricks needed, while warding off the "blows" of his opponents. Then we will survey the situation from the viewpoint of the partner of the opening leader. He is the first defender to see more than his own thirteen cards. We are going to be interested in knowing whether he does or does not approve of the opening lead, and it is quite likely that he will signal his feelings in the matter. Finally, when we have laid this groundwork of what the various combatants seem to have in mind, we are going to go into the techniques of the declarer in more detail to see just what he can do to develop the tricks he needs. I hope I may be able to throw some new light on this struggle for tricks.

IN the old days of whist, when there was no bidding, they used to call the opening lead a "blind" lead. Some people still call it that. But whether it is a blind lead or not, bridge players are not deaf. They have heard the bidding, and that gives them something to go on.

You may have noticed that seven of the twelve ancient "axioms" I listed in the introduction refer to leads. While they do not specifically state that they refer to opening leads, it is obvious that the majority of them do. Apparently, opening leads were causing a lot of trouble a half century ago; they still do. How often have you made an opening lead and then, when you saw the dummy, wished you could take it back! "If only," you say to yourself, "I had been able to see the dummy before I led, I would have led an entirely different card." Nevertheless, while we don't expect the opening lead to be as wise a choice as subsequent plays will be (remember—the opening lead is the only lead made by a player who sees only thirteen cards), we do think that opening leads made today should be better than those made at whist when there was no bidding.

The very first thing we have to study in play of the hand by either the declarer or defender is the opening lead and its implications. The declarer does not plan his play of the hand until he has examined the opening lead and the dummy, and the dummy does not come down until after the opening lead has been made. The defenders also do their major planning after they have seen the dummy, and, of course, by the time they have seen the dummy, they have also seen the opening lead.

First of all, it should be realized that the opening lead is not only an attempt to attack the declarer at his weakest point, it is also a signal. It nearly always reveals something about the distribution or general makeup of the opening leader's hand. This signal can be read by the declarer, as well as by the leader's partner, but the theory is that the information given by the opening lead will be more helpful in the long run to one's partner than it will be to the declarer.

The goal of the opening leader will vary from hand to hand. Occasionally he will be trying to destroy the declarer—to set him a large number of tricks. This nearly always occurs when the declarer has made some injudicious overcall or when he has taken a deliberate sacrifice. Under these circumstances, the goal is usually to roll up a very large score. More often than not, however, the goal is simply to set the declarer one trick and worry about additional tricks after that has been accomplished. This is the type of opening lead we will be most concerned with here.

We will start by taking up the opening lead when the adverse contract is something less than a slam—that is, when more than one or two tricks are required. In considering what to lead, it should immediately be recognized that there is a difference between defending a trump contract and a defending a no-trump contract.

At no-trump, the defender's purpose is usually to establish his long suit so that when he regains the lead, he can take tricks with all small cards in that suit. Consequently, the opening leader's longest suit is normally led in the hopes of driving out whatever high cards the opponents have in that suit. On occasion, when the bidding tells you that you have virtually all the high cards that your side holds and you have no promising suit to lead from, your purpose will merely be to get off lead and let the declarer play into your hand.

When the opponents are playing under the protection of a trump suit, however, you obviously must adopt a different approach. Small cards in long suits are not nearly as likely to take tricks. When the declarer has complete control of the trump suit, as is the usual case, he can simply trump your small cards. Therefore, as the opening leader, you must decide which of several courses offers the best possibilities for your side. You might:

1. Simply try to set up or take your high cards before the declarer has time to establish a side suit of his own on which he can discard his losers.

2. Play to eventually take tricks with your small cards by destroying declarer's control of the trump suit. For example, whenever you hold four trumps and the declarer holds only five, if you can make him trump just one time, you will then have as many trumps as he. This leaves him in a position where he can no longer pull all of your trumps without exhausting all of his. If you suspect that such a situation exists, you should lead a suit that will force declarer to ruff himself "down to your size." In general, the lead would be in your longest suit.

3. Lead a short suit in an effort to convert your useless small trumps into winners via ruffs.

4. Lead a trump to disrupt declarer's apparent plan to crossruff or trump his losers in dummy.

5. Make a purely "passive" lead so as not to give declarer a trick that he otherwise cannot make.

Figure 1-1 illustrates the essential difference between leading against no-trump contracts and leading against suit contracts.

Fig. 1-1

First let us suppose that the declarer (South) is in five clubs. (It is unimportant for our purposes to show how he arrived at that contract.) If we were to consult our list of axioms to determine what to lead, we would immediately run into a series of contradictions. Rule 1 tells us to lead an ace to see the dummy; Rule 2 advises leading fourth best from our longest and strongest suit; Rule 3 warns us not to underlead tenaces.

Observe that on this deal if either of the first two rules were followed, declarer would make his contract. A diamond lead, either the ace or a low one, allows South to score the king (or jack) of diamonds, and he winds up losing only a diamond and a club. However, if West chooses to apply Rule 3 and does not lead a diamond at all, declarer will eventually lose two diamonds and a club to go down one.

How West should know which of the three rules to apply does not matter at the moment. Suffice it to say that leading or underleading an ace against a suit contract is generally a poor policy. The main point of the deal is that, if South were playing in three no-trump, leading a low diamond (Rule 2) would be the only way to defeat the contract! Against any other lead, South has time to take the losing club finesse to set up his long suit, and, even if East switches to a diamond, the defense cannot take more than two diamond tricks before declarer regains the lead to make his contract.

After a low diamond lead, however, declarer can take only eight tricks no matter what he does. East will play the ten, and declarer must win that trick, or the defense will take the first five tricks. When East next gains the lead with the king of clubs, he will return a diamond, and West will take four diamond tricks. Note that lead of neither the ace nor the queen of diamonds would enable you to take four tricks in that suit. The lead must be specifically a small diamond.

This hand dramatically shows the advantage of leading away from a long suit at no-trump, and not doing so at a suit contract. The difference lies in the fact that at no-trump, small cards can take tricks, while against a trump contract, they usually can't. It is almost like playing two entirely different games. In the defense against the three no-trump contract, the opening diamond lead gave declarer a trick he would not have been likely to make if left to his own devices. But by sacrificing this one trick, the defenders were able to take four later on. Conversely, against the five club contract, a diamond lead was the only way to let the declarer make eleven tricks.

It should be pointed out that the lead of a small card from your longest suit will not always work out as well as in the illustration given. Bridge is a game of probabilities, and every once in a while what would normally seem to be the best lead turns out not to be. But in the hand given, West should have every reason to believe that a low diamond lead offers the best chance for his side. If the opponents are in three no-trump, they probably arrived there on an auction of one no-trump by South and three no-trump by North. (North might have used Stayman in between.) West can credit the opponents with at least 26 high-card points, and since he has only 8 points himself, he can hope that his partner has 5 or 6. If so, his partner is likely to gain the lead before declarer can score nine tricks. On this reasoning, it is clearly right to attempt to establish the diamond suit, so that when East wins a trick and returns a diamond, West can collect four more tricks. In this deal, West's hopes are realized.

There are times, though, when it is possible to judge that leading your longest suit against no-trump may not be the best approach. For example, let's say you are West and are on lead against a three no-trump contract with this hand:

♠ 74 ♡ 653 ◇ J9742 ♣ 742

The bidding:

SOUTH	WEST	NORTH	EAST
1 NT	Pass	2 NT	Pass
3 NT	Pass	Pass	Pass

Would you lead a small diamond? Remember that the purpose of leading against no-trump is to establish your long suit, then to regain the lead and take tricks with the small cards in the suit. Now just how good do you think your chances are to drive out all of the high cards the opponents have in diamonds and then to gain the lead so that you can take some tricks with your small diamonds? Of course, it is always possible that the cards will be distributed in such a way that you can do this, but it is most unlikely. Some other lead might prove much more effective.

What lead? Well, let's take a look at the bidding again. Judging from the auction, the opponents hold somewhere between 25 and 27 high-card points (something like 17 points opposite 9). This means your side has about 14 points, but with you holding only 1, your partner must hold approximately 13. So why not lead what he probably would have led if he had been on lead, so that *his* long suit can become established? With all his high cards, he certainly has a better chance of regaining the lead to run his suit than you do.

You hold only two spades and three hearts. Your right-hand opponent did not bid spades or hearts. Your left-hand opponent not only did not bid a major, he did not even employ the Stayman Convention, which he presumably would have done had he held four cards in either hearts or spades. The best possibility, then, is that your partner's long suit is a major, with the odds slightly favoring spades. You must be careful to lead the seven of spades (top of nothing) and not the four-spot. You needn't worry that your partner will interpret this as coming from a long suit. He can be sure by applying the Rule of Eleven (which we will discuss later on), but the chances are he can work out from the cards he holds that you are simply trying to find his long suit, and he will carry the ball from there.

THE OPENING LEAD AS A SIGNAL

Once we have decided which suit to lead, we choose a card with which we hope to give our partner some useful information about our holding in that suit. Sometimes the opening lead itself will give the desired information. Sometimes it takes two or more plays from the suit to get the message over.

The Opening Lead of Honor Cards When your partner leads an ace, he tells you he does not have the king of the suit led. The standard lead with the two top honors of a suit being held is the king. There are, however, some exceptions. Your partner, when he has a doubleton ace and king, will first lead the ace against a suit contract. Your first impression will be that he does not have the king, but if he corrects that impression by leading the king, he has told you in no uncertain terms that he has no more cards in that suit. This play tells you that if you gain a lead, he can trump the next card led in that suit.

There is another exception when playing no-trump. It does not occur very often, but it is standard, and you should know about it. If your partner leads the ace of a suit you have not bid against no-trump, he is asking you to play your highest card in the suit. This lead is made when he has a very long suit which will "run" if you happen to have the right high cards, but which might block if you don't play it at once. Look at the following example. South is declarer. Your partner is West and holds the A K J 10 7 5 2 of one suit. With his holding, he will lead the ace, and let's say he sees the cards shown here:

	3	
A K J 10 7 5 2		6
	8	

One thing is sure: you hold neither the nine nor the queen. If you had held either, you would have played it. So South holds both of these cards. Your partner will switch suits in the hope that you have the four-spot to lead back and that you have some card with which you can gain the lead. Of course, if you had the queen and had played it at trick one, your partner would have known that he could go ahead and take seven tricks before giving up the lead.

While the lead of the king from a suit holding the ace-king is still the standard lead, there are players who are copying the British system of leading the ace from the holding of ace-king. However, unless you and your partner have an understanding to the contrary, you will always lead the king when you have the ace and the king with additional cards.

If your partner leads the king of a suit you have not bid, he is probably telling you that he has either the ace or the queen, or conceivably both. After the dummy goes down, examine it and your hand to see whether you or the dummy has the ace or the queen. Should you see either card, it is a good assumption that your partner has the one you do not see.

When there is a sequence headed by the king, the king is always led, whether it be an opening lead or a subsequent lead of the suit. The lead of the king from a three-card solid sequence—K Q J x (x)—is nearly always an excellent lead. It gives the opponents no tricks they could not have won otherwise and it establishes a trick for your side quickly. It is a lead you will find well recommended in most of the textbooks. I have only one fault to find with it—it is not held often enough.

Should it be on a two-card sequence—K Q x—the king is a proper lead against either a suit contract or a no-trump contract. Should it be a four card or longer suit, the king is still led against a suit contract where the purpose of the opening lead is to establish tricks quickly. Against no-trump, it generally will work out better to lead the fourth best of the suit.

Where there is a broken sequence, such as K Q 10 x or K Q 10 9 x, and the suit is to be led against either no-trump or a suit contract, the king is still the proper card to lead. This is a more hazardous lead, for when the jack and two or more small ones appear in the dummy and the declarer has the ace and one or more small ones, it may well enable him to take two tricks in the suit where otherwise he would get only one.

Very occasionally, the king will be led when it is accompanied by only one small card, even though the suit is not bid. This tends to be a desperation lead, and the odds are against it. When your partner has made this lead, it is in the hope that you have the ace and can give him a ruff, or, hopefully, that you have the queen of the suit, will be able to get the lead before trumps are extracted, and can cash your queen and then give him a ruff.

When your partner leads the king of the suit you have bid and does not have the ace, it usually means that he has the queen to go with it, or that he has not more than one small card in the suit. There are some exceptions where he might lead the king of your suit with three or more small ones, but they will be discussed later.

When your partner leads the queen of a suit, he positively denies holding the king. If you don't see the king in either your hand or the dummy, you will know that the declarer has it.

This lead also is generally from a sequence, and experience teaches us that the lead of the queen with one or more small cards is not often a paying proposition. As in the case of the king, the top of a sequence is the proper lead with any three-card holding such as Q J x. In a four card or longer suit, if only small cards are held in addition to the queen-jack, the queen is the proper lead against a trump contract, and the fourth best against a no-trump contract.

The queen is also led from a broken sequence such as Q J 9 x (x). Like the lead of the king from a broken sequence, this is both an attacking and a hazardous lead. When you happen to find the A 10 x or the K 10 x at your left and the other high honor at your right, you have given up a trick you did not have to lose. However, if you feel the bidding calls for the lead of this suit, the queen is usually the best card to lead.

The queen could conceivably be the top of an interior sequence, such as A Q J 10 x (x) if the lead is against a no-trump contract. Of course, at a suit contract, if that suit must be led, the ace would be the proper lead.

When your partner leads the queen of a suit you have bid, it probably means that he holds the jack or that he holds not more than one small card with the queen. Again, there are a few exceptional cases where your partner might lead the queen of your suit without the jack even though he holds three or more cards, just as he might sometimes lead the king of your suit with three or more cards. Like the king, the lead of the queen with this holding will be discussed later.

When your partner leads the jack, he positively denies holding the queen. This holding is likely to be very similar to that which he has when he leads the queen, except one step lower. With the J 10 x, he will lead the jack against either a suit or a no-trump contract. With only a two-card sequence and four or more cards, he will lead the jack against a suit contract and the fourth best against no-trump. His broken sequence is still a dangerous lead, but not quite so dangerous as the lead of the queen from a broken sequence. His broken sequence might be J 10 8 x (x).

Against no-trump he might lead the jack from an interior sequence where his sequence is three cards long. The jack would be the proper lead from either K J 10 9 x or A J 10 9 x. One trouble with the lead is that it is difficult for the partner to "read" it, and you will find too often that your partner does not return the suit when he regains the lead, even though that would have been the killing play. The suit is almost never led against a suit contract unless you have bid the suit and your partner has raised, or your partner has bid the suit.

If your partner leads the jack of the suit you have bid, he should either have the ten-spot with it or it should be a singleton or doubleton. It almost never pays to lead the jack in your partner's suit from a three card or longer suit when the jack is supported only by small cards. With only three, lead the small one. With four or more, lead fourth best.

The Opening Lead To Show Length When honor cards (ten through ace) are led, they tend to say something about what high cards are held in the suit led. When smaller cards are led, the emphasis is more often on telling us how many cards are held in the suit led. Sometimes two or more cards in a suit have to be played before the story is told.

We are going to take a look at the manner in which a signal with small cards is given by choosing the specific cards played or the order in which these small cards are played. These leads of small cards are made with a suit which is not headed by a three card or longer sequence, for when such a sequence is held, it is more important to tell your partner about the high cards held in a suit by leading one of them than it is to tell him how many cards you have in the suit. As for leading suits headed by two-card honor sequences missing the ace, your decision usually depends upon the number of cards held in the suit and whether you are defending a suit or a no-trump contract. Also, a different procedure is used when you are leading trumps from those used when you are leading a side suit. As most leads are from side suits, we shall consider those first.

Obviously, when you have decided to lead a singleton, there is no problem about which card to select. With a doubleton, the universally accepted lead is the top one. It does not matter what the two cards are—with ace-king or ace-two you lead the ace: with three-two, you lead the three.

This brings us to three-card holdings. With a three-card holding to the ace, should you decide that you will lead the suit against a suit contract, you lay down the ace. You never—*never*—underlead an ace against a suit contract. One time out of forty or fifty that lead might be the killing lead. If you had seen the dummy and a few plays, or even if you had just seen the dummy before you led, you might have been able to determine that the hand was one where the exception held and the underlead of the ace would be a good lead. However, there is no player alive who can find these exceptions before he has seen the dummy. For this reason, if the bidding and the balance of your hand tell you that the suit where you hold A x x is the proper one to lead, lead the ace.

Should you lead from this holding against a no-trump contract, you would lead the smallest card. This lead does not often work out too well against no-trump unless your partner has bid the suit.

If your holding is A K x, you would lead the king against either a suit or no-trump. It would be most unusual for a lead from this holding to be the best bet against a no-trump contract, as it is more likely that when you lead this suit you are helping the declarer (who probably has the missing honors) establish the lower honors in the suit.

Against a suit contract, the lead of the king from A K x has a bit more going for it, but not that much more. There is little chance that you can give your partner a ruff in this suit (which would be a possibility if you had a greater length), and so the likelihood is that you are helping the declarer set up his minor honors in the suit. And, if declarer happens to have the Q J x in his hand, you will not only set up a trick for him, but he may be able to throw a loser away from the dummy on his queen later on or ruff out your ace if dummy holds a singleton in the suit. Another reason for not leading from A K x against either a suit or no-trump contract is that if declarer or dummy has the queen, your lead shows him where seven of the missing high-card points are. This may be all the information he needs to find the right line of play.

When leading from a three-card suit which holds two touching honors not including the ace (such as K Q x or J 10 x), the higher honor card is always led, regardless of the contract. Where a three-card suit has two honor cards not touching (such as K J x or Q 10 x), the small card is the proper lead.

Where there is one honor card in a three-card holding other than the ace, it usually works out best to lead the smallest card.

With three small cards, where the highest card is the nine-spot or a lower card, the standard lead is called "the top of nothing." Obviously that is the highest card in the suit. Your partner will not always be able to tell whether you are leading from a three-card holding or a two-card suit, and you must be alert to any opportunity to clarify the situation. You do this by playing, at the first opportunity, the original middle card from the same suit (not your lowest). Thus, if you led the eight-spot from 8 5 2, you will play the five on the second round, not the deuce. The deuce would definitely announce that it was a doubleton. After your partner has seen your five-spot, he can allow for the possibility that you started with three small, since the deuce will not have appeared on the first two rounds.

I must warn you, however, that there is no unanimity among leading players concerning the proper card to lead from a worthless three-card suit. The great advantage of leading the highest card is that it serves to inform your partner right off the bat that you hold no honors in the suit. However, your partner will not always be able to tell in time whether you are leading from a two- or three-card suit. Because of this, there are players who prefer for their partner to lead the smallest card from a worthless three-card holding, and there is another school of thought that believes leading the middle card is the proper procedure.

However, the lead of the highest card is still standard and, in my opinion, superior, and I recommend you use it unless you and your partner come to a definite understanding concerning other methods.

The more cards you have in a suit, the better the lead of the king from the ace-king becomes against a suit contract. Not only are the chances less that you will be establishing lower honors for your opponents, but the chances are also greater that someone might be trumping that suit, and it might be your partner. However, with four or more cards headed by the ace-king, if you are going to lead the suit against no-trump, the fourth highest card is the best lead.

A K J (x) (x). Now we have strengthened the suit by adding the jack. Against a suit contract, the king remains the best lead. Against no-trump, when your suit gets up to six or seven cards in length, it gets very close. Probably with seven your best play would be the ace, asking your partner to play his highest card in the suit. With six cards defending against no-trump, my own policy is to lay down the ace, provided I have a sure entry into my hand. I may be willing to go ahead with the king and give them one trick to get my suit established. It is not often that you are leading such a suit against no-trump with a sure entry, and unless those exact conditions prevail, I think the fourth best card has the best chance.

Of course, if the suit is headed by the A K Q (x) (x), you lead a card from the sequence as you do whenever you have a three-card honor sequence. The king is the proper lead from this holding, rather than the ace. With any three-card solid sequence which does not include the ace, you lead the highest.

With a two-card sequence missing the ace, and with four or more cards —K Q x x (x) Q J x x (x)—you lead the highest card against a suit contract and specifically the fourth best card against a no-trump contract.

If you decide to lead a four card or longer suit against a trump contract and your suit contains the ace but not the king, for an opening lead you always lead the ace. Once more, I repeat, it is not wise to underlead aces against trump contracts. If you lead this suit against no-trump, you lead the fourth best in the suit.

The rules concerning solid sequences, broken sequences, and interior sequences already explained under "honor cards" hold true when leading four card or longer suits. In all other cases, whether the suit is headed by one or two honors lower than the ace or by no honors at all, the normal lead from a four card or longer suit is the fourth best in the suit.

The Opening Lead of a Trump Different procedures are used when leading trumps because when you do so you are trying to accomplish something altogether different than when you lead a side suit. Usually, you are not trying to knock out the declarer's high cards to establish your high cards, nor do you have a suit sufficiently long to be trying to knock out his high cards in the suit to take tricks with your small cards. A trump lead can be very effective on a hand where it is obvious the declarer intends to play a crossruff or where it appears he is going to trump several losers in the dummy. Your purpose in leading trumps is to try to frustrate his plan.

In selecting which trump to lead, many players attempt to give their partner a count on how many trumps they hold. Thus, while leads from three to an honor or sequences would remain the same, leads from small card holdings change somewhat: from four small, you lead fourth best; from three small, the middle card (planning to play the lowest on the next round); and from two small, the lower card.

If you should happen to hold precisely the A x x of trumps and would like to lead this suit, it is usually best to start with a small one. If the opponents are playing in an eight-card fit, this lead will make it possible for your partner to return a second trump, if he happens to gain the lead before you do. When he does, you can win and play a third round. Note, however, that if you lead the ace and another trump, your partner will have no trump to return when he gets in. Then the third round cannot be played until you gain the lead, and that may be too late. The only time it would be right to lead the Ace from A x x would be when your partner cannot have two trumps or when you are certain he can never gain the lead to return a second trump.

The next time you have A Q x of your opponents' suit, try leading the ace. If the king does not show up in the dummy, you can then lead something else, and your queen will take a trick in due course.

If you happen to run into the following layout, you are going to have some fun:

K 10 7 5

A Q 2 43

J 9 8 6

After you take the first trick with the ace, you next play the deuce of trumps. On rare occasions, you will find the declarer guesses what you are up to and takes the finesse. However, if you don't start off leading the ace, declarer is almost sure to take the percentage play of the finesse, and you will end up with exactly one trump trick.

Of course, if you happen to catch your partner with a singleton king—??!! I'm sorry I thought about that.

An Exception to the General Rule Now let us take a look at exceptions to the general rule on opening leads. The cases we will consider here concern themselves with the proper lead from three to an honor *when your partner has bid the suit.* You may have noticed that the recommended lead of a *low* card from such a holding is in itself a violation of the old auction bridge Rule 4, which stipulated "lead the *highest* card of the suit bid by your partner." But following that advice turned out to be a losing proposition more often than not when the highest card was an honor, and so that rule has since been changed. Perhaps it would help to take a look at a common situation to see why this is so.

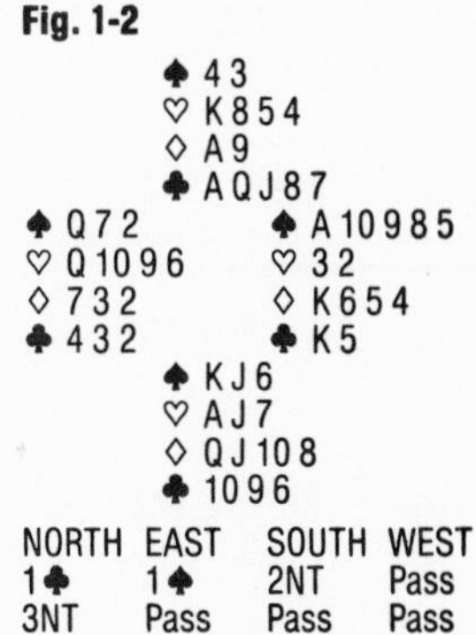

Here you can see that if you lead the queen of spades, the declarer can take two tricks in spades no matter what your partner does: If East takes his ace, South immediately has two spade tricks established; if East does not take his ace, South will win with the king and later can lead a small spade from dummy toward his jack so that it too will take a trick. Once the declarer has two spade tricks, he can add those to his two heart tricks, one diamond trick, and four club tricks (after taking a losing club finesse) and come to nine tricks. But if you can hold the declarer to one spade trick, as you will if you lead a *low* spade originally, retaining your queen behind declarer's jack, then, no matter how he plays, your side will come to at least five tricks and defeat him.

The fact that there are so many situations similar to this one is the reason that the old Rule 4 was changed. Nevertheless, there are cases where, curiously enough, the old rule works out better than the new one, and to recognize such exceptions, it is necessary to apply that one rule that supercedes all others, Rule 13. Suppose you were sitting West and held

♠ 10 9 ♡ K 8 2 ◇ 8 5 2 ♣ 8 7 6 3 2

and you heard the following bidding:

SOUTH	WEST	NORTH	EAST
1♣	Pass	1◇	1♡
1♠	Pass	2♠	Pass
4♠	Pass	Pass	Pass

If you follow the new Rule 4 and lead the deuce of hearts, your partner will probably be on lead at trick two. Since you have absolutely no suit, other than hearts, which you would want your partner to shift to, having him on lead at trick two may leave your side badly placed. But if you can keep the lead in your own hand until the dummy has been exposed, you may find something there that will indicate an effective shift from your hand. So, applying the Thirteenth Rule, you lay down the king of hearts, and here is what you see:

DUMMY
♠ Q 8 5 3
♡ Q 7 4
◇ K J 9 6 4
♣ 5

WEST
♠ 10 9
♡ K 8 2
◇ 8 5 2
♣ 8 7 6 3 2

Dummy plays low, partner follows with the three, and declarer plays the five. Partner has played the smallest heart he can, even though he obviously holds the ace in the suit; this means he is asking you to lead something other than another heart. Before deciding what to shift to, however, you review the bidding and what you have learned so far. You hold only three high-card points, and dummy only eight, yet South never made a move toward slam. Therefore he cannot have a powerhouse, meaning your partner must have a pretty good hand. Since declarer showed no interest in diamonds during the auction, and since it is unlikely your partner could want a club lead (in declarer's first-bid suit *and* with a singleton club in dummy), you elect to shift to the eight of diamonds (remember—lead *top* from three small). Now this is what East sees:

DUMMY
♠ Q 8 5 3
♡ Q 7 4
◊ K J 9 6 4
♣ 5

EAST
♠ 7 4
♡ A J 10 9 6 3
◊ A Q 7
♣ A 4

As soon as your eight of diamonds hits the table, East knows he has the contract beaten—the only question is by how much. Declarer plays low from dummy, finessing you for the queen, but it is all for naught. East wins with the queen and can count four certain winners—your king of hearts and his ace-queen of diamonds and ace of clubs. Note that he does not count his ace of hearts as a sure trick, since it is conceivable that you have indeed led the king of hearts from a three-card holding. But, by the same token, he can count two diamond winners, as your eight-spot shows at most a three-card suit, marking the declarer with at least two originally. So he cashes his ace of clubs and ace of diamonds (on which you play the five) before trying his heart ace. South ruffs this, but the defense has gained a one-trick set. Fig. 1-3 shows the full deal.

Fig. 1-3

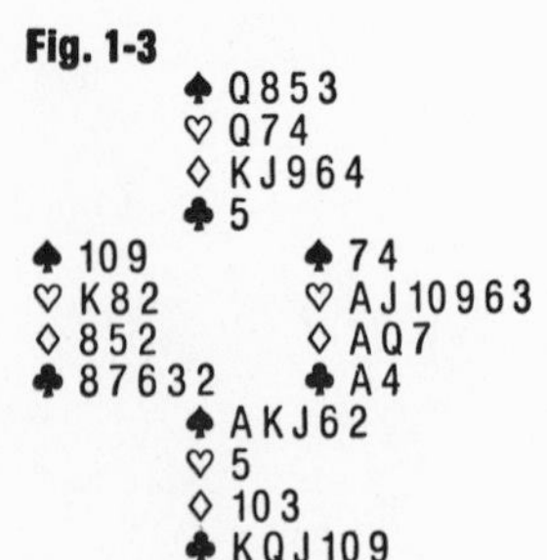

Note that if you had led the two of hearts, East would have won the first trick with the nine (figuring that your two was from three of an honor), but there would then have been no way to beat the contract. If East tried leading a second heart, declarer would simply trump, pull trumps in two rounds, and start leading clubs. East could win with the ace, but without West on lead, he couldn't score the queen of diamonds. Whatever his return, South can eventually discard four of dummy's diamonds on his good club suit, surrender a diamond, and trump a diamond in dummy for his tenth trick.

Here is another example where you could consider leading your honor from a three-card holding (again,you are West):

♠ 4 2 ♡ Q 6 4 ◊ 7 4 3 2 ♣ Q 10 5 4

The bidding:

NORTH	EAST	SOUTH	WEST
1 ◇	1 ♡	1 ♠	Pass
1 NT	Pass	3 ♠	Pass
4 ♠	Pass	Pass	Pass

In this case, the dummy has bid no-trump, indicating that he holds something in your partner's suit—very possibly the king unsupported by any lower honors. In addition, this figures to be your only time on lead, although you may eventually win a club trick. Taking the bidding and your hand into account, I would recommend leading the queen of hearts through dummy's holding at trick one. Although this runs the risk of your partner's concluding that you hold a doubleton in the suit, I think there is a greater risk of his finding himself saddled with an impossible lead at trick two if he has to win the first trick with the jack or ten. Besides, after the dummy is in view, your partner may be able to assess what he sees there in combination with the bidding and conclude that you might well have led the heart queen from a three-card suit.

In closing, I must remind you that the two foregoing examples are exceptions to the rule; when you have no clearcut indication that the lead of an honor from three in your partner's suit is best, you should lead a small one to protect the honor and to indicate to partner length and some strength in the suit.

The Rule of Eleven In our discussion of opening leads to this point, you will have noticed that I have recommended (as do nearly all experts) the lead of the fourth best card from a long broken suit (one not headed by a touching honor sequence). You might have wondered why specifically the fourth best card and not the third or fifth best is selected—after all, you may have asked yourself, when one is leading a low card, what difference can it make which one you choose?

The answer is that, so long as you lead the fourth best card *consistently* from a long suit, it is an important signal for your partner. If he sees you lead a deuce, or if you lead a four and he can see the three and deuce in the dummy or his own hand, he can assume that you hold *no more than four cards in that suit* (although you could hold three and be leading low from an honor). How can he tell this? Well, if you always led fourth best and held a five card or longer suit, the deuce could not possibly be your fourth best card. If you can find an example where it would be, I would like to know about it.

This kind of information can be very helpful to your partner, who may have to decide whether to win, play low, or cover dummy's honor at the first trick. It comes in handiest against no-trump contracts, if for no other reason than that against no-trump, one usually leads his longest suit. If partner can depend on you to follow the fourth best rule religiously, he can draw all kinds of inferences about the distribution of not only the suit you have led, but of other suits as well.

There is yet another reason for leading fourth best, and that is that it permits the partner of the opening leader (and, incidentally, the declarer, too) to apply the well-known "Rule of Eleven." This rule, the development of which is most often credited to British whist expert R.F. Foster, has been in existence since the 1890's and is universally used today. The rule states that (provided the opening lead is indeed fourth best) when the pip on the card led is subtracted from the number eleven, the resulting figure will reveal how many cards *higher* than the one led are held in the *other three hands* of that suit. The player applying the rule then has only to look at the cards in his own hand and in the dummy to determine how many cards higher than the one led are in the fourth player's hand (remember—the opening leader himself is not included in this deduction).

Take a look at the hand in Fig. 1-4.

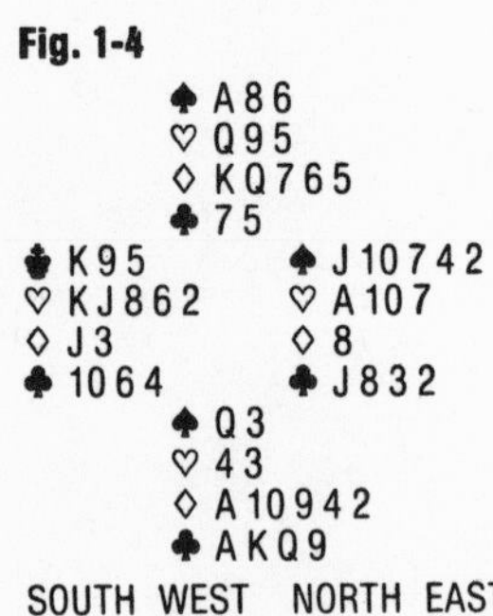

South's rebid of three no-trump is not so foolish as the opening lead of the six of hearts makes it appear. Had the East and West hands been reversed, the opening lead would have been the four of spades, and three no-trump would be home by simply taking the first trick with the ace and then cashing five diamond tricks and three club tricks. Even with the heart lead, the hand would still be makable if the ten of hearts were in West's hand instead of East's hand because dummy could simply insert the nine-spot and force out the ace from East's hand, making the queen a stopper. But with the distribution as it is, declarer is doomed, if East applies the Rule of Eleven. Eleven minus six comes to five. That means that in the other three hands, the north, east, and south hands, there are exactly five hearts which are higher than the six spot. East sees two of these in the dummy; in his own hand, he sees three of them. There is no reason for East to decide that West has not led fourth best, and he knows that all he has to do is cover whatever card dummy plays to take the first heart trick. If dummy plays the five, then East's seven will win; if dummy plays the nine, then East's ten will win; if dummy plays the queen, East's ace will take the trick. So East ignores the old rule about "third-hand high" and instead applies the Rule of Eleven plus Rule 13. As it turns out, with West holding a five-card heart suit, the defense can take five tricks before the declarer even gains the lead. Had East followed the old adage of third-hand high and played the ace, dummy's queen would have stopped the suit, and the declarer could have scored game.

Application of the Rule of Eleven is not restricted solely to the opening lead—it can be used any time partner is known to be leading fourth best. In this connection, it should be noted that when a player returns his partner's suit, at any stage of the proceedings, he should always be careful to select the original fourth best card in that suit. Should he have been dealt only three cards in the suit, he must be equally careful not to return the lowest one, lest partner think he is leading fourth best. Instead, from an original holding of, say, K 7 2, the defender, having put up the king the first time, should return the seven to *deny* holding length in the suit. An alert partner, putting the missing and already played pieces of this suit together, should then be able to work out that the seven-spot has been returned from either an original three-card or doubleton holding, but not from a four-card or longer suit.

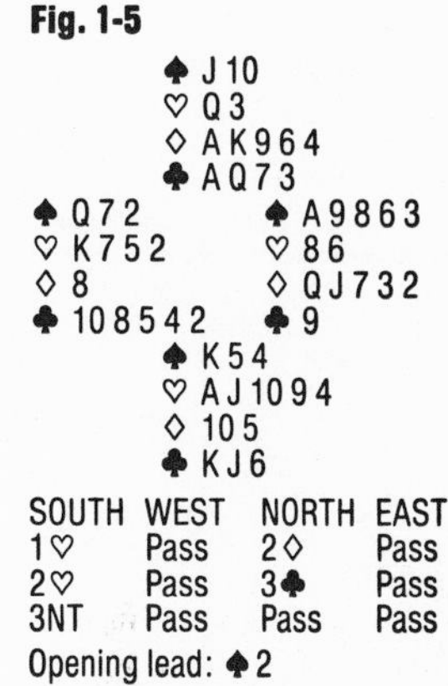

Let's take a look at Fig. 1-5 to see how this principle works in actual practice.

Since the opponents had bid both clubs and hearts, West decided not to lead either of his long suits. Instead he selected the spade deuce (low from three to an honor) in the hope of finding his partner with length in that suit.

East won with the ace and, in accordance with the principle just discussed, returned his original fourth best spade, the six. Declarer, seeing that he was going to have to take the heart finesse to establish his ninth trick, and observing that if East held the K x or K x x of hearts he could make twelve tricks, saw no reason why he should duck a round of spades. "After all," he reasoned, "if the heart finesse loses to West, he is going to be able to cash his spades anyway—ducking one round now won't stop that. Besides, didn't West lead the spade deuce, indicating a four-card holding and marking each opponent with four spades? The worst that can happen to me if I go up with the king of spades now is that the heart finesse will fail and the opponents will then take two more spades. I'll still make nine tricks in that case, so I'm not going to duck when, with a little bit of luck, I might make twelve."

But the declarer was wrong in his assessment of the situation, and he lived just long enough to regret it. However, it first took a good play by West to do South in. When declarer went up with the spade king at trick two, West paused to do a bit of computation. Applying the Rule of Eleven to East's return of the six-spot, West determined that the three remaining hands (exclusive of East) had begun with five cards higher than the six. Since the dummy had started with the J 10, the declarer had just played the king, and he himself still held the Q 7, he was able to conclude that declarer had no cards left higher than East's six. This meant that East was prepared to run the spade suit the next time the defense gained the lead. But before East could do this, West had to get rid of his queen of spades, which was blocking the suit. Thanks to the Rule of Eleven, West was able to dump his queen under declarer's king with the total certainty that this would not cost his side a trick.

No doubt as soon as West's queen hit the table, South realized the error he had made, but it was too late for him to do anything about it. He crossed to dummy with a diamond and tried the heart finesse, but West won and returned the spade seven. East duly overtook with the eight and proceeded to cash the rest of the suit for down one. Another triumph for the Rule of Eleven and Blackwood's Thirteenth Rule.

Intercepting Defenders' Signals As we have seen, the messages the defenders can send to each other by adhering to the rules governing opening or subsequent leads can be very helpful to their cause. Occasionally, however, these signals can be turned by the declarer to his own advantage. Now, we will examine two deals where a defender's opening lead of fourth best in a suit was instrumental in enabling declarer to find the winning line of play.

West had a choice of three four-card suits to lead from on hand 1-6.

Fig. 1-6 Dlr: E

West	North	East
	♠ 8 4	
	♡ 6 3 2	
	◇ K J 4	
	♣ A Q 10 7 4	
♠ A Q 5 3		♠ 10 9 7 6 2
♡ Q 10 8 4		♡ K 9 5
◇ 10		◇ 7 6 5 2
♣ 8 6 3 2		♣ K
	♠ K J	
	♡ A J 7	
	◇ A Q 9 8 3	
	♣ J 9 5	

EAST	SOUTH	WEST	NORTH
Pass	1 NT	Pass	3 NT
Pass	Pass	Pass	

Opening lead: ♡4

He decided that the club suit was too weak to establish and that a spade lead might give away a trick, so he chose the middle road by leading a heart. Declarer played low from the dummy and could not afford to duck East's king, as a spade shift by East might prove most embarrassing.

In assessing his chances, South could see that he had only seven sure tricks and that his only real hope appeared to be a successful club finesse. Of course, if the finesse worked, declarer would make eleven tricks, but if it lost, the floodgates would open to the defenders. However, there was no rush to try the club play, and South decided to cash his diamonds first to see what, if anything, he could learn about the opposing hands.

On the first four rounds of diamonds, West had no problem discarding a spade and two clubs, but on the fifth diamond, West imagined he was in dire straits. He did not want to throw a heart, since if East ever gained the lead, a heart return through declarer would yield three tricks. And he also (for reasons best known to himself) did not want to blank down to the A Q of spades. So he decided to part with a third club, reasoning that if South had the club king, it did not matter what he discarded, while if East had the club king, declarer would lose a finesse to him. After all, West thought, if South had only two clubs, East's king was guarded, and even if South had three clubs, he would never be able to guess that East's king was a singleton.

But West did not realize that declarer had at this point gained a great deal of information about his hand. After cashing the fifth diamond and seeing West throw a third club, South paused to consider what he had learned thus far. Going back to the opening lead—the heart four—declarer was able to conclude that West had led from precisely a four-card suit. This deduction was based on the assumption that against no-trump, a defender normally leads the fourth best card in his longest suit. However, since the three and two of hearts were in dummy, it was clear that the four was West's lowest heart, and it was equally obvious that if West had held more than four hearts, his fourth best card would have to have been a higher spot card than the four.

Once South decided that West had indeed led from a long suit, and that that suit was only four cards long, the rest was easy. West had shown up with a singleton diamond, and the only hand that can contain a singleton and yet have no longer than a four-card suit is a hand with a 4-4-4-1 distribution. Therefore, South was able to place West with four spades and four clubs originally, along with his four hearts—and West had already thrown three of the clubs away! So, after cashing his last diamond, South led a club toward dummy. When West followed with the eight, dummy's ace was put up, felling East's king, and declarer had eleven tricks in the bank.

South's success on this deal can be attributed to two factors: first, his alert interception of a signal intended to aid the defense; and second, his application of an age-old bridge principle that your granddaddy should have taught you before you left the farm for the big city—"give the suckers a chance to go wrong."

Now let's take a look at another case where a fourth best lead backfired on the defenders. Fig. 1-7 comes from an actual duplicate game.

Fig. 1-7

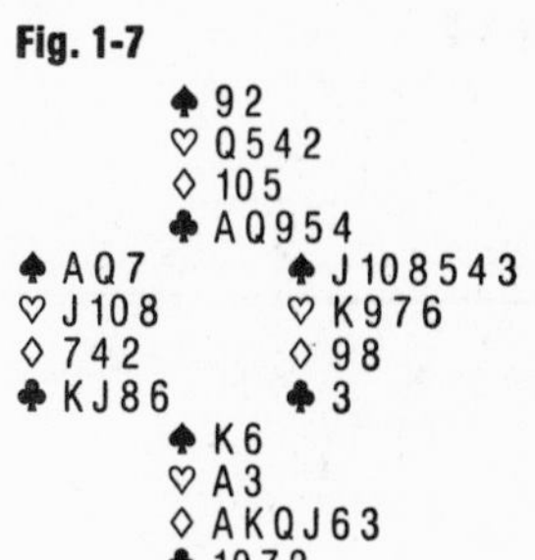

The auctions varied from table to table, but most of the time South wound up playing three no-trump. Whenever West selected the heart jack as his opening lead, South had to sweat for nine tricks. Every declarer who received this lead was understandably afraid to gamble on a double club finesse in an attempt to make overtricks—they were more concerned with trying to keep East out of the lead so he could not shift to a spade. So instead of playing for the unlikely (25 percent) possibility of finding both the king and jack of clubs onside, they took a simple finesse against the club king and, when it worked, emerged with nine tricks. (We will not go into the gory details of what happened when one misguided soul tried for his ninth trick by crossing to dummy's diamond ten at trick two and then leading a spade to his king.)

At some tables, however, the opening lead was the club six, and this made all the difference in the world—three tricks difference, to be exact. Those declarers fortunate enough to receive this lead had only to apply the Rule of Eleven to determine that East could not hold a club high enough to beat their seven-spot. This conclusion was arrived at by first assuming that West was making a normal fourth best lead; then, since there was no reason to think he wasn't, West's six-spot was subtracted from eleven, leaving five cards outside of the opening leader's hand that were higher than the six. Since declarer could see all five of these cards in his own hand and dummy, there was no way East could win the trick if South let the six ride around to his hand. Furthermore, once these declarers had won the first trick with the seven, it was a simple matter for them to repeat the deep finesse in clubs, pick up the whole suit, and wind up with twelve tricks in all. (Incidentally, observe that if declarer has to break this club suit himself, West's club spots will prevent him from scoring all five tricks.)

Despite what we have seen here, the fact is that in the great majority of cases, the defenders stand to benefit more from following the general rules we have established about leads. Remember—they cannot see each other's hands, while declarer can see the dummy and plan his plays accordingly. Consistently leading in the same fashion is one way the defenders can help overcome declarer's advantage.

SELECTING WHICH SUIT TO LEAD

In previous sections, we have concentrated mainly on the proper card to lead *once you have decided to lead a particular suit.* We have examined the advantages (and occasional disadvantages) these more or less standard leads offer the defenders and have even included a few deals where it was right to violate the normal procedure.

One major area, however, has not been covered to any great extent thus far: how does one select which suit to lead in the first place? Although it is granted that every hand presents a new problem, there are nevertheless some leads that are nearly always right, some that stand to gain more than they lose over the long run, and some that should be avoided at all costs.

Let us begin by discussing some "good" leads—those that figure to be both safe and effective for the defense. First off, any suit your partner has bid is certainly entitled to serious consideration. This is true even though your opponent may have bid no-trump directly over your partner's bid. It is even truer when your partner has opened the bidding in a major suit, since major-suit openings tend to show longer and stronger holdings than minor-suit openings. If your partner's bid has been an overcall, you should definitely favor leading that suit, as he may have made this bid for the specific purpose of indicating a good lead to you. (Of course, in choosing *which card* to lead, you should adhere to the principles set forth earlier, i.e., low from four, low from three to an honor, high from a doubleton, etc.)

Naturally, there are always exceptions to such rules. For example, if the opponents have arrived at a suit contract and you hold five or more cards in a suit your partner has bid, your side doesn't figure to take more than one trick in your suit. In this case you might look for some other lead that might help establish tricks elsewhere, such as a lead from a high honor sequence. Another reason for not leading your long suit in this situation is that, even if partner wins the first trick, he may be at a loss as to what to do next.

A second possible exception to leading your partner's suit is when you happen to hold the ace and two or three other cards in the suit, and the opponents are in a trump contract. Even though your partner has bid this suit, leading it will often present declarer with a trick he could not have made if left to his own devices. Of course, if you *must* lead the suit, you should lead the ace first—underleading aces against suit contracts is a very dangerous proposition.

Another good lead is from any touching three card honor sequence, such as Q J 10 (x) or K Q J (x). Not only does this lead start your side off to establishing some winners, but it is completely safe in the sense that you have not given declarer a trick he could not otherwise make. Leading the top honor from suits with broken sequences, such as K Q 10 (x) or Q J 9 (x), is not as safe, but turns out right more often than not.

Now let us look at a few "sometimes" leads. We have previously discussed the matter of leading trumps. This is often the most effective lead when the auction has made it apparent that declarer will play to cross-ruff the hand or is planning to ruff losers in the dummy.

The blind lead of a singleton against a suit contract is at best a doubtful proposition. When such a lead succeeds, it is spectacularly evident. When it fails, however, the failure may be much harder to spot. If you are playing rubber bridge, where the cards are thrown in after the hand is over, the fact that you may have made the only lead to give declarer his contract may never be realized, unless you have watched the play very carefully. Your lead may have picked up an honor in your partner's hand which declarer would never have picked up on his own; or it may simply have put declarer on notice that this particular suit (and, therefore, perhaps some others) was not breaking, enabling him to succeed via an otherwise abnormal line of play. Often a singleton lead helps declarer establish his side suit.

Nevertheless, there are circumstances in which a singleton lead has much to recommend it. Among the factors that must be present are (1) the trumps you hold are virtually worthless (you do not have a holding such as Q J 10, which will produce a trump trick anyway); (2) your partner stands a good chance of gaining the lead before your trumps are exhausted; and (3) you don't have length (four or five cards) in the trump suit, in which case it is usually best to try to force the declarer to ruff by leading a long side suit in the hopes that he will eventually lose control of the hand.

The ideal situation in which to lead a singleton is where you hold the guarded ace or king of trumps and have reason to believe you can put your partner in the lead after you win your trump honor. It is reasonable to expect that your partner has at least one entry if he has entered the auction at some stage, or if the opponents' bidding has made it clear that your partner must have some high cards. In this latter regard, you can frequently tell from the opponents' auction just about how many high cards they hold, and if you yourself do not hold many of the missing honors, then your partner has to have them. By the same token, if you *do* hold nearly all of the outstanding honors, then your chances of putting partner on lead later become very slim, so the singleton lead may not be best.

Strangely enough, for much the same reasons as those just discussed, a singleton lead will often work out well when you have a very weak hand, with or without a trump honor. Indeed, some players will nearly always lead a singleton from a weak hand when the opponents have not bid too vigorously, figuring that their partner must have at least one—if not several—entries. This used to be called a desperation lead, but whatever you call it, it will succeed more often than one would think, particularly when the opponents have stopped in game without having made a single move toward slam.

Another "sometimes" lead is one where you suspect that your *partner* is short in a certain suit, and you are planning to give *him* a ruff when *you* gain the lead. Suppose you (West) hold the following hand:

♠ Q 10 x x ♡ A x ◊ x x x ♣ x x x x

The bidding:

SOUTH	WEST	NORTH	EAST
1 ♡	Pass	2 ♣	Pass
4 ♣	Pass	4 ♡	Pass
4 NT	Pass	5 ◊	Pass
6 ♡	Pass	Pass	Pass

Unless the opponents are kidding with their club bids, your partner has to be very short in clubs. He could have none at all, but at most he is holding a singleton. Since you have the ace of trumps—a card which the declarer is going to have to knock out before he can do much else—it is not difficult to envision that if you lead a club, you will be able to give your partner a club ruff when you win the ace of hearts. All he needs for this plan to succeed is two trumps.

One more point about leading singletons: it is not wise to lead a singleton against a small slam when you happen to hold an ace. The fact that the opponents have bid a slam missing an ace means it is extremely unlikely that your partner has an immediate entry also. Your side may eventually defeat the contract, but it won't be because of a ruff given to you by your partner.

However, leading a singleton against a slam when you do not hold an ace and you think your partner might is a horse of a different color. If the ace is in either your singleton suit or in the trump suit, you can secure a ruff to defeat the contract by leading your singleton initially.

Leading away from an unsupported king in a suit that your side has not bid is another "sometimes" lead, but although it is dangerous, it is sometimes necessary. The lead is usually tipped off by the opponents' auction, which discloses that they cannot be very well heeled in that suit. For example, suppose you (West) hold the following hand,

♠ K J x x ♡ x x x ◊ Q x ♣ J x x x

and the bidding goes:

NORTH	EAST	SOUTH	WEST
1 ◊	Pass	1 ♡	Pass
3 ◊	Pass	3 ♡	Pass
4 ♡	Pass	Pass	Pass

North does not appear to have too many black cards, and South cannot be very strong, since he made no move toward slam. However, any trump honors your partner may hold are badly placed for your side, and your queen of diamonds in front of dummy's long suit is not going to help your cause either. Given time, declarer will be able to pick up the heart and the diamond suits and dispose of some or all of his black-suit losers. Therefore, if you have any club or spade winners, you'd better get them in a hurry. I recommend a spade lead, since that is where you can give your partner the most help—for a club lead to be right, your partner would have to hold ace-king or ace-queen over dummy's king.

Similarly, the following auction calls for a spade lead regardless of West's holding in the suit:

SOUTH	WEST	NORTH	EAST
1 ♡	Pass	3 ♡	Pass
4 ♣	Pass	4 ◊	Pass
5 ♡	Pass	Pass	Pass

Here, the opponents have shown control of three suits, and South has said additionally—by his five heart bid—that his only worry is the spade suit. Since North could not continue further, he too has denied any control in spades. Therefore, West must try to gather his side's spade tricks before the mice get at them.

Incidentally, while it does not apply to the above deals, when you have to choose between underleading a king and underleading a queen, the former will prove disastrous less frequently. This might sound peculiar to some, but the fact is that when your underlead of the king fails to find your

partner with the ace or queen, you will often get your king anyway later in the play. Should your underlead of the queen turn out to be wrong, though, you are very unlikely to regain that trick later on.

Occasionally, the opponents' auction makes it obvious that your best lead is a passive one—that is, a lead from a worthless suit rather than from any honor card. Such leads are called for when your own holding, combined with the opposing auction, indicates that you possess virtually all of the outstanding high cards and you have no honor sequence to lead from. Your best bet in such a case is to get out of your own way with a lead in your weakest suit and hope declarer has to break the other suits for you.

When you hold four of declarer's trumps, you frequently will find it better to lead your long suit rather than your singleton (Fig. 1-8).

In the north-south hands you can find five spade winners, three heart winners, and three club winners. This comes to a total of eleven winners, and that is exactly what declarer could take if he had the opening lead. But West has the opening lead. If he chooses to lead his singleton heart, one of South's heart winners will disappear. West will find just what he ordered—his partner will hold the ace of the suit, and he can get an immediate ruff and the defenders can take the first three tricks. The trouble with this defense is that the declarer will take the last ten tricks. But let's see what happens if West takes advantage of his good luck in holding four trumps and, instead of leading a short suit, leads his long suit.

South, unaware that he is going to get a 4–1 break in spades will certainly trump the second diamond. At this point, West will have as many trumps as he has. South will find this out when he leads trumps twice. Whenever he decides to quit leading trumps and give up a heart trick, East will lead a third diamond, and when South trumps that, West will have more trumps than South has. This passing of trump control to West will prevent South from taking even ten tricks. Even if South could see West's hands and knew he held four trumps, he cannot take ten tricks against this defense. If he decides, for instance, to discard on the second diamond trick and trump the third one so that East will be out of diamonds and have none to return, West can, after winning his diamond trick, switch to his singleton heart and get his ruff after all.

The lead of the long suit by West in the hope that he can reduce declarer's trump length to his own is called "forcing the declarer." In some circles they call it "punching the declarer," while in some of the back rooms where some of us have played at one time or another, it is called "pumping the chump."

DANGEROUS OPENING LEADS

We have discussed "good" opening leads—those that figure to be both safe and effective on most deals. We also covered a few "sometimes" leads—normally risky leads that could work out well because of a special set of circumstances. Now we will examine leads that should be avoided in all but the most unusual situations.

We will begin with what I consider the "least worst" first, progressively working down to the worst of all at the bottom of the list.

1. The lead of an ace in an unbid suit (unless you happen to also hold the king). Aces are best saved to capture opposing honors, and not the twos and threes you will collect if you lead them.

2. The blind lead of a short suit—a singleton or doubleton—except under the conditions described previously, where they have a better chance of succeeding.

3. The lead of a suit bid by the dummy. Beginning players seem to like such leads, confusing it with the old maxim of "leading through strength." There is a difference, however, between leading through strength and leading through *length*. The former refers to leads through short suits such as A Q x or K J x and is often an effective tactic once the play has begun. Leading through an opponent's five- or six-card suit, though, serves only to do declarer's work for him by helping him to get the suit established.

4. The lead of a doubleton queen or jack in a suit your partner has not bid. A blind lead from either of these holdings seems to cost a trick about three times as often as it gains one.

5. The lead of a suit (not trumps) bid on your right. This is even worse than leading through a suit bid on your left, since, in this instance, you are not only leading the opponent's length, but *into* his strength.

6. The underlead of an ace against a suit contract. As stated earlier, leading away from an ace against a trump contract will lose many more times than it will gain, one reason being that your partner, who will not be expecting such a lead, may make the wrong play to the first trick (and maybe even subsequently). If you feel you simply must (in direct opposition to No. 1 above) lead a suit which contains the ace unsupported by the king, then the ace is the proper choice at trick one.

LEAD DIRECTING DOUBLES

Now we come to those special situations where your partner requests that you lead specific suits. If during the bidding procedure your partner has named a suit and you have not and the opponents end up at three no-trump, your partner's double practically demands that you lead his suit. Of course, you might wait until trick two to do so, if you have the ace and king of a side suit, so that your partner will know where to get the extra trick after he has run his suit, but this happening will be extremely rare.

If the opponents have reached three no-trump when you have bid a suit and your partner has not and he doubles their three no-trump bid, he is telling you to go ahead and lead the suit you have bid, he has a supporting honor in the suit.

Sometimes the opponents will reach three no-trump after you and your partner have each bid a suit. Under these circumstances, when my partner does not double, my normal tendency is to show him the courtesy of leading his suit unless mine is practically established after trick one. If, therefore, he does make a penalty double after we have each bid a suit, I assume he is asking me to do what I would not normally do—lead my suit and not his.

When, however, the opponents reach three no-trump and neither of us has bid and my partner doubles, he is asking me to lead the first suit bid by the dummy and to lead the highest card I hold in that suit. For example:

SOUTH	WEST	NORTH	EAST
1 ♢	Pass	1 ♠	Pass
2 NT	Pass	3 NT	Double
all pass			

In this bidding my partner has asked me to lead a spade. He may hold something like the K Q J 10 9 in spades plus a quick entry; but he could hold the A K Q 10 with one or two small cards.

If your partner doubles three no-trump when nobody has bid any suit, this is known as a double "out of the blue." This occurs when your right-hand opponent has opened one no-trump and your left-hand opponent has either gone directly to three no-trump or has given a single raise, and your right-hand opponent has carried on to three no-trump. This double states that if your partner himself had the lead, he could set the hand before the opponents could get the lead, and generally indicates a solid running suit. It asks you to lead a suit where you have no high cards and, preferably, to lead a short suit. For example, with the holding

♠ x x x x x
♡ x x
♢ Q x x
♣ Q J 10

all signs are that your partner has solid hearts. He cannot have a solid suit in either diamonds or clubs where you hold some honors, and his long suit is much more likely to be hearts than spades. Yes, opponents sometimes do get into three no-trump with one suit completely unstopped, especially today when a number of players are inclined to go ahead and bid one no-trump even though they hold a worthless doubleton in some suit or another. The opening bidder's partner can have ample high cards and bid the three no-trump although he holds no stopper in the same suit.

The double of an artificial or conventional bid is frequently made to indicate a lead. The double of a two club response to an opening bid of one no-trump says, in effect, "Partner, no matter what they end up playing I have indicated to you that a club lead will be a good lead."

The double of an artificial response to a Blackwood four no-trump bid likewise asks for that suit to be led. Unfortunately, this double in my opinion is made too often by a player who happens to hold only an unsupported king or ace, with length in the suit. This situation sometimes guides the declarer into deciding whether or not to contract for a slam. The double is best made when the holding is some sort of a sequence, such as K Q x x.

And, finally, we come to the Lightner double. This is a double of a slam bid which the opponents have made not as a sacrifice but in the hopes of fulfilling it. This double says, "Partner, do not lead trumps. Do not lead what you have bid. Do not lead what I have bid. Lead something else." It frequently indicates that the doubler has a void suit in his hand somewhere which he asks you to locate so that he can trump the opening lead. With some players today the tendency is to take this request to lead the first bid suit by the dummy. While I personally think this is a doubtful interpretation of such a double, when there are no indications that will guide you to locate your partner's void suit, this might be the best shot.

There are times when the Lightner Double is of doubtful value because it might allow your opponents to escape from a contract which they cannot make into one they can make. Hand 1-9 is an example where East can double with a secure feeling declarer would have no place to run.

Fig. 1-9 Dlr: S Vul: N-S

North: ♠ 9 7 5 3 ♡ Q 9 7 6 3 2 ◇ A ♣ 9 8

West: ♠ 8 6 2 ♡ — ◇ 8 6 3 2 ♣ 10 6 5 4 3 2

East: ♠ A K Q J 10 4 ♡ A 5 ◇ Q 10 9 5 4 ♣ —

South: ♠ — ♡ K J 10 8 4 ◇ K J 7 ♣ A K Q J 7

SOUTH	WEST	NORTH	EAST
1♡	Pass	4♡	4♠
6♡	Pass	Double	All Pass

Opening Lead: ♣ 10

The double told West not to lead spades, and not to lead trumps. This left only the minor suits. West had no trouble deciding that if his partner had a void suit it was more likely to be in clubs than in diamonds. The opening lead of a club set a hand which could not otherwise have been set.

OPENING LEADS AGAINST SLAMS

Before concluding our discussion on opening leads, I'd like to make some comments about the specialized area of leading against slams. Against a small slam being played in a suit, it frequently pays to make an attacking lead from an honor in an unbid suit (or in a suit cue-bid by an opponent), except where you have reason to believe that you hold all of your side's high cards. No guarantee goes with underleading a king against a small slam, but, under the right circumstances, I have found it to be a winning play more often than not. Against a small slam in no-trump or any grand slam, however, the best chance is to play passive by not leading any suit in which you hold an honor (unless, of course, you hold an honor sequence).

This brings us to the subject of leading aces against slams—a tactic that would appear to be in violation of the advice given earlier. Nevertheless, I find that in this area I am not in agreement with the leading authorities and must contradict my own rule. When I was learning bridge, I had a mentor who told me, "Easley, if they bid a small slam, and you have an ace, don't think—just lead it." Although I think he overstated the case somewhat for bridge in general, I am still inclined to do exactly as he said at matchpoints, where an extra trick can make the difference between a good and bad result.

In particular, I have found it profitable to lay down an ace against a small slam when the opponents have indicated that they hold strong trumps plus a long solid side suit. On occasion, the ace lead has actually brought about the defeat of the slam, even though my intention at the time was merely to hold the opponents to their contract. The few instances when I have lost on this lead have been more than compensated for by the extra matchpoints earned on deals where cashing the ace was right.

At any variation of total point scoring, however, the situation is not so clear. In this case, I find that an important factor to consider is the quality of the opposition. When the players are known to be of the highest caliber, and especially when they have all sorts of conventions for locating controls, I am a bit more cautious about laying down an ace against a slam. Otherwise, I still tend to follow my mentor's advice.

The foregoing naturally assumes that you have no other obvious course to follow in selecting your lead against a slam. However, sometimes when you hold a side ace, you are fortunate enough to hold a king-queen in another suit, or maybe you have good reason to believe you can establish a second-round winner for your partner in another suit. In such cases, the best approach is, of course, to retain your ace and lead the other suit, in the hopes that the contract cannot be made without surrendering a trick to your ace first.

HAVING concluded our discussion of opening leads from the viewpoint of both the defenders and the declarer, we will now turn our attention to the next phase of the play—the planning by the declarer when the dummy is tabled and his subsequent implementation of that plan.

Once the dummy goes down, declarer has the only opportunity given in contract bridge for a solo performance. Bidding and defense are purely partnership operations, while playing the dummy offers declarer the chance to be a star in his own right. To make the most of his unique position, however, declarer must possess the knowledge of how to assess his chances for success after he first views the dummy. He must formulate some plan of attack, and to do so he has to know what to look for.

Over the years, many bridge writers have attempted to make the declarer's lot an easier one by offering simple mnemonic devices designed to help him remember the steps he must go through before he plays to the first trick. My own device is the word "COB," which stands for the following:

C = Count your tricks.
O = Opening lead—what does it tell you?
B = Bidding (or lack of it) by the opponents.

A bit of elaboration on counting tricks: in general, you count winners at no-trump; then, should you discover that you don't have enough of them, you try to find a way to develop the necessary additional tricks. At a suit contract, you usually count losers and look for a way to dispose of them if you find you have too many. Sometimes, though, it is wise to count both winners and losers. There are hands where you can count, say, nine winners at a no-trump game, but only after the opponents have taken five tricks. In such cases, the problem becomes the development of nine winners *before* the defenders can cash the setting trick.

Some of the books I have read leave one with the impression that the initial assessment procedure is always a difficult task for the declarer. This is not so. On more hands than these writers would seem to realize, you simply do not have to go through the second and third ("O" and "B") processes at all. You merely count your winners (or losers), discover that you have enough tricks for your contract, with no chance of developing any others, and so can skip any thoughts about the significance of the opening lead or the bidding.

In addition, there are many deals where only a single, simple problem exists. The contract may depend solely on a straightforward finesse or a favorable suit break. If it is your day, the cards will be kind to you. If it is not, you will go down, and that will be that. As before, in such instances it is not necessary to go further than counting your tricks—but my one caution is that you be sure you have no other alternatives that may offer additional chances.

There are hands, though, where the situation is much more complicated, and it is on these that the declarer must avail himself of the complete COB procedure. It may, for example, be necessary to gain a count on the opponents' hands, and here the opening lead and any bidding could play important roles. It is for deals like these that your heavy thinking should be reserved, since a great deal of planning may be required. However, if you have worn yourself out on simple deals, you may not be up to making the winning decisions on the difficult ones.

There are twelve standard plays and procedures which are well known to experienced players:

1. The finesse
2. Suit establishment
3. Trump management
4. Unblocking and creating entries
5. Throw-in plays
6. The squeeze
7. Counting
8. Loser-on-loser
9. Safety plays
10. Hold-up plays and defensive entry plays
11. Avoidance
12. Deception

The first eight of these aim primarily at developing additional tricks. The next three are principally defensive maneuvers to frustrate your opponents. Deception is usually an attempt to "con" them out of what is rightfully theirs.

Once you know these techniques, you will examine the combined assets of your own and the dummy's hands to see whether you can isolate the problem so that you can apply one of them, or whether the problem is more complex. Even in the case of a simple finesse, you may have to decide which of two finesses to take, or which to take first. Occasionally you may have to choose between which of two standard plays offers the best chance. It may be necessary to go through the complete COB procedure before you can make an intelligent choice.

In this chapter I will examine the more frequent of these plays available to declarers and give an easy—but not too easy—illustration of each. They will be examined in greater detail later in the book.

THE FINESSE

In Fig. 2-1, you play low from dummy, East wins the ace of spades and returns the four. A count of your sure winners reveals that you have two spade tricks, three hearts, three clubs and a diamond. Obviously, you cannot make your contract unless you can come up with three more tricks, and your only source of those extra tricks lies in the diamond suit.

That takes care of step one, but on this deal there is no need to review the bidding or examine the meaning of the opening lead. Clearly, these are extraneous matters which cannot help you here. Your concentration should center solely on the best way to bring home the diamond suit without the loss of a trick.

It should not take you more than a moment to realize that your best chance is that East has the king of diamonds. If he does, you can lead through him—toward your A Q J—and eventually pick up his king. This is known as a simple finesse, but don't let the word "simple" fool you. There is a danger in the diamond suit brought about by the fact that neither your hand nor the dummy's contains the nine of diamonds, and this leaves the suit with a weakness. Therefore, you are going to have to call on Blackwood's Thirteenth Rule before you can proceed.

What bearing can the nine-spot have on the outcome? Well, suppose you win East's spade return in dummy and begin your finessing operation by leading the ten of diamonds. Then suppose East has the king, as you had hoped, but it is *singleton* (a 2.8%-chance). You can win with your ace, all right, but in the meantime you have established West's nine as a fourth-round winner and the slam has gone kaput.

Thus, your first step, to protect against such an eventuality, is to lead a *low* diamond from dummy to your jack. This wins, but it is not yet time to abandon Rule 13. One more pitfall still exists—that East began with four diamonds (as in the actual deal) and is presently holding the K 9 7. If so, you cannot simply return to dummy and carelessly lead a diamond to your queen. This would leave East with the king-nine of diamonds, dummy with the ten-six, and you with the ace-eight, and whatever you did next, East would have a trick in the suit.

How can you overcome this possibility? The answer is to cross to dummy after winning the first diamond finesse and then lead the ten through East. If he plays low, you will take the next two tricks with the ace-queen; if he covers, you will win with the ace and, when West shows out, return to dummy to lead a third diamond up to your queen-eight, picking up his nine-seven in the process and making the slam.

Fig. 2-2 Dlr: N Vul:0

West	North	East
	♠ K	
	♡ J 5	
	◇ Q J 10 8 4	
	♣ A K 9 7 5	
♠ 10 9 6 5 2		♠ J 8 7 3
♡ K Q 7		♡ 9 8 4
◇ K 3 2		◇ A 7 5
♣ Q 6		♣ J 10 4
	♠ A Q 4	
	♡ A 10 6 3 2	
	◇ 9 6	
	♣ 8 3 2	

NORTH	EAST	SOUTH	WEST
1◇	Pass	1♡	Pass
2♣	Pass	2 NT	Pass
3 NT	Pass	Pass	Pass

Opening lead: ♠5

SUIT ESTABLISHMENT

There is more than one way to establish the small cards in your long suit so that they will become tricks. At a trump contract, for example, you can ruff a round or two of a side suit to set up spot cards as winners. At no-trump, however, the usual way to establish a suit is to drive out the missing honors so that the suit can be run. Fig. 2-2 illustrates just how this is done.

As declarer, your first duty is to count your sure winners to determine how many more tricks will be needed to make the contract. You can count three spade tricks, two clubs, and a heart, so you are going to have to find three more. In such cases, you should first look for a long suit to establish, but in the hand given, there are three suits—diamonds, hearts, and clubs—that might be developed. So the question is, which one do you attack?

Here we run into two contradictory bridge principles. The first one states that in trying to develop small cards in long suits, you should choose the suit in which you and the dummy hold the greatest number of cards. In this instance, that would be clubs. The second principle, however, holds that you should first set up the suit in which you do not have the top cards, rather than the suit in which you do. In the present case, this would apply to the diamond suit rather than the heart suit, since the diamonds are more solid.

The answer to the problem lies in the number of tricks you actually need to make your contract. If you play on clubs and the suit divides 3–2 in the opposing hands, you will gain two extra tricks, but that will still leave you one trick short. If you go after diamonds instead, though, you will have three tricks once the ace and king are knocked out. True, this means having to give up the lead twice, but since you have every suit double-stopped, there is no danger that the opponents will collect five tricks before you can muster nine.

Therefore, you should start by winning the king of spades in dummy and leading a diamond to the nine. If this holds the trick, you continue playing diamonds until you have forced out the two high honors, preserving the ace and king of clubs as entries to the dummy. It is even possible that once your work in diamonds is done, you will make an overtrick if the opponents are not careful or if their cards are distributed unfavorably for them, but this should not be your prime concern. Your first obligation is to make sure of your contract—even at match-point scoring.

TRUMP MANAGEMENT

In Fig. 2-3, after the dummy is tabled, you once again count your sure tricks and find that you have only nine—five spades, two hearts, and two

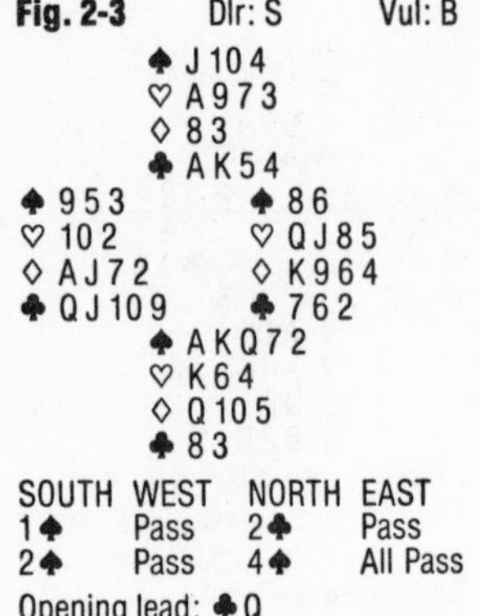

clubs. The same result is obtained by counting your losers, the usual procedure in a suit contract. Looking at it this way, you are certain to lose a heart and possibly three diamonds. Therefore, you are going to have to find a way to make an extra trick.

Unfortunately, the remaining parts of the COB formula for assessing your position will be of little help here. West's opening lead appears to be perfectly normal, and the opponents never entered the auction. Their failure to bid is not surprising, though, since your side holds 26 high-card points and some length in every suit.

About the only inference you can draw is that West does not hold the ace-king of diamonds. If he did, he would probably have laid down a top diamond at trick one, rather than leading a club. This increases the chances that East may hold both high diamonds, in which case you can establish your queen as a trick by leading diamonds twice from the dummy toward your hand.

The likelihood, however, is that the ace and king of diamonds are in separate hands. Even if this is the case, the fact that you hold the diamond ten gives you yet another chance to score a diamond trick. If East happens to have the jack, you can lead a diamond from dummy, insert the ten when East plays low, and force West's high honor. Later, a second lead from dummy will force East to rise with his ace or king, setting up your queen.

Barring such favorable developments, you have a third string to your bow. If the diamond trick fails to materialize, you can *trump* your third diamond in dummy. This means, though, that you *cannot draw any trumps* until the diamond suit has been tested. Playing even one round of trumps would enable the defense to win a diamond, return a trump, win the second diamond, and return another trump to fully deplete dummy's trump holding. Indeed, now that you think about it, you are happy that West did not lead a trump to begin with, since this would have given the defenders the timing to remove all of dummy's trumps before you could ruff a diamond on the table.

But back to the problem at hand. With your planning now completed, you win West's club lead with dummy's king and lead a diamond. East follows low, so you finesse the ten, hoping West will have to win with the ace or king. When West produces the jack, however, you are not overjoyed, but you are still in control. It is too late for the enemy to extract all three of dummy's trumps, even if West shifts to that suit. If he does, you win in dummy, lead another diamond, win the trump return in your hand, and ruff your third diamond on the table. It is then a simple matter to enter the closed hand with a club ruff to draw the remaining trump, after which you can claim ten tricks.

UNBLOCKING

In Fig. 2-4, against your (South's) three no-trump contract, West leads the eight of spades. You count your tricks: two spades, one heart, one diamond, and three clubs—seven tricks. You analyze the opening lead to see

Fig. 2-4

if you can gain a clue as to how to come by the two tricks you need. West has obviously led from a short suit—you apply the Rule of Eleven after one glance at dummy, and you know this cannot be a fourth best card.

Here is something to remember: a short suit lead against no-trump sometimes means the player on lead has a near-worthless hand with no entries to his long suit; he is probably trying to find partner's long suit, expecting the missing high cards to be in partner's hand where they can be used for entries once the long suit is established.

This line of thought is encouraging—if East has the king of hearts, two finesses through him will bring in the necessary eighth and ninth tricks. But, to take two finesses through East, you must have two entries to dummy, and the only possibilities are the king and ten of spades plus the queen of diamonds.

You try spades first by playing low from dummy, hoping East will rise with his ace. Let's say East does play his ace, failing to notice your lack of entries to dummy—a very thoughtless play. However, this error does not help you one bit if you are equally thoughtless. You must drop either the *queen* or the *jack* of spades under East's ace. The play of the nine-spot at trick one would prove a very false economy because you need that precious card to lead to dummy's spade ten as one of your two entries to finesse against the heart king.

When East returns a spade at trick two, you overtake your spade nine with dummy's ten to finesse the heart jack, then lead your remaining top spade to dummy's king to finesse the heart queen. Now when you cash your red suit aces and three top clubs, you have taken a total of nine tricks. You have made not only your contract, but your first unblocking play as well.

Unblocking plays have many variations, and we will explore this subject more thoroughly with other illustrations later.

THROW-IN PLAYS

In bridge jargon, throw-in plays sometimes are called "end plays." This is not always an accurate description because throw-in plays frequently occur long before the end of the hand.

You are playing in a Swiss team with IMP scoring and have bid six spades on the following hands:

DUMMY
♠ Q J 8 5 2
♡ A Q 4
◇ A 10 6
♣ 7 5
DECLARER
♠ A K 9 6 3
♡ K 8 2
◇ K J 4
♣ A Q

You get the opening lead of the jack of hearts, and when the dummy goes down, you count your winning tricks. You have five spades, three hearts, two diamonds, and one club, for a total of eleven. If either minor suit finesse wins, you will make your slam, so your first impulse is to draw trumps and take the club finesse, expecting—if that fails—to try to guess which opponent has the diamond queen.

You realize that West would have solved all your problems if he had led either a diamond or a club, but a 75 percent chance doesn't seem too bad—that's the percentage when you have to make only one successful finesse out of two for your contract. Still, wouldn't you rather have a sure thing than a 75 percent shot? The fact is that if you play this hand correctly you can't go down—six spades is ironclad.

You are planning to lose one trick, but you must arrange things so that whichever opponent wins the trick has no safe return. First you draw trumps, which removes one safe exit. Then you cash out the A K Q of hearts, leaving no hearts in either your hand or dummy. This takes care of the second suit. Now you must forgo the club finesse—you play the *ace* and then the *queen* of clubs, taking care of the third suit. Your hand and the dummy now contain only spades and diamonds, so you don't care which opponent wins the club king. If the return is a diamond, you will have you a free finesse for the queen. If the lead is a club or a heart, you will discard a diamond from one hand, while trumping in the other.

Remember, you are playing IMPs! If you guess correctly and manage to locate both minor suit honors, you will make seven for an occasional 1-IMP pickup. But how important is the possibility of picking up an occasional overtrick compared to taking out a 100 percent sure insurance policy on your slam contract?

Try this strip and throw-in play for yourself. Lay out the cards and move the club king and diamond queen wherever you wish. The suggested play *always* works.

This technique also is called an elimination play. This procedure of voiding both your hand and dummy of a suit is a frequently used device to prepare for the throw-in play. You are making sure that when you present an opponent with a trick, he will have to make a return that is advantageous to you.

THE SIMPLE SQUEEZE

There are many complex variations of squeeze plays. One of them is called the "simple squeeze." It is aptly named because this play is frequently simple to execute, even though inexperienced players feel it is enshrouded in mystery. Usually these three conditions must exist:

1. You must be able to win all the remaining tricks but one, and one of your winning cards (the *squeeze card*) must be played at such a time as to force a fatal discard.

2. One opponent must guard two suits where you have potential winners.

3. You must have an *entry* and a potential winner in the hand *opposite* the squeeze card.

Here is a classic example:

♠ J (potential winner)
◊ K 6 (◊ 6 potential winner, ◊ K entry)

West	East
♠ A (guards ♠ J)	♠ 9
◊ J 10 (guards ◊ 6)	♣ 10 7

♡ K (squeeze card)
◊ 7
♣ 5

Let's check the above steps:

1. Since you have two sure tricks (the heart king and the diamond king), you can win all the remaining tricks but one. To win all three remaining tricks and force a fatal discard from West, you must play your *squeeze card* at the right time—and that is *now* at trick eleven.

2. West holds guards in two suits (spades and diamonds) where you have potential tricks, so he is the opponent to be squeezed.

3. The king of diamonds is an *entry* to the spade jack and diamond six, potential winners in the *opposite* hand (dummy). If you had not saved your diamond king, you could not reach your established winner after the squeeze is executed.

Once you see that all conditions are fulfilled, play your *squeeze card* and watch West squirm. He probably will save the spade ace because he will be looking at that jack in dummy. So when he parts with a diamond, you toss the spade jack (it is worthless now), lead your seven of diamonds to dummy's king as West's last diamond falls, and claim the thirteenth trick with dummy's lowly diamond six.

Now that you have the end position well in mind, let's go back to the beginning and see how the whole hand developed, as we follow the evolution of the simple positional squeeze in Fig. 2-5.

Fig. 2-5 Dlr: W Vul: 0

North: ♠ J 5 4 ♡ A Q 3 ◊ A K 6 5 ♣ 8 3 2

West: ♠ A K Q 10 2 ♡ 2 ◊ J 10 4 3 ♣ Q J 9

East: ♠ 9 8 6 3 ♡ 7 6 4 ◊ 9 8 ♣ 10 7 6 4

South: ♠ 7 ♡ K J 10 9 8 5 ◊ Q 7 2 ♣ A K 5

WEST	NORTH	EAST	SOUTH
1♠	Dbl	Pass	2♠
Pass	3◊	Pass	3♡
Pass	4♡	Pass	4 NT
Pass	5♡	Pass	6♡
Pass	Pass	Pass	

Opening lead: ♠K

As soon as the opening lead is made and dummy is spread, you count the high-card points. You have 13 high-card points, and your partner has 14, so there are 13 points left, and West (who opened the bidding) surely has most, if not all, of those. When he leads the spade queen to trick two (which you ruff), you are sure he has the ace, so dummy's spade jack is a potential winner or a one-card *menace* against West's ace. You count up your tricks and realize you have six winners in hearts, three in diamonds, and two in clubs, for a total of eleven. You need twelve to make your contract, and the opponents already have their one trick, so you have complied with condition 1.

If the diamonds are kindly divided, three in each hand, you have your extra trick, but now you can add to that the possibility that West started with *four or more* diamonds. If he did, you will have condition 2 under control. While running your good cards, you may cash two diamond honors, being sure to leave one in dummy along with the potential trick-winning spade jack. We will call the diamond king your *"get-there card,"* so now condition 3 obtains.

After drawing trumps in three rounds, tricks six through ten are two top clubs, two top diamonds, and one more top heart. That brings you to the three-card position shown at the start of this topic.

COUNTING

Fig. 2-6 Dlr: N Vul: 0

DUMMY
♠ 3 2
♡ A J 6
◇ A K 7 6
♣ K J 6 5

DECLARER
♠ 9 7 6
♡ K 10 9 3
◇ 3
♣ A Q 10 9 3

NORTH	EAST	SOUTH	WEST
1◇	1♠	2♣	Pass
4♣	Pass	5♣	All Pass

Opening lead: ♠A

We now come to a form of standard play considered to be most difficult. Many players mistakenly think counting is the exclusive province of experts and near-experts. Counting the unseen hands can be a most profitable operation on many deals and is well worth the trouble. It requires a little concentration, the ability to count to thirteen, and an occasional mental review of the bidding.

You have two fast spade losers (your third spade can be ruffed in dummy), but you will go down if you lose a trick to the heart queen. You can finesse either opponent for that card, so this is obviously one of those hands where getting the count in the various suits is going to give you a picture of the unseen hands and help you decide who holds the vital red queen.

The spade ace wins the first trick, and East overtakes the spade ten with the jack at trick two to lead his diamond queen to dummy's king. Now you are starting to get a count of the hand. You lead a diamond and ruff it (there is no danger, you have plenty of high trumps)—now you can start getting a count of the missing clubs. Play the club ace, then a small club to dummy's king. When both opponents follow, you have that suit counted—each opponent held exactly two clubs.

You now try to complete the count of the diamond suit—cash the diamond ace, discarding a heart from your hand, and ruff dummy's fourth diamond. When West shows out on the last diamond, you have the suit counted: West had only three, and since you and the dummy had five between you, you know that East started with five.

Now you ruff your last spade in dummy, West following suit with the five. East therefore must have had exactly five spades for his overcall—he probably wouldn't overcall with fewer, and he can't have more. Since he has shown up with five diamonds and two clubs, you know twelve of his original thirteen cards. Thus, he must have exactly one heart. Since that singleton could be the queen, you return to your hand with the heart king, as East follows with the four-spot. Then you confidently finesse against West's heart queen. You have *counted* your first hand.

This may seem a trying job, but it requires only that you adopt Blackwood's Thirteenth Rule—theenk. You are playing bridge because you like a "thinking-person's game" so hands like this should be both a challenge and a pleasure to you.

LOSER-ON-LOSER PLAYS

Fig. 2-6A Dlr: S Vul: N-S

North:
♠ K 8 4
♡ 10 6 5 2
◇ K 9 5 3
♣ 8 6

West:
♠ J 7 5 3
♡ 9
◇ 8 4
♣ K Q 7 5 4 3

East:
♠ Q 10 9
♡ J 8 4
◇ Q J 10 6 2
♣ A 2

South:
♠ A 6 2
♡ A K Q 7 3
◇ A 7
♣ J 10 9

SOUTH	WEST	NORTH	EAST
1♡	Pass	2♡	Pass
4♡	Pass	Pass	Pass

One of the more pleasant plays available to a declarer is the loser-on-loser play. It seems so artistic. Let me illustrate what I am saying with Fig. 2-6A.

When the declarer first got a look at the dummy, it looked like he had one loser in spades and two in clubs. West's opening lead was the king of clubs and East overtook that with the ace and then returned the two spot. West won that with the queen and came on with a third club.

Now it looked like another loser had been uncovered. East was acting like a man who started with exactly two clubs and who could overruff the dummy. Declarer simply could not afford to lose a trump in addition to two clubs and a spade, but he had available a way to get along without any spade losers at all. He simply resigned himself to losing a trump ruff to East but discarded a spade from the dummy instead of trumping himself. Now East got in his ruff all right, but declarer's spade loser had disappeared in smoke. When he regained the lead, he simply pulled trumps and then cashed the king and ace of spades and trumped a spade.

One of the nice things about the loser-on-loser play is that it seems perfectly willing to act as an assistant to many other forms of play. It can help the declarer frustrate the opponents in their efforts to get a ruff, as in Fig. 2-6A and, at times, it can help him execute a squeeze play, act as an avoidance play, help establish a side suit, or aid in the execution of a throw-in play. Let's look at Fig. 2-6B, where the loser-on-loser enabled the declarer to triumph in spite of the fact that all finesses were wrong.

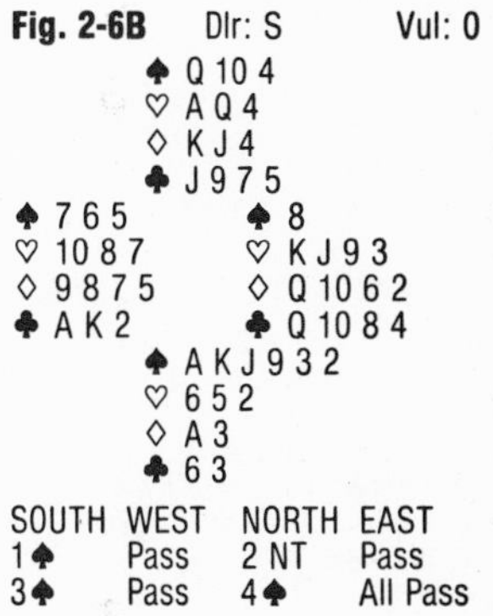

The club king was opened and declarer had no difficulty in finding two losers in the club suit. Diamonds seemed to be in good shape, and hearts would be in good shape if the heart finesse would only work. If the heart finesse failed, there would be two losers in hearts. Of course, one way to get rid of one of those heart losers is to finesse diamonds, but suppose that one failed?

Our hero found a way. East duly signaled with the eight of clubs and West went ahead and cashed the ace and then led the two spot. Dummy's nine was covered by the ten and declarer ruffed. This sequence of plays made it pretty clear who had the queen of clubs. Declarer pulled trumps in three rounds, ending in the dummy, and then led the jack of clubs. When East covered with the queen, declarer knew that that was all thirteen of the clubs. But, he didn't trump it. On that loser, he just threw away a losing heart and saddled East with the lead. East could either lead a heart to end the misery at once or could lead a diamond. In that event, dummy's jack would win, declarer would return to his hand with the ace of diamonds and then go over with the ace of hearts and discard his second losing heart on the king of diamonds.

THE SAFETY PLAY

The *safety play* is an insurance policy against a bad suit break. It is employed when necessary to eliminate or minimize the danger of your contract's being beaten.

Until recently, safety plays had been receiving scant attention in duplicate circles because they are used so rarely at match-point scoring. However, with the increased popularity of Swiss team games, safety plays are becoming more and more important to duplicate players. This makes them worthy of our careful attention.

The play of the heart suit in Fig. 2-7 illustrates graphically the principle of the safety play.

Fig. 2-7 Dlr: S Vul: N-S

North: ♠ A 7 5 3 ♡ A 10 8 4 ◇ K 5 ♣ Q 6 2

West: ♠ K 8 ♡ Q J 5 3 ◇ Q J 10 8 4 ♣ 10 3

East: ♠ 10 9 6 4 2 ♡ — ◇ A 9 6 2 ♣ 9 7 5 4

South: ♠ Q J ♡ K 9 7 6 2 ◇ 7 3 ♣ A K J 8

SOUTH	WEST	NORTH	EAST
1♡	Pass	3♡	Pass
4♡	Pass	Pass	Pass

Opening lead: ◇Q

East and West capture two fast diamond tricks, and West gets out with the ten of clubs which you win in your hand. When you assess your losers, you see that you may or may not have to lose a spade, and your heart losers may be zero, one, or two. You don't know how many hearts you can afford to lose until you discover who has the king of spades (so you take the spade finesse at trick four). When that works, you see that you can afford one heart loser.

If East had won the spade king, you would have had to go all out to take five heart tricks to make your contract, but now you can afford the luxury of a *safety play.* You are willing to lose one heart trick to be sure that you do not lose two tricks.

If you lead the first heart from the south hand and west plays low, simply put in the eight-spot. If East wins with an honor, only two hearts will remain outstanding, and they must fall when the ace and king are led. When East shows out in the actual hand, your two top hearts will pick up all but one of West's trumps, whereas, if you had banged down the ace and king of hearts, you would have had to lose to both the queen and the jack.

If you start the hearts from the north hand, lead a low one, and when East shows out, you can take either of two lines. You can go up with your king and take the marked double finesse through West's remaining Q J 5. Or you can put in the nine to lose to the jack, setting up the marked finesse against the queen when you regain the lead.

Fig. 2-8 Dlr: N Vul: 0

West	North	East
	♠ K 9 2 ♡ K 9 8 ◇ 5 3 2 ♣ A Q J 8	
♠ 10 8 3 ♡ J 6 3 ◇ A 10 8 6 4 ♣ 7 5		♠ J 7 6 4 ♡ Q 10 7 4 ◇ Q 9 ♣ K 4 3
	♠ A Q 5 ♡ A 5 2 ◇ K J 7 ♣ 10 9 6 2	

NORTH	EAST	SOUTH	WEST
1♣	Pass	2 NT	Pass
3 NT	Pass	Pass	Pass

Opening lead: ◇ 6

THE HOLD-UP PLAY

In Fig. 2-8, your first step after dummy goes down is to count your sure tricks. West's diamond lead has guaranteed you a trick in that suit, and, in addition, you have three spade tricks, two hearts, and the club ace —seven in all. This leaves you two short, but that should be no problem: the club suit, once the king is dislodged, will furnish the extra winners you need. Furthermore, if West happens to have the club king, there will be no need to lose a trick in that suit at all, since repeated finesses will pick up four tricks. So is there anything to fear?

The answer is yes. If East happens to have the club king and West has led from a five-card diamond suit, there is a good chance that the defense will be able to score five tricks (four diamonds and a club) before you can come to nine. West's lead of the six-spot certainly looks like a perfectly normal fourth best lead against no-trump, and the absence of the four-spot in either your hand or the dummy's opens the possibility that West could have that card, giving him five altogether.

Can you overcome such a distribution of the cards? The answer to this is also yes, but first let's see what East plays to the first trick. You call for a low diamond from dummy, and East produces the queen. Do you win with the king?

If you do, you are doomed, for East will win the club king when you finesse and return a diamond through your jack-seven. West, holding the A 10 8 4, will then cover whatever you play and cash four more diamonds to defeat the contract. Therefore, the proper play by you at trick one is to permit East's queen to hold!

Now you are entirely safe. You have not lost a diamond trick, since you still have the king-jack, and with the queen already gone, you can build this into a trick later. In practice, East will probably return a diamond after winning the queen, so your diamond trick will come home to roost right away, but this is of no real significance. What is significant is that when you lose the club finesse, East will have no more diamonds to return to West's established suit. You can then collect your nine top tricks at your leisure.

It is entirely possible, of course, that the diamonds could be divided 4-3 originally, and not 5–2 as in the diagram. In this case, when you let East hold the queen and he continues with a diamond at trick two, West can duck so as to leave East with a diamond to return later on. But if that is the actual distribution, the opponents can never take more than three diamonds and a club, so the contract is always safe, and allowing East to hold the queen at trick one will have absolutely no bearing on the outcome. Since the hold up will make all the difference in the world against a 5–2 break, however, it is clearly the only correct play.

THE AVOIDANCE PLAY

Fig. 2-9 Dlr: S Vul: N-S
DUMMY
♠ K 6 4
♡ K 8
◇ J 6 4 3
♣ A 10 8 7
DECLARER
♠ A 5 2
♡ Q 7 2
◇ A K
♣ K J 9 6 3
SOUTH WEST NORTH EAST
1 NT Pass 3 NT Pass
Pass Pass
Opening lead: ♡ 5

Once again, as illustrated in Fig. 2-9, you count your sure tricks and this time come up with a total of seven—two spades, two clubs, two diamonds, and the heart trick you are certain to have after the first trick is completed. You also observe that you can take an additional two or three tricks in clubs, depending on whether or not you lose a trick to the club queen.

Now examine the opening lead: it would appear to be a normal fourth best card from a long suit. It is easy to see that if you play a small heart from dummy to start with, East will be able to play a card high enough to force your queen. This will leave the heart king as a singleton in dummy, and should you subsequently fail to guess the position of the club queen, forcing you to give up the lead in that suit in order to develop your game-going tricks, either opponent can cash the heart ace to fell the king. Should this happen, you would then be at the mercy of the opposing heart division, and if the suit were not divided 4–4, you would go down.

Clearly, you can gain much more flexibility in the heart suit if you put up dummy's king at trick one. First of all, it may win the trick, leaving you with the guarded queen and marking West with the ace. Secondly, even if the king loses to East's ace, you can then duck a round of hearts before being forced to take the queen.

What does all this have to do with the crucial club suit? The answer is everything. What happens on the first heart is going to determine how you attack the clubs! Obviously, the only danger to your contract is in a 5–3 or 6–2 heart division, and you are going to protect against it. Let's see how it works.

Suppose the king of hearts holds the first trick. Then your next move would be to cash dummy's club ace, lead the ten and, if it is not covered, let it ride to West. Even if the finesse loses, West cannot hurt you in hearts, since you hold the queen doubleton as a stopper. As soon as you regain the lead, you can cash nine tricks for your contract (and, if West makes the mistake of returning a heart, you will make ten). Of course, if East covers the club ten, or the ten holds the trick, you will make an overtrick in the process.

Now suppose East wins dummy's king with the ace at trick one. A heart is returned, you duck, and a third heart forces your queen. This time, you take the club finesse the other way, into the *East* hand. If the finesse loses and East has a fourth heart, he will be able to cash it, but you will have the rest of the tricks, losing three hearts and a club in all. However, if East has no more hearts—meaning that he started with three and his partner with five—the defense will be unable to cash their established suit because you have been careful to keep the longer hand—West—out of the lead. Such a maneuver is called, quite aptly, an avoidance play.

The only way this play could backfire on you would be in the unlikely circumstance that West's original lead came from a three-card suit. If an opponent happens to hit on such a lead and it causes you to go wrong, you simply have to pay off. Fortunately, nobody is that smart too often. Note also that in playing the club suit as advised, you give up the normal percentage play of cashing the ace and king to try to drop the queen, but this is not the prime consideration on this deal. Ensuring the contract is.

DECEPTION

Along with all of the standard plays, the wise declarer will use a little guile. It is usually wise for the defense to refrain from falsecarding, but no such inhibition binds the declarer. He has no partner to fool, so if he deceives anyone, it must be his opponents. Fig. 2-10 is an example that tickled my funnybone.

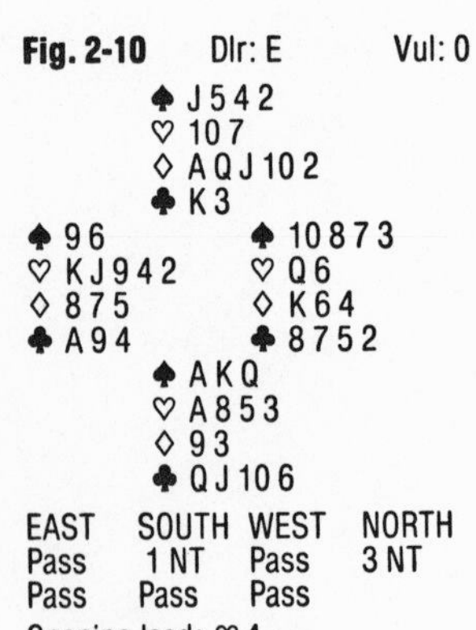

Declarer quickly realized that if West held five hearts and the ace of clubs and East the king of diamonds, the contract was doomed to failure.

East played the queen on his partner's opening lead of the four of hearts, and South ducked, smoothly playing the *five* of hearts. When East returned the six of hearts, South played the *eight*, and West won the jack. Notice how this sequence of plays appeared to West: he placed South with an original heart holding of A 8 5 and his partner with Q 6 3. It happened that West was a suit-preference nut, so at trick three he returned the *deuce* of hearts to tell his partner he had the ace of clubs for an entry. South collected this trick with his *three*, and proceeded to make the "impossible" contract even though West held a five-card heart suit and the ace of clubs, and even though the diamond king was offside.

Go ahead and fault West for falling into South's trap, but when he won the jack of hearts at trick two, his remaining cards in that suit were the K 9 2. He was absolutely *sure* that declarer's ace was now blank. It was understandable gullibility that led him to return the heart deuce to tell his partner about the club ace.

But don't take any credit away from the subtlety of South's play. He made no wild discards—he didn't play the eight and then the five to wake everybody up to the fact that something funny was going on. He just played naturally and smoothly up the line, concealing his three-spot and arousing no suspicion. He deserves A-plus for giving West the opportunity to misread the holdings.

FROM time to time, you will meet someone who claims to have an uncle who can tell you, after the opening lead is made, the location of every card held in the concealed hands, whether he is the declarer or a defender. You will, naturally, never meet the uncle himself, but you will (more frequently than you would like), meet the person who knows the person who can perform this feat. Of course, the story is so much hogwash, because the uncle, and anyone like him, does not really exist.

Nevertheless, the fact is that a player can often learn a great deal from the opening lead; indeed, sometimes he can draw enough conclusions so that it may seem that he *is* able to see every card in the concealed hands. In general, it is the opening leader's partner who is in a better position to make such judgments, but the declarer can usually draw some important inferences of his own.

We will examine a single hand at length to see just what each of the players can in turn deduce from a single opening lead and the subsequent play, in combination with the bidding that has taken place. In so doing, we will make use of some of the points we have covered in the preceding chapter on opening leads.

Let us first suppose you are West and you hold the following cards:

♠ A 9 5 3 ♡ Q 10 2 ◇ 7 2 ♣ K 10 8 5

The bidding:

SOUTH	WEST	NORTH	EAST
1 NT*	Pass	2 NT	Pass
3 NT	Pass	Pass	Pass

It is your lead, and, as is often the case, you have no long and strong suit to lead from. It appears that you are on a guess as to which suit to attack, but before making a final decision, it is wise to review what you have learned from the bidding. You should realize right away that the opponents have between 25 and 27 high-card points—North has 9 or 10 for his invitational two no-trump bid, and South has 16 or 17 for his acceptance. Going one step further, you can conclude that, since you have nine high-card points of your own, partner has either 4, 5, or 6. This would seem to make it unlikely that partner could have both a long and strong suit *and* the necessary entry to run that suit once it has become established. Therefore, the situation would appear to dictate against a short-suit lead designed to set up a suit in partner's hand.

So you decide to lead one of your own four card suits, but the question is, which one? To answer this, you must try to picture the distribution of the north-south hands. South has advertised either a 4–3–3–3, a 4–4–3–2, or a 5–3–3–2 pattern with his opening no-trump. If he happens to hold the last of these, it is more likely in practice that he will hold a five-card minor than a five-card major. North, for his part, did not use Stayman, so it is improbable that he holds a four-card major suit.

All of this would seem to indicate that if the opponents have a weak spot anywhere, it is most likely in spades. Accordingly, you lead your fourth best spade—the three—as the least of evils, and dummy tables his cards. Now we shift our perspective to the South hand; this is what declarer sees:

DUMMY
♠ J 10 2
♡ A 6 4
◇ A 10 9 6 3
♣ 6 4

Opening lead: ♠ 3

DECLARER
♠ K 6
♡ K 5 3
◇ Q J 4
♣ A Q J 9 7

South can draw an immediate conclusion of his own: with the two of spades in dummy and the three led, he can assume that West has no more than four spades—from a five card or longer suit, the fourth best card would have to be something higher than the three-spot. And while it is possible that West could be leading from a three-card suit to an honor, it is

*15–17 high-card points.

best to assume, when playing a no-trump contract, that the opponent has led from a long suit. For this reason, South can also conclude that West probably does not hold another suit longer than four cards, or else he would have led it.

With these initial inferences tucked away in his mind, South now begins to count his tricks. He can see that he is sure to make one spade trick and that if every missing card is well placed, he can score five diamonds, five clubs and two hearts besides. But this is not the way one assesses a hand—declarer's first concern should be to make sure he has nine tricks before he tries for more, and in so doing he should ask himself whether he can make his contract if all the missing key cards are badly placed. From that viewpoint declarer can see that if both the king of diamonds and the king of clubs are adversely located, he may go down, losing three spade tricks and both minor suit kings before he can set up nine tricks. In counting his tricks, he can come to only eight if the diamond finesse loses—one spade, two hearts, four diamonds, and the club ace—leaving him with the necessity of trying the club finesee for his contract.

However, on reexamining the spade suit, South sees there is a possibility that he can score two spade tricks, if a certain lie of the cards exists and if he can induce East to make a mistake. The situation needed is for East to hold specifically the queen without the ace. If the suit actually lies this way, the play of the jack from dummy at trick one might provoke East into covering with the queen, after which dummy's ten would become a stopper behind West's ace. Since this play can cost nothing, declarer decides to try it.

Now let us move into the East seat to see how things look to this player. This is the layout from his position:

DUMMY
♠ J 10 2
♡ A 6 4
◇ A 10 9 6 3
♣ 6 4

Opening lead: ♠ 3

EAST
♠ Q 8 7 4
♡ J 9 8 7
◇ K 8 5
♣ 3 2

When declarer has been thinking, East has been doing some thinking of his own. He too has decided that West has led from a four-card suit, leaving declarer with only two spades. In addition, while it may be relatively unimportant to this hand, he has been able to come to another conclusion—namely, that South has five clubs! This seemingly remarkable deduction is not really difficult to arrive at—it merely requires that East apply the same type of reasoning we saw the declarer apply earlier; that is, that West does not have more than four cards in any suit. If this is true, then West cannot have more than four clubs, marking South with five. (Of course, South could have *six* clubs, in which case he has opened an off-shape no-trump, but while this has been known to happen, it is wrong to count on it.)

Taking everything into account, it seems likely to East that South has precisely a 2-3-3-5 distribution, a standard no-trump pattern. Once having placed declarer with this distribution, it is easy for East to add his red-suit cards to those in the dummy and in declarer's hand and conclude that West has precisely three hearts and two diamonds, or a 4-3-2-4 pattern. Finally, East does the same kind of arithmetic that West did when he was considering his opening lead, and, adding his points to those in dummy and those presumed to be in declarer's hand, he places West with 8 or 9 high-card points.

It is hoped that the reader will forgive the foregoing deviation from the main point of the hand—what East is supposed to play at trick one—but it was included to show the wealth of information that can be gleaned from a perfectly ordinary opening lead. It may not be quite the same as the uncle who can tell you exactly where every card is as soon as the dummy goes down, but it comes close to it!

And now to the crux of the matter: should East cover the jack of spades or not? His first impulse may be to follow the old rule of "cover an honor with an honor," but he should restrain himself momentarily and ask whether this could be a situation where Blackwood's all-important Rule 13 applies. A brief review of what he has deduced thus far about the deal should provide him with a quick answer. He knows that South has only two spades, and these are either the ace and king alone, the ace and a low card, the king and a low card, or two low cards.

In the first case, putting up the queen would give declarer three spade tricks when he is entitled to only two, so East should not cover the jack. In the second case, it does not make any difference whether East covers or not, since South will always make two spade tricks if he holds the ace doubleton. In the third (and actual) case, covering with the queen will enable declarer to score his king in his hand and eventually the ten in dummy, while playing low will hold him to one trick. (Although dummy's jack wins at trick one, the king later falls to West's ace, and the ten then falls to East's queen.) Thus, only in the last case, where declarer holds two small spades, is it right to put up the queen. And since this is a very unlikely holding for an opening no-trump bidder to have, the odds clearly favor the play of the eight-spot (as a signal) at trick one, and not the queen.

Once East has refused to fall into South's trap, declarer is helpless.

Fig. 3-1 shows the entire hand.

Fig. 3-1

West	North	East
	♠ J 10 2 ♡ A 6 4 ◇ A 10 9 6 3 ♣ 6 4	
♠ A 9 5 3 ♡ Q 10 2 ◇ 7 2 ♣ K 10 8 5		♠ Q 8 7 4 ♡ J 9 8 7 ◇ K 8 5 ♣ 3 2
	♠ K 6 ♡ K 5 3 ◇ Q J 4 ♣ A Q J 9 7	

After winning the opening spade lead, declarer comes to his hand and tries the diamond finesse. East's spade return then enables the defense to take three tricks in that suit. Upon regaining the lead, declarer has no recourse but to try the club finesse, and goes down one when it fails.

On this deal, the information given by the opening lead—which is a form of signal—was more helpful to East than it was to the declarer, which is usually the case. South, looking at both his hand and the dummy's, knew exactly how many high-card points the opponents held and had a pretty good notion as to how the spade suit was divided. However, he knew less about the *distribution* of those high-card points and all four suits than did East. If there was an "uncle" present at this table at all, he was certainly seated in the East chair.

In the last chapter, I gave to the declarers of the world my favorite mnemonic device—COB—to help them with steps they should go through before they play to the first trick. The device can be just as useful to the defenders.

In my opinion, declarer's play and defender's play should be studied simultaneously, and the strategy employed by both sides should be carefully analyzed in order to learn the game well.

It is true that declarer has certain advantages because he is looking directly at twenty-six of the fifty-two cards. If he holds in his hand the K J 4 2 of a suit and sees in the dummy the Q 10 3, he knows he can knock out the enemy's ace and establish three tricks for himself by so doing. The *defenders* might not establish their tricks in this suit so quickly because each will be afraid to break the suit for fear of giving the declarer a soft trick. By the time it is obvious that such a suit must be led, it is frequently too late.

The defense has some advantages, however, and these become more evident when the COB procedure is applied. It is more difficult for the defenders to count the number of tricks they can win, but they *can* count points and they *can* count distribution. A defender can count the high-card points in the dummy and his own hand (C), review the bidding in his mind (B), and come close to visualizing the unseen hands so he will have a much better idea than declarer how the defenders' high cards are distributed.

The most powerful advantage that accrues to the defense is the privilege of making the opening lead (O). Being able to strike the first blow sometimes will enable a defender to destroy a declarer.

Both the declarer and the defender whose partner makes the opening lead have the opportunity, as soon as dummy is spread, to make assumptions as to what cards are in the unseen hands. First, let us examine a hand from declarer's point of view.

The bidding:

SOUTH	WEST	NORTH	EAST
1 ♡	Pass	2 ♣	Pass
2 ♡	Pass	3 ♡	Pass
4 ♡	Pass	Pass	Pass

Opening lead: ♠ 8

Declarer sees these 26 cards in his hand and the dummy:

DUMMY
♠ Q 9 5
♡ 9 7 5 2
◇ A 3 2
♣ A Q 2

DECLARER
♠ A J 2
♡ A Q 10 8 6
◇ Q 9
♣ 8 6 4

First, he examines the lead: It is not a fourth best lead, as there are four spades higher than the eight in his hand and the dummy. Low from three to an honor? That would give West the K 10 8. A most unlikely lead. A short suit lead? It appears to be either a singleton, a doubleton, or "top of nothing" from three. If this is true, it is almost a sure thing that South will have to lose one spade trick—unless East makes a mistake and puts up the king at trick one.

As for losers in the other suits—there may be as many as two heart losers, depending on the location of the king and jack of trumps. There is a sure diamond loser, but if the king of diamonds lies to the East, the queen may be established and the ace of diamonds used for a club or spade discard. Clubs? The club king had *better* be with West, or declarer is not going to reach dummy enough times to do all the work there is to be done on this hand.

There is a further possibility of saving a trick in the minors: if the club finesse works and the heart finesse works, West may be stripped of trumps and his other spade (if he led from a doubleton) and thrown on play with the third round of clubs. *Then,* if he had the king of diamonds, he would be end-played and have to lead away from that card or give a sluff and ruff late in the hand. So already, at trick one, declarer is visualizing the play of the entire hand.

He hopes West holds a hand such as:

♠ 8 4
♡ J 4
◇ K J 5 4
♣ K J 10 5 3

Meanwhile, East is also studying the dummy, analyzing the opening lead, and thinking as he looks at these cards:

DUMMY
♠ Q 9 5
♡ 9 7 5 2
◇ A 3 2
♣ A Q 2

EAST
♠ K 10 7 6
♡ J
◇ 10 8 7 6 5
♣ 10 9 5

"I have 4 high-card points, the dummy has 12, and declarer made no really strong bid during the auction, so he should have between 13 and 15 points . . . that leaves 9 to 11 points for my partner.

"The opening lead of the eight of spades is not a fourth best because I see the K Q 10 9 in my hand and the dummy. Partner does not have the ace of spades, for he does not underlead aces on opening leads against suit contracts. He cannot be leading from three to the jack because I can see the ten and the nine, therefore, declarer has both the ace and the jack of spades. Partner's lead is either singleton, doubleton, or high from three small. I don't believe it is a singleton, for that would give declarer an unmentioned five-card spade suit. If it is a doubleton, declarer has four spades and might well have opened the bidding with one spade with his minimum hand and four spades to the ace-jack. It is most likely that West and South have exactly three spades."

Having come to this conclusion, East does not have to be a genius to see that if he plays the king, South is going to take *three* tricks in spades and the defense will take *none.* If, on the other hand, he simply covers whatever card the dummy plays, South can take only *two* spade tricks, and the defense will take *one.* If dummy plays the five to trick one, East signals with the seven to encourage partner to lead spades again when he regains the lead.

Looking at the dummy and knowing partner has some 9 to 11 points, East feels reasonably certain that partner will be on lead again before long.

Fig. 3-2

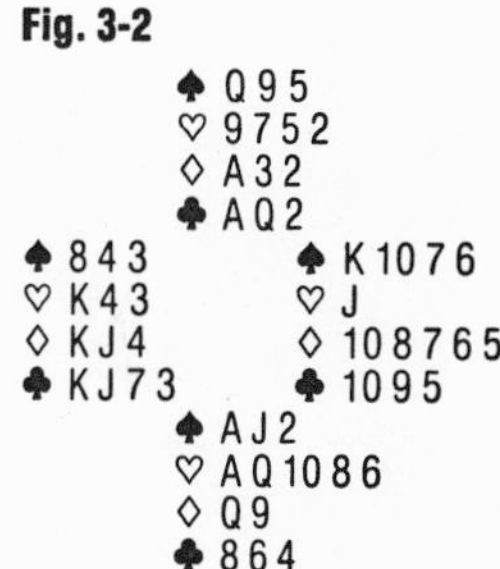

East also places South with a five- or six-card heart suit and four or five cards in the minors. A finesse in clubs will likely work, but any diamond finesse seems doomed to failure.

All this goes through East's mind while he looks at the dummy and before he plays to trick one. Most of the information is filed back in his memory for use later in the hand, but he must ferret out the details about the spade suit immediately because if he carelessly plays third-hand high, the contract will not be defeated. Fig. 3-2 illustrates the whole deal.

As you can see, declarer's dreams were not realized except for the club finesse. He had to lose a spade, a trump, a diamond, and a club. West had spades to get out with and could not be end-played. And East—holding the worst hand at the table—was the real hero because he applied Blackwood's thirteenth rule at trick one concerning the spade suit instead of following the ancient rule of third-hand high.

We hope we have convinced you that it is incorrect to play third-hand high in certain cases, and that by following blindly such old rules you will fail to defeat a large number of contracts.

Let us go into the subject with another hand. This hand deals with an instance where you are given the opportunity to win the first trick. There are times when you should defer winning until later. It is your choice, and certainly no blind following of an old saw from whist days is going to supplant your *theenking* out what is to your advantage.

You are East and have heard this bidding:

NORTH	EAST	SOUTH	WEST
1 ♢	1 ♠	2 ♣	Pass
3 ♣	Pass	3 NT	All Pass

Your partner leads the nine of spades and you are looking at your hand and this dummy:

DUMMY
♠ A 4
♡ K 6 4
♢ Q 10 9 5 3
♣ K Q 7

EAST
♠ K 8 7 6 3 2
♡ Q J 2
♢ A 2
♣ 10 9

Declarer calls for the low card from dummy and you have the choice of winning the trick or playing low. If you rush right in with your king of spades and continue the suit to knock out dummy's ace of spades, either you earn a very bad score at duplicate or you cost your side a bundle of points at rubber bridge. North-South will make four no-trump via two spades, two hearts, three diamonds, and three clubs.

Thinking at trick one would prevent this disaster, but what should you think about? Remember COB. Count the outstanding points; analyze the Opening lead; mentally review the Bidding.

Look back at the North and East hands and the bidding box given above and figure what point count South has for his bids of two clubs and three no-trump. It looks as if he has 10 to 13 high-card points (he went to the two level and took another bid, but he never made a really ambitious bid—like two no-trump at his first opportunity.) Give him 11 or 12 high-card points. Since the dummy has 14 and you have 10, your partner can have only 3 or 4.

You quickly realize after the dummy goes down that there are only four more spades you cannot see—the queen, jack, ten and five. Partner cannot have any of the first three (you surely can figure out why not), so he has led from the nine-five doubleton or the nine singleton. If the nine of spades is a singleton, you are probably not going to defeat the contract no matter what card you play at trick one. If the nine of spades is from the nine-five doubleton, you would like partner to be able to lead a second round of spades before your ace of diamonds is knocked out, in order to keep your entry for the long spade suit.

Therefore, when declarer calls for a low card from dummy at trick one, you preserve your king of spades, but you signal with the highest spade you can afford—in this case the eight—to tell partner to continue with spades if and when he gains the lead. Declarer wins the opening lead with the ten of spades (or jack or queen—it doesn't matter, *you* know he has all three of those cards) and leads a diamond toward dummy. Your partner wins the king of diamonds (hmmmm, there's 3 of his 3 or 4 high-card points) and leads the five of spades to dummy's blank ace. Now when a diamond is led from dummy, you will win your ace and your king of spades will drop South's last stopper in the suit. Your three small spades then will be good, and you will defeat the contract by two tricks.

Declarer will have seen through your strategy, however, and probably will try to salvage what he can by cashing out his club tricks. This is the whole hand:

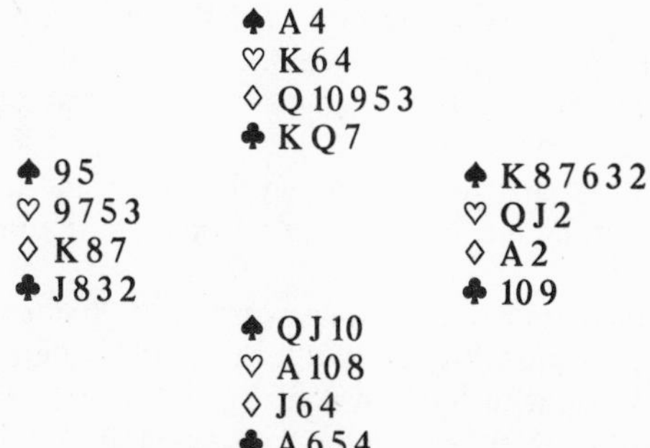

Declarer will be disappointed that clubs do not break, but notice that you have to discard a spade on the third lead of clubs (a heart pitch, of course, would give North-South three heart tricks). Now when South knocks out your ace of diamonds you have only the king of spades and two small spades to cash. However, you will still defeat the contract one trick.

Can you spot the other hero in this defensive saga? *West* also broke an old rule that goes all the way back to whist. When South led a diamond toward dummy at trick two, West flew right up there with his king of diamonds. If he had followed the rule of thumb from olden times, "second-hand low," declarer would have made ten tricks just as surely as he would have if you had played third-hand high at trick one.

THE OPENING LEAD—"WHAT IS IT?"

The opening leader's partner will be the first member of his team who can seriously apply the COB procedure because he is the first to get a look at the dummy and the opening lead, together with his hand. The first question he should ask himself is, "What is it?" This question applies to the opening lead. If the lead is an honor card, it does not tell much about how many cards there are in the suit, but it usually does tell something about what other honor cards are held, especially when it is not the lead of a suit you have bid. We have gone over the opening lead signals, and you are acquainted with them. For example, you will remember that when the queen is led, the possession of the king is denied, but usually the queen will be accompanied by the jack and often the ten-spot as well. For a review of the other possibilities, you may refer back to the chapter on opening leads.

When the card is a spot card (from the deuce through the nine), you, as the opening leader's partner, must try to put all of the pieces together to decide whether the card led is the highest card your partner holds in the suit (top of nothing) or whether it is a low card, implying that he holds some honors. Could it be a fourth best? Could it possibly be a lead from a three-card suit headed by an honor other than the ace? Usually, by studying the dummy and the bidding, you can come to some conclusion about this. That conclusion is very likely to tell you what you should play, and especially whether you should or should not play third-hand high.

Let us try to lay down some general rules that will be true more often than not concerning your actions once you have decided whether your partner's lead of a small card is the highest card he has in a suit or is a low card from either length or an honor.

First, let us assume that you decide that the lead is not the underlead of a four-card suit or an honor, but is either a singleton, doubleton, or a top of nothing.

You know immediately that whatever cards you do not see in that suit in your hand or the dummy higher than the one led by your partner are in the declarer's hand right in back of you. You usually do not play third-hand high unless you can either win the trick or establish the possibility of promoting a trick in your hand. You do know that you are not going to promote any tricks in your partner's hand by playing third-hand high. Of course, if you happen to hold the K Q x, you will play the queen because, after the ace is gone, your king will take a trick.

You will notice that when you are leading a card in a sequence, such as K Q x or K Q J, you always lead the highest card in the suit. When you are following suit you do exactly the opposite, and, if you are going to play a high card from a solid sequence, always play the card which is lowest in the sequence.

Now let us see what you do when you decide that the lead IS fourth best or a lead from three to an honor.

A great deal depends upon what you see in the dummy. If the dummy has no honor card at all, it usually pays to play your highest card. Your purpose is to promote the high cards in your partner's hand. If you held the king-queen yourself, you would automatically play the queen to make the king worth a trick. In the cases where your partner holds the king and you hold the queen, you must play the queen for exactly the same reason.

Fig. 3-3

DUMMY
♠ 4 2
♡ J 7 6
◇ A 7 6
♣ K 10 9 8 6

EAST
♠ 10 8 3
♡ K 9
◇ 9 8 5
♣ A Q 7 4 3

SOUTH	WEST	NORTH	EAST
1♠	Pass	1 NT	Pass
3♠	Pass	4♠	All Pass

Opening lead: ♡5

When the dummy does hold some honor cards, you may be able to promote your partner's high cards by not playing your highest, but by finding a lower card that will force declarer to play his high ones if he wishes to win the trick. Sometimes when you are convinced your partner has led fourth best, you can tell exactly what three cards your partner has which are higher than the one he had, and you can be guided accordingly.

Let's put ourselves in the position of the partner of the opening leader and see just what we can learn by applying the COB procedure (Fig. 3-3).

You look at the five of hearts, your hand, and the dummy, and the first question you ask yourself about your partner's lead is, "What is it?"

One thing you can be sure of—it is not a singleton. You are looking at exactly six hearts: the three in the dummy, the two in your hand, and the lead. If it is a singleton, South has seven hearts. Players with seven hearts don't bid one spade and then jump to three spades.

If it is the highest card in a suit, then your partner has either two or three hearts. Crediting him with three would still leave South with five cards in the suit, and I think you would agree that that holding is most unlikely.

No, the lead of the five of hearts is almost certainly the fourth best from a broken suit, and the Rule of Eleven will apply. There are six hearts higher than the five-spot in the three hands. In your hand and the dummy, you see five of these. This leaves the declarer with one heart higher than the five-spot. What is that card?

Your partner does not underlead aces against suit contracts, and so the one other card higher than the five is the ace. Presto, you know that declarer holds the ace of hearts.

Now, if you want to, you can tell exactly what three cards higher than the five-spot your partner holds. He does not hold the six-seven—you see those in the dummy. He holds those which you do not see between your hand and the dummy, and so his high cards must be exactly the Q 10 8.

Even before you decide which card to play on the first trick, there is another little bit of information which you really ought to tuck away in your memory, as it will be useful later on. South's jump is usually made with around 19 total points, of which about 17 are high cards. You know that between your hand and the dummy there are an additional 17 high-card points. This means your partner has about 6 high-card points, maybe 1 or 2 more or less, depending on the exact composition of South's hand. Now back to your play at trick one.

It is obvious that, if a low card is played from the dummy, your nine will force South to play the ace to win the trick. If dummy plays the jack, you can play the king, and your partner will have in his hand the two high cards in hearts. It is also obvious that, if dummy plays low and you play third-hand high, declarer will win the trick with the ace (which you know he holds) and later on his jack will become a trick. So at trick one, you just force him to win his ace of hearts, leaving your partner with two good hearts, and, as it happens, your application of the COB procedure will prevent declarer from making his contract.

Fig. 3-4 shows the entire setup.

Fig. 3-4

South should wind up winning six spade tricks, two diamond tricks, and one heart trick, for a total of nine—one short of the contract. Had you played third-hand high, he would have gotten an extra heart trick and would have come home with ten tricks.

Let's look at Fig. 3-5 for another one (you are still East).

Fig. 3-5 Dlr: S Vul: N-S

DUMMY
♠ K 7 6
♡ K J 4
♢ A 6 3 2
♣ K 7 2

EAST
♠ J 5 3
♡ 10 7 2
♢ K 9 5 4
♣ A 10 9

SOUTH	WEST	NORTH	EAST
2♡	Pass	4♡	All Pass

Opening lead: ♣4

South is using the so-called "weak" two bid. What is your partner's four of clubs? It certainly is not a singleton, for in that instance South would have started with six clubs. On the same reasoning, it probably is not the highest card of a doubleton, which would leave South with five clubs. And it positively is not the top of a three-card suit, as you see the two-spot in the dummy, making it impossible for your partner to hold two clubs smaller than the four-spot. No, almost certainly it is a fourth best. You know it is not fourth best from the ace or king because you see both of those cards. Neither is his suit headed by the queen and jack because when you lead a two-card sequence against a suit contract, you lead the highest card in the sequence, not fourth best. The most likely holding is that your partner has led from four or five cards, including either the queen or jack, but not both.

When dummy plays low as you put on your nine-spot, is there any chance that declarer will win this trick with a singleton queen or jack? You know this is impossible because your partner simply cannot hold the six cards which he would have to hold for South to hold a singleton—if the four-spot is his fourth best and he holds six cards, he would have to hold two cards smaller than the four-spot, and we have decided that cannot be.

Knowing the declarer has either the queen or jack and either one or two more cards, you can figure he is going to take at least one trick in clubs no matter how you play. You can also figure that, if he has the queen rather than the jack, he will take two tricks in the suit if you win with the ace, but only one trick if you play the nine keeping the ace-ten over his king.

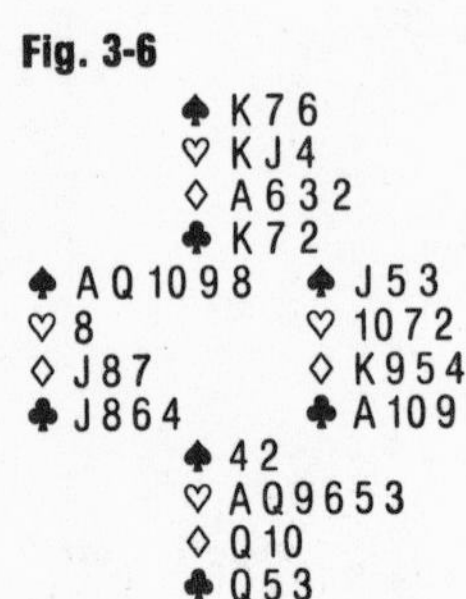

There seems to be no place to take any discards, so you decide your club trick will never get away, and you play the nine.

While you are at it, it will only take a second to tell about how strong your partner's hand is in high cards. Your vulnerable opponent's weak two bid indicated he had about 10 or 11 high-card points. Between your hand and the dummy, you are looking at 22 high-card points. This means that your partner has about 7 or 8 high-card points. Fig. 3-6 indicates the entire deal.

You put in the nine-spot, and the declarer wins with the queen, meaning that the only high card your partner had in the club suit was the jack. This increases the chance that among his 7 or 8 high-card points is an ace. If so, he can regain the lead and lead another club. With you and the dummy holding three of the honor cards in the trump suit, it seems more likely that declarer's weak two bid included the ace of trumps, leaving your partner with the ace of spades.

Fig. 3-7

DUMMY
♠ A 7 2
♡ 7 3 2
◇ A 10 5
♣ 7 6 4 2

EAST
♠ Q J 10 9 6
♡ J
◇ K 8 3
♣ J 10 8 5

SOUTH	WEST	NORTH	EAST
1♡	Pass	1 NT	Pass
2◇	Pass	2♡	Pass
3♡	Pass	4♡	All Pass

Opening lead: ♣K

At trick two, declarer goes to the dummy with the king of hearts, and leads the two of diamonds. You rise with the king and reach your partner's hand with the ace of spades. He leads another club, giving your side two club tricks, a diamond trick, and a spade trick.

Fig. 3-7 is another hand.

On this hand, your partner's lead of the king of clubs shows that he has either the queen or the ace. If he is leading from the ace-king, you do not want him to continue the suit in case South happens to hold three cards to the queen. On reflection, you come to the conclusion that, if your partner has both the ace and the king, South can not hold three cards to the queen. For South to have this holding, your partner would have had to start with only two clubs, and if his two clubs are the ace and king, his lead would have been the ace and not the king. If South does have the queen of clubs, it is either a singleton or a doubleton.

Reviewing the bidding should give you a bit more information. South certainly bid like a man who had exactly five hearts. If this is true, your partner has four hearts in his hand, and there is always the chance that by encouraging your partner to continue leading clubs, you can shorten declarer and promote a small trump trick in your partner's hand. South bid like a man who had about 16 high-card points, which added to the 16 you see in your hand and the dummy comes to 32. This means your partner has about 8 high-card points. So whether your partner has led from the king-queen or the ace-king, you want to encourage the continuation of the suit, so you play the eight-spot.

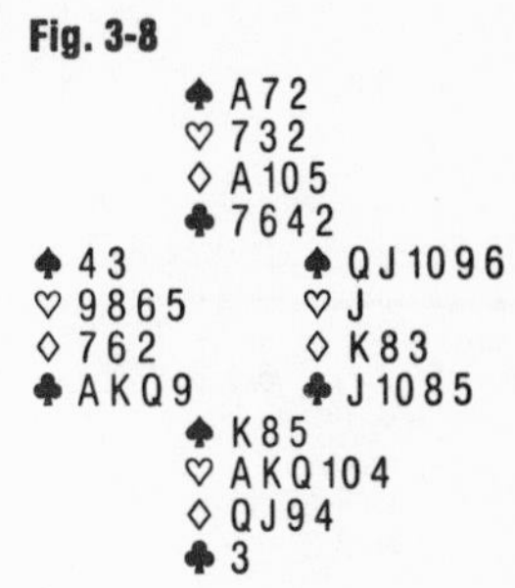

Let's look at the entire deal in Fig. 3-8.

Looking at the north and south hands, it is hard to see how declarer is going to lose more than three tricks. With your jack falling helplessly when the ace is played, it looks like he has five heart tricks plus two spade tricks plus three diamond tricks, leaving for your side only one club trick, one diamond trick, and one spade trick. However, if you and your partner continue leading clubs every time you gain the lead, you will finally reach the point where your partner has more trumps than declarer, and he will come to the setting trick in the trump suit. The key decision in this hand was not difficult to make: it was deciding that it was impossible for South to hold three clubs to the queen.

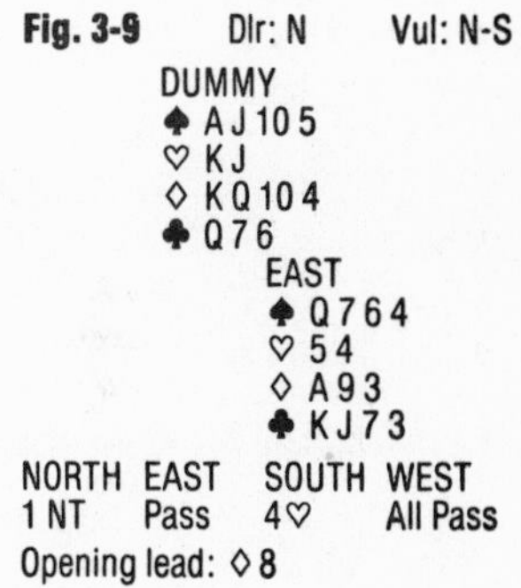

Fig. 3-9 is another example.

South's jump to four hearts was not very helpful. We do know he almost certainly has six or more hearts, and he has advertised a distributional hand. This sort of bidding is usually made with between 7 and 10 high-card points, depending on how long the trump suit is. Looking at the 26 points in the dummy and your hand, you can at least come to the conclusion that your partner must have from 4 to 7 high-card points.

The important problem, however, concerns itself not with how many high-card points your partner has, but with his lead of the eight of diamonds. WHAT IS IT?

You can easily be sure that it is the highest diamond your partner holds—the only honor card you do not see is the jack, and the eight cannot be low from three to the jack because you are looking at the nine and ten. It must therefore be either a singleton or the highest card of a two- or three-card suit.

Should it be a singleton, you want to play the ace and give your partner an immediate ruff. However, if that eight of diamonds is a singleton, then South has not only an awful lot of hearts, but he also has a five-card diamond suit. While it is possible that this is his holding, it is a better view that he does not have as many as five diamonds, since he jumped straight to four hearts. He might easily have four of them, however, in which event your partner has led from a doubleton.

Partners who lead short suits often have quick tricks in trumps. There is no reason why among your partner's collection of high cards there cannot be included the ace of trump. If so, you do not want to take the ace of diamonds at the first trick because your partner, with a doubleton, cannot trump your return. Having no quick entry elsewhere, you want to

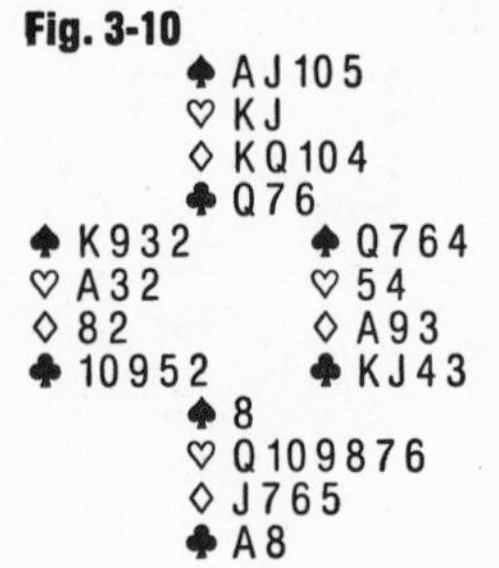

maintain communication and urge your partner to lead diamonds again, if he does indeed gain the lead before his trumps are exhausted. And, knowing that South almost certainly has at least three diamonds, it is unlikely that your ace of diamonds is going to get lost if you don't take it at trick one.

You play the nine-spot to encourage your partner to continue diamonds when and if he gains the lead.

South wins the first trick with the jack of diamonds and leads a heart. Your partner promptly jumps up with the ace of hearts and leads the two of diamonds. That lead of the two-spot takes all questions out of the diamond suit. With a short suit, your partner plays the two-spot on the second lead of the suit only when he started with only two cards. You take the ace and return a diamond for your partner to trump.

You will take two trump tricks in addition to your ace of diamonds, and, eventually, you must come to a club trick.

Fig. 3-11 is another one.

Fig. 3-11 Dlr: E Vul: N-S

North: ♠ 8 ♡ A 10 8 7 ◇ Q 8 7 ♣ 8 7 6 5 4

West: ♠ 6 4 3 ♡ K J 9 4 3 ◇ J 10 9 6 ♣ 9

East: ♠ K 10 9 7 5 2 ♡ Q 2 ◇ A K 2 ♣ 3 2

South: ♠ A Q J ♡ 6 5 ◇ 5 4 3 ♣ A K Q J 10

EAST	SOUTH	WEST	NORTH
1 ♠	Dbl	2♠	3♡
Pass	Pass	Dbl	Pass
Pass	4♣	Pass	5♣
Pass	Pass	Dbl	All Pass

Opening lead: ♠6

It is a good thing that this chapter is not on the subject of bidding, or I might have a lot of explaining to do about the above hand. Let's just say that you and I do not agree with all of it and get on with the important question of how East knows not to play his king of spades after West opens with the six. As you and I can plainly see, if East does play his king, South will get two discards, and, if he is able to get rid of two diamonds in the dummy, he is going to make five clubs. After all, East knows that West raised spades, and, assuming that East and West are bidding four-card majors, it is not *altogether usual* for your partner to give a raise with three small trumps. And, in case West has underled the queen, it is essential for East to go up with his king to promote that card and keep South from winning a cheap trick with the jack.

However, if East believes the signal given by West's lead of the six of spades, he knows that South is sitting there with exactly three spades and that they are precisely the A Q J. Obviously, the six is not a fourth best, as East can see five spades higher than the six-spot in his hand and the dummy, and, were it the fourth best, West would have all of the spades higher than the six-spot. This would include the ace. Holding it, West would have led it.

Looking at all intermediate cards between the six and jack, East can tell that the six-spot is not small from three to the jack, nor is it from three to the queen. And, of course, if West held the Q J 6, his opening lead would be the queen. However, West did raise, and he must have at least three spades to do this. This leaves South with exactly three, and, since West has neither the ace, the queen, nor the jack, those are the three cards South holds.

So East carefully preserves his king of spades, leaving South with only one discard from dummy. Eventually, South will lose a heart and two diamonds.

The proper time for you to apply the COB procedure is after you see the dummy and *before* you play at trick one. No matter how quickly the declarer plays from the dummy, take your time.

South bid like a man with about 18 to 19 high-card points. Add this to the 16 high-card points you see, and you can decide your partner has about 4 or 5 high-card points. Now take a good look at that lead of the seven of spades. What is it?

For sure, it is not the highest card of a short suit. If your partner started with three spades, South started with seven of them. No, that seven of spades is a fourth best. The Rule of Eleven tells you that South has exactly one spade higher than the seven-spot. He did jump to two no-trump for his second bid, and so that one card is much more likely to be the ace or the queen than the ten or eight. With this information, you know that your partner's three top spades are either the Q 10 8 or the A 10 8.

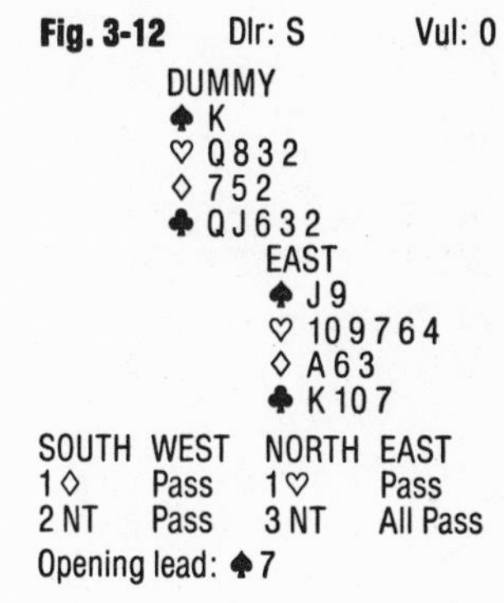

Fig. 3-12 Dlr: S Vul: 0
DUMMY
♠ K
♡ Q 8 3 2
◊ 7 5 2
♣ Q J 6 3 2
EAST
♠ J 9
♡ 10 9 7 6 4
◊ A 6 3
♣ K 10 7
SOUTH WEST NORTH EAST
1 ◊ Pass 1 ♡ Pass
2 NT Pass 3 NT All Pass
Opening lead: ♠ 7

But, for heaven sakes, how many spades does your partner have? Of course, South might have overlooked a four-card spade suit and jumped to two no-trump, but it isn't often done. If we give South three spades, West has led from a seven-card suit! Do you have partners who refuse to bid with seven-card suits?

Now, if South has the ace of spades, it makes not a bit of difference which one you play at trick one. But, if your partner has the ace and South has three to the queen, it makes all the difference in the world. You had better get that jack out of your hand, so that you will have the nine-spot to lead to your partner's ace-ten. Otherwise, South can let your jack hold the next spade trick and block the suit.

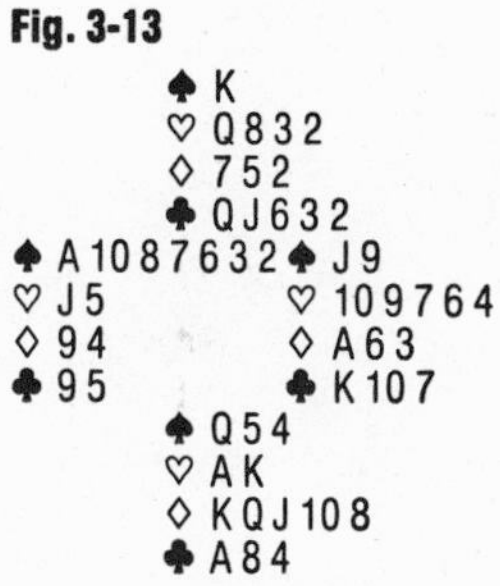

Poor South! He should either hate me for writing this book or hate you for reading it. You have played the jack on the first trick, and, before he has taken too many tricks, you are going to get into the lead and lead your nine of spades. In spite of the fact that he and his side held 27 high-card points, you and your partner are going to take more tricks than he does. And, of course, if you had not stopped to think at trick one, but had simply dropped your nine under the king it looks like he could have ended up with about ten tricks to your three.

But the opening lead is only the first of many signals which the two defenders may give to each other during the play of the hand. These other signals can sometimes prove just as effective as the opening lead signals. Let's have a look at them.

SIGNAL CARDS

Among the thirteen cards held by a defender, there are a number with which he cannot expect to take tricks. A wise defender will try to put these cards to work by using them as signals to his partner. He will use them to tell partner what suit to lead or not to lead, and he will describe his distribution or high-card holding so that, as play progresses, each defender may gain for himself the advantages the declarer automatically has by seeing his twenty-six cards in combination.

Usually these cards that cannot be expected to take tricks will be smaller ones, and we will refer to them as "signal cards." Only in rare instances will a card higher than a jack be used to give a signal.

Signals frequently involve not only the *size* of the card played, but in many instances the *order* in which they are played. There are six signals which are standard the world over. They are

1. The echo
2. The trump echo
3. The length signal
4. The down-and-out signal
5. The queen signal
6. The suit preference signal

Declarer, as well as the partner of the signaler, will be watching these signals and there are times when the information given will be more helpful to the declarer than to the defense. Most of the time, however, the signals will be more helpful to the defenders. If a defender determines that declarer might be helped more by the signal than his partner, he should not give the signal. There is no formula for deciding whether a signal should or should not be given—you must use judgment. In other words, theenk.

The opening lead is the first signal given by a defender. This really should be considered the seventh signal. We have already discussed it at length, and will not take it up again at this time. We will discuss, in turn, each of the six standard signals.

The Echo The oldest and most generally understood signal is the echo. Giving your partner an echo means playing (to two rounds of one suit) your signal cards in a particular order—a higher one followed by a lower one. For example, these could be the nine-spot followed by the deuce, or the trey followed by the deuce. The echo in this sense applies to any suit which is not trump. The echo in the trump suit has a different meaning which will be discussed separately.

The echo can be used either in following suit or discarding. It simply says, "Partner, please lead the suit in which I gave an echo."

It is not always possible to complete an echo, as there may be times when you will be able to discard or follow with only one card in the suit. In this instance, you simply play the highest card you can afford without costing a defensive trick. If you are able to make only one discard, the play of a high spot will suggest to partner that you have done your best by starting an echo. Likewise, the discard of a deuce would tell your partner you are not interested in having that particular suit led.

Fig. 3-14

When your partner leads the king of a suit from the ace-king, you do not echo simply because you have a doubleton in the suit. You echo only if you want him to continue the suit. Take the hand in Fig. 3-14.

Sitting East against a four heart contract, your partner leads the king of diamonds. You know the lead of the king is from the ace-king because you can see the queen in the dummy. However, you also notice that you have a sure trump trick whether you trump a diamond or not. If the ten of hearts is led from the board, you simply cover with the jack and guarantee yourself a trump trick. Therefore, trumping a diamond will gain you nothing—but you are most anxious for partner to lead a spade. So you play the three of diamonds, telling partner not to cash his ace. Looking at dummy, West does not have to be a genius to know his best chance is to lead spades. He will lead the ten of spades, and now you're going to set the hand. If declarer finesses the queen, you will collect one spade trick, two diamonds, and a trump. Declarer may rise with the ace of spades, hoping to cash two hearts and then discard a spade on dummy's high clubs. This will not work either, as West will be able to trump the third club, and your side will have not only your trump trick, but also partner's ruffing trick.

Had you played the eight of diamonds and had your partner continued with the ace of diamonds, you could then have trumped the third diamond, but that would have been all the tricks your side would have taken. Declarer would regain the lead, no matter what you returned. His trumps would be solid, and his losing spade could be discarded on a club or a diamond after your side was exhausted of trumps.

Fig. 3-15 is an example of the echo in its simplest form.

Fig. 3-15

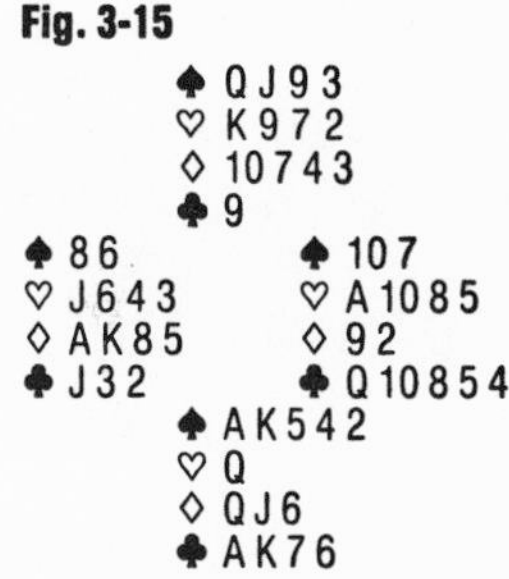

South opens one spade and, after partner bids two spades, jumps to game. West leads the king of diamonds, and you, East, have to decide whether you want the suit continued. In this case you *do* want diamonds continued. Hopefully your partner has no more than four diamonds and you can trump the third round of the suit. Note you have no natural trump trick this time. A smart declarer may try to confuse the issue by dropping the jack of diamonds under the king, but partner should believe you and continue with the ace of diamonds. When you play the two of diamonds, West should not be fooled, even if declarer now drops his queen of diamonds. Since he knows you want the suit continued, he leads a third diamond which you ruff. Then you must cash the ace of hearts to set the contract because, if you wait for two heart tricks, South's losing heart will disappear on dummy's good ten of diamonds.

There are times when you don't have a useless high card in the suit you want partner to lead, but you can still tell him what *not* to lead. For example, look at Fig. 3-16.

The defenders' problem is to defeat a five club contract. West leads the ten of diamonds. Declarer tries a deceptive play by winning with dummy's ace. East plays the two of diamonds, saying, "Partner, please don't lead that again!" At the second trick, a club is led to South's king. West decides South must have five clubs for his bidding, so he delays taking his ace to see what sort of signal he can get from his partner concerning the major suits. South continues with a small club, and this time West wins with the ace. If East had time to discard the three and two of spades in that order, he could ask for a spade lead. However, East figures he will not have a chance to play both of these cards before declarer regains the lead, and the three-spot certainly would not look like a come-on. But he does

Fig. 3-16

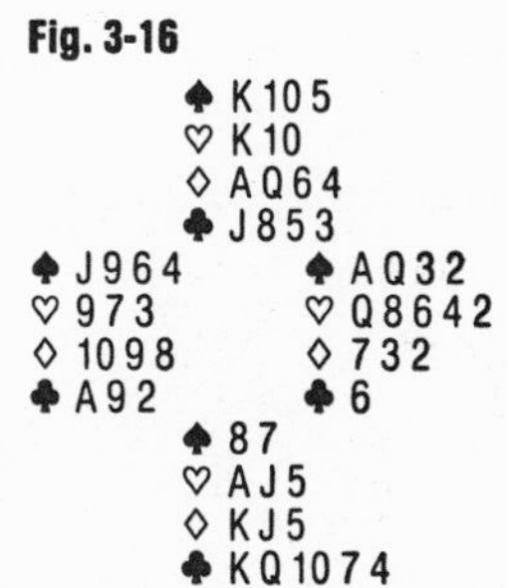

have an alternative—he discards the two of hearts, saying "Partner, do not lead the heart suit!" West gets the message. He knows that to lead a third trump would accomplish nothing, so he leads the four of spades, allowing East to win his two tricks in that suit and set the contract.

As previously pointed out, these regular classic echoes apply only to suits which are not trump. An echo in the trump suit is for an entirely different purpose, which will be discussed next.

The Trump Echo Playing first a middle card and following with a low one in the trump suit says, "Partner, I have a trump left." Usually it also says, "Furthermore, I can trump something, and the trump I have left is otherwise useless."

Fig. 3-17

After South opened the bidding with one spade, North-South bid briskly to get to four spades and then ran out of gas. West made the desperation lead of his singleton club and struck gold.

East won the ace of clubs and led back a club for West to trump. Not knowing whether information about his trump holding would be of value to partner or not, but knowing it could not possibly hurt, West carefully trumped with the four of spades. He got out with a diamond, and East's queen of diamonds fell to declarer's ace. South led the king of spades next, and East was in with the ace. On this trick West carefully played his three of spades. This play of the four followed by the three told East that his partner still had a trump left, so he led another club for West to ruff for the setting trick.

Had West carelessly trumped with the three and then followed suit with the four, he would have guaranteed that he had no more trumps. East, when in with the ace of spades, would have led the ten of diamonds, hoping against hope that his partner held the king of diamonds.

The trump echo is usually made when holding exactly three trumps. Some signal-mad players show high-low in trumps every time they hold three trumps, even when there is no suit they can ruff. This is not recommended because the information given is likely to be more useful to the declarer than to your partner. Unless you are quite sure it will help your partner to know you have three trumps, I recommend that you reserve this signal for those times when you can use an otherwise worthless trump to ruff something.

As I noted, this signal is usually employed when you hold exactly three trumps, but it may be used in some rare cases when you have four small trumps which will not otherwise be of value to you. Generally speaking, when a defender holds four trumps, he is better off to play a forcing game —that is, he should try to locate declarer's short suit and force him to ruff. But say you hold the 6 4 3 2 of trumps and want to ruff something. You should carefully trump first with the four, then with the three, and then with the two. When the two finally shows up, your partner will realize that you still have one more trump.

The Length Signal Under proper circumstances, the high-low play ceases to be an echo or a come-on and becomes an integral part of the length signal. There is a conventional situation in which a high-low signal is given not to denote an interest in the suit, but to indicate an *even number* of cards in that suit.

A rather simple convention, it is most useful when a defensive holdup play must be employed. When it is obvious, for example, that declarer is trying to establish a long suit in the dummy (which has no outside entries) and that one defender is going to have a problem as to when he should take his ace, the other defender gives a *high-low* signal when holding *two* or *four* cards of that suit; where he has *three* cards of that suit, he plays his *lowest* card on the first lead of the suit.

This signal is normally used to enable a partnership to destroy communications between declarer's and dummy's hands. Fig. 3-18 is a typical case.

Fig. 3-18

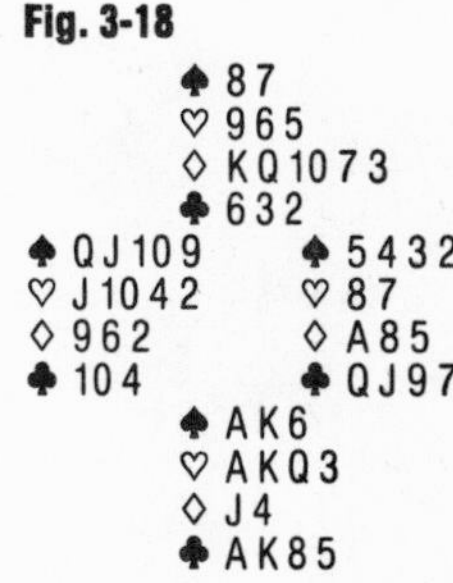

South, declarer at three no-trump, wins the opening spade lead and attacks diamonds. East can see that the only possible entry to dummy is the diamond suit itself. He wants to take his ace of diamonds at the precise trick when South runs out of diamonds. To do this he needs to know South's length in diamonds. The responsibility is on West to give the answer to that question. When he has an even number of cards in the key suit, he plays high-low; when he has an odd number, he plays low-high. When the jack of diamonds is led, West plays the two of diamonds, a guarantee of an odd number of diamonds. East knows that odd number has to be one or three. If West holds a singleton diamond, then South has four cards in the suit and communications cannot be broken. However, if West holds three diamonds, South has to have precisely two, so the second diamond should be taken. If East takes the first diamond or waits for the third one, South will come to his nine tricks.

This length signal is used more often at no-trump than where there is a trump suit, but there are exceptions. If dummy is entryless or if entries have been removed, one of the defenders still may need to know when to taken his high card of a long running suit in the dummy. Fig. 3-19 is an example.

Fig. 3-19 Dlr: S Vul: B

North: ♠ K 6 5 ♡ 10 9 ◊ 8 7 4 ♣ K Q J 10 7

West: ♠ 9 2 ♡ K Q J 6 4 ◊ Q 9 3 2 ♣ 8 2

East: ♠ A 7 3 ♡ 8 7 5 3 ◊ 10 6 5 ♣ A 9 4

South: ♠ Q J 10 8 4 ♡ A 2 ◊ A K J ♣ 6 5 3

SOUTH	WEST	NORTH	EAST
1♠	Pass	2♣	Pass
2 NT	Pass	3♠	Pass
4♠	Pass	Pass	Pass

Opening lead: ♡ K

South wins the first heart lead with the ace of hearts and—trying to preserve the king of spades as an entry to dummy—leads the queen of spades. East refuses to go for this. He wants to take his ace of trumps only when the king of spades is gone from dummy or when he can remove it, so he ducks. South continues with the jack of spades. East wins and returns a spade to dummy's king of spades. Dummy leads the king of clubs. East ducks, and West plays the eight of clubs. East knows this is the start of a signal showing an *even* number of cards in the suit. If that even number is *four,* South not only has played the suit in a strange fashion, but has bid two no trump with a singleton club. It appears that West is showing precisely two clubs. That means South holds three clubs, and East should not take his ace until the third lead of the suit. When East refuses to take the second club, South abandons the suit and tries the losing diamond finesse, but has to lose one trick in each suit for down one. If East wins the first or second club lead, South can win the diamond or heart return, enter dummy with a club, and shed his jack of diamonds to make the contract.

Fig. 3-20

```
            ♠ J 10 8
            ♡ 9 3 2
            ◇ Q J 10
            ♣ A K 8 3
♠ 6 5                 ♠ 7 3
♡ 10 8 7 6 4          ♡ K Q J
◇ 9 2                 ◇ A K 7 6 5
♣ Q 10 9 6            ♣ J 7 5
            ♠ A K Q 9 4 2
            ♡ A 5
            ◇ 8 4 3
            ♣ 4 2
```

The Down-and-Out Signal Whenever a defender, for any reason, has played his highest card from a three-card suit, his subsequent play in the same suit should always be the middle card and not the lowest one.

This differs from the procedure with a four-card suit where his second play, had he played the highest one on an earlier trick, would be his original fourth best. This play from a three-card holding is known as the *down and out signal.* It is used to help your partner count the unseen hands.

East dealt and opened the bidding with one diamond. In short order, South became declarer at four spades. West duly opened his partner's suit and, holding only two diamonds, properly led the nine of diamonds. East won with the king, and South, in an effort to deceive someone, dropped his eight of diamonds. This was really a foolish play and made his probable defeat almost a certainty. Consider how this play appeared to East:

If South really had the singleton eight of diamonds, West held 9 4 3 2 and would have led his fourth best, not the nine-spot. East therefore continued with the ace of diamonds. South played the four, and West played the deuce. The three-spot was missing, but East *knew* his partner was now out of diamonds. *How?* Had West started with the 9 3 2 of diamonds, his second play would have been the missing *three-spot*—remember the second play from a three-card holding is the middle card, not the lowest.

West ruffed East's diamond continuation, and South still had to lose a heart.

The play probably would have taken the same form had South not made that foolish falsecard of the eight of diamonds at trick one. However, East might have had some concern about leading the ace of diamonds because he would not have known before trick two whether his partner started with a doubleton diamond or three of them. East might have considered the necessity for establishing a heart trick before he set up a diamond in dummy. It was declarer's apparent determination to deceive him that made him feel more secure in continuing with the second diamond.

Both defenders, not just the opening leader, should follow this down-and-out policy. When either has played his highest card from a three-card holding, the next play in the same suit should be the middle one.

Let us examine in Fig. 3-21 the various things a thoughtful defender can learn about a hand from the clues he gathers.

Fig. 3-21 Dlr: S Vul: 0

```
         NORTH
         ♠ Q 5 2
         ♡ 10
         ◇ K Q J 7
         ♣ K Q 5 4 3
WEST
♠ J 9 6 4
♡ K J 8 7 3
◇ 9 3
♣ J 6
```

SOUTH	WEST	NORTH	EAST
1♣	Pass	1◇	Pass
1 NT	Pass	3♣	Pass
3 NT	Pass	Pass	Pass

Opening lead: ♡7

East won the ace of hearts, as South played the four of hearts. East returned with the six of hearts, covered by the nine, and West won the jack of hearts. Dummy discarded a small spade. At first glance it looks as if declarer has the lone queen of hearts because he might have bid hearts at the one level if he had four of them. If declarer does in fact have the lone queen of hearts, then West should take the balance of his heart tricks and set the hand before giving up the lead. But it is a better policy to put more trust in messages sent by your partner than in the opponent's bidding. Let's work out what the holding is likely to be considering that East returned specifically the six of hearts.

So far you have seen, in your own hand and the quitted tricks, ten of the thirteen hearts in the deck. The missing cards are the queen, the five, and the two. There is no possible way you can place any combination of these cards in your partner's hand to make the six a fourth best lead. (With A Q 6 5 or A Q 6 5 2, he would lead back the five; with A Q 6 2 or A 6 5 2 he would lead back the deuce.) Therefore, East has *at most* three hearts. That means South *has* bypassed a four-card heart suit to rebid one no-trump, but it's not likely he passed up the chance to show a *five-card* heart suit at the one-level. So we are morally certain the heart suit was distributed 5–4–3–1, and that partner has exactly one more heart.

Because of these calculations, we cannot affort to lay down the king of hearts in the hope of dropping the queen and running the suit, for we have definitely concluded that South started with four hearts, including the queen. Cashing the king of hearts now would establish South's queen for a trick and would take the last heart out of partner's hand. You want your partner to get in again so he can lead through declarer's queen. Is it going to be possible?

Go back and remember that South's first rebid was one no-trump. This would show 12, 13, or 14 high-card points, since the modern tendency is to open one no-trump with a balanced hand and 15 high-card points. Looking at dummy, you see 13 high-card points, so, if South has 12 or 13, the opponents have 25 or 26. The six points in your own hand bring the total to 31 or 32. That leaves your partner with eight or nine points. He has already played the ace of hearts, so he has four or five points left. If South started with 14, then your partner will have only three points left.

You can see by checking the dummy that your partner can hold no high card in the minors save the ace. If the ace of diamonds or the ace of clubs is in partner's hand, it is not likely to get shut out, as you do not see where declarer can possibly bring in nine tricks without finally giving your partner the lead with whichever minor suit ace he happens to hold. If declarer holds both of these aces, it is virtually certain that he will run nine tricks in the minors as soon as he obtains the lead. So you decide to hope your partner has the ace of spades. If he holds not the ace but the king, then South has all three aces and is going to make his game no matter what you do. Fig. 3-22 is the entire setup.

Fig. 3-22

The Suit Preference Signal The suit preference signal is a defensive device that enables a player to indicate a desire to have his partner lead one suit rather than another when his partner has a choice. This signal has been a great help to players who thoroughly understand it and use it properly, but it has been a disaster to those who try to use it without full understanding.

The suit preference signal allows you to tell partner the suit you would like him to lead even when you are unable to play a card from that particular suit as a come-on. In this situation your partner usually will have a choice of exactly two suits. *(The signal never applies to the trump suit or to the suit led to the current trick, so it is designed to guide partner's choice strictly between the other two suits.)* Your play of a conspicuously high card in a suit your partner has led (when it is not conceivably the start of an echo) asks partner to choose the higher ranking of these two suits. The

Fig. 3-23

West	North	East
	♠ Q 7	
	♡ Q 5 4	
	◇ K Q J 10	
	♣ K Q J 10	
♠ J 8 2		♠ 10 6
♡ A K 9 6 3		♡ 8 7
◇ 4 2		◇ 9 8 7 6 3
♣ A 4 2		♣ 9 8 7 6
	♠ A K 9 5 4 3	
	♡ J 10 2	
	◇ A 5	
	♣ 5 3	

play of a conspicuously low card asks partner to lead the lower ranking suit. Note the emphasis on the word "conspicuous." The use of suit preference signals is not a substitution for the old-fashioned echo. The echo is by far the more important signal because it comes up more often. The suit preference signal supplements the echo—it does not replace it.

With South playing four spades, West led the king of hearts. Partner started an echo by playing the eight of hearts, and so West continued with the ace of hearts, and, when East followed with the seven of hearts, completing the echo, West felt certain his partner could trump the third heart. Before the days of the suit preference signal, West would have done well to lay down his ace of clubs before leading a heart for his partner to trump. Otherwise, after partner trumped the heart, he would see identical holdings in dummy's minor suits and he could not possibly have the slightest idea whether to lead a club or a diamond. However, since the days of suit preference, West can lead the third heart and tell East what suit to return just by taking care which heart he leads.

If West had no preference, he would lead his regular fourth best, the six of hearts, for East to ruff. However, West had a decided choice. Only clubs and diamonds were considered, since neither the suit in play nor trumps ever is involved. In order to get a diamond return, West would play his highest heart. In this case, the play of the nine, the most conspicuous heart West could play, would send the message: "Return the *higher ranking* of the two suits we are considering." In reality, he wanted clubs returned, so he led the three of hearts, a conspicuously low heart. East trumped this with the six of spades and, thankful for the suit preference signal, returned a club. West continued with a fourth heart that East trumped with the 10 of spades, forcing out declarer's king of spades. This eventually promoted a trump trick for West's jack of spades. The suit preference signal enabled the defenders to defeat the hand two tricks.

Fig. 3-24

West	North	East
	♠ K 9 7 6	
	♡ J 6 3	
	◇ 7 6	
	♣ Q J 4 3	
♠ 10 8 5		♠ 3
♡ 9 8 7 4		♡ A Q 5 2
◇ 10 8 4 3		◇ Q 9 5 2
♣ A K		♣ 10 9 6 5
	♠ A Q J 4 2	
	♡ K 10	
	◇ A K J	
	♣ 8 7 2	

Fig. 3-24 is a hand where a combination of signals enabled the defenders to find the right plays to break what looked like an ironclad contract.

You sit East defending against four spades, and partner leads the ace of clubs. When dummy comes down, you wonder what has happened to those good leads your partner has been making. It appears he is off on the wrong foot this time, so you play the five of clubs, showing no interest in the suit. Then your partner ignores you and leads the king of clubs! Partner's play guarantees he is now void in clubs. If you can gain the lead, you can return a club for partner to trump. But how can partner find out what suit to lead? The answer is—you must tell him.

On the king of clubs, you play a conspicuously high club—the highest one you have—the ten-spot. The only suits under consideration are hearts and diamonds because the suit preference signal applies neither to the suit being led nor to trumps. Since the play of a conspicuously high card says lead the higher ranking of the other two suits, your partner leads a heart to your ace. You win and lead back a club for him to trump, setting the contract.

I have already mentioned the danger that arises in using suit preference signals. Some partners may take every card you play as a suit preference signal. They may even think suit preference has replaced the old-fashioned echo—not so. Properly used, the suit preference signal does not interfere with conventional encouraging and discouraging plays and discards. The signal is a suit preference signal only when it could not conceivably be the start of an echo.

How can you and partner tell the difference? Review the bidding in your mind, consider all the cards you can see, and usually you can work it out.

The Queen Signal While the queen should never be used to start an echo, the queen *can* be a signal card under very special circumstances. When you play a queen under partner's lead of the king, you are delivering a precise message. You are asking partner not to cash his ace, but to lead a small card so you can ruff it or win it with the jack. In any event, you will gain the lead. Obviously this play of the queen under your partner's king is made only when the queen is a singleton or when you have the jack of the suit to assure that you take the second trick when a low card is led. It is best made when you think a lead from your side of the table will be advantageous. Take the hand in Fig. 3-25.

The bidding makes it obvious to East that a club lead from his side might be highly advantageous. Since South can't have more than two hearts, East needs to deliver his message in a hurry. The play of the queen of hearts under partner's king of hearts guarantees he holds either the jack of hearts or no more hearts, and it urges partner to lead a small heart so East can obtain the lead.

When *East* wins the second heart and switches to clubs, the defenders take four tricks before declarer ever gains the lead. If *West* holds the second heart, partner never gets the chance to lead through clubs. So the defenders get only one club trick because two of South's club losers go off on dummy's long diamonds.

WE now begin a detailed study of the various techniques declarer uses to develop tricks not available from high cards and long solid suits. The first technique is our old friend, the finesse. No matter what the books tell you about avoiding finesses, the finesse is still the greatest little trick-taker of all. The same writers who tell you how to avoid taking finesses use them like crazy themselves. Of course, whenever there's a play that gives you a *better* chance of developing tricks, the superior play should be used. But you shouldn't rely on such plays on *most* hands.

Some players regard the finesse as the simplest of all bridge plays. In some circumstances it is exactly that, but the technique can become complex and difficult.

Let's start by defining the finesse and then look at the various forms it takes.

A finesse is an attempt to win a trick with a card lower ranking than one held by an opponent. Sometimes you may hope to win all the tricks available in a suit; on other occasions you hope to gain a trick with a lower ranking card after giving up one (or more).

1.	DUMMY A Q	2.	DUMMY K 3
	DECLARER 3 2		DECLARER 4 2

1. By leading a small card from your hand and inserting the queen when West plays low, you hope to win both tricks, and you will whenever your left-hand opponent holds the king.

2. Many beginners do not realize this holding is as much a finessing situation as the first. You hope West holds the ace, for you will inevitably win a trick with your king whenever you lead through West's ace. Observe that in both cases the lead must be made from the hand without the high cards toward the hand with them. If the lead is not in the hand with the low cards, you have to find an entry in another suit to get to the correct hand to originate the finesse.

3.	DUMMY	4.	DUMMY
	Q 3		Q 5 3
	DECLARER		DECLARER
	A 5 4 2		A 4 2

3. By leading low from South, you can take two tricks if West has the king, but of course you have to give up a trick to earn an extra one. With this holding you cannot afford to lay down the ace and then lead toward the queen because (unless the king falls singleton) your queen will never take a trick—it will fall under the opponent's king.

4. This time you may cash the ace before taking the finesse because the queen in dummy has an extra guard. However, with your side holding only six cards in the suit, the chance the king is singleton is slight—actually less than 1 percent. For tactical reasons you probably will choose to lead small toward dummy before laying down the ace.

The more cards your side holds in a suit the greater the chance of catching a singleton king. If your side has seven cards, the chance of catching a singleton king is 2.4 percent. If your side holds eight cards, the chance of catching a singleton king jumps to 5.7 percent.

5.	DUMMY	6.	DUMMY
	Q 7 5 3		Q 10 4 2
	DECLARER		DECLARER
	A 6 4 2		A 6 5 3

5. With eight cards you should consider the possibility that East started with the king doubleton. This means you should lead the ace first and then lead low and duck in dummy. East will hold the doubleton king slightly more than 13.5 percent of the time. However, West will hold the king and two small cards much more often (in excess of 20 percent). If West is the sort of player who will duck with the king whenever it is guarded, the mathematical favorite is to lead the ace first and then a low card to dummy's queen.

Another situation occurs when West starts with four to the king and ducks the second lead from South. His spot card will hold the trick, but you can still get your two tricks in the suit if you can get back to the closed hand to lead the suit a third time.

6. Add a ten to dummy and the problem changes again. After you lead the ace and a small card (if West has played nothing but spot cards), the play of the ten rather than the queen becomes superior. Only if you are convinced West holds the king should you play the queen because (a) you need two tricks in a hurry or (b) you hope East will have nothing left but the jack which will now drop.

Weighing these various factors becomes a matter of judgment. You have to take into consideration the bidding you have heard, what you know about the distribution of the opponents' hands, and even the competence, personality, and playing habits of the opposing players before coming to a winning decision.

The Official Encyclopedia of Bridge contains a classified analysis covering 53 pages of suit combinations broken down in sections according to the number of *high-card points* held by the defense in the crucial suit, and subdivided to account for the number of *cards* in the suit held by the declaring side. It is not my intention here to repeat information available from that source or to use so much space to give these tables and analyze the percentages. I will, however, cover some typical situations. Then we will get on to more serious matters concerning the finesse and its nature.

7.	DUMMY	8.	DUMMY
	J 2		J 3 2
	DECLARER		DECLARER
	A K 4 3		A K 5 4

7. This is another example of a finesse that occurs frequently. You try to get three tricks in the suit at the cost of one by leading small toward dummy's jack. This play will succeed whenever West holds the queen.

8. This differs from No. 7 in that dummy's jack is doubly protected. Here the technically correct play is to lay down the ace or king before leading to the jack to cater to the almost 2.5 times in 100 that the queen will be singleton. With this holding, though, arithmetic has to be weighed against strategy. If West holds the queen, will he play it when you lead small? Or will he, for reasons best known to himself, hold up the queen and let your jack win the trick? Almost certainly he will play the queen if it is a doubleton, but more than 40 percent of the time he will hold the queen with two or more guards.

If you hold *five* cards in South and three in the dummy, the odds change somewhat. Now the queen will fall singleton almost 5.7 percent of the time, and the queen with two or more guards will be with West 33.6 percent of the time. But when West is holding three or more cards to the queen, he will have a problem when you lead low toward the jack. For all he knows, you may hold not the ace-king, but the ace-ten five or six long. It would be embarrassing for him to fly with the queen and find that his partner started with the singleton or doubleton king. Bridge is played by people and not by calculating machines, and in this as in many other finessing situations, your best procedure may depend not on the simple arithmetic of the matter, but upon your estimate of what your opponents are likely to do.

9.	DUMMY	10.	DUMMY
	A K J 4 2		A K J 10 4 3
	DECLARER		DECLARER
	6 5 3		5 2

9. One of the first things new bridge players learn is the old saying, "eight ever; nine never." This means that when the combined holding in your hand and dummy is eight cards and you are missing the queen, you always finesse for the queen, but, when your combined holding is nine cards, you never finesse for the queen. "Eight ever" is nearer the truth than "nine never," for the odds in favor of a finesse in No. 9 compared with playing for the drop is successful only when East holds precisely the queen doubleton. Playing the finesse works whenever West has either three or four cards that include the queen. West will hold Q x x or Q x x x 233 times during the time East holds the queen doubleton 100 times. With the setup the way it is in No. 9, and assuming plenty of entries in South, the ace or king should be led before the finesse is taken. This will take care of that almost 3 percent of the time when East holds the singleton queen.

10. This looks similar, but it requires different treatment. There are still eight cards in the combined hands, but now there are six in North and only two in South—and North has been fortified with the ten-spot. This extra ten makes it possible to bring in the entire suit without loss whenever West holds four cards in the suit to the queen, as well as on those occasions where the distribution is more favorable. However, to bring in the suit with West holding Q x x x, it is necessary to lead twice from the South hand. If you lay down the ace or king and then come to the South hand to finesse, you will protect yourself against the singleton queen in East's hand, but you no longer will be able to handle Q x x x in West's. As the Q x x x in West is exactly four times as frequent as the queen singleton in East, it is obvious that with this holding you cannot afford the luxury of laying down the ace or king. You must lead small from South and take a first-round finesse of the jack or ten. Should it lose to a singleton queen with East, you will have to console yourself with the thought that you made the proper play. I hate to tell you this, but virtue does not always receive a proper reward in bridge.

11.	DUMMY	12.	DUMMY
	K Q 5		K Q 10
	DECLARER		DECLARER
	4 3 2		4 3 2

11. On this deal, you lead small from South toward the dummy and win two tricks whenever West has the ace, always assuming you have another entry to get into the South hand to lead again. If East has the ace, you will win only one trick.

12. On No. 12, however, the ten has been added to the North hand. You can win two tricks even where East has the ace, provided West has the jack. You first lead low from South and play the king. If it loses to East, you come back and lead low and finesse the ten-spot. If the king *wins* the

first trick, you come back and lead low again. Then (unless you have reason to believe that East has been clever enough to refuse to play his ace) you play the queen when West again plays low.

13.	DUMMY	14.	DUMMY
	K J 5		K J 10
	DECLARER		DECLARER
	4 3 2		4 3 2

13. Here you lead low from South, and, when West plays low, you insert the jack. If East wins the ace, you have your one trick. If East wins the queen, you must come back to your hand and lead the suit again. When East holds both the ace and the queen, you will take no tricks in the suit. You may lose two tricks in the process of doing so, but you will always get one trick as long as West holds either the ace or the queen.

14. You make the same play with 14, leading low from your hand and inserting the ten-spot, but the difference here is that eventually you will win a trick no matter how the cards are divided. Of course, if East holds the queen, you will have to lose two tricks before you can get one, but one is assured.

15.	DUMMY	16.	DUMMY
	Q J 2		Q 10 2
	DECLARER		DECLARER
	5 4 3		5 4 3

15. By leading low toward dummy twice, you get one trick whenever West holds either the ace or king or both.

16. If West follows low, you play dummy's ten-spot. This maneuver will win a trick when West started with the jack and either the ace or king. There is also the chance that West holds both the ace and the king and will play one of them when you lead low toward the queen.

17.	DUMMY	18.	DUMMY
	A 3 2		A 3 2
	DECLARER		DECLARER
	Q J 4		Q J 5 4

17. With this holding, you can always take two tricks no matter how you play the combination. Laying down the ace first will be the better play in the few cases where the king is singleton. This does not give you much edge, since when you hold six cards in the suit, the king will be singleton slightly less than 1 time in 100. If there is any chance you may be able to discard a small card from either your hand or dummy's on another suit, your better play is to forget about dropping the singleton king and lead the queen from your hand toward the dummy. If it holds the trick, or if West plays the king and you win the ace, you can then go about your other business.

I hope it is becoming increasingly evident that an important factor in considering the feasibility of a finesse is the number of cards you hold in the suit. Sometimes this translates into a study of the number of cards the opponents hold. These factors will become more apparent as we go along.

18. Here your best play usually is to lay down the ace first. Holding seven cards in the suit, your chances of dropping a singleton king increase to almost 2.5 times out of 100. But that is not the important factor. The important factor is that, if East holds the king, you can take three tricks in the suit, as you have two more cards in dummy to lead toward your queen-jack. Also, if you lead the queen from your hand, you can take three tricks in the suit only when the outstanding cards are divided 3–3.

19. DUMMY	20. DUMMY
A J 10	A J 9
DECLARER	DECLARER
5 3 2	5 3 2

19. With this deal, you lead low from your hand toward dummy and take two tricks whenever West has either the king or the queen or both.

20. This holding is similar, except you lead low from your hand and put in dummy's nine-spot. You will win two tricks whenever West has the ten-spot with either the king or the queen. Of course, if it turns out that West ducks holding the king-queen and East has the ten, your play will lose. However, West is twice as likely to hold the ten with either the king or queen as he is to hold both the king and the queen, so the nine becomes the proper play, except in those cases where you have overwhelming evidence that West holds both the king and the queen.

Here are eight more typical finessing situations. The last two are almost in the "safety play" zone, a subject that will be taken up in detail later.

21. DUMMY	22. DUMMY
A Q 10 3	A Q 9 3
DECLARER	DECLARER
5 4 2	5 4 2

21. Here your best play to bring in the maximum number of tricks is to lead small from your hand, put in the ten, and repeat the process, leading small and putting in the queen the second time. The only way this loses a trick you would not otherwise lose is when East holds the doubleton king-jack.

22. Similar, though not so easy to recognize, is 22. The best chance of bringing in two tricks is to lead small from your hand and, if West plays low, play dummy's nine. If that loses to the ten or jack, play the ace next. If the king does not fall, reenter your hand and lead toward the queen. (If you need three tricks, your best shot is to finesse the nine and, if it loses, next finesse the queen.) The play of the nine wins on those occasions where West has both the jack and the ten. West will hold the jack and ten with one or more small cards more than 1 time out of 5. It does West no good to split his honors when he holds both of these—you play your queen, and, if that loses to the king, you return to your hand and lead toward dummy's ace-nine through West's jack doubleton.

23.	DUMMY	24.	DUMMY
	J 5 3		7 5 3
	DECLARER		DECLARER
	A Q 6 4 2		A Q 6 4 2

23. In 23, you lead small from dummy and, if East plays small, play your queen. If this holds the trick, you then lay down your ace. You will win all five tricks whenever East started with the king and only one other card. The best play for four tricks is to play the ace and lead toward the jack, in case West has the singleton king.

24. The situation is different in this case. The opponents hold all the cards from the eight through the king, with the exception of the queen. If you finesse the queen and lose to a singleton king, you still have to lose two more tricks to East. When the opponents have five cards in the suit, West will hold the singleton king almost 3 percent of the time. Your better play is to lead the ace first. Most of the time the king will not fall singleton, but you then go to the dummy and lead low toward your hand. If the king does not appear from East, you have two choices. You may play low from your hand if you think West started with the king doubleton. If West shows out, you can still return to dummy and lead toward your queen again to ensure your three tricks in the suit. However, if you think East has three to the king, you may put up the queen to hold the trick. A third round then drives out the king.

25.	DUMMY	26.	DUMMY
	A K 10 2		K J 4 2
	DECLARER		DECLARER
	9 4 3		A 5 3

25. This combination is frequently misplayed. If you must bring in three tricks without losing any, you lead low from your hand, hoping to find both the queen and the jack with West. If West plays low, put in dummy's ten-spot. The odds are 3 to 1 that West will not hold both these cards. Of course, if he does hold both of them (alone or with exactly one more), you can bring in four tricks in the suit—but he will have this holding less than 9 percent of the time.

When you need three tricks in the suit and are willing to give up one to get the three, the best play is to lay down the ace. If no honor drops, lead small to the ten. This is slightly better than playing the ace and king, which succeeds when either opponent has a doubleton honor or when the opposing cards are split 3–3.

26. This combination is less frequently misplayed. Of course, if you need four tricks in the suit, your only play is to take the ace and lead low toward the dummy, finessing the jack. This will bring you four tricks only 18 percent of the time. If you can afford to lose one trick in the suit and want to have the best chance possible of taking three tricks, the proper play is to cash dummy's king and your ace, then lead toward the jack. This will work when West started with the queen, when the suit splits 3–3, and when East started with a doubleton queen. Your chances of taking three tricks have jumped to 77 percent.

27.	DUMMY	28.	DUMMY
	A 3 2		A 3 2
	DECLARER		DECLARER
	K Q 10 5 4		K Q 9 6 5 4

27. Here you would like to finesse against the jack whenever the east hand holds four to the jack. You can discover whether this distribution exists only if you are sure to cash one high honor from *each* hand. Then, if East started with four to the jack, West will show out, and you will be able to finesse against the jack.

28. In this case, you are missing both the jack and the ten. Should West hold all four of the missing cards, there is no way to avoid losing a trick to him. However, if East holds all four, you can finesse through his jack-ten twice. You should cash the ace first, and, when West shows out, you will be able to take two finesses against the jack-ten.

These last two plays might be described as "no lose" safety plays. The subject of finesses does meet the subject of safety plays at about this stage.

While the possession of intermediate cards such as nines and eights will, in some of these cases, alter the odds somewhat and make a different line of play preferable, the positions we have examined so far are the basic setups. Experienced players become so familiar with them that they recognize them on sight. Any variations caused by the possession of intermediate cards or by a decision to go for all possible tricks (or taking the best chances to collect a smaller number of tricks) can be determined if you possess a sound knowledge of these typical situations.

Sometimes when you hold the A Q 10 you take the double finesse and sometimes you don't—it all depends.

DUMMY
♠ 9 7 4 3
♡ A Q 10
♢ A K Q J
♣ 9 3

DECLARER
♠ A Q 10 5
♡ 6 2
♢ 10 7 6 2
♣ J 7 2

After some aggressive bidding, South got into a four spade contract. West took the first two tricks with the ace and king of clubs and switched to a small heart.

In spades, South has the A Q 10, and in hearts North has the A Q 10, but you don't handle the two suits the same way. You are striving to lose no tricks at all in hearts, and your best chance to do that is to play the queen. Let's say that it holds the trick. Now your next goal is to limit yourself to one loser in spades. Your best play here is to lead a small spade and, if East plays low, to put in the ten-spot. This could bring in the spade suit without losers if East happens to hold K J x, and it will limit your losses to one spade if East holds either the king or the jack. Should the ten lose to the jack, the proper play would be to return to the dummy with the ace of hearts and take a finesse against the queen this time.

WHEN TO LEAD HIGH

The study of the mathematical probabilities as applied to bridge hands is fascinating. It is also useful, provided that you know its limitations. These limitations are not always properly appreciated by those who become enamored with the subject. Nonetheless, I am going to give you a table here which should be labeled "a priori." That means that these figures have validity before you know anything about the distribution of the twenty-six cards held by the opponents. In this particular case, the figures would not change a great deal, even if you did know something about the distribution of the opposing hands. Anyway, I give you this table, not hoping that you can remember it (as I certainly cannot), but rather to illustrate my point.

Cards Held	*East Has Singleton King*	*East Has Doubleton King*	*East Has One or The Other*
4	0.67	1.95	1.01
5	0.18	2.13	2.31
6	0.48	4.36	4.85
7	1.21	8.07	9.29
8	2.83	13.57	16.39
9	6.22	20.35	26.57
10	13.00	26.00	39.00
11	26.00	24.00	50.00

Column one represents the total number of cards you and dummy have in any one suit. We are assuming neither you nor the dummy has the king of the suit.

Column two represents the frequency with which the player in the east seat will hold the singleton king. Of course, this also represents how often West will hold the singleton king.

Column three represents how often East will hold the king doubleton, and column four represents how often East will hold the king either doubleton or singleton.

In the following examples, you and dummy have certain key high cards. For the purpose of illustrating my point, you hold (outside of those high cards) the smallest cards in the suit. I have done this to avoid complicating the problem with higher intermediate cards.

1. DUMMY
J 5 3

DECLARER
A Q 6 4 2

2. DUMMY
J 3 2

DECLARER
A Q 10 9 4

When we looked at hand No. 1 in the last section, we saw that where East has the king doubleton, you can bring in the entire suit without loss, provided you lead small from the dummy, insert the queen, and lay down the ace. The table tells us East will hold the doubleton king a little more than 13.5 percent of the time when you and dummy hold eight of a suit. This is worth playing for. Besides, if you lead the jack from dummy, there is no possible distribution that will allow you to bring in the suit without loss (assuming the opponents play correctly). If East has the king, he must play it when you lead your jack. There is no way you can *gain* a trick by leading the jack, but there are ways you can *lose* a trick. Notice that if East holds the singleton king, leaving West with the 10 9 8 7, you can get by with the loss of *one* trick if you lead small the first time; if you lead the jack the first time, you must lose *two* tricks.

2. You are in the dummy and want to take the finesse. Since we have added the ten-nine to your holding, you will take the same number of tricks whether you lead the jack first or a low card. If you have entry problems, you can take the finesse by leading the jack from dummy at no cost.

3.	DUMMY	4.	DUMMY
	J 3 2		J 2
	DECLARER		DECLARER
	A Q 8 7 6 5 4		A Q 7 6 5 4 3

3. Here we have removed the ten-nine, but your suit is seven cards long instead of five. Don't give even a fleeting thought to playing the ace to drop the singleton king in West, unless something in the bidding indicated West is almost sure to have the king. The table shows that when you and dummy hold ten cards, the chance that either opponent holds a singleton king is 13 percent. You can run the suit without loss if East has either the singleton or doubleton king (but not if he has K 10 9), and that is a 39 percent chance, or just three times as good as trying to drop the singleton king with West. It makes no difference whether you start off by leading the jack or the deuce from the dummy.

4. Now we have shortened dummy to a doubleton, and it does make a difference whether you lead the jack from the dummy. It will cost you a trick whenever East holds the singleton king. You stand to lose a little more than 6 percent of the time by leading the jack, and you never stand to gain by doing so.

5.	DUMMY	6.	DUMMY
	J 4 3 2		J 4 3 2
	DECLARER		DECLARER
	A Q 8 7 6 5		A Q 9 7 6 5

5. In No. 5 it makes no difference whether you take your first finesse by leading the jack or by leading small, for, if you must lose a trick, it will be lost either way. The only time it makes a difference is when East holds the K 10 9 and erroneously fails to cover your jack. It doesn't cost anything to give East an opportunity to make a mistake, so why not lead the jack?

6. This holding, however, is an entirely different case. Your eight has been replaced by the nine, making the lead of the jack from dummy a must play. The missing three cards held by the opposition are the K 10 8. East will hold all three of these cards 11 percent of the time. The only reasonable way to bring in the entire suit when this occurs is to lead the jack from the dummy. Whatever East does, West will show out on the first trick, and, if East has covered, you will then enter the dummy and take a second finesse in the suit.

We have looked at some hands where it is a technical error to lead high from the dummy, at some others where it makes no difference but does give your right-hand opponent the opportunity to make a mistake, and at still others where the only proper lead is high from the dummy. This could be worked out at the table—a tiresome and time-consuming process—but we will look at some easy formulas that should help you solve the problem almost automatically.

Formulas for Leading High When you are missing the king or the queen of a suit and need to take a first-round finesse, it is safe to lead high toward the hand with the top honors, whenever you fulfill one of these requirements:

I. The cards you and dummy hold just above and just below the missing cards are one more in number than the total number of cards in the hand where you have the greater number.

1.	DUMMY Q 10 2	2.	DUMMY J 9 2
	DECLARER A J 3		DECLARER A Q 10 3

1. This is an illustration of the first of our formulas. Your longest holding is three cards, and you hold four of the high cards, missing the king. You have one more of these high cards than your greater length, so you have nothing to lose by leading high from the dummy. It is simply a matter of where you would like to have the lead, should the finesse lose. If you wish to be able to get the lead next in the hand of your choice, you will lead the ten from dummy. Should West win the king, you can take the next trick in that suit in whichever hand you prefer.

2. In this hand you have five of the high cards, missing the king, and the longer holding is four cards long, so this also qualifies under the first of our formulas. Should East hold four or more to the king, you would need to be able to lead three times from dummy. Should dummy be short of entries, you must be careful to lead the nine from dummy the first time. For your second lead, you can lead the jack from the dummy and drop the ten under the jack if the king does not appear. If East did in fact start with four or more to the king, you still have the deuce in dummy to take the final finesse to your ace-queen. It will not avail you to lead the jack first and underplay the ten when East plays low. If you do this, you have reduced your high-card holding to only three—the A Q 9, and your greater length is three cards. Thus the second lead (of the nine) will fall under the first formula.

II. The number of cards you hold (that surround the missing card) are equal in number to the total number of cards held by the opponents.

To lose no tricks at all where a card is finessable, you need one more surrounding card than the number of cards held by the player holding the finessable card. Where he might hold all of the missing cards, this means that it takes one more than the total number of cards held by the opponents. However, to be sure you do not lose a trick *because* you lead high, it is only necessary to have as many of the surrounding cards as the total number the opponents have. It is true that if the player with the finessable card holds all of the missing cards you are going to lose a trick when you lead high. It is also true that under these circumstances you are going to lose a trick no matter what you lead. So, let's look at some examples:

3. DUMMY
J 9 4

DECLARER
A Q 10 3 2

4. DUMMY
J 5 4

DECLARER
A Q 10 3 2

3. This does not qualify under our first formula, but does qualify under our second. The opponents hold five cards in the suit, and you hold five cards missing the king. Leading high from the dummy cannot cause you to lose a trick you would not otherwise lose. If you are going to lose the trick, it will be either because West has the king or because East has all five missing cards in the suit.

4. This hand does not immediately qualify under the second formula. The opponents have five cards between them, and you have only four of the high cards. Observe, though, what will happen if you lead low from dummy and insert the ten or queen from your hand and it holds the trick. If both opponents follow suit, the number of cards they hold between them is now reduced to three. You still have three of the high cards left between your hand and the dummy. The second formula, not effective when you first led the suit, has become effective. When you return to dummy in some other suit, leading the jack cannot cause you to lose any trick you would not otherwise lose. However, doing so has little to gain. If East started with the doubleton king, your jack will become another entry to the dummy after you lead low from the dummy again. If the extra entry to the dummy may be of value to you,it is recommended to lead low the second time.

5. DUMMY
Q 10 2

DECLARER
A J 6 5 4 3

6. DUMMY
Q J 5 4

DECLARER
A 9 8 6 3 2

5. This hand also qualifies under our second formula. The opponents have four cards between them, and you have four of the high cards. Leading high from dummy cannot cost a trick you would not otherwise lose. However, it will preserve the lead in dummy in those cases where East started with three to the king. The recommended lead is one of the high cards.

6. This also qualifies under the second formula. The opponents hold three cards, and you hold three high cards. With only three cards missing, you might be tempted to lay down the ace hoping to drop the singleton king with West. Take a look at our table and you will see that a singleton king in one of the hands is only a 13 percent chance, while a singleton or doubleton in the East hand is 39 percent. This should convince you the proper play from dummy is the queen . . . and this brings us to my third formula:

III. Leading the top card from the weaker hand is an absolute must whenever the opponents hold only three cards which are precisely the second highest, the fifth highest, and one smaller spot card not adjacent to the fifth highest.

To help myself remember these numbers, I call it my "bargain lead—my three candy bars for 25¢ lead." By remembering three for a quarter, I remember the critical numbers: "3" for the total number of opponents' cards; "2" and "5" for the rank of the cards they hold. Remember hand No. 6 from the preceding subsection.

DUMMY
J 4 3 2

DECLARER
A Q 9 7 6 5

The opponents hold the K 10 8. The king is the second highest; the ten is the fifth highest. You should lead the jack in an attempt to pick up the K 10 8 on your right.

7.	8.
DUMMY 10 4 2	DUMMY 10 4 2
DECLARER A K J 5 3	DECLARER A K J 8 3

7. This hand does not meet the requirements of our formulas. The opponents hold five cards between them, and we hold only four of the high cards. However, if we lay down the ace and both opponents follow, the second formula becomes applicable. The opponents will be left with three cards, and you will have three of the high cards. So far as taking tricks is concerned, it makes no difference whether you go to the dummy and lead the ten-spot or go to the dummy and lead small. It might, however, make a difference in entries into the dummy. If East started with a doubleton queen, your lead of the small card from the dummy will give dummy an additional entry.

8. This deal is quite different. Again, the formula does not at first work because the opponents hold a total of five cards and you hold only four high ones. After you lay down the ace and both follow, the hand falls under the third formula, and the lead of the ten-spot from the dummy becomes a "must" play. The queen has become the 2 card, and the nine has become the 5 card. There are three cards outstanding, and they include the queen and the nine. Now you go to the dummy, but lead the ten-spot. If East has been left the queen, the nine, and the small card,

West will show out, and whatever East does, you will bring in the entire suit.

9.	DUMMY	10.	DUMMY
	10 6 4 2		10 3 2
	DECLARER		DECLARER
	A Q J 8		A Q J 8 4

9. Hand number 9 is the diamond suit in the hand I showed you when I made my introductory remarks about finessing. With ample entries in the dummy, I pointed out that the first time the finesse is taken, the small card must be led from the dummy. By either of the first two formulas, leading the ten-spot from the dummy would be incorrect. Should East happen to have the singleton king, the nine in the west hand would be promoted to a high card. However, if the finesse of the jack wins the first trick, I pointed out that the next time the suit is led from the dummy, the ten must be led. This is because the third formula applies after the jack has won the trick. There are exactly three cards outstanding in the opposing hands, and they consist of the king, the nine, and a smaller card. The king is the second highest card, and the nine, after the jack has been played, becomes the fifth highest.

10. Here is another illustration of the same thing. The small card from the dummy is a must the first time, but if the jack holds the trick, when you return to the dummy, the ten is a must lead because the cards left outstanding include the second and fifth highest cards.

11.	DUMMY	12.	DUMMY
	J 2		J 3 2
	DECLARER		DECLARER
	A Q 3		A Q 4

11. In this hand you take three tricks by leading low from the dummy and playing your ace, if either of your opponents has a singleton king. The percentage tables will show you how slim a chance this is. I hope my past and future opponents will forgive me for what I am about to say, but with this particular holding, I lead the jack from dummy on the theory that East will fail to cover at least as often as one of my opponents will hold a singleton king. I now apologize to anyone whom I have insulted and go on.

12. Here you can take three tricks by leading low from the dummy whenever East has the king doubleton or singleton. Now we are up to chances that are almost 5 in 100, and my opponents are not that bad. I always make the normal play—lead a low card and finesse the queen, if the king does not appear from East.

It is, however, necessary to look at the whole hand, rather than to look at one suit. Sometimes it is essential that you lead high even though you do not have the number of surrounding cards given in our three examples.

Let us look at the problem in Fig. 4-1. In three no-trump, West has led the queen of diamonds, and East has gone up with the king. It would

Fig. 4-1

West	North	East
	♠ A K 4 ♡ A K Q ◇ 7 5 ♣ A Q 10 6 3	
♠ 10 8 3 ♡ 10 8 ◇ Q J 10 9 6 ♣ K 9 5		♠ Q J 9 6 ♡ 9 7 6 5 2 ◇ K 8 ♣ 8 7
	♠ 7 5 2 ♡ J 4 3 ◇ A 4 3 2 ♣ J 4 2	

be proper to let them hold this trick but then, when the eight is returned, to win it with the ace. If we don't win it, we may never get to the south hand.

Now we don't have to have the five club tricks, or even four. Three club tricks will bring our total up to nine, and we should make every effort to be sure we get three club tricks. We are not worried about losing a finesse —should East win with the king of clubs and should he have a diamond left, our losses are probably limited to one club and three diamond tricks. If, as we suspect, he has no diamonds left, there is nothing he can do to harm us when he wins the king of clubs. So all we have to worry about is the king of clubs' being in West's hand. Sure enough, if it is a singleton there or even a doubleton, we can run the entire suit by leading low toward the queen. But suppose West holds the king three long or four long? Now if we lead low toward the queen, we are going to get exactly two tricks without giving him the lead, and we have reason to believe that giving him the lead will be fatal. On the other hand, should he have the king, we can make sure of taking three tricks without giving up the lead by leading the jack, no matter how many clubs he has. We have four of the cards surrounding the king, and, even if we have to waste two of them on one trick, we will still get three tricks out of the suit. And should it turn out that West has the king either doubleton or tripleton, we still will bring in the entire suit by leading the jack.

Leading High for a Smother Play Unless you and dummy have sufficient high cards in a suit, you usually lead low toward your tenace position when taking a finesse. This is because the finessable honor may be so thinly guarded that it will fall of its own accord under one of your high cards. We have been studying those situations where it can't cost a trick to lead a high card toward the tenace because your side has enough high cards in a suit to afford the luxury of spending two of your high cards to capture one of theirs.

Now we come to a variation where we have reason to believe the finessable honor is well protected, but where intermediate cards in the hand opposite the finessable honor may be insufficiently protected. In this circumstance, it may become mandatory to lead high toward the tenace position in an attempt to "smother" the thinly guarded intermediate card. Fig. 4-2 is a simple example.

East opened the bidding with one no-trump, and South ended up playing four hearts. The opening lead was the queen of clubs, and, when the dummy came down, it was obvious that three aces would be lost, so the problem was to avoid losing a trump trick.

Fig. 4-2

West	North	East
	♠ K Q J ♡ Q 10 8 4 ◇ 7 4 ♣ 8 7 3 2	
♠ 8 6 5 4 3 2 ♡ J ◇ 10 9 8 ♣ Q J 10		♠ A 9 7 ♡ K 5 ◇ A J 6 3 ♣ A 9 5 4
	♠ 10 ♡ A 9 7 6 3 2 ◇ K Q 5 2 ♣ K 6	

East-West were playing 16- to 18-point no-trumps, so it figured that East had the king of hearts. South therefore had these possibilities to consider:

1. The king of hearts is singleton in East. If so, the winning play would be to lead the ace or lead low toward the ace. In view of the opening bid of one no-trump, it is unlikely East's king of hearts is a singleton.

2. East has the doubleton king-jack of hearts. If so, a trump trick has to be lost no matter how declarer plays the suit.

3. East has all three missing hearts. Now the lead of the ace of hearts

would lose *two* trump tricks. Declarer needs to lead hearts from the dummy and cover whatever East plays.

4. East has the king and five of hearts, leaving West with the singleton jack. With this holding, the lead of the queen from the dummy would "smother" the jack.

East won the ace of clubs and returned a club. South eventually got to dummy to lead trumps by ruffing a diamond, so the story ended happily when the queen of hearts dropped the singleton jack from West.

Fig. 4-3 is a further illustration where the quality of the intermediate cards is of importance to this type of finesse.

Fig. 4-3

North: ♠ K Q 6 2 ♡ J 8 6 2 ♢ K Q J ♣ K 4
West: ♠ 10 9 8 5 ♡ 10 ♢ 10 8 5 3 ♣ 9 8 3 2
East: ♠ A 3 ♡ K 9 3 ♢ 9 7 6 4 ♣ A Q 7 6
South: ♠ J 7 4 ♡ A Q 7 5 4 ♢ A 2 ♣ J 10 5

On this hand, after East opened the bidding with one club and South again reached four hearts, West opened the two of clubs. East cashed the ace-queen of clubs and switched to a diamond. As South was looking at 27 high-card points and East had opened the bidding, he must have the missing 13 high-card points, so there was no question where the king of hearts reposed. The playing of the club suit indicated that East did not have very long clubs, as West had led the two and followed with the three. If East held the K 10 9 of hearts, he was going to get a trump trick unless some way could be found to make him lead hearts, and that seemed most unlikely. South considered it also unlikely that East held the singleton king of hearts, as he might not have opened the bidding with that flawed minimum.

Exchange North's eight of hearts for East's three of hearts, and the only thing you can protect against is a singleton or doubleton king of hearts in East's hand. To do that you must lead small from the dummy. However, North *does* have the eight-spot, and the possession of these intermediate cards often makes a big difference. Even if South has no idea where the king of hearts is and whether or not it is protected, the lead of the jack is slightly better than leading small when you have that eight-spot. However, once you assume that East not only has the king of hearts, but that it is not singleton, the lead of the jack becomes an absolute must. If East covers and West drops either the ten or the nine, the proper play is to return to the dummy and take a finesse of the seven-spot. This loses a trick that would not otherwise be lost only when West has specifically the ten-nine doubleton. In all other cases, the lead of the jack either makes no difference at all or saves a trick that otherwise would be lost.

Determining when the situation is ripe for a smother finesse is not always simple, but you frequently find excellent clues in the bidding (Fig. 4-4).

Fig. 4-4 Dlr: N Vul. E-W

North: ♠ 4 2 ♡ 10 7 2 ♢ K Q J ♣ A Q J 7 2
West: ♠ A J 8 6 3 ♡ 9 ♢ 10 9 8 3 ♣ 8 6 5
East: ♠ K Q 7 5 ♡ K J 6 4 ♢ A 6 5 ♣ 9 4
South: ♠ 10 9 ♡ A Q 8 5 3 ♢ 7 4 2 ♣ K 10 3

NORTH	EAST	SOUTH	WEST
1♣	Dbl	1♡	1♠
Pass	Pass	2♡	2♠
Pass	Pass	3♣	Pass
4♡	Pass	Pass	Pass

Opening lead: ♠A

North got a little frisky in the bidding after he found out that his partner had a five-card heart suit and a club fit. His confidence in South was well repaid. After the opponents cashed two spade tricks, East missed the best defense when he failed to lead a third spade instead of the ace and a small diamond. East's takeout double seemed to indicate length in the major suits, so the chance of finding the king of hearts singleton or doubleton in his hand was remote. Actually, the chances were better than if he had four (hopefully not five). If he did have four, then West had a singleton, and if the singleton turned out to be the nine-spot, then the setup was perfect to blotter it out. South won the second diamond lead in dummy and led the ten of hearts. He was able to get back twice more to lead

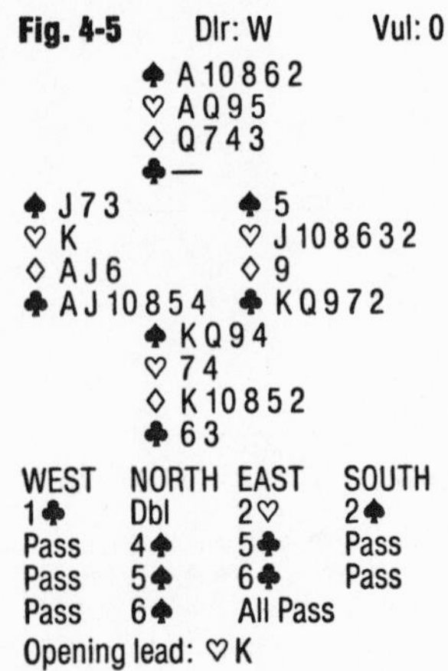

through East and to bring home his contract without losing a trump trick.

Fig. 4-5 Dlr: W Vul: 0
♠ A 10 8 6 2
♡ A Q 9 5
◇ Q 7 4 3
♣ —
♠ J 7 3
♡ K
◇ A J 6
♣ A J 10 8 5 4
♠ 5
♡ J 10 8 6 3 2
◇ 9
♣ K Q 9 7 2
♠ K Q 9 4
♡ 7 4
◇ K 10 8 5 2
♣ 6 3
WEST NORTH EAST SOUTH
1♣ Dbl 2♡ 2♠
Pass 4♠ 5♣ Pass
Pass 5♠ 6♣ Pass
Pass 6♠ All Pass
Opening lead: ♡K

On this hand (Fig. 4-5) a foolish East talked too much. He not only pushed his opponents into a slam they did not seem to want to bid, but also he told them how to play it. A more sensible preemptive effort after the takeout double would have been an immediate bid of five clubs. But had he done so, I would not have this story for you.

West led the king of hearts, causing South no anguish at all. After pulling trumps in three rounds, declarer stopped to reflect.

East had bid like a man with many cards in hearts and clubs, and this was confirmed when dummy's queen of hearts was cashed and West discarded a club. South suspected that East, having winged his way to six clubs almost unaided, had at least five clubs, and, therefore, a singleton diamond. South had to hold his diamond losers to one trick. The missing diamonds were the A J 9 6. Could East hold either the jack of diamonds or the nine of diamonds singleton? As the lead was in dummy, declarer called for a small diamond, losing the king of diamonds to West's ace of diamonds, as East's nine fell. The club return was ruffed in dummy, and declarer ruffed a heart back to his hand to lead the ten of diamonds. West played the six of diamonds, but South resolutely took the finesse and brought home his contract.

In Fig. 4-6 is an example where you have to plan ahead to blotter out an honor in a finessing situation.

After taking the ace-king of diamonds, West switched to hearts. Declarer won the king of hearts and realized that he had to avoid losing two trump tricks if he was going to bring home his contract. Only if West had a doubleton consisting of the ten-spot and one of the higher honors was success assured.

South led a small spade toward dummy, and West had to play his queen of spades or lose it. Declarer then entered dummy and led the jack of spades through East's king of spades, blotting out West's ten-spot.

Sometimes you have to go pretty deep to find these "smothering finesses."

In Fig. 4-7, West led the jack of hearts, and South held off to the third round, discarding a small club from dummy.

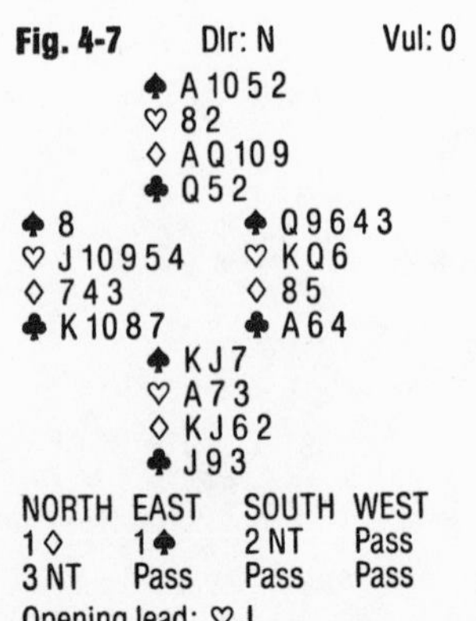

East had overcalled with one spade, so it seemed likely he had the queen of spades. With a finesse for that card, declarer could count eight tricks. Unless West started with five hearts and both high club honors were in East's hand, declarer could not afford losing the lead. But our declarer had read about my "smother finesses," so he opined: if West has a singleton spade, and that singleton is either the nine or the eight, I can win four spade tricks! So he crossed to dummy with a diamond and led the ten of spades. East covered with the queen (playing low does not help), and South won with the king, noting with satisfaction the fall of the eight from West. It was elementary to go back to dummy, lead a small spade, and finesse the seven. Then he cashed the jack of spades, returned to dummy one more time to take the ace of spades, and so collected four diamonds, four spades, and one heart to solve his problem nicely.

Another reason for trying a smother finesse is that if it doesn't work, nothing will.

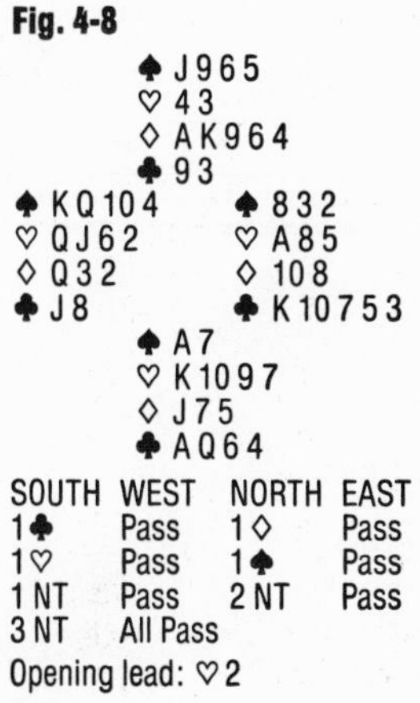

It is too late to give your partner a lesson about the values required for a raise from one no-trump to two no-trump. The best thing to do in circumstances like Fig. 4-8 is to consider his raise a compliment and see whether there is any combination of cards that will bring home the total contract.

West led the two of hearts, and East took the ace and returned the eight-spot. South covered with the nine, and West won with the jack. He found the best return of the jack of clubs. South had been having trouble counting more than about five sure tricks, and at least this lead brought his total up to six. He won the queen and saw that it was going to be necessary to bring in a lot of diamond tricks. He led a small diamond and played dummy's ace. If East had had a singleton queen, five tricks in diamonds would have been available by winning and then taking the finesse through West. Had West played the queen, South's best play would have been to let him hold the trick. He then would have had four diamond tricks and would have had to hope for manna from heaven to get one more trick to bring his total up to nine. But neither player played the queen, and so declarer returned to his hand with the ace of clubs. Now there was only one holding which would bring in the entire suit. If he laid down the king and picked up the now singleton queen, the suit would be blocked by his jack. But with East holding the singleton ten and West the queen, the lead of the jack did the job and brought in the five diamond tricks needed.

Now if you were South, aren't you glad you didn't bawl your partner out when he gave you that raise in no-trump?

The card to be smothered is usually a singleton, but not always.

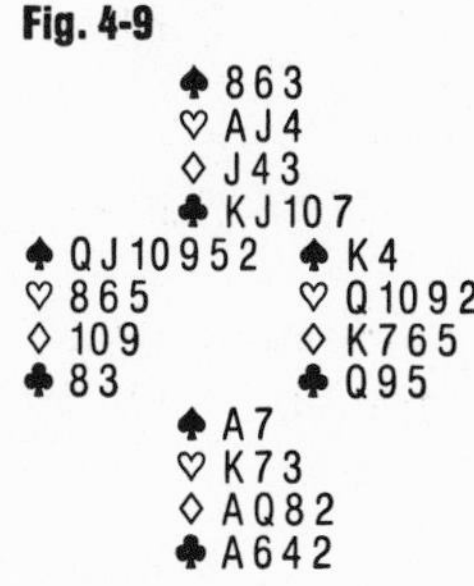

South opened the bidding in Fig. 4-9 with one no-trump, and North bid three no-trump. West led the queen of spades. East put up the king, and South let it hold the trick, but had to capture the return of the four-spot. Declarer cashed the ace of clubs and lost a finesse to East's queen. East got off lead with a small club, and South had no trouble deciding that East was out of spades. West discarded a heart. Declarer returned to his hand with the king of hearts and next tried the heart finesse. East won this queen and put South back in the dummy by leading another heart. This time West discarded a spade.

By now it had become obvious to South that he was going to win one spade, two hearts, and three clubs. If he was going to bring in nine tricks total, he had to bring in three tricks in diamonds. Furthermore, he had to bring in those three tricks without letting West gain the lead to cash the balance of his spades. This meant that East had to have the king of diamonds. If East did hold the king of diamonds and it was either alone or doubleton, then declarer would have to lead low from the dummy to finesse when East played low and then lead the ace to drop East's king. But South knew that East held more than two diamonds. West had shown up with six spades, three hearts, and two clubs, leaving him with two diamonds. This meant that East had four diamonds.

So far, all of South's chances for extra tricks had failed. The only chance remaining was a remote one. That was that East had the king of diamonds and that the doubleton which West held consisted of exactly the ten and nine. A remote chance is better than no chance at all, so South led dummy's jack of diamonds for a smother play of a doubleton in West. To give this story a happy ending (and to illustrate my point), these are exactly the cards that I have chosen to give to West.

None of the textbooks I have read have given proper coverage to the matter of leading an honor toward the tenace when taking a finesse. Louis Watson, in his classic 1934 book, *The Play of the Hand,* wrote, "It is possible to finesse by leading an honor in such a way that it may be covered, only if the next lower card is held." Since then textbooks have meticulously copied Mr. Watson's statement without bothering to check its validity. On the hand just shown, the next lower card than the jack of diamonds certainly was not held, but the lead of the jack was mandatory.

The queen doubleton opposite a long suit headed by the ace-ten and other high intermediate cards is a special case which all bridge players should tuck away in their memories. How you handle the suit and what your chances are depend on the total number of cards you and dummy have in this suit, plus the quality of the intermediate cards.

DUMMY
Q x

DECLARER
A 10 9 x x x x

With a total of nine cards, the best play is to lead the queen from the dummy. Chances are better than 6 percent that West will have the singleton jack, and, in that event, you will bring in all seven tricks in the suit. Leading the ace and dropping a singleton king will not bring in all seven tricks, as one player would be left with three to the jack. Leading the queen will not cost a trick should East have the singleton king, nor will it cost a trick where East has all four of the suit's outstanding cards. Of course, if you have good reason to believe that West has the king, you should lead low toward dummy's queen in case West has three of the cards.

Although you are missing the king and the jack, you do have four of the cards surrounding these two, and that is as many as the total number of cards in the suit held by the opposition. You always give some thought to leading high for the finesse when you have this many surrounding cards, as it is not disastrous to find a singleton king in the second hand. However, if you shorten your holding by one card and have only six of them in the south hand, the lead of the queen is still the percentage play. There is, however, no way you can take all of the tricks with this holding when you have only eight cards if the defenders play properly.

Q 2
J — K 7 6 5
A 10 9 8 4 3

Here you have five surrounding cards, and the opponents have a total of five. The lead of the queen is still the proper play, although you do not expect it to give you six tricks in the suit. After all, West will hold the singleton jack something less than 3 percent of the time. And, of course, if East does not cover the queen when you lead it, there is no way you can bring in all six tricks.

On those rare occasions where you hold eight opposite two,

DUMMY
Q x

DECLARER
A 10 x x x x x x

the situation is vastly changed, and, if you must take eight tricks in the suit, it is better to lay down the ace than to lead the queen from the dummy, in spite of the fact that you have three of the surrounding cards—the same as the total number of the cards in the suit held by your opponents. The lead of the ace will bring you the entire suit if either hand has a singleton king, while the lead of the queen will bring you the entire suit only if West has the singleton jack.

However, trying for eight tricks in the suit may result in losing two. If you want to be sure to take seven tricks against any distribution, lead low toward the queen. Should East have all three missing cards, you will go to the dummy and finesse him from there for his jack after he has won his king. Should West have all three of them, the low lead toward the queen guarantees you seven tricks.

Put three cards to the queen in place of the doubleton, and the situation is different.

DUMMY
Q 3 2

DECLARER
A 10 9 6 5 4

To take six tricks in the suit, it is purely an even proposition whether you should lead the ace, hoping East has the singleton king, or lead the queen from the dummy, hoping West has the singleton jack. The way to give yourself a maximum chance of taking five tricks is to lead the ace and then lead small toward the queen.

Change it just a little, and you have a different story.

DUMMY
Q 6 2

DECLARER
A 10 8 5 4 3

Your chances of taking six tricks by force are pretty slim, but the only chance is to lead the queen from the dummy hoping to smother the singleton jack in West's hand. If East covers the queen with the king, you can return to the dummy and finesse against his nine-spot. However, the play which gives you the best chance to bring in five tricks in the suit is the lead of the ace and then play small to the queen, just as though you did not have the eight-spot.

Let us see what we have learned in these studies. When there is a choice whether to lead an honor or a low card toward a tenace in taking a finesse, the lead of the low card may be proper when the finessable honor might be doomed to fall anyway because it is not accompanied by a sufficient number of small cards to give it protection. In such a case, leading an honor would simply result in the next hand's covering the honor and using up two honor cards to capture one. It also might promote winning cards in the hand opposite the finessable card.

When you have sufficient high cards, you may be able to afford the luxury of leading the honor toward the tenace without risking losing a trick which would not otherwise be lost.

When the opponents have only three cards in the suit, or when a suit has been reduced to where the opponents have only three cards, if a finesse is to be taken and high cards are available to lead toward the finesse, the high card should be led when the opponents hold specifically the second and the fifth highest cards remaining outstanding in the suit.

When you can judge from the bidding or from the play that the finessable card is accompanied by a sufficient number of low cards so that it is adequately guarded, there is nothing to lose by leading an honor toward the tenace. This gives the opponent an opportunity to go wrong by failing to cover. In addition, when this situation exists, you should always consider the possibility that the hand opposite the finessable card has intermediate cards which might be smothered, provided the honor is led toward the tenace.

I hope that this study has thrown new light on what previously were dark corners concerning the matter of leading high for a finesse.

THE RUFFING FINESSE

With a singleton opposite a holding of A Q J, a simple finesse is taken by leading the singleton and playing the jack, providing for an immediate discard on the ace. The ruffing finesse works when the king is offside (or behind the A Q J) by playing the ace first, then leading the queen, planning to ruff if the queen is covered and to discard if it is not covered. With no information as a guide, declarer should choose the ruffing finesse in preference to the simple finesse for the reason that the ruffing finesse will lose one less trick when it fails.

DUMMY
♠ A 6 2
♡ K 9 4
◇ A Q J 10
♣ K J 3

DECLARER
♠ 9 5 4
♡ A Q J 10 6 3
◇ 4
♣ A Q 8

Six hearts is a cinch if you don't get a spade lead. You take a ruffing finesse in diamonds, discarding both spade losers, while your ace of spades still controls the suit. Even if the opening lead is a spade, the ruffing finesse is still the superior play. If West holds the king of diamonds tripleton, the regular finesse enables you to get rid of one spade loser on the ace of diamonds immediately, and, perhaps, another on the fourth diamond honor after you have ruffed once. But when East holds the king of diamonds, you get rid of two losing spades no matter how many times the king is guarded. Your chances are 50 percent that East holds the king of diamonds, and they are only slightly better than 33 percent that West holds the king of diamonds doubleton or tripleton. Change the hand slightly and decide how you would play a seven hearts contract:

DUMMY
♠ A 3 2
♡ K 9 4 2
◊ A Q J
♣ K J 3

DECLARER
♠ 5 4
♡ A Q J 10 6 3
◊ 4
♣ A Q 8 7

You have a choice of plays. If West has the king of diamonds, you take a simple finesse and throw your losing spade on dummy's ace of diamonds. If East has the king of diamonds, you play the ace of diamonds first and discard the spade on the queen of diamonds unless East covers, in which case you return to dummy and discard a spade on the jack of diamonds.

On this particular hand, whether to take the plain finesse or the ruffing finesse is largely a guess. I suppose you might run a lot of tricks in hearts and clubs to try to discover who started with the fewer number of cards in those suits, then guess that the player holding more cards in spades and diamonds would be more likely to hold the king of diamonds. Personally, I am not impressed by this procedure. You cannot approach a complete count because you cannot play on either spades or diamonds and must keep at least one high club in dummy for a reentry. That would leave four or five unknown cards in each opponent's hand, and, assuming they have given nothing away with their discarding, the odds about the location of the king of diamonds would be 50–50. I suppose someone could prove me wrong, but for myself, I would rather depend on intuition, or a hunch, or what is commonly called table presence.

If you stopped at six hearts, you have twelve tricks off the top, even when the opponents get off to their best opening lead of a spade. The ruffing finesse is the safe one to take because you get rid of your losing spade, even when the finesse loses to West. If East has the king of diamonds and you lose a finesse to that card, the opposition will also cash a spade to set you one at six.

Sometimes the ruffing finesse can involve two cards and be, in effect, a double finesse, as in Fig. 4-10.

Fig. 4-10

	North	
	♠ J 10 9 2 ♡ 10 8 7 ◇ 7 5 2 ♣ 9 3 2	
♠ K 7 5 4 ♡ 4 2 ◇ K 9 8 ♣ Q J 10 8		♠ Q 8 6 3 ♡ 3 ◇ Q 10 6 3 ♣ 7 6 5 4
	♠ A ♡ A K Q J 9 6 5 ◇ A J 4 ♣ A K	

South, playing six hearts, gets the club queen opening lead. His problem is what to do about his two diamond losers. At first glance it looks as if the only chance is to lead a small diamond from dummy and hope the king-queen of diamonds are both with East. The odds against East's holding both the king and the queen are 3 to 1. Take a second look. If the spade honors are split, the hand can be made with a ruffing finesse—and the odds are 3 to 1 against West's holding both the king and queen of spades (guarded, of course. If he has king-queen doubleton we are still okay).

So, by going for the ruffing finesse, South can change the odds from 3 to 1 against him to 3 to 1 in his favor. He should win the ace of clubs and lay down the ace of spades. To preserve entries to dummy, he must lead the nine of hearts and overtake it with dummy's ten. Now the lead is the jack of spades. If East covers this, declarer should trump with a heart honor, return to dummy by leading a small trump, and lead the ten of spades.

If East covers again, declarer will return to the dummy once more to discard a diamond on dummy's good spade. Whenever East fails to cover, South simply discards one of his diamonds.

When the hand in Fig. 4-11 appeared in a duplicate game, the number of tricks taken by South in a spade contract ran all the way from nine to twelve.

Fig. 4-11

	North	
	♠ A J 3 ♡ 5 4 3 ◇ A Q 10 9 ♣ A Q J	
♠ 8 ♡ A Q 9 6 ◇ 8 4 2 ♣ 10 8 5 4 3		♠ 6 4 ♡ J 10 7 ◇ K 7 5 3 ♣ K 9 6 2
	♠ K Q 10 9 7 5 2 ♡ K 8 2 ◇ J 6 ♣ 7	

Those players in a four spade contract who took the straight diamond finesse soon discovered how unlucky they were when East switched to a heart, and the defenders won not only the king of diamonds, but also three heart tricks. Other players better acquainted with the ruffing finesse generally managed to take twelve tricks. Let us follow the play, assuming an opening lead of the eight of spades. To preserve the trump entries in the dummy, declarer won this in his own hand and then led to the ace of clubs for a ruffing finesse. East's best play, when declarer led the queen of clubs, was to cover with the king, which South trumped. Declarer then returned to the dummy with a trump and discarded a small diamond on the jack of clubs. Next he led the ace of diamonds, followed by the queen. Again, East could gain nothing by not covering, and, after trumping that, South was able to go to the dummy with the remaining trump and discard two hearts on dummy's good diamonds, losing only one heart trick.

THE BACKWARD FINESSE

Fig. 4-12

	North	
	♠ Q 8 7 ♡ A Q 10 ◇ 7 6 5 2 ♣ K J 9	
♠ 3 2 ♡ 7 5 4 3 ◇ Q J 10 4 ♣ 10 7 5		♠ A 5 ♡ K 8 2 ◇ A K 8 3 ♣ Q 8 4 2
	♠ K J 10 9 6 4 ♡ J 9 6 ◇ 9 ♣ A 6 3	

In Fig. 4-12, East opened one no-trump, and South overcalled two spades. North, the enthusiastic type, jumped to the spade game.

West led the queen of diamonds and continued with the jack of diamonds after East played the eight-spot. South trumped, led a spade to East's ace of spades, and ruffed the diamond return. A top spade revealed the 2–2 trump break, so South led the jack of hearts and finessed to East's king of hearts, losing his third trick. As South trumped the fourth diamond, he realized he had to decide how to handle the club suit. North and

South together had a total of 21 high-card points; West showed three high-card points when he led the queen and jack of diamonds, for a total of 24. This left just 16 points for East who had opened the bidding with one no-trump. Therefore, *East held the queen of clubs, and the normal finesse would fail.*

While it was evident East held the queen of clubs, it was far from clear who held the ten of clubs. A play was available by which South could finesse for the ten of clubs rather than the queen of clubs, and this play is called the backward finesse. It is a play you make when the bidding tells you the normal finesse will fail.

South crossed to the dummy with a heart and led the jack of clubs, intending to let it ride if East did not cover. East had no better play than to cover, so South won the ace of clubs and led small toward the king-nine. When West played low, he finessed the nine. This way, he brought in three club tricks without loss and fulfilled his contract.

Sometimes you can spot the situation for a backward finesse not because your opponents bid something, but because they did not bid at all.

In Fig. 4-13, West opened the jack of hearts, and East continued the suit, South trumping the third round. South pulled trump in three rounds and led the ten of clubs for a finesse. East won the king and returned a club. At this stage of the game, South had seen East play the A K Q of hearts and the king of clubs. This came to a total of 12 high-card points, and East, with a chance to open the bidding, had not done so. If East had the queen of diamonds in addition to his other high-card points, he would have had 14 and certainly would have bid something.

Based on this reasoning, South decided East did not have the queen of diamonds but might have the ten of diamonds. The nine-eight of diamonds in dummy would give him a chance to try the backward finesse. South won the queen of clubs, led the jack of diamonds, and, whether West covered or not, South was sure to bring in the diamond suit without loss because a finesse against the ten of diamonds in the East hand was going to work.

Sometimes the backward finesse is used as an "avoidance play" to keep a dangerous hand from gaining the lead:

In Fig. 4-14, with South playing three no-trump, West opened his fourth best heart. South held up his ace until the third round, noting from the play of the spot cards that West probably had started with five hearts. In counting his tricks South saw he had five tricks outside the club suit, so had to have the four clubs to bring his total to nine. He hoped to develop the club suit without letting West in, so planned to take any finesse into East.

However, when South led the jack of clubs, intending to pass it to East, West covered with the queen, and North won the ace of clubs. Had South seen all the cards, he would have taken the backward finesse on the return and ended up with ten tricks, but declarer couldn't risk the chance that West had started with the queen-ten doubleton, so he next played the king of clubs. When the ten of clubs did not drop, declarer just had to hold his

Fig. 4-15 Dlr: N Vul: 0

	North	
	♠ A 6 5 3 ♡ Q 9 ◇ A 10 9 7 2 ♣ A 7	
West		**East**
♠ Q 8 2 ♡ 10 6 4 3 ◇ J 5 3 ♣ 8 6 5		♠ 10 ♡ A K J 8 5 ◇ Q 6 ♣ Q J 10 9 2
	South	
	♠ K J 9 7 4 ♡ 7 2 ◇ K 8 4 ♣ K 4 3	

NORTH	EAST	SOUTH	WEST
1◇	1♡	1♠	Pass
2♠	3♣	4♠	All Pass

breath and play another club. Since all these stories are used to illustrate a point, it was fitting that South enjoyed a happy ending, as West showed out on the third club. East won with the ten, but could do no further harm.

THE DISCOVERY FINESSE

Sometimes the opponents bid too much and help you out, as in Fig. 4-15.

West led the three of hearts, and East won the first two heart tricks before switching to a club. It sounded on the bidding as if East had two suits of five or more cards and, therefore, not more than three cards in diamonds and spades. Declarer set out to find out how many diamonds East had. He won the club in dummy and laid down the ace of diamonds. He then led a small diamond toward the closed hand so that, if East were out of diamonds and wanted to trump, he would be ruffing a losing diamond rather than declarer's king of diamonds. However, when East followed to the second diamond, declarer expected to find him with only one spade. There was nothing declarer could do if West's three trumps included both the queen and ten—West was going to get a trick no matter what—but if East's singleton was either the queen or the ten, the suit could be brought in without loss. Declarer laid down the king of spades, and when he saw East drop the ten he led the jack of spades for a backward-type discovery finesse through West.

THE OBLIGATORY FINESSE

All the books I have give a combination something like this:

DUMMY
K 6 4 2

DECLARER
Q 7 5 3

They tell you that you can take three tricks with this combination provided you can guess who has the ace and provided the ace is doubleton. If you think East has the ace, you should lead low from the North hand and play South's queen. If this holds the trick, you then lead low from the South hand and play low from North as well. If East started with the doubleton ace, the ace will have to fall, and the balance of the suit will belong to you. If you make this play with nothing to guide you as to who has the ace, you just have to guess one way or the other.

Authors of the books who give you this advice are not paying enough attention to McTavish's Rule, "Give the suckers a chance to go wrong."

Using McTavish's Rule, if you have no idea who has the ace, you lead toward the closed hand *twice.* Of course, this assumes you have plenty of entries to dummy. This works just as well as the textbook procedure when the setup happens to be

K 6 4 2
J 10 9 A 8
Q 7 5 3

But suppose the setup happens to be

K 6 4 2
J 9 A 10 8
Q 7 5 3

You lead low from the dummy toward the South hand, and, when the queen holds the trick, you come to the conclusion you have guessed right as to who has the ace of the suit. Now you return to the dummy and again lead low from the key suit. Of course, East has seen West play the nine and ought to have some idea about your distribution which would convince him you are not down to the singleton jack, but after all, there is McTavish's admonition. I have known East players who forgot whether their partner played the nine and who had trouble enough ducking an ace one time, let alone ducking twice in a row. Believe it or not, some of them are not as bad players as you think they are.

But I notice the textbooks always give you, in addition to your king and queen, the lowest spot cards in the suit. In actual play, you don't often get those particular cards. Frequently your holding is more like this:

K 6 4 2
J 5 A 10 8
Q 9 7 3

Once more, you make a good guess and lead low from North toward your hand, and the queen holds the trick. This time East has only the play of the five-spot by West to guide him. When you get back to the dummy and lead the four-spot, he is more likely to play the ace than he would have been had West played the nine. You and I know he should have some idea about our distribution and should not make this play, but you have nothing to lose. If East started with the ace doubleton, it will now fall. If he started with the A J x, nothing would bring in three tricks for you.

Another distribution might be the following:

K 9 4 3 2
J 5 A 10 8 6
Q 7

Now when you lead toward the closed hand the second time, East may really have a problem. If you started with a singleton queen, he does not want to play his ace. If you started with the queen-jack doubleton, he may have to play it now or lose it forever. Leading low toward the closed hand when the ace is just ahead of the closed hand is technically just as good as leading once from the dummy and once from the closed hand and gives you whatever advantage may accrue to you from the application of McTavish's admonition.

WHICH FINESSE TO TAKE FIRST

So far in our studies we have considered the proper handling of finessing situations in a single unit. In playing the dummy, however, where we have four suits to manipulate, problems may arise in more than one suit.

First, let's look at situations where two or more finesses can be tried. Let's see which one we should take first, or perhaps which one we should forgo in order to take a finesse in a different suit.

DUMMY
♠ 8 4
♡ A K 6 2
♢ A K Q
♣ J 10 4 2

DECLARER
♠ A Q 5
♡ J 4
♢ J 10 9 4
♣ A K Q 5

You play six no-trump from the south hand and receive an opening club lead. You have eight winners in the minors and three in the majors, for a total of eleven, so you must develop one more trick. Which of the two possible finesses, spades or hearts, should you try first? If you lead a spade to the queen and the king is on your right, you obviously get your twelfth trick in spades. Or you can lead a small heart from North toward the jack of hearts, taking an indirect finesse against the queen. If East holds the queen, your jack of hearts will provide the twelfth trick.

But the question remains: which finesse—and why? If the direct finesse in spades is right, it makes no difference which finesse you take first.

But beware if the spade finesse is a loser and the heart finesse a winner! If you lose to the king of spades, you still have to lose a trick to the queen of hearts in order to establish a heart trick. That's why it is essential to take the indirect finesse first. If it wins, you will never have to take the spade finesse because you will have your twelve tricks. Should the heart finesse fail, you will still have the direct finesse in spades to fall back on. With the direct finesse, you do not have to lose a trick when the finesse is successful, but with an indirect finesse you must automatically allow for the loss of one trick in order to establish another.

Here is a general rule to tuck away in your memory: *Other things being equal, when both a direct finesse and an indirect finesse are available and the success of one will make the other unnecessary, take the indirect finesse first. In other words, first take the finesse which must lose a trick, even though it is successful.*

This hand is based on the same principle with a slight variation: You are in six spades and get a trump opening:

DUMMY
♠ J 10 9 8 6 2
♡ 7 4
♢ 8 5
♣ 9 6 4

DECLARER
♠ A K Q 4 3
♡ K 6
♢ A Q
♣ A K Q J

When East follows suit, you win the first trick with a top spade in your hand, as you might need those small spades as entries to the dummy.

It is not hard to isolate the problem. You have six tricks in spades, four in clubs, and one in diamonds, for a total of eleven. To develop the twelfth trick you may take either the indirect finesse in hearts or the direct finesse in diamonds. The general principle just established stated that the indirect finesse should be taken first. However, if the heart finesse is taken early and fails, the opponents can cash two heart tricks.

So here's the cure for that. After winning the spade, cash four clubs, discarding one of dummy's hearts. Now, even if the indirect finesse in hearts fails, we lose only one trick in that suit and still have the direct finesse in diamonds left as a final resort. At trick six, cross to the dummy with a small trump and lead the heart. If *East* turns up with the ace of hearts, the hand is over because the king of hearts provides a parking place for one of North's small diamonds. If *West* wins the ace of hearts, you enter dummy by trumping a heart or leading a trump and have the diamond finesse in reserve. If either finesse is right, you will have twelve tricks . . . and the odds are 3 to 1 that at least one of the finesses will be right.

In the next hand finesses are available in each of the four suits.

DUMMY
♠ A Q 4 3
♡ 3
♢ 9 8 4 2
♣ 10 9 5 4

DECLARER
♠ 2
♡ A K J 10 9 8 4
♢ A Q J
♣ K 6

South is playing four hearts and gets the lead of the jack of spades. Should he take the spade finesse? The heart finesse? The diamond finesse? Or lead up to his king of clubs?

South decides West is not the sort of player who would lead the jack of spades if he also held the king of spades, so he rules out the spade finesse and wins with dummy's ace. In dummy for the only time, his next decision is which of the other three finesses to take. In the end he has nothing to go on except probability. If he leads a club and finds the ace in East's hand, his problems are immediately solved, as he will lose at most one trick in each red suit.

If he finesses either of the red suits at trick two, he will eventually have to lead clubs from his hand and lose two clubs. That means he will have to bring in one of the red suits without loss. If he tries the diamond finesse and it works, he will still have a diamond loser unless East started with only one guard for his king. The situation is a little better in hearts, where a winning finesse against the queen is likely to bring in that suit without a loss.

The best percentage play is the lead of the club at trick two. This has a 50–50 chance. If it loses, there is still a reasonable chance of bringing in the heart suit without loss, since either opponent can hold the queen alone or with only one guard. One or the other of the opponents will have this holding one time out of three. This combination chance is better than any single chance. The odds that either the ace of clubs will be right or the heart suit can be brought in without loss are approximately 2 to 1.

Fig. 4-16

Often it is necessary to take a finesse that will lose a trick even when it succeeds rather than a direct finesse that will lose no tricks if it wins, but may not produce enough tricks to bring home the contract.

Consider the hand in Fig. 4-16.

North opened the bidding with one diamond, East overcalled one spade, and you, as South, eventually became declarer at three no-trump. West opened the eight of spades in response to his partner's overcall. Declarer let the king win the first trick, and won the continuation. Since you can count on five tricks in the majors, you need four in the minors. Which suit do you attack first?

A successful finesse in diamonds will bring in the four additional tricks required. A successful finesse against the queen of clubs will bring in three tricks, and the ace of diamonds will provide the fourth one. Which finesse do you take first?

As we described previously, you first take the finesse where you may lose a trick in order to gain one.

The proper play is to lead the ten of clubs and let it ride if it is not covered. If it loses to the queen and the defenders take an additional club trick, you still can try the diamond finesse for your ninth trick.

Fig. 4-17

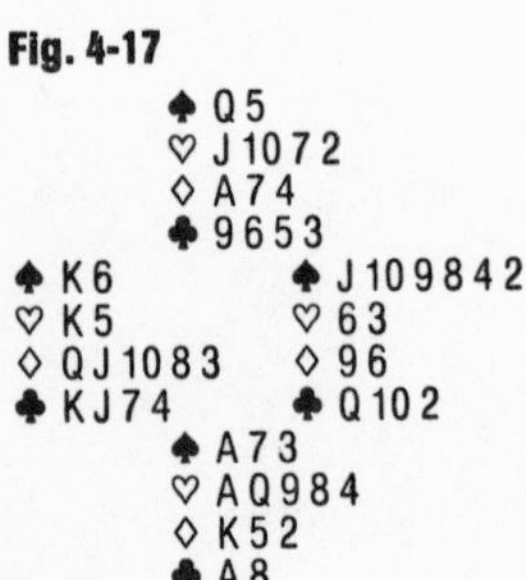

If you take the diamond finesse first and lose to the king, East can establish his spades while he has the ace of clubs for an entry. The favorable location of the queen of clubs then would be of no value to you. You would win only eight tricks.

If both finesses fail—well, tough luck!

On the next hand, in Fig. 4-17, we are playing four hearts, and the queen of diamonds is led.

Examining the dummy, we see two losers in the minor suits, a possible loser in hearts, and one spade loser.

If the king of spades is with West, we can shed a diamond loser from dummy on the ace of spades, but it is necessary to do this before the defenders establish diamonds, so the proper play is not to win the diamond lead in dummy and promptly finesse hearts, but to win the king of diamonds in the South hand and lead a low spade. West will win the king of spades and lead back the jack of diamonds. If you are not playing match-point duplicate and want to play as safely as possible to ensure your contract, win dummy's ace of diamonds, cash the queen of spades and forgo the heart finesse altogether. Lead the jack of hearts in case East has the king and decides to cover, but go up with the ace. (You still may drop a singleton king in West's hand, as he will have this holding something better than 6 percent of the time.)

You will receive dividends from this play, for when you lead your ace of spades, West can trump—but only with the king of hearts—as you proceed to discard dummy's diamond loser.

Here is a different situation:

DUMMY
♠ 7 3 2
♡ A 4 3 2
◇ A 9 4
♣ 8 5 4

DECLARER
♠ A Q J 10 9
♡ 7 5
◇ K 6 3
♣ A Q J

You are playing four spades and West has led the king of hearts. There is no trouble isolating the problem: you have a potential loser in each of the four suits. You have exactly two entries to dummy. Two successful finesses in clubs will eliminate the club loser, while two successful finesses in spades will eliminate the spade loser, provided East has not more than two guards on his king of spades. In spite of this, the club finesse should be taken first.

If you take the club finesse and it loses, you will have to use dummy's remaining entry to take the spade finesse, but you can still bring in the spade suit without loss, provided East has the king of spades and not more than one other spade. East is much more likely to have a singleton or doubleton king of spades than he is to have a singleton or doubleton king of clubs. As a matter of fact, when you and the dummy hold only six cards of a suit, the chances of the king's being singleton or doubleton in a specific hand are only 4.85 percent, but when you and the dummy hold eight cards of a suit, the chances the king will be singleton or doubleton in a specific hand rise to 16.39 percent. So, if you take the club finesse first and it loses, you still have a reasonable chance to bring home your contract. If you take the spade finesse first and it loses, your chances are very slim.

On some hands, selecting the proper finesse is simply a matter of odds,

Fig. 4-18

	North	
	♠ K J 8 6 2 ♡ J 9 4 2 ◇ 4 3 2 ♣ K	
♠ 7 ♡ K 8 5 3 ◇ K J 9 6 ♣ J 10 9 8		♠ 5 3 ♡ 10 7 6 ◇ 8 7 ♣ A Q 7 6 3 2
	♠ A Q 10 9 4 ♡ A Q ◇ A Q 10 5 ♣ 5 4	

but on others, you can add to your chances by selecting the finesse in a suit which may become established.

In Fig. 4-18, West leads the jack of clubs against your four spades contract. East wins the ace of clubs and returns the eight of diamonds.

In addition to the ace of clubs, you have a potential heart loser and two potential diamond losers. While it would be most unlucky to lose all three finesses, the lead of the ominous eight of diamonds makes it appear that both diamond finesses will fail. However, time is on your side, so you insert the ten of diamonds, losing to West's jack of diamonds. You win the trump return with the ace in your hand, ruff a club, and lead the dummy's jack of spades, underplaying the ten of spades to preserve entries both ways. Now you take the heart finesse and not a second diamond finesse—not only because of the lead of the eight of diamonds by East, but because the heart suit has some potential even if the finesse loses. Your queen of hearts loses to West's king of hearts, but you are now able to discard one diamond loser on the jack of hearts, and, when the ten of hearts falls, the nine of hearts provides a parking place for your last diamond loser. Of course, the ten of hearts might not drop, but a declarer should be rewarded with *some* luck when three finesses fail.

On the next deal declarer refused to take the finesse offered him at trick one because he had a finesse to take later that guaranteed his contract whether it succeeded or not.

DUMMY
♠ A 9 5 2
♡ K 7 4 2
◇ A Q
♣ 7 4 2

DECLARER
♠ Q J
♡ A Q J 9 6 5
◇ 7 3
♣ A 6 5

South was playing a four hearts contract, and the opening lead was the six of diamonds. Declarer counted one spade loser, one diamond loser, and two club losers. If the diamond finesse worked, he would have only three losers. However, if the diamond finesse lost, East was almost sure to find the switch to clubs—where there were two losers. If this was South's unlucky day and the spade finesse also lost, the contract would be sunk.

Declarer was not playing match-point duplicate, however, and he decided to guarantee his contract. He won the ace of diamonds, pulled trumps with the ace and queen, and led the queen of spades. If that finesse lost, he planned to cash the jack of spades and go to the dummy with a trump to discard one of his losing clubs on the ace of spades. At the worst, he would lose one trick each in spades, diamonds, and clubs. If the ten of spades should fall tripleton, he would take eleven tricks.

On the next hand, South found a play that would secure his slam 100 percent of the time, so long as he chose to take the right finesse first.

DUMMY
♠ K 10 6 4
♡ K 5 2
◇ A Q 3
♣ A Q 9

DECLARER
♠ A Q J 8 7 3 2
♡ A 6
◇ 7 4 2
♣ 8

Against a six spades contract, West led the queen of hearts, and South won the ace. One spade lead extracted trumps. South then cashed the king of hearts and trumped a heart to eliminate all the cards of that suit from his hand and dummy's. Now it was time to finesse in one of the minor suits. A success in either would give him his twelfth trick, but a *failure* in clubs would also give him his twelfth trick! South chose to finesse the suit where he had no losers—the eight of clubs was led, and dummy played the nine of clubs. Whatever East played, South had his contract. Declarer had three small diamonds in his hand, and, if East returned a minor suit card, there would be three winners in dummy to take care of the losers. If East preferred to commit suicide on a different road, he would lead a heart. South would discard one of his diamonds as dummy ruffed, and the minor suit aces would take care of the other two. If West played to split the jack-ten of clubs when the suit was first led, South would play dummy's queen. Whether East won the king of clubs or not, the contract was assured.

In the next hand, all the finesses fail, but the contract succeeds.

DUMMY
♠ A Q J 3
♡ 6 4 3
◇ 7 3
♣ A Q J 4

DECLARER
♠ K 10 9 8 5
♡ A Q 10
◇ A Q
♣ K 10 5

South plays at six spades and receives the opening lead of the eight of clubs. He wins in the closed hand and leads trumps. It takes three leads to clear the trump suit, and declarer still has a high trump in dummy. He cashes two more clubs, ending in dummy, and does not know what to discard on the fourth club. As both opponents have followed to three rounds of clubs, declarer knows they are down to all red cards and he can finesse for the king of diamonds, the king of hearts, or the jack of hearts. If all three of these cards are behind him, he can still make the hand. He leads a heart from dummy and puts in the ten-spot. West wins the jack, but he has had it. Whichever suit he returns, declarer wins the queen, goes to dummy with the high trump, and discards his other queen on the thirteenth club.

This hand appears in the collection of practically every bridge teacher I know. If it doesn't, it should, for it is a good one:

DUMMY
♠ 8 7 4 2
♡ A 10 9
◊ 8 5 2
♣ 6 5 4

DECLARER
♠ A 5
♡ K Q J
◊ A Q J 10
♣ A Q 3 2

South plays three no-trump, and West leads the three of spades, giving declarer hope that, since the two of spades is visible in the dummy, the lead is from a four-card suit. South counts six winners in top cards, and the other tricks will have to come from diamonds or clubs. Which minor suit finesse should he attempt when he makes use of his one entry to dummy?

Note that declarer can take three diamond tricks even if the finesse loses—but he has no guarantee he can take *four* diamond tricks if the finesse wins. East would have to have a singleton or doubleton king of diamonds for that approach to succeed. South should play for the three diamond tricks he can achieve by leading that suit directly from his own hand and save that one precious entry for a subsequent club finesse.

His best play, therefore, after winning the ace of spades at trick two, is to lead the ace of diamonds, followed by the queen of diamonds to get his three diamond tricks established. Eventually he will lead to dummy's ace of hearts and take the club finesse. If West's spade lead *was* from a four-card suit, South will have a 50–50 chance of fulfilling his contract by banking on the club finesse. There is less than 1 chance in 10 of picking up the diamond suit without loss.

Deals where most of the strength is concentrated in one hand create problems because of the shortage of entries into the opposite hand. On the next deal, South solved this problem by a judicious use of the finesse in Fig. 4-19.

Fig. 4-19

	North	
	♠ 9 6 4 ♡ 6 2 ◊ 7 5 3 ♣ A J 10 9 8	
♠ Q J 10 3 ♡ Q 9 5 4 ◊ 8 4 ♣ 6 5 3		♠ 8 7 2 ♡ J 10 8 ◊ K 10 9 6 ♣ Q 7 4
	♠ A K 5 ♡ A K 7 3 ◊ A Q J 2 ♣ K 2	

Against three no-trump, West led the queen of spades. South won the first trick and led the two of clubs to dummy's jack. If East wins this trick, South makes his contract with four clubs, one diamond, and two tricks in each of the major suits. But this particular East had been there before, so he ducked with his queen of clubs. South took advantage of this opportunity to lead a diamond from the dummy for a finesse. When the jack of diamonds held the trick, he led the king of clubs and overtook with dummy's ace of clubs (after all, East could have had the queen of clubs doubleton). The queen did not fall, so South abandoned clubs and took another diamond finesse. He hoped diamonds would break 3–3, with the king of diamonds onside, so he could take all four diamond tricks, but this didn't work either. However, his skill paid off, as the second diamond finesse provided three tricks in that suit which, with the two tricks in each of the other suits, brought his total to nine.

The next hand was played by Dick Frey, successful author, journalist, columnist, and champion player. He was No. 8 in the first group of players to be named Life Master when that designation was created, and he won most of the major national championships in the 30's and 40's.

In a contract of six hearts on this deal, it looked as though it all depended on the diamond finesse (Fig. 4-20).

Fig 4-20

West	North	East
	♠ 10 9 2 ♡ K 10 7 2 ◇ A Q ♣ A 10 5 2	
♠ 8 7 ♡ J 6 4 ◇ J 7 6 2 ♣ Q 9 6 4		♠ Q J 5 3 ♡ 9 ◇ K 10 9 4 3 ♣ J 7 3
	♠ A K 6 4 ♡ A Q 8 5 3 ◇ 8 5 ♣ K 8	

Frey decided in favor of the finesse of the four of spades! No, that is not a misprint—Dick finessed the four of spades. Here is how it happened. The opening lead was the eight of spades, and it was covered by the nine, jack, and king. Frey pulled three rounds of trumps, ending in the dummy, and led the ten of spades. East covered with the queen, and South won the ace, as West dropped his seven-spot.

Lesser mortals such as you and I might not have noticed that South now had a tenace position over East, but noticing such things is what makes champions. Dick went to dummy with the ace of clubs and led his two of spades, finessing the four-spot when East followed with the three of spades. On the established six of spades, he discarded dummy's queen of diamonds and subsequently ruffed his diamond loser in dummy, ending up with an overtrick!

Not all finesses are against kings and queens. By watching the spots, Frey was able to find one of the smallest finesses on record.

WHICH WAY TO FINESSE

One recurring problem is deciding which way to go when you have a two-way finesse for a queen.

With a combined holding of eight cards, the problem is simply "which way?" With nine cards, as in the diamond suit in this hand, the odds are very close to even. If you cash a top card from either hand and then lead low, the opponents following with small cards, it actually is only 52+ percent in favor of going up and playing for the drop. There are times, however, when you can get a count which will tell you which way to go.

Fig. 4-21

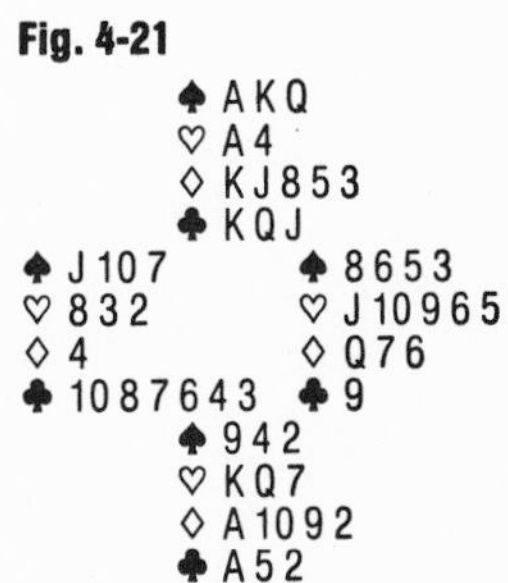

On Fig. 4-21, South had gotten himself to a seven no-trump and did not like any 52 percent odds on a grand slam. He received the opening lead of the jack of spades and decided to find out what he could about the adverse distribution. He found out that the spades were split 4–3, though he did not learn which opponent had four. He cashed three hearts, discarding a diamond from dummy, and learned that each of his opponents had three or more hearts. Now he tried clubs and quickly found out what he needed to know: East showed out on the second club, so West started with six of them. West had shown up with at least three spades and at least three hearts, so there was room in his hand for no more than one diamond. Declarer played dummy's king of diamonds first and then, with full assurance that his finesse would work, led the jack of diamonds for a successful finesse.

Sometimes there is a good reason to take a finesse a certain way other than knowing that your finesse is bound to win.

DUMMY
♠ K J 8 2
♡ Q 6 3
♢ K 8 7
♣ K J 2

DECLARER
♠ A 10 9 7 6 3
♡ 5 4
♢ A J 4
♣ A 6

With no opposing bidding, South got into a contract of four spades and received the opening lead of the jack of hearts which held the trick. The ten of hearts followed, and a third heart was covered by the queen, East's king, and ruffed by South. It looks like the extra trick depends only on a winning finesse in either clubs or diamonds.

BUT WAIT! There are three spades including the queen of spades outstanding, and if either opponent holds all three of them, a finesse will also be necessary in the trump suit. Which way? Does South start with the ace from his own hand or the king from dummy?

After checking out the trump situation, South finds a play that will guarantee his contract if all finesses fail. To give himself this protection, he wins the first spade in the North hand. If both opponents follow suit, declarer simply pulls the second spade and proceeds to finesse clubs or diamonds for an overtrick. If *West* shows out of spades, South takes the marked trump finesse against East with the same result. If *East* shows out of spades, South plans a throw-in play against West. He cashes the ace of spades, the ace of clubs, and the king of clubs, and trumps a club. Now a spade is led to West's queen, and he has to lead a diamond into South's ace-jack or lead a heart or a club, which will allow South to discard one of his diamonds while he ruffs in the dummy.

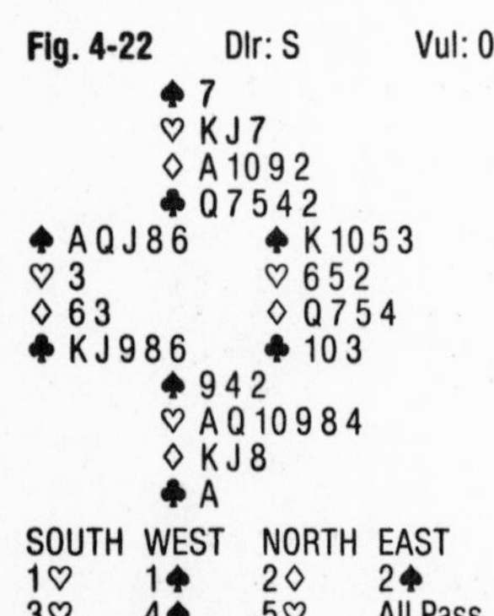

Fig. 4-22 is another one where knowing which way to finesse helped bring home the contract.

West led a trump—the only lead likely to give declarer a problem. It would be dangerous to pull trumps and then try to guess which way to finesse diamonds. If trumps are 3–1 and the diamond guess turns out bad, the defense will cash three spade tricks. Declarer might try the diamond finesse at trick two, while holding trumps in dummy as policemen against the run of the spades. However, if declarer misguesses the diamond, a second trump might be led at trick three and a third when a spade is conceded—leaving dummy without a trump for even one spade loser.

Our hero in the South seat found a way to handle the diamond guess. At trick two, a spade was led from dummy. East bounced up with the king of spades and led a second trump as *West showed out.* Dummy won the trick and led the small diamonds for a finesse into the "safe" West hand. If West won the queen of diamonds, he could not lead a trump, and declarer would win any return, ruff a spade, and eventually discard his other spade on dummy's fourth diamond. When the jack of diamonds held the trick, declarer trumped a spade with dummy's last trump. It was tempting to finesse diamonds again, but declarer decided to play it safe. West could have held up the queen with Q x x x. So declarer just came to his hand with the ace of clubs and took East's last trump away from him. When diamonds didn't break, he was unable to dispose of his last spade, but he had taken eleven tricks and fulfilled his contract.

Sometimes you decide which way to finesse after you know how many tricks you require from a certain suit. Here is a combination to illustrate this point:

DUMMY
A 9 4 2

DECLARER
K J 5 3

Notice that nine-spot in the North hand. It is an important card. If you want to play as safe as possible to take *three* tricks in the suit, your 100 percent play is to lead the king first and then lead low toward the dummy, inserting the nine if West plays low.

But suppose you have already lost your book and must take *four* tricks with this holding. You should now play *East* for the queen, as West will hold the queen doubleton only 13.5 percent of the time—so it is not good business to cash the king as before. You can make your contract if East has the queen, provided it is singleton, doubleton, or tripleton. However, in case East's queen is singleton, you don't play the ace first. You must lead low from North toward your hand so that if the queen comes down, singleton, you will be able to cash the jack and finesse against the 10 X X X in the West hand.

On hand 4-23, South can play West for the king of hearts and take an indirect finesse or he can play East for that card and take a direct finesse. If he guesses right, he makes his contract.

West did not find the killing lead of a spade, but got off to the lead of the queen of diamonds, indicating he did not have the ace or king. South trumped the diamond and won the next two tricks with the ace-king of clubs. Next came the decision about the heart suit. The thing that tipped the odds in favor of the indirect finesse was the fact that West had made a vulnerable overcall on a queen-high suit. South decided he would be more likely to hold either or both major-suit kings than would East, so a diamond was ruffed in the closed hand. Declarer's next lead of a small heart toward dummy's jack proved to be just what was needed to make the contract. West won and belatedly made the spade switch, but it was too late. Declarer won the ace of spades, cashed dummy's jack of hearts, and returned to his hand by ruffing another diamond. On the ace-queen of hearts, he discarded two of dummy's small spades and so conceded only the king of hearts and one spade trick.

On the next hand, declarer came to the conclusion that the indirect finesse was an odds-on favorite compared to the direct finesse.

Fig. 4-23 Dlr: S Vul: B

North: ♠ 6 5 3 2 ♡ J 6 ◇ 7 5 2 ♣ K Q J 4

West: ♠ K J 10 ♡ K 10 9 4 ◇ Q J 10 9 3 ♣ 2

East: ♠ Q 8 7 ♡ 7 3 2 ◇ A K 8 6 4 ♣ 7 6

South: ♠ A 9 4 ♡ A Q 8 5 ◇ — ♣ A 10 9 8 5 3

SOUTH	WEST	NORTH	EAST
1♣	1◇	2♣	3◇
5♣	Pass	Pass	Pass

Opening lead: ◇ Q

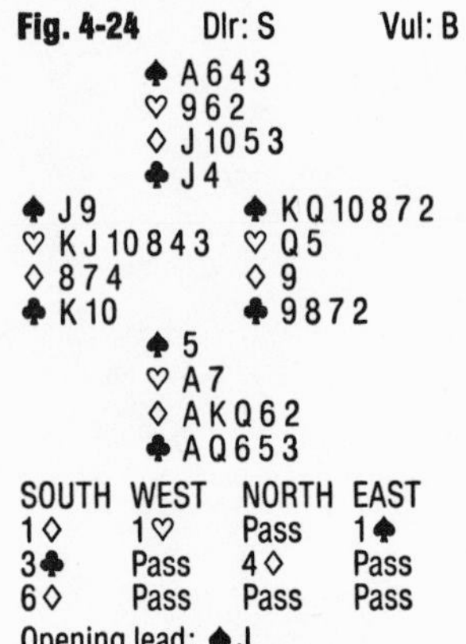

In Fig. 4-24, North's delayed jump raise encouraged South to try for a slam. East's doubtful call of a spade saw to it that West did not find the killing heart lead. After the opening lead of the jack of spades won by the ace in the North hand, South calculated his chances of going for a direct club finesse followed by a crossruff versus the chances of establishing the club suit to discard a couple of hearts from the North hand. In view of what seemed on the bidding to be wild distribution on the part of the opponents he decided that establishing the club suit offered the best bet.

Once he came to that conclusion, he next decided that the best way to approach the club suit was to take the indirect finesse. In keeping with these plans, he exhausted the opponents' trumps in three leads, ending in his own hand. The indirect finesse of clubs looked like a winner whenever West had the king, and even if East had the king with only two others, the discards would be available. West won the club trick with the king, but South could not be prevented from cashing dummy's jack of clubs and discarding dummy's heart losers on his good clubs.

Finally he took the ace of hearts and trumped his seven of hearts with dummy's last trump to come home with one spade, one heart, five diamonds in the closed hand, one ruff in dummy, and four clubs.

AVOIDING A FINESSE

In a six diamond contract on this hand, South got the opening lead of the queen of spades:

DUMMY
♠ 7 5
♡ Q 9 7
◇ A 9 8 6 2
♣ A J 6

DECLARER
♠ A K
♡ A K J 10
◇ K J 10 7 4
♣ Q 4

South sees one (highly improbable) loser in diamonds and a possible club loser. With a little care, he can be sure that he does not lose both of these tricks, even if everything is wrong. He takes the first diamond trick with the king in his own hand. If everyone follows suit, he goes ahead, pulls trump, and ends up taking the club finesse. If *East* shows out of diamonds, the marked diamond finesse is taken against West's queen with the same result.

However, if *West* shows out of diamonds, South cashes the ace of diamonds, leaving East with the singleton queen. Now he takes his other spade trick, as well as his four heart tricks, throwing away dummy's six of clubs. Now a diamond to East forces a club return or a sluff-ruff—in either event the club loser is avoided.

Had South carelessly taken the first diamond with dummy's ace, he would have been in trouble if *West* had Q x x in diamonds, and *East* the king of clubs.

THE FINESSE VERSUS SUIT ESTABLISHMENT

Some writers go to great lengths to tell you to try all sorts of fancy plays to avoid taking a finesse. That is not always the best way.

Playing three no-trump in the South seat, you get an opening lead of the six of hearts on this hand:

DUMMY
♠ 5 3
♡ A 5 4
◇ 6 5 3
♣ 9 7 6 4 2

DECLARER
♠ A K Q 4
♡ 10 7
◇ A K Q 2
♣ A Q 8

After you win the first or second heart lead, you have exactly seven more tricks off the top. The ninth trick can come either from the club finesse or from a 3–3 break in diamonds. If you are going to take the club finesse, you are going to have to take it right now. There are no more dummy entries, and it is unlikely an attractive end-play position will develop.

The club finesse is an even chance, while the 3–3 diamond break is only slightly better than one chance in three (35.53 percent if you want me to be exact). So you should take the club finesse. If that fails and West runs enough hearts to set you, and you later discover that diamonds broke 3–3 after all . . . just reflect it wasn't your lucky day.

Sometimes it is not all that easy:

DUMMY
♠ K 9 3
♡ A 7 4
◇ K 6 3 2
♣ A 9 2

DECLARER
♠ Q J 10 8 7
♡ K 6 2
◇ A 7 4
♣ Q 5

Instead of being in the ironclad contract of three no-trump, you play in four spades, getting a heart opening lead. Since you have a loser in each suit, you have to eliminate one of them. One way is to pull trumps and hope you can establish a thirteenth diamond on which to discard a loser. The superior play is to win the opening lead in dummy and promptly lead a small club toward your queen of clubs, taking the indirect finesse against the king. If East wins the king, you take the heart return, drive out the trump ace, cash the queen of clubs, go to the dummy with a diamond, and throw away a loser on the ace of clubs. This play is superior to banking everything on the 3–3 diamond break.

But there are times when you can try both plays:

DUMMY
♠ A 4
♡ 7 4 3
◇ K Q 7 4
♣ A 9 6 3

DECLARER
♠ K 7 3
♡ A Q 5
◇ A 8 2
♣ K 8 4 2

Playing three no-trump with the South hand, you get an opening lead of the queen of spades. You can count eight tricks off the top. For additional tricks you have chances in hearts, diamonds, and clubs. Can you try all three suits? You can if it proves necessary. There is no hurry about winning the first trick, and who knows what will develop if you don't? West probably will continue spades, win dummy's ace, and try the ace and king of clubs where you have the best chances. If both opponents follow, the game going trick has materialized. Just give them a club trick and you will have one. If either fails to follow to the first or second club, try the heart finesse. If that fails, you have as a last resort a possible 3–3 diamond break to fall back on.

On this hand you are playing three no-trump, and you can count eleven eventual winners. So what's the problem?

DUMMY
♠ Q 4 3
♡ J 3
◇ A Q 10
♣ J 10 9 8 5

DECLARER
♠ A 7
♡ A K
◇ K J 9 6 4
♣ Q 6 4 2

Given plenty of time, you simply concede two club tricks and take the rest, but plenty of time you don't have. Since West's opening lead was a heart, nine tricks are in jeopardy if you carelessly go about setting up the club suit to get them. The opponents will establish and run their hearts first, using the clubs for entries. They almost surely will take five or six tricks by the time you get the club suit established.

So what do you do? You have to fall back on that old friend, the indirect finesse, rather than try to establish the club suit. You win the first heart and lead the seven of spades toward dummy. If the king of spades is not with West, at least you get home with eight tricks by cashing out when they lead another heart.

Playing six spades on the next hand, you have eleven tricks off the top:

DUMMY
♠ K Q 4
♡ J 6 4 2
♢ A 9 6 2
♣ K Q

DECLARER
♠ A J 10 9 8
♡ A K 10
♢ K 7 4 3
♣ A

West opens a club or a diamond, and you can count on taking five spades, two hearts, two diamonds, and two clubs. You can establish your twelfth trick by conceding a diamond if the suit breaks 3–2. The odds are better than 2 to 1 that five outstanding cards will be divided 3–2.

A successful finesse of the ten of hearts would also bring in the twelfth trick, and that finesse is a 50–50 shot. In some cases a *losing* heart finesse will bring in twelve tricks just as surely as a winning heart finesse. If the ten of hearts loses to the queen of hearts, the jack of hearts in dummy becomes your twelfth trick *if you can reach it.* But say West has opened a diamond and continues that suit when he wins the queen of hearts—you are in dummy for the last time, and the ace-king of hearts irrevocably block the run of the suit.

Now it becomes obvious that your best shot is to take no heart finesse at all, but to win the diamond in your hand with the king, draw trumps, cash the ace of clubs, and develop hearts by banging down the A K 10. If the queen of hearts drops singleton or doubleton, you have thirteen tricks, but you always have your twelve and an entry to cash the jack of hearts which will take care of one of your diamond losers, while the king of clubs affords a parking place for the other.

Do you take a finesse or do you establish a suit? On the hand in Fig. 4-25, you have to do both, but you have to be careful which you do first.

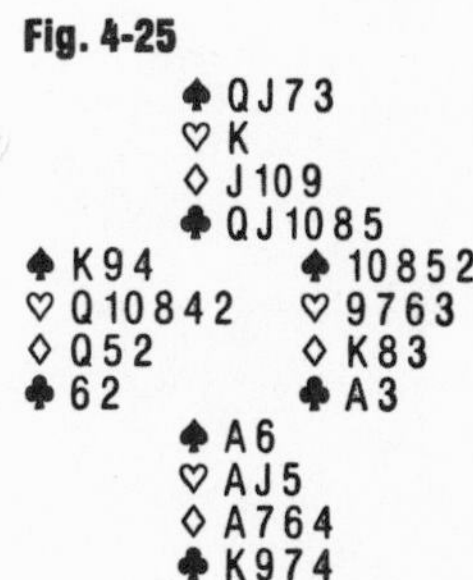

Fig. 4-25

West led the four of hearts against South's three no-trump contract, and dummy's lone king captured the first trick. With only four tricks off the top, South obviously has to develop some additional tricks. Four of these will come from the club suit, and here is another case where a *losing* finesse will develop the game-going trick. The catch is that South must establish this trick before touching clubs. The proper play is to lead the queen of spades at trick two and let it ride. West cannot do any damage by continuing hearts—or by doing anything else! South wins any return and knocks out the ace of clubs. Four clubs, one diamond, two hearts, and two spades make a total of nine tricks. If South carelessly goes about establishing the clubs first, East wins his ace of clubs and leads a heart through the ace-jack of hearts for an unhappy result for declarer.

Fig. 4-26

	North	
	♠ J 9 7 ♡ J 7 2 ◇ 7 3 ♣ K Q 10 9 5	
West ♠ K 10 6 5 ♡ Q 10 8 4 3 ◇ 9 4 ♣ 8 2		**East** ♠ Q 4 2 ♡ 9 6 5 ◇ K 10 8 2 ♣ A 6 3
	♠ A 8 3 ♡ A K ◇ A Q J 6 5 ♣ J 7 4	

Fig. 4-26 is a classic hand where you work on finesses and suit establishment at the same time.

South plays three no-trump, and West leads the four of hearts. South starts on the clubs by leading the four of clubs toward dummy, and West, seeing what looks like an entryless North hand, signals that he has an even number of clubs by playing the eight-spot. East declines the trick, so declarer leads a diamond, finessing the jack. When that holds, he leads the jack of clubs as if that is the only one he has left, overtaking with dummy's queen. But East is not fooled! His partner has played the eight and then the two of clubs, so East knows South has a club left.

But declarer is now home. He finesses the diamond again, then leads the ace of diamonds and concedes a diamond. This gives him four diamond tricks, two club tricks, two heart tricks, and a spade trick for a total of nine. There was nothing the defense could do because declarer timed his suit establishment plays and finesses exactly right.

South plays three no-trump with the cards below. West leads the seven of hearts, and East puts up the queen. How would you plan to take nine tricks?

DUMMY
♠ 10 2
♡ 8 3
◇ K J 2
♣ K Q 10 7 6 5

DECLARER
♠ K J 6
♡ K 5 2
◇ A 8 7 6 5
♣ A 2

Those clubs in dummy look mighty pretty, and South just might consider running off six of them which, with the ace-king of diamonds and the king of hearts, comes to nine tricks. Suppose declarer cashes the ace of clubs and leads a club toward dummy. West shows out, and the hand falls apart. South should have taken better care—after all, the 4–1 club break, though unexpected, is not all that unusual. He could have checked out the clubs while still preserving a second shot—diamonds. As it is, declarer can get back to his hand to take the diamond finesse, but can't get back again to run the fourth and fifth diamonds.

A painstaking declarer, visualizing a possible bad break, would start off by leading the two of clubs to dummy's king and then a club back to the ace. If both players follow, or if the jack of clubs falls, well and good. The king of diamonds is an entry to the dummy to take the balance of the clubs—and six clubs, two diamonds, and one heart account for nine tricks. When declarer plays this way and gets the bad news that East has four clubs, he is in his hand with the ace of clubs and tries his other shot—he must play on diamonds for five tricks. To do this, South falls back on the friendly finesse to save the hand from the bad suit break. He plays the jack of diamonds, the king of diamonds, the other top club, and returns to his hand with the ace of diamonds to take the eight-seven of diamonds. He is suitably rewarded, of course, for the West hand is:

♠ A 8 4 3 ♡ A J 9 7 4 ◇ Q 10 4 ♣ 3

The books tell us the odds slightly favor playing for the drop when you have eleven cards in a suit missing the king. Nevertheless, there are occasions when you take the finesse to insure making your contract.

DUMMY
♠ A 9 8 7 4 2
♡ K 7
◇ 10 4
♣ J 7 2

DECLARER
♠ Q J 10 6 3
♡ A 4 2
◇ 9 7
♣ A Q 5

Against a four spades contract, the defenders promptly cash two diamond tricks and switch to a heart. The best play is to win the king of hearts, cash the ace of hearts, and ruff a heart. After these preparations, lead a small club and put in the queen. If West wins the king of clubs, you will go with the book and bang down the ace of trumps when you regain the lead. However, the situation is entirely different if the club finesse wins. Now you lead the queen of spades and, if West plays low, let it ride. If East wins with the singleton king, he is end-played—he must either allow you a sluff-and-ruff, or he must lead a club that you will allow to ride to dummy's jack. If West shows out when you lead the queen of spades, you go up with the ace and lead a spade right back, putting East in with his king, thereby placing him in the same predicament.

TIMING THE FINESSE

Timing the finesse sounds like high-level stuff. Actually, all we are saying is, "Should we do something else *before* we take the finesse?"

Often there is something that must be considered before taking a finesse.

DUMMY
♠ K J 8
♡ K 5 2
◇ K J 5
♣ Q 10 5 4

DECLARER
♠ A 10 9 6 4
♡ A 7 3
◇ Q 10
♣ K J 7

At four spades you get the opening lead of the jack of hearts. I don't know which way you plan to finesse spades, but I do know you have some

Fig. 4-27

Fig. 4-28

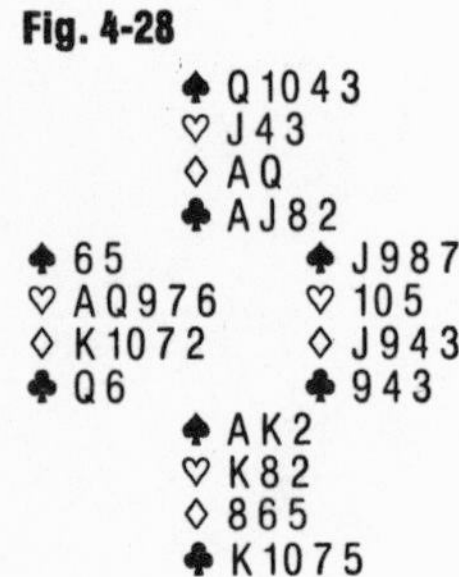

important business to transact before you finesse at all. First, you had better establish a diamond for a discard of your heart loser. Win the ace of hearts in your hand, then lead the queen of diamonds. Once that's out of the way you can start worrying about the queen of spades and the ace of clubs.

On hand 4-27 West opened the queen of clubs against South's contract of four spades. East won the ace of clubs and shifted to the jack of hearts. The finesse in trumps is certainly going to be a key play in the hand, and the odds overwhelmingly favor the finesse rather than the drop of a singleton king of spades with West. However, the trump finesse should be postponed and the indirect diamond finesse taken first. Declarer should win the second trick in dummy, lead to the ace of diamonds, and play back the small diamond toward the queen. If West holds the king of diamonds, declarer will have a parking place for his heart loser. If the king of diamonds shows up in the East hand, declarer still has the finesse against the king of spades for his tenth trick. In other words, if the spade finesse loses and the diamond finesse wins, it is essential that the diamond finesse be taken first.

In Fig. 4-28, playing three no-trump, South got the opening lead of the seven of hearts. He was not displeased when dummy's jack held the trick. It was obvious clubs could be finessed into West from whom another heart lead could do no harm. So South cashed dummy's ace of clubs and ran the jack of clubs. West, in with the queen of clubs, proved he was no friend of South's by leading the two of diamonds. This play definitely sent South to the library. He counted his tricks—three spades, one heart, one diamond, and three clubs. He needed another trick from somewhere.

There were two "somewheres" among his assets—spades and diamonds. If the diamond finesse failed and a heart came back, South knew he was sunk immediately, so he considered the spade situation. There was a chance spades would split 3–3. There was a chance the jack of spades was singleton or doubleton. There was even an off chance that East started with a singleton spade which would show up after South had cashed the ace-king, so he would know to take a successful finesse of dummy's ten of spades. Or, if it turned out that West had four spades to the jack, South might even be a genius and figure out on the third spade lead to finesse the ten-spot. So he rose with dummy's ace of diamonds. Of course, when he got around to leading spades, he found out on the third lead that nothing he had hoped would happen had happened and he got home with only eight tricks.

South was in too big a hurry to take the "safe" club finesse. Had he delayed doing so, he could have found out whether the diamond finesse was necessary. After winning the first trick with the jack of hearts, he should simply lead three rounds of spades to find out the story in that suit. Now he would know he could not bring in more than three spade tricks, and he would go ahead with the club finesse. When the diamond came back, he would know he had to take that finesse for his game-going trick.

On this hand, declarer took his finesse a trick too late. On the next hand, he took it too soon.

In a six spades contract, South got the queen of hearts as the opening lead. He trumped that and laid down the ace of spades. When East showed out, declarer led a small trump toward dummy. That was a mistake. He should never have led the second trump. While in dummy, he took the losing club finesse, and West fired back a third round of spades, cutting dummy's trumps down to one. Declarer was able to discard one of dummy's diamonds on a top club, but the queen of diamonds was offside and there weren't enough trumps in dummy to handle two diamond losers, so he had to go down one.

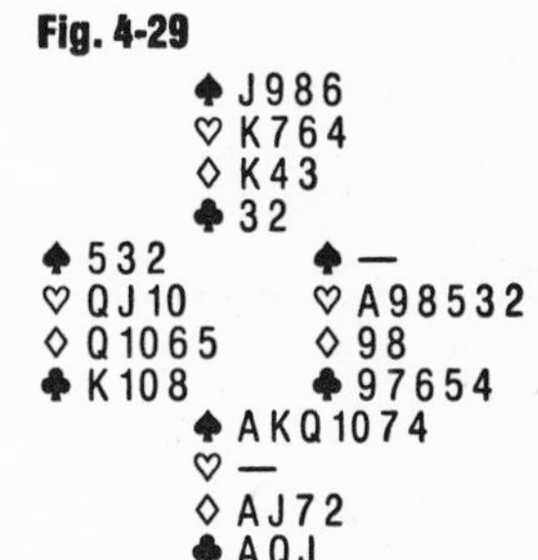

Once declarer discovers West has all three trumps, he should finesse clubs before leading a second trump. His best bet is probably to win the first spade trick in dummy and immediately come off with a club. But even after leading the trump ace, he can go to dummy with the king of diamonds and finesse clubs. When that fails, he gets rid of one of dummy's diamonds on the long club and crossruffs hearts and diamonds to bring home an easy twelve tricks.

Sometimes the finesse should be deferred as a sort of hold-up play. Look at the hand in Fig. 4-30.

Against South's three no-trump contract, West led the ten of hearts. Declarer was in a hurry to test the heart suit finesse, so he played the jack of hearts to the first trick. East covered with the queen of hearts, and South won his ace, but lost his contract. West, holding both missing aces, was able to gain the lead often enough to establish and run his hearts.

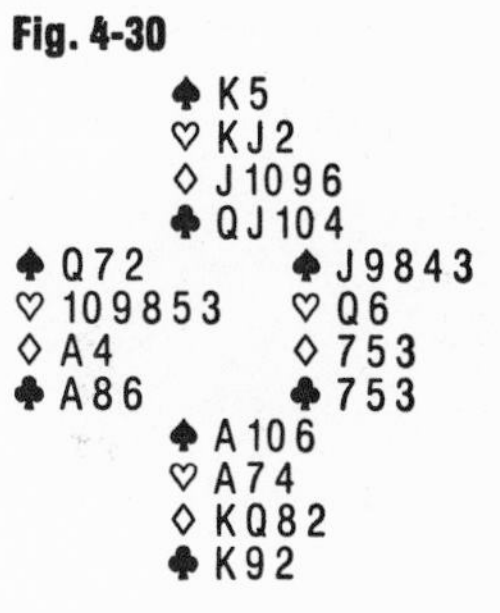

It was all right to take the heart finesse, but the play should have been deferred. Declarer should play low from dummy on the first trick, winning the ace of hearts. After he tackles a minor suit and gets another heart lead from West, he can try the finesse. When East wins his queen of hearts, he has no heart left to return. Whatever he leads back, declarer knocks out the other ace and takes ten tricks, still holding the king of hearts to control that suit.

[*Yes, we noticed that, in the given hand, South can drop East's queen of hearts and take eleven tricks. Since this section is about timing the finesse, however, we just want to point out that this is a time when the finesse, if taken, should be later rather than at the first opportunity.*]

True, the finesse is one of the greatest devices known to bridge players for developing those extra tricks, but it is not as simple as the textbooks make it appear. It is well to know the various ways it can be used and to know at what moment in the play it can be used to best advantage.

FINESSES BASED ON ACTIONS TAKEN BY THE OPPONENTS

There are hands where the opponents make exactly the right bids to guide you down the road to success (Fig. 4-31).

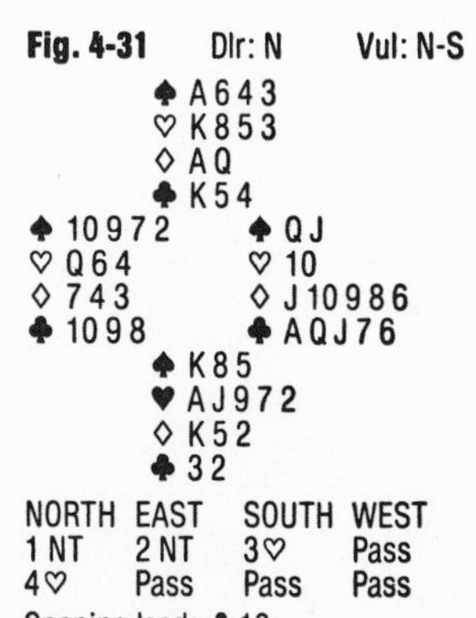

West led the ten of clubs, and declarer trumped the third round of the suit.

The use of the unusual two no-trump bid by East indicated to South that East had a lot of cards in the minor suits and very few cards in the major suits. Declarer decided to find out how those major cards were distributed. He led small to dummy's ace of spades, as East dropped the queen. Well, if East really had one spade and two hearts, then let him use one of his trumps to ruff a loser and declarer might still win ten tricks. So a second spade was led from the dummy. When East sheepishly produced the jack of spades, declarer won the king and decided that East likely had at most one heart. Just in case East had made a foolhardy two no-trump overcall on a 2–2–4–5 shape, declarer took the safeguard of leading to the ace-queen of diamonds before cashing his ace of hearts. When East produced the ten of hearts, declarer was reasonably sure it was a singleton. First he played the king of diamonds, throwing a spade from dummy, then he confidently passed the jack of hearts. Even if, by weird chance, East had started with the queen-ten of hearts doubleton, he would now be end-played, and the ensuing sluff-ruff would eliminate South's spade loser. As it was, the heart finesse against West was successful, and declarer ended up with ten tricks—a feat he would not have been likely to accomplish without the two no-trump bid from East.

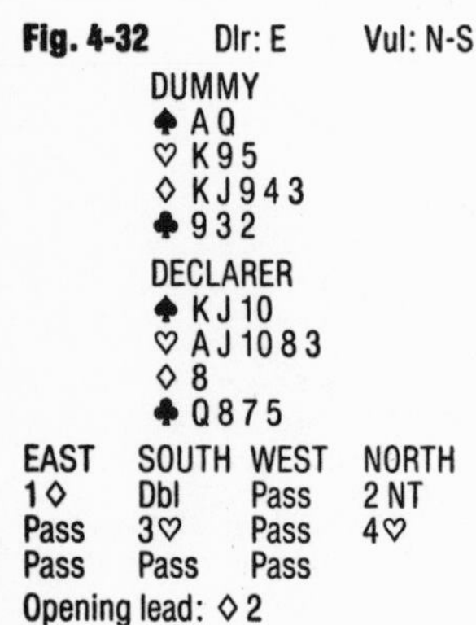

Fig. 4-32 is a more subtle example taken from Dorothy Hayden's book, *Winning Declarer Play.*

West led the two of diamonds, declarer played low from dummy, and East won the *queen.* East cashed the king and ace of clubs and led the jack to South's queen, West following to three rounds. It seemed sure that East did not have the ten of diamonds, or else he would have won with that card. So, if West had the ten of diamonds, he had at least three diamonds to begin with, for with ten-two he would have led the ten rather than the deuce. This left East with at most four diamonds to the ace-queen. He had shown up with precisely the A K J of clubs, so he probably started with six cards in the major suits, divided either 3–3 or 4–2, for, if East held a five-card major suit, he would have opened one heart or one spade instead of one diamond. East's distribution therefore must be either 4–3–3–3 or 4–4–3–2.

All of this is leading up to deciding who has the queen of hearts. East held 6 high-card points in diamonds and 8 high-card points in clubs, for a total of 14. Dorothy points out that if East had the queen of hearts, he had a balanced hand of 16 points and a perfect opening bid of one no-trump. Therefore she concludes that East does *not* have the queen of hearts, so a finesse should be taken against West who surely holds that card. (Ed. note: conversely, if East-West are playing weak no-trumps, East *must* have the queen of hearts, else he would have opened a balanced 14 with one no-trump.)

Of course there are isolated cases where East will not open one no-trump holding a useless doubleton. While this is possible, it is the most unlikely of all possibilities, and Dorothy is entirely correct that the percentage play is to finesse against West for that vital queen of hearts.

Sometimes the fact that your opponents do not bid tells you what to do about your finesses (Fig. 4-33).

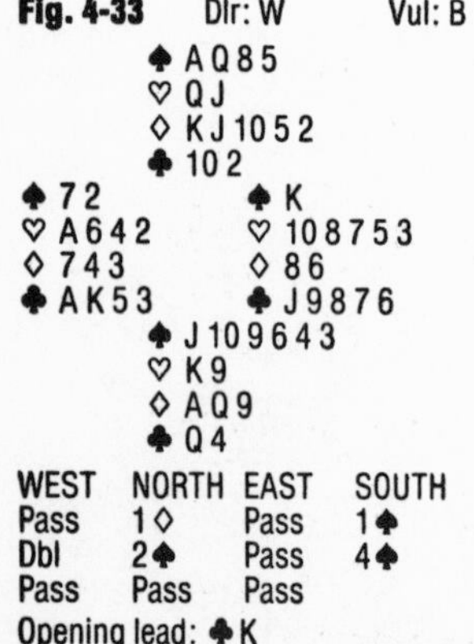

West started the defense by cashing the king-ace of clubs, followed by the ace and another heart. West was not the sort of player to pass as dealer holding 14 high-card points, so he almost surely did not hold the king of spades. Therefore, East had the king, and if it was guarded, East was going to take a trick with it. So declarer won the second heart and made the gesture of leading the jack of spades, but when West played low, he went right up with the ace from dummy. The most startling effect of this play was on East, who promptly clutched his hand closer to his chest and muttered something unintelligible.

Sometimes the opponents will tell you by the way they defend a hand exactly how you should play to be sure of success.

East won the ace of clubs (Fig. 4-34) and returned the three of clubs, a suit preference signal indicating a diamond reentry. West ruffed and led a diamond to his partner's ace. East studied the dummy and his own hand and led back the nine of diamonds! This strange play by East did not go unnoticed by declarer. He won the diamond in dummy, led the jack of spades, and finessed against East's queen of spades. Yes, he knew there were only four spades out at this point and that he might very well be able to drop a doubleton queen—but he *knew* East had the queen! If East did not have the queen, he would surely have returned another club in the hope that West could ruff higher than dummy. East's diamond return was a dead giveaway, but another club was just as bad—and a careless declarer might ignore the inference implicit in the diamond return.

Fig. 4-34 Dlr: S Vul: B

North: ♠ J 10 5 ♡ A Q 8 3 ◊ K Q 10 7 ♣ 9 4

West: ♠ 7 3 ♡ J 9 6 4 2 ◊ 8 6 5 4 3 ♣ 2

East: ♠ Q 6 2 ♡ 10 5 ◊ A 9 2 ♣ A 8 6 5 3

South: ♠ A K 9 8 4 ♡ K 7 ◊ J ♣ K Q J 10 7

SOUTH	WEST	NORTH	EAST
1♣	Pass	1◊	Pass
1♠	Pass	2 NT	Pass
3♣	Pass	4♠	All Pass

Opening lead: ♣2

Sometimes just knowing where the cards lie may not be enough—you have to know what to do about it. The bidding will tell you some things, but you may need a little luck besides (Fig. 4-35).

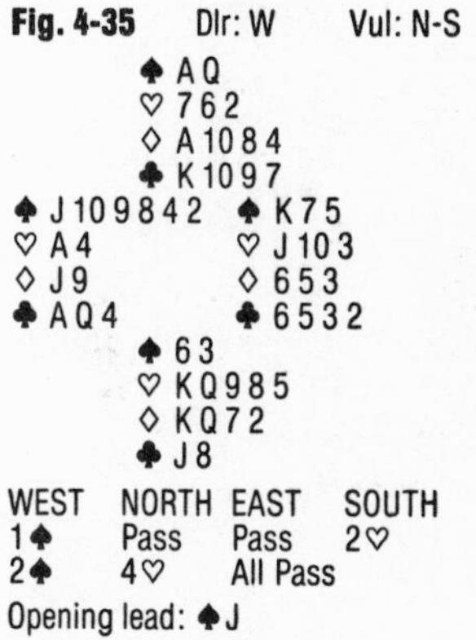

When the dummy came down, a warm glow came over declarer as he examined the layout. West must have the preponderance of the outstanding high cards for his opening bid, so South expected to lose no spades, no diamonds, and no more than one club—so he could afford two trump losers if necessary.

When dummy's queen of spades lost to East's king, declarer had to reconsider. Hoping to find the ace of hearts with East was now an exercise in futility, as West had to have the two outstanding aces for his opening bid. Besides, East would have taken action holding an ace and a king. If West also had the jack or ten of hearts along with his ace, the contract was doomed. South considered all this and then gave his kibitzers a thrill by winning the second spade in dummy, leading the two of hearts, and covering East's three-spot with the five! Had East split his trump honors, South of course would have played the queen of hearts and later returned to dummy to take a finesse against the other honor.

The bidding on the hand in Fig. 4-36 may make you wonder about the condition of the players, but you will agree that at least the declarer was sober!

Fig. 4-36 Dlr: S Vul: N-S

North: ♠ Q 8 7 ♡ Q J 9 5 ◊ K 9 7 ♣ Q 9 6

West: ♠ K 9 6 5 2 ♡ 7 4 ◊ 10 5 3 ♣ A 10 2

East: ♠ 3 ♡ 8 6 2 ◊ 8 4 ♣ K J 8 7 5 4 3

South: ♠ A J 10 4 ♡ A K 10 3 ◊ A Q J 6 2 ♣ —

SOUTH	WEST	NORTH	EAST
1◊	1♠	1 NT	2♣
3♡	4♣	4♡	Pass
5♣	Pass	5◊	6♣
6◊	Pass	6♡	7♣
7♡	Dbl	All Pass	

Opening lead: ♣A

South must have expected his partner to hold the king of spades for his first round response of one no-trump—and, if partner had that card, South was not willing to settle for doubling the opponents at seven clubs. West opened the ace of clubs, and when declarer examined dummy, he recognized that the spade finesse was a loser and that the best chance for his slam was to reverse the dummy, i.e., ruff three clubs in the closed hand, draw trumps from the dummy, and throw his spade losers on dummy's trumps.

Accordingly, he ruffed the opening club lead high, led a small heart to dummy, and ruffed another club high. Now he needed two more non-trump entries to dummy—one to get over there to ruff the last club and one to get back to draw the opponent's trumps—and he needed his last trump to ruff the third club.

Obviously the only other entries to dummy were in the diamond suit. If he used the king of diamonds, he could trump the last club all right, but then he would have no way to get back to dummy to draw trumps. So to have the extra entry to dummy, it was necessary to lead the two of diamonds and finesse dummy's nine of diamonds! When that worked, declarer had his extra entry. He trumped dummy's last club with his last trump and returned to dummy with the king of diamonds. On dummy's trumps he discarded spades, then he returned to his hand to cash three diamonds and the ace of spades. In all he took one spade, four hearts in dummy, five diamonds, and three club ruffs for thirteen tricks, but he could not have negotiated all that without finessing the nine of diamonds!

In my final example of a finesse based on action taken by the opponents, South had to find a smother finesse (Fig. 4-37).

Fig. 4-37 Dlr: W Vul: E-W

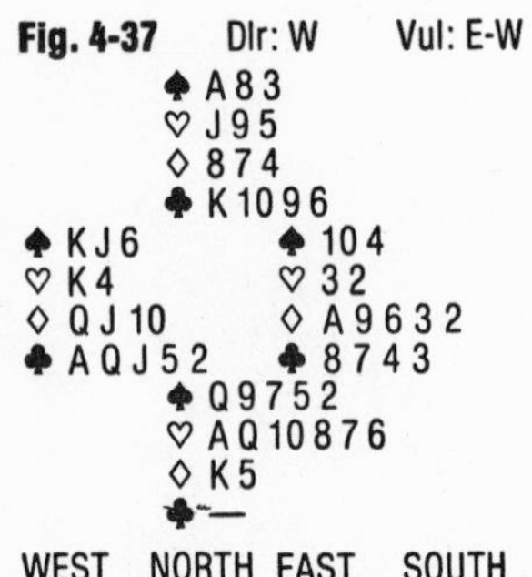
♠ A 8 3
♡ J 9 5
◇ 8 7 4
♣ K 10 9 6

♠ K J 6 ♠ 10 4
♡ K 4 ♡ 3 2
◇ Q J 10 ◇ A 9 6 3 2
♣ A Q J 5 2 ♣ 8 7 4 3

♠ Q 9 7 5 2
♡ A Q 10 8 7 6
◇ K 5
♣ —

WEST	NORTH	EAST	SOUTH
1 NT	Pass	2◇	2♡
3◇	3♡	Pass	4♡
Pass	Pass	Pass	

Opening lead: ◇ Q

West's opening lead was the queen of diamonds, and when East won this with the ace, South knew East couldn't have much else in the way of high cards. If West had a minimum one no-trump bid, East could not have the king of hearts in addition to the ace of diamonds, so declarer had to resign himself to a trump loser. This meant that if he was going to make his contract, he had to hold his spade losers to one trick. He laid down the ace of hearts and a small heart. West won the king of hearts and got out with a diamond, ruffed by South.

Proper action on the spade suit had to come from the dummy, so declarer led a heart to the jack and called for a low spade. South decided that as West had already shown up with a doubleton heart the odds were against his holding a second doubleton in spades for his no-trump opening bid. Hoping that East held either the jack or ten of spades and that either card was doubleton, he inserted his nine-spot, losing to West's jack. But now declarer was in control. He ruffed the club return and led the queen of spades through West's king. This successfully blotted out the ten in the East hand.

ENTRIES AND THE FINESSE

The proper procedure with the following holding is well advertised in all textbooks.

◇ A Q 10 4
◇ K 8 7 3 ◇ 6 2
◇ J 9 5

South, on lead, wants to take as many diamond tricks as possible. If he needs to conserve entries to his hand, the proper card to lead from South is precisely the *nine-spot*—not the jack or five. Should West cover the nine of diamonds with the king, South's purpose has been achieved—four diamond tricks are available for cashing. If West does not cover, South next leads the jack of diamonds and, if West again plays low, dummy underplays with the ten! South is still in his hand for a third finesse to the ace-queen and succeeds in taking four diamond tricks without using up a single entry in other suits.

Not so well known is the situation where declarer has to take a double finesse and is short of entries (Fig. 4-38).

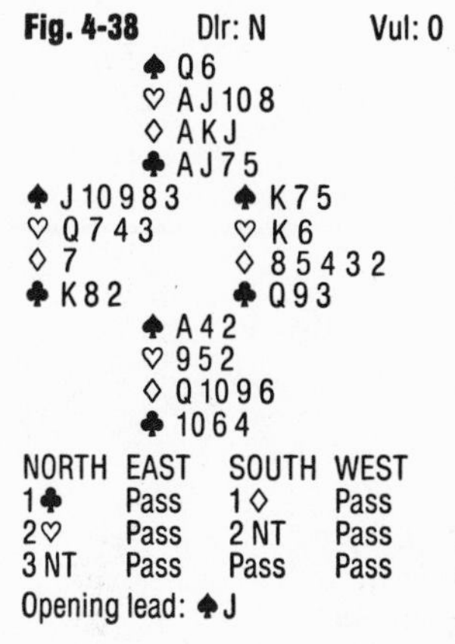

When West opened the jack of spades, South tried dummy's queen of spades and ducked when East produced the king. East continued spades, and South won the third round, discarding a club from dummy. Now it appeared he had to take three heart tricks to make his contract. He started his entry-preserving procedure by leading a small heart from his hand and playing the ten of hearts from dummy, carefully keeping the nine in his hand and the eight on the table. South hoped the heart he lost to East's king was the last heart he would have to lose. East, now out of spades, returned a diamond. South won two top diamonds in dummy, overtook the jack of diamonds with the queen of diamonds, and cashed his last diamond. Now was the time to lead the nine of hearts—and as long as West held the king of hearts, it was all over. Of course West did not cover with his king, but the eight of hearts was still in dummy to drop under the nine so that South could take the final essential finesse. Note that South did not waste his nine on the finesse he expected to lose—the first heart finesse—but saved it to lead for the finesse he hoped to win so he could stay in his hand and repeat the process.

On the hand in Fig. 4-39, playing a contract of four spades, declarer got the opening lead of the four of clubs.

When the dummy came down, declarer counted nine tricks off the top. It appeared that the tenth trick must come from the club suit. Hopefully, declarer played small from dummy on the opening club lead to see if his queen of clubs would win the trick. No luck—East won the king of clubs. Had there been no entry problem, the opening lead would have assured declarer two club tricks, for he could cash the queen and ace separately. But in this case there definitely was an entry problem. South's best chance to take two club tricks now was to find West with the jack of clubs. Therefore, South unblocked by playing the queen of clubs under East's king. He won the diamond return, pulled trumps, led the three of clubs, and crossed his fingers when he inserted dummy's ten of clubs. Like all careful declarers in bridge literature, this one was also rewarded with a happy ending.

Did you ever face a situation where you have a lot of winners in dummy and no way to get there? So have I. In this hand, South found a way to avoid this horrible situation:

DUMMY
♠ 9 7 5
♡ J 3
◇ 7 5
♣ A K 6 5 4 2

DECLARER
♠ A 4 3
♡ A 10 5
◇ A K 2
♣ J 10 9 7

South plays three no-trump, and West opens the six of spades. (Declarer should wait and win the second spade. If East obtains the lead and has another spade, presumably West started with a four-card suit, and declarer would lose only three spade tricks.) After winning the second spade, the club situation must be taken care of. All is well, for you bring in all six club tricks if the queen of clubs drops singleton. But what if the queen of clubs is doubleton or tripleton? The suit will be hopelessly blocked if you play the ace and king too early. The way to overcome the blockage is to lead the jack of clubs and let it ride if it is not covered. If East wins the queen of clubs, the suit is no longer blocked. If West has the queen you will bring in all six club tricks.

Sometimes drastic actions are necessary (Fig. 4-40).

South opened the bidding with one diamond and, when North bid one heart, he jumped directly to three no-trump. West chose the jack of spades for his opening lead. When dummy came down, declarer saw that he had nine tricks provided he could win four club tricks. This meant that he had to have a successful club finesse, then another, and possibly even a third. For this he might need as many as three entries to the dummy. If the jack of spades was backed up by the ten of spades as seemed likely from the opening lead, these entries were all available in the spade suit so long as South unblocked. Therefore, he won the first trick with dummy's ace of spades, carefully underplaying the king of spades. The finesse of the ten of clubs was successful, and the queen-nine of spades were there over West's ten-eight to provide two more entries to dummy so declarer could finesse clubs twice more.

Fig. 4-40

GOLD-BOND, 100-PERCENT GUARANTEED FINESSES

We hear a lot about finesses that have a 50-percent chance to succeed, double finesses that have a 75-percent chance to succeed, and some poor finesses that have only a 25-percent chance to succeed. If you search around, you will surely find someone to disagree with such figures. However, I want to show you some finesses that are 100-percent winners—finesses that carry an absolute guarantee whether they succeed or fail—for the contract always comes home. You can't do any better than to go with such absolute guarantees as these:

South is declarer at three no-trump, and West opens the eight of spades. South correctly plays the queen of spades from dummy, and this holds the trick. South now has one of those gold-bond finesses available, provided he chooses the right suit to finesse. Other things being equal, the primary finesse would seem to be diamonds, as that is the longer suit and produces five tricks if successful. However, other things are *not* equal.

Fig. 4-41

♠ Q 5
♡ A 10 2
◇ A K J 8 4
♣ 10 9 2

♠ A J 9 8 3
♡ J 7 3
◇ 6 5
♣ K 7 6

♠ 10 7 4
♡ 9 8 6 5
◇ Q 7 2
♣ 8 5 3

♠ K 6 2
♡ K Q 4
◇ 10 9 3
♣ A Q J 4

(It has been some time since I reminded you of Blackwood's thirteenth rule. In case you have forgotten, here it is again: theenk!)

If South goes to his hand with a heart to finesse diamonds, East will win and return a spade, and the defense will immediately cash five tricks. But suppose you choose the club finesse. Now you are guaranteed at least nine tricks whether the club finesse wins or loses. If West has the king of clubs, he cannot successfully continue spades, and you come home with one spade trick, three hearts, three clubs, and two diamonds. On the hand shown above, the queen of diamonds does not fall doubleton, so only nine tricks would be made (unless West continues spades and gives you ten). However, when the queen of diamonds is doubleton, eleven or twelve tricks are your reward for correct play.

On the hand in Fig. 4-42, South plays three no-trump, and West opens the nine of hearts.

Fig. 4-42

Declarer has one of those gold-bond finesses, but it is *not* in the heart suit! If declarer plays the queen of hearts, East wins the king and continues hearts until the ace is driven out. Eventually South has to try the diamond finesse, and, when East wins the king of diamonds, he cashes enough hearts to defeat the contract. It is the *diamond finesse* that is of the gold-bond variety, but first declarer must make the proper play in hearts. Win the ace of hearts at trick one, go to the South hand with a club, and lead the ten of diamonds. Whether it wins or loses, South has his contract. If East has the king of diamonds, he cannot pursue the attack on the heart suit without giving dummy the queen of hearts. So declarer runs five diamonds, two spades, a heart, and two clubs. But he must take the gold-bond diamond finesse rather than the speculative heart finesse.

Sometimes the odds on ways to play a single suit are quite different from odds on the way to play an entire hand (Fig. 4-43).

Against South's four spades contract, West leads the king of hearts and continues the suit. Declarer ruffs the second heart and leads two trumps, ending in the dummy. As a matter of good technique, he ruffs dummy's last heart.

Fig. 4-43

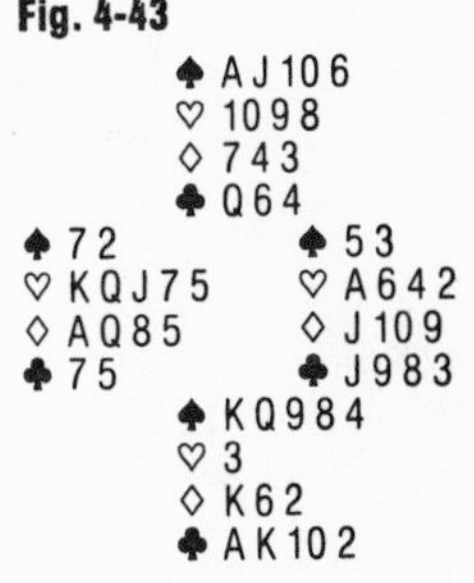

Now I want to introduce you to a way of thinking and counting which is not sufficiently emphasized in any textbook I have seen, but which is terribly important. You are going to use this technique when we get to the subjects of suit establishment and safety plays. In anticipation of that, let me digress right now.

As declarer, most of us count the number of cards of a suit in our own hand and in the dummy. When we add them together, we may be slightly conscious of the number the opponents have between them, but after a trick or two is played, our awareness of the number still held by the opponents is vague at best. Believe me, it will simplify your task as declarer if you keep in mind the number of cards the opponents hold *after* a trick or two in a suit has been played.

For example, look at the club suit in the above hand. Between them North and South hold seven clubs; obviously East-West hold six. When we cash the ace of clubs and they both follow, they now hold four. When we lead small to the queen and they both follow suit, they now hold only two. When we lead a small one from dummy and East follows suit, there is only one club outstanding! So far as the club suit itself is concerned, the odds at this point very slightly favor playing the king of clubs rather than taking the finesse.

But so far as this hand is concerned, the finesse is of the gold-bond variety. If the club finesse wins, you can discard one of dummy's diamonds—limiting your loss in that suit to two tricks. If the finesse loses, West, now stripped of black cards, must lead a diamond to your king or lead a heart which you ruff in your hand, as dummy discards a diamond. Another diamond goes off on your king of clubs. In either event you will lose only three tricks.

Fig. 4-44

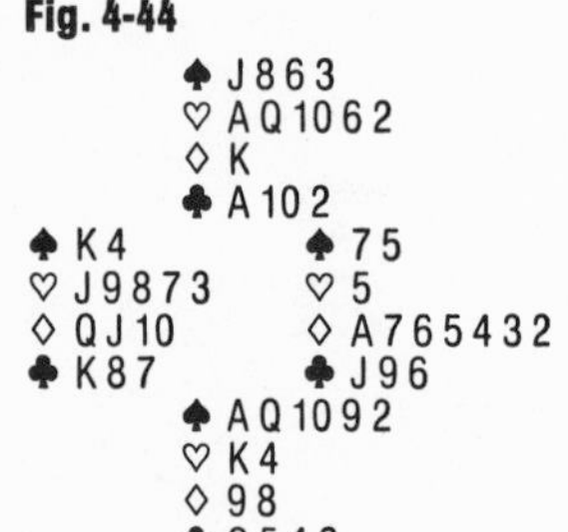

Let's look at a hand where seven cards of a suit are divided differently in your two hands (Fig. 4-44).

Against a four spade contract, West opens the queen of diamonds. East wins the ace and switches to a spade. West wins the king of spades and continues trumps. South wins and ruffs his remaining diamond. Next he leads the two of hearts to his king and notes that both opponents follow suit. They had started with six hearts between them, so now they hold four distributed some way. When South leads the four of hearts toward dummy and West follows suit, he realizes he has one of those 100-percent finesses available.

He inserts the ten of hearts and, when that wins the trick, he has two good hearts on which to discard two clubs, so he loses in all one trump, one diamond, and one club.

But suppose the heart finesse loses? In that event, the opponents have played four of their six hearts, and only two are outstanding. Dummy has three hearts, all of which are guaranteed winners, so South can discard all three of his clubs. He thus makes his contract by losing only one spade, one heart, and one diamond.

Did you ever hear that little ditty, "eight ever, nine never?" That is supposed to mean that when you are missing the queen of a suit, you are supposed to finesse with eight cards in the suit, but *not* with nine. I am not qualified to judge that little ditty as poetry, but bridgewise you'd better forget it. There are too many exceptions.

Fig. 4-45

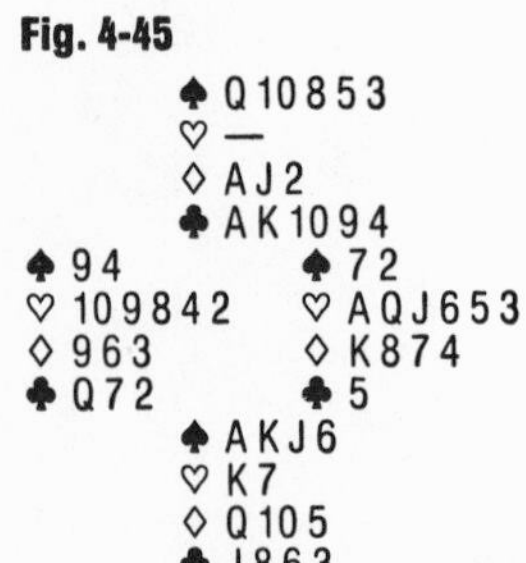

After North opened the bidding with one club, South got to a six spades contract despite East-West's competitive bidding in hearts. West led the ten of hearts, and when declarer trumped in dummy, he came to his hand with a spade to ruff his other heart. South won the next spade in his hand, cashed dummy's ace of clubs, and led one more trump to the closed hand.

He now had one of those guaranteed 100-percent finesses available. Both opponents had followed to the lead of the ace of clubs, so since they had started with only four clubs between them, there were only two outstanding. South led a small club and took the finesse! If this won, he would discard a diamond on dummy's long club and make his contract regardless of the location of the king of diamonds. If the finesse lost, East would be out of clubs and spades, so would have to return a red card. On the lead of a heart, declarer would discard a diamond from his hand, ruff in the dummy, and then throw his other diamond loser on the fifth club. If East led a diamond, of course, declarer would have two diamond tricks and would still throw his third diamond on the long club.

If declarer had banged the ace-king of clubs, he would have lost a club and a diamond to go set.

On the hand in Fig. 4-46, declarer found his gold-bond finesse in the trump suit.

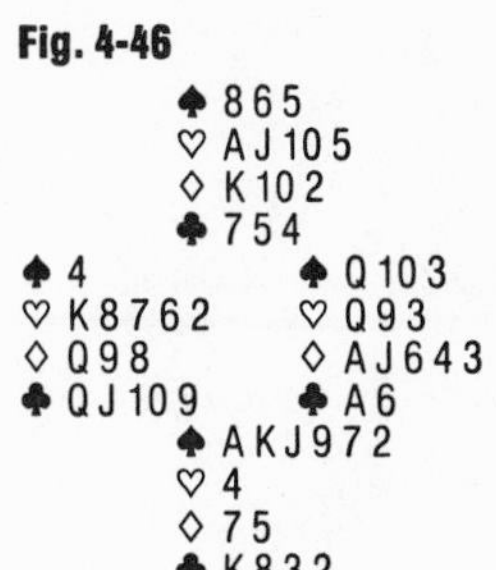

South was playing weak two bids, and though his hand was pretty sturdy for an opening two spade bid, that was the action he chose. As both sides were vulnerable, he succeeded in silencing his opponents and buying the contract. West's opening lead was the queen of clubs, won by the ace, and East's club return was taken by declarer's king. South laid down the ace of spades, and when both opponents followed, his guaranteed finesse was waiting for him. He went to dummy with the ace of hearts, led a spade, and finessed it! When the jack of spades held, he romped home with six spade tricks, one heart trick, and one club trick.

But suppose the finesse had lost. Then both opponents would have been exhausted of trumps, and, since one trump would still remain in the dummy to ruff a club, declarer would still make eight tricks.

Sometimes it is our old friend, the ruffing finesse, that can give us the security of a sure thing.

DUMMY
♠ 4
♡ A 8 6 5 2
◇ A Q 10 4 3
♣ A 6

DECLARER
♠ A 8 5
♡ K Q J 10 7 3
◇ 9 5
♣ 8 2

South got to six hearts, and, luckily, West led the king of spades. South now had a sure thing, no matter how the opponents' cards were distributed. Proper procedure is to win the ace of spades and extract the two outstanding trumps. Next declarer should cash the ace of diamonds! Let's see what happens if an opponent shows out of diamonds.

If East shows out, South returns to his hand with a trump and leads the nine of diamonds. West will have to play his king to win the trick, and dummy's queen will provide a place for declarer's club loser.

If West shows out, declarer simply leads a small diamond from dummy. East has to play the jack of diamonds or let the nine-spot win. Declarer gets back to dummy by trumping spades to play the queen of diamonds for a ruffing finesse against East's king, establishing the ten for a club discard.

But let's suppose (as is most likely) both opponents follow suit to the ace of diamonds. Declarer returns to his hand with a trump and leads the nine of diamonds. If West plays an honor, declarer now has no trouble finding a parking place for the club. Should West show out at this point, declarer simply lets East win with his jack and, again, he can reach the dummy to lead the queen and force out the king to establish the ten-spot. If West follows with a small diamond, declarer lets the nine ride. If East can win this, the opponents will have played four of their six diamonds.

Fig. 4-47

	♠ 8 6 5 ♡ 7 5 4 ◊ A J 9 6 2 ♣ 6 3	
♠ K J 7 ♡ 8 3 ◊ Q 10 8 3 ♣ Q J 10 9		♠ Q 4 3 2 ♡ Q J 10 6 2 ◊ 4 ♣ 7 5 2
	♠ A 10 9 ♡ A K 9 ◊ K 7 5 ♣ A K 8 4	

Since dummy will still have three diamonds left, one can be established easily, and there are plenty of entries to bring in the suit and to discard a club on the long diamond.

In Fig. 4-47, West led the queen of clubs against three no-trump. Looking at all four hands, we can see that declarer has seven top tricks and needs only two more. We can also see that the diamond suit will provide those tricks if declarer cashes the king of diamonds and then leads low toward the dummy and just covers whatever card West plays. West is most likely to play the eight, and North should cover with the nine.

As declarer cannot see into the West hand, let's seek information as to how he determined that this finesse is the proper play. What makes it one of those 100-percent gold-bond plays?

First he counts the diamonds he sees: eight. This means that the opponents have five between them. After both follow suit to the king of diamonds, they have three left. When South leads the five and West plays the eight, there are two out. South does not know whether East is going to follow suit, but, if he does, there will be only one outstanding diamond, and it will fall under the ace. Whether the finesse of the nine wins or loses, the contract is guaranteed. If the finesse loses to East, there are three more diamond tricks available, and South has a diamond left for entry purposes. If the finesse of the nine of diamonds succeeds and East shows out, it is a simple matter to return to the South hand to lead the diamonds once more and bring in all five diamond tricks.

On the next hand, South didn't care if his finesse won or lost. Either way he was assured of the twelve tricks he needed to make his six spades contract.

DUMMY
♠ K 4
♡ J 6 3
◊ A Q 10 9 3
♣ 10 9 4

DECLARER
♠ A Q J 10 9 6 3
♡ —
◊ J 5
♣ A K J 8

West led the king of hearts. South ruffed and played the king, ace, and queen of spades, as it took three leads to extract the opponents' trumps. Next South led the jack of diamonds—if East won the king of diamonds, there would be club discards available on dummy's diamonds, and South would have no further problems. Both opponents played small, and the jack of diamonds held the trick. The fact that East played low did not prove he did not have the king of diamonds. He might well be one of those fiends who withholds a king trying to lead you into a trap, thinking your finesse has worked. So while he was waiting, South looked again and suddenly he saw that he now had a gold-bond finesse, but not in diamonds —in clubs! So he led the five of diamonds, played dummy's ace of diamonds, and pulled dummy's ten of clubs off the board. No matter who had the queen of clubs, his contract was now assured. Fig. 4-48 shows the entire hand.

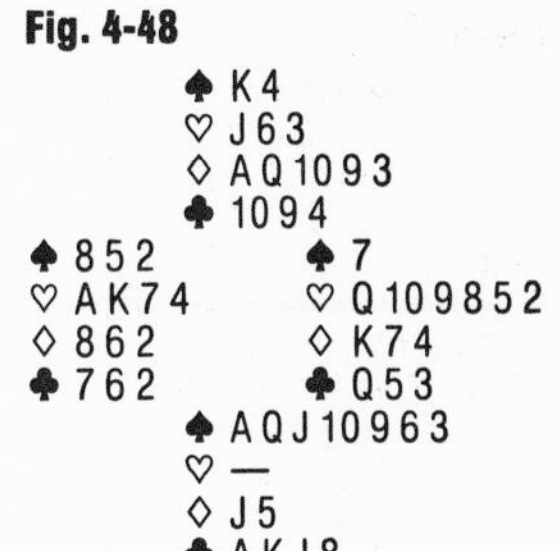

To put some icing on the cake I have put the queen of clubs in the East hand so that South makes a grand slam. But even had West had the queen of clubs, twelve tricks still would have been made.

In the next hand, declarer found a spectacular 100-percent play in the trump suit and what was for all practical purposes a gold-edged bond for a slam contract.

West felt pretty smug when South got to a contract of six hearts. He led the jack of spades and settled back to see the surprised look on South's face when he discovered the bad trump split. It was West who was in for a surprise. South won the king of spades, led the two of hearts, and, when West followed with the three, called for dummy's four of hearts! Needless to say, this development left West badly shaken up.

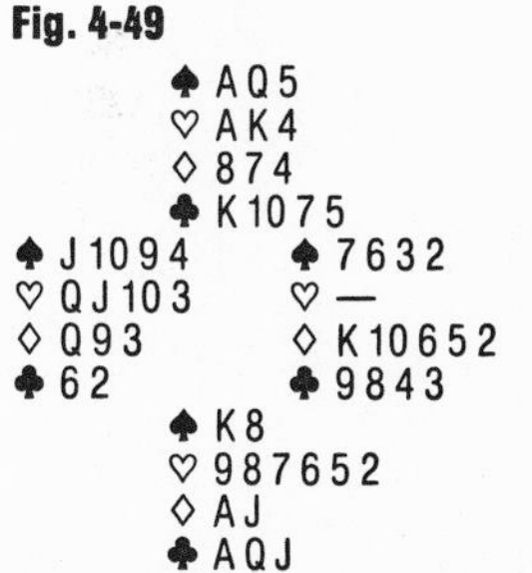

But what did South have to fear? It didn't look as if he had anything to fear, but if he did, it would be the loss of two trump tricks. Of course, there was theoretically some chance that if he let the defenders win a trick they were not entitled to they might be able to bring about a ruff of something. However, this was more remote than the chance of finding all four trumps in one hand. As it was, when South led the two of hearts and West followed suit, South knew he would lose not more than one trump trick if he finessed dummy's four. This play would not have looked so spectacular if North had had the A K 9, but actually it is the same play. All of the cards in the north-south hands from the four to the nine are equal, so any one of them in the north hand has the same trick-taking potential. Since declarer and dummy hold nine hearts between them, the opponents have four. When West followed suit, there were only three left. If East followed suit to the four of hearts, then the opponents would have only two trumps left, and they would fall under the ace-king. As sensational as the play looked, upon examination it turns out to be the only safe play once West followed to the heart lead.

This hand concludes our study of finesses as such. It easily could have been included in the chapter on safety plays rather than the chapter on finesses, because it really is a finesse used to make a safety play. Don't think we are going to forget about the finesse for the balance of our discussion on declarer's play, however. The finesse will put in many appearances in future chapters. They have a great part to play in establishing small cards in long suits, safety plays, avoidance plays, hold-up plays, end-plays, squeeze plays—in fact just about every aspect of declarer's play. And so to the bridge declarer's best friend we are not saying "farewell," but only "au revoir."

AN established suit is a long suit in which a player holds all the remaining high cards. At no-trump (or after trumps have been drawn at a suit contract), these cards will all be winners when the suit is led and run. One makes a suit good—or *establishes a suit* —by forcing out the opponents' guards or winners. You establish K Q J 10 9 of a suit for four tricks by conceding one trick to the ace.

1. DUMMY	2. DUMMY
4 3 2	K Q 3
DECLARER	DECLARER
A K Q J 10	A J 10 4 2

1. It is obvious that with this hand you can take five tricks in the suit at no-trump or at a suit contract after the opponents' trumps have been extracted. It is an *established suit,* as you have a five-card sequence ready-made—the ace through the ten in consecutive order of rank.

2. It is almost as clear in this hand that you can take five tricks. Between you and the dummy you have one high card for every round of the suit, and the ace and the ten are exactly equal in trick-taking value. However, there is a difference in entry values. While the ace and the queen (for example) are exactly equal in trick-taking value, the ace is higher when they are both played on the same trick. It is usually advisable when running such a suit to take the first tricks in the "short hand"—the hand with the fewer number of cards—to avoid later entry problems.

3. DUMMY	4. DUMMY
4 3 2	A K Q
DECLARER	DECLARER
A K Q J 5	J 10 4 3 2

3. With this deal you can take five tricks provided neither opponent holds all five of the outstanding cards of the suit. However, the suit is *established* if both opponents follow to the first round, because that means the outstanding cards can split no worse than 4–1. Only about 1 time in 25 will all five cards be in one of the opponents' hands. You don't have to hold a high card for every round of the suit to take all the tricks with your long-suit cards—you just have to have more high cards in the suit than the total number of cards held by either of your opponents.

4. This hand illustrates the embarrassment that may be caused by the difference in entry value of the five cards in sequence. After cashing the A K Q in dummy, it is necessary that you have an outside entry to enjoy the jack-ten in your hand.

5. DUMMY	6. DUMMY
K Q	K J
DECLARER	DECLARER
A J 10 4 3 2	A Q 10 3 2

5. You and dummy hold eight cards in the suit, leaving only five for the opponents. If you cash your five top cards separately, you will surely be able to take all six tricks in the suit because the opponents will be exhausted of the suit after five leads. If both opponents follow when you lead the king, you can safely overtake the queen, as there are now only three cards outstanding, and they will fall safely under the A J 10 of the suit. But if one of the opponents shows out when you lead the king, complications have arisen. You cannot overtake your queen and cash out the suit because the opponent with 9 x x x x will stop the run. So once again it is necessary that you have an outside entry to your hand after the king-queen of the suit have been played.

6. In this hand you have seven cards between you and the dummy, leaving six for the opponents. If the opposing cards split 4–2 or 3–3, you are safe to lead the king from dummy and overtake the jack with your queen. If you must have five tricks from the suit and someone shows out on the lead of the king or the jack, revealing a 5–1 or 5–0 split, it will be necessary for you to have an entry elsewhere to complete the run of the suit.

7. DUMMY	8. DUMMY
4 3 2	Q J 3
DECLARER	DECLARER
K Q J 10 9	K 10 9 4 2

7. Here your cards are solid except for the ace. Any card you lead will be equally efficient for forcing out the opponents' ace, so that you are assured of four tricks as long as you have an entry in your hand. If you lack

an entry, clever opponents will wait to take their ace until the third round of the suit and so limit you to two tricks. Of course, if the opponent who holds the ace has it singleton or only once guarded, he will be forced to win while you have a small card or two left in the dummy. In most circumstances you cheerfully give up one trick to gain four.

8. You have the same five-card sequence—one high card for each round of the suit to be played. In forcing out the opposing ace, it is usually wise to take the first trick in the "short hand," thus conserving entries to your long cards. So if you are in your hand when you first attack the suit, lead a low one toward dummy's queen-jack. If dummy is on lead, you are safe to lead a top card. This hand is similar to number seven except the sequential cards are split between the two hands. Again, if the opponent holding the ace can wait for the third round to win it, you must have an outside entry to finish the run of the suit.

In considering card promotion and suit establishment we want to remember the worth of cards in a sequence. The *Official Encyclopedia of Bridge* says a sequence is "two or more cards in consecutive order of rank, as A K Q (three-card sequence) or Q J 10 9 (four-card sequence). Regardless of length, we want to keep in mind the equal trick-taking value of each card in a sequence. A solid sequence provides as many tricks as you have cards in whichever of your hands holds the greater length minus the number of top cards missing from your sequence.

9. DUMMY	10. DUMMY
4 3 2	J 8 2
DECLARER	DECLARER
Q J 10 9 8	Q 10 9 4 3

9., 10. In both 9 and 10, you have a solid five-card sequence. As the queen is the third-ranking card of the suit, the J 10 9 8 also rank as the third card of the suit in trick-taking value. Once the ace and king are gone, the remainder of the cards in the suit are good for three tricks. In 9 it doesn't matter which card you play to force out the top cards. In 10 you should lead to dummy's jack-eight or lead the jack-eight if you start from dummy. It is good technique to lead "equal" cards from the "short hand" to conserve entries to the "long cards."

There is another element to trick taking with cards in a sequence that might not occur to the inexperienced player. That is the *number* of cards held by the opponents.

11. DUMMY	12. DUMMY
6 5 4 3	K J 4
DECLARER	DECLARER
A K Q J 2	A Q 6 5 3 2

11., 12. In both examples you have a solid four-card sequence (A K Q J) and nine cards of the suit between you and the dummy. That means the opponents have four cards of the suit between them, and, even if all four are in the same hand, they must fall under your top card leads.

Thus, in 11, you come home with five tricks and in 12 you win all six, provided you play dummy's king-jack early, retaining the four-spot as an entry to your "long cards." Give the six-spot to the opponents, and let one opponent hold all the outstanding cards—the 10 9 8 7 6, and you will be able to take (immediately) only your four top cards in the suit.

13. DUMMY	14. DUMMY
Q 10 4 2	K 10 2
DECLARER	DECLARER
K J 6 5 3	Q J 6 5 4 3

13., 14. Again you hold as many cards in your (split) sequence as the opponents could possibly have in their hands, but as you are missing the ace, you must give up a trick to garner your winners.

15. DUMMY	16. DUMMY
Q 7 4 2	Q 9 4 2
DECLARER	DECLARER
K J 8 6 5 3	K 8 7 6 5 3

15. Here you have only three cards in your sequence, but your opponents hold only three cards total, so you are assured of completing the run of your suit after you give up a trick to the ace.

16. In this hand you have only the king-queen for a sequence, and the opponents hold the A J 10. Whether you can bring in the suit for five tricks depends on whether the three cards are all in one hand or whether they split 2–1. They will split 78 percent of the time, so your chances are pretty good, but this is not a sure thing. If all three are in one hand, you will have to give up two tricks before you can run four.

An experienced player will quickly evaluate the trick-taking potential of any hand that has a long suit containing cards in sequence. That evaluation will take into consideration whether the lead must be given up to establish the suit, the opening lead, and the importance of the suit in the context of the whole hand. Here you are playing three no-trump and the opening lead is the five of spades.

DUMMY
♠ Q 6 2
♡ 9 4 2
♢ A J 4 2
♣ Q J 3

DECLARER
♠ A 10
♡ A K J
♢ K 6 3
♣ K 10 9 4 2

A quick look at the dummy reveals only five top tricks. While there are less inviting possibilities, the club suit provides four sure tricks. You have a five-card sequence with five-card length in the South hand, and no entry problems. The ace of clubs is knocked out, and declarer runs his tricks unless the opponents can run enough tricks of their own when they obtain the lead with the ace of clubs. The red suits are double-stopped, so there is no danger there. That brings the experienced declarer back to the problem of the opening lead and what he should do at trick one. What card do you play to absolutely guarantee a second stopper in spades? A little thought and you will surely see the value of that ten of spades in your hand, so you play low from the dummy and cover whatever East plays. Say he plays the jack of spades, you win the ace, knock out the ace of clubs, and, when the opponents pursue spades, your ten is good enough to force the king, and your queen is a second stopper. Of course if East plays the king of spades at trick one, your queen is immediately established as a second stopper. You go wrong *only* if you rise with the queen on the first trick.

Let us summarize all of the above and see what conclusions we can draw from it:

With a solid sequence that includes as many cards as you hold in whichever of your hands holds the greater length, you can take one trick for each round, after giving up a trick to any of the top cards which are missing in your sequence.

You can accomplish the same thing if your sequence holds as many cards as are in the hand of the opponent who holds the greater length in this suit. As you have no way of knowing how the opponents' cards will split, you cannot count on this as a sure thing unless you have as many cards in your sequence as the opponents hold all together. That is because it is entirely possible that all of these cards will be in one hand.

When you are trying to establish a suit and your solid sequence is long enough, you can lead high from either hand without fear of its costing a trick. But if your sequence is not long enough to be established on sheer power, there frequently are ways to attack the suit without taking the chance of losing a trick unnecessarily.

17. DUMMY	18. DUMMY
Q J 3	Q 8 4
DECLARER	DECLARER
K 10 5 4 2	K J 6 5 3 2

17. In this hand you have a four-card sequence, the K Q J 10, and you want four tricks out of this suit. They are readily available if neither opponent has all the missing cards—the A 9 8 7 6. You should lead low from your hand, and, if dummy's jack holds the trick and both opponents follow suit, you will achieve your aim. You can now lead high from either hand to knock out the opponent's ace, and your suit will come in for four tricks.

18. Here your three-card sequence, K Q J, is adequate if neither opponent holds the A 10 9 7 of the suit. When you lead low toward the dummy and the queen holds the trick, both opponents following, you know the suit can be established at your pleasure and will come home for five tricks. In

fact, you may even use the extra entry to dummy for some other purpose if needed, as you are perfectly safe to pursue the development of this suit by leading the king or jack from your own hand.

On other hands it is the *location* of the high card held by your opponent that enables you to bring in a suit with minimum loss.

19. DUMMY	20. DUMMY
K Q J 2	Q J 4 2
DECLARER	DECLARER
6 5 4 3	K 5 3

19. If you have plenty of entries to your hand, you lead toward dummy at every opportunity and you will always get three tricks in the suit if *West* has the ace—even if he holds A 10 9 8 7. However, if East has the A 10 9 8 7, the A 10 9 8, or the ace alone, you will be able to establish only two winners in the suit. In other words, if the ace is offside, the outstanding cards must split 3–2 for you to achieve your goal of three tricks in the suit.

20. When you have a three-card sequence split between you and dummy, it frequently is better to make your first lead toward the two-card sequence. (This presumes you have no definite idea from the bidding as to which of your opponents holds the ace.) In 20, if you make your first and second leads toward dummy, you will take three tricks in the suit whenever West holds the ace singleton, doubleton, or tripleton. If dummy wins the first trick, you return to your hand and lead toward dummy again. If West has the doubleton ace, it will show up when he drops his ace on your small cards, and your high ones will be winners.

21. DUMMY	22. DUMMY
Q 4 3	K Q 4 2
DECLARER	DECLARER
K J 6 5 2	J 8 6 5

21. If you know which player has the ace, you should lead through that hand. Here your three-card sequence, K Q J, is adequate so long as the opponents' A 10 9 8 7 is divided 3–2. Should one player hold all five, you would find it impossible to take four tricks in the suit, no matter which hand you lead from. But you can protect yourself against a 4–1 break where the ace is singleton. If you are convinced West holds the ace, lead small from your hand toward dummy. If West produces the ace and East follows, you can bring in the suit for four tricks just by leading out your top cards when you regain the lead. If the ace does not appear, the queen holding the trick, you are well placed to bring the suit in for four tricks so long as West does not have four or five cards in the suit.

22. On hand 22, if you have no idea who has the ace, by all means lead low from your hand toward the king-queen. If dummy holds the trick, you cannot be sure who has the ace—but more than likely it will be friend West. You still are not safe if West started with A x x x, so you should return to your hand to lead the suit again. Whether the ace appears this time is unimportant so long as both opponents follow suit.

Fig. 5-1

```
            ♠ A 5
            ♡ 7 4 2
            ◇ K J 7 3
            ♣ K Q 4 2
♠ Q J 10 9 4       ♠ 8 7 2
♡ A J 3            ♡ 10 9 8 5
◇ 6                ◇ 10 9 8 4 2
♣ A 10 9 7         ♣ 3
            ♠ K 6 3
            ♡ K Q 6
            ◇ A Q 5
            ♣ J 8 6 5
```

Occasionally this precaution will pay handsome dividends. Look at this deal (Fig. 5-1).

You play three no-trump, and West opens the queen of spades. You win the king in your hand and promptly lead a low club toward dummy. West correctly plays low, and the queen wins the trick. If the opponents' clubs split 3-2, you are home free with two spade tricks, four diamonds, and three clubs, but with the hand above you are far from safe. You return to your hand with a diamond and lead a second club toward dummy. Now West has had it. If he plays his ace, you get your three club tricks. If he ducks again, you win dummy's king and East shows out. You have collected only two club tricks, but you know where to go now to establish your ninth trick—you abandon clubs and lead a heart to your king-queen.

Aside: I suggest that the first club you lead from South be the six of clubs and the second one be the eight of clubs. On the given deal, it makes no difference whether West takes his ace or not, but West does not know that. And there are hands where it does make a difference. No harm can come from a simple deception—and you may gain from West's having to work out the distribution from the fall of the club spots on the first round. It does no harm to keep your opponents under pressure trying to figure out what is going on. So I recommend—when you are playing the dummy and have no partner to mislead—that you make it standard to muddy the waters as often as possible.

Fig. 5-2 Dlr: W Vul: N-S

```
            ♠ 6 2
            ♡ A Q 10
            ◇ K Q 7
            ♣ K J 5 3 2
♠ Q J 10 9 5       ♠ 7 3
♡ J 5              ♡ 8 7 6 3 2
◇ A 9              ◇ 8 6 5 3
♣ A 10 8 4         ♣ 9 6
            ♠ A K 8 4
            ♡ K 9 4
            ◇ J 10 4 2
            ♣ Q 7
```

WEST	NORTH	EAST	SOUTH
1♠	Dbl	Pass	2 NT
Pass	3 NT	All Pass	

Opening lead: ♠Q

On the hand in Fig. 5-2, declarer felt sure he knew where the aces were. That information told him not only which hand he should lead from, but also which suit he should work on first.

When the dummy came down, declarer could count only five immediate tricks, all in the major suits. To make his contract, he needed to get four tricks from the minors, and, as he was missing the aces in those suits, he had first to establish them.

However, as soon as he won the lead with a high spade, the opponents were within one trick of establishing their long suit, and declarer could see that it was going to be a race to see who got there first.

Naturally, he turned his attention first to clubs where he had the greater length.

With a total of seven cards in a suit, the opponents had six. The most likely distribution of those six cards was four in one hand and two in the other. The sequence in the suit which declarer held between his and the dummy was only three cards long, so if he led the queen of clubs, it was unlikely that he could bring in the entire suit.

Between his hand and the dummy, declarer saw 28 high-card points, leaving only 12 for the opponents, and West had opened the bidding. It looked as though West had every missing high card, and this meant that he had the aces in both minor suits. Declarer thought he saw a solution to his problem.

He won the first trick with the ace of spades and led a low club. Now, should West play his presumed ace, declarer would have his three-card sequence intact, and, if either opponent had no more than three cards left, he could bring in the entire suit. This plan looked sure to work unless one of the opponents had started with five or more clubs.

West knew about these things, too, and played a small club. Now if declarer continued clubs, he would have to play his queen from the south hand, as that was the only one left. But, having one club trick under his belt, he could now turn his attention to diamonds where there were three more tricks available. In that suit, there was a sequence four cards long between his hand and the dummy. This made it perfectly safe for him to start proceedings by leading high diamonds, and he did not have to go to the trouble of leading up toward anything. He simply led the king of diamonds and was sure to bring in three diamond tricks, making nine total tricks.

Let's take another look at this setup:

DUMMY
K 5 3

DECLARER
Q J 4 2

If you have no definite idea from the bidding which opponent holds the ace, you should lead low toward the queen-jack. But what if you *know* (or at least have excellent reason to believe) that *West* has the ace? Not only the location of the ace, but also the number of small cards guarding that ace, is now all important.

If you are able to determine who has the ace of a suit you are trying to establish, and can count how many cards the player has in that suit, an "obligatory finesse" may bring in extra tricks—even though you and the dummy combined have only a three-card sequence, as above.

Let's follow declarer's reasoning on 5-3.

Fig. 5-3 Dlr: W Vul: B

NORTH
♠ K J 10 6
♡ A K 4
◇ Q 7 5
♣ 7 6 4

SOUTH
♠ A Q 9 3
♡ 8 6
◇ K J 6 4
♣ Q 9 2

WEST	NORTH	EAST	SOUTH
1♡	Pass	Pass	Dbl
Pass	2♡	Pass	2♠
Pass	3♠	Pass	4♠
Pass	Pass	Pass	

Opening lead: ♣K

Although I am reporting the bidding, I'm not especially recommending it. However, since South made his contract, I would not presume to criticize. East-West, incidentally, were playing a system whereby a major-suit opening bid guaranteed at least a five-card suit.

Declarer counted three club losers and one diamond loser. There was some chance of getting rid of one club loser on the fourth diamond, if that suit behaved well, and declarer could get a count on the distribution of the suit.

I suppose West led the king of clubs so that he could "see the dummy." After taking a look, he switched to the queen of hearts. Declarer won the ace of hearts and pulled three rounds of trump, ending in the closed hand. On the third trump, *East* discarded a small heart.

Declarer thought he knew who had the ace of diamonds. He was looking at 25 high-card points in his hand and the dummy. If West had opened the bidding without the ace of diamonds, he had opened with only 11 high-card points and in a suit missing both the ace and king. Declarer therefore led the four of diamonds toward dummy's queen of diamonds, leading through the presumed ace in the West hand. The queen held the trick, and now it was time to reconnoiter.

West started with exactly three spades; his opening one heart bid guaranteed at least five hearts, so he had at most five minor suit cards. The ill-advised lead of the king of clubs indicated to South that West probably had three clubs to the ace-king, for with the doubleton ace-king, he would play first the ace and then the king. So if West started with three spades, five hearts and three clubs, he had only two diamonds. A small one had been played to the previous trick, so the ace was now alone!

Declarer, trusting this analysis, called the five of diamonds and played the six from his hand. West had to drop the ace of diamonds "on air," promoting South's king-jack. One of dummy's clubs went away on the high diamond, so declarer lost only two clubs and one diamond to make his bid. Fig. 5-4 shows the full deal.

Fig. 5-4

Note also that the "obligatory finesse" is made to avoid two losers from this type of holding:

Q542
A7 J109
K863

If the position of the ace is marked with West, you lead low toward dummy. If West does not put up the ace, you win the queen and duck all around on the next lead of the suit. The play costs nothing, for if the cards are otherwise distributed, at least two tricks must be lost in the suit in any event.

What you are trying to do in suit promotion is to elevate a card of lower rank up to the position of highest rank so that it can take a trick. Before we go further into the subject, let's take a look at the principle of promotion.

PROMOTION OF INTERMEDIATE CARDS

How many cards are there in a suit higher than the eight-spot? If you want to, you can count them on your fingers and see that there are six. If you want to take a shortcut, you can subtract eight from fourteen and come up with the same answer. Let's call this the "Rule of Fourteen." (Honor cards are actually numbers, and the ace is number fourteen—there are thirteen cards in each suit, and no number one.)

What is the smallest card that can become elevated to the highest rank after two leads to a suit? The six-spot. Assuming no one has discarded from the suit, the greatest number of higher cards that can be played on two leads is eight—one from each of the four hands—and eight from fourteen is six. If the eight higher cards have been played, the remaining highest card would be the six-spot. The entire distribution of the suit might look like this:

J8
Q9 107
AK65432

West, North, and East have to play their high cards because they have no smaller ones to go with them. In other words, such high cards as they have are insufficiently guarded.

Now this little bit of information that the six-spot can become established in two leads of a suit may not be of great practical value, but the mathematics of promotion and the importance of guards can be tremendously important in practical play. Tremendously important also is the possession of intermediate cards.

Take a solid sequence of A K Q in one hand and consider the difference in that suit when the remaining cards are the smallest possible spots and when one of the remaining cards is the ten.

	Col. 1	*Col. 2*
1. A K Q 4 3 2	0	27%
2. A K Q 5 4 3 2	36%	62%
3. A K Q 6 5 4 3 2	68%	73%

Column one gives your mathematical chances of taking a trick with each card held with the suit shown, assuming dummy is void in the suit. Column two shows your chances of taking a trick with each card held if you simply substitute the ten-spot for a small card. This illustration highlights the tremendous impact of that ten. In addition, it shows the importance of having guards for your own cards. When you hold the ten, one of your opponents holds the jack—really the eleven-spot. When subtracting eleven from fourteen, we see that there are three cards higher than the jack. When the jack has three guards, it cannot be felled by one of the higher cards. But, obviously, the greater your own length in your suit, the smaller the chance that your opponent who has the jack has sufficient guards to go with it.

Now for one final illustration before we start looking for ways to apply this knowledge:

DUMMY
J 9 3 2

DECLARER
A Q 5

How important is that nine-spot in the dummy? How many times will you take a trick with this combination that you would not take if dummy had the four instead of the nine?

Of the four cards higher than the ten, you and the dummy have three. Whenever the ten is part of a doubleton, it will fall on your honors, and the nine will be promoted to take a trick. There are other chances. If the king is singleton or doubleton in the East, you can play West for the ten and finesse to your jack-nine.

Here are the combinations that will allow you to take a trick when you have the nine rather than a small spot card. (1) Whenever the ten is doubleton in either hand. (2) Whenever there is any singleton in the East hand. (3) Whenever the ten is singleton in the West hand. (4) Whenever the ten is four long in the West hand, with the king doubleton in the East. In (4) the finesse to the queen works, and when the king falls under the ace, you finesse dummy's nine over the ten presumed to be in the West hand and take all four tricks in the suit. I figure this at nearly 33 percent.

Fig. 5-5

	North	
	♠ K ♡ K J 6 5 3 ◇ A K 4 ♣ Q 10 4 2	
♠ Q J 10 9 2 ♡ 9 8 ◇ Q 8 7 5 ♣ 9 5		♠ 8 7 5 4 ♡ A Q 10 7 ◇ 10 2 ♣ 8 7 3
	♠ A 6 3 ♡ 4 2 ◇ J 9 6 3 ♣ A K J 6	

Let's look at a practical application of this theory of promotion of intermediate cards (Fig. 5-5).

The diamond combination here is similar to the situation shown above, with the short hand holding ace-king rather than ace-queen. At a recent tournament the opening lead against South's three no-trump contract was (inevitably) the queen of spades. The players who counted their tricks immediately found they had two spades, two diamonds, and four clubs, for a total of eight tricks. About a third of the field went set, and we can only assume that they found the heart suit too seductive. They came to their hand with a club and tried to get the ninth trick by finding West with either the ace or queen and hoping they could guess which. Obviously that did not turn out well—they had to collect their eight tricks in a hurry when East returned a spade.

Some players found the diamond suit more interesting than the hearts because of the presence of that nine-spot in the South hand. They figured that if the ace-king of diamonds dropped a doubleton ten or queen or if West showed out on either the first or second lead of the suit, they would know precisely where to get their ninth trick. It was not necessary to know the exact odds of having one of these favorable things happen, but I think that if they paused to think about it, most players would have decided the chances were about 1 in 3, and they would have been right.

If nothing good happened after the lead of the ace-king of diamonds, they could then decide whether to continue diamonds (hoping East had the queen or that the suit broke 3–3) or whether to try for a heart trick with no more danger than would have been involved if they had never tested diamonds at all. Obviously, when the ten of diamonds fell on the second lead, these declarers had no trouble establishing their ninth trick in the diamond suit.

Whenever I have a class with brand new players, I have a favorite hand that I give them near the beginning of the first lesson. At this point they have had instruction only in the mechanical basics of the game. They know the requirement to follow suit, that the person who plays the highest card of the suit led wins the trick, that the ace is the highest card, and that one of the players gets to see his partner's hand face up on the table. They also know that bridge is a partnership game, but they know nothing as yet about the bidding, nor do they know that there is such a thing as trumps.

They are told that West has the opening lead and that North will put his hand down as dummy after the opening lead. Then they are cut loose with these cards (Fig. 5-6).

Fig. 5-6

	North	
	♠ K 6 ♡ A 4 ◇ Q J 10 8 ♣ Q J 9 4 3	
♠ Q J 10 9 3 ♡ J 9 8 ◇ A 3 2 ♣ A 6		♠ 8 5 4 2 ♡ 10 7 6 5 ◇ 5 4 ♣ 7 5 2
	♠ A 7 ♡ K Q 3 2 ◇ K 10 7 6 ♣ K 10 8	

The usual procedure is for West to cash his two aces and then look around for new worlds to conquer. Declarer will obtain the lead in any event, and, as a general rule, will cash his top tricks in spades and hearts, and then try to decide where to go from there. Don't laugh. The chances are that you and I could have done no better the very first time we saw a bridge hand.

Occasionally I have a West player who starts off leading the queen of spades. Once in awhile a South player will lead the diamond suit when he obtains the lead, and sometimes a declarer will lead the club suit at the first opportunity. If I find two or three players such as this in a class, I know I probably will have some students who will be hard to beat within a year or two. New players who don't need to be told about the concept of establishing tricks are almost certainly future champions.

Through the play of the above hand, pupils learn that it is not essential to take the current trick, but that sometimes by giving up an immediate trick they guarantee several tricks in the future. They soon recognize that giving up one trick for four, as South can do in the club suit above, is an excellent bargain. Once they have grasped this idea, they have a fundamental aspect of play—the establishment of suits.

Shortly thereafter I introduce the feature of playing with a trump suit, at which time I give them the hand in Fig. 5-7.

Fig. 5-7

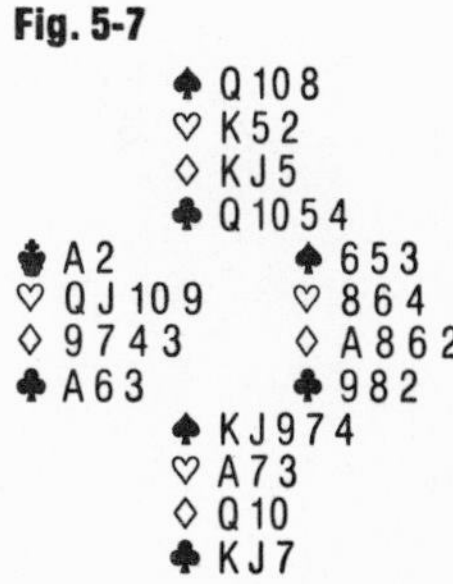

The contract is four spades, and West is instructed to start proceedings by leading the queen of hearts. South is told he must take ten tricks with spades as trump and that he should count his losers as soon as he sees the dummy. He finds one loser in each suit. That is one too many. So the job is to find a way to get rid of one loser. The heart loser can be discarded on a diamond, but only after the diamond has become *established.* The diamond must be established before the defenders have established their heart trick, so there is no time to go after trumps. To do so would surrender the lead and give the defenders time to set up their heart winner before South has any place to get rid of his heart loser. Therefore, diamonds must be led before trumps.

We also face the problem of getting to the good diamond after it is established. Therefore, the first heart should be won in the South hand so the king will remain in North as a sure entry to dummy after diamonds are established.

When my pupils are convinced that diamonds must be led at the second trick, I hope that they have gained some knowledge of establishing tricks and that this magic works with short suits as well as with long suits. As a bonus, they have been introduced to the element of timing in the play of the hand.

An establishment play is nicely illustrated in C. Jack Bonney's *Master Bridge Teaching Guide* (Fig. 5-8).

Fig. 5-8

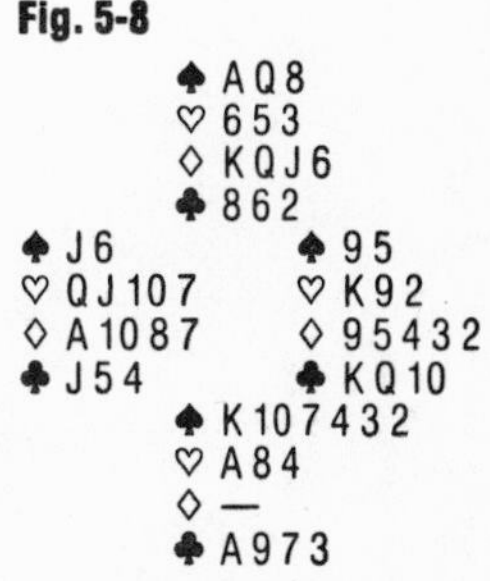

South plays a contract of four spades and gets the opening lead of the queen of hearts. There are two heart losers and two or three club losers—depending on whether the clubs break 3-3 or declarer is able to trump the last club in dummy. Anyway you look at it, there are too many losers. But what about those diamonds in dummy? Once the ace of diamonds is forced out, top diamonds will afford discards for losers. As we have no diamonds in our hand, we will just take *three* discards on the diamond suit!

We win the ace of hearts and lead a small spade to dummy's ace or queen. We lead the king of diamonds and discard a heart. The opponents can cash a heart trick, but then have to give us the lead. We draw trumps, ending in the dummy, then discard two clubs on the queen-jack of diamonds, leaving only one club loser. In all we lose only the ace of diamonds. one heart, and one club.

Fig. 5-9

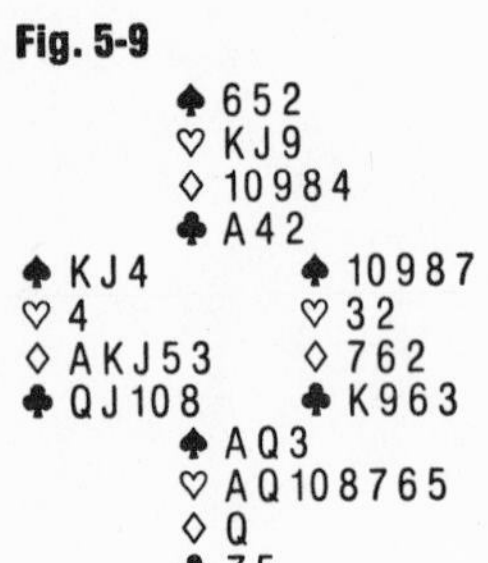

In Fig. 5-9, after West opened one diamond, South ended up playing four hearts. West led the king of diamonds and, after a look at the dummy, switched to the queen of clubs. The lead of the queen of clubs seemed to indicate West did not have the king and, lacking the king of clubs, he just about had to have the king of spades for an opening bid. This left declarer with one club loser, two spade losers, and the diamond trick he had already lost.

However, the sequence of intermediate diamond cards started him thinking. There were four cards higher than the ten of diamonds before the opening lead, but only two remained outstanding after the first trick. So, by giving up *two* diamond tricks, *three* losers could be discarded.

The best play, therefore, is to take the ace of clubs and then just one top trump in dummy, as the others might be needed for entries. After the king of hearts, lead the ten of diamonds, discarding a club. West wins and continues clubs. After trumping, declarer returns to dummy with a trump and throws the three of spades on the nine of diamonds, letting West win the ace. Now the good eight of diamonds provides a discard for the queen of spades. Instead of losing two spades, a club, and a diamond, only three diamond tricks are lost.

Fig. 5-10

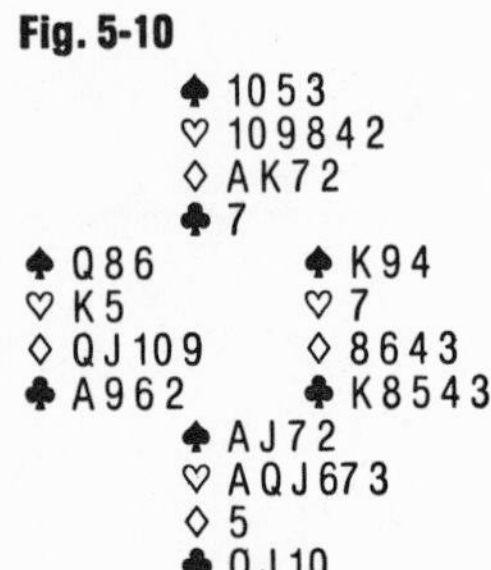

On the deal in Fig. 5-10, South opened one heart. North brought proceedings to a halt by jumping straight to four hearts.

West led the queen of diamonds, and declarer counted one club loser, as well as two probable spade losers, and a possible heart loser. There was a faint chance he would escape with only one spade loser—if East had the king or queen doubleton. Declarer could lead low from the dummy and put in his jack, losing to an honor in the West hand. Then, if he was lucky, the ace would drop the other honor and his ten-spot would be promoted to being a winner.

He won with dummy's king of diamonds, and tried the heart finesse. Nothing good happened as West took the trick with his king and continued diamonds. Declarer won the ace of diamonds in the dummy and then took another look. Suddenly he saw a play that offered better prospects than trying to find a doubleton spade honor in the East hand. There in his own hand was a nice little three-card club sequence. He saw that if he gave up two club tricks, he could discard two spades from the North hand, one of them while he was losing the unnecessary second club, and the other when the ten-spot was established. This would leave no spade losers. So he discarded a spade, came to his hand with a trump, and led a club. When West won with the ace, he led another diamond (if he had returned a spade, declarer would have abandoned clubs, for there would have been only one spade loser). Declarer trumped the diamond and led a second club, discarding one of dummy's spades, letting East win his king of clubs. Then he had a place to dispose of another spade, and he ended up losing only two clubs and a trump.

Fig. 5-11

The contract in Fig. 5-11 is four hearts. The opening lead of the eight of clubs would be good news if West had the king, but players don't often lead eight-spots when they have kings, so it looks as if declarer has a club loser. In addition, he has a diamond loser and two possible spade losers.

But what about the three-card diamond sequence split between declarer's hand and dummy? When the ace is gone the king of diamonds will give a discard for one of the spade losers. However, declarer has to time this right to get his tricks set up before they get theirs. If he takes the club finesse at trick one, East will almost certainly switch to spades—if he does not have the king at any rate. East-West could get their two spade tricks established before declarer gets his diamonds going, and that would put him down one.

Since a club loser seems inevitable, he decides to lose it at a time to suit *his* convenience. He plays the ace of clubs at trick one and draws three rounds of trumps. Then he leads the queen of diamonds, and the timing is all his, as he is going to get his diamonds established and take his discard before the defenders can get their spades established. East wins the ace of diamonds and does the best he can by leading the jack of spades. Since declarer can afford one spade loser, he plays the queen. Sure enough, it loses to the king. He wins the next spade with the ace and cashes the jack of diamonds. Then he goes to dummy with a trump and discards the three of spades on the king of diamonds. Finally he gives them their club trick and ends up losing only one spade, one diamond, and one club.

Fig. 5-12

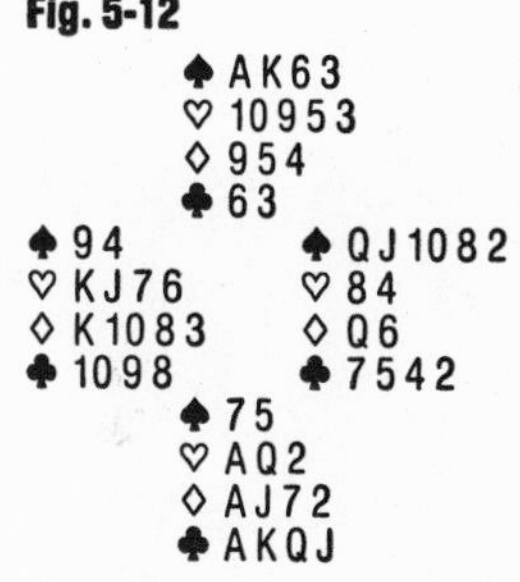

This hand was played in real life by Bruce Gowdy of Toronto (5-12).

Bruce, playing three no-trump, got an opening lead of the ten of clubs. When he counted his winners, he found only eight: four clubs, two spades, and the two red aces. Of course, he could go for his ninth trick by going to the dummy with spades and trying heart finesses, but Bruce thought he saw a surer way. Had he gone to dummy with the ace-king of spades to take finesses for the king of hearts and jack of hearts, he would almost surely have failed to find his ninth trick.

He took a look at that two-card heart sequence in the dummy. There were only four hearts higher than that ten-spot, and Bruce held two of those, leaving only two with the enemy. He started by leading the ace of hearts. When the king failed to fall, he led the queen of hearts, and West won the king of hearts.

Now Bruce was in control—no switch could hurt him. Actually, West continued clubs. Bruce won and led the two of hearts toward the dummy. After West won with his jack of hearts, the ten of hearts became the game-going trick, and the spades were there to provide the entry.

Fig. 5-13

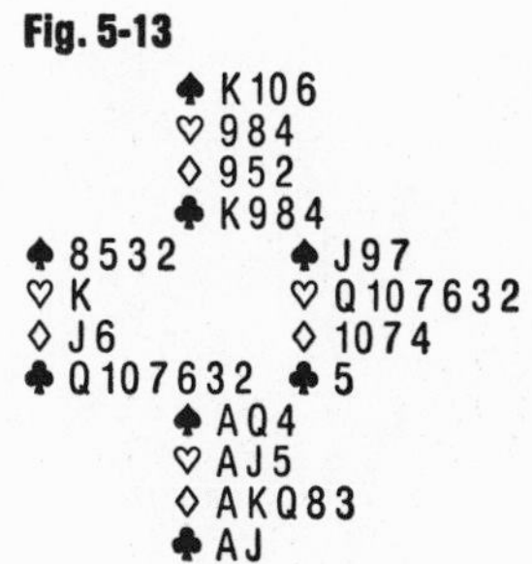

In the Vanderbilt Cup championship a number of years ago, both Howard Schenken and Edgar Kaplan had a chance to show their skill in Fig. 5-13.

In Room One, Schenken, playing six no-trump from the South hand, got the opening lead of the two of spades. He noted that even if diamonds broke favorably, he had only 11 tricks. Hoping to find an extra entry to dummy so that he could finesse the jack of clubs and get back to cash the king of clubs, he put up dummy's ten of spades. If East had only known! All East had to do was let the ten of spades hold the trick and almost certainly the next play would have been a finesse of the jack of clubs—a losing finesse.

But East, not a genius, duly played his jack of spades. This put Schenken in his own hand, and he did not have sufficient entries to get to the dummy to finesse the jack of clubs, cash the ace, and then get back to the dummy to cash the king.

But there was still hope. In dummy were two beautiful intermediate cards in the club suit. Schenken won the first spade and then the ace-king of diamonds to be sure that suit was breaking properly. He then laid down the ace of clubs and followed with the jack. West had to cover, or declarer would have his twelfth trick immediately, but then Schenken simply won the king of clubs, led the nine of clubs, and discarded a heart. West won the ten-spot, but that was the only trick for the defense. Declarer was now able to return to the dummy with the king of spades and discard his other heart on dummy's established eight of clubs.

The situation was a little different in the other room as Edgar Kaplan was playing six no-trump from the North hand. He had his opportunity to finesse the jack of clubs on the very first trick, as the opening lead from East was the five of clubs. A lesser player probably would have done just that, but Kaplan did not think a good defender was underleading the queen of clubs against a six no-trump contract. He had to make his decision at trick one. He won the ace of clubs and promptly played the jack of clubs. This was covered by the queen and king. The nine-eight of clubs in the closed hand gave him heart discards, and he came home with twelve tricks.

Double dummy advocates will point out that the hand is simple if South simply leads the ace of hearts, dropping the singleton king from West, and then goes to North and leads up to the jack of hearts. The mathematicians tell us that when seven cards are outstanding, the chances of finding a singleton king or queen in a specific opponent's hand are something less than 1 percent.

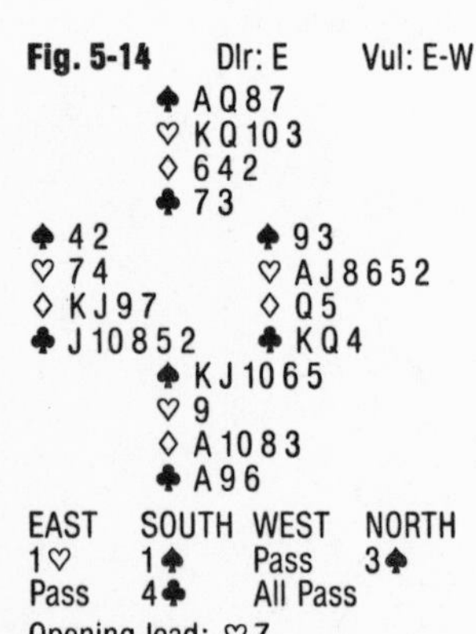

On the hand in Fig. 5-14, West led the seven of hearts—his partner's bid suit—and South took a look at the dummy to view his prospects.

No matter how South counted, there seemed to be more than three losers. Even if diamonds were 3–3 so that he could discard one of dummy's clubs on the thirteenth diamond, this was going to work out only if the opponents delayed playing clubs. As he examined the hand, however, that nine of hearts caught his attention. The more he looked at it, the larger it seemed to be. It was obvious the seven of hearts was the highest of West's hearts. If declarer called for the king or queen from dummy, he would win exactly one heart trick.

If, however, he played low from the dummy and let East win the jack of hearts, South saw he had a pretty good chance to win *two* heart tricks, and on each of them he could discard a minor suit loser. He therefore played the three of hearts from dummy, and East switched to the king of clubs after winning the jack. But declarer had everything under control. He led the king of spades and then the jack, which he overtook in the dummy. He was gratified to see that his opponents were now out of trump.

His king of hearts was covered by the ace, so he trumped it. He returned to dummy with a trump and discarded both his clubs on the two good hearts. He eventually conceded two diamond tricks and ruffed a diamond in dummy to claim his contract, losing only one heart and two diamonds.

In Fig. 5-15, a modern lead calculated to help the defenders helped the declarer more.

Fig. 5-15

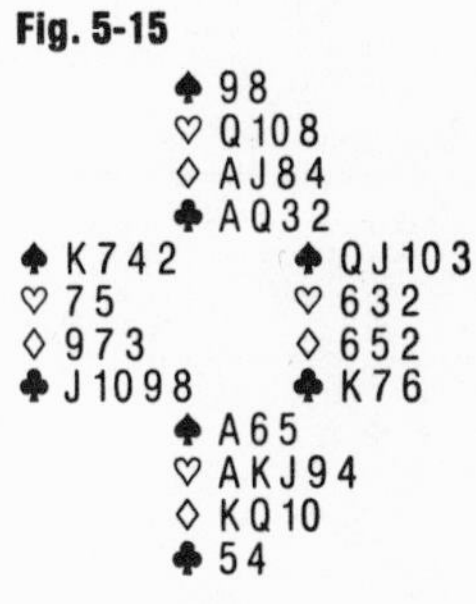

South was declarer at six hearts, and West opened the jack of clubs. East and West were playing a system of opening leads where the jack guaranteed no higher cards. Had West held an interior sequence such as K J 10, he would have led the ten-spot, which would have indicated either no higher cards or two higher. The lead told South that a finesse of the queen of clubs was bound to fail. He counted and found one spade trick, five hearts, four diamonds, and one club, for a total of eleven. Had he been given time, he could have conceded one spade trick, trumped a spade in dummy, pulled trump, and discarded a club on the long diamond, claiming twelve tricks. But the opening lead had closed that line of play.

However, it was still possible the queen of clubs could take a trick if East's king of clubs were poorly guarded. South took the ace of clubs and promptly led the two of clubs. He was on his way to recovery from the unfavorable lead. West won the eight of clubs and, no matter what action he took, declarer was going to ruff out East's king of clubs on the next lead. After drawing trumps, he would discard a spade from his hand on the queen of clubs, and the other spade would go off on dummy's fourth diamond.

In all, declarer would limit his losers to that one club trick.

Often the opening lead and the fall of the spot cards will give declarer a clue as to the successful route to follow in developing tricks with intermediate cards. One South, enamored of his success in ruffing out the king-third of *clubs* on the previous hand decided to try for the king-third of *spades* on this deal in Fig. 5-16.

Fig. 5-16

Playing five diamonds, South received the opening lead of the jack of spades. When he studied the dummy, it appeared he had a sure heart loser, a spade loser if East held the king, and a club loser unless he could find a place to dispose of it. There were two possibilities: build the heart suit if he had time, or try to drop East's king of spades or ruff it out. Testing spades first, declarer went up with the ace of spades and led the deuce, East played the seven of spades and then the five—but declarer noticed something peculiar. East had won the trick, yet West overtook with the nine-spot. A new plan began to form. West switched to a club, and South "knew" West had played the nine of spades because he had none smaller. South won the queen of clubs with his ace and led a trump to dummy. Now, instead of leading the eight of spades, hoping to drop the king-third from East, declarer led the *queen of spades,* hoping to blotter out West's ten and establish dummy's eight-spot. When East covered the queen of spades with the king, declarer trumped and was delighted to see West's ten of spades come tumbling down. A diamond to dummy exhausted the opponents' trumps, and there sat the eight of spades for South's discard of the jack of clubs. Now it was time to establish a heart trick, and there was still a trump left in the South hand to take care of North's losing club.

Fig. 5-17

```
            ♠ A Q J 9 4
            ♡ K 10
            ◇ A 5
            ♣ Q 9 3 2
♠ 8 3                 ♠ K 7 6 2
♡ 6                   ♡ 5 4
◇ 10 9 8 3            ◇ K Q J 7 4
♣ K 8 7 6 5 4         ♣ J 10
            ♠ 10 5
            ♡ A Q J 9 8 7 3 2
            ◇ 6 2
            ♣ A
```

On the hand in Fig. 5-17, declarer had to deal with the most damaging opening lead, but a nine-spot saved the day.

South was playing six hearts and West opened the ten of diamonds. Against any lead but a diamond, he would have had time to pull trumps and try the spade finesse, eventually establishing a place to dispose of his losing diamond. However, South was faced with a more severe problem.

Declarer could count only eleven tricks without the spade finesse, and if it worked, he would take thirteen. However, if East had the king of spades, South would take only eleven tricks. At first glance it looked as if it had to be the spade finesse or nothing, but declarer looked again and decided to see if he could ruff out the king of clubs. Kings have been known to have so few guards that they fall after two or three leads. If this did not work, South could still fall back on the spade finesse.

He won the ace of diamonds, took his ace of clubs, and returned to dummy with a trump. He led the three of clubs, trumping with the seven of hearts. Now he took another look. So far, he had not been able to ruff out the king of clubs, but the jack of clubs and ten of clubs had fallen from the East hand, making dummy's queen and nine equals. Of the five clubs higher than the nine-spot, three had been played, and one was in the dummy, leaving only one for the defenders. By giving up *one* club trick, South would be able to take *two* discards, and that suited him just fine.

He went back to dummy with the last trump and led the queen of clubs on which he discarded his diamond loser. West won with the king of clubs, but there was nothing he could do. He continued diamonds, but declarer trumped, went to the dummy with the ace of spades, and discarded the ten of spades on dummy's nine of clubs.

These intermediate cards that become established seem to get smaller and smaller. Let's see how the declarer in Fig. 5-18 made out with a six-spot.

Fig. 5-18 Dlr: E Vul: 0

```
            ♠ Q 10 2
            ♡ A J 7
            ◇ A K 10
            ♣ Q J 7 6
♠ 6 3                 ♠ 7 4
♡ 8 6 3               ♡ K Q 10 9
◇ J 9 5 2             ◇ Q 8 7
♣ 10 9 5 3            ♣ A K 4 2
            ♠ A K J 9 8 5
            ♡ 5 4 2
            ◇ 6 4 3
            ♣ 8
```

EAST	SOUTH	WEST	NORTH
1♣	1♠	Pass	2 NT
Pass	4♠	All Pass	

Opening lead: ♣10

West duly led the ten of clubs, and declarer paused to count his losers —two hearts, one diamond, one club. One too many. Of course, if West had the king-queen of hearts or the queen-jack of diamonds, South could hold his heart losers to one or his diamond losers to none. But East had opened the bidding, so he probably had most, if not all, of the missing high cards. There was another chance—establish the intermediate cards in the club suit. It is not often that you can establish a suit the opponents have bid, but that is exactly what South proceeded to do on this hand.

He covered the opening lead of the ten of clubs with dummy's jack, and East won the king. Eyeing the seven of clubs in dummy, declarer first applied the Rule of 14, which told him there were seven clubs higher than the seven-spot. Four of these had been played already, counting his own singleton eight of clubs. This left three outstanding, and since dummy had one of those, the opponents had only two. After winning the king of clubs, East led the king of hearts which declarer allowed to hold the trick.

Obviously, East could not continue hearts, and he was afraid to lead diamonds because of the ten in dummy, so he got out with a trump. Declarer won the ten in dummy, and led the jack of clubs. East covered, and declarer trumped. Now there was only one club outstanding higher than the seven-six sequence. By giving up one club trick, declarer could take two discards. By discarding one diamond and one heart, he would have no losers left in those suits.

He cashed a high spade, to be sure the opponents would be exhausted of trumps, before he returned to dummy with the queen of spades. He led the seven of clubs, discarding a heart, and permitting West to win the nine-spot. West led hearts through, but it was too late. Declarer went up with dummy's ace and led the six of clubs to discard his losing diamond.

How do you establish a six-spot in just two leads? Well, here's one way:

10 9 2
8 7 QJ 3
A K 6 5 4

Let's assume you had a peek at the East-West hands. By leading dummy's ten-nine through East, you could win all five tricks in the suit—and that would establish the six-spot after two leads. When East covered the ten, you would win with the king, return to dummy with another suit, and lead the nine. With East covering, you pin the eight-seven in the West hand, and the six is good. Of course, for this unlikely play to work, you have to find the doubleton eight-seven with West. You would not make such a play unless you had information about the hand. If the queen-jack is doubleton in *either* hand, you win all the tricks by laying down the ace-king (finding the queen-jack doubleton in either of two hands happens twice as often as finding the eight-seven doubleton in a specific hand).

Fig. 5-19 is a hand where close attention to the quick promotion of the six could have made a contract otherwise doomed to failure.

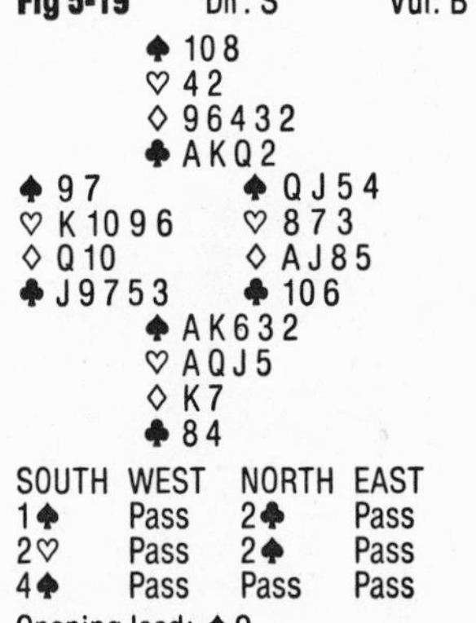

North seemed a bit aggressive on the bidding, but I am told that is the way it went. In view of South's heart bid, West decided to cut down on dummy's ruffing power by leading the nine of spades. That achieved the purpose of stopping heart ruffs, but it also made possible the quick promotion of the six of spades. The nine was covered by the ten and jack before being won by the king. Declarer crossed to dummy with a club to take the losing heart finesse. West won the king of hearts and continued with the seven of spades—covered by the eight, queen, and ace.

I regret to tell you that my reporter now states that South, no spot-watcher, did not realize that his six of spades was good and thought his best chance was to find the two remaining spades evenly divided. He carelessly led the deuce. East won the four of spades and returned a club, putting dummy on play for the last time. Declarer continued with a third club, but East ruffed. Although South overruffed, he ended up going down two tricks, losing in all one spade, two hearts, and two diamonds.

Had declarer noticed that his six was high, he could have extracted one of East's spades, conceded a trick to the other, and kept control of the hand. When in dummy, he can discard the five of hearts on dummy's high club and then lead toward his king of diamonds—losing only one spade, one heart, and one diamond.

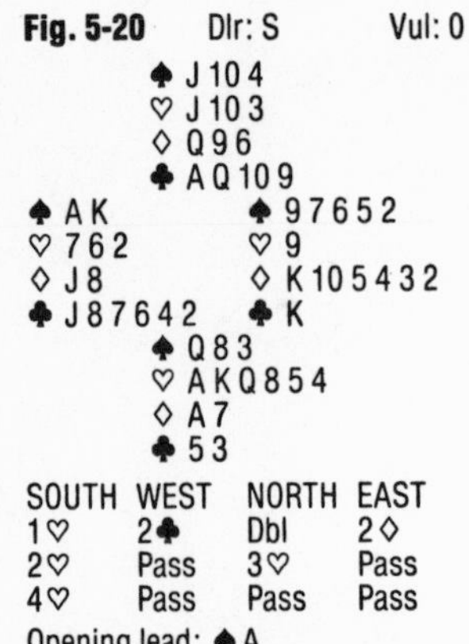

Before we get on to more serious things, let's look at one more six-spot promotion—this from the land of exotica (Fig. 5-20).

You can judge from the bidding that the game was of a jovial nature. However, I wish to proclaim that whatever the condition of the other three players, South had his wits about him.

West led the ace-king of spades, advertising to all that he was now void in the suit. All he needed to beat the contract was a quick entry to his partner's hand so he could ruff a spade. His partner had bid diamonds, so West led the jack of diamonds to trick three. It was covered by the queen-king and won by South's ace. Declarer now thwarted West's ruff by leading three quick rounds of hearts. Then he got out with his last diamond, and it went 7 8 9 10 of diamonds.

A spade was returned to declarer's queen. He led a club, paused to think for a moment as West followed low. East, sitting there with the bare king, put on an expression of great innocence. Suddenly the declarer reached over to dummy and played the ace! A howl went up from East. "Don't you have two clubs? How could you possibly decide not to take the finesse? My partner bid clubs—and missing the A Q 10 9! To play me for the king of clubs you must have peeked."

"I didn't peek," replied South, smiling. "The play of the ace was an absolutely sure thing—and without seeing your hand."

"Just tell me how you know this," said East, no longer jovial about the whole thing.

"Because the six of diamonds in dummy is good for a club discard," answered South quietly.

Just how small an intermediate card can be established in a four-card suit? Shall we try for a three-spot?

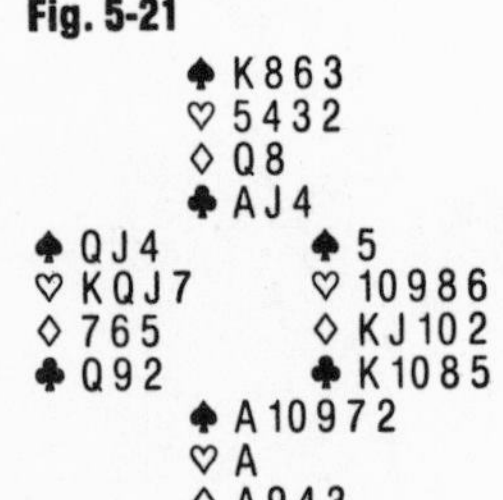

By bidding to the hilt, South got to a four spades contract that appeared to need a lot of breaks. When he didn't get the breaks he needed, declarer made up for the misfortune with sufficiently adept dummy play to bring home ten tricks. His only real break was that East-West did not realize the urgency of leading clubs soon enough, and declarer took full advantage.

After West made the natural lead of the king of hearts, South won the ace and surveyed his prospects. If trumps were 2–2, it appeared that he would lose only three tricks, but like a good declarer, he decided to prepare for the worst by starting on a side suit before he tackled spades. This is generally a good idea. If you start trumps first and they don't break and you have to give up a trick in the development of your side suit, often the opponent with the master trump will be able to draw two of your trumps for one of his and prevent their use in a better cause.

At trick two, declarer led a small diamond toward dummy's queen. To make my story a little better than it might otherwise be, let's say he leads the four-spot and not the three. If the king of diamonds is in the West hand, a lot of problems are solved. But it wasn't—the queen fell to the king in East's hand. East returned a heart, and declarer ruffed. Next he laid down the trump ace and then led to dummy's king of spades, getting the bad news about the break in that suit. It looked almost certain that he would have to lose a spade, a diamond, and two clubs. But all was not yet lost. From the dummy he led the eight of diamonds—I don't know if he intended to let it ride if East did not cover. The problem did not arise because East was afraid he might let it ride and played the ten of diamonds. Declarer won the ace. He had noticed that West followed with the five of diamonds and the six of diamonds. Could it be that West had the seven of diamonds as well? And was it now all alone?

Before trying the "last resort" play of trying to find West with king-queen of clubs, declarer led the nine of diamonds just to see what would happen. Sure enough, he pinned the seven in the West hand, so he made the loser-on-loser play of throwing a small club from dummy, as East won the jack of diamonds. East now shifted to a club, but declarer was in control. He won dummy's ace, ruffed another heart to get to his hand, and discarded dummy's jack of clubs on the established three of diamonds. It mattered not whether West ruffed in—South would just crossruff the hand and let West make his trump whenever he liked. The defenders took one trump trick and two diamonds, but never got a club trick.

When the play seems obvious, good players will nonetheless examine the spot cards to see if there is an alternative play that offers a better chance (Fig. 5-22).

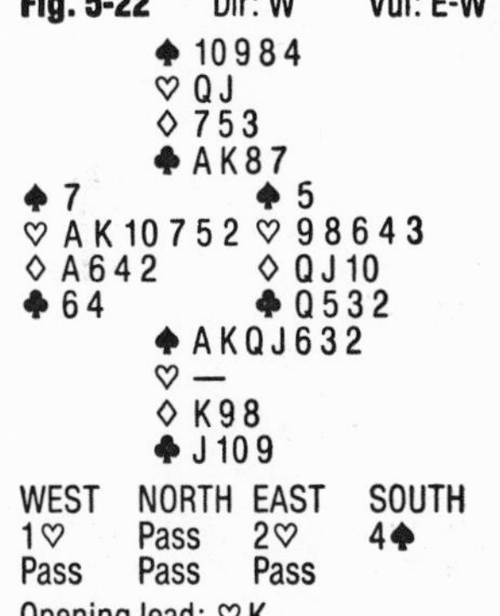

Had East-West not been vulnerable, they might have found the save at five hearts, but then I would not have this story to tell.

As the hand actually was, West led the king of hearts, and South studied the dummy to decide whether he had made a good sacrifice or whether there was a chance to come home with ten tricks.

He soon figured that if East obtained the lead, a diamond through his king would be disastrous. The club suit was intriguing—solid except for the queen. If West had the queen of clubs, a successful finesse would bring in four tricks for a total of eleven—an overtrick, hmmmm. Of course, if *East* had the guarded queen of clubs, the finesse would fail and only nine tricks would be available because the defenders would gobble up the queen of clubs and three fast diamonds.

In examining those club spots, South found a way to make the hand no matter who had the queen of clubs! He decided it was better to go for the 100-percent guaranteed ten tricks than take a chance on eleven. So instead of ruffing the king of hearts, he simply discarded a club! He gave his kibitzers a thrill by discarding the jack of clubs to make it look dashing. West gave some thought to the defense, but could find no better line than to continue with a second heart. South ruffed, pulled the two outstanding trumps, and cashed the ace-king of clubs. When he led the eight of clubs from dummy and East produced the queen, all declarer's pains were justified. He trumped the queen of clubs, returned to dummy with a spade, and discarded a diamond on the seven of clubs. So instead of losing three diamonds and one club, declarer ended up losing one heart and two diamonds—which from his viewpoint was much better.

The newest thing in the play of the hand has the mysterious sounding name of "Discovery." Bridge players seem to like these cryptic names for their play, as it may give them a sense of knowing things that common people cannot know. What Discovery means is finding out who's got what —it's as old as the game—only the name is new. It also is sometimes a pretty good idea.

Fig. 5-23

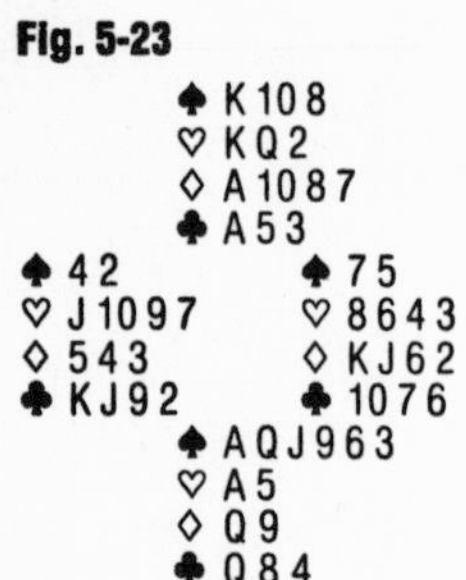

After North opened the bidding with one no-trump, South ended up playing six spades. The opening lead was the jack of hearts. At first glance, it appeared that a diamond could be discarded on dummy's third heart and that the slam would depend on the club situation—making if East held the king of clubs. But South decided to try some of this "who's got what" thinking. He won the first trick in the closed hand and allowed himself the luxury of one trump lead before going on his hunting expedition. After the ace of spades, declarer led the queen of diamonds. When West played low, South decided he had made a discovery. West might have either the king of diamonds or the jack of diamonds, but he most certainly did not have both. That was all South needed to know. From here on in, he had a 99 percent chance to make the hand.

He went up with dummy's ace and then cashed the king and queen of hearts, discarding the nine of diamonds from his hand. With the nine gone, the three cards in dummy were equals, topped only by the king-jack. Declarer led the ten of diamonds from North, planning to discard if East played low. When East produced the jack of diamonds, South ruffed, entered dummy with a second trump lead, and led the eight of diamonds, intending once again to let it ride if East did not cover. East covered with the king of diamonds, South ruffed again, reentered dummy, and led the seven of diamonds to discard a club. His play to find out "Who's got what" turned out to be considerably better than trying to find the king of clubs in the East hand.

Many people consider Georgio Belladonna of Italy the greatest player in the world. On the hand in Fig. 5-24, from the qualifying round of the World Championship in Bermuda in 1975 against the Indonesian team, Belladonna showed how he earned that reputation.

Fig. 5-24

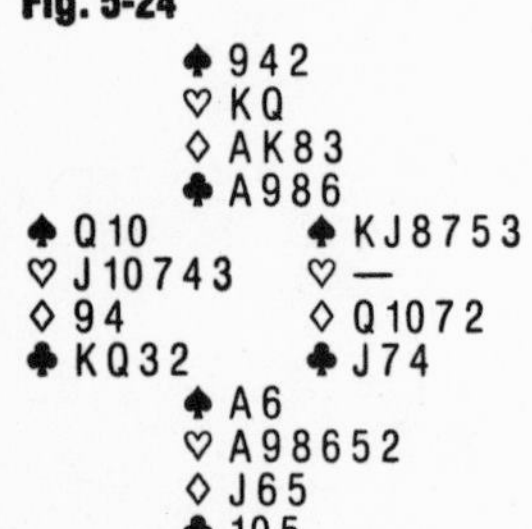

Playing four hearts, Belladonna got the opening lead of the king of clubs. He examined the dummy and noted that there might be a loser in each of the side suits—but no trump losers if the suit broke 3–2. He won the first trick with dummy's ace of clubs and laid down the king of hearts to discover the miserable trump break; in addition to losers in spades, diamonds, and clubs, it looked as though there might be two trump losers. If the queen of diamonds should fall doubleton, that would do away with the diamond loser, but it would not go very far toward solving the other problems engulfing the hand. Belladonna, seeing a chance to utilize the good intermediate cards in the club suit, realized he had received a favorable opening lead in the king of clubs. That left only the queen-jack of clubs in the opposing hands higher than his "solid" three-card sequence of the 10 9 8. Properly handled, this combination would provide some salubrious discards.

At trick three he led the six of clubs. East rose with the jack of clubs and led a spade, but it was too late. Belladonna won the ace of spades and returned to dummy with the queen of hearts. On the nine of clubs he discarded a spade, as West won the queen of clubs. There was nothing West could do. Actually, he returned a spade, which Belladonna trumped. He then cashed the ace-king of diamonds and led the eight of clubs, discarding the jack of diamonds. Declarer had won eight tricks, and his last three cards were the A 9 8 of trumps, while West was behind him with the J 10 7. A diamond was led from dummy, ruffed with the eight of hearts, and, no matter what West did, Belladonna was going to get two trump tricks. So he ended up losing no spades and no diamonds—just two clubs and one heart.

When you can't establish intermediate cards by force, there is no regulation that prevents use of a little guile.

Some years ago, the late Sidney Silodor found himself in six diamonds on the hand in Fig. 5-25.

Fig. 5-25

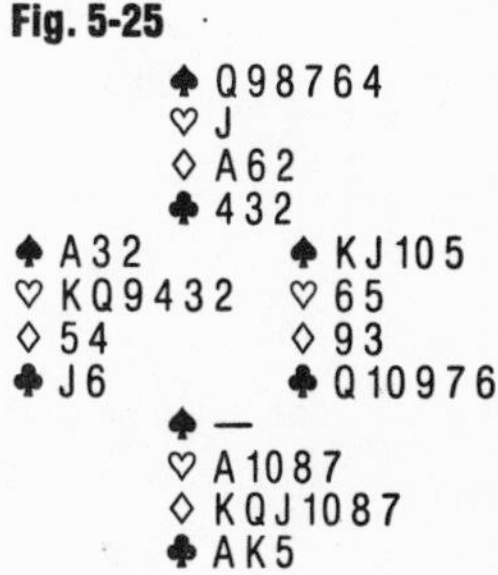

The bidding is not given, but the report I have says that—playing in the national team championship of 1943—Silodor got to six diamonds after West had competed in hearts. The opening lead was the king of hearts. Down came the dummy, and it must have appeared that there was a sure club loser and one or more heart losers—either by West's winning with his high cards or by East's overruffing dummy. That doesn't seem to be the way it appeared to Silodor.

He won the ace of hearts and led a small heart to dummy to trump it. Wait a minute! That's just the way it seemed to the West player. After West played a small heart, he heard Silodor call for the two of clubs. Look again and you will see that the small heart that Silodor had led was the seven-spot which duly won the trick. I suppose West thought there was no reason to cover a small heart which was going to be trumped in dummy anyway. From there on, it was a breeze. Silodor next led the ace-king of clubs, ruffed a club in dummy, ruffed a spade back to his hand, and ruffed another heart with the ace of diamonds. He then took out the opponent's trumps and conceded a heart trick.

In some cases we can attempt a suit promotion while keeping a finesse in reserve in case our primary plan fails. Fig. 5-26 is such a hand.

Fig. 5-26

North-South reached four spades, and West led the king of clubs. After taking a look at dummy, he switched to a trump.

Declarer surveyed the hand and saw another loser in clubs and one in diamonds, as well as a possible heart loser if that finesse failed. However, there were some chances in the diamond suit, and declarer set out to see whether he could examine those before taking the heart finesse. After all, one of the opponents had to have three or fewer diamonds, and that opponent might well be the one who had the ace. Although the odds were against it, it was worth a try if it did not involve too much risk.

Declarer won the trump lead in dummy and led the three of diamonds toward his queen. Had East played the ace, the ball game would have been over, as the queen of hearts eventually could have been discarded on the king of diamonds, but East was too smart for that and the queen won.

Declarer next led a small diamond toward the dummy, and when West played the 9, let it hold the trick.

West exited with a trump, and declarer played the queen. When East followed suit, declarer carefully unblocked by playing the eight so that he would be able to enter dummy with a trump. Once more he led a small diamond, and, as East had nothing left but the ace, declarer was able to ruff it, establishing the king for a discard. He never did have to try the heart finesse.

Fig. 5-27

On the hand we just looked at, the diamond suit had both the king and the queen. Let's take a look at one where the diamond suit is even weaker, but the declarer was still able to put the defenders in an impossible situation.

When West led the Jack of spades against four hearts, declarer saw two sure diamond losers and the possibility of two losers in clubs. If worst came to worst, he could try the indirect finesse in clubs by taking his ace and leading toward the queen, but he decided to try everything else first.

He won the opening lead with the king, led to the ace of spades, and ruffed a spade with the ace of hearts just to be safe.

Next he drew two rounds of trumps from his hand. When this gathered all the opposing trumps, he next led a diamond. When West played low, he inserted the nine from dummy, giving the trick to East with the jack. It also gave East an impossible problem. If he led a club, declarer would be sure to lose at most one club trick. So East did the best he could—he played the king of diamonds, which won the trick. Along came a third diamond, but declarer didn't trump. He simply discarded one of his losing clubs, and let West win with the ace. Now the queen of diamonds was established for a discard of the other club loser, and a high trump remained in dummy to reach it. West's club lead was too late, so declarer wound up losing three diamond tricks, but no other tricks at all.

Fig. 5-28

The hand in Fig. 5-28 comes from Robert Darvas, who was a great Hungarian player, writer, and composer of bridge hands which delight the connoisseur.

According to Darvas, South was in three no-trump, with the ten of spades as the opening lead. In spite of his 26 high-card points, South had only seven tricks in his hand. The jack of spades in dummy could be another trick. So, after he cashed three top spades, declarer crossed to dummy with the five of clubs to take the jack of spades.

I believe I got ahead of my story a little bit. Declarer, after winning three spades in his hand, led the ten of clubs. West covered with the jack, and dummy's queen went to East's king. East's diamond return was won by the king. Now the six of clubs was led and covered in turn by the seven, eight, and nine.

Let's stop and apply our rule of 14. There are nine clubs in the deck higher than the five-spot. Two rounds of clubs had been played, and every club played so far was higher than the five. This meant that only one higher remained unplayed, and declarer had that in his own hand.

So, after East won the nine of clubs, he shifted to a heart, but South put up the ace, entered dummy with the five of clubs, cashed the jack of spades, and returned to his hand with the king of diamonds to cash the ace of clubs for the ninth trick.

Did any bridge player ever play this hand in real life? I don't know, I said in the introduction to this hand that Darvas was a composer of delightful bridge hands. Whether he made it up or whether it was actually dealt, it beautifully illustrates the principle of promotion.

It is obvious that master players have long known of the value of establishing intermediate cards. For some reason, the literature on this subject is extremely limited. So far as I know, the hands I have shown you represent the first full study of this important subject. Briefly, here are some of the points that have been raised.

1. Sometimes intermediate cards can be promoted to top rank very quickly. Cards from the six-spot up can get to be boss of a suit in as few as two leads. (There are eight cards in each suit higher than the 6, and under some circumstances they will all be played by the time the suit has been led twice.)

2. Some of my pupils tell me they watch the growth of these spots best by referring to the Rule of 14. Others tell me they find it easier simply to watch the spots that have been played. The best thing for you to do is whatever seems easier to you. There is nothing sacred about the use of the Rule of 14.

3. Where a sequence is solid, the play can become a cinch, so long as (a) declarer can afford to lose tricks to get rid of losers, (b) declarer has all other suits under control so the defenders cannot cash enough to defeat the hand when they secure the lead, and (c) the hand with the sequence has sufficient entries to enable declarer to get back there to take his winners.

4. Sometimes the establishment can work only because of favorable distribution in the opponents' hands.

5. Sometimes quick promotion is possible only because you have received a favorable lead. That usually is a high card which would not have had to be played if the defender were merely following suit.

6. If all else fails, there are times when you can get by with a very pleasant theft.

I hope this study will enable you to find some of the pleasure I have found from time to time in bringing home those little seven and eight-spots in what looked like an otherwise hopeless contract.

ESTABLISHMENT OF LONG SUITS

We have studied the promotion of intermediate cards in cases where, after a few rounds have been played, our remaining cards are higher in rank than those of the defenders. We now come to the matter of establishing small cards simply because the opponents are exhausted of cards in a suit where we still have cards. It is obvious that if our small cards are to be established in such a suit, we must start with more cards in one of our two hands than either defender has in the same suit.

32
J 109876
AKQ54

In this example, our small cards will never take a trick if East can hang onto the five he holds. Don't worry about that too much because the odds are better than 5 to 1 that the six cards held by the defenders will not be so distributed. They are more likely to be:

32
J10 9876
AKQ54

Here, the declarer has more in his hand than either of the opponents and he can finally make one of his "long cards" good. In the process of doing so, he will take his A K Q and then do something about one of the spot cards. If he is playing no-trump (or with no trumps available in dummy), he will have to give up a trick in order to take his fifth card. Of course, if he has a trump in the dummy and entries back to his hand, he will trump one small card and then return to his hand to cash the other. A player will usually be able to get four tricks out of this combination one way or the other. On a lucky day, declarer may run into this distribution:

32
J109 876
AKQ54

With this holding, the defenders will have no cards left in the suit when the A K Q have been played, and declarer will take all five tricks in the suit. This will have to be a lucky day, as the odds are almost 2 to 1 that the six cards held by the defenders will not be evenly divided.

Sometimes declarer needs to establish a suit without such a fine holding as A K Q and must decide how to develop a suit like this:

32
J10 KQ98
A7654

After four leads to the suit, the fifth card in declarer's hand will be good. Meanwhile, the declarer is going to be busy giving up three tricks or managing to trump some of the low cards with dummy's trumps.

There are many variations of this theme which depend on the high cards held in the suit we are trying to establish.

The question of how many cards you and the dummy hold in a suit and the related question of how many are held by the opponents are important in the matter of knowing when you can lead high to finesse and when you can lead high to establish intermediate cards in a suit. In trying to establish long cards because the opponents have none left, how many your side has and how many the opponents have and how they are divided becomes basic and essential.

Beginning players almost immediately sense the importance of long suits in their own hand. Before too long, they are giving consideration not only to the length in their own hand, but also to the combined length with their dummy. The next step is to pay more attention to the number of cards held by the opponents and, finally, as they progress, bridge players learn the importance of considering the distribution of the cards held both in their own and their opponents' hands.

Practically every book on play of the hand has, or should have, the following table showing the probable distribution of cards in the two hands held by the opponents, depending on the number of cards held together by you and the dummy. Here is the most important part of the table.

The first column shows the total number of cards held by your side; the second column shows the number held by the opponents; column three shows possible distributions; and the last column shows the frequency of each distribution on a percentage basis.

Probable Distribution

No. of N-S Cards	*No. of E-W Cards*	*E-W Cards Distributed*	*Percentage of Time*
5	8	5-3	47.1
		4-4	32.7
		6-2	17.1
		7-1	2.9
		8-0	0.2
6	7	4-3	62.2
		5-2	30.5
		6-1	6.8
		7-0	0.5
7	6	4-2	48.5
		3-3	35.5
		5-1	14.5
		6-0	1.5
8	5	3-2	67.8
		4-1	28.3
		5-0	3.9
9	4	3-1	49.7
		2-2	40.7
		4-0	9.6
10	3	2-1	78.0
		3-0	22.0
11	2	1-1	52.0
		2-0	48.0

I have extracted some figures from this table which might be easier to use. The first column below shows the total number of cards your opponents hold in the key suit. The next five columns indicate the likelihood, in terms of percentages, that your lead will win that trick because the opponents' cards have been eliminated.

Likelihood That Your Long Card Will Win the Trick (in percentages)

Opponents' holding	*2nd trick*	*3rd trick*	*4th trick*	*5th trick*	*6th trick*
8	0	0	0	32.7	impossible
7	0	0	0	62.2	92.7
6	0	0	35.5	84.0	98.5
5	0	0	67.8	96.1	100.0
4	0	40.7	90.4	100.0	100.0
3	0	78.0	100.0	100.0	100.0
2	52.0	100.0	100.0	100.0	100.0

For example, if you need a long suit trick and you have to choose between attacking a suit of A K Q x x opposite a void or A K x x opposite three small, you can see that you will win the fifth lead only 32.7 percent of the time with the first holding, whereas the last card from the A K x x holding will be good 35.5 percent of the time. Clearly it is better to attack the A K x x suit.

These are a priori tables, assuming you do not know the distribution of any suit in the opposing hands. For example, if you take twenty-six cards which include precisely five hearts and put them into two groups of thirteen each in a random manner, they will come out four in one hand and one in the other 28.3 percent of the time, as shown in the tables. Of course, if you discover that another suit—say diamonds—is split 4–4 between the hands, you no longer have twenty-six unknown cards. You now have only eighteen and it can be shown that the 4–1 split will occur only 26.5 percent of the time. However, if those eight diamonds are found to be six in West and two in East, you have a different problem. Of the eighteen cards left, you are going to give West only seven and East eleven. Now the 4–1 split will occur 31.4 percent of the time. The difference between these figures and the a priori figures are modest enough to ignore in this discussion of suit establishment. The big difference is whether the four-card holding will be with East or West, which could be terribly important in deciding which way to finesse, but not in suit establishment. For a further discussion of this subject, see Appendix A.

If the cards are hand dealt instead of computer dealt, they are not truly random, unless you shuffle much more carefully than most people do. This tends to make the distributional pattern of hand-dealt hands more erratic than that of computer-dealt hands. The long-term result is likely to be that suits will become established more often than as shown in the table when hands are hand dealt.

You Hold 4–3; They Hold 6 If you and partner together hold only six cards in a suit—three each—the opponents have seven. It is therefore impossible for you to draw all of their cards and have a good one remaining in either of your own hands; one of the opponents *has* to have as many as four.

However, where your four-card length is faced by three cards in the opposite hand, it is possible to establish one by length. Reference to the table (p. 148) will tell you that the fourth card will become established a little better than 35 percent of the time. That is still almost 2 to 1 against you, but if there is no other choice, that is much better than nothing. Sometimes when you *have* a choice it is quite clear what you should do first.

Fig. 5-29

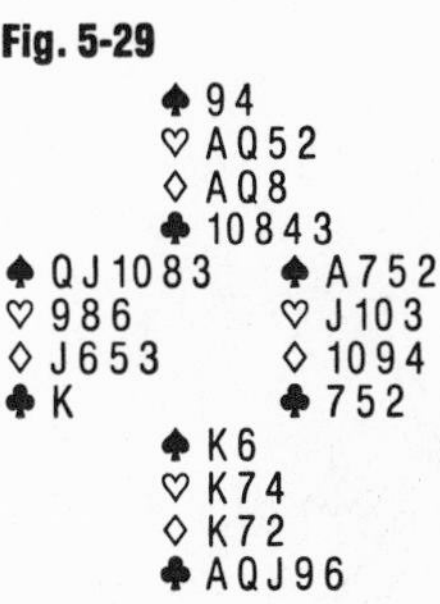

South opened one no-trump and, after North used Stayman to see whether South had four hearts, wound up in three no-trump. West led the queen of spades, overtaken by East's ace, and, when the suit was returned, South was in with the king.

In addition to the trick he had already taken, declarer could see seven additional tricks in aces and kings. That made eight, and he needed one more. Several more could come from the club suit if the finesse worked, but only one more could come from the heart suit—if the fourth heart could take a trick. The finesse was obviously a 50–50 chance, and establishing the fourth heart trick was not. Nonetheless, declarer wisely chose to try for the heart trick first. If he tried the club finesse and lost the lead to West, that player might have any number of spades to cash—he could have started with seven! So South led hearts, holding the club finesse in reserve if hearts did not break. When they did break, the fourth heart brought in his ninth trick provided he refused to finesse clubs. Caring more about fulfilling his contract than making extra tricks, declarer led a club and went up with the ace. *In real life, virtue is not always adequately rewarded, so I try to make up for it as best I can in the world of cards.* South got his full reward when West's king of clubs fell, and declarer ended up taking 12 tricks. Of course, if he had tried the club finesse, West would have won and cashed three more spades to put him down one.

There are times when it is necessary to get a favorable break with a four-card suit opposite three (Fig. 5-30).

Fig. 5-30

Against a contract of three no-trump, South received the opening lead of the jack of spades. There were four-card holdings in both black suits, but neither had a "long card" that could be established. With only two in the opposite hand, one of the opponents was sure to have four of each suit. There were also four-card holdings in the red suits, and there the total holding was at least seven cards, making a "long card" establishable in one of these or both, provided the opposing cards were divided 3–3.

To establish hearts would require that the lead be relinquished twice, so declarer properly decided to try diamonds first. To try to keep everything under control as well as possible, he won the first spade trick and promptly played a small diamond from each hand. When he regained the lead with a spade, he next ducked a round of hearts. When West persisted with yet another spade and East followed, it was safe to give up the lead again, so declarer ducked another heart. East returned a club, but declarer was in control. He first tried the ace of hearts, but that suit didn't break. Now he played the ace and king of diamonds and was a happy man

Fig. 5-31

when both opponents followed suit and the five of diamonds became his ninth trick.

Frequently, in establishing a suit, it pays to lose whatever tricks you have to lose early.

With South playing four spades, West started by leading three rounds of diamonds. It was easy to count the winners in this hand. Unless there was a terrible distribution in spades, there were five spade tricks, two hearts, and two clubs, for a total of nine. The tenth trick could come either from an established heart—provided that suit split favorably—or from a club finesse. By playing his cards in the correct order, declarer reserved the chance to take both plays so that if either of them should work, he would make his contract. Instead of trumping the third diamond, declarer discarded the four of hearts!

Now any further diamond leads could be trumped in dummy. West switched to a trump, and declarer proceeded to pull the remaining trumps. Next he cashed the king of hearts, crossed to the ace of hearts, and ruffed a heart. When that suit broke, his problem was solved. Instead of taking the club finesse, he crossed to the ace of clubs and discarded his seven of clubs on the established nine of hearts.

Fig. 5-32

♠ A K 9
♡ 8 2
◇ K Q 5 2
♣ 7 5 4 2

♠ 8 6 3
♡ K Q J 9 4 3
◇ J 4
♣ Q 3

♠ Q J 10
♡ 7 6
◇ 10 9 8 6
♣ 10 9 8 6

♠ 7 5 4 2
♡ A 10 5
◇ A 7 3
♣ A K J

Once in a while you will have time to test two four-card suits in trying to develop your game-going trick (Fig. 5-32).

Against three no-trump, the opening lead was the king of hearts. Declarer counted eight tricks off the top and needed a ninth one. This could come from the fourth diamond in dummy, the fourth spade in his hand, or from the club suit. Declarer set out to see whether he could try both suit breaks and still have in reserve a club finesse if neither broke favorably. To exhaust East of hearts, South ducked two rounds, winning the third as North and East discarded small clubs.

To establish spades, South would have to lose one trick in the suit, and he wanted to lose that trick to East who was now void of hearts. So after winning the ace of hearts, declarer played a small spade and inserted dummy's nine. East won and returned the ten of clubs. South won with the ace and cashed the ace-king of spades. When both followed suit, he had his ninth trick, without taking a finesse. Next he crossed to the ace of diamonds to cash the thirteenth spade. Diamonds might break also, to give him an extra trick, so he tried the king-queen of diamonds. When East proved to have diamonds stopped, he could have only one club left, and since West started with two, declarer's king-jack of clubs had to take the last two tricks. By timing his plays correctly, declarer was rewarded with his overtrick.

Fig. 5-33

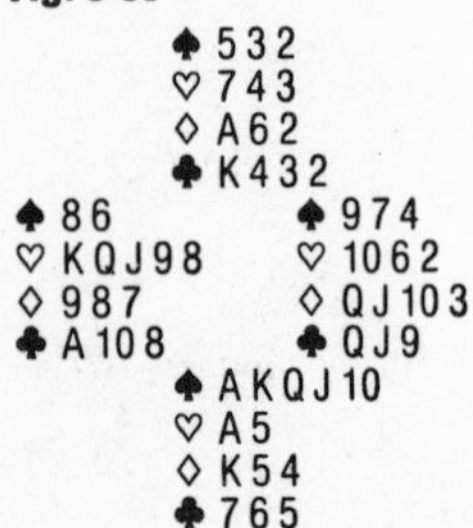

South needed a lot of luck to make four spades on this deal in Fig. 5-33.

For ten tricks, not only did declarer need an even break in the club suit, but West had to have the ace of clubs. The odds against this were something like 4½ to 1, but it was too late to worry about the odds—the time had come to play.

As declarer won the opening heart lead with the ace, he saw that outside of the club suit he had exactly eight tricks. Unless he could take two club tricks, he would go set. That meant that both the king of clubs and one small club would have to take tricks. It also meant there was an entry problem because clubs had to be led three times before the fourth one would become good.

South pulled three rounds of trumps and led the five of clubs, ducking all around. East saw what was going on and led back the queen of diamonds to see if there was a chance to eliminate the dummy entry. Declarer rose with the king, however, and led another club. West was helpless. If he rose with the ace, there would be two good clubs in dummy. If he played low, dummy would play the king of clubs and another club, which West would have to win. The ace of diamonds would provide an entry for the good club.

On the next hand, declarer was afraid to give East the lead. However, he managed to develop his hand without doing so.

Fig. 5-34

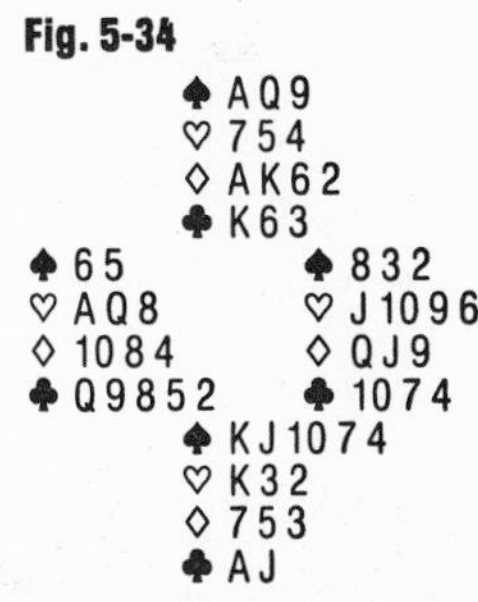

Again South arrived at a four spade contract. West led a trump, and declarer counted nine tricks off the top. The finesse of the jack of clubs might bring a tenth; if it didn't, the establishment of a small diamond might bring in the needed trick. If both failed, then the ace of hearts might be in the East hand.

By taking these plays in the proper order, declarer would be able to test all of them. He won the opening lead with the trump ace in the dummy and led a small club to the jack. That did not work too well, West winning with the queen. West shifted to the four of diamonds. Declarer won the king of diamonds and came to his hand with the ace of clubs. He now led the ten of spades and overtook it with dummy's queen of spades, preserving a small trump for an additional dummy entry. Pleased to see that both defenders followed suit to the second trump lead, he realized that one more lead would exhaust the enemy's trumps. Next declarer cashed the king of clubs, discarding a diamond. When the ace of diamonds fetched a diamond from each opponent, declarer led a small diamond and trumped it with the jack of spades. When both opponents followed suit, the fourth diamond was established in dummy, and declarer had the nine of spades as a final entry to discard a heart on that diamond. Next he led a heart, trying for an extra trick in case East has the ace of hearts, but that was not to be.

Occasionally you will be able to establish the fourth card of a 4–3 suit without ever giving up a trick in the suit—even when the opponents have most of the high cards in the suit. On this example in Fig. 5-35, the "thirteenth" diamond provided the slam-going trick.

Fig. 5-35 Dlr: N Vul: N-S

North:
♠ K 8 6
♡ A K 8
◇ A 6 4 3
♣ 10 9 4

West:
♠ 2
♡ Q J 10 9 7 4
◇ K J 8
♣ A J 3

East:
♠ 4 3
♡ 6 5 3 2
◇ Q 10 9
♣ 8 7 5 2

South:
♠ A Q J 10 9 7 5
♡ —
◇ 7 5 2
♣ K Q 6

NORTH	EAST	SOUTH	WEST
1◇	Pass	1♠	2♡
2♠	Pass	6♠	All Pass

Opening lead: ♡Q

Declarer won the heart lead in the dummy, discarding a diamond from his hand, and led the four of clubs. He played his queen, and West, with a look of great innocence, dropped the three of clubs. This did not lull our declarer. If West didn't have that ace of clubs, he had bid two hearts on a piece of cheese. South decided if all else failed, he would eventually lead the ten of clubs from dummy and finesse East for the jack of clubs.

But first he thought he'd better see whether "all else" would fail.

Guaranteeing three entries to dummy, he led the nine of spades to the king and threw away another diamond on the king of hearts. Next he cashed the ace of diamonds and led a small diamond which he trumped with an honor. The seven of spades to dummy's eight-spot provided another dummy entry, and another diamond was led and trumped high. With both opponents following suit to three diamond leads, the six-spot in dummy was a "thirteener"—the only diamond left. Now the carefully preserved five of spades was played to dummy's six of spades, and declarer discarded a club on the good diamond. He eventually conceded one club trick to the opponents, but he made his slam.

As a final hand in this group where you have a 4–3 fit in a suit where you want to establish a long card, I want to show you one frequently misplayed combination (Fig. 5-36).

Fig. 5-36

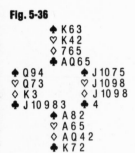

♠ K 6 3
♥ K 4 2
♦ 7 6 5
♣ A Q 6 5

♠ Q 9 4 | ♠ J 10 7 5
♥ Q 7 3 | ♥ J 10 9 8
♦ K 3 | ♦ J 10 9 8
♣ J 10 9 8 3 | ♣ 4

♠ A 8 2
♥ A 6 5
♦ A Q 4 2
♣ K 7 2

Against a three no-trump contract, West led the jack of clubs. This was one of South's 4–3 fit suits, but the club lead by West made it seem rather unlikely that this suit would break so that the long club would become established. Declarer could count eight tricks off the top, and needed only one additional trick.

He decided to try for an extra trick in diamonds. If he had taken a simple diamond finesse to the queen he would have lost the extra trick—but he didn't do that. As he had double stoppers in the other three suits, he played diamonds safely and in such a fashion that he could win two diamond tricks (1) whenever the suit broke 3–3, (2) whenever the king was singleton or doubleton with West, and (3) whenever East held the king (with any number of guards). This certainly was better than the 50–50 chance provided by the direct finesse of the queen.

Declarer won the first club in the South hand and led a small diamond, West playing low and East winning the eight of diamonds. East had no more clubs, so he returned a heart. Declarer won with the ace and laid down the ace of diamonds. When the king fell, his problem was solved. Had the king *not* fallen, he would have gone to dummy with a spade and led the last diamond from the dummy toward the queen-four in the closed hand. If East started with K x x, the king would now fall. If East followed low, declarer would go up with the queen because, if *West* had the king, the suit would be breaking 3–3 and the small diamond would be established for the game-going trick.

You Hold 4–4; They Hold 5 We have added one card to your holding, and there has been a dramatic improvement in your fortune. Reference to our table says that now the fourth card in the suit will find the defenders exhausted of the suit more than two times out of three.

Fig. 5-37

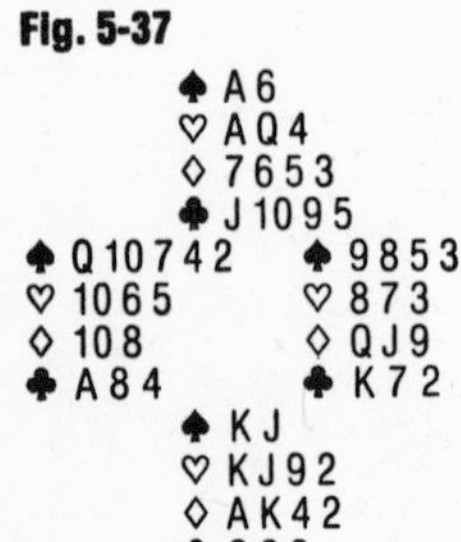

In the next hand, that holding in the diamond suit enables the declarer to overcome a bad holding in the spade suit.

Playing three no-trump, South received an opening lead of the four of spades. Now, in spite of the fact that this gave him a free finesse, he was going to take only two spade tricks out of the A K J. With one small spade added to either the dummy's hand or his own in place of one small diamond, he would have had three spade tricks after the opening lead. He also would have had time enough to lead clubs, getting rid of the ace and king, and would have been assured of eleven tricks.

As it was, he couldn't even come up with a sure nine tricks. In addition to the two spade tricks, he had four in hearts and two in diamonds. He didn't have time to develop two club tricks, as that would have involved losing the lead two times, and the defenders could certainly cash three spades along with two clubs. But, while he didn't have a sure thing, he did have a 2 to 1 shot in the diamond suit.

He won the opening lead with the king of spades and then cashed four heart tricks, discarding a small diamond from the dummy. If either opponent wished to turn loose of a diamond, thinking the diamond suit he saw in the dummy was too pitifully small to be of value, that would be all right with declarer. Neither saw fit to discard a diamond.

So, the declarer led a small diamond to make sure he kept communication, won the spade return with dummy's ace, took his nine tricks, and folded up his tent and went home.

Sometimes there is a play to fall back on if the five outstanding cards do not split 3–2 (Fig. 5-38).

Fig. 5-38

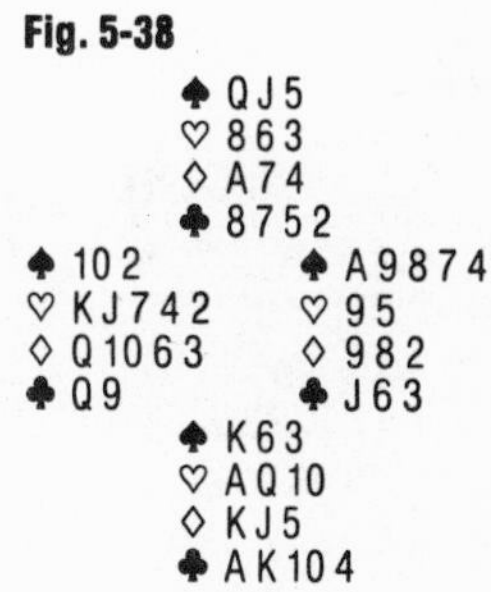

Against a three no-trump contract, West led the four of hearts. South could now count on two sure winners in hearts, but he could find only four others without taking a chance on losing the lead, so he needed to develop three more. It looked as though if he handled things well he would be able to get one additional club trick and two additional spade tricks. Having to establish tricks in both of the black suits, he decided to go after clubs first because he might be able to control which of the defenders won the club trick that he probably was going to have to surrender. If he could lose this trick to West, West could not continue the attack on hearts successfully. So, declarer crossed to dummy with the ace of diamonds and led the two of clubs. When East played low, he put in the ten-spot. Had East held both the queen and jack, this would have provided a trick, but West duly won with the queen. West now decided that his best chance was to work on spades, and he led the ten. East won with the ace and returned a heart. It was too late; South now had his nine tricks without trying the diamond finesse.

On this hand, an unexpected response led declarer to believe that the odds favored a grand slam. He was right—the odds did favor a grand slam.

Fig. 5-39 Dlr: S Vul: B

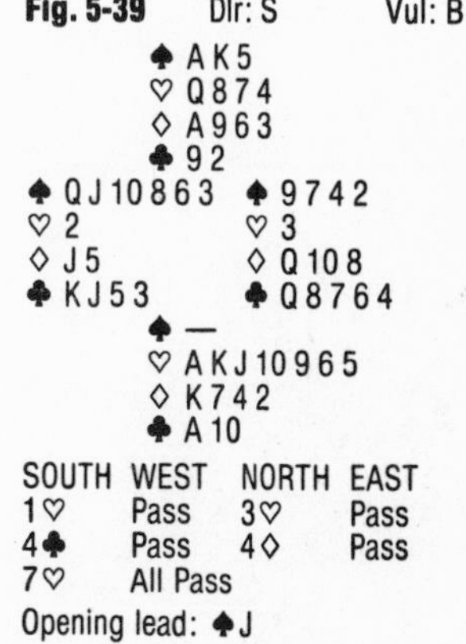

SOUTH	WEST	NORTH	EAST
1♡	Pass	3♡	Pass
4♣	Pass	4◇	Pass
7♡	All Pass		

Opening lead: ♠J

When South picked up his hand, he found it quite exciting. He wondered whether he should open with one heart, two hearts, or four hearts. He strongly suspected that his partner had a singleton heart and doubted that he would ever be able to convince him that his heart suit was as strong as it was. However, he knew that the proper bid was one heart, and so he restrained himself and made that bid. Imagine his surprise when his partner jumped to three hearts!

After cue bidding clubs and finding his partner had control of diamonds, he went to seven. The queen of spades was led, and the dummy came down. Somehow, the dummy looked a little disappointing. In diamonds and clubs there were three losers. In the north hand, there were two winners in the spade suit, but, if he sluffed a club and diamond on the ace and king, he would still have a diamond loser. But the declarer had been studying ways to establish suits without losing a trick, and he saw a play which was a favorite to win. On the ace of spades he discarded a diamond. He led the four of hearts to the ace in his hand and knew the trumps were gone. He cashed the king of diamonds and led a diamond to dummy's ace. On the ace of spades, he discarded his other diamond. Now he had two small diamonds in the dummy and none in his hand. He led one, trumping it high enough to provide an entry back to dummy, and led the jack of hearts to dummy's queen. Now on the fourth diamond he discarded the ten of clubs.

They tell us you should bid a grand slam when the odds are any better than 2 to 1 that it will make. A percentage of 67.8 percent is not much better than 2 to 1, but it is better. There was, however, one more consideration in the hand above. Odds favored bidding the slam only providing the declarer knew about suit establishment.

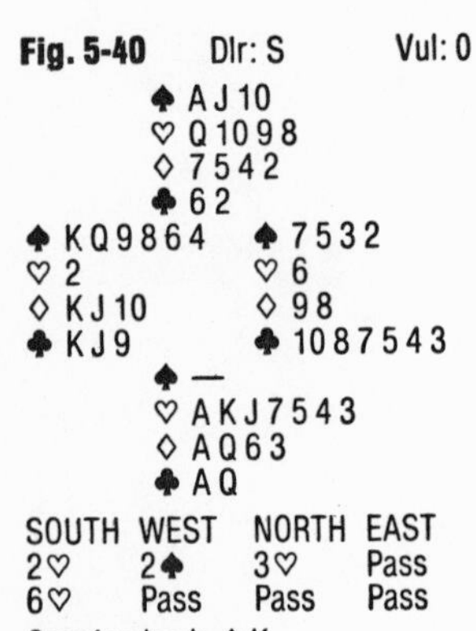

Sometimes the play is not so easy to see.

West led the king of spades, and declarer surveyed the dummy. He would gladly have traded the five points dummy had in spades for the king of diamonds. But, he knew no way to do that, so he had to make do with what he had.

Declarer considered it likely that West, who had overcalled two spades, had most or all of the high cards outstanding, so the finesses in the minor suits did not look too good. While there was some slight chance of a throw-in play, West had to have just the right cards. Declarer saw a much better chance to establish the diamond suit without loss in spite of the fact that the finesse would probably fail. To compensate somewhat for the fact that North's high-card points were mostly in the defenders' suit, he did have both the jack and ten with his ace. He decided he had received a favorable lead. Declarer took the ace of spades and discarded a diamond on it. Next, he played the jack of spades, letting West win with the queen, and discarded another diamond. West thought the safest way to get off the lead was to lead a trump. Declarer won that in the dummy and discarded his queen of diamonds on the ten of spades. His next step was to win the ace of diamonds and return to the dummy with a trump. He trumped dummy's four of diamonds high and returned once more to trump the five of diamonds with an honor. The seven was now high, and there was a trump to get back to the dummy. On the seven he discarded his queen of clubs.

Fig. 5-41

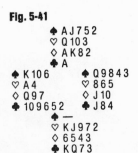

	North	
	♠ A J 7 5 2 ♡ Q 10 3 ◇ A K 8 2 ♣ A	
♠ K 10 6 ♡ A 4 ◇ Q 9 7 ♣ 10 9 6 5 2		♠ Q 9 8 4 3 ♡ 8 6 5 ◇ J 10 ♣ J 8 4
	♠ — ♡ K J 9 7 2 ◇ 6 5 4 3 ♣ K Q 7 3	

On the hand in Fig. 5-41, the problem looked a little different, but it really was not.

South got all the way up to six hearts in the bidding, and West led the ace and another trump. This meant that declarer had four trump winners in his own hand. He had one trump left in the dummy with which to trump a club, and that would bring his trump winners to five. The ace of spades made six, two winners in diamonds and three in clubs came to a total of eleven. One more trick was needed from somewhere.

The first suit declarer examined was spades—the opponents had eight spades, and if there were four of these in each hand, the long spade in the dummy could become the twelfth trick. There were plenty of entries in the dummy to take the spades and try to establish them, but the odds were considerably against the defenders' spades breaking 4–4.

He and dummy had eight diamonds, and the odds were very much in favor of their breaking 3–2, so that a long diamond could be established, but the trouble with that procedure was that it involved giving up a diamond trick, and, as the ace of trumps was already lost, declarer could not afford to lose a trick to establish a trick. Neither could he find any way to discard two of the diamonds in his hand so that he could establish the suit without losing a trick. But this train of thought led to something better. While there was no way to discard two diamonds from his own hand to establish those in North, declarer did see a way to discard two in the north hand and then establish one in his own hand, provided the diamonds broke 3–2. This procedure involved having clubs led three times without being trumped, but since the opponents held eight clubs, declarer knew the odds were excellent that each held as many as three. He therefore embarked upon the procedure of establishing a diamond in his hand without losing a diamond.

After winning the second trick in the dummy, he cashed the ace of clubs and the ace and king of diamonds. He then cashed the ace of spades, on which he discarded a club from his hand, and trumped a spade to return to his hand. On the king and queen of clubs, he discarded the two small diamonds in the dummy. He was then able to lead the five of diamonds and trump it with the queen of trumps. He returned once more to his hand by trumping a spade, finally pulled the last trump, and played his six of diamonds, which stood up for the twelfth trick.

How did South calculate that the chances of getting a favorable distribution in both clubs and diamonds was better than getting a favorable distribution in the spade suit? Well, it's not necessary to calculate these things exactly in the middle of play; however, if you like to be your own mathematician, here is the way it is done.

The eight diamonds will break favorably 67.8 percent of the time. We will consider that clubs are favorable whenever they are 4–4 or 5–3. This comes to 47.1 percent plus 32.7 percent, or a total of 79.8 percent.

It is a good rule of thumb to consider that whenever each of two favorable events is better than 70 percent, the chances that both of them will be favorable is better than even. The chances that diamonds would break favorably did not quite come to 70 percent, but the chances in clubs greatly exceeded 70 percent, making the combination better than an even chance. Here is the formula. When the odds on each of two events are known, if you will multiply them by each other, you will have the chances that both of them will be favorable. My trusty hand calculator tells me that 79.8 x 67.8 comes to something better than 54 percent of the time, which means that more than half of the time, both diamonds and clubs will break favorably. This is considerably better than the chances that the spade suit will break 4–4.

DUMMY
♠ K 6 4
♡ A 7 3
◇ K 9 5
♣ 7 6 5 3

DECLARER
♠ A Q
♡ K J 4
◇ A 6 4 3
♣ A Q 4 2

Just how you play these 4–4 fits when you have the tenace situations may depend on how many tricks you need in the suit. With the illustration shown above, after you receive an opening lead of a spade, you have seven sure tricks outside of the club suit, and two club tricks will give you your nine in three no-trump. You also have plenty of stoppers in all suits, so your opponents cannot get their suit established before you get yours. Your best play is to lay down the ace of clubs. If the king does not fall, go to the dummy with the ace of hearts and lead a club toward your hand. If East follows low, play the queen, and you are assured of two tricks. If East does not follow suit, you could never have taken two club tricks no matter how you played. By playing this way, you will win two tricks whenever your opponents' cards are divided 3–2, whenever West has the singleton king, or whenever East has the king of clubs with any number.

But with the following holding, you have a different problem.

DUMMY
♠ K 6 4
♡ A 7 3
◇ K 9 5
♣ 7 6 5 3

DECLARER
♠ A 3
♡ K 6 4
◇ A 6 4 3
♣ A Q 4 2

Again, you are playing three no-trump and get the lead of a spade. Now you have seven tricks off the top and need two additional tricks. In addition, the defenders are within one lead of getting their suit established.

Your best chance to get the two additional tricks is to play for three tricks in the club suit. Were it not for the fact that the defenders were about to get their suit established, you could consider laying down the ace of clubs, going to the dummy, leading a club, and then, if East plays low, playing the queen unless you are a good guesser and can guess that West started with the king doubleton. However, if the suit did not break too well, you might find that they could establish their spades while you are fooling with clubs. Under these circumstances, your best play is to rise with the king of spades, promptly lead a small club, and finesse the queen. This will bring in three tricks whenever East has the king doubleton or the king three times. It is not a 50–50 chance, but it is the best chance you have.

But, let's try establishing suits that are longer than four cards. It ought to be easier.

You Hold 5–0; They Hold 8 Obviously, unless the opponents' cards are split 4–4, one of them will hold as many cards in this suit as you do, and, if that player hangs onto all of his, your fifth one can never become a winner unless it is high. The chances that they will have this specific holding, which allows your fifth one to be the one remaining, are something less than 1 out of 3. Sometimes, however, there will be several plays available to you, any one of which will bring in the contract, provided these plays are made in the right order, where one of these plays is going for a 4–4 break.

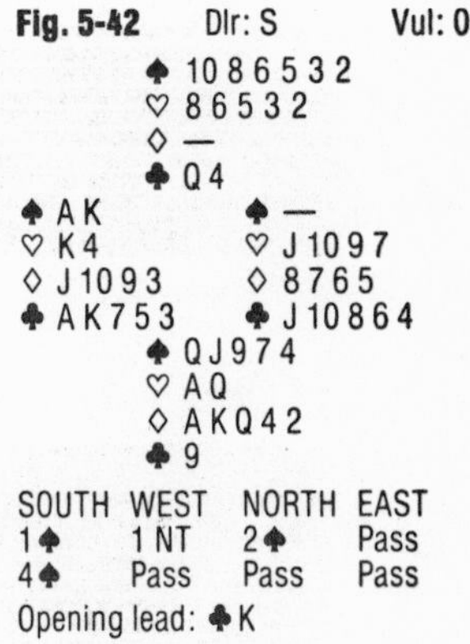

West opened the king of clubs, and South had a chance to survey the dummy. He commented that he was pleased that his partner did not underbid the hand. Unless West had bid one no-trump with a singleton, he had both the ace and king of spades, making two losers in that suit, in addition to the club loser. The heart finesse didn't look like much of a chance, with West overcalling one no-trump. And, it was a little late for a throw-in play, with the defenders having three pretty obvious tricks. It didn't seem likely to unscramble some sort of a squeeze situation, as West, who had all the high cards, would always be playing after the declarer. So, it looked like it was a 4–4 break in diamonds or nothing. As this hand is used to illustrate the point, it was a 4–4 break in diamonds.

West continued with the second club, which South trumped. He then led trump. West, not liking to lead too often, cashed both the ace and king of trumps and got off lead with the jack of diamonds. Declarer won the A K Q of diamonds, discarding three of dummy's hearts, and then led a small diamond, which he trumped. This exhausted all the diamonds and made the fifth diamond good. He returned with a trump and, on the four of diamonds, discarded the fourth heart, leaving a singleton in the dummy. The ace of hearts, followed by the trumping of a heart, gave declarer his ten tricks.

On this hand in Fig. 5-43, declarer had two suits to work on. He could try them both, provided he took them in the right order.

South opened four spades, and North bid six. West opened the queen of diamonds, and South surveyed his prospects. Between himself and the dummy, there were nine clubs. If the opponents clubs would break 2–2, he could simply cash the ace of clubs, give them one, and then his hand would be good. In addition, there was a 5–0 holding in hearts. If the opponents' hearts would split 4–4, then the dummy could win three heart tricks—the ace, the king, and the long one. That would allow three clubs to be discarded from South's hand, and then, no matter how clubs split, declarer would lose only one club trick. Declarer properly decided to explore the possibilities of establishing a heart first, as that would not immediately result in going set if it failed, whereas, if the ace of clubs and another club were led, school would be out if they did not break 2-2. Nor would it be proper after pulling trumps to surrender a club trick by playing low from both hands, planning then to lay down the ace and see how the suit broke before trying the hearts, since, if clubs did not break, the opponents, after winning the club trick, could return a club and take the extra entry out of the dummy.

We are getting more and more involved in the matter of entries as we go along, and as the subject is going to become increasingly important, it is time we paused a few moments to see how the declarer estimates his chances of having enough entries to establish his suit.

If the fifth heart is going to be established and win a trick, the suit will have to be led five times. The opening lead has taken one of dummy's entries out. Leading the ace and king of hearts and trumping a heart makes a total of three leads of hearts. The ten of spades would provide a fourth entry lead, and then, if the ace of clubs is still there, it would provide the entry for the fifth lead of hearts. However, it is not necessary to take the ace and king of hearts before trumping one, and, while the chances that the king of hearts will be trumped are remote, why take any chance at all?

After winning the ace of diamonds, declarer led a small heart and trumped it with a high spade. He then laid down the ace of trumps and saw that with one more lead all trumps would be exhausted in the opponents' hands. He used up the trump entry by leading a small trump to dummy's ten, and laid down the ace and king of hearts, discarding two clubs. Next he led the fourth heart from the dummy and trumped it. When the opponents followed to that one, the fifth heart was the only heart outstanding, and the ace of clubs provided the entry to dummy so it could be cashed and another club discarded. This left only one club loser. Had the hearts failed to break to suit the declarer, he would have had the club suit to fall back on.

On the next hand, West, with his 17 high-card points, was quite surprised to hear South open with a forcing two spade bid.

If West was only surprised when South opened two spades, he was so mad when they reached seven spades that he doubled. Unfortunately for him, he made the only opening lead which allowed declarer to make his contract.

After the king of clubs opening lead, declarer saw that his only possible loser was the ten of diamonds. The jack was favored to fall after three diamond leads, but that was not guaranteed. With the king of clubs led, declarer saw a way to have two strings to his bow.

For the fifth club to win a trick, not only was it necessary that the opposing clubs broke 4–4, but also that clubs be led five times. West had made one of those leads—was there a way to get to the dummy to lead clubs four more times?

Properly handled, spades should provide three entries, and the ace of hearts was the fourth one, so the answer was yes, provided the declarer kept three small trumps in his hand. He trumped the king of clubs with the ten of spades and led the seven of spades to dummy's eight. The second club was trumped high, and the four of spades to dummy's nine made it possible to trump a third club. The two of trumps to dummy's three provided the entry for trumping the fourth club, and the six of hearts to dummy's ace provided the final entry, so that the ten of diamonds could be discarded on the fifth club.

Sometimes it is better to trump the small card first before cashing the high card in the suit, as in Fig. 5-45.

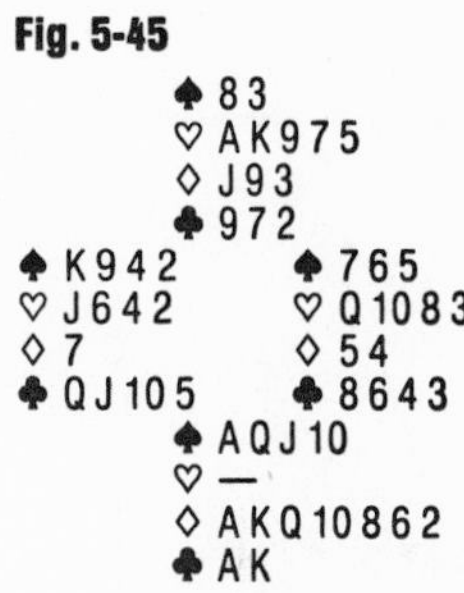

Fig. 5-45

This hand was played by David Carter of St. Louis in a contract of seven diamonds. Carter demonstrated how an old master gives himself every chance.

The opening lead was the queen of clubs. If North had had the king of spades instead of the king of hearts, the hand would have been cold. Of course, a successful spade finesse would bring in the contract, as two of declarer's spades could have been discarded on the ace and king of hearts, and the trump suit seemed to offer adequate entries. However, Carter saw another chance that he should take before trying the spade finesse.

Should the hearts break 4–4, he could discard not two spades on the heart suit, but three spades. For this to work, he would need three entries into the dummy. By careful conservation of his trumps, he saw he could probably manage that. Saving the two of diamonds in his hand for later on, he led the eight and overtook with dummy's nine. When both followed, he knew the three-spot would provide the necessary entry. He led a small heart and trumped it with an honor. The six of diamonds to dummy's jack provided the second entry, and another small heart was trumped high. The carefully preserved two was led to the three, and now Carter laid down the ace and king of hearts, discarding two spades. Had either opponent shown out, he would have had to fall back on the spade finesse, but when the defenders followed to the ace and king of hearts, all hearts were accounted for, and Carter discarded the queen of spades on the nine-spot.

You Hold 5–1; They Hold 7 Once more, we see the magic of that one additional card. The defenders hold seven cards, so that one of them is bound to have at least four, and we can't count on our fourth card to take a trick. But the chances that our fifth card will take a trick have improved drastically—jumping from 32.7 percent when we had only five cards between us and the dummy to 62.2 percent now that we have a total of six cards.

We often have entry problems when we have this holding. Let us first take a simple example and see just how the declarer would calculate his chances before we go on to more complex entry problems.

Fig. 5-46

Playing four hearts, West opened the queen of spades. Declarer played low in case West had started with a five-card suit, leaving only a doubleton in the East hand, in which even the ace would have to be played on the second lead, and the king would be good. No such luck. The defenders cashed three spade tricks, and East returned the king of diamonds.

It wasn't difficult to see that there remained a diamond loser that could only be disposed of on dummy's long clubs. This could be accomplished, provided clubs were divided 4–3 and also provided clubs could be led often enough. For the fifth club to become established and win a trick, clubs would have to be led five times. The club suit would provide two of these leads, as the dummy had the ace which could take a trick and another could be led and trumped. That left three more times for clubs to be led before the fifth one could become a winner, and the dummy had to have three more entries. There were entries in the trump suit, provided declarer was smart enough to keep three small trumps in his hand so that the suit would not block. While the four heart contract was not a cinch, since there could be five clubs in one hand, declarer felt he was a favorite to bring home ten tricks consisting of seven in hearts, one in diamonds, and two in clubs. On the last club he would drop his losing diamond.

From here on, the play is simple. Take the ace of clubs and trump a club high. Lead low to the trump in the dummy, trump a third club high. Lead low to the trump in dummy; lead a fourth club and trump it high. A small trump to the dummy makes it possible to cash the fifth club.

Fig. 5-47

On the next hand in Fig. 5-47, declarer found exactly the right number of entries in the dummy to try to get his suit established and cash tricks with it.

Against a four spade contract, West opened the jack of hearts, and East won the first two heart tricks, switching to the jack of clubs, going along with the lead-up-to-weakness theory. South took a look then at the five-card diamond suit in the dummy which would provide a discard. To get this done, diamonds had to be led five times. With a singleton in his hand and the ace in the dummy, the suit itself would allow two leads of diamonds, and there were three high trumps in the dummy which would give him entries for the balance of the five diamond leads. He decided not to go for the club finesse because, if it lost and somebody changed his mind about leading trump, one of dummy's entries might be removed prematurely and he might not be able to establish the diamond suit and cash the small diamond trick. So, he played the ace of clubs. If diamonds turned sour, he could always lead up the queen of clubs later for an indirect finesse.

From there on, it was easy sailing, and things went according to plan: a diamond to the ace, and a diamond ruff with the nine of spades; a small trump to dummy's eight, and another diamond trumped. Another trump lead to dummy's jack allowed the fourth diamond to be trumped with an honor, and the preserved small trump to dummy's queen was the entry to the now good fifth diamond on which a club was discarded.

Now I think it is time for us to see that declarer got a little help from the opposition. Let's take a look at what East might have done. After he cashed his two heart tricks, the dummy was plainly visible to him, as well as to the declarer. He also could see that long diamond suit with a dearth of entries outside of the trump suit. Had he thought just a little longer, instead of leading the jack of clubs up to weakness, he would have led a trump. The play in clubs could wait. A wise defender, seeing a long suit in the dummy and knowing himself just how many entries are required to establish such a suit, could always consider the possibility of prematurely removing some of those entries from the dummy. In this case, if a trump entry had been removed from the dummy *before* the diamond suit was played, there simply would not have been enough entries to establish the diamond suit and still cash the long diamond. Declarer would have had to fall back on the club suit, and his total would have come to only nine tricks.

The fact that the dummy held both the ace and king of this 5–1 split made it possible to handle the next hand a little differently.

Playing six hearts, declarer got an opening lead of the queen of spades. It looked like the only possible losers in the hand were in the diamond suit. A count of the winners showed eleven—one short of the total needed. If West had either the king or jack of diamonds, the declarer would be able to get his twelfth trick by leading a small diamond and putting in the nine from dummy at the appropriate moment (either losing to the jack and repeating the finesse or losing to the king and having his twelfth trick established immediately). The odds greatly favored West's holding at least one of these key cards.

Fig. 5-48

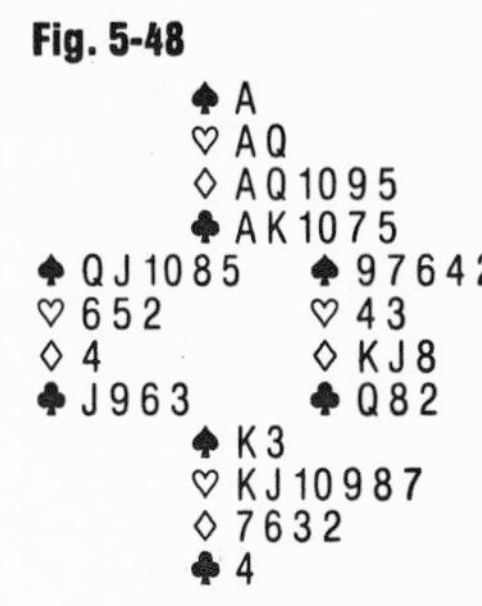

However, there were plenty of entries to get clubs established if that suit would behave, and if declarer could establish a fifth club, he would be able to discard two diamonds from his hand—one on the king and one on the long club. This would reduce his possible losers to one, and, if that failed, he would still have the diamond play to fall back upon. All he had to do was handle his transportation problem.

He won the ace of spades in dummy and led the ace of clubs. Next he led a small club and trumped it. A trump then went to dummy's ace, preserving the queen in the dummy so the suit would not block, and a third club was led and trumped. Declarer noted before he led any clubs that the opponents had seven between them. After they both followed to the ace and one small club, they had three left. After he trumped the next small club, they were down to one between them, and he had the king and the ten-spot. He could now sluff the two diamonds whenever he wanted to, as the last club would fall under the king. First, he pulled their teeth by leading the king of hearts and taking their hearts away. Finally, he led a small diamond and finessed the queen. Had West had the king, declarer would have made seven, but East won that, and declarer still had the ace of diamonds to get to the dummy to discard his last two diamonds on dummy's clubs. A diamond back to his last trump let him cash the king of spades for the twelfth trick.

Declarer is not always blessed with high cards in his five-card suit. On the next hand in Fig. 5-49, North opened two no-trump, but South insisted on playing in spades and reached game in that suit.

West opened a small spade, and declarer saw one loser in clubs, one in hearts, and probably two in diamonds. There was a slight chance that West held the king and queen of diamonds, making only one loser in that suit, but declarer properly figured there was a better chance of establishing a long club in the dummy for a discard of one of his losers, provided his entries and trumps both held out. Clubs were going to have to be led five times, and one of dummy's entries was gone. The club suit itself would provide one lead, and declarer noted with satisfaction that there were still four entries into the dummy. He could not afford to waste one of them by leading the ace of trumps. At trick two, he led a small club, and West won this and led a second trump. Declarer was happy to see that East followed suit. He had to trump three clubs and draw their trumps, and it took exactly six trumps to do that job. He won in the dummy and trumped the club. He returned to the dummy with the king of hearts and trumped another club. When both opponents followed suit, the declarer knew that

Fig. 5-49

clubs were going to become established. To be sure no accident occurred, he led a trump, extracting West's, and then returned to the dummy with the king of hearts to trump the fourth club. The ace of diamonds provided the final entry, and the queen of clubs provided the tenth trick.

Now I have a sad story to tell you. Not all hands end happily, and a reporter whom I trust implicitly tells me that there was not a happy ending on the next one in Fig. 5-50—at least, so far as declarer was concerned.

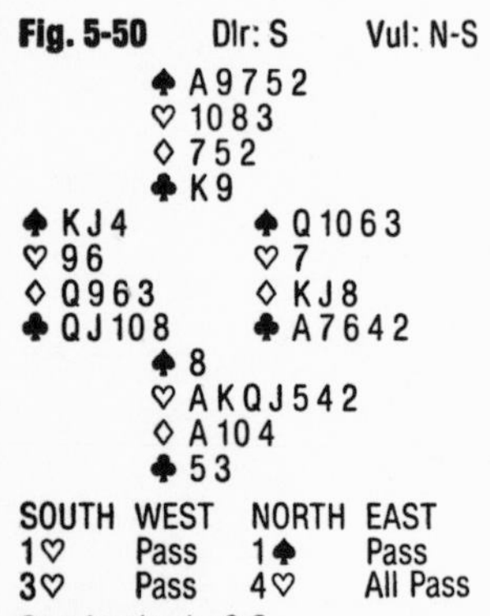

After receiving the opening lead of the queen of clubs, declarer studied things carefully and shrugged his shoulders and played the king, which duly lost to the ace. Another club came back, and West won, shifting to a small diamond. Declarer shrugged his shoulders again, but said, "I give you two diamond tricks. Don't feel too badly about it, partner, we didn't lose a thing, I had 100 honors—I can take nine tricks, and don't even need a finesse."

What North said to his partner I am not sure—if he noticed that the hand could be made, he probably had a lot to say. The worst statement of all was South's that he did not need a finesse—he needed a finesse of the nine of hearts, and it was there. That five-card spade suit in the dummy could be established and provide a place for discards, provided that spades could be led five times. Proper handling of the trump suit would make it possible if only West had the nine, or if East should happen to have the singleton nine. The nine's being with West was more probable, and declarer should have played accordingly.

Proper play was to win the diamond and lead a spade to dummy's ace. A small spade back could be trumped with one of the honors. Now declarer should preserve the two of trumps in his hand as an entry and lead the four. When West played the six, declarer should have played the eight-spot. This would hold the trick, and a third spade could be led and trumped high. Now, the four of trumps to dummy's ten would not only pick up all of the trumps, but would allow a fourth spade to be led and trumped high. Finally, the two of trumps to dummy's three-spot would allow the established spade to be led and a losing diamond to be discarded from South's hand.

Don Krauss played the next hand in a national tournament.

West opened the ace of spades and led a second spade. Krauss saw about three ways to play the hand, but one of these procedures was better than the others. Krauss picked it and succeeded in taking twelve tricks.

One plan was to leave the two trumps at large and try to cash three club tricks and then cash the aces and kings of the red suits and crossruff the hand. This plan, if it worked, would bring in three tricks in clubs, two in diamonds, two in hearts, and four in spades, plus the trick already won, for a total of twelve. Another procedure was to try to establish one of the red suits.

Whichever suit Krauss went after, the success of his contract depended on finding the seven cards held by the opponents in that suit split 4–3. The odds on this are pretty good, but, after all, 30.5 percent of the time they will split 5–2.

Even if the heart suit split favorably, Krauss would run out of entries by the time he got them established and could never bring in a long card in that suit. On the other hand, the extra club entry in the south hand made it plausible to go after diamonds. If they split 4–3, there would be sufficient entries to establish the suit, return to the south hand, pull the opponents' trumps, and cash the winners.

The problem was whether it would be better to try diamonds first or go for the crossruff. If clubs were tried first and they did break 5–2, it could be fatal to the contract, as the defenders already had one trick. On the other hand, if the diamonds broke 5–2, the situation would not be hopeless.

So he won the second trick with the ten of spades and led to the ace of diamonds. He led a small diamond and trumped it with dummy's queen of spades. A small club to the jack put him back in his hand, and another small diamond was trumped with the king. That round showed that the diamond suit would break favorably. Krauss had the king and a little one left, and there was only one diamond outstanding. Now if he could get back to his hand, he would be in good shape. The club back to his queen did put him in his hand. At long last, he extracted the remaining trumps which West held and now had a trick to burn.

Those players who did not look as deep as Krauss did and tried to cash three quick clubs before starting a crossruff obviously did not do so well.

You Hold 5–2; They Hold 6 Again we have added just one card, and let us see what magical results that has brought about. As long as we were dealing with a 5–1 situation, it was impossible for us to establish a small fourth card if the opponents held onto all their cards in the suit. Suddenly, with the addition of one card, the fourth card in the suit can become established almost 36 percent of the time. Establishment of the fifth card has gone from 62 percent to 84 percent.

In addition, that extra card has made the hand much more manageable, as it sometimes provides the extra entry to get our suit established.

In a three no-trump contract, South got the opening lead of the queen of diamonds. He was looking at eight tricks in top cards. He needed to establish one of his suits for the ninth trick.

In both black suits, he had 4–3 fits. Clubs looked more promising than spades, but in either suit the odds did not favor the establishment of the fourth trick.

While he had only seven hearts in the combined hand, they were divided so that there was a fifth card available to be established. As a matter of fact, if the six cards the opponents held were three in each hand, declarer could bring in the entire heart suit, which would give him ten tricks altogether. The odds favored a 4–2 break, and by taking out a tiny bit of insurance, declarer could more than double his chances of taking nine tricks. That insurance consisted of simply leading the first heart and playing low from north. Upon regaining the lead, he could get to dummy with his remaining heart, and now he had four tricks in that suit, bringing his total to an easy nine.

Fig. 5-52

West	North	East
	♠ 10 7 6 2 ♡ A K Q 3 2 ◇ 7 ♣ 8 6 4	
♠ Q 8 ♡ J 10 9 6 ◇ Q J 10 9 2 ♣ Q 5		♠ K 9 5 3 ♡ 8 7 ◇ 8 6 5 ♣ J 10 9 3
	♠ A J 4 ♡ 5 4 ◇ A K 4 3 ♣ A K 7 2	

He was able to take out this insurance because he had all other suits under control. The defenders could not, upon obtaining the lead, run away with any of the other three suits. The lack of entries in the north hand was the determining factor in deciding to concede a heart trick early. Had declarer had an extra entry in the north hand, this would not have been necessary.

Fig. 5-53

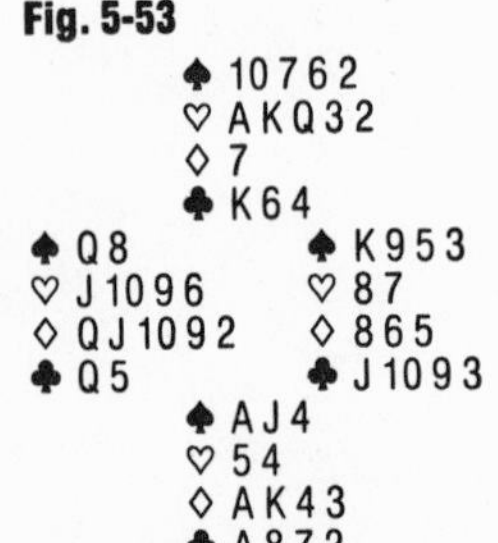

In the deal in Fig. 5-53, the twenty-six cards in the north and south hands have not been changed, but their location has. The king of clubs which was in the south hand has been swapped for the eight of clubs and is in the north hand. Now the declarer does not have to take the extra precaution he took in the preceding hand. After winning the first trick with a diamond, he can simply cash the A K Q of hearts, and, had they broken 3–3, he would have taken his extra trick. When they failed to do so, he simply conceded the fourth heart trick because he still had all suits under control and an extra entry into the dummy to get back to cash the fifth heart.

In Fig. 5-54 is another example of that extra small card which enables you to fulfill contracts.

Fig. 5-54

At a six heart contract, declarer can see a loser in clubs and another in diamonds. By establishing the long spade in the north hand, one of these losers can be discarded. The problem is finding enough entries in the north hand to lead spades five times.

Declarer got the opening lead of the queen of diamonds. Let's go through his mental processes and see how he can arrive at a plan to lead spades five times—four times to get rid of all of theirs (assuming they would break 4–2 as expected) and the fifth time to cash the winning spade. Laying down the ace and king of spades and then trumping one would involve leading spades only three times, and getting to the dummy with the ace of clubs would allow only four times. This would not be enough, unless spades were kind enough to break 3–3. But look at the miracle that declarer can perform by simply leading a spade at the proper moment and conceding a spade to the opposition! Now, when he takes the ace and king of spades, they will be the second and third leads. The small one he trumps will be the fourth one, and he will still have the ace of clubs in the dummy to get there to cash the fifth one.

Entry problems frequently arise in establishing and cashing suits. A good declarer learns how to determine how many entries he has before embarking on his plans for bringing home his contract. It is worth emphasizing that when everything is under control and when the long suit is headed by the ace and king opposite two small, four leads in that suit can be accomplished without touching any other suit, provided the first trick is conceded. Of course, declarer had best be sure that his plans cannot be interrupted by the opponents' trumping, and, in this case, he was lucky that the opening lead was a diamond and not a club because a club would have destroyed his dummy entry prematurely. But, with the diamond lead, he immediately pulled trumps. He had to lead them four times to accomplish this, and that meant that North had to discard twice. Of course, he could not discard one of the small spades, so instead he discarded one diamond and one club. Then he led a spade, playing low from the dummy, and East won the trick. East returned a diamond, but it was too late—declarer then led his remaining spade to the dummy's ace, cashed the king, discarding a diamond, and trumped the four-spot. This exhausted not only his trumps but the opponents' spades. Now he went back to the dummy with the ace of clubs and discarded his losing club on the established spade.

Let's see what declarer can do when the suit to be established is not headed by the ace-king.

Fig. 5-55

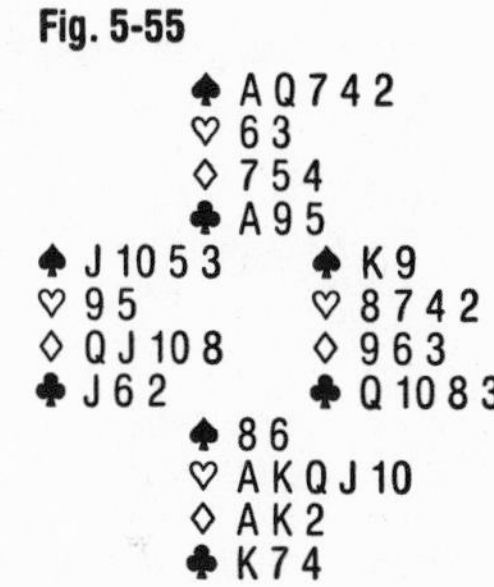

Our first comment on seeing South in six hearts is "He shouldn't be there." However, it is not all that bad. After a diamond lead, he could proceed by pulling trumps, finessing a spade, cashing the ace, trumping one, and hoping the suit breaks 3–3. Should that work, he would have thirteen tricks, but West would have to have exactly three hearts including the king.

The chances for that were not so good, so declarer looked for the best line to bring in twelve tricks. He needed only three heart tricks.

He won the diamond trick and led a heart, playing small from the dummy. East saw what he was up to, and led a club in case there was a chance to remove an entry from the dummy. But declarer won in his hand with the king, and led a heart to dummy's ace. When East played his king, South had his three heart tricks. He trumped a heart with his last trump and went to the dummy with the ace of clubs, and there were two good heart tricks there to take care of his two minor suit losers.

By giving up the finesse altogether declarer was going to win three heart tricks whenever the suit divided 3–3, no matter which opponent had the king, and also when either had a doubleton king. A little arithmetic tells this comes to almost 52 percent. Not so bad, after all.

At times, the matter of entries is pretty delicate (Fig. 5-56).

Fig. 5-56

In a six no-trump contract, South received the opening lead of the ten of diamonds. He saw four tricks in spades, provided he took them in the right order, plus three in hearts, three in diamonds, and one in clubs, for a total of eleven. The twelfth trick could come from establishing the fifth heart or from a successful club finesse. The odds on establishing the fifth heart are much better than the odds of the finesse, and that is the route the declarer should take. However, he must take it with care. If he first takes the queen and jack of spades, goes to the dummy with the queen of hearts to cash the ace-king of spades, and then plans to concede a heart trick, the opponents might well be able to cash a spade trick while they have the lead. However, by careful timing, the declarer could avoid that possibility. After winning the opening diamond lead, declarer should cash his queen and jack of spades and then lead a small heart, playing low from the dummy. Now, no matter what is returned, declarer can win the trick, go to the dummy with the queen of hearts, take the ace and king of spades while discarding both losing clubs, return to his hand with a diamond, and find all winners there. The small heart will take the twelfth trick.

When you have trumps, you may be able to establish a trick without losing any tricks in the suit. See how the declarer handles that on this next hand in Fig. 5-57.

Looking at the dummy, declarer saw no losers in any suit except diamonds. A diamond from his hand could be discarded on an established

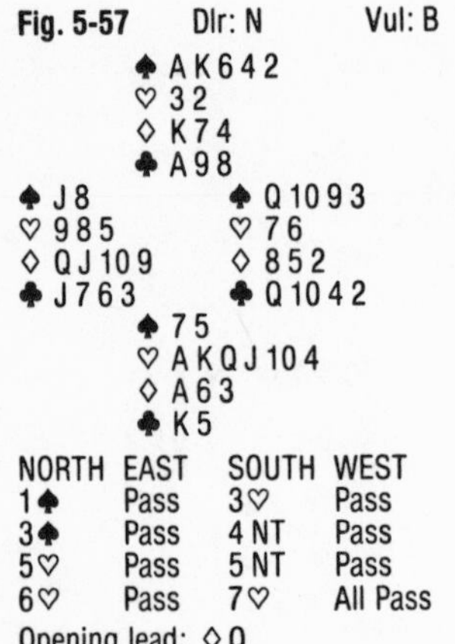
Fig. 5-57 Dlr: N Vul: B
♠ A K 6 4 2
♡ 3 2
◇ K 7 4
♣ A 9 8
♠ J 8 ♠ Q 10 9 3
♡ 9 8 5 ♡ 7 6
◇ Q J 10 9 ◇ 8 5 2
♣ J 7 6 3 ♣ Q 10 4 2
♠ 7 5
♡ A K Q J 10 4
◇ A 6 3
♣ K 5

NORTH	EAST	SOUTH	WEST
1♠	Pass	3♡	Pass
3♠	Pass	4 NT	Pass
5♡	Pass	5 NT	Pass
6♡	Pass	7♡	All Pass

Opening lead: ◇Q

spade in North's hand, provided he could get that suit established and have plenty of entries. He could not afford in a grand slam the luxury of giving up a spade trick so that he would be able to lead the spades four times without using up additional entries. However, he could take the ace and king, lead a third one, and still have two entries in the dummy, provided he took the opening lead in his own hand instead of in the dummy. There was the matter of exhausting the opponents' trumps before he ventured upon his establishment of spades. That did not prove too difficult, since the opponents showed out after three rounds. Of course, he could not discard a spade on the third trump, but he could sluff one of the diamonds. Now it was a simple matter to take the ace-king of spades and trump a third one. A club to the dummy made it possible to lead the fourth spade and trump it, and this took away all the opponents' spades. A diamond back to the dummy enabled him to cash the fifth spade and discard his losing diamond on it, leaving him with nothing but winners.

On the next hand, declarer had to use the trumps themselves as entries.

Fig. 5-58 Dlr: S Vul: N-S
♠ A 4
♡ A 5 3
◇ 8 7 5
♣ A K Q 6 3
♠ 10 9 5 2 ♠ K Q J 6 3
♡ 9 2 ♡ 8 7 4
◇ A 9 3 ◇ Q J 10
♣ J 10 9 7 ♣ 8 4
♠ 8 7
♡ K Q J 10 6
◇ K 6 4 2
♣ 5 2

SOUTH	WEST	NORTH	EAST
Pass	Pass	1♣	1♠
2♡	Pass	4♡	All Pass

Opening lead: ♠10

After the opening lead of the ten of spades, declarer could see one spade loser and, if he pulled trumps, as many as three or four diamond losers if the diamond suit lay badly for him. This came to five possible losers. Of course, if the club suit broke properly, he could get rid of one loser on the queen of clubs and another loser on the fifth club; or, if they should break 3-3, he could get rid of three losers. However, he decided not to count on the 3-3 split. One trouble was that he could not afford to pull trumps because the opening lead had taken out one of dummy's entries, and the only one left outside of clubs was the ace of trumps. So, declarer rose with the ace of spades, led a small heart, and took two rounds of trumps in his own hand. Then he cashed the ace and king of clubs, but not the queen. Instead, he led a small club, and, when East could only discard on it, he trumped it. Back to the dummy he went with the ace of trumps, and on the last two clubs—queen and six—he discarded the losing spade and a small diamond. He then led a diamond in case East had started with the ace, but when he quickly lost three diamond tricks, he realized how important the knowledge of suit establishment was to him.

When the trumps themselves are going to provide the entries for establishing a suit and cashing it after it is established, drawing the trumps must often be deferred.

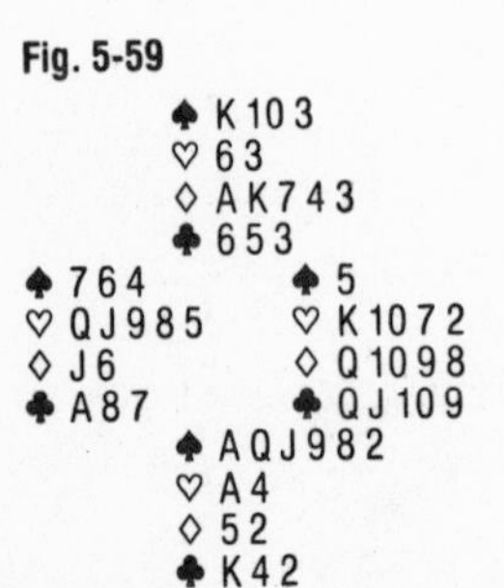
Fig. 5-59
♠ K 10 3
♡ 6 3
◇ A K 7 4 3
♣ 6 5 3
♠ 7 6 4 ♠ 5
♡ Q J 9 8 5 ♡ K 10 7 2
◇ J 6 ◇ Q 10 9 8
♣ A 8 7 ♣ Q J 10 9
♠ A Q J 9 8 2
♡ A 4
◇ 5 2
♣ K 4 2

Against a contract of four spades, South got the opening lead of the queen of hearts. He saw four possible losers—one in hearts and three in clubs—and had to see what to do about it. Leading up toward the king of clubs might get rid of one loser if East had the ace, but the diamond suit seemed to offer better possibilities. Diamonds probably would break 4-2, and it would be necessary to lead diamonds five times to get a discard. Declarer could not afford to lose a diamond while establishing them, so it was not possible to use diamonds themselves for four leads by first leading a small one and conceding a trick. That would leave too many loose tricks lying around for the opponents to pick up. This meant that diamonds themselves would only allow three leads—the ace, the king, and one to be trumped. However, if the king and ten-spot of spades were retained in the dummy, they would provide the two entries necessary to trump the fourth diamond and then return to the dummy to cash the established diamond.

Declarer won the first trick with the ace of hearts and laid down the ace of trumps to be sure all trumps were not in one hand. After both followed, he knew that when he led trumps two more times there would be none left, and the established diamond in the dummy, if plans worked out, would be there to take its trick unmolested. He could not afford a second trump lead at this point because of the needed entry to dummy. Instead, he cashed the ace-king of diamonds and then trumped a diamond with the eight-spot. West discarded, and declarer knew that he had played the hand correctly and that success was assured. A small trump returned him to dummy, and then he trumped the fourth diamond, establishing the fifth diamond. A trump lead to dummy's king extracted the last trump held by the defenders and provided the entry to the fifth diamond. A small club was discarded on this. Declarer then led a club because, if the ace had been with East, he would have had an extra trick, but that was not the case.

On the next hand (Fig. 5-60), declarer had to decide whether to take the simple finesse or try to establish a suit.

Fig. 5-60

South had a minimum hand in high cards, but after he opened the bidding, his partner would sit for nothing less than a small slam in spades. West led the queen of hearts.

No matter what happened, there was going to be a trump loser, and there was also a diamond loser. There was nothing to do with the trump loser, but the diamond loser could be disposed of either by finessing the club or establishing the club suit. As always, when considering the establishment of a suit, the question must be asked, "Are there sufficient entries?" Declarer decided that by leading clubs twice and then trumping one, there were sure to be two entries in North, with the king and queen of trumps plus a diamond. In addition, there was always a chance that the long club might not have to be established, as the queen might fall out sometime during the first three leads of the suit. South rightly decided that the club establishment play had better chances than the finesse. He won the ace of hearts and cashed the ace-king of clubs. When both followed suit, it looked like his troubles were probably over. He led another club and trumped it with the eight-spot so that, if it were overtrumped, only the ace could do the job. West couldn't see using his ace for that purpose and discarded a heart. South then led a low trump toward the dummy, and West had no better play than to rise with the ace and exit with a diamond. The declarer won it in the dummy, trumped another club high, and a trump lead back to the dummy pulled the opponents' last trumps and allowed declarer to discard a diamond on the established jack of clubs.

Fig. 5-61

Look at another example in Fig. 5-61.

After North opened the bidding with one spade, South lost little time in verifying that North had two aces and a king and bid seven hearts. West missed the killing opening lead of a trump and led the queen of diamonds. A quick check of the dummy showed declarer that he had a diamond loser. But he also saw our old friend, the 5–2 fit with a five-card holding having the ace and king. If the spades in the opponents' hands split normally, there would be a 4–2 distribution, and they would have to be led five times for the little spade to take a trick. Obviously, in a grand slam you cannot concede a trick, so declarer had to count his entries by starting off with the ace and king of spades and then trumping one. That made three leads. Now the ten of hearts in the dummy and the ace of diamonds made it possible to lead the fourth and fifth spades. There were two little items of timing to watch: the opening diamond lead had to be won by South, and the trumps could not be pulled, but the risk of a spade ruff on the second lead was slight. South could breathe easily after the ace-king of spades were played. He trumped a low spade, led a small heart to the ten of hearts, so that when another spade was trumped, declarer would be in his hand to pull the balance of the opponents' trumps and then lead a diamond back to the dummy to cash the good spade, discarding a losing diamond on it.

Fig. 5-62

Now let's look at some other hands where the five-card suit is not conveniently headed by the two high cards.

The contract was six spades, and the opening lead was the queen of hearts. Declarer saw a loser in hearts and a loser in diamonds. One or the other had to be disposed of. He would have been happy to add a little club to the north hand or to have one heart less there so that he could trump a heart, but he had to make do with what the dealer had given him. Obviously, he had to establish the diamonds to discard a heart.

Now let's see how many times you can lead the diamonds with a 5–2 holding where the five-card suit is headed by the ace only. If you take the ace of diamonds and then give them one, that will be only two, and you'll need three more entries to dummy. However, if you concede a diamond, then take the ace and trump one, you will have three diamond leads out of the suit and need only two more entries, and those are there in the trump suit.

At first glance, it looks like you might be able to afford one trump lead as extra insurance, but don't believe it. Once you concede the diamond, one of your opponents might be smart enough to lead a second trump, and there will go one of dummy's precious entries. Never give an opponent an opportunity to be a genius if you don't have to do it.

So, declarer won the first trick with the king of hearts and graciously gave the opponents trick number two by leading a small diamond and playing a small one from dummy. A surprised East won that and found that it made no difference what he returned. Actually, he returned a second heart, which declarer won. Then declarer crossed his fingers and led a small diamond to the ace. When that won, his troubles were over unless all four trump were in one hand. Back came the third diamond which was trumped high. A small trump to dummy's queen eliminated the trump distribution worries and provided access to another diamond to again be trumped high. Now declarer cashed one trump in his hand and led to dummy's last trump to cash the good diamond and discard his losing heart.

Sometimes a losing trick has to be conceded "right now," as in Fig. 5-63.

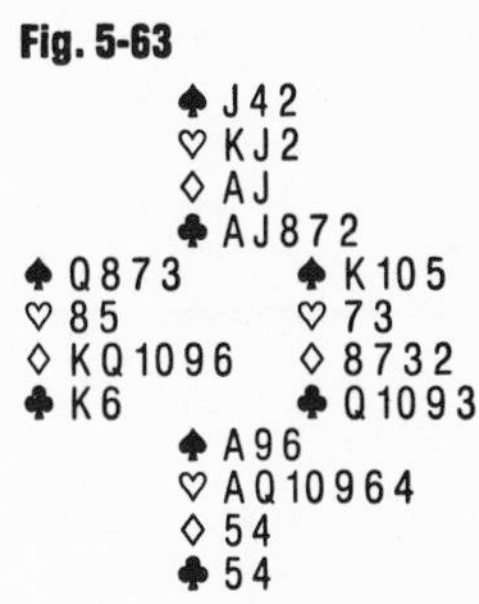

After North opened the bidding with one club, South reached four hearts. The opening lead was the king of diamonds.

Down came the dummy, and a survey of losers indicated two in spades and one each in diamonds and clubs. Unless something strange and unexpected happened in spades, this meant that clubs had to be established for the discard of a spade.

We have all been trained so long to lead from the weak toward the strong hand that the thought went through South's mind to come to his hand and lead a club toward the dummy. After all, the king and queen might both be with West. But a little reflection told him this could be a grievous error. The king of diamonds lead had taken away one of dummy's precious entries. There were only two entries left in trumps, and clubs had to be established with these two entries. Of course, it is always possible that six outstanding cards will be divided 3–3, but as long as you can prepare for the more probable 4–2 division, you should do so. That meant that the declarer wanted to lead clubs five times. As he could not accomplish this by leading the ace of clubs and then a small one, he had to try to concede a club and then lead the ace and trump a small one. This would be three club leads, and the two trump entries would make it possible to lead the fourth one and then return to cash the fifth one, provided the opponents were by this time out of trump.

A small trump could be led to the south hand to allow clubs to be led toward dummy, but if the opponent who won the conceded club trick chose to continue with trumps, declarer would be one entry short. Neither could declarer come to his hand with the ace of spades and then concede a club—that simply would be leaving too many tricks for the defenders to pick up. They could take two more spades and a diamond upon winning the conceded club.

No—clubs had to be led immediately. At trick two, declarer led the two of clubs, and West won a club trick with a much smaller card than he expected to win with. He cashed his queen of diamonds and switched to spades. South won with the ace and cashed the ace of clubs. The third club he trumped with the nine of hearts. He led a small trump to dummy's king, trumped another club high (the fourth club), then led the ace and a small trump to dummy. The opponents' trumps were exhausted, and the fifth club took care of one of his losing spades.

Let's look at Fig. 5-64, where the high cards are in the short hand and not the long hand.

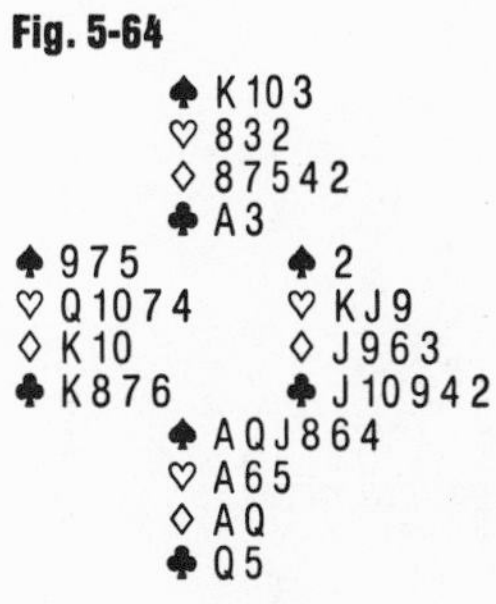

With no adverse bidding, South arrived at four spades and received the four of hearts as an opening lead. This seemed to leave him with two heart losers, a club loser, unless some sort of end play could be maneuvered, and a diamond loser, if the diamond finesse failed. The finesse looked attractive, but a 5–2 suit looked prettier. Was there any way to combine the two? A careful examination convinced declarer that there was not. The dummy had exactly three entries—one in clubs and two in trumps. If one of these were used for a finesse entry and if that finesse failed, the defenders might knock out an entry, and the diamond suit would be dead. Declarer decided that his best chance was to go after his diamonds right away without using up any of dummy's entries.

As a result of this wise decision, he laid down the ace and queen of diamonds. This totaled two leads, with the three entries still intact. West won the king and led a heart. The opponents cashed two heart tricks, ending with East. East led the jack of clubs which declarer covered with the queen. West's king forced dummy's ace. Those two trump entries were still in the dummy. Declarer led a third diamond, trumped it high, and could now afford to lay down the ace of spades. When both sides followed suit, his problems were over. A small trump to North let him lead the fourth diamond and trump it high. Another spade to dummy pulled West's last trump and provided the fifth diamond for discarding the small losing club.

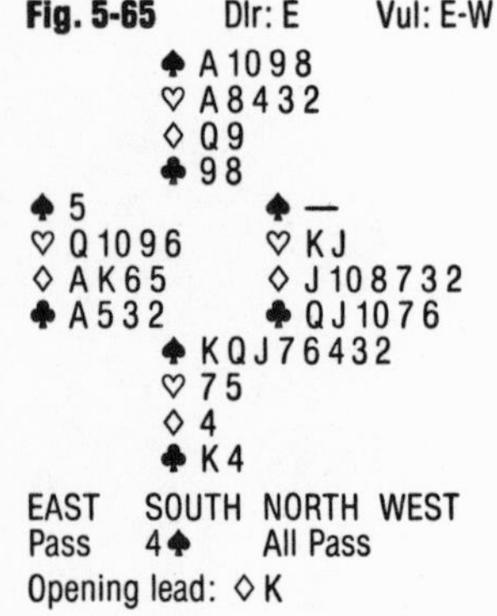

In Fig. 5-65, South solved the problem with help from the opposition. South's non-vulnerable opening bid of four spades talked the opponents out of a slam they could have made and the game they certainly would have bid, had he given them time to get together. Now his problem was to take ten tricks, after West led the king of diamonds.

South was looking at one loser in each of the red suits, and there might be two losers in clubs unless East held the ace. How about establishing the hearts? That was very fine, as there were plenty of entries to get the job done, but it involved conceding a trick which might well be won by East. Surely East would lead a club then if he didn't have the ace. South simply followed suit to the first trick and awaited developments. West decided to try to cash a second diamond before looking for new worlds to conquer and led the ace. South didn't trump this one high. He didn't even trump it. He discarded a heart. Now, if the hearts were establishable, he would establish them while not conceding a trick in the suit. If they could not be established, he still had his plan of leading toward the king of clubs.

West thought over this development and switched to a trump. Declarer still had plenty of time. He won that trick in the dummy, led the ace of hearts, and then a small heart which he trumped. That made two heart leads, and there were still three entries in the dummy to allow for the other three heart leads. On the fifth and last one, the declarer discarded a club.

The next hand (Fig. 5-66) is taken from an intercollegiate tournament back in the 1950's.

Fig. 5-66

♠ Q 9 8 4 3
♡ A 7
◇ K 3
♣ K 4 3 2

West	East
♠ A 10 2	♠ K J 7 5
♡ K Q J 8 3	♡ 10 9 4 2
◇ Q 10 6 5	◇ 9 2
♣ 8	♣ 9 7 5

♠ 6
♡ 6 5
◇ A J 8 7 4
♣ A Q J 10 6

The experts who prepared these hands for intercollegiate play wanted South to get into a contract of five clubs and make it. Reports show that quite a few got into a contract of three no-trump and somehow or other made it. Just how the bidding was supposed to go, I don't know, for it looks like East and West could do well in hearts provided they guess everything right and the defenders don't find the spade ruff. Maybe East and West pushed to four hearts and that's the reason North-South were supposed to be in five clubs.

Anyway, what we are concerned with is the play at five clubs after a lead of the king of hearts. At first glance, it looks like one heart loser and one spade loser, but what are we going to do with all of those diamonds? Trying to establish spades obviously gets us nowhere, so the problem is to establish diamonds. Against a 4–2 break, diamonds cannot be established after three trumps are led, as there would be only one trump in the dummy for the purpose of trumping diamonds. So the play is to go about establishing diamonds before pulling trumps.

After winning the first trick with the ace of hearts declarer plays the king of diamonds and a small one to his ace. He then leads a small diamond. Trumping this doesn't seem to work out. To avoid being overtrumped, he will have to trump with the king, and then he can come back to trump the fourth one and find it inevitably overtrumped. So, on the third diamond, declarer simply discards the losing heart. By this loser-on-loser play, he takes care of most eventualities.

West wins this third diamond and now, if he wants to, can cash a spade or lead a heart to shorten dummy, but nothing he does will get him anywhere. South will return to his hand, lead a fourth diamond, and trump with the king which cannot be overtrumped. He will still be able to return to his hand, pulling trumps, and his fifth diamond will be a winner.

While we are digging up these old hands, let's take a look at one of them which was part of the 1942 bridge examination put out by the Eli Culbertson Studios. It will show you the sort of bridge problems the older generation was supposed to be able to solve.

We can only assume that East and West had taken some sort of sedative when South jumped to five clubs. I suppose the Culbertson Studios overlooked the fact that a small slam is on for the defenders in one of the major suits. However, the problem was to play five clubs in the South hand against an opening lead of the queen of spades.

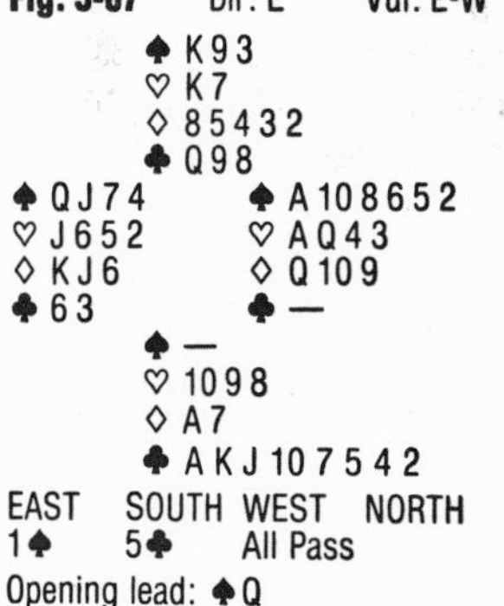

One thing declarer did not want was for West to have a chance to lead again because he might lead through the king of hearts. So he covered the queen of spades with the king, not in the hopes of winning a trick, but to transfer the lead to East. He wanted to see if he could establish that five-card diamond suit for a discard, and, if he could not, to reserve the possibility that West had the ace of hearts by being able, at the proper moment, to lead a heart toward the dummy. And all of this had to be done without letting West get the lead. So, instead of trumping the opening spade lead, declarer discarded the seven of diamonds on it. Now, with plenty of entries in the dummy, he was going to get that diamond suit established if it broke 3–3, particularly if East did not have a trump to lead to remove one of dummy's entries.

Well, everything worked out, and while the whole scenario is improbable, it does illustrate a point. East, after winning the ace of spades led a diamond, and South won. A small club to North pulled one round of trump and made it possible to lead one diamond to ruff. Declarer led another club and a third diamond, and, when both followed to the third diamond lead, there were two good diamonds in the dummy and an entry to reach them. Two hearts from the South hand were discarded on the two good diamonds.

We needed to use this hand because, on all of the hands I have been showing you, the six cards held by the defenders have been splitting 4–2. Of course, in real life it doesn't always work out that way. A little better than 1 time in 3, they will split 3–3, and about 1 time in 6 they will be 5–1 or 6–0. In actual play, you prepare for a 4–2 split whenever you can manage to do so.

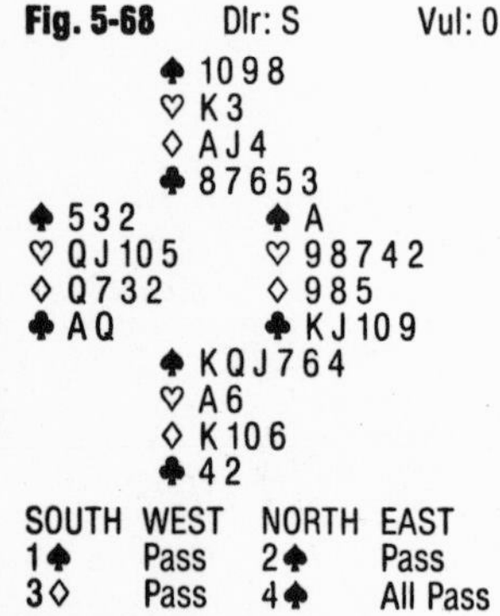

On the next hand (Fig. 5-68), declarer did not have any high cards in his long side suit. Nonetheless, he was able to establish a trick in it.

A look at the dummy showed declarer that his sole problem was avoiding a diamond loser. He had three losers in the black suits about which there seemed to be nothing he could do. Declarer was not sure whether this day was a good guessing day or not, and he decided he'd better try to establish the weak club suit, holding the diamond guess in reserve in case the clubs did not work out. He figured he had enough entries to establish the suit if it broke 3–3, and that he might be able to establish it if it broke 4–2, provided the opponents didn't or couldn't take entries out of the dummy fast enough.

South won the opening lead in his hand and led a club. West didn't have to have second sight to see what was going on, and he decided a good return at this time was a trump. East won this with the ace, but had no trump to return. He did the best he could and returned a heart. Dummy won that and led a second club. When both followed suit, declarer was on his way to victory. Neither opponent could afford to lead a diamond, the clubs were going to be at least as good as 4–2, and the opponents couldn't remove dummy's entries fast enough. West won the second club and led another spade. Declarer won, trumped a third club with an honor, and then went to the dummy with a third spade to lead the fourth club. Now he had the fifth club established and still had the ace of diamonds in the dummy to get there to cash it and discard a diamond from his hand.

You Hold 5–3; They Hold 5 The last time we cut our opponents down to a five-card holding, we increased our own 4–3 to 4–4. We saw a startling change in the probabilities that our fourth card would take a trick. That probability increased from slightly better than 1 time in 3 to slightly better than 2 times in 3. Now that we have divided our own cards 5–3 instead of 4–4, we find that we have a fifth card to work with and that our chances that neither opponent will hold more than four cards so that our fifth can take a trick (provided we can withstand the onslaught of the opponents while we are getting it established) are a startling 96 percent. That is not quite as good as an ace, but almost.

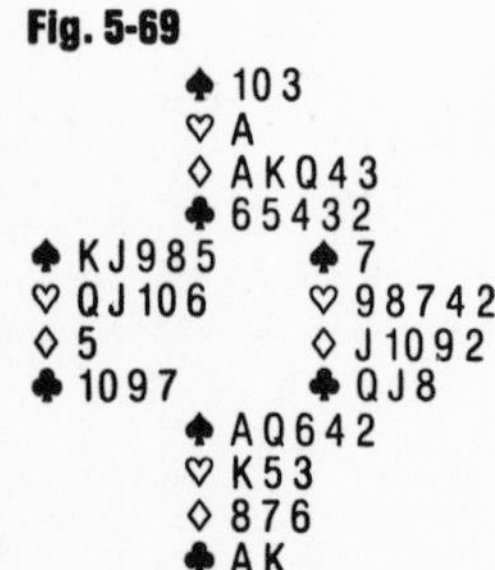

The minute declarer got a look at the dummy in the hand in Fig. 5-69, he felt very optimistic about his contract of three no-trump.

After the opening lead of the queen of hearts, declarer counted that he had eight tricks off the top. He had all sorts of chances for his ninth trick. These included a spade finesse, the establishment of a club trick, and a throw-in play. But the best chance of all was the establishment of one of those small diamonds in the dummy.

However, the opening lead had removed the only side entry the dummy had. To get diamonds properly established, declarer had to keep in touch with the dummy. His best play was to lead the ace of diamonds. When both opponents followed suit, the hand became a 100 percent hand. However, he could not afford to cash another high diamond because, if this was one of those cases where the diamonds broke 4–1, he would be unable to surrender a diamond and still get back to the dummy to cash one. He knew that if he led a small diamond and let them have a diamond, he would still have one left to get back to the dummy and would be assured of four diamond tricks. These plus two hearts, two clubs, and one sure spade came to nine. If after winning his diamond tricks, the declarer felt he could work out the holding in the opposing hands and try either the spade finesse or the throw-in play, that was up to him.

You don't always have a suit headed by the A K Q to work with.

Fig. 5-70

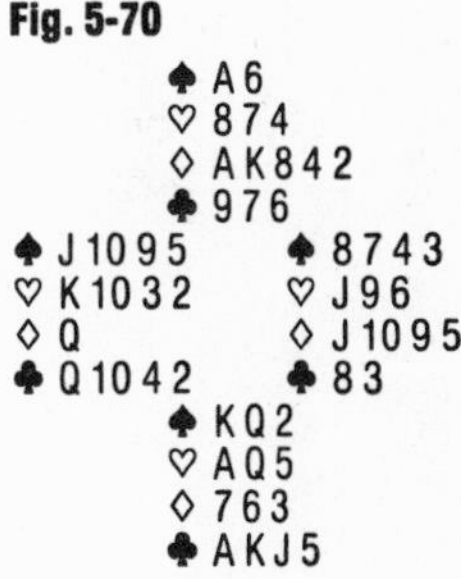

In South's three no-trump contract, he got an opening lead of the jack of spades. Again, he had eight sure tricks and all sorts of plays for his ninth one. His best play was the establishment of his fifth diamond, a 96-percent play, which was surely better than any other he had. However, he had to keep in touch with the dummy to do this, and the enemy was attacking dummy's only entry.

He won the opening spade lead in his hand and led a small diamond. When West played the queen, it became obvious that declarer was not going to be up against an embarrassing heart lead from East, and so he simply let West have that trick. West continued with a small spade, and declarer was in the dummy with the ace. He now had a better than 68-percent play by laying down the ace of diamonds, as he would now take four diamonds if the suit broke 3–2. If it didn't, he could go for some finesse. However, why monkey with that sort of a play when he had a 100-percent play. Of the five diamonds the opponents had started with, they had only three left. All he had to do was take out a bit of insurance and concede them one more diamond and he would still have a small diamond in his hand to get to the dummy, guaranteeing three tricks in that suit. These, added to three spades, two clubs, and one heart, guaranteed him a total of nine.

In Fig. 5-71, declarer was in three no-trump, but in his long suit he held only the ace, and that was in his three-card holding.

Fig. 5-71

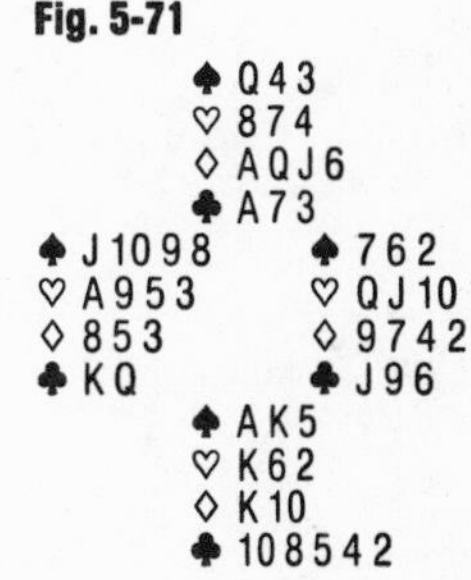

Declarer could see eight of the nine tricks he needed when he got a look at the dummy. If West would lead hearts, or if declarer had to lead hearts and East had the ace, that would be his ninth trick. However, there was an additional possibility of establishing a long club. Declarer won the opening lead of the jack of spades with the king and led a club to see how things would work out. He was delighted when West played the queen because it made it look possible to work on clubs without surrendering the lead to East. Declarer rightly felt that a heart lead from East might make him nervous. West persisted with a spade which South won with his ace. Declarer then tested another club lead. When West played the king, it was all over. Declarer simply let him hold that trick also, and when East followed suit, the remaining jack of clubs was bound to fall under dummy's ace. There was no way that West could harm the declarer, as

South had all suits properly covered and could cash the ace of clubs and return to his hand to win tricks with two small clubs for a total of ten.

Fig. 5-72

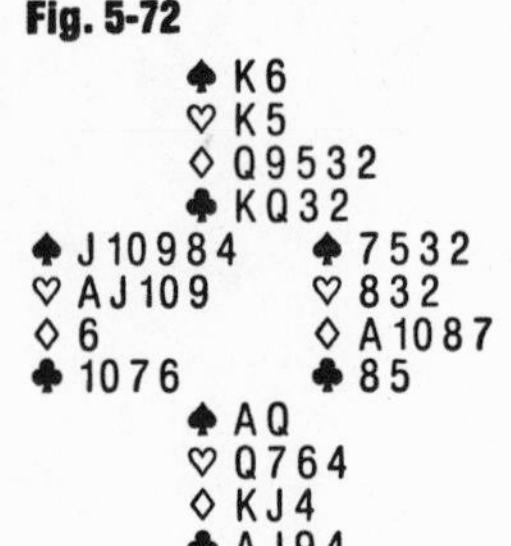

On the next hand, declarer had to overcome the disability of not having the two of spades in either hand.

South was in a three no-trump contract, and, after an opening lead of the jack of spades, he could see only six sure tricks; he needed three more. With declarer and dummy each holding exactly two spades, the A K Q could take only two tricks. His 5–3 diamond holding seemed to give him the best opportunity.

There was, however, one thing which was extremely important to declarer: he had to be sure to lead the first diamond from the correct hand.

If the outstanding five diamonds broke 3–2, it didn't make any difference. But if they did not and if either defender held four or five diamonds including the ace and ten, the first diamond had to be led from the north hand. If it were West with the long diamond holding, whenever he won the ace (provided diamonds were led only from the north hand), declarer would have a natural finesse against the ten-spot to bring in three diamonds. If, as really happened, East held four of them, repeated leads from North would put East on the spot.

So, declarer won the opening lead with the king of spades and promptly led a small diamond. East could not go up with the ace without conceding the whole suit to declarer, so he played small. Declarer then returned to the dummy with a club and led another diamond. Now East was faced with a choice of plays, both of them suicidal. If he took his ace, declarer would still have his diamond tricks. If he did not, West would show out, and declarer would have two diamond tricks and would immediately lead a small heart to establish his ninth trick in that suit.

Fig. 5-73 Dlr: S Vul: B

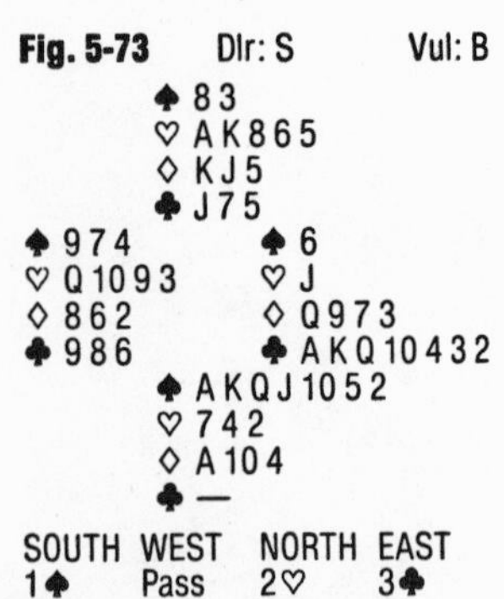

SOUTH	WEST	NORTH	EAST
1♠	Pass	2♡	3♣
4♣	Pass	4♡	Pass
6♠	Pass	Pass	Pass

Opening lead: ♣9

When you are playing trumps, you have an added dimension, as ruffing can frequently help establish the long suit (Fig. 5-73).

In his six spade contract, South saw eleven tricks. Best chances for the twelfth were a diamond finesse or the establishment of a small heart. The establishment of the fifth heart was by all odds the better shot. It was something better than 96 percent. To establish the fifth one, hearts would have to be led five times. By proper handling of the heart suit, that suit itself would allow hearts to be led four times, and the king of diamonds would be the entry for the fifth heart, if necessary.

Declarer trumped the club and extracted trumps. Now he led a small heart and ducked it in the dummy. He was going to have to concede a heart in any event, and, by doing so immediately, he was able to use the heart suit for four heart leads. East returned a club which declarer ruffed. He then cashed the ace and king of hearts and trumped a small heart. That left a good heart in the dummy and the king of diamonds for an entry so that the small diamond in the declarer's hand could be disposed of on the good heart.

In the next hand, East opened one heart, and South wound up playing four spades.

East won the opening heart lead with the jack and, after considering the matter carefully, decided to lead a trump to keep the declarer from trumping hearts in the dummy. Declarer was not too much concerned with this, as he could handle the hand without trumping a heart, provided the black suits broke in some reasonable manner. He won the spade lead with the ace in dummy and fell back on his club suit where the odds were better than 2 to 1 that he could bring in the fourth club. However, to do so, he had to concede a club, and to do that while keeping in contact with the dummy and before anybody got any idea about the clubs, he immediately led a small club. Now the defenders could continue with trump if they wanted to. In that event, he would simply pull trumps and discard a losing heart on dummy's long club if clubs broke. If they decided to continue hearts, dummy would trump the third heart, and then declarer could come to his hand with a diamond and claim the balance of the tricks.

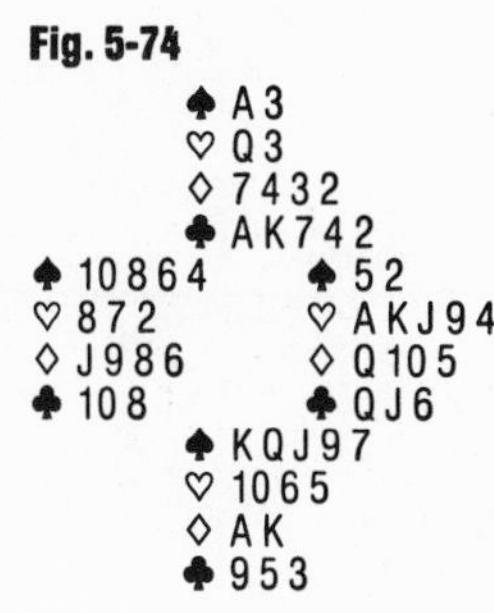
Fig. 5-74

In Fig. 5-75, declarer had to find a way to establish his suit without letting East gain the lead.

After West opened the bidding with one spade, South bought the contract for four hearts.

After the opening lead of the king of spades, the dummy came down, and declarer saw what looked like one loser in spades, one in clubs, and almost certainly two in diamonds. The chances were almost overwhelming that West had the ace of diamonds, in view of his opening bid. A club could be established if the suit broke normally, but the trouble was that a trick had to be surrendered to get the suit established, and, if East should win it, a diamond lead-through would be fatal. While it was possible that West would have to win the club trick, declarer thought he saw a way to handle the hand.

Fig. 5-75

After East followed suit with the two of spades, West switched to a trump which was won in the dummy with a seven-spot. Then declarer led the queen of spades and, instead of trumping it, discarded a club. This loser-on-loser play made it possible for him to establish the club tricks without losing a trick in clubs at all. West returned a heart which declarer won in his hand, preserving the ten-spot in dummy for an entry. When both opponents followed suit, he was getting closer to the solution of his problems. Then, when both followed to the ace and king of clubs, his problems were solved. He led a third club and trumped it high. He returned to the dummy by overtaking the nine of hearts and discarded two diamonds on dummy's two good clubs. He wound up losing two tricks in spades and one in diamonds, but none in clubs.

When you bid a grand slam, it pays handsomely to be as careful as possible. On the next hand, declarer was extremely careful, and it paid off.

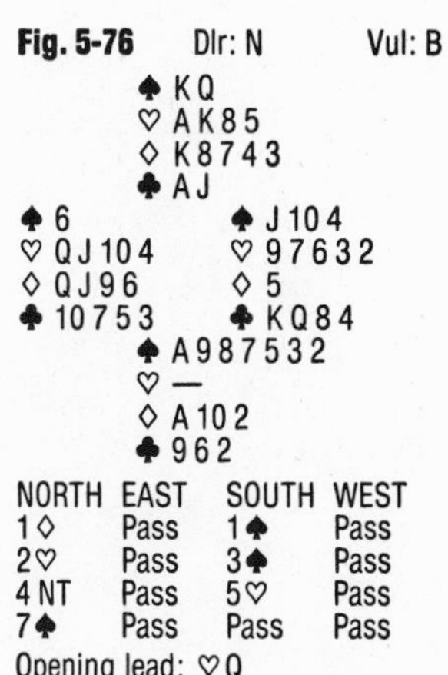
Fig. 5-76

West led the queen of hearts. In grand slams, there is no way to give up a trick to establish another, and so South discarded a small diamond on dummy's king of hearts. After thinking that over, he decided to take additional precautions against an unfavorable break and cashed the ace of hearts and discarded a second diamond. Next, he won the ace of diamonds in his hand and returned to the dummy with a trump. Now he led a small diamond, and East went into a huddle. At this point declarer knew his precautions had been well taken. East finally decided it would do no good to trump this diamond with one of his spades, and he was right, so he discarded a heart. Declarer won that in his hand with a trump and returned to the dummy with the king of spades. On came another small diamond. East again saw the futility of trumping that with his remaining spade and discarded another heart. Declarer trumped the diamond and led the ace of spades, taking East's last trump. A small club let him get to the dummy, and now the king of diamonds was waiting there to take the final diamond away from West and allow declarer to discard a club. The eight of diamonds was now good, so he could discard his other losing club.

Fig. 5-77 Dlr: S Vul: B

North: ♠ 74 ♡ A3 ♢ KJ82 ♣ A7652
West: ♠ AQJ63 ♡ KQJ42 ♢ 10 ♣ 94
East: ♠ 1095 ♡ 109865 ♢ 53 ♣ QJ10
South: ♠ K82 ♡ 7 ♢ AQ9764 ♣ K83

SOUTH	WEST	NORTH	EAST
1♢	1♠	2♣	Pass
2♢	2♡	5♢	All Pass

Opening lead: ♡K

On the next hand (Fig. 5-77), the problem was to find the way to establish the club suit without having East in the lead. Declarer found a neat solution.

When West led the king of hearts, it looked like declarer had two losers in spades and another in clubs. However, he thought he saw a way out, provided West held as many as two clubs. The bidding indicated that West had ten cards in the major suits, but that still allowed for two or three clubs. Declarer simply let West hold the trick, and that left declarer in charge. No matter what West now did, declarer was going to be able to discard a club on dummy's ace of hearts and get the suit established without loss. Actually, West continued with a second heart, and declarer won that with dummy's ace and discarded a club from his hand. Two trump leads exhausted the opponents' trumps. He then led the king of clubs and his remaining club to the ace, and then he trumped a club. This left two good clubs in the dummy, and a trump was there for an entry. On these two clubs, South discarded two of his spades and scored a well-earned game.

On the next hand we take a look at a new and important principle in suit establishment.

Fig. 5-78 Dlr: S Vul: B

North: ♠ K63 ♡ K73 ♢ KJ52 ♣ K62
West: ♠ J ♡ 865 ♢ 109843 ♣ Q1075
East: ♠ Q1094 ♡ 10 ♢ AQ76 ♣ J983
South: ♠ A8752 ♡ AQJ942 ♢ — ♣ A4

SOUTH	WEST	NORTH	EAST
1♡	Pass	2 NT	Pass
3♠	Pass	4♡	Pass
6♡	Pass	Pass	Pass

Opening lead: ♢10

The principle has its application in a number of situations and is particularly important in suit establishment: "If you must offer the opponents an opportunity to trump something, offer them the opportunity to trump a loser and not a winner."

Let's see how this works out. The opening lead of the ten of diamonds was trumped. If spades broke 3–2, there would be one spade loser and that would be all there was to the hand. The only thing to protect against was a 4–1 break, but as that happens more often than one time in four, why not try to take out insurance against it? Especially since the insurance is free.

After winning the opening lead, declarer won two trump tricks with the queen and jack. Had trumps broken 2–2, he could have gone about his business, and the 4–1 break in spades would not have bothered him. He could simply concede one spade, trump one in the dummy, and limit his losses to one spade. However, trumps had not broken; nonetheless, he quit leading trumps. If spades broke 4–1, he would need a trump in the dummy to trump a spade.

Let us assume for a moment that it is West who has shown out of trump so that East has a trump left. Declarer would have then won the first spade trick with the king, to protect against East's having a singleton spade. He would then make a lead from the north hand toward his ace through the hand that had a trump left. Should East trump this, he would trump a loser, as South would simply play a small spade, and now the defenders would have no trumps left. When South regained the lead, he could lead the ace of spades, trump a spade, and, when he returned to his hand, the fifth spade would be good. If East should refuse to trump, declarer would win with the ace, and then lead a third spade, conceding the trick to West. When he regained the lead, he would trump his fourth spade with dummy's king, come back to his hand to draw the last trump from East, and claim the balance of the tricks.

However, it was West who was left with a trump after the two had been led, so declarer first cashed the spade ace and, following the general principle of leading through the hand that has a trump left, led a small spade. West was in the same situation: if he trumped with his last trump, South would play a small spade from the dummy. With both defenders out of trumps, declarer would win any return and still have time to go to the dummy with the king of spades and get back to his hand to trump a spade with the king of hearts and return to his hand once more, with the five of spades becoming a winner.

Should West refuse to trump, declarer would win with dummy's king, and concede a spade to East. He would regain the lead to trump a spade with dummy's king, and get his fifth spade established as his twelfth trick.

On the next hand, let's give up the luxury of seeing all four hands and, as in real play, see only our own hand and the dummy.

DUMMY
♠ A 6
♡ A J 6 4 3
♢ Q J 9 7
♣ A 8

DECLARER
♠ 7 4
♡ K 5 2
♢ A K 10 8 5 4 3 2
♣ —

You have gotten into a contract of seven diamonds, your left-hand opponent has led the king of clubs, and you assume the ace will take the trick right now, as West did not bid like a man who had eleven clubs in his hand to the K Q J. They tell us you should be in a grand slam when the odds are better than 2 to 1 that it will make. The question is: Do you belong in a grand slam?

There is a potential loser in spades which can be discarded on the ace of clubs. If that is the best we can do, we are going to have to bring in the heart suit without losing a trick, and the odds that we can do this are not much better than even. But we do have a play which will succeed more than 98 times out of 100, and, if we can find it, we should be in this grand slam. The answer is to discard not a spade on the ace of clubs, but a heart. Lead one trump, and the opponents have no more. Now, the heart trick can be established, provided that East does not have all five of them.

Should West have all five, we will discover that as we lead the king and will have an automatic finesse of dummy's jack. If the suit breaks 3–2, it is simple. If it breaks 4–1, we can still establish the fifth heart without losing a trick—by ruffing. We have to lead hearts five times, and there are ample entries in the dummy. By leading the king, the ace, and then trumping one, we get three entries. A trump lets us get back to lead the fourth heart, and then we can go back with either the ace of spades or a trump to lead the fifth heart and discard a spade from South.

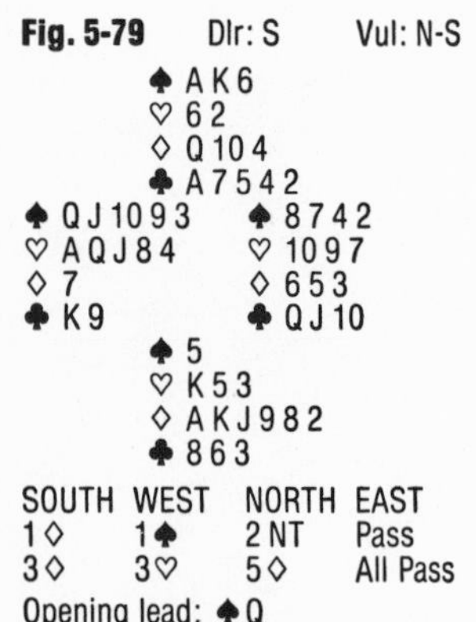

Fig. 5-79 Dlr: S Vul: N-S

On the next hand in Fig. 5-79, declarer had only the ace of the suit where he had a 5–3 fit. He was faced with a problem of establishing that suit without letting East get the lead. He found the way.

Unfortunately for the declarer, North got in the first no-trump bid. South would have had no trouble taking nine tricks at no-trump, but with North playing, a heart lead would have defeated the hand right away. South got into the only contract he had a chance to make. It seemed that he was looking at two club losers, as well as two heart losers, if East ever managed to get the lead. Of course, if clubs would break 3–2, he could get two discards on the established clubs in the dummy and that would be helpful. The trouble was that East almost certainly would get the lead while declarer was trying to establish clubs and, judging from the bidding, for East to be able to lead hearts almost certainly would be fatal.

Declarer found a way that had a chance. He let the queen of spades hold the trick. So far as the defenders were concerned, that could only be what is known as a revolting development. West had a sorry lot to make his next lead from and finally settled on a trump. Declarer won that in his hand and carefully preserved the two high trumps in the dummy for entries. He went to the dummy with the ace of clubs. On the ace and king of spades, he discarded two clubs. Now he was able to lead a second club and trump it high, and when both opponents followed, he was home free. A small diamond to the ten let him lead a third club, and a diamond to dummy's queen eliminated East's last trump and let declarer reach the dummy to discard two hearts on dummy's last clubs. He ended up losing his trick in a strange place, as he lost a spade trick, but only one heart trick.

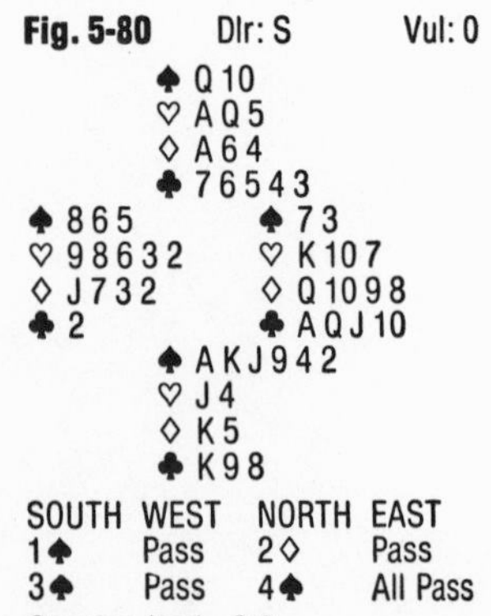

Fig. 5-80 Dlr: S Vul: 0

There is an old saying that the defenders should not monkey with the dummy's long suit, no matter how weak it is. That is often true, especially if dummy has plenty of entries to go along with that long suit. Unfortunately, the player on opening lead does not always know what dummy's long suit is.

After South opened the bidding with one spade, North thought he was a little weak to reply immediately with two no-trump, but decided to bid the minor suit where he had an ace rather than his weak five-card club suit. He thought the ace of diamonds might be more important to his partner than the five-card suit. He was wrong. A small club became just as good a trick as the ace of diamonds.

The opening lead of the two of clubs had all the earmarks of a singleton. East pounced on it with the ace and led back the queen of clubs. West got all set to trump this when suddenly he found it was not necessary to do so. South didn't play his king—he played the nine. Now East had a problem with no solution. If he quit leading clubs, declarer could pull trumps, and the king of clubs would be a trick. This one trick, added to six in spades, two in diamonds, and one in hearts, made a total of ten. On the other hand, if East persisted and led a third club, he would leave the fifth club in North within one trick of establishment. West could trump the king of clubs and switch to the heart, but declarer would rise with the ace of hearts, lead a fourth club, trump it high, pull trumps, and go to the dummy with the ace of diamonds where the fifth club was waiting to take a trick. On that trick he could discard his heart.

You Hold 6–0; They Hold 7 It is very discouraging to hold a nice six-card suit and find that your partner has none at all. Fortunately, this does not happen too often. When it does, those third and fourth cards in your suit will not take tricks unless they happen to be high cards. The fifth card will hold up better than 3 times out of 5, and the sixth card up to better than 9 out of 10, provided you can keep everything under control while you are getting the suit established and have plenty of entries to the hand with the six-card suit. Obviously the entries have to be in some suit other than the six-card suit itself, which means the chances to cash those long cards when the six-card suit is not rich in high cards become rather slim. However, it can be done, particularly when entries are in good supply, as in Fig. 5-81.

You should not be in a grand slam in hearts on this hand: both red suits have to break reasonably for you to take thirteen tricks, and the odds that both will do so are not enough to justify a grand slam bid. However, if you struggle up to a small slam in hearts, you might consider trying to take all thirteen tricks if you are playing match-point duplicate where the extra tricks cound much more than in rubber bridge. The chances that both red suits will behave reasonably well are better than 50–50.

Fig. 5-81

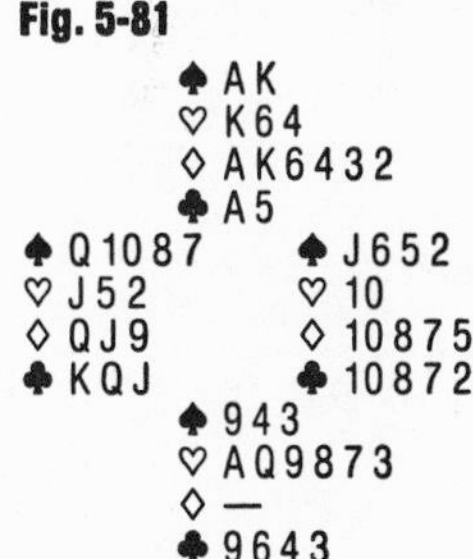

Let us say you get the opening lead of the king of clubs. If diamonds break 4–3, you can win tricks with both the two big diamonds and the two small ones. Adding four diamond tricks to two in spades, six in hearts, and one in clubs, you come to thirteen. North, the hand with the six diamonds, is rich in entries, so there is no problem there. However, there is danger of an overruff if you take too many diamonds. The safest bet is to start trumping diamonds before you take the ace and king and not after. So you will win the king of clubs with the ace and promptly lead a small diamond, trumping it. Here, it might be a good idea to lay down the ace and queen of trumps. When that turns out all right, you can go to the dummy with a spade and lead another diamond, trumping it. With things going along so nicely, lead a heart to dummy's king, extracting all of the opponents' trumps. On the four good diamonds in the dummy, you will discard three clubs and one spade, and you will still have a trump in your hand to take care of dummy's small club.

Mrs. Rixi Markus of Great Britain is recognized as one of the world's great players. On the hand in Fig. 5-82, she got to a contract of six clubs

Fig. 5-82

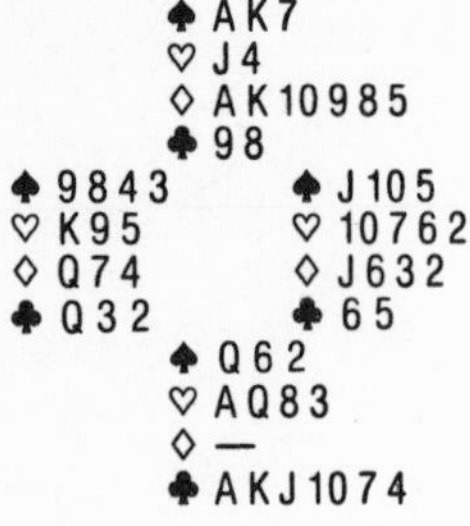

and had a more complicated problem in negotiating tricks with a 6–0 break.

Mrs. Markus got an opening lead of a spade. Either a heart finesse or a club finesse might or might not solve all her problems. Mrs. Markus thought she had a better chance to bring in the diamond suit. Dummy didn't have too many entries to get this suit established and cashed, but Mrs. Markus decided to force an extra entry not immediately apparent. She won the opening lead with dummy's ace and, due to the scarcity of entries, decided to cash the ace and king of diamonds, discarding two hearts, before she led diamonds to trump. She led a third diamond and trumped it with the jack of clubs. When both opponents followed suit, she knew she was going to be able to get the diamond suit established for another discard. She led a small club toward dummy. West rose with the queen and led a second spade. Mrs. Markus won that in her own hand and led a second club toward dummy. This put her in the dummy and gave her the opportunity to lead another diamond and trump it. She pulled the one oustanding trump and went back to the dummy with a high spade to take the good diamond on which she discarded her queen of hearts.

The entry problem, with a 6–0 hand, can sometimes cause declarers to find some exotic solution. George S. Coffin, in his classic book, *Bridge Play From A to Z,* reports this hand (Fig. 5-83) played by Frederick E. Taylor of Lincoln, Massachusetts.

Fig. 5-83

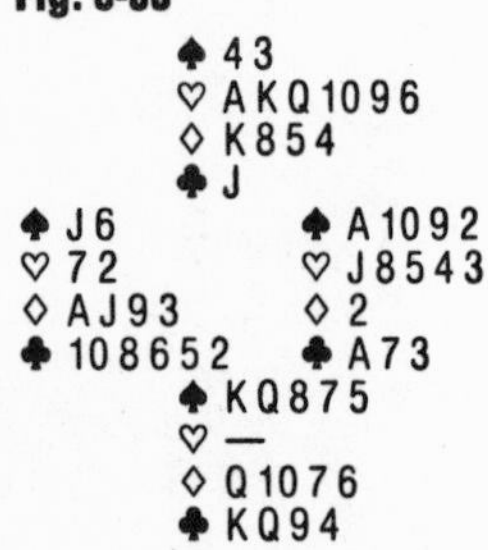

Playing in three no-trump, Taylor got an opening lead of the three of diamonds. The Rule of Eleven told him that if this was a fourth best lead, dummy's eight would win the trick, and, since the dummy needed all the entries he could get, he played dummy's eight. It did win the trick. Taylor was looking at a lovely heart suit which should bring in a lot of tricks, especially if the jack would fall out in three leads. Even if it did not, the diamond suit seemed to offer a second entry after a trick had been surrendered to the jack.

This presented two problems. In the first place, Taylor knew that the chances that the jack would fall out in three leads were not good. He didn't need to know that they were slightly more than 36 percent—all he needed to know was that the play was not favorable. With the opponents holding seven cards, one of them had at least four, and, obviously, the jack was more likely to be with the long hand than with the short hand. In addition, if Taylor started leading hearts right now, what the devil was he going to discard from his hand on that long run of hearts?

This line of thought led him to make a play which had all of the odds in its favor: he led the ten of hearts, willing to give up a trick to the jack now while he still had his entry left in dummy and before he had to take a lot of discards. Should East hold the jack of hearts, he would have no diamonds left to prematurely take out dummy's entry. Should West have the jack of hearts, he could not lead a diamond without giving up an additional diamond trick. Taylor felt that the chances were excellent that he could establish two tricks in the black suits before using up dummy's diamond entry to run his hearts and that, with two diamond tricks and two tricks from the black suits, he could get five tricks in hearts to bring home his nine tricks.

Taylor's farseeing plan paid off, as the defenders were not able to find any sequence which might frustrate his plan.

You Hold 6–1; They Hold 6 When you add one card opposite a six-card length, you have improved your chances considerably. The opponents no longer have seven cards; they now have only six. Establishment of the fourth card has stopped being inpossible and has become a reasonable chance. Chances to establish the fifth card have been considerably enhanced.

I am making a distinction between the words "promoted" and "established." A card becomes promoted to the top rank when the opponents have some cards left, but none higher than the card in question; it becomes established when the opponents are out of any cards in the suit.

In addition to the value of your small cards having increased considerably, your entry problems have been alleviated. The hand with six cards no longer needs quite so many entries—the mere presence of the singleton in the opposing hand makes it possible to lead the suit at least once without using up an entry, and where the six-card suit is headed by the ace, it makes it possible to lead the suit twice without using up a side.

The particular combination of 6-1 does have some problems which belong largely to it alone. Look at the problem existing in Fig. 5-84.

Fig. 5-84

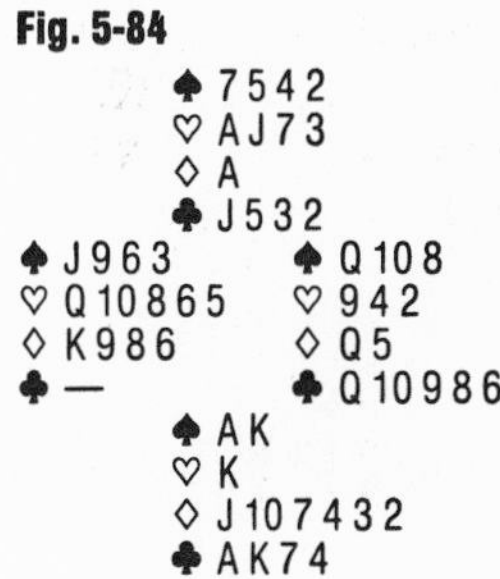

Playing at three no-trump, the declarer got an opening lead of the six of hearts. A count showed that he had seven tricks off the top. This presumed that he would cash his ace of hearts when he was in the dummy with the ace of diamonds, and he was afraid this play might lead to complications. Declarer thought it might be wise to leave the ace and jack of hearts in the dummy for protection, provided he could take nine tricks without a second heart trick. He could do this if he could bring in four tricks in diamonds.

With four entries in the south hand, declarer thought he had a pretty good chance to bring in a trick with the ace of diamonds, another with the jack-ten combination, and two more with the two small diamonds. At trick two, he led to dummy's ace of diamonds and, at trick three, to his king of clubs.

West showed out, discarding a small spade. Declarer saw two things about the club suit. First, West was not going to be able to lead them if he got the lead; second, East could not afford to do so without surrendering a trick. Thus, declarer turned his attention to the diamond suit. Before he had taken the ace of diamonds, the opponents had held six cards in the suit; now they held four. These four could be all in one hand, they could be 3–1, or they could be 2–2. If they were 2–2, his two cards in sequence consisting of the jack and ten were good enough to lead the jack, and he had nothing to lose by doing so. However, if there were three in one hand, he could only afford to lead high if he had a sequence of three cards; if there were four in one hand, he could afford to lead high only with a four-card sequence. Declarer could figure that the most likely distribution at the start was for the diamonds to be 4–2; this would leave 3–1. If one held all four diamonds, he was not going to establish the tricks he wanted in the suit, no matter how he played. If the hand holding three diamonds had both the king and queen, the situation was still bad, and he was going to have to try for some sort of end play in clubs or hearts. But, if the king or queen was now alone in one hand, he could accomplish his purposes by leading a small diamond—the hand with a singleton honor would have to play it. This would also work if, at the beginning, each opponent had three diamonds. Were that the case, they each had two left, and it made no difference whether he led the jack or a small one.

If, at the beginning, the diamonds were 4–2, the odds favored finding one of the honors in the hand with the doubleton. Declarer led the two of diamonds and discarded a spade from dummy. East had to win it with his lone queen.

A look at the dummy told East it would be folly to return the heart suit or to lead a club, so he led a small spade. It was too late; declarer won that and led the jack of diamonds, forcing the king from West. When he recovered the lead with the ace of spades, the ten of diamonds took the nine out of West's hand, and the two diamonds were good for the eighth and ninth tricks.

Back in the 1930's and 1940's, serious bridge players were just as interested in finding new angles for play of the hand as they were in finding the utopian bidding system which would inevitably get you to the right spot. Regretfully, in late years, interest in advancing bridge seems to belong to the romantics who are still looking for that perfect bidding system. The realists who are trying to find ways to improve play of the hand have receded into the background. It is a shame; there is a lot to be learned about dummy play and defense.

Back in those days, a great deal was made out of a situation where there was a six-card suit headed by the ace-king opposite a singleton and the winning play was still to lead small and surrender a trick before cashing either the ace or king. The literature had a number of examples of such a hand, but the hand was first played by Alfred Sheinwold and was a prototype of all of the others. The clarity and precision of Sheinwold's writing makes all of us in the bridge writing business jealous; but, by the play of this hand, he showed that he can play them as well as write about them.

Sheinwold won the opening trump lead with dummy's jack and, at trick two he led the two of diamonds! Any kibitzers he had must have thought he pulled the wrong card. On the contrary, the play of a small diamond was the one card to play to increase his prospects for a slam. Let us see whether we can try to reconstruct his reasoning. Counting five probable trump tricks and six additional tricks in aces and kings brought his total to eleven. Trying to trump a club in the dummy was a dubious way to try for the twelfth trick, as both the queen and jack of hearts were necessary to protect the trump suit against a probable 4–2 break of the six trump held by the opponents. The spade finesse was a 50–50 chance, and, as with all fine players, Sheinwold wanted a better chance than that if it were available. Diamonds offered a better chance provided he could get them established and retain an entry to the dummy to reach them after they were established. The danger of laying down even one before trumping a small one was that he might get overruffed. He couldn't afford to pull a second trump before leading the diamonds, as trumps furnished an entry to the suit. His best chance was to establish diamonds by trumping once and leaving enough trumps to pull the opponents'.

Once Sheinwold had led a small diamond, the hand was a cinch with the cards as they were. When next he reached the dummy with the high trump, he would trump a small diamond and then return to his hand with a black suit to finish pulling trump. The king of spades in the dummy would provide an entry, and the ace-king of diamonds would drop the two outstanding diamonds, making the small diamonds good for tricks.

It is nice when you have one of those long solid trump suits that permit you to first cash an ace and king and then trump high. On the next hand (Fig. 5-86), declarer had that trump suit, but the six-card suit which he was trying to establish left something to be desired.

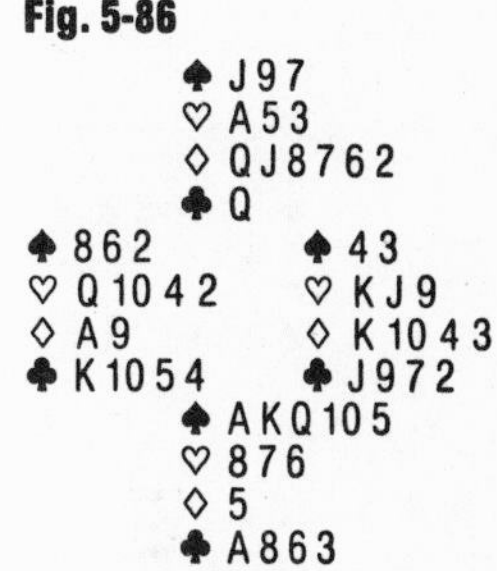

Fig. 5-86

Declarer got himself into an aggressive four spade contract, and West got off the good lead of a trump. In addition to his obvious five trump tricks, declarer had only two other tricks in aces. Whatever chance he had at the beginning to trump three clubs in the dummy was certainly already gone with the trump lead from West, and so declarer had to fall back on trying to establish the diamond suit.

The dummy didn't seem to offer too many entries, and to preserve them as best he could, declarer won the opening trump lead with the queen. At trick two, he led his small diamond. West had to play his ace on that or have it ruffed out. He went up with the ace and, seeing what declarer was after, led a small heart to remove one of dummy's entries. He succeeded admirably, as declarer played the ace in dummy and led the queen of diamonds, meaning to trump that high if East covered. East saw no reason to make things easy for declarer and didn't cover. Declarer discarded a small heart. Next, he led a third diamond and trumped it with the king of spades. A small trump to the nine put dummy back in the lead for a fourth diamond which he would trump with the ace of trumps. The ten of trumps to dummy's jack furnished the final entry and collected the last trumps from the opponents. In the dummy then sat the two good diamond tricks. These, together with the queen of diamonds which had already won a trick, gave declarer three tricks out of that ragged diamond suit and brought his total up to ten.

You Hold 6–2; They Hold 5 A 6–2 suit has a lot going for it. It has become better than 2 to 1 that the suit will be established after three leads. The 6–2 suit is generally better than the 5–3 suit, despite the fact that in both cases the opponents hold five cards. With the 6–2 fit, there is the extra trick represented by the sixth card in the long hand. And, the fact that the opposing hand has two cards, frequently decreases the problem of entries. When the suit contains both the ace and king and you have trumps, it frequently will become possible to establish the suit without losing a trick.

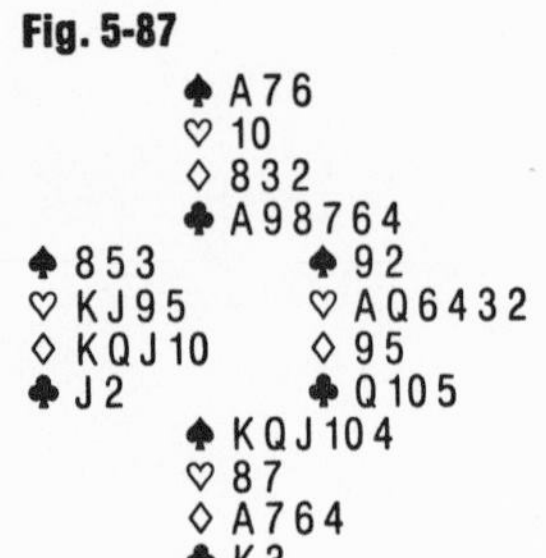

Fig. 5-87

Against a four spade contract, West opened the king of diamonds. At first glance, there appeared to be four losers in the red suits, unless the declarer could manage to trump both a diamond and a heart in the dummy. That would involve giving up the lead three times and was a little too much to expect. On the other hand, there was that beautiful six-card club suit in the dummy and, between them, the two hands had both the ace and king. There was a little entry problem in the dummy, but if both black suits behaved well, declarer would be able to capitalize on the club suit. He won the opening lead with the ace and laid down the king and queen of spades. He had to leave the ace in the dummy for entry purposes. When both opponents followed to the two spade leads, he saw that the suit was behaving. He led next the king of clubs and a small club to the ace, and both opponents followed to the leads. Then he led a small club and trumped it with an honor to avoid an overruff. He then led to the ace of trumps, picking up the one outstanding spade, and threw away three of the five losers he had in the red suits on the three clubs, ending up with eleven tricks.

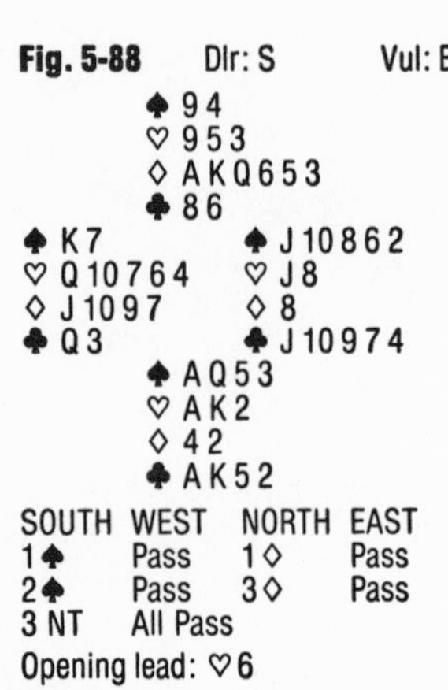

Fig. 5-88

On the hand in Fig. 5-88, the declarer took out some cheap insurance against a bad break.

Against a three no-trump contract, West led the six of hearts. Declarer could count eight tricks off the top and needed only one additional one to fulfill his contract. He decided to take the first heart trick with the king of hearts because he didn't fancy a spade shift. You and I could see that he would be able to take the ace of spades and then lead a small one to get his ninth trick established, but he couldn't see that. He decided to try to get the extra trick from the diamond suit.

Had he not been a careful man, he would have laid down the ace and king of diamonds and then seen that he was going to come to grief. After all, they should split 3–2 more than 67 percent of the time; but on the other hand, they split 4–1 more than 28 percent of the time. Having two diamonds in his hand to lead, declarer decided to give them a diamond trick. He led small and then played small from the dummy. Now he was going to take five diamonds, two hearts, two clubs, and the ace of spades, for a total of ten.

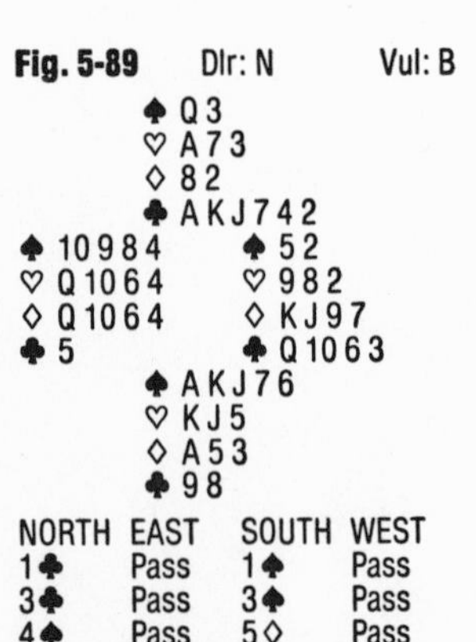

Fig. 5-89

On the next hand, North's rebid of three clubs was not the best bid he ever made, and South's final contract of six spades was not the best contract he was ever in. However, it all worked out because West chose the ten of spades for his opening lead, and that was not the best opening lead he ever made.

The opening trump lead persuaded the declarer that he was not going to use any of dummy's trumps for ruffing, and he soon decided that his best chance was to develop the club suit. So he rose with dummy's queen of trumps and then led three more rounds of trumps, leaving himself with just one. With an entry still in the dummy and with two clubs in his own hand, he could take a few precautions, and he did so. He led the nine of clubs, and, when West followed suit, he lit a cigar and played small from the dummy. Once West followed suit, he was going to take twelve tricks no matter how the remaining clubs lay. If West had them all, the nine would hold the trick, and he would be assured of four club tricks. If East won the trick, it would be demonstrated that clubs wouldn't break worse than 4–1.

East won the trick and switched to the nine of hearts. Declarer was not about to give up the ace of hearts entry in the dummy and rose with the king. He led the eight of clubs to dummy's ace. Then he discarded a diamond on the king of clubs and trumped the next club. Now he used dummy's ace of hearts to get to the two good clubs in the dummy on which he threw away another diamond and the losing heart.

The next 6–2 combination (Fig. 5-90) has been around a long time, but I haven't seen much of it lately. Let's take a fresh look at it.

Fig. 5-90

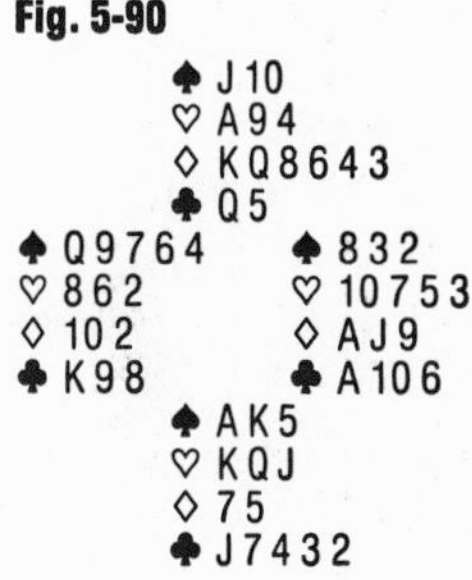

Against three no-trump, West led the six of spades, and dummy's ten won the trick. The old-timers had a lot of fun with this particular setup, showing that declarer might come to his hand with a heart honor and lead toward dummy's diamond holding, putting up dummy's queen. East could frustrate declarer's plan by playing a small diamond. Now there was no way to establish diamonds in the dummy and also get there. However, it was shown that South's proper play was simply to play a small diamond from each hand and concede the trick. The simplest way is to lead a diamond from the dummy at trick two. He now could win the lead in the major suits at once or eventually in clubs, lead a small diamond, and play the queen. This way he would be able not only to establish the diamond suit, but also to have the ace of hearts in the dummy for an entry once he got it established.

The key to the hand is that the declarer is missing the A J 10 of the suit, with the ace-jack and another following dummy's long suit. I don't know how soon this hand will come up again in actual play, but the next time it does—have fun. Of course, you will need plenty of stoppers in all the other suits.

When you don't have all of those nice high honors in your six card suit, you may be more hard pressed to find the winning play.

Fig. 5-91

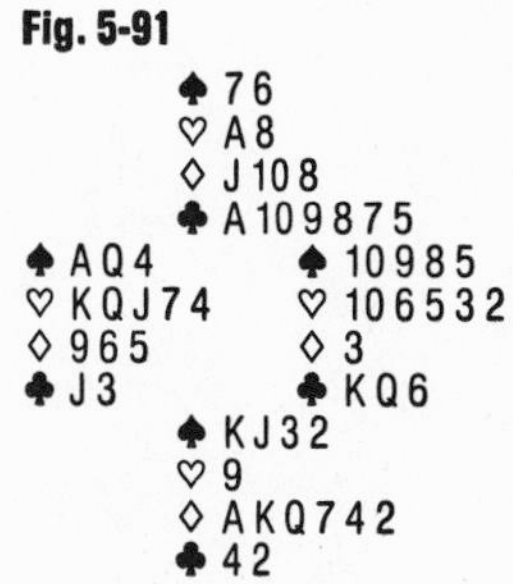

Against a heart overcall by West and a lot of heart bidding by the opponents, South finally reached a contract of five diamonds. The opening lead was the king of hearts. South didn't fancy his prospects in spades, as it looked like two spade losers; he also had a club loser. Of course, it would be nice if he could get the club suit established without losing the lead, but it was not immediately apparent how that was to be done. After looking the hand over, declarer thought he saw a way. He let the king of hearts hold the first trick. West switched to the jack of clubs, but declarer had everything under control if the two minor suits broke normally. He won with dummy's ace and discarded a club on the heart ace. He led a small club and trumped it with an honor. When both followed suit, he knew the club suit was breaking 3–2. Next he laid down the ace of diamonds and saw that the diamond suit was going to behave as well. A small diamond to dummy's jack let him lead a third club, which he also trumped with a high honor. A small diamond to dummy's ten pulled the last trump and provided the entry to the three good clubs waiting. On these he discarded three of his spades. He ended up losing one heart and one spade trick.

On the next hand (Fig. 5-92), both minor suits broke badly for the declarer. With a little luck and a lot of perseverance, he prevailed.

Warned away from the club lead by the bidding, West tried the five of

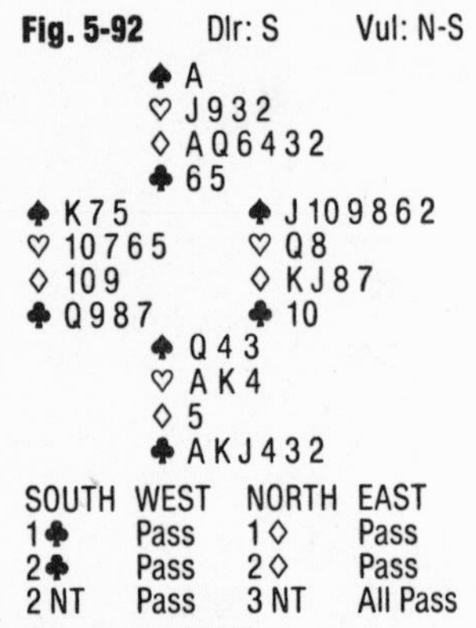

hearts. The nine from the dummy brought East's queen; declarer won with the king and saw that he had three heart tricks. Added to these was one in spades, one in diamonds, and two in clubs. There were still two missing for game. In diamonds there was a 6–1 fit, and in clubs a 6–2 fit. It was obvious the 6–2 fit was the better to go after, not only because the opponents had fewer cards in the suit, but also because declarer had more high cards there. He decided against using up too many of dummy's entries to lead clubs from the dummy and simply led a small club at trick two.

East won it with the ten and switched to the jack of spades. Declarer won the ace and led another club from the dummy, intending to finesse the jack. When East showed out and played the eight of diamonds, declarer simply took the ace-king of clubs and then put West in with his queen by leading a small club. This established two good clubs in his hand. West duly led the ten of diamonds, but declarer wasn't having any of that. He rose with the ace to avoid a possible spade lead from East and then came to his own hand with the ace of hearts to cash his two clubs. Dummy's jack of hearts was the ninth trick.

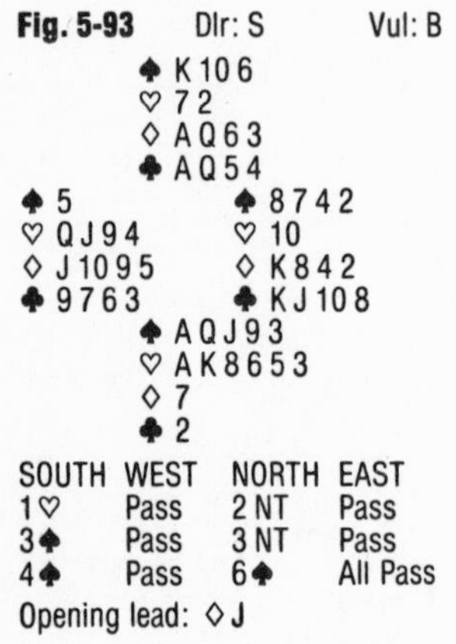

Playing six spades on the next hand, it appeared to declarer that all he had to bother about was a bad break in both major suits. He took what precautions he could against that, and came out in fine shape.

Against the six spade contract, West led the jack of diamonds after hearing South open hearts and rebid spades. Declarer put dummy's ace on it and led a small heart. The play of the ten-spot by East warned South to play carefully. He won that with the king and then led a small trump to dummy's ten. He was following the very fine old precept of leading toward the high cards instead of away from them, and he led a second heart from dummy. Had East followed suit to that, declarer intended to duck it himself and later on to trump a heart with dummy's king of spades. East decided that a bird in the hand was worth two in the bush and trumped the heart lead. He didn't think South had another diamond, but decided he would look like a fool if declarer did have one and he didn't cash his king. Declarer trumped the king and led another small heart, trumping with dummy's king. He led a spade back to his hand and then took East's last trump away. The play of the ace of hearts made the balance of that suit good, and dummy had the ace of clubs for the twelfth trick.

Sometimes, the situation looks a little different when you have to make the first lead in the suit from the long hand, but it really is the same.

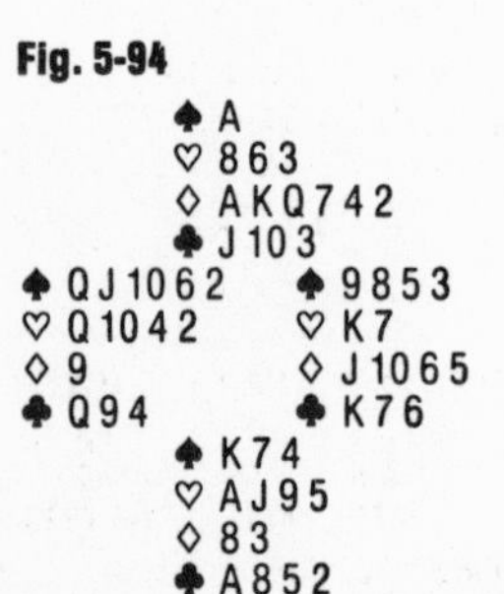

South got to three no-trump, and the queen of spades lead removed one of the entries in the dummy. Outside of the diamond suit, there were just four tricks off the top. Five diamond tricks would bring the total to nine. Of course, if the diamond suit broke 3–2, there would be six diamond tricks, for a total of ten. A wise declarer would forget all about that and lead the two of diamonds at trick two to pick up the game contract, since 28 percent of the time the diamonds will break 4–1.

On the next hand (Fig. 5-95), declarer took a deep finesse to protect himself from a 4–1 break; and unless East had all five diamonds, he was going to make his contract whether the finesse won or lost.

Again the contract was three no-trump. West opened the four of hearts. With this particular heart holding, unless the queen can win trick one, it is not likely to win a trick at all, so declarer played it. He now counted two spades, one club, and the heart trick already won. If diamonds broke normally, he would have six diamond tricks, for a total of ten. At trick two, declarer led a small diamond from the dummy, and, when East followed, he took a deep finesse of the eight-spot for two reasons: if it lost the trick, neither opponent could have more than four to begin with and he would have nine tricks and would be protected against a heart lead by East; if it won and West was able to follow suit, he would have the six tricks, bringing his total up to ten.

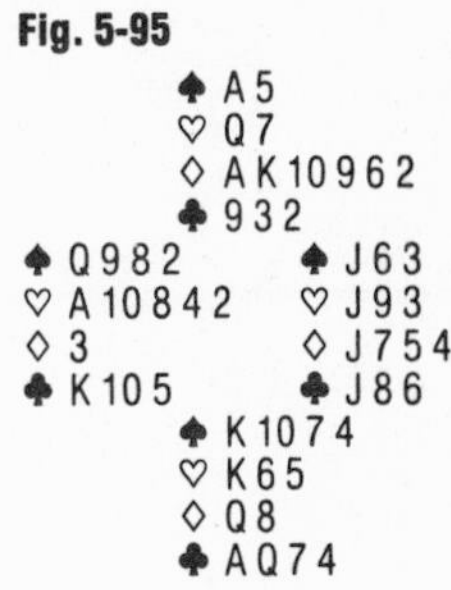

Fig. 5-95

A very wise bridge teacher once said, "Nothing that I say is absolutely true." Even that statement probably is not absolutely true. There are exceptions to nearly everything, but not quite everything. So, let me show you when the proper procedure with six headed by the A K Q is to start cashing them right away without monkeying around.

Against four spades, West led the jack of diamonds. When declarer played the queen from the dummy, he found that it was not going to take a trick at all. East played the king, and declarer the ace. Now declarer was looking at a diamond loser, a heart loser, and two spade losers. The minute he let them in while trying to establish hearts, they could cash their diamond winner, and then, no matter what he did, he had two spade losers. So, declarer tried to see whether he could do a little horsetrading. He went after clubs and led them three times. On the third club lead he planned to discard a diamond, no matter who did what. East trumped and led a diamond, but South trumped it. He then laid down the ace and another spade. In effect, he had discarded his losing diamond on one of the defenders' trump winners, and thus wound up losing two spades and one heart, but no diamonds.

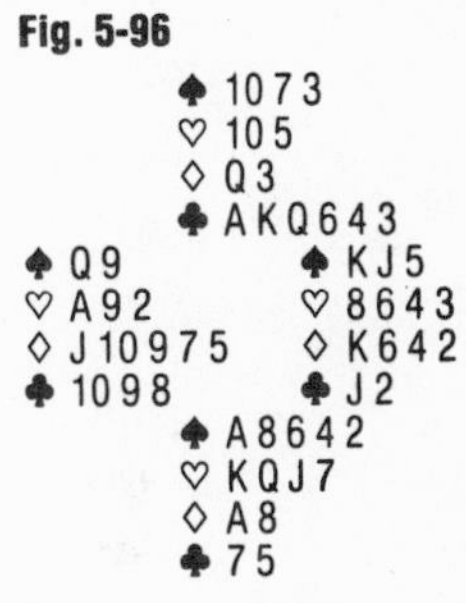

Fig. 5-96

The next hand (Fig. 5-97) shows another example of a declarer willing to let the opponents take a trump trick to keep them from taking any other tricks at all.

It looks to me as though North and South were overly aggressive to reach their small slam contract. The bidding indicated to South that his honors in diamonds were probably worthless to him, and it is difficult to see what made North think there were twelve tricks available. However, the more I talk about this, the worse I look, for they made twelve tricks.

West led the jack of hearts, which was covered by the queen, king, and ace. The defenders had one defensive trick established. Our hero in the South seat didn't have that king and queen of clubs to try for a quick discard. If West had the king of spades, the hand was going to be defeated. The fact that he overcalled didn't guarantee that he had it. South led to dummy's high club and took the spade finesse. When this won, he was delighted and was on the verge of going back to the dummy to repeat the finesse when it occurred to him that he had a lot of losing diamonds in his hand he had to do something about. So, he abandoned that idea and laid down the ace of spades. Had East started with only two spades, the trump situation would have been taken care of, but it didn't

Fig. 5-97

turn out that way. East had a sure trump trick, but South was still very much in the running for twelve tricks. As a matter of fact, if clubs broke normally, he would take twelve tricks. He led a second club to the dummy and then a third one. If East trumped that with the king, he could have discarded his losing heart. Of course, East followed suit, so the declarer trumped that and then trumped a diamond to get back to the dummy. He now started leading clubs, and East could trump with his king whenever he wanted to do so. Whether he did or not, declarer was going to throw away from his hand first the small heart and then two small diamonds. The only trick he lost was to the king of spades.

Now let's give our declarer a solid trump suit and show how he can utilize that to his advantage in suit establishment.

Fig. 5-98

This time, the six spade contract which South reached seems more reasonable than the last one I showed you. This South was an exceedingly cautious player, and this hand was one where caution paid off.

The opening lead was the queen of hearts, which was won by the king. Something now had to be done with the four little diamonds in declarer's hand, and he didn't fancy his prospects of trying to trump them in the dummy. As soon as he led a diamond, the opponents would see what he was up to and would probably return a trump to disrupt his plans. If they did, he saw he would end up in the dummy with no way to return to his hand after disposing of his diamonds. So, he went for the suit establishment, and at trick two led a small club to dummy's king. He didn't hurry about his next play. His trumps were solid and he had quite a few of them, so it occurred to him that he might be able to protect himself against a bad break in clubs. He remembered that five cards outstanding would break 4–1 almost 10 percent of the time. He led the ace of hearts and discarded the second small club from his own hand. Now he led a small club from the dummy and trumped it, seeing that it was well he had done so when West discarded a heart. Next he led the ace and another trump to dummy's queen and saw that trumps were behaving. Another club was trumped and he extracted West's last trump and led a diamond. This forced an entry into the dummy, and, on the king and small clubs, he had plenty of discards to take care of the diamonds.

Your Side Holds 9; They Hold 4 When you get to where you and the dummy have nine cards in any suit, that suit likely is trumps, and we are going to have a whole chapter on trump control. There are times when you have a completely solid suit and it becomes obvious you can take as many tricks at no-trump as you can at trump, but establishing such a suit creates no problems and needs no discussion here. What we are going to talk about in this section are those few times when your nine-card holding is not trump and when there are problems about getting it established. This will usually happen when the nine-card holding is a minor suit and you go for the bargain game of nine tricks at no-trump rather than the eleven trick minor suit game.

You are entitled to a few hands on this subject, pointing out problems that may arise in establishing the long cards, and I shall see to it that you have them.

In Fig. 5-99, when declarer first counted his tricks, it looked too easy to be true. There were two spades, one heart, five diamonds, if they broke normally, and one club. But, on a closer look, declarer saw a horrible thing: he was going to have to take the fourth diamond in his own hand, and, if the defenders persisted on knocking out the ace of hearts in dummy, he would have no way back to the long diamond. Surely West had the king of clubs for his overcall. But declarer found a way out. As a matter of fact, he soon decided that after the king of hearts opening, he was a cinch to make the hand unless one of the defenders had all four diamonds. He simply let West hold the king of hearts. West continued with the queen, which also held the trick, and finally led a third heart, which forced dummy's ace. On that declarer discarded the offending five of diamonds. He now had his five diamond tricks when the suit broke normally.

Fig. 5-99 Dlr: N Vul: 0

North: ♠ 8 7 2 / ♡ A 7 6 / ◇ A K Q 4 3 / ♣ 10 2

West: ♠ Q 3 / ♡ K Q J 8 5 / ◇ J 10 2 / ♣ K J 8

East: ♠ J 10 9 6 4 / ♡ 9 4 3 / ◇ 9 / ♣ 7 6 4 3

South: ♠ A K 5 / ♡ 10 2 / ◇ 8 7 6 5 / ♣ A Q 9 5

NORTH	EAST	SOUTH	WEST
1◇	Pass	2♣	2♡
Pass	Pass	3◇	Pass
3♡	Pass	3 NT	All Pass

Opening lead: ♡K

But suppose West, after leading the king of hearts, had switched—say—to the queen of spades. Now South could win it with the king and lead the ten of hearts and duck it. He was determined to lose two heart tricks so he could discard a diamond on the third heart, and no lead West made after the opening lead could have stopped him from doing so.

South took his nine tricks and got on to the next hand where he got into a grand slam in hearts.

Fig. 5-100

After some exuberant bidding, South got the lead of the king of diamonds. He could count only ten tricks in straight leads. If he could trump three diamonds in the dummy, that would make thirteen, but he couldn't figure out any way to keep getting back to his hand to do this. Finally he had to fall back on the club suit. In that suit, it was necessary to bring in two extra tricks without losing any, and this might require some handling. First, he led three rounds of trumps, ending in the dummy. He was vastly relieved when that suit broke 3–2. Next, he laid down the ace and king of clubs. If that suit had broken 2–2, school would have been out. On the fifth club he could have discarded one of his losing diamonds, and the other two could have gone on dummy's two spades. But when West showed out on the second lead, declarer brought his secret weapon into play. He led the three spades from the dummy and discarded the two remaining clubs on the king and queen. Next, he trumped a small club, establishing two in the dummy for discards. He returned to the dummy by trumping a small diamond, and the two good clubs let him discard his remaining diamonds.

Fig. 5-101

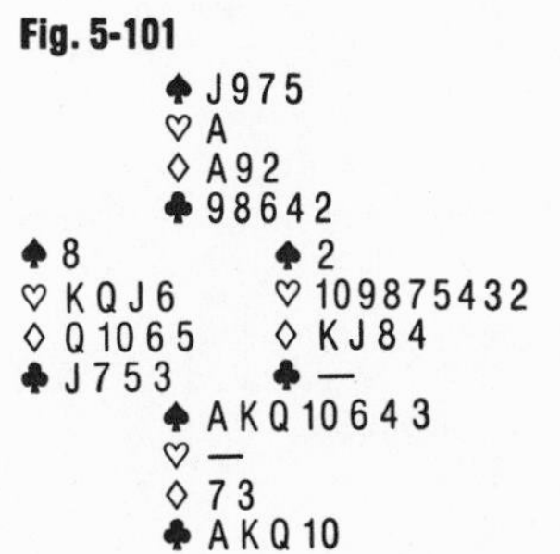

Grand slams are fun. Let's try another one (Fig. 5-101).

South duly got to a seven spade contract. When West led the king of hearts, he had a 100-percent play, unless West had started with 12 hearts. This did not involve discarding a diamond on the ace of hearts. Instead, declarer discarded the ten of clubs.

Now he was going to get that fifth club in the dummy established no matter how the opposing clubs broke. Remember, when you have a 5–4 fit, the fifth card becomes a 100-percent card provided you can establish and reach it. The lead of the ace of trumps cleared the suit. Next, declarer cashed his high clubs, finding the 4–0 break, and went to the dummy with a trump to lead the fourth club and trump it. Back he went to the dummy with the ace of diamonds to cash the fifth club, on which he discarded the offending diamond.

Of course, the chances that all four of the clubs would be in one hand were only 9.6 percent, so the chances they would all be with West were only half that or 4.8 percent. Those were pretty good odds, but why go for a 95-percent chance when you have a 100-percent chance?

With the nine cards, you are likely to have at least one of the four high ones, but you don't have to. Even when you have the nine smallest cards in a 6–3 suit, chances are still excellent that you can take three tricks in the suit if you can hold off the opponents while you are getting the suit established.

Fig. 5-102

At three no-trump, declarer got an opening lead of the jack of hearts. He had eight tricks off the top and did not see any way to develop a ninth trick in any suit except the diamond suit. Should the outstanding diamonds break 2–2, he could establish four tricks by giving them two, provided he could keep them from getting their suit established while he was giving up his tricks. The chances that he could do that looked good. In the more likely event that diamonds broke 3–1, he would have to give up three tricks to establish three in diamonds, and, should they break 4–0, he would have to give up four tricks to win two. No matter how they broke, he would have enough tricks, provided he could get his tricks in before the defenders got their tricks established.

He won the heart lead in his hand with the king and led a small diamond. West won and continued with a heart (a spade switch would have been better). Declarer won with the queen and led a second diamond. East won and had no hearts to return, so he did the best he could and led a club. Declarer won it with the king and gave East his third diamond. He ended up losing only three diamond tricks.

On the next hand (Fig. 5-103), declarer had an option of two plays. One looked like it would not work; the other looked like it probably would. He had to think awhile to decide which one to choose.

Fig. 5-103 Dlr: W Vul: 0

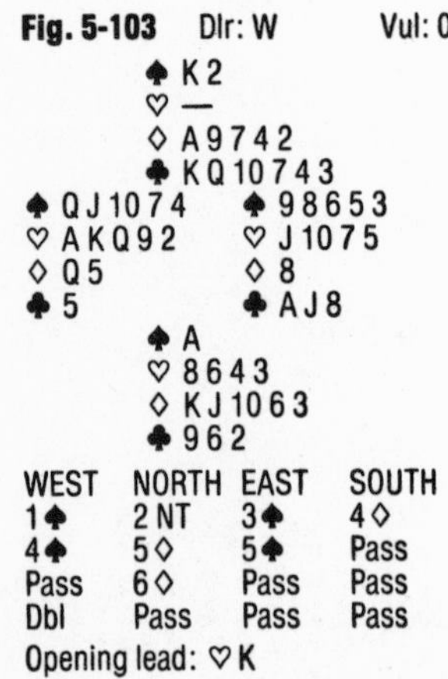

It looked as though one way to try to bring in twelve tricks was to trump four hearts in the dummy. Declarer tried to figure out how he might have enough entries into his hand to do this, and couldn't come up with an answer. The alternative play was to try to establish the club suit with the loss of not more than one club trick. This would prove easy if West had the ace of clubs, but was not quite so easy should East hold the ace, jack, and another. While West had opened the bidding and was more likely to have the ace of clubs than East, East had to have something for his bidding. Declarer decided his best chance was to go after clubs. He trumped the opening lead in the dummy and pulled trump in two leads, ending in his hand. Before tackling the clubs, he led the ace of spades to unblock that suit. Next he led a small club toward the king, and, although East won with the ace, declarer had his contract after both opponents followed to one round of clubs. East returned a heart which was trumped in the dummy. Declarer played the queen of clubs, and, when West showed out, led the king of spades and discarded the last club from his hand on it. Another club from the dummy cleared the suit as it was trumped. He was able to return to the good clubs in the dummy by trumping a heart with dummy's last trump.

South did not quite know how to be scientific in bidding the next hand, so when his partner opened with two no-trump, he went directly to six spades.

The opening lead was the jack of hearts. When the dummy came down, trumps seemed solid enough, and the only losers seemed to be in diamonds. Should that suit break 2-2, there would be only one loser in the hand. The odds did not favor that break, and declarer found a way to improve his chances. He played the ace of hearts and trumped a heart. Next he cashed two trump tricks, ending in the dummy, and then led the A K Q of clubs. On these he discarded three diamonds. He then led the five of clubs and trumped it.

Now the time had come to tackle the diamonds. He led a small diamond, and, when West played the eight, he simply played the nine. If East had started with three diamonds, he was going to go set, and that was all there was to it. Should the diamonds be 2-2, he was only going to lose one diamond trick, and whether he lost it now or after taking his ace made no difference. The difference was when East held a singleton honor. He would have to win the trick with that, and whatever he led back, declarer would be able to discard a diamond from the dummy while trumping in his own hand.

It would have done West no good to play one of his honors when the diamonds were led. Declarer would simply have gone up with the ace, and East's queen would have fallen. The spot cards in diamonds would make it possible for declarer to lose only one trick in that suit.

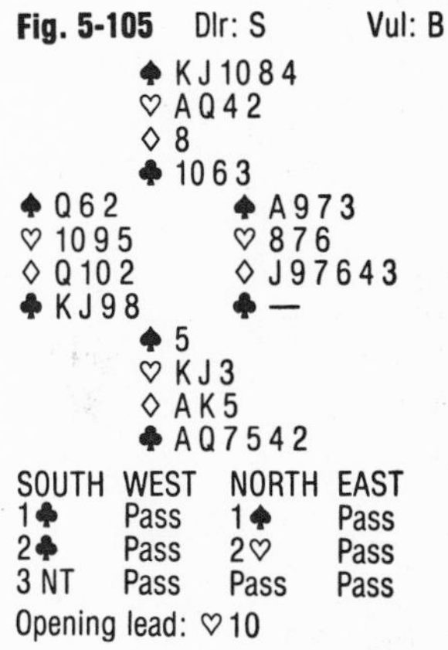

On the next hand (Fig. 5-105), entries looked rather awkward, and declarer decided to play it safe in taking his nine tricks.

Declarer was looking at seven tricks off the top and decided the club suit offered the best possibility for developing two more. He properly decided that the entry situation required that he go ahead and start leading clubs from his hand instead of trying to get into the dummy for that purpose. Having made that decision, he next decided that he should not lay down the ace, but should lead a small club to see what he could learn about the club division. West had to play the jack to keep dummy's ten from winning the trick, and declarer knew right away what was required in the club suit.

After declarer had decided to lead a small club at trick two, there was no way to keep him from developing the two tricks that he needed while keeping control of the hand. This would have been equally true if it had been East who held all four clubs.

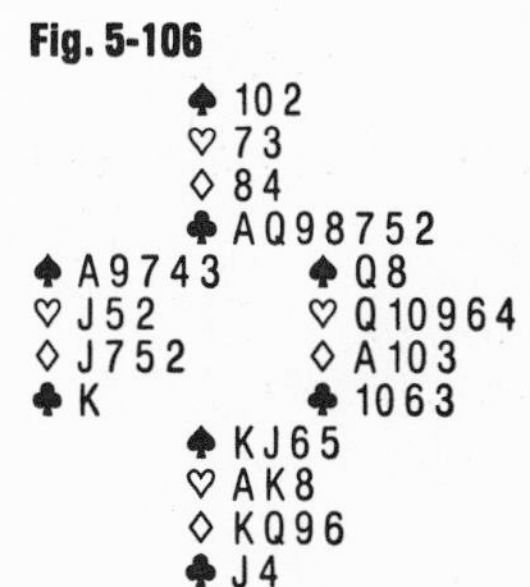

With a 7-2 holding, about the only problem that can arise is that of entries.

Against three no-trump, West opened the four of spades. Dummy played low, East played the queen, and declarer the king. All he had to do to be sure of his contract was to bring in six club tricks.

Should East hold three or four to the king, East might give declarer problems, but when declarer played the jack and West had to play the king, there were no problems left. Declarer simply played the two-spot and let West win with the king. Not only did declarer have six club tricks sitting there waiting for him, but any lead West made was going to allow declarer to get in an extra trick. A spade lead would give him the extra trick right away. A heart lead would give him ample time to establish a trick either in spades or diamonds, as suited his convenience. A diamond lead would also put declarer in fine shape.

Your Side Holds 9, but Is Missing the Queen About the silliest notion ever sold to the bridge playing public is the idea that when you have nine cards with all of the high cards except the queen, you should play for the drop of the queen rather than finesse. This is an area where mathematics give way to the imperfect shuffle, except in those cases where computers have dealt the cards. Even when the mathematical probabilities hold, they are not so hot; neither has the full story yet been told. It is time to place all the facts on the table.

First, let's take a look at the arithmetic itself.

DUMMY
♠ K J 9 6
♡ 10 9
◇ Q
♣ 10 9 8 6 3 2

DECLARER
♠ A 10 8 7 4
♡ K Q J 5
◇ A 5
♣ 5 4

In a spade contract, it appears you have two losers in clubs and one in hearts. The only problem is how to play the spade suit to avoid losing any tricks in it.

From what I have told you, it is pure guess whether you win the first spade trick with your ace or dummy's king. Let's say you lay down the ace and everyone follows suit with a small card. You then lead the four of spades, and West plays a small card. This is the moment when you have to decide whether to play the king or to take a finesse.

Of all of the possible distributions of the four outstanding spades in the hands of the opponents, only two possibilities are left: either West started with only two small cards or he started with a total of three, including the queen. The mathematical question is "Which is more likely?" The answer is that West would have started with the queen and two small cards 18.6 percent of the time, while he would have started with just two small cards, leaving the queen and one in the East hand, 20.35 percent of the time. Translating this into comparative odds, the mathematical answer is that playing for the drop will succeed 52.2 percent of the time, while the finesse will succeed only 47.8 percent of the time. Those decimals don't make that much difference, so let's call it 52 to 48 in favor of the drop. Big Deal! Among other things, this means that nearly half the time you will go up with the king, and East will discard something, while West sits smugly with his queen.

Of course, if you are a bridge player rather than a mathematician, you might have tried leading the jack from dummy, intending to play the ace if East did not cover, just to see if you have any foolish players in your game. But that has become sort of a futile thing to do. However, it's just about as good as playing the mathematical odds.

That's not all the story. In this mathematical analysis, we have assumed that you know absolutely nothing about distribution of the cards held by the opponents. This is almost never true, as they have bid something, or failed to bid, or played a card or two before you tackled spades in nearly all instances. Let us bring the scenario back to real life and see just what the mathematical chances are after you have seen a few cards. We will now assume that West led the king and ace of clubs, in that order, and that East discarded on the second club lead. West then led a heart, which East won with the ace. He returned the heart, and you are in the lead.

Now, you do know something about the hand—something very important. Of the five clubs, West started with four, and East with only one. The mathematical odds have undergone a dramatic change.

It is now essential that you win the first spade trick with dummy's king, keeping your tenace position over East, the player who had fewer clubs than his partner had. Would you believe that if either of your opponents is void in spades, it is four times as likely to be West as East? And that is not all. Let us say that both opponents follow with small cards and you have duly won the trick with dummy's king and have led a small spade toward your hand, with East following suit again. That moment of decision has come again. But the mathematical odds have changed. Now the odds favor the finesse 56 percent to 44 percent.

Let's see what general principles we can draw from this. When you get a precise count on the number of cards each of your opponents started with in a specific suit, you will also know the number of cards they started with in the other three suits combined. On the hand above, when you found that East started with one club, you knew he started with twelve cards in the other suits, while West, who started with four clubs, started with only nine cards in the other suits. In all cases, as in the one shown above, when there is a difference in the number of cards in the "other suits" held by your opponents and you reach the moment of decision, you should take a finesse through the hand which has the greater number of cards in the other suits; that means through the hand which had the smaller number of cards in the suit you have counted. The only exception is when you have found in the known suit that one of your opponents has exactly one more card than the other. This will only be when your opponents have an odd number of cards in the suit. In this situation, the odds become 50–50 on the finesse as compared with the drop, provided you can finesse through the hand which is short in the known suit. If you have to finesse through the hand which is long in the known suit, it is another story. Look at these two hands:

1. DUMMY	2. DUMMY
♠ 642	♠ 642
♡ KQ54	♡ A5
◇ AK5	◇ 74
♣ K53	♣ AJ7642
DECLARER	DECLARER
♠ Q105	♠ Q105
♡ A3	♡ K96
◇ 32	◇ AK63
♣ AJ7642	♣ K53

On both hands you have bid three no-trump. West has opened a small spade, and the defenders have cashed four spade tricks. West is known to have started with four spades, and East with three. With both hands you have to bring in the club suit without losing a trick. With hand 1, you lead the king and a small club; both follow to the king, and East follows small to the second club. I wish you good guessing. It is 50–50 whether you finesse or play for the drop.

With hand 2, you arrive at the same situation, but now the odds favor the play of the ace 56 to 44 percent.

Just to give you an idea how the odds change as one of your opponents' hands is shown to have considerably more cards than the other, I am attaching here another table for you.

Division of Opponents' Cards in a Given Suit	*Finesse (%)*	*Play for Drop (%)*
2–1	50.0	50.0
3–1	52.6	47.4
4–1	55.6	44.4
5–1	58.8	41.2
6–1	62.5	37.5
7–1	66.7	33.3

Of course, in these cases, the finesse is always taken through the hand that holds the singleton. This excludes the hands that divide 2–1 where the angels will have to take care of you. I hope you don't try to remember these numbers. I don't. All that is necessary is to remember the general principle. Some of the tables could easily be made up for other distributions where the short hand is void or where it has the doubleton, but the principle remains the same. If either the bidding or play or both have indicated to you that one of your opponents is long in a suit so that you, after seeing the dummy, know that his partner is short in that suit, try to take the first trick in the hand in front of the one that is short in the suit and then, when you lead again and the moment of decision arrives (because only small cards have been played), take the finesse.

Let's have a look at a different hand.

East overtakes the opening lead of the king of hearts with his ace and returns a small heart, which is won by West with the ten. West switches to a diamond, and you have a lead with one of the honors in your hand. In addition to the tricks already lost, there is a club trick to lose, and spades must be brought in without a loss.

Having graduated beyond the phase of always playing for the drop, you lead the seven of spades to the king and carefully keep a tenace over East. All signs are that West started with seven hearts and East with two. Assuming both players followed small when you played the king, you lead another spade, and now, if East also plays small, you have reached that moment of decision. Obviously, the finesse must be taken. Outside of the heart suit, East had eleven other cards, and West had only six other cards. It really isn't necessary to know the figures; however, for the curious, they are roughly 64 percent in favor of the finesse to 36 percent for the drop.

Fig. 5-107 Dlr: W Vul: 0

DUMMY
♠ K 8 6
♡ 4 2
◊ K 9 7 4
♣ K Q J 5

DECLARER
♠ A J 10 9 7 5
♡ 7 5
◊ A Q J 10
♣ 8

WEST	NORTH	EAST	SOUTH
3♡	Pass	Pass	3♠
Pass	4♠	All Pass	

Opening lead: ♡ K

Actually, you can be your own mathematician when you are trying to determine the whereabouts of the only card left for the opponents in a suit, and there is no reason why you shouldn't be. Let me show you how:

DUMMY
♠ K 7 3 2
♡ 7 4 3
◊ K 5 4
♣ A 4 2

DECLARER
♠ A J 6 5 4
♡ 8 6 2
◊ A Q 9
♣ K 6

It is a matter of determining how many cards each opponent has in suits where the distribution is *unknown.* To determine that, you have to know how many cards each opponent had in suits where the distribution was *known,* or, assumed to be *known.* To simplify matters, let me refer to cards in the suits where the distribution is not known as unknown cards. Let us say on this hand that West has cashed three heart tricks and that on the third one East had discarded a diamond. Now hearts are "known." West started with exactly five, and East with exactly two. The fact that East played a diamond on trick three tells us nothing about the diamond suit, except that he wasn't void in diamonds, and that fact is of no value. The diamond suit remains one of the unknown suits.

Obviously the only problem declarer now has is avoiding the loss of a spade trick. He would now lead a small spade toward dummy's king and then a spade back toward his ace. Let's say that West followed to the first spade, and East followed suit to the first and second leads. Now here is the gimmick: when there is only one card left outstanding in a suit, you can consider those which have been played as known cards. You now know that of the three small spades the opponents had, East had two and West had one. So, we know that of the known cards West had five hearts and one spade for a total of six. That leaves him with seven unknown cards. East had two hearts and two spades, leaving him nine unknown cards. At this point, the odds are 9 to 7 that East still has the queen, and so the finesse is definitely in order. That is a lot easier than breaking it down to percentages, but if you did so, you would find it is 56.25 percent to 43.75 percent that East has the queen of spades—or any other specific card that you wanted to mention, for that matter.

But now let's change the story a little bit. Let's say that West opened a heart, but East cashed the A K Q of hearts, and, on the third one, West showed out. Let East then lead the queen of clubs. Again, our only problem is to avoid losing a spade trick. We win the club, cash the spade king, and then lead one toward our hand. Again, West has followed to the first one, and East has followed to both. But now we have a quite different story. The known cards in the East hand are five hearts and two spades, coming to seven, leaving six unknown cards. In the West hand, the known cards are two hearts and one spade, leaving ten unknown cards. Now the chances are 10 to 6 that West has the last one outstanding—the queen—and the proper play is the ace. Again, if you want to change that to a percentage basis, it is 62.5 percent that West has the queen, against 37.5 percent that East has the queen. However, I recommend the 10 to 6 odds as being all that is really needed.

If it were as easy to figure all the odds as it is to figure the odds on one outstanding card, it would save all of us a lot of money. We wouldn't buy all of those books with all of those columns of figures in them. However, if you simply must know more about this in detail, I refer you to Appendix A, where there are a lot of figures on this subject.

Does what you learn about the distribution of the cards held by the opponents ever improve the odds of the drop as compared to the odds for the finesse? The answer is yes, but not a great deal. For example,

DUMMY
♠ Q 7 6
♡ 9 4
♢ K 6 2
♣ A J 7 6 2

DECLARER
♠ A K 4
♡ 8 6 2
♢ A Q 7
♣ K 10 9 5

After you opened the bidding at one no-trump, your partner jumped to three no-trump. Your opponents promptly led hearts. They always do. Some of these days, if you wait long enough, they might make a friendly opening lead like a club. But, then, you're not so unlucky after all, as they win four heart tricks and both follow suit four times.

They switch to a spade, and you have the lead. Now that you know that each opponent started with exactly four hearts and each had nine cards in the other suits, the odds in favor of playing for the drop in clubs have improved, but only slightly; they have gone up to approximately 53 to 47.

So much for the math. If you're playing in a tournament where the cards are dealt by computers, it will all hold true in the long run, but it may be a long, long run. The odds are so close that you will often be disappointed and find that when playing for the drop, the finesse would have been successful, and vice versa. However, if you will keep a record long enough, you will find that you come out slightly ahead by following the mathematical principles.

But, it is a different matter if the cards are "people" dealt, as a great majority of them are. Back as early as 1934, Ely Culbertson sensed that cards do not always follow the mathematical laws of probability. He attributed this to the imperfect shuffle of cards and, in his famous *Red Book on Play* published in that year, wrote quite a chapter on distribution and symmetry, in which he propounded his laws of symmetry. In it, he said, "The factor X—the artificially formed patterns and the imperfect shuffle—must be seriously reckoned with in calculation and forms the basis of the law of symmetry." He went so far as to say, "If a player holds a singleton king, it will happen much more often than probability warrants that another singleton king is in the offing." It is at least implicit in his writings on the subject that if you have a singleton in your hand or the dummy, you would be wise to expect a singleton in one of the hands held by your opponents.

The only way to verify Culbertson's intuitive feeling about this was to make a statistical study of a very large number of hands. Records of such hands were hard to come by, and, so far as I know, I made the first statistical study of any size in 1952. By that time, book records of matches were being published that contained a number of hands dealt in sequence, making them appropriate for a statistical study. There were 300 hands played by Mr. Culbertson and Mrs. Culbertson against Sidney Lenz and his partners available, along with some others, and altogether I made a study of 448 deals. This is not a great number, in view of the studies which have been made subsequently, but it was enough to be significant.

I came to the conclusion that Culbertson had great insight, but that he had not gone into the matter quite deeply enough. These statistics, I discovered, have particular relevance to the distribution of four cards known to be held by the opponents where we held nine cards in a given suit. Let us call our nine-card suit the critical suit. If, in another suit, we held the singleton in one of our hands, and if, in the companion hand, there were three cards or fewer, then there were considerably more 3–1 breaks of the opponents' four cards than could be justified mathematically. This increase of 3–1 breaks seemed to apply only when the cards held by the opponents totaled nine or more in a suit other than the critical suit. But here was the strangest part of all: when the opponents held nine cards in some suit other than the critical suit, leaving us with four, if the four which we had broke 2–2, then the four cards in the critical suit held by the opponents seemed also to break 2–2. On the other hand, if we held 3–1 or 4–0 in our four-card holding, then the opponents seemed to have more 3–1 or 4–0 distributions in the critical suit than could possibly be justified.

Let us call all hands where the shortest suit we have, outside the critical suit, is five cards long or where the shortest suit we have is four cards long and split 2–2 *balanced* hands. Let us call all hands where we have a four-card suit, which divided between us and the dummy is split 3–1 or 4–0, or where we have a suit with three cards or fewer *unbalanced* hands. Of course, we are talking in terms of twenty-six cards. Both our hand and dummy's hand can be extremely unbalanced, but the total of the two hands can be balanced. There have been many statistical studies made since 1952, and they have all come up with approximately the same conclusions. Wherever the hands are balanced (in the sense mentioned above) and where no other information is available, then the odds do, in fact, favor the drop over the finesse. Where, however, the hands are unbalanced (as described above), the odds favor the finesse anywhere from a low of 54 percent to a high of 60 percent. There is, very simply, no way to justify this mathematically; however, the mathematicians tell us that when statistical findings do not conform with probabilities, either the probability theory is incorrect or the items under consideration have not been randomly selected. The only answer that I can see is that a deck of cards has a pattern before it is shuffled and that some of this pattern remains when it is shuffled, so that cards which are shuffled by people never, or seldom, are distributed in a random manner.

I hope I have not overemphasized the importance of these mathematics. The odds are not all that great. These probabilities should only be used when you have nothing better to go on, and that does not occur too often. Let us look at a hand that tells us when and how to use these odds and when not to use them.

DUMMY
♠ 10 6
♡ A 5 3
♢ Q 10 7 4
♣ A 10 8 5

DECLARER
♠ Q J 3
♡ K 6
♢ A K 5
♣ K J 9 4 2

Against no adverse bidding, you reach a contract of three no-trump from the south hand, and the opening lead is the five of spades. Dummy plays small, East plays the nine, and you win the trick.

You are looking at somewhere between eight and twelve tricks. In addition to the spade trick you have won, you have an additional seven off the top. If clubs behave and diamonds as well, you will take five club tricks, four diamond tricks, two heart tricks, and the one spade trick.

How are the spades in the opponents' hands divided? Let's face it—we just don't know. It is likely that West has both the ace and king, but it is not certain. He could hold anywhere from four to seven of them. I believe, if I had to guess, he probably holds five headed by the ace and king, leaving three in the East hand. At any rate, I am not so interested in taking twelve tricks as I am taking nine before they can regain the lead. The odds are just too good that, if they can regain the lead, they can take enough tricks to set me. For just a moment, I am going to use my arithmetic and start on clubs. But I will carefully take the first club with dummy's ace and not with my king. If my guess is right—that West holds five or more spades—I know without knowing the numbers that the odds that clubs will break 4–0 have increased somewhat. In addition, I know that if either of my opponents should be void in clubs, with West having a long suit in spades, West is much more likely to have a club void than is East. Without bothering with the arithmetic, I protect myself against a 4–0 break with all of them in the East hand rather than the West. Let us say that nothing spectacular happens on the ace of clubs and that I then lead small toward my hand, and East plays small. Again, if my guess that West started with five or more spades is right, the odds on the club suit slightly favor a finesse, but I'm not going to take the finesse. Even though the odds might be 3–2 in favor of a finesse and even better if West had more spades, I still am going to play the king of clubs. I think that should I lose the lead at this point, the chances are good that I will go set before I regain the lead. And, if West shows out when I play the king of clubs, I still have the diamond suit to fall back on, and the odds are better than even that I can bring in four diamond tricks. So I am going to forget about the odds in the club suit alone and think about the hand as a whole, as though I never knew that the possession of a long spade suit by West would increase the odds in favor of a finesse against East in the club suit.

There are a number of circumstances where you should take the finesse, no matter what the odds are. Here is one of them:

DUMMY
♠ Q J 10 3 2
♡ A Q 7
◇ K 10 9 7 4
♣ —

DECLARER
♠ A K 9 4
♡ 9 3 2
◇ A J 8 6
♣ K 5

After you open one no-trump with the south hand, your partner decides to invoke the Stayman convention, and you arrive at a contract of six spades.

The opening lead is the queen of clubs. You trump it, lead a trump to your hand, and then lead the king of clubs, which you trump. You return to your hand with another trump, and both of your opponents follow suit. The time has come to consider the situation in the red suits. It happens that you are playing in a tournament with computer-dealt hands, and you expect them to follow the laws of probabilities, so you ignore the fact that you and dummy started with only two clubs. The only suit which you have really counted is the spade suit, and you know they have each started with two spades.

You win the next trick with the ace of diamonds, and both opponents follow with small diamonds. You lead a small diamond from your hand, and West plays small. The moment of decision has come.

You know that with computer-dealt hands, the original odds in favor of playing for the drop were 52 percent. You also know when each of your opponents started with two spades, these odds increased slightly. Forget it! The time has come to quit being a mathematician and be a bridge player. If you finesse, you can't lose! If the finesse holds, you can discard one of your hearts on dummy's long diamond and limit your loses to not more than one heart trick. If the finesse fails and East wins with the queen, he can't possibly have any diamonds left, and you know that he is out of spades. He will have to lead a heart or club because that is all he has. If he leads a club, you can discard a heart from your hand while you trump in the dummy, then you can discard a second heart on dummy's long diamond. Should he lead a heart, that obviously takes care of the situation as well.

It seems that no matter what way we twist and turn in studying play of the hand, we sooner or later come back to Blackwood's Rule 13, which takes precedence over all other rules—*theenk.*

SIMULTANEOUS PROMOTION AND ESTABLISHMENT

We have talked about promoting cards which are something less than high until they can take tricks. We have also talked about trying to establish small cards in a suit by exhausting the opponents of all of the cards they hold in that suit. Often you will be trying to do both of these things at the same time. Let me show you some examples.

Some of these situations have been well covered in the literature. Others have not received the attention they surely deserve. Let me show you first examples of those which have been well covered, in case you have overlooked any of them.

In a three no-trump contract (Fig. 5-108), you get the opening lead of the six of spades, and dummy's ten-spot holds the trick. This has given you three spade tricks for sure, plus three heart tricks. You need three others, and, obviously, the club suit offers a better chance than any other suit.

Fig. 5-108

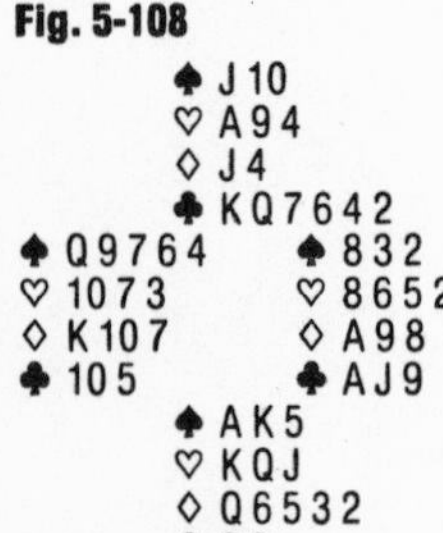

There is nothing wrong with coming to your hand with a small heart to lead a small club toward the dummy in case West has a singleton ace or decides to play it for his own reasons. When, however, he plays low, your proper play is to play a small club from the dummy.

Should you play the queen, East can simply let you hold the trick. Now, you're not going to get your three club tricks. Presumably, you will return to your hand with a second heart to lead a second club, and, when you play dummy's king, East will win it with the ace. He will have the high jack of clubs left. Your club suit will not be established, and, while you can get there with the ace of hearts to establish it, you then cannot get back to take your winners after it is established.

By playing low, you force East to take one of his tricks now. You will have a club left to lead to give him his second trick, and can keep the heart ace to get back to the established suit.

Fig. 5-109 is another classic situation.

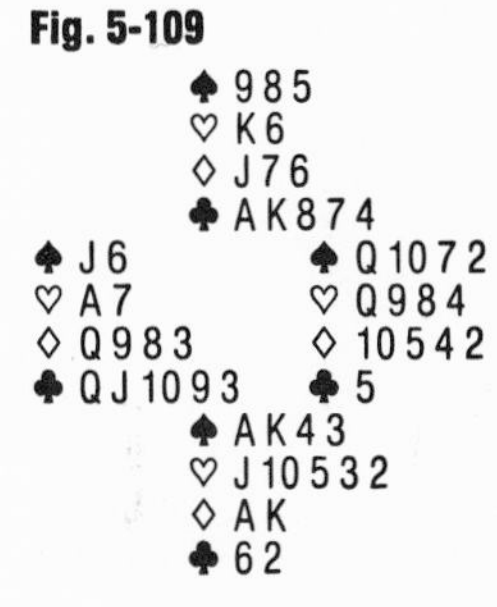

Fig. 5-109

Again, South was playing three no-trump. The opening lead was the queen of clubs. Three ace-king combinations were immediately available, making a total of six tricks and leaving three to be developed. The fact that West had led clubs reduced considerably prospects in that suit. Even had clubs not been led, hearts would have offered the best prospects. Declarer won in the dummy with the king and came to his hand with the ace of spades to lead a small heart. West played low, and dummy's king won. Declarer led back the six of hearts, and East played the eight-spot. Declarer had arrived at the Rubicon. If the six missing hearts were divided 3–3, it didn't make much difference what declarer played—he would lose exactly two heart tricks. However, if they divided 4–2, his only chance was to play low on the second heart trick. West would have no hearts left except the ace and would have to play it, leaving the jack-ten intact in his hand to knock out the queen and bring the total number of hearts won up to three.

Back in the 1930's, the situation in the next hand must have just been discovered, as it appeared in some of the literature about once a month. I haven't seen it for some time now, so here it is (Fig. 5-110).

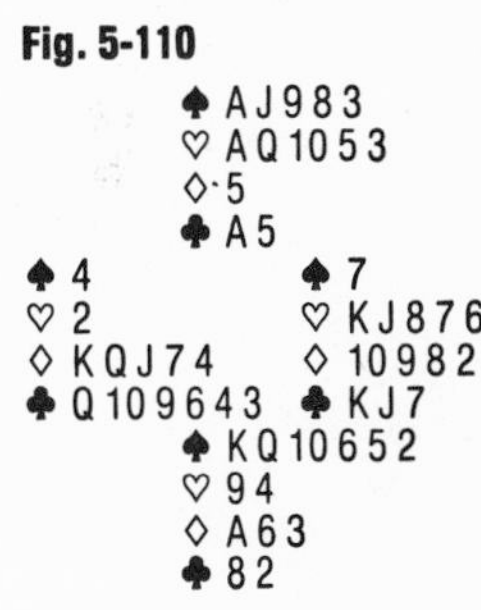

Fig. 5-110

The bidding is not given. The hand was published before the use of the unusual no-trump convention, but I suspect the bidding was pretty wild. The report I have is that the final contract was six spades by South, and he was fortunate enough to get an opening lead of the king of diamonds. A club lead would have caused him more problems.

He won with the ace and led the king of spades, which exhausted trumps in the hands of his opponents. He was now going to be able to discard a club on one of dummy's hearts no matter how the suit broke. He led small to the ace of hearts. Had East shown out, it would have been a simple matter to come back to the south hand and lead a second heart to establish them for a discard of a club. Had West shown out, declarer could have led small from the dummy toward his nine-spot. East could win this, but now he would have only one honor left, and dummy would sit with the queen and ten. By going to the dummy and leading the queen, he could force out the last honor East had, ruff it, and then return to the dummy to discard a club on the established heart. When both opponents followed small to the ace of hearts, the proper play was to return to the south hand and lead the nine. If West played an honor, the problem would obviously be solved. If West followed with a small card, declarer would simply let the nine ride. If East could win that trick, it would be established that hearts were going to break no worse than 4–2, and the fifth heart could finally be established for a discard. When, in fact, West showed out on the second heart lead, declarer let it ride, let East win, and again was able to establish one of dummy's intermediate hearts for a club discard.

It was the possession of the intermediate cards which made this play

Fig. 5-111

possible. Of the five hearts higher than the nine-spot, dummy held three. In addition, dummy's ten with declarer's nine made a nice little sequence.

On the next hand, the sequence was not immediately apparent, but it showed up after the lead of the ace of diamonds.

In a contract of six clubs, South got the opening lead of a spade. His possible losers were one in hearts and one in diamonds. His best chance was to handle the diamonds in such a manner that he could discard a heart on that suit, while losing not more than one diamond trick.

He won the ace of spades and exhausted the opponents' trumps by leading them twice. Now, while he did not have the magic holding in the diamond suit of the ten in one hand and the nine in another, the play of the ace at the first trick was still the proper play. However, when the ten fell from the East, the nine and eight he held were promoted to the magic holding, and he was going to make his contract no matter how the suit divided. He went to the dummy and led the nine of diamonds. When East showed out, he let it ride, and West had to play the jack to win the trick. Now declarer had the queen-eight with all cards in between missing. These were good enough to make West play his king, while declarer trumped and got the eight-spot established for the necessary heart discard.

Fig. 5-112

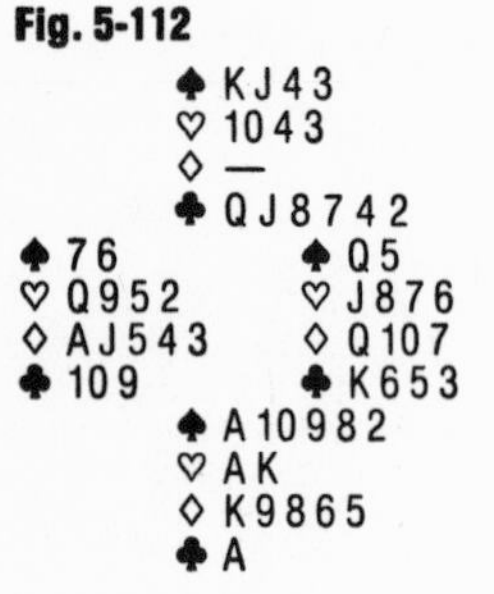

In the 1974 World Championship, Pietro Forquet of the famous Italian Blue Team had a chance to develop the intermediate cards in a long suit, while at the same time promoting the small cards (Fig. 5-112).

Forquet reached a contract of six spades. The opening lead was a trump, and that solved one of his problems immediately. At trick two he laid down the ace of clubs. The play of the nine by West showed him that he was on the right track in deciding to develop dummy's hand. He crossed to the dummy with the king of trumps and led the queen of clubs. East refused to cover, but Forquet discarded a small diamond anyway. He ended up taking all thirteen tricks.

Fig. 5-113

Jim Jacoby of the North American Team is the hero on Fig. 5-113.

This hand was played in the World Championship in 1971. The opening lead against the six spade contract was the king of clubs. Jacoby won with the ace and then led four rounds of trumps. This still left him with three trumps.

He was now faced with a probable loser in hearts and a possible loser in diamonds. Rather than trying to guess the diamond situation, he simply went to work on the hearts. He led the queen and let it ride. East won this with the king and returned a club. Jacoby trumped it, led a heart to dummy's ace, and a small heart back, which he trumped. This made all of the remaining three hearts in the dummy good, giving dummy more discards than he needed, and the ace of diamonds was there as an entry to the hearts.

This next hand (Fig. 5-114) is from England where they seem to deal some pretty wild hands at times.

It seems that South tried so hard to reach a slam that he finally got to the awkward contract of five spades. This turned out to be almost too high. But, declarer's knowledge of suit establishment saved the day for him.

The opening lead was the ten of clubs. When dummy's jack forced East's queen, declarer trumped. He then pulled trumps in three leads, and it became time to tackle the heart suit. He had seven hearts between himself and the dummy. If the opponents' six hearts broke 3–3, he could get by with losing only two hearts. This was against the odds, but the little sequence of the 9 8 7 gave him hope that there was another distribution which would prove favorable. If either opponent held the king and only one small card, declarer could limit his heart losses to one by playing a small heart. If either opponent held the jack or ten with only one small card, declarer could accomplish the same thing by leading first the ace and then the queen. As it was twice as likely that an opponent held either the jack or ten doubleton as it was for one to hold the king doubleton, declarer decided to go for the former play. He led the ace of hearts and then the queen. He did find the expected 4–2 distribution, and his luck held when East played the ten. Now he could get the heart suit established with a loss of only one more trick.

On the following hand, at first glance declarer thought he saw only eight tricks with reasonably good breaks. On a closer look, he saw that with a little luck, he could bring in the nine needed.

With his 21 high-card points, South got to a contract of three notrump, and West led the ten of spades. Even with clubs breaking normally, declarer could see only four club tricks plus two in each of the major suits without letting the opponents lead often enough to cash whatever tricks they had in spades. Since they held nine spades, it was certain that one of them held five or more. So they could get three spade tricks, and, if they also got a club and a diamond, that would be one too many. But declarer looked a little deeper. He won the spade trick and deferred playing clubs. Instead, he led a small diamond.

Yes, if East held the ace of diamonds, things were not going to turn out too well. South must have been a good boy for some time, for Lady Luck had placed the ace three times in the West hand. If West went up with the ace of diamonds, then South could take four diamond tricks. These would bring his total to nine, with only one club trick. West knew something about bridge, too, so he did not play the ace. Now when the king of diamonds won the trick, declarer promptly reverted to clubs. Clubs broke well, and he got his four club tricks to go with two spades, two hearts, and one diamond, for a total of nine.

On the next hand (Fig. 5-116), West painted an accurate picture of his hand in the bidding process. The trouble was, this accurate picture helped South as declarer choose the right line of play. Maybe it is not wise to paint an accurate picture of your hand when you only hold two queens and a jack.

The declarer had no trouble at all deciding that the jack of hearts was a singleton. To avoid going set at once, it was necessary to win this trick with dummy's ace. Now the simple way to play the hand would be to try to ruff a diamond in the dummy. If this could be accomplished, trumps could be pulled, the heart could finally be given to the opponent's king, and that would be the end of that. But with West advertising some ten or eleven cards in the minor suits, declarer decided that the attempt to trump a diamond wasn't safe and he'd better look for a different way to take twelve tricks, even if it were a bit more complicated. It took a little study, but the answer was there waiting for him. He won that trick with the ace and was not surprised when he had to lead four rounds of trumps to clear the suit. Now his situation was that he would give the queen of hearts to the king held by the opponent, and his ten of hearts would then take a trick. He had plenty of entries to go to the board and lead a small heart and trump it. As this was the fourth heart that had been led, East was now out of hearts. There was still an entry to the board to cash the fifth heart on which the seven of diamonds was discarded.

The game of bridge is made fascinating by the fact that a hand that seems to follow a certain theme sometimes has a different twist. For example, South guessed on the following hand that West's lead of the ten of diamonds was a singleton, but the hand required a different treatment from the preceding one.

Fig. 5-117

West got in his overcall of one spade, but that did not keep North and South from reaching a normal contract of four hearts.

South did not really care whether or not the lead of the diamond ten was a singleton—he was willing, in any event, to lose two diamond tricks, provided he didn't lose a spade trick. If West had somehow opened from a doubleton diamond, declarer was going to limit his losses to one diamond trick, and he was going to lose it right now. He simply let the diamond hold the trick. If he had two to lose, he wanted to lose them at his own convenience. As you will see, had declarer played the queen, East would still have held two diamond tricks. Worse than that, the diamond suit could not have been established in time to discard a spade before East regained the lead and could lead spades.

West was a little surprised to win the trick with his singleton ten, but knew he couldn't lead spades, so he led a trump. Declarer won that, pulled a second round of trumps, and led his ace of diamonds. This cut East down to the singleton king, and declarer led another diamond, giving him that trick. East returned a spade, but declarer didn't go for the finesse. He rose with the ace, crossed to the dummy with a diamond, and discarded his queen of spades on the fifth diamond. He ended up losing one club trick and two diamond tricks, but he didn't lose any spade tricks at all.

Fig. 5-118

	North	
	♠ A 10 ♡ K Q 4 ◇ Q 6 5 4 3 2 ♣ 10 4	
♠ 8 6 3 ♡ J 10 9 6 ◇ K 10 9 7 ♣ 9 8		♠ K 7 5 4 2 ♡ 8 5 3 2 ◇ — ♣ 6 5 3 2
	♠ Q J 9 ♡ A 7 ◇ A J 8 ♣ A K Q J 7	

On the next hand (Fig. 5-118), declarer had a choice: he could curse his luck, or he could make six no-trump.

South opened the bidding with two no-trump, and North promptly took him to six no-trump. The opening lead was the jack of hearts. Declarer won that in the dummy so that he could take a diamond finesse. If East followed suit to the diamond lead, South could claim twelve tricks. If the finesse lost, there would still be five diamond tricks for the taking, as West could not have more than three of them after East followed suit. Should the finesse win and West show out, South would have two diamond tricks in the bag to add to his five sure club tricks and his three sure heart tricks. Two spade tricks would bring his total to twelve, and he could get that simply by finessing spades, whether the spade finesse won or lost. But East didn't follow to the diamond, and now declarer had a different problem.

Let us hope that after his feeling of dismay when he got this terrible break he pulled himself together and found that twelve tricks were still a cinch, provided he did not take the finesse. He should rise with the ace and then lead a small diamond toward the dummy. If West took that, there would still be five diamond tricks for the declarer. If West did not take it, the queen of diamonds would win, and, again, declarer would have two diamond tricks and would only have to come to his hand and take the spade finesse to total twelve tricks. Even if the finesse lost, East would not have a diamond to return to his partner's king.

Burt Marks is the lawyer who pled the case when the California Supreme Court ruled that bridge is a game of skill and not a game of chance. Alfred Sheinwold reports this hand which Marks played and which could well be used to prove his point.

Fig. 5-119

In the contract of four hearts, Marks got an opening lead of a small trump. He had a spade loser, which could easily be disposed of on the ace of diamonds, but what was he going to do with all those clubs? If the opponents hadn't led trumps, he could have given them two clubs and then trumped at least one. But it looked like they would lead hearts every time they got the chance, and in the rather likely event that either of them had three trumps, he was never going to get to trump a club. So, he decided to parlay his chances and play both minor suits at once.

He won the opening lead in his hand, led the king of diamonds, and then a small club. West won that, but there was nothing he could do. Marks figured that if West had started with only two hearts and led one of this point, that would take all of the hearts out of the opponents' hands, and he would get to trump his club after all. If West held all of the remaining hearts, the nine of hearts would provide an extra entry into the dummy. He could use that to cash the ace of diamonds and then trump a diamond. The ace of trumps would be the entry to the dummy to trump the fourth diamond, and the ace of spades would be there so the fifth diamond would take a trick.

On the other hand, if West led a spade at trick three, Marks would put up dummy's ace, discard a spade on the ace of diamonds, and then lead a second club. Nothing could then keep him from trumping a club, which is all he needed for his tenth trick.

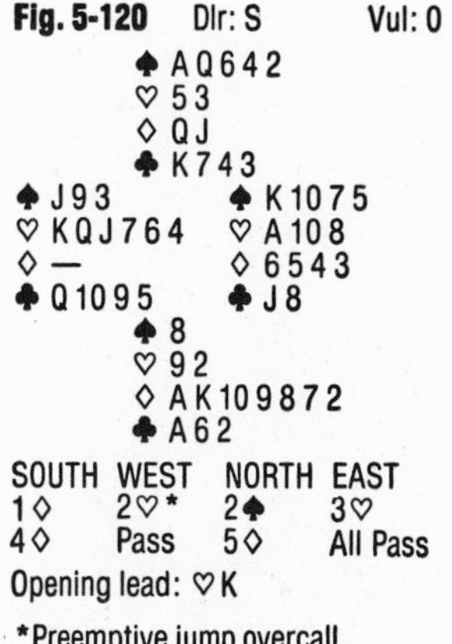

Fig. 5-120

On the next hand (Fig. 5-120), declarer had to decide whether to take a finesse or play for the establishment of a suit where he was missing seven cards.

West cashed two heart tricks and switched to a small spade. There was a club loser to be disposed of, one way or the other, and this could be done by a successful finesse of the queen of spades or by finding the spades distributed 4-3 between the opponents. There were just enough entries in the dummy to get the fifth spade established and get back to the dummy to use it for a discard. As the 4–3 break is a better chance than a finesse, declarer rose with the ace of spades and promptly led a small spade and trumped it. He went back to the dummy with a trump and led a third spade, trumping it. He again crossed with a trump, led a fourth spade, and trumped it. This exhausted the opponents' spades, but left declarer with one. He pulled East's last trumps and then used dummy's king of clubs to enter the dummy, cash the fifth spade, and discard his losing club.

Someone is going to say to me, "But you said the odds are different when the distribution of one suit was known. On this bidding, it seems obvious that West has long hearts, and doesn't that change the probabilities of a 4–3 split?" Well, it doesn't exactly change the odds, but, if we assume that West was dealt six hearts and East three, then the probabilities that the spades will split 4–3 are only 59 percent instead of 62 percent. On that same basis, the odds on finding the spade king in West are only 41 percent. Ignoring any chance that West started with the king doubleton of spades, the best play is still to go for the 4–3 split.

But suppose the finesse, if taken, had to be taken the other way?

DUMMY
♠ A Q 6 4 2
♡ 5 3
♢ Q J 5 4
♣ 4 3

DECLARER
♣ 8
♡ 9 4 2
♢ A K 10 9 8 7 2
♣ A Q

On the same bidding, suppose West opened the king of hearts and continued the suit. This time East overtook the second trick with the ace and led back a small club. Now what about the odds? Again, assuming the action taken by the defenders had told us nothing about the distribution of any suit except hearts but that it has told us the hearts are split 6–2, then the odds for a 4–3 break are nearly the same as the odds that the finesse will work, and the difference is not worth mentioning. Leaving out the psychology of the situation, the better play is still to go up with the ace of clubs because the additional small chance is that the king of spades will fall out while you are in the process of ruffing spades. But, I think the best thing to do is to quit being a mathematician and become a psychologist. Has your friend East thrown you a curve ball or a straight ball? Has he put the heat on you by underleading the king of clubs because he knows that spades will break unfavorably for you? If you can solve questions like that, you don't need too much arithmetic anyway.

Let's take the queen of spades out of the north hand and get the problem down to a simple one of the probabilities that the finesse will succeed, as compared with the probabilities that the spades will break 4–3.

Here is what we will have:

DUMMY
♠ A 6 4 3 2
♡ 5 3
◊ Q J 6 4
♣ 4 3

DECLARER
♠ 8
♡ 7 4 2
◊ A K 10 9 8 7 2
♣ A Q

Let us assume that the bidding and play made by the opponents have guaranteed that their eight cards in hearts were dealt six to West and two to East, but have given no information whatsoever concerning the location of the king of clubs. Now the arithmetic is that the finesse will succeed 61 percent of the time, while a 4–3 break will materialize only slightly over 54 percent of the time. Are we going to take the finesse or not? In my opinion, this is what bridge players mean when they say they would have to be "at the table" to make a decision. It is not mathematical, but I, and many others, would consider some factors which have nothing to do with arithmetic. Who is East? Is he the sort of player who likes to keep you under constant pressure when he is defending? Is he alert at the moment so he would see the danger of the five-card spade suit in the dummy with four trumps to use as entries? And, before I came to a decision, I would go so far as to consider whether the last several hands had been breaking normally or whether there had been wilder than usual distribution.

Let's see what general principles we can learn concerning the discovery that one of our opponents has considerably more cards in a given suit or suits than has the other. For purposes of illustration, let's consider the last hand where we had reason to believe that West had started with six hearts and East with only two.

Contrary to an opinion many people hold, the odds have not changed as a result of this discovery. The odds were established once the hand was dealt. What has changed is our knowledge of what was dealt in the first place.

With West's having been dealt only seven cards that we don't know about and East's having been dealt eleven, the odds are, and have been, 11 to 7 that any specific given card will be with East. This applies to the king of clubs, as well as any other cards, and means that the way the cards were dealt, the odds are 61 percent that the club finesse will work. These have been the odds from the beginning, the only new thing is that we have just discovered something about how the cards were dealt at the beginning.

This assumed knowledge about the split of the heart suit has also enhanced our knowledge about the probable distribution of all other suits. Whatever number of cards they hold in any other suit, the odds in favor of the most even possible distribution are not as high as the books tell us they should be. Where they have seven cards, as in the spade suit, the probabilities of a 4–3 split are less than we have been told. If there is a suit where they hold only four cards, the probabilities of a 2–2 split are not as great as those shown in the tables we are used to looking at, with, of course, the longer segment being more likely to appear in the hand with one heart than in the hand with six hearts.

If there is a lesson to learn from this study, I believe it is this: where the odds are reasonably even, don't count too much on arithmetic. Try to find some other clue in the bidding and play and use this arithmetic only as a last resort.

ENTRY PROBLEMS IN SUIT ESTABLISHMENT

Sometimes getting the suit established is not as difficult as finding an entry to get there once it is established. Let's take a look at some of these hands where the main problem seems to be the entry problem.

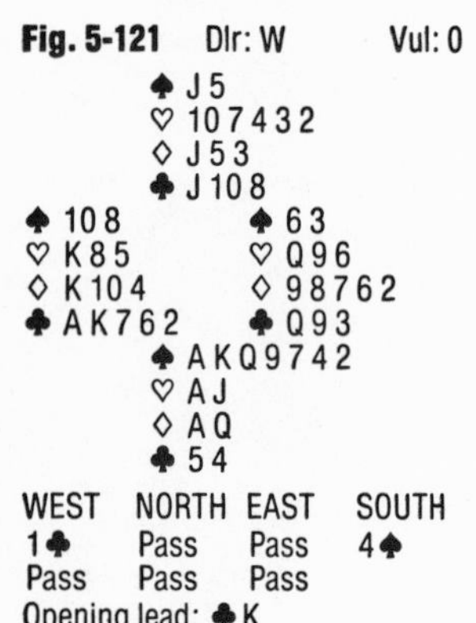

Fig. 5-121 Dlr: W Vul: 0

North: ♠ J 5 ♡ 10 7 4 3 2 ♢ J 5 3 ♣ J 10 8
West: ♠ 10 8 ♡ K 8 5 ♢ K 10 4 ♣ A K 7 6 2
East: ♠ 6 3 ♡ Q 9 6 ♢ 9 8 7 6 2 ♣ Q 9 3
South: ♠ A K Q 9 7 4 2 ♡ A J ♢ A Q ♣ 5 4

WEST	NORTH	EAST	SOUTH
1♣	Pass	Pass	4♠
Pass	Pass	Pass	

Opening lead: ♣K

West opened the king of clubs and continued the suit when East played the nine followed by the three. Declarer trumped the third round. There was one lone entry in the dummy. Declarer could get there to take a diamond finesse, and, if the finesse lost, the jack of diamonds in the dummy could be used to discard a losing heart, provided declarer could get back to the dummy. He didn't just quite see how he could get there twice. The diamond finesse didn't look too good anyway, since East had passed West's opening bid.

Declarer decided that he was very fortunate that his defenders did not lead a major suit which might have caused him more difficulty. He decided to take as little chance as possible, and so, after trumping the third club, he didn't lead trumps. He wanted to preserve that entry in the north hand until it could be useful. Neither did he lead the ace of diamonds. To be as safe as possible he led the queen of diamonds.

West won with the king and, after thinking it over, decided to lead a trump. South won in his hand, cashed the ace of diamonds, and then led a small trump to the entry he had carefully preserved in the dummy. When both opponents followed suit to the second round of trumps, it made no difference how diamonds were divided. On the jack of diamonds he was able to discard his jack of hearts.

On the next hand (Fig. 5-122), you would have to look a little harder to see the entry into the north hand, but it is there.

Fig. 5-122

North: ♠ Q 4 ♡ 10 8 7 2 ♢ 7 5 4 3 2 ♣ A 5
West: ♠ J 10 9 8 6 5 ♡ 3 ♢ Q 8 ♣ K 8 7 3
East: ♠ 3 2 ♡ 6 5 4 ♢ K J 10 9 ♣ J 10 9 4
South: ♠ A K 7 ♡ A K Q J 9 ♢ A 6 ♣ Q 6 2

West made a weak jump overcall of two spades, but that didn't keep South from getting to six hearts. West led the jack of spades, the dummy went down, and declarer took a good look at his combined assets. It looked like he had to lose a diamond trick no matter what he did, and, in addition, he had to do something about his club suit. No matter how many times he counted his quick winners, he came up with only ten, leaving him needing two more. These had to be won while losing no more than one trick.

If diamonds would only break 3–3, two of the losing clubs could be discarded on that suit, provided there were enough entries to the dummy to get there after three diamond leads. That seemed to pose no problem—leading the ace and another diamond from South would be two diamond leads, and declarer could leave the queen of spades in North to have another entry, together with the ace of clubs. But, suppose the diamond suit had taken the more normal break of 4–2; now there could be only one discard on the diamond suit. Furthermore, diamonds would have to be led five times, and just how was declarer going to get into dummy often enough to achieve that? He saw a way, provided that all four trumps were not in one hand. He won the opening spade lead in his own hand with the ace and led three trumps. So far things were going along just fine. Next he led the ace and one diamond. East won that and led the jack of clubs. The play went jack, queen, king, ace. Declarer was off and running. He led the third diamond from the dummy and trumped it. He went back to the dummy with the carefully preserved queen of spades to lead the fourth diamond, and he trumped it with his last trump. At the same time, he exhausted East of diamonds. Now he led his top spade and discarded a club from the dummy on it. A club was led and trumped with dummy's last trump. On the good seven of diamonds, declarer discarded his club. Altogether he won three spade tricks, six heart tricks, two diamond tricks, and one club trick, losing in the process only one diamond trick.

On the next hand, declarer had to look very hard to find the needed entries into the dummy's hand.

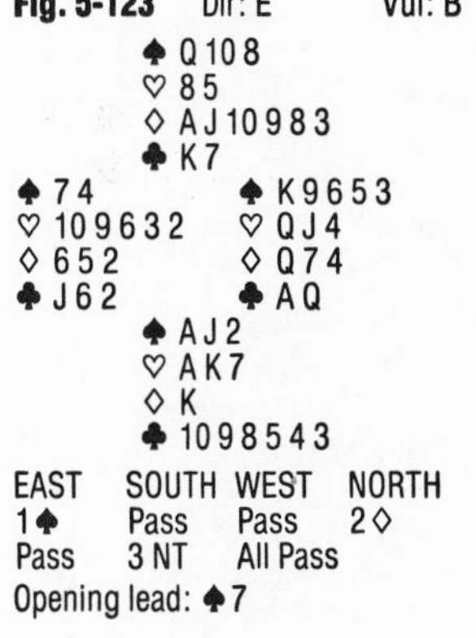

West led the seven of spades, which was covered by dummy's eight-spot. East was not willing to relinquish control at this point and played the nine, making it possible for South to win a cheap trick with his jack. But South had to look beyond this trick. Somehow he had to win nine, if he was going to fulfill his contract, and he certainly could see no way to get these unless he could bring in the diamond suit. He had no trouble deciding that East had the king of spades, and he saw that if he wanted to use the spades as a way to get to the north hand, he had to get rid of that ace.

Even after he played the ace of spades at trick one, he was not out of the woods. He had a delayed entry to the dummy, but he didn't think the king of clubs would turn out to be an entry. Of course, the fact that East bid did not prove he had the ace of clubs—players have been known to open without the ace of clubs; but, in this case, it seemed more likely that he had it. South was looking at 15 high-card points in his own hand and 10 in the dummy, for a total of 25; that left only 15 for the opponents. If East had opened the bidding without the ace of clubs, he had opened the hand with only 11 high-card points, and a look at dummy's and declarer's hands showed that he had opened it on a pretty bad suit besides. So, declarer decided not to count on using the king of clubs to reach the north hand. Still, he needed an entry not only to get to diamonds and get rid of the queen which was obviously held by one of the opponents, but to reenter the dummy after the queen had been played. Of course, it would be very nice if the queen were doubleton, but declarer thought he had a better chance.

So, after winning the first trick with the ace of spades, he led the king of diamonds and overtook it with dummy's ace. Now all he had to do was continue leading diamonds until the queen was played and then give up a spade trick to ensure an entry. He would be assured of five diamond tricks, two heart tricks, and two spade tricks. That gave him nine tricks. In addition, East was going to have to be mighty careful not to wind up in the lead with nothing left but clubs.

Fig. 5-124

```
          ♠ 6 5 4 2
          ♡ A K 8 6
          ◇ 10 2
          ♣ 6 3 2
♠ Q J 10 9          ♠ 8 7
♡ 9 4 2             ♡ J 10 7 3
◇ A J 9 6           ◇ 8 7 5
♣ 10 8              ♣ K J 9 4
          ♠ A K 3
          ♡ Q 5
          ◇ K Q 4 3
          ♣ A Q 7 5
```

When a hand (Fig. 5-124) doesn't have as many entries as you need, you have to decide what you are going to do with the ones you do have.

Against three no-trump, West opened the queen of spades, and declarer thought he needed to lead both diamonds and clubs from the dummy.

Unless he wanted to overtake the queen of hearts, he didn't have two entries to the dummy. He wasn't rich enough in tricks to give up his third heart trick. As a matter of fact, he saw that in spite of his 27 high-card points, he was going to have to be pretty lucky to take nine tricks.

After looking it over carefully, he saw a way to take two diamond tricks if the cards were right for him, so he decided to reserve the one entry in the dummy for the club finesse. He let the queen of spades hold the trick. When West persisted in spades and East followed suit, declarer saw that there would be only two spade losers, even if West gained the lead two times. Now all he needed was to find the jack of diamonds in the West hand. If West held that card, declarer was going to take two diamond tricks, no matter who had the ace.

After winning the second trick with the king of spades, he led a small diamond toward dummy's ten-spot. So that neither South nor you would be disappointed, I have arranged the key card in West's hand so that South's scheme works. With the jack of diamonds in west and the king of clubs with East, declarer winds up with two spades, three hearts, two diamonds, and two clubs. West had to be happy with only two spade tricks and two diamond tricks.

On the next hand, the opening lead knocked out the chief entry the declarer had for his suit, and so he had to find his entry in that suit itself.

Fig. 5-125

```
          ♠ A 5
          ♡ K 9 7
          ◇ 6 4 3
          ♣ A Q 7 4 3
♠ K J 7             ♠ 10 9 6 4
♡ Q J 10 8 6        ♡ 5 4 3 2
◇ K 8 7             ◇ 5
♣ 9 6               ♣ K J 10 8
          ♠ Q 8 3 2
          ♡ A
          ◇ A Q J 10 9 2
          ♣ 5 2
```

Declarer found himself in a contract of three no-trump with an opening lead of the queen of hearts. Obviously, the diamond suit with nine cards, including five of the six highest, offered better prospects for development than the club suit, with only seven cards and two of the top ones.

Declarer could get to the dummy with the two black aces to finesse the diamonds, but he had every reason to fear that, should West hold the king of diamonds three times, he would not win the first trick, and then declarer didn't know what would happen to the two black suits with the aces gone out of both of them. You can see from the whole layout that it would not have been good.

How about laying down the ace and then the queen of diamonds? That would be fine if either player held the king doubleton or singleton, but if either opponent held the king three times, the declarer might find that he would win a total of two diamond tricks from his beautiful suit.

He found a way which would guarantee his contract, unless one of his opponents held all four diamonds. Outside of the diamond suit, he had exactly four tricks off the top. He needed five diamond tricks. At trick two, he led the queen of diamonds. If West won his king, everything was under control. If he did not win the king, declarer would lead the jack of diamonds, still offering the king to West, while there was a diamond left in the dummy. Of course, if West did not take the king now, declarer would lay down the ace and win six diamond tricks. Whenever West did take his king, South would still have five diamond tricks to add to the four tricks he had in the other three suits.

I like what Freddie Sheinwold says about the way South played the next hand. Sheinwold says that if South's play had been as accurate as his mathematics, he would have had nothing to apologize for.

Fig. 5-126

South reached a contract of six spades and got an opening lead of the jack of hearts. Declarer won this and led five rounds of trumps, hoping someone might discard a club. Nobody did, so he next cashed the king of diamonds, led a club to the ace of clubs, cashed the ace of diamonds, and returned a club. West took two club tricks, and that was it.

Declarer pointed out that had the clubs split 2–2, or had West had either the singleton king or the singleton queen, the hand would have been made, and he quoted the mathematical odds that one of these good things would happen. It was this explanation that occasioned the comment made by Sheinwold.

Declarer should have tried out the diamonds to see whether the opposing diamonds would break 4–3, in which case he could discard one of his clubs on the ace of diamonds, and another on the fifth diamond and lose only one club trick. The trouble was that there seemed to be a shortage of entries for this play. Had South been a little more resourceful, he could have found enough.

At trick two, he should have cashed the king of diamonds and gone to the dummy with the ten of spades. He could then lead the ace of diamonds. If East could trump this, declarer could overruff and still have his club play to fall back on. The only risk was that West could trump it. That risk was small indeed, so he should have discarded a club on the ace of diamonds. Next he would lead a small diamond and trump it, and as soon as the opponents followed suit, there would be only one diamond outstanding. He still would have to get to dummy twice—once to establish the fifth diamond and once to cash it. He could get there once by trumping his good queen of hearts, then he could trump one more diamond, and finally pull trumps. He still would have the ace of clubs as his final entry to the dummy, and, once there, he would discard another club on the good small diamond. This would leave him with only one club, but that was the only loser in the hand.

Fig. 5-127

You well may have seen the next hand (Fig. 5-127) before. It has been published in a number of places. It is a good one and deserves repeating.

I don't know what bidding was originally given with the hand, but the above seems to me to be reasonable. The opening bid by West warned South that all finesses were likely to fail. As he was automatically off a club trick, he somehow had to get rid of no fewer than four diamonds from his own hand. In the dummy were three discards on clubs and one on a heart, but how in the world was declarer going to reach the dummy?

The key to the hand is that he does not play his ace on the opening lead of the king of hearts. He leaves it in the dummy as one of his potential entries. Instead, he simply trumps the first heart, and then leads three rounds of trumps, discarding a small heart on the third one. Next he leads the king of clubs. Whether West takes that club trick or the following one, he is going to have to lead something that will give the lead to the dummy. Had the ace of hearts not remained in the dummy, West could have waited and taken the second club and then gotten off the hook with a lead of the the queen.

Mr. Johannes Brun of Norway was a co-founder of the European Bridge League. He played the following hand in 1933. To a bridge player, a beautifully played hand is an artistic masterpiece and deserves to live forever. I trust I may add to the longevity of this hand.

Fig. 5-128

Mr. Brun had arrived at a four heart contract from the south position. West led the king of diamonds and then shifted to a trump. East won with the ace of hearts and led a second heart, which was won in dummy with the queeen.

Mr. Brun had lost two tricks and had five bad diamonds to dispose of. Three of these could go on the top spades and top clubs in the dummy, but that would still leave him two losing diamonds. If he tried to establish the long clubs for a discard, he would have no way to reach the dummy once he got them established. The best he could hope for in the spade suit was a 4–4 break, but where were the entries to come from to get back and cash the fifth spade?

Mr. Brun found a way. On the ace and king of spades, he discarded two of the offending diamonds, leaving him only three. He led the third spade and trumped it. Then he led a trump to exhaust East of trumps. He went back to dummy by leading his singleton to dummy's king of clubs and led a fourth spade. When East played the queen, Mr. Brun did not trump it, but discarded one of the offending diamonds. This left East in the lead with nothing but clubs, and his club lead provided the entry to the dummy which Mr. Brun needed. On the club, Mr. Brun discarded his next to last diamond, and, on dummy's fifth spade, he discarded the final diamond. He thus held his losses to one trump, one diamond, and the one spade trick he gave to East when he turned the lead over to him.

When you can't find a sure way to force an entry into a hand that has the tricks, there is nothing left but hope that the cards are distributed to suit you.

Fig. 5-129

In Fig. 5-129, South had no trouble getting to three no-trump—he just dealt and bid three no-trump. The trouble he had was finding a way to take nine tricks, even after receiving the friendly lead of the four of spades. Dummy played the seven; East played the queen; and South won with the king. He looked as hard as he could, but could only find seven additional tricks which he could take. There were four more in the dummy if he could find a way to get to them.

As usual, I started this section with some simple, illustrative hands, and have now arrived at some pretty exotic situations. As usual, I want my story to have a happy ending. So, let's let South win his three diamonds and two clubs and then lead the ace and king of hearts and a small spade.

West can win three spade tricks and one heart trick, but after that he is going to have only one card left, and that will be the eight of clubs. Of course, South is a very clever fellow who noticed that West couldn't have any diamonds after he had followed to three diamond leads, and he carefully saved the queen of clubs in the dummy for the ninth trick.

HINTS OF THINGS TO COME—THE SQUEEZE PLAY

Throughout this discussion of establishing small cards in long suits, I have said that under some circumstances these small cards cannot be established if the opponents will hang on to the cards they have in that suit, or words to that effect.

I am well aware of the fact that there are times when the opponents cannot hold on to all of the cards they have in the critical suits.

Here is a simple example. Let us say that South is playing in some number of no-trump. In both clubs and diamonds, he has a seven-card holding, but if East can hold on to all four cards in both suits, the two-spots will never take tricks. The trouble is that after declarer takes the A K Q of spades and the A K Q of hearts, there will be only seven cards left in each hand. This will make it impossible for East to hold all of his clubs and diamonds because he has eight cards in those two suits. The two-spot the declarer holds will become good in whichever of those two suits East makes a fourth discard.

Fig. 5-130

I find it necessary to mention this subject here because there are times when one side or the other has to discard, allowing the other side to establish small cards in long suits. However, this subject properly belongs under the heading of "squeeze plays." All squeeze plays are based on variations and elaborations of this same theme. We have to postpone until the proper time a detailed discussion of these variations and elaborations.

TRUMPS can do a lot of things for you which could not be done if you did not have trumps. That is why you get the same bonus for taking nine tricks without trumps that is awarded if you take ten tricks with a major suit as trumps, or even eleven tricks, if trump happens to be a minor suit. Among other things, trumps can prevent the high cards held by your opponents from taking tricks. One look at the old Duke of Cumberland hand is worth a thousand words in making this clear, so let's take a look at Fig. 6-1.

Fig. 6-1

	North	
	♠ 9 8 5 2 ♡ 10 4 3 2 ◇ — ♣ 6 5 4 3 2	
West ♠ 10 7 6 4 3 ♡ J 9 8 7 6 5 ◇ J 10 ♣ —		**East** ♠ A K Q J ♡ A K Q ◇ A K Q ♣ K J 9
	♠ — ♡ — ◇ 9 8 7 6 5 4 3 2 ♣ A Q 10 8 7	

I have seen several versions of this hand, but this one will do. Apparently it was already old when it was first published in a book by Edmond Hoyle in 1750.

The Duke was a "patsy." He bet on the other man's game. The story is that he made a wager of 20,000 pounds that, holding the East hand, he would take at least one trick with clubs as trumps. Of course, in spite of his 32 high-card points as opposed to the 8 held by his combined opponents, he took nary a trick. The *Official Encyclopedia of Bridge* assures us that the 20,000 pounds at the time the good Duke lived is the equivalent of $750,000 today.

No matter what the opening lead was, declarer could establish diamonds by trumping three in the dummy and could take advantage of his opportunities to lead clubs and take finesses from the dummy.

But trumps are not always a blessing. The opponents have the opening lead and there are times when they can get a crossruff established before you can even gain the lead and take enough tricks to set you before you have a chance. Not only that, if they have too many trumps, or even if their trumps are bunched in one hand, they can bring you to grief. An example of this is the famous Mississippi heart hand, on which it is claimed Charles M. Schwab lost a bet of $10,000. Let's take a look at Fig. 6-2.

Fig. 6-2

According to the story, the sharpsters would bet South that with hearts as trumps, they would take more tricks than he would take. South would take tricks with each of his six trumps, but that was all. West opened a diamond, of course, and when South trumped, already had two more trumps than South had. Whenever South led a black card, West simply trumped it and led another diamond. Of course, declarer couldn't take all of West's hearts away from him, and, if he tried that, he would take whatever heart tricks he could and every card in West's hand would be good.

So let's try to take a good look at some of the things that trumps can do for—and to—us.

WHEN TO LEAD TRUMPS

A story is told of a successful bridge player who saw two former members of his bridge club begging for enough to buy a cup of coffee. He stopped to ask them what had happened to bring them to this predicament.

"I never learned to lead trumps," said the first.

The successful bridge player then asked the second beggar what happened to him.

"I always led trumps," he replied.

So, to be successful and maintain our memberships, I suppose what we need to learn is *when* to lead trumps.

The situation where trumps must be led is the more obvious one, so let's study it first.

It is obvious that you would like to take away from them any small trumps your opponents might hold, lest they manage to take tricks with them by trumping some of your high cards. So, we well might say that you lead trumps except on those hands where trumps have more important duties to perform and you cannot spare your own trumps which would be lost by the process of leading them. These exceptions are not all that rare, but at the moment we are looking at those cases where you should lead trumps at once.

DUMMY	DUMMY
♠ J 5	♠ 8 4 3
♡ Q 6 3	♡ 9 6
◊ K J 10 6 5	◊ 7 5 4
♣ 7 6 2	♣ A K Q 6 2
DECLARER	DECLARER
♠ A K Q 10 4 2	♠ A K Q J 10
♡ A K 5	♡ A Q 10
◊ 7 4 3	◊ A K 2
♣ 8	♣ 5 4

In the first hand, you are in a contract of four spades, and the opening lead is the jack of hearts. East follows suit, and you win that trick with a high heart. You can afford to lose one trick in clubs and two in diamonds and still make your contract, but you cannot afford to let your opponents trump anything. Be thankful they did not lead a club, which could have caused you more problems had the trump suit broken badly, and get busy taking their trumps away from them before anything bad happens. Don't monkey with diamonds yet. Not only will you be running the risk that someone might be able to trump hearts, but you are adding to this the risk that someone might be able to trump a winning diamond. In going after trumps, follow one of the oldest rules in bridge. Win the first trump trick in the short hand; that is, in the dummy. This saves any entry problems in case there is a freakish distribution in either spades or hearts. Continue with trumps, and unless one of your opponents has all five of them, you are assured you will not lose more than three tricks. Once they have run out of trumps, lead a diamond and, if West plays low, put in the ten-spot. If it loses to the queen, it won't be tragic. You can win whatever they lead back and lead a second diamond, letting them have their ace. That will be the end of the ball game.

On the second hand, you have arrived at a contract of six spades, and West leads the queen of diamonds. Counting your possible losers, we see one in diamonds and two in hearts. The club suit will take care of at least one of those losers, and there is an excellent chance it will take care of another as well. If you will just give them a club trick and if the clubs break no worse than 4–2, you will be able to discard two of your losers in the red suits on dummy's clubs. And, by giving them a club trick, you will retain a club in your hand to reach the dummy.

Of course, you will have to pull trumps before you go through this procedure, so you simply win the first trick and lead trumps until they are exhausted. Then, lead a club and duck it. If East wins and returns his partner's lead, you will still have available the heart finesse, should one of the players show up with five clubs. If, however, when East wins he leads a heart, your best play is to go up with the ace. The odds are against one of your opponent's holding five clubs.

DUMMY	DUMMY
♠ A 8 6 3	♠ 7 6 2
♡ 10 9 7 5	♡ 7 6 5
◇ A 9 4	◇ 6 5 3 2
♣ K 7	♣ K Q J
DECLARER	DECLARER
♠ Q J 5	♠ K 10 5
♡ A Q J 8 5	♡ A K Q J 9
◇ Q J 10 6 3	◇ A K Q 4
♣ —	♣ A

On the first hand above, you have reached a contract of four hearts. After you opened the bidding with one heart, West overcalled two clubs, and his opening lead is the two of diamonds.

When a defender bids one suit and then leads a small card from another, wise declarers become very suspicious that the opening lead is a short suit. This suspicion becomes acute when the declarer sees between his hand and the dummy's as many as eight cards. The problem is just how short a suit has been opened? The lead of the two-spot certainly suggests that West did not start wtih a doubleton diamond, and the best guess is that it is a singleton.

So, you should conclude that you can afford to lose one trick in spades, one in hearts, and one in diamonds, but that you cannot afford to let West get in an additional small trump by trumping a diamond. So, you decide that this is no time for a diamond finesse or any other kind of a finesse for that matter. You rise with dummy's ace of diamonds and lead a small trump to your ace. Then you come back with a trump, and, sure enough, West wins with the king, and East shows out. West's next lead is a spade. With a trump still outstanding, you are in no mood to take the spade finesse either. You go up with the ace and then take West's last trump away from him. Finally, you go ahead with establishing your diamonds, secure in the knowledge that your opponents will win three tricks with kings, but no others.

On the second hand, you arrive at a contract of six hearts, and the opening lead is a club. If both red suits break even halfway decently, you are looking at five heart tricks, and four diamond tricks, in addition to the club tricks, provided you can get to the dummy to take the two good clubs. The six of diamonds should be an entry to the dummy after you have cashed the A K Q, but, of course, not until you have extracted trump. So, again, you simply lead trumps until they are exhausted or, if you want to, go ahead and lead all of them, giving your opponents the opportunity to sluff a diamond if they wish to avail themselves of it. The chances are that they will be out of diamonds after you have led them three times, and you will be able to reach the dummy to cash the queen-jack of clubs, on which you will discard two of your spades, leaving the king of spades as the only loser.

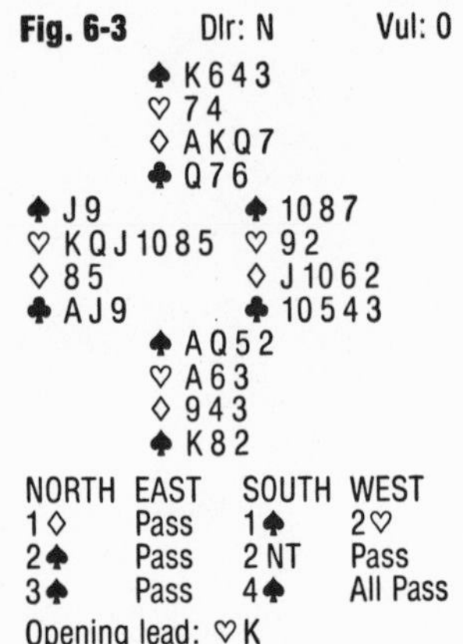

You don't always have those nice long strong trump suits, and, when you have less, you have to make do with what you have.

West led the king of hearts, and declarer looked the dummy over to assess his prospects. It looked like the trumps had to break 3–2 to be comfortable, and it also looked like he had to get the lead really fast to take the opponents' trumps away from them.

It was pretty obvious he had two losers in clubs and one in hearts, unless he was able to trump a heart. He did not feel he could trump a heart as long as his opponents had trumps, especially when East followed suit on the first trick with the nine of hearts. Should he try to trump with the king of spades, he would automatically establish a spade winner for his opponents. If he wished to safely trump with a small spade, he had to pull trumps at once. That way he would reduce his losers to only one heart. Looking at it another way, he would win five tricks in spades (counting the spade in the dummy used to trump a heart), one heart, and three diamonds, assuming they did not break evenly. To these he could always add a trick in clubs. He won with the ace of hearts and pulled three quick rounds of trumps, leaving one in his hand and one in the dummy. Next he gave them a heart trick and was in business. He trumped the heart continuation in the dummy, led a club to his king, and got his tenth trick established. Diamonds did not break for him, but he still had that small trump in South's hand so that everything was under control.

Sometimes, when you lead trumps, you are trying to get the suit established just as you have to establish suits which are not trump (Fig. 6-4).

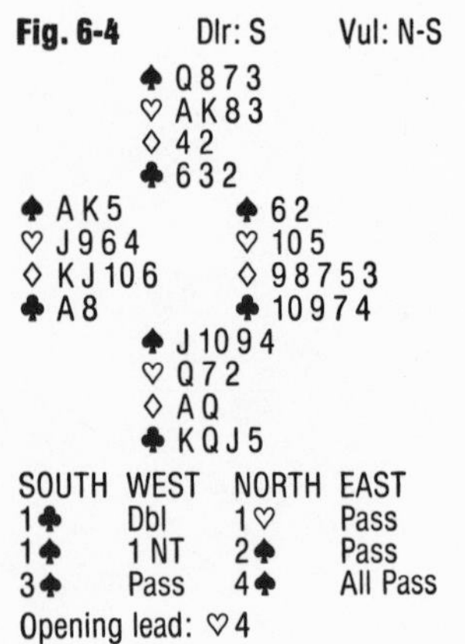

Maybe you think North and South bid too aggressively, but with a slight assist from West, they brought in ten tricks, so let's not be too critical.

The slight assist was the opening lead of the four of hearts. When the dummy came down, declarer saw no way to avoid losing tricks to the ace and king of trumps and the ace of clubs. What he couldn't afford to do was to lose a trick to a small trump, so he knew he had to start leading trumps as soon as possible. In addition, he had a probable loser in diamonds to dispose of, but that could wait.

The ten of hearts from East forced the queen from South, and South promptly led a small trump. West saw that he was going to be embarrassed leading all of the time, so he rose with the ace of spades, cashed the king, and led the five. Declarer won that in his hand and led a small heart, ready to finesse the eight-spot in case West played low, figuring that West was likely to have four hearts to the jack for his active bidding. It really makes no difference what West did, but let's say he played the nine to stop the deep finesse. Declarer won that in the dummy with the king and led a club. willing to give up his club trick now. West won with the ace and had no better lead than to return the eight of clubs. South could go ahead and cash his two club tricks on the off chance that the suit would break, but when it did not, he could finally lead another heart and again finesse the eight, if West played low. The queen of diamonds could then be discarded on dummy's heart.

Before we go on with more complicated matters, let's take a look at one more hand where simply counting tricks gives you the answer.

Fig. 6-5

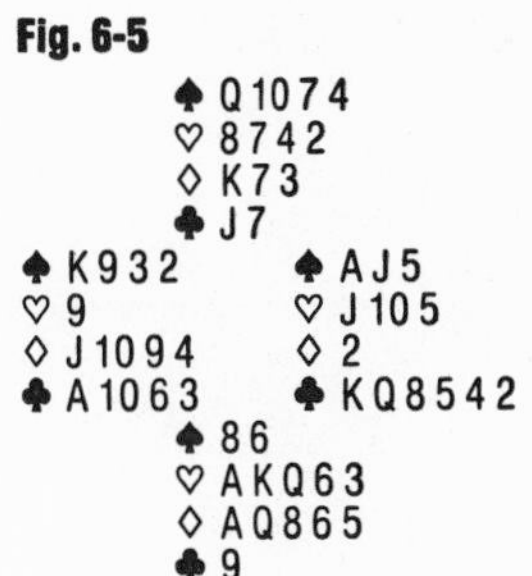

In a contract of four hearts, South got the lead of the jack of diamonds. Of course, declarer played low from dummy, for if anybody could trump diamonds, it would be East, and if East did so, he would be trumping only worthless diamonds. When East followed suit, the declarer stopped to count. Unless one of his opponents had all of the trumps, he was a cinch to take ten tricks. Let's count them up. There would be five tricks in hearts taken by the South hand at one time or another. In addition, the fact that both opponents had played diamonds on the first trick guaranteed that this suit would not break worse than 4–1. If it broke as badly as possible, there would still be three diamond tricks in top cards; there would be a trump left in the dummy to trump the fourth diamond; and doing that would establish the fifth diamond for a trick. Once declarer laid down the ace of trumps and both opponents followed suit, he knew he would lose, at the most, two tricks in spades and one in clubs. He went ahead and cashed his three heart tricks and then proceeded to take the king of diamonds, come back to his hand with an honor, and trump a small diamond.

Then there is the situation where the dummy has a solid suit which will take a lot of tricks, but has no entry outside the suit itself. In these cases, the opponents' trumps must be exhausted before you start running the suit, even though you have to sacrifice a possible trump trick (Fig. 6-6).

Fig. 6-6

In a contract of four spades, West led the A K Q of diamonds. Declarer trumped the third diamond and simply could not afford to go to the dummy and take a spade finesse. If the finesse failed, he would have no way back to the dummy to take those nice looking club tricks. So, he must lay down the ace and king of spades. There are times when the queen will be doubleton and that will take care of the matter, but on the hand as given, that would not occur. Often it is advisable when there is only one trump outstanding, and that is the high trump, to go about your business and leave it there. But that is not true with an entryless dummy and a running suit. In this case, when the queen of spades does not fall, South must lead the jack of spades to get the queen out of the opponent's hand before he starts leading clubs to get rid of two hearts out of his own hand.

On the next hand, declarer learned at once that West started with six clubs and East with only two. This made it obvious to him that there was an excellent chance that in any one of the other three suits, or even in each of them, East would hold more cards than West. That fact made it likely that any given card in one of the other three suits was with East. The conclusion of this was that the heart finesse for the queen was not a play which was favored to win; however, declarer found a way to avoid that finesse.

Fig. 6-7

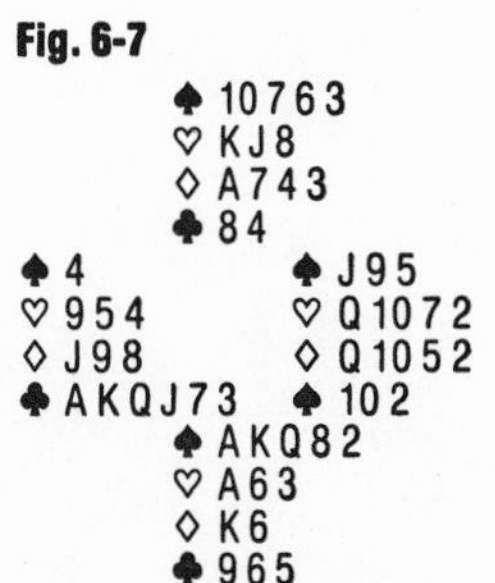

With South playing four spades, West started with two high clubs. East signaled vigorously with the ten and two-spot. West continued with the third high club, and declarer decided he knew where his best chances were.

East's vigorous signaling indicated that he must be able to overtrump dummy, and that placed the jack of spades in his hand. It also indicated that he had started with only two clubs and, therefore, had eleven cards in the other three suits. All of this leads to the conclusion that trying to take ten tricks by finessing for the queen of hearts was not too good a proposition. So, if declarer trumped in the dummy, he would have two club losers, plus the overruff that East had advertised, plus a heart loser. That was too many.

He avoided that by simply discarding the eight of hearts on the third club and letting the defenders take the first three tricks, believing he could then take the balance. If the fourth club came on, he could ruff in the dummy and, whatever East trumped with, he could overruff. He thought he could even handle the hand if East had all four of the missing trumps. It would not have been an outlandish distribution in view of the fact that East started with only two clubs.

Declarer gained the lead on the next trick and was able to draw spades in three leads and trump a losing heart with dummy's fourth trump. In effect, he took six tricks with trumps, two with hearts, and two with diamonds, losing three tricks in clubs only.

On the next hand (Fig. 6-8), declarer knew he had to lead trumps as soon as possible to keep his right-hand opponent from taking tricks with some small trumps. He knew he had to lead as many as possible before giving up the lead.

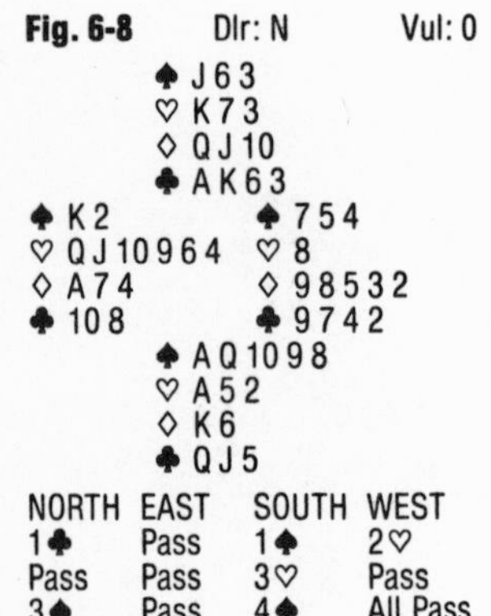

NORTH	EAST	SOUTH	WEST
1♣	Pass	1♠	2♡
Pass	Pass	3♡	Pass
3♠	Pass	4♠	All Pass

Opening lead: ♡Q

West led the queen of hearts, and declarer played the king from the dummy, hoping that East had at least one heart. So far, so good; East followed suit. Declarer thought he might have to give up the lead before pulling trumps, and, had he won the first trick with his ace of hearts, East well might have ruffed out dummy's king. Now, if East did get to trump any hearts, it would be small hearts in both hands and not one of the high ones. Furthermore, declarer was now in the dummy for a spade finesse, and he led the jack for that purpose.

When East followed suit with the five-spot, declarer gave the matter second thoughts. Suppose the finesse lost, and further suppose East had started with three trumps. This seemed quite likely, with West showing a long heart suit, thus increasing the chances that East had more cards in any one of the other suits than West did. With three trump, East could not only trump the next heart lead, but would have a trump left. In addition, he would probably be able to give West the lead again with the ace of diamonds and use his third trump to trump another heart—thus getting South's ace. This would give the defenders three trump tricks, and they were sure to get the ace of diamonds. That would be one too many tricks.

Declarer decided he could afford to lose two trump tricks and the ace of diamonds, but not three and the ace. So, he played the ace of spades on the jack and continued with the queen. West did win this with the king, but now East had only one trump left. He was able to trump what amounted to South's loser, which otherwise would have been discarded on one of dummy's clubs, but declarer had limited his loses to three tricks.

I have been saving bridge hands since the early days of contract, and in my files are many, many hands. In many instances, I have indicated the date on which I got the hand. Some of them are quite old. My next exhibit goes back to 1940.

If you asked me what system North and South were playing which justified the pass by South on the first round and the bid on the second round, I would have to tell you that I don't know. I would think that today immediate action would be natural with eleven cards in the majors, but the way I show the bidding above is the way I have it recorded.

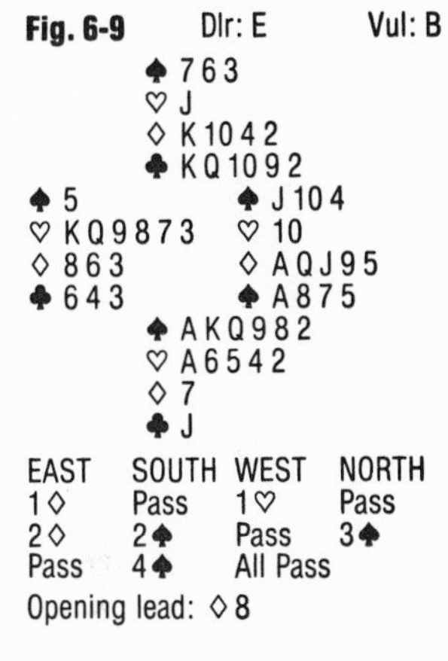

West led the eight of diamonds, and dummy's ten lost to the jack. Back came the ten of hearts. Declarer was sure East had noticed the singleton in the dummy, and could only account for this play if East had a singleton heart and could overruff the dummy. So he decided to play on that assumption. He won the ace of hearts and led three rounds of trumps. West discarded two clubs on the last two trumps, so declarer felt pretty good about the whole thing when he led the jack of clubs and overtook with dummy's queen.

East had no better play than to win this with the ace and then play the ace of diamonds. Declarer decided he enjoyed having East on lead, so he didn't trump the ace of diamonds—he just threw off the two of hearts. Now any card East led would turn the lead over to the dummy where there were plenty of high cards to get rid of the bad hearts in the south hand.

On the next hand (Fig. 6-10), a wise declarer led trumps fast to try to avoid having to face any future complications.

Our hero in South got into a contract of four spades with the opening lead of the queen of hearts. He won in the dummy and led the queen of spades. When East played low, he thought a minute and then played the ace. Can you see why he did that?

It looked like he might have one losing trump trick and two losing club tricks. Having bid only four spades, he did not particularly object to losing those three tricks. What he did object to was losing the finesse and giving West another chance to lead a small club. He didn't relish the idea of trying to guess the club situation while there were still trumps outstanding. The best way to arrange that was to guess the club suit after the trumps were all gone. As long as he had the lead himself, he could lead trumps. If and when he surrendered the lead to the opponents, he was not sure what they would lead.

Of course, he might not have had to guess if he had gone ahead with the trump finesse. But suppose the East-West setup had been as shown above and he had taken the finesse when West led the three of clubs. What would you have plaed from the dummy? Our South was not faced with that dilemma. He played a second trump, and then could afford to lose two club tricks.

RUFFING TRICKS

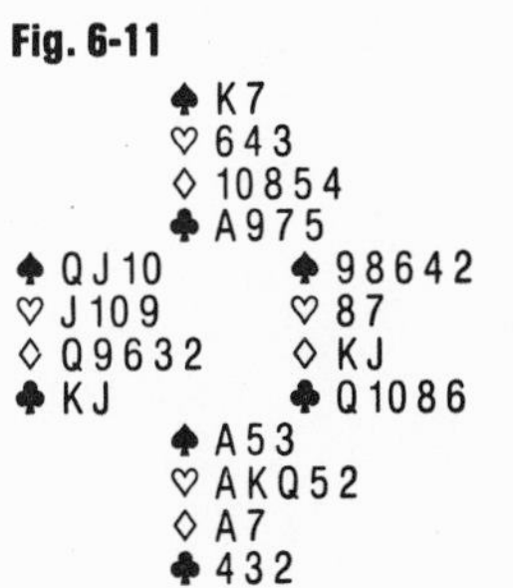

One of the reasons for deferring the lead of trumps is to enable short trumps in the dummy to take extra tricks.

South arrived at a contract of four hearts, received the opening lead of the queen of spades, and took a count of his potential losers to see what his prospects were. It was not certain that he was going to make his contract, but prospects were good. Starting from the bottom suit, it looked like he had two losers in clubs and one in diamonds which he could do nothing about. If he could limit himself to only those three losers, everything would be fine. He would have to hope for a 3–2 break in hearts, or else his efforts would be in vain. He had one loser in spades unless he could trump a spade in the dummy. It was obvious that he could not trump a spade in the dummy unless there were some trumps left in the dummy. So, he simply could not afford to draw three rounds of trumps.

Declarer won the king of spades in the dummy and led exactly two rounds of trumps. Next he cashed the ace of spades and led a small spade. Unless the player who had the one outstanding trump could trump that trick, he was as good as home. When West, who had the outstanding trump, had to follow suit, declarer was able to trump the losing spade in the dummy and then return to his hand with the ace of diamonds and complete the job of pulling trumps. If we want to count the tricks declarer took, we will see that he took four outside of trumps—two in spades and one each in diamonds and clubs. Looking at the trump suit, we see that he took six tricks with trumps. It was the ruffing trick that brought his total up to ten. A ruffing trick has been defined as a trick won by a trump, which could not have been won had the trump been led.

Usually, but not always, the symptom that indicates ruffing tricks can be made is that some short suit, other than trumps, shows up in a dummy which itself does not have as many trumps as are in the declarer's hand. This hand I have just shown you is a typical case. Experienced players immediately spot the doubleton spade in the north hand, along with the three small trumps, and set out to make up their shortage of tricks by making an extra trick with one of those small trumps in the dummy. Usually, but not always, these extra ruffing tricks are available only in the hand that is short in trumps. It seldom gains to trump in the hand that is long in trumps, as those trumps are likely to take tricks without trumping. At times, it might even be disastrous to do so.

Fig. 6-12

West	North	East
	♠ K 7 ♡ 6 4 3 ♢ A 8 5 4 ♣ A 9 7 5	
♠ Q J 10 ♡ J 10 9 ♢ Q 9 6 3 2 ♣ K J		♠ 9 8 6 4 2 ♡ Q 8 ♢ J 10 ♣ Q 10 8 6
	♠ A 5 3 ♡ A K 7 5 2 ♢ K 7 ♣ 4 3 2	

As you can see in Fig. 6-12, we have taken the previous hand and given the declarer one less trump trick. To compensate for that, we have given him an extra trick in diamonds. In the dummy he has a doubleton spade and should go about trying to trump a spade in the dummy, just as in the previous hand. However, you will notice that he also has a doubleton in the south hand where, after cashing the ace and king of diamonds, he can start ruffing. Let's see what would happen should he elect to do so. Let him win the first spade in the hand with the ace and then lead the king and ace of diamonds and another diamond to trump. East can trump this, and now, to win the trick, South is going to have to overtrump with his king. He started out with only one trump loser, and now he has two trump losers, as West is sure to get two trump tricks, and he still has to face the problem of those losers in clubs and spades. But let's say that friend South is a stubborn fellow, determined to trump diamonds, and so he returns to the dummy with the king of spades and leads another diamond. East can trump this one also, and to win it, South will have to overtrump with his ace. Now he is faced with three trump losers and still has done nothing about his clubs and spades. He can get rid of his spade, all right, by trumping it now, but now it is West who is going to get the lead. Who is going to be drawing trumps? The shoe is on the other foot. West is now going to pull trumps and take the balance of the tricks.

Ruffing tricks can make a lot of difference.

DUMMY
♠ 4 3 2
♡ J 8 5 4 3
◇ 9 8 7 4 2
♣ —

DECLARER
♠ A K Q J 10
♡ A K
◇ A K 5
♣ 8 7 5

Without a trump lead, South stands an excellent chance of taking twelve tricks by using those small spade trumps in the north hand to trump clubs. Should he decide to pull trumps instead of trumping clubs, every trump he pulls is going to cost him a trick because he will have to play one from the dummy on each one he leads from his hand. If he takes all of the opponents' trumps away from them, he not only won't take twelve tricks, he won't even take ten. He will end up losing three clubs and a diamond. Had the opponents known to lead trumps, declarer's maximum would have been eleven tricks.

This all seems very simple and basic, but it will get more complicated as we go along.

Fig. 6-13

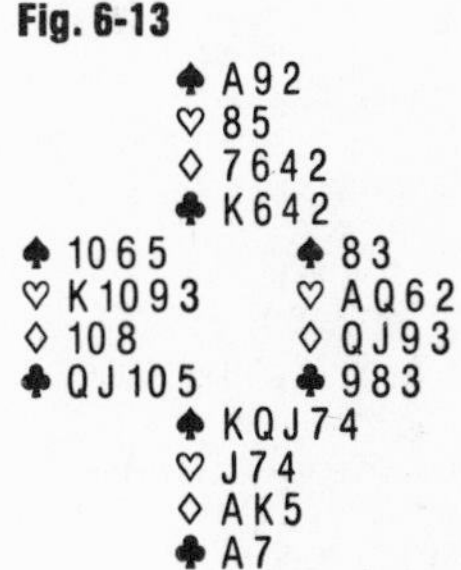

Fig. 6-13 is another case where the declarer cannot afford a single trump lead.

With South playing four spades, West failed to get off to the killing lead of a trump, but led the more natural queen of clubs. With a sure diamond loser, declarer can afford to lose only two hearts. He can do this provided he can trump one heart in the dummy. But he dare not lead a single spade before he leads hearts. Should he lead a spade, he would have to lead hearts twice before he could trump one, and each time the opponents took a heart trick, they would be able to lead a spade, and dummy's spades would be exhausted before declarer could trump with one. However, after he leads the first heart, the defenders can shift to trumps if they want to, but they are one tempo behind. Declarer will be able to win the trump return and lead a second heart. Even though the defenders lead a second trump, he will still have one left in the dummy to take care of the losing heart.

There is a disease inexperienced and sometimes thoughtless players get. It is called "thistrickitis." If you haven't played a lot of bridge, it is easy to feel that you should exercise all of your strength in taking the current trick. Of course, if you could do that thirteen times in a row, you would take them all. Obviously, there aren't many hands where you can do this. There are times where you have to refuse to take this trick because the chances are that by giving up this trick you will take more tricks later on.

Players who play "thistrickitis" with the above hand are almost certainly going to end up with nine tricks. The way to have an excellent chance to take the tenth one is to be sure after winning the first club trick that you do not take the next one—you lead hearts. As soon as you regain the lead, don't win the next trick. Lead another heart. Now chances are excellent you can trump a heart in the dummy, and that will be your tenth and game-going trick.

If the opponents miss the killing opening lead of a trump, don't give them another chance.

Fig. 6-14

♠ 9 4
♡ A Q 8
◇ Q 7 5 4
♣ 9 5 4 2

♠ A Q 10 5 ♡ 6 5 2 ◇ 9 3 ♣ Q 8 7 3 (West)
♠ J 8 6 3 ♡ 7 3 ◇ K 10 8 6 2 ♣ J 10 (East)

♠ K 7 2
♡ K J 10 9 4
◇ A J
♣ A K 6

I watched the declarer go wrong on this hand. The opening lead against a contract of four hearts was the nine of diamonds. This solved one of declarer's problems and must have given him a false sense of security. East was too wise to play the king, so the first trick was won by South with the jack. South then went to the dummy with a trump so that he could lead toward his king of spades. That would have been a winning play had East had the ace, but West had the ace. He took the king with his ace, and he had noticed something that declarer had overlooked. He had seen that doubleton spade in the dummy. He knew about ruffing tricks, so he led a trump. That left the dummy with only one trump, and the dummy also still had a spade. Desperately, declarer led a second spade, but West could not be denied. He won that trick and led a third trump, denuding the dummy of trumps. Declarer ended up losing three spade tricks and a club trick for down one.

The declarer should have been more impressed by the doubleton spade in the dummy than by the possibilities of leading up to the king of spades in his hand. He simply could not afford that trump lead to try to reach the dummy. All he had to do after winning the jack of diamonds was to lead a spade from his hand. Now he would have the timing; nothing the defenders could do would keep him from trumping a spade with one of dummy's trumps, thereby limiting his losses to two spades and one club trick.

Fig. 6-15 Dlr: N Vul: B

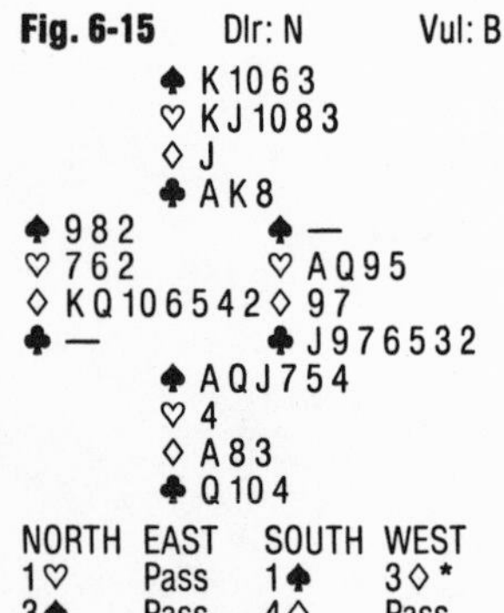

NORTH	EAST	SOUTH	WEST
1♡	Pass	1♠	3◇*
3♠	Pass	4◇	Pass
6♠	Pass	Pass	Pass

Opening lead: ◇ K

*Preemptive jump overcall.

I can't account for the play by declarer on the hand in Fig. 6-15 either, unless he simply suffered a temporary blackout.

This declarer was lucky, as many declarers are, that the hand is not played double dummy, for an opening lead of a heart from West and a club return from East would have settled his hash at once. But, West led the king of diamonds, and that gave declarer a way to commit suicide himself. He won that with the ace and laid down the ace of trumps. He still had two diamonds to trump, and so he discontinued trump leads for the moment and trumped a diamond. He then returned to his hand with a second trump and ruffed the last diamond. Now he tried to return to his hand by leading to the queen of clubs, but West had a trump left and trumped that. Given his second chance, West led a heart, and it was all over, with the defense getting two tricks.

After the diamond ace won the trick, the hand was an absolute cinch. However, trumps could not be led yet. The proper play was to lead a small diamond immediately and trump it with one of dummy's honors. The south hand could be reentered by leading a small trump, and a final diamond led. This could be trumped with the remaining honor in dummy, then a small trump in the dummy could be used to return to the south hand, and declarer could finish pulling trump. Finally, a lone heart trick could be ceded to the opponents.

Of course, when you can see only six cards in a suit, you do not exactly expect one of your opponents to be void. However, West, with his preemptive jump overcall, had told all who were willing to listen that his hand was a distributional freak. When your opponents have notified you of this, it is a poor time to get careless. It is, instead, a time when every precaution should be taken.

Fig. 6-16

On the next hand, the ruffing trick is there, but you have to look carefully to see it.

The report that I have on this hand says that, against a four spade contract, the opening lead was the king of clubs, and that South won that and promptly led the ace and king of diamonds to discard a club. He preserved dummy's ace of spades as another entry to dummy, and led a heart to finesse the ten-spot. That lost, and West continued clubs. Declarer trumped the third club and then pulled trumps, ending in the dummy. He led another heart, and, again, the finesse failed him. He had one chance remaining—the nine of hearts might have been only three long and might fall on his ace, in which case his eight would become established. No luck. The declarer ended up losing three heart tricks and a club trick.

Of course, he was terribly unlucky. Odds greatly favored finding either one of the heart honors in the East hand or having the nine of hearts fall out. But declarer had a better method.

After winning the ace of clubs, he should go ahead and cash his ace and king of diamonds to discard a club. Then he should simply lay down the ace of hearts and lead a second heart. Now, no matter what the opponents do, he is going to be able to lead another heart, regain the lead, and finally trump a heart with dummy's ace of spades. That will give him four tricks outside the trump suit, plus a total of six tricks from trumps, leaving him with one club loser and two heart losers.

Sometimes you have to be lucky to get in your ruffing tricks. But, if it takes luck to make your contract, you'd better give it every possible chance to perform for you (Fig. 6-17).

Fig. 6-17

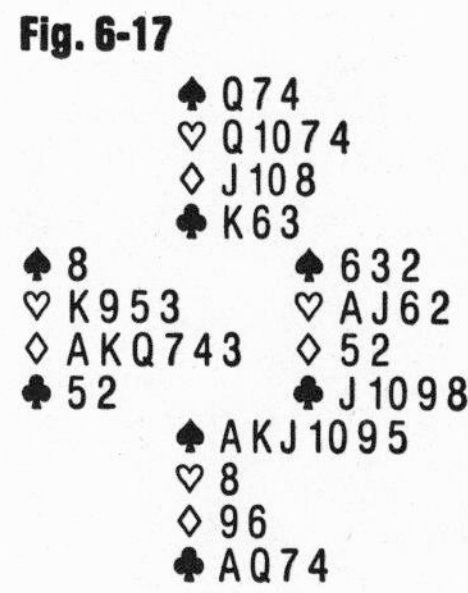

West competed in diamonds, but South ended up playing four spades. West led diamonds, and declarer trumped the third one. Now, if he was going to be lucky, spades would break 2–2, and the hand would be over, as he could trump a club in the dummy and would lose only one additional trick to the top heart. He cashed the ace and king of spades, but luck was not with him in the spade department. On the lead of the second trump, West showed out. Now declarer needed some luck in the club department. He took the A K Q of clubs. Had they broken 3–3, he would have gone ahead and pulled the other trump, as his small club would be good. He didn't have that sort of luck in the club suit, but he was lucky nonetheless, as East, who had the long clubs, also had the last trump. So declarer still got to trump his club and make his contract.

This sort of situation occurs rather frequently: all you can do is leave a trump in the dummy and hope for the best. Some you will win, some you will lose.

Generally speaking, a three-card suit in the dummy is not considered a short suit, but it can be when you in the south hand have four bad ones.

After North opened the bidding with one no-trump, South ended up playing four spades. The opening lead was the queen of diamonds. The only probable losers declarer could see were in clubs and hearts. If the ace of hearts turned out to be with West, there would be only one loser. If the ace turned out to be in East and hearts broke 3–3, there would be two losers. But if the ace turned out to be with East and the six outstanding hearts had the more likely distribution of 4–2, there well might be three losers.

Analyzing the problems practically gives you the answer. The way is to trump one heart in the dummy. To do this, you cannot even afford one round of trumps. Should you do so, the defenders might catch on to what you are doing when you lead hearts, and, each of the two times they get in, they might add a trump lead to the one you made. Three leads would exhaust the dummy of trumps. The proper play is to win a diamond in your hand with the king and promptly lead a heart. East can win this with the ace, but now it is too late for the defenders to lead trumps. The best he can do is return his partner's diamond lead. Now you are going to cash the queen of hearts and then, after giving up a small heart, ruff a small heart with your king of trumps. The extra ruffing trick will bring you up to ten tricks.

Fig. 6-19

North: ♠ 8 4 3 ♡ K 5 3 ◇ A 7 5 2 ♣ A 6 3

West: ♠ Q 10 6 ♡ Q 10 8 2 ◇ K J ♣ Q J 10 2

East: ♠ J 9 ♡ J 9 ◇ Q 10 9 8 4 3 ♣ 9 8 7

South: ♠ A K 7 5 2 ♡ A 7 6 4 ◇ 6 ♣ K 5 4

On the next hand (Fig. 6-19), declarer had a four-card holding in his hand opposite three in the dummy and needed to trump one in the dummy to bring home his contract. He had to make his plays in just the right order to get this done.

In four spades, South got the opening lead of the queen of clubs. He had one sure loser in clubs and only one in spades, provided that suit would behave properly. He had one in hearts, if the suit would break 3–3 or if he could maneuver it so that he could trump a heart in the dummy. Taking the ace and king of spades and then the ace and king of hearts and then giving up a heart would prove fatal, as West would win the third heart and simply take the last trump off the board. Neither would it work to take the ace and king of hearts, and then lead a third heart. West would win this, lead a fourth heart, and East could overruff the dummy. South solved this problem by losing his heart trick right away. He won the ace of clubs in the dummy, and then led a small heart and played low from his hand. West let East hold the trick with the nine-spot, in case East had any bright ideas about defense. But the best East could do was to continue his partner's clubs. Now declarer laid down the ace and king of trumps and then took the king and ace of hearts.

He led his last heart toward dummy's trump, not caring whether anybody could trump that or not. If anybody did trump it, it would be with the last outstanding trump, and declarer would still limit his losses to one trump trick, one heart trick, and one club trick.

In Fig. 6-20 South got to a contract of six spades. Not wishing to underlead any of his high cards, West led the nine of trumps. In approved fashion declarer took a count of possible losers, and found one in diamonds and one in clubs. There were several possibilities for getting rid of one of the losers. Diamonds might break 3–3. If they did not, he might be able to trump a diamond in the dummy. Or, it might be possible to trump a club in the dummy. That last option didn't look likely, but that is the way it turned out.

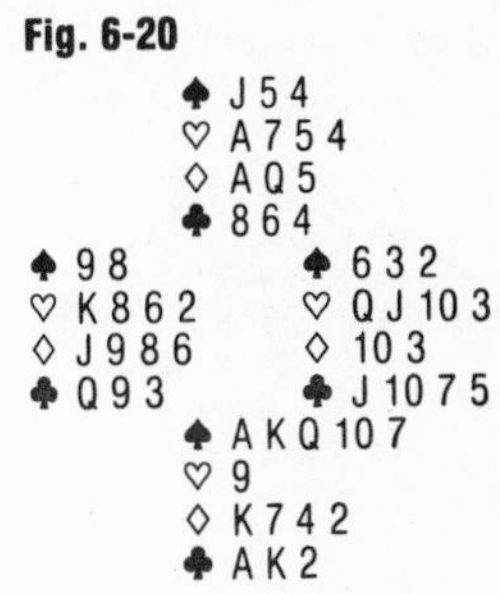

You can't trump anything in the dummy unless there is a trump in the dummy, so declarer took two trumps in his own hand, left his opponents with one, but kept the jack in the dummy. Next he gave his attention to diamonds. Being a good technician, he led dummy's high diamonds first so that if it turned out East could trump the third diamond, his problems would be solved. East could trump the third diamond, but there was no solution for his problems. If he did trump, declarer would just play low. On regaining the lead, with the defenders holding no more trumps, he could discard one of dummy's clubs on the king of diamonds, and trump his losing club with dummy's jack. If East didn't trump the third diamond, declarer would win with the king, and trump his losing diamond with dummy's jack. Either way, he was going to trump one of his two losers.

There are times when the ruffing tricks serve the double purpose of helping you establish long cards in the suit which you are ruffing.

South had trouble maintaining his composure when West opened one heart, with South's seven-card suit, and North made a takeout double. I don't know exactly what led South to jump straight to six spades, but I rather imagine he considered simply passing, but decided he could get a larger plus than he would get setting a nonvulnerable West if he went all the way to a slam in spades. Whether that was the best way to bid the hand or not, I don't know, but we, like South, are now concerned with making the hand rather than worrying about whether or not it was properly bid.

The opening lead was the queen of hearts, and when declarer got a look at the dummy, he decided there was no particular reason for thinking that West had made a psychic bid. He further decided that West did not have all of the outstanding hearts, for had he held them all, his opening lead would have been the king. In addition to his ace of hearts, South had small ones to get rid of somehow, and it looked as though he was going to have to take some tricks with some of them. If he wanted to get any tricks with the small trumps in the dummy hand, he decided he had to get them right away because, if he waited awhile, East would be overtrumping the dummy. So, instead of letting the queen of hearts ride to his ace, he trumped it with the two of spades. The play of the king by East confirmed his suspicions about the heart suit.

As the four of spades in the dummy was of no further use for ruffing, he led it to get to his hand. Then he led the three of hearts, which he trumped with the queen of spades. Back he came to his hand with the ace of clubs and led another heart, which he trumped with the king of spades. This left him with four hearts and West with two. He trumped a diamond to return to his hand, and one more trump lead cleared the trump suit. Finally, he cashed the ace of hearts, reducing West to a singleton, conceded one heart trick to West, and the balance of his hand was good.

When you have to trump with small trumps, there is always the chance

Fig. 6-22

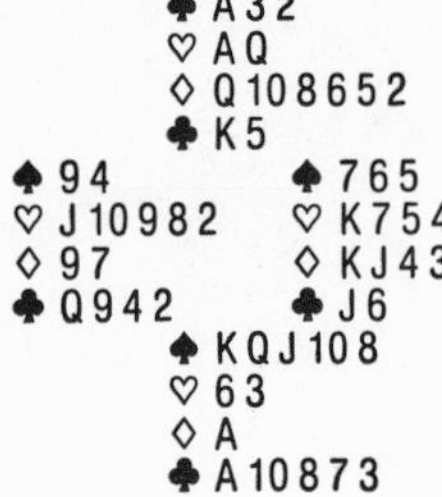

that your opponents will be able to overtrump. On the next hand (Fig. 6-22), declarer found a clever way to avoid that fate.

In a contract of six spades, declarer got an opening lead of the jack of hearts. In addition to the possible heart loser, he had three club losers unless he could do something about them.

Establishing the dummy's diamonds didn't seem to be the right line, so declarer examined the possibility of establishing the clubs. The danger was that he would have to trump two clubs to get them established, and that meant that once he would have to trump with a very small trump. He decided, instead, to trump a heart with the smaller trump and a club with dummy's big trump and to concede one club trick, but no more. If all suits broke reasonably well, it looked like it would work.

You are going to say, "How can he trump a heart in the dummy when he has only two hearts in each hand?" Well, he found a way.

He won the first trick with dummy's ace of hearts and then cashed the king and ace of clubs. He led a third club and simply discarded dummy's queen of hearts on it. Now nothing could keep him from trumping one of his small hearts with dummy's two of spades and the fourth club with the ace of spades, after which he would have a good fifth club for the twelfth trick.

Fig. 6-23 Dlr: W Vul: Unknown

DUMMY
♠ 10 5
♡ Q 2
◇ 9 5 3 2
♣ J 9 5 4 3

DECLARER
♠ A K 4 2
♡ A K J 10 9 8 6 5
◇ A
♣ —

WEST	NORTH	EAST	SOUTH
1◇	Pass	1♠	2♠
Pass	3♣	Pass	3♡
Pass	4♡	Pass	5◇
Pass	5♡	Pass	6♡
Pass	Pass	Pass	

Opening lead: ◇ K

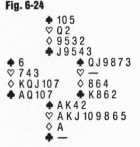

My final hand on ruffing is from the Culbertson Bridge Examination of 1941.

You get the opening lead of the king of diamonds which you win with your ace. You lay down the ace of spades, and it takes a trick. At this point, the Bridge Examiner (or should I say inquisitor) wishes to know what play you must make to ensure your contract against any lay of the cards and any defense?

Really, you have a choice of two cards. To accomplish this desirable end, you could lead either the two of spades or the four of spades, but no other cards. If you lead the king of spades, it will be trumped, leaving you with two losers, and whether the opponents lead a trump or continue hearts, you are going to lose another trick. Obviously, you can't lead trumps and still dispose of two spades. But once you have led a small spade, you are assured that no matter what they lead back, you can trump a spade with dummy's queen of hearts and then pull trumps and claim the balance. Fig. 6-24 is the entire setup.

I would say that any player who made this play at the table would be a very cautious bridge player. Of course, when you look at it, the play should be made. It is so logical.

Fig. 6-24

North:
♠ 10 5
♡ Q 2
◇ 9 5 3 2
♣ J 9 5 4 3

West:
♠ 6
♡ 7 4 3
◇ K Q J 10 7
♣ A Q 10 7

East:
♠ Q J 9 8 7 3
♡ —
◇ 8 6 4
♣ K 8 6 2

South:
♠ A K 4 2
♡ A K J 10 9 8 6 5
◇ A
♣ —

THE CROSSRUFF

Some people call the crossruff the rambler's delight. You sit there with dummy short in one suit and your hand short in another. With plenty of trumps in each hand, you proceed to make each of your trumps take a trick all by itself. Fig. 6-25 is an example.

There are two special things to learn about crossruff hands.

1. While usually when playing with trumps it is better in planning your play to count losers, it often will work out better when planning a crossruff to count winners. Sometimes it pays to count both ways.

2. Unless your high cards in side suits are needed as entries, it is often important that you cash your high-card tricks in the side suits before embarking on the crossruff.

Fig. 6-25 Dlr: S Vul: B

North: ♠ 6 ♡ K J 8 ◇ 8 5 3 ♣ A 10 8 5 3 2

West: ♠ K J 10 8 5 2 ♡ — ◇ A Q J 2 ♣ 9 7 6

East: ♠ 7 3 ♡ 9 6 4 3 2 ◇ 10 4 ♣ K Q J 4

South: ♠ A Q 9 4 ♡ A Q 10 7 5 ◇ K 9 7 6 ♣ —

SOUTH	WEST	NORTH	EAST
1♡	1♠	2♡	Pass
3♡	Pass	4♡	All Pass

Opening lead: ♣9

The hand above is a clear example of the first principle. In a contract of four hearts, South received an opening lead of the nine of clubs. The spade overcall by West made the spade finesse appear doomed to failure. and it did not add any glamor to the king of diamonds in declarer's hand, as West seemed likely to hold both of these important cards. Outside of the trump suit, declarer could see exactly two winning tricks—the two black aces. However, he and dummy together had eight trumps, and it looked like he had a pretty good chance to have each of these trumps take a trick. If he could only avoid being overruffed, he could bring in eight trump tricks by a crossruff.

He won the ace of clubs and promptly trumped a club with the five of hearts. Next he laid down the ace of spades and trumped a small spade with the eight of hearts. Then he led a club and trumped it with the seven of hearts. When that did not get overruffed, his problems were solved. His six remaining hearts were all high, and nothing could keep him from making a trick with each of them by simply continuing the crossruff.

My second hand is an example of the second crossruff principle already stated above.

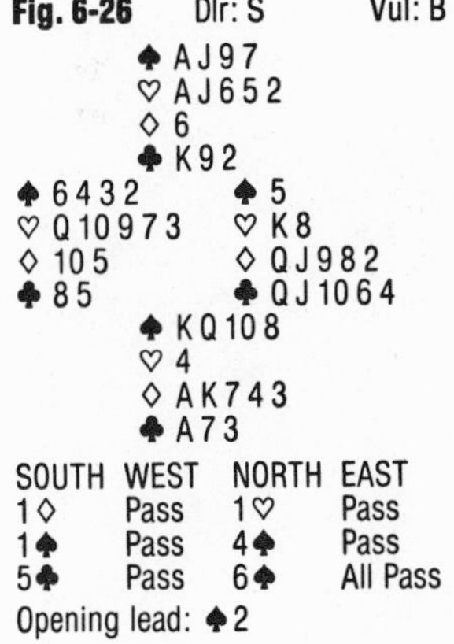

West had listened to the bidding, and it sounded like a crossruff hand to him. The way to stop a crossruff is to lead trumps, and so that is what West did.

Declarer now counted his tricks. Outside of the trump suit, he had five of them in aces and kings. He would have to expend two trumps to take the first trick, which would bring it up to six. That left three trumps in each hand, and, if he could make each of these good separately, it would bring his total up to twelve.

However, this is the hand where the declarer needs to do first things first. Suppose he lays down the ace and king of diamonds and then leads a diamond to trump it. West wasn't born yesterday or he wouldn't have led trumps in the first place. He will give further demonstration of it by simply discarding a club on the third diamond lead. Now, the declarer no longer has two club tricks. If he persists in his crossruff by taking the ace of hearts, trumping a heart, and then leading another diamond to trump it, West will get rid of his last club, and now declarer won't have any club tricks left.

He could have avoided this sad result by simply cashing the ace and king of clubs before starting out with his crossruff. Yes, there was some chance that one of the high clubs would get trumped, but it must be regarded as a very small chance.

On the next hand (Fig. 6-27), the high card has to be established before it can be cashed.

Fig. 6-27 Dlr: E Vul: 0

	North	
	♠ K Q 4 ♡ 5 ◇ Q 7 4 3 2 ♣ A Q 10 3	
West ♠ J 10 7 5 3 ♡ Q 10 8 7 3 ◇ 10 9 6 ♣ —		East ♠ A 9 ♥ 9 4 ◇ A K J 8 5 ♣ 9 5 4 2
	South ♠ 8 6 2 ♡ A K J 6 2 ◇ — ♣ K J 8 7 6	

EAST	SOUTH	WEST	NORTH
1◇	1♡	Pass	1 NT
Pass	2♣	Pass	4♣
Pass	5♣	All Pass	

Opening lead: ◇ 10

West led the ten of diamonds, and when declarer got a look at the dummy, he saw a typical crossruff situation, with lots of trumps in both hands and short suits in both hands. In the way of tricks in the side suits, declarer saw the ace and king of hearts, leaving him needing nine more tricks. Between his hand and the dummy, he had nine clubs, and if he could find four cards to trump in the dummy so that each of those trumps would take a trick, plus five to trump in his own hand so that each there would take a trick, and if he could do this without being overruffed, he could bring in eleven tricks.

The trouble was, he didn't have four bad cards in his hand to trump. So, he decided he would have to establish a spade trick. In addition to doing that, he could discard dummy's small spade on the king of hearts and have plenty of losing cards in his hand to trump in the dummy.

However, he had to time all of this just right. After trumping the opening diamond lead, he could lay down the ace and king of hearts, discarding the small spade from the dummy, and then lead the third heart and trump it high. East could not overtrump it, but he could discard a spade. Now declarer would find it impossible to get his spade trick. Remembering that the first principle is to take the side tricks first, declarer carried this one step further and made it the first principle to establish the side tricks first. So, before he touched hearts, he led a small spade toward the dummy. East took that with the ace and returned a trump. South's six-spot held the trick, and, when West showed out, all chances that West would be able to overruff anything disappeared.

So for that matter had the chance that East would be able to overruff dummy, because dummy's three remaining trumps were now high. Declarer now cashed the two hearts, discarding the small spade from the dummy, and then cashed the king of spades before anything bad happened. Now he got the crossruff rolling. He took eight trump tricks: five in his own hand and three in the dummy. These, added to two heart tricks and one spade trick, came to a total of eleven.

Remember that a wise bridge teacher once said, "Nothing I tell you is absolutely true." I wouldn't go quite that far, but I would say that there are exceptions to most so-called rules of play.

I have warned you, as other people have warned you, about the necessity of cashing your high cards before you start your crossruff. Now I had better tell you about the exception. There are times when it is not only not necessary, but when it is not wise.

DUMMY
♠ 7
♡ K 10 7 5 2
◇ A K 4 3
♣ 7 6 3

DECLARER
♠ A 6 2
♡ A Q 6 4 3
◇ 9 2
♣ A K 5

These instances generally occur when your side has a great many of the thirteen trumps, so that you can afford to use up a few trumps before you start your crossruff. On the hand above, you are playing six hearts and get the opening lead of the king of spades. Off the top, you can count only ten tricks, but you immediately notice that all of the requirements for a crossruff are there, for the dummy is short in spades, and your hand is short in diamonds. You do not cash the two club tricks before you start your crossruff. Admittedly, the chance that the king of clubs will be trumped are very slight indeed, but why take any chance at all when it is not necessary. You will need to trump two spades in the dummy and two diamonds in your hand. Even if one opponent holds all three of the outstanding trumps, you can pull their trumps in three leads and still have two trumps in each hand for purposes of the crossruff. So, you simply take the ace of spades and lead trumps until the opponents have no more. Then you go ahead with your crossruff, cashing the ace and king of clubs at your pleasure.

In the next hand, there is still another lesson to be learned:

DUMMY
♠ A 7 4
♡ J 10 8 7
◊ 9
♣ K Q 7 4 2

DECLARER
♠ 3
♡ A K Q 9 6 5
◊ A Q 4 2
♣ 8 5

Again you are playing six hearts, and the opening lead is the king of spades. On these hands that look like a crossruff, you first count your sure winners and find eight right off the top, plus another sure one by establishing a club trick. You can pick up the extra three tricks by trumping three diamonds in the dummy, but your way back to your hand to accomplish this will be to trump spades in your hand, so the need for entries in your hand makes this a crossruff hand. This time you can't afford to pull trumps right away, because then you won't have enough left in the dummy to trump those three diamonds. So, the question arises, just when should you establish the club trick? There is more danger that there will be a singleton club in one of the opponents' hands now than there was in the last hand. Here you hold seven clubs. While that danger is not very great, is there a way to avoid whatever danger there is?

Yes, there is. You plan to trump three diamonds in the dummy. That will leave you a heart for an entry back to your hand. You plan to trump two spades in your own hand. That will leave you with four trumps so that, even if one opponent should hold all three outstanding trumps, you can still pull them and have one left. Therefore, you will have the hand under full control if you proceed with your crossruff first, planning after you complete it to return to your hand by leading a trump and then finally taking away from the opponents whatever trumps they have. After all of this is done, you can establish your club trick for your twelfth trick.

But there is a danger to be avoided, and the lesson I mentioned to be learned is still lurking there. If you start your crossruff by first trumping a spade in your hand and then leading the ace of diamonds and trumping a diamond, you are going to have to run that risk after all. You will end up in the dummy with no more spades to lead, while you still have a diamond in your hand to trump, and the only way you can get to your hand to accomplish that will be to lead a trump from the dummy and then trump a diamond with dummy's last trump. Now you will still face whatever danger there is that one of your opponents will have a singleton club.

So here is the lesson which has general application. Don't start trumping spades first. Lead a small diamond to the ace and start trumping diamonds first. Other things being equal, start your crossruff by first trumping the suit where you have the greater length. With three diamonds and two spades to trump, keep your entries nice and neat by starting out trumping diamonds.

More often than not, when you embark on a crossruff, your trumps are not all high ones. There is always the danger that one of your opponents will overruff you. At times, when they do overruff you, they can still further disrupt your plans by leading trumps.

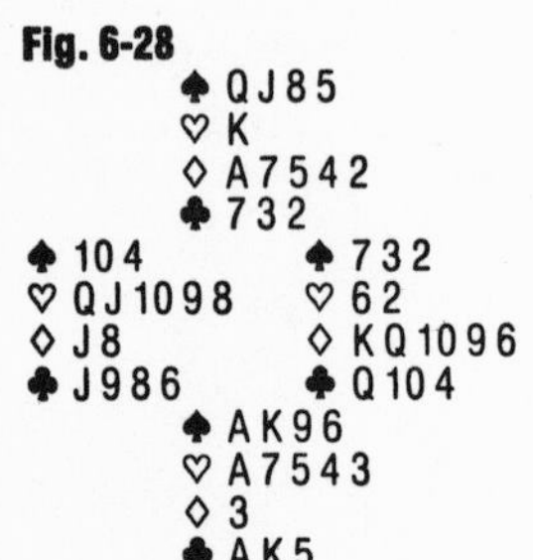

With the proper holding, you can lessen the possibility of an overruff.

South got to a contract of six spades and got the opening lead of the queen of hearts. He saw that he would need seven tricks from the trump suit, as he had only five tricks from the other three suits. It looked like the best way to get seven tricks out of the trump suit was to crossruff.

Of course, if he could take all eight of his trumps separately, he would take thirteen tricks, but that specter of an overruff was staring him in the face. Should one of his opponents overruff him, that would cut him down from eight trump tricks to seven, and should that person who overruffed then lead a trump so that two had to fall together, that would cut him down to six trump tricks, and that wasn't enough.

The chances that the first small trump played would not be overruffed would be pretty good, and declarer found a way so that, should he be able to get by with taking tricks with the five and six of spades, he could then assure himself of seven trump tricks.

He won the first trick in the dummy with the king of hearts and then went to his hand with the king of clubs. The opening lead of a heart rather indicated length, and the declarer decided that he might get by with two heart leads, but that it would be dangerous to trump the third heart with the five of spades and that trumping the third club would be a safer proposition. Should West turn out to be short in clubs, declarer could handle the situation. So, he took the ace of hearts and discarded a small club from the dummy. Next he led to the ace of diamonds and trumped a diamond in his hand with the six of spades. So far, so good. The king of clubs took the next trick, and he trumped a small club with dummy's five of spades. When that held the trick, he was home. He trumped a diamond with the king of spades. Then he trumped a heart with the queen of spades, another diamond with the ace of spades, and his last heart with the jack of spades. This brought him up to eleven tricks. Then he led a diamond and trumped it with his nine of spades. If West did not overtrump, that would be declarer's twelfth trick. When West did overruff, the eight of spades in the dummy was promoted to the twelfth trick. It was the holding of both the eight and nine of spades which made this play possible after declarer got by with ruffing with small trumps in both his hand and the dummy.

There are times when you have enough trumps to stand the overruff and the trump lead.

On hand 6-29 the bidding led South to suspect that West had most of the high cards. With the three top tricks in the minor suits, it was likely there would also be one in hearts, so declarer postponed counting his tricks until he discovered for sure that the heart trick was available. He won the lead with the ace of clubs and then led the ten of hearts. West rose with the ace of hearts and led a heart back. Now declarer could count four tricks outside the trump suit. That made him need a minimum of six tricks from the trump suit.

There were several ways he could accomplish this. One was simply to concede a trick, sooner or later, to the king of trumps, but to trump clubs in the dummy, giving him four trump tricks in his own hand and at least two in the dummy. This involved returning to his hand to lead clubs and suggested a crossruff as the way to find these entries. Declarer decided that the crossruff gave him the best chance to take the maximum number of tricks with the greatest amount of safety.

He and dummy together held nine trumps. With the king of trumps outstanding, there was no way to take nine trump tricks if the king was with West, but if West would overruff with the king, that would merely cut declarer down to eight trump tricks. And, if West should then lead a trump, making declarer play one from each hand, that would still leave him seven. This, with his high cards in side suits, brought his total to eleven.

Declarer took the customary safety precaution of cashing the ace and king of diamonds before anything had happened and then led the king of hearts and discarded a diamond. He now had two hearts and two diamonds to ruff, or a total length of four cards from the north hand and three from his hand, so he was in the right hand to start the crossruff. He led a small heart and trumped it with the five of trumps, then a small club which he trumped with the four of trumps. From there on it was clear sailing. He took another heart with the seven of trumps and another club with the eight of trumps. He then trumped a diamond with the nine of trumps. West did overtrump that and led back his three of trumps, but declarer still had his eleven tricks.

A very fine player is reported to have gone set on the hand in Fig. 6-30. Let's see whether you and I, based on what we know about crossruffing, can do better.

The declarer got to a very fine contract. West led a small heart, and

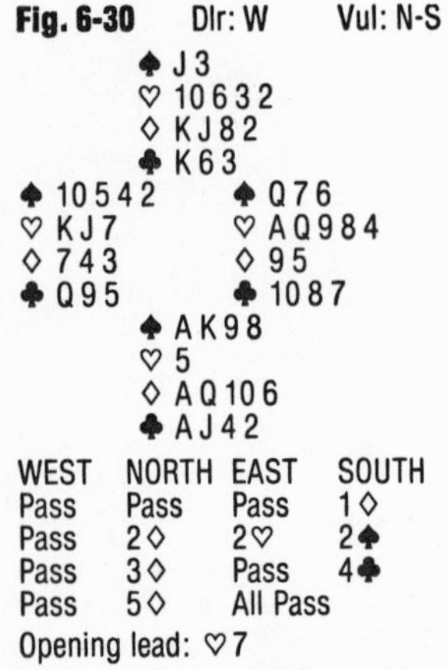

East won and returned the suit. Declarer trumped this and then led the three top diamonds. Next he led to the king of clubs and then returned a club and finessed the jack. The queen won the trick. West was then able to cash the king of hearts for the setting trick.

Declarer had two spade tricks off the top. After he had trumped a heart, he had another four trump tricks, bringing him up to a total of seven. For his plan to work, he would have had to take four club tricks. He just about had to have the queen of clubs with East and, not only that, have it precisely three cards long. That would give him four club tricks to add to his five trump tricks and two spade tricks.

Let's see how you and I can get along by taking only two club tricks, but by setting up a crossruff. If we take the ace of spades and the ace-king of clubs, we will need seven tricks from the trump suit.

We have eight trumps between us and the dummy and can afford to have trumps led exactly once and still have seven tricks, if we can make the rest of them separately. Our chances are pretty good.

We trump the second heart and next cash the ace and king of spades. We do this before monkeying with clubs to keep someone from finding a way to discard a spade on clubs while we are fooling with them. Next we lead a small spade and trump it with the eight of diamonds. For this play to fail, East would have to have started with only two spades and also with the nine of diamonds. The odds were that East did not have this combination. Having accomplished this, we are almost home free. We now cash the king of clubs and then take the ace of clubs. Then we lead another club, and this gives them their second trick, but they are now through.

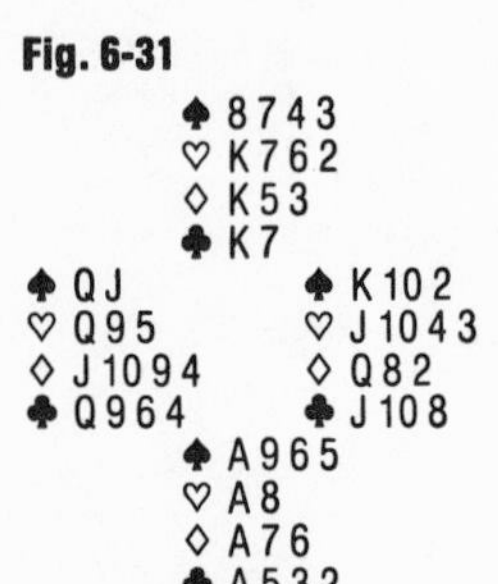

We have now won six tricks, and lost two. We still have three trumps in each hand, and can take five tricks with them on a cross ruff, no matter what West leads.

When the trump suit is weak, it may require special handling (Fig. 6-31).

When West led the jack of diamonds against a four spade contract, the makings of a crossruff were there, with a doubleton heart in the south hand and a doubleton club in the north hand. Declarer and dummy between them held the ace and king of both suits. Unless somebody could trump something very fast, declarer had six tricks outside the trump suit. That left him needing four tricks in the trump suit. He had a way to practically guarantee this result, provided the trumps broke 3–2.

He won the first diamond trick in the North hand and led a trump from the dummy and ducked it. He was bound to regain the lead whatever the opponents led and when he did so, he played the spade ace. When both followed suit, he had it made. He cashed the ace and king of both hearts and clubs, and started crossruffing. He had four small trumps, and expected someone to overruff with the king somewhere along the line. That would still give him a total of three trump tricks to add to the trick he took with the ace of trumps. Those four plus the six side suit tricks gave him a neat batch of ten.

We are South playing a contract of four hearts, and we have received an opening lead of the king of spades. A quick count of losers might make us a little too optimistic. We could, for example, say that we have one spade loser and two trump losers and that's it. That assumes a 3–2 trump break, which is not unlikely, and it also assumes that the opponents cannot make their trumps separately, but that we can.

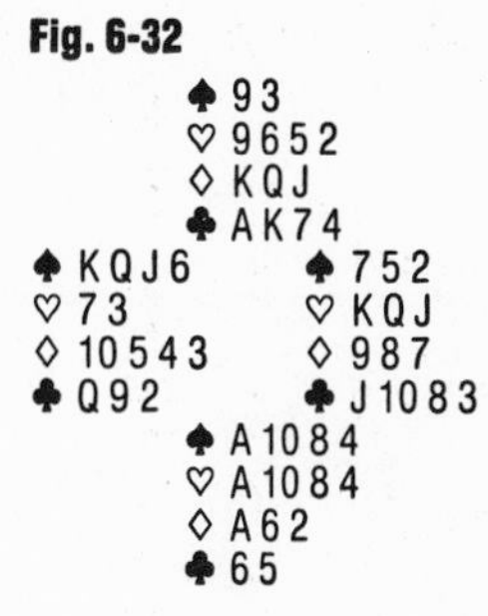

Let's examine this last supposition. Suppose we win the ace of spades and then lead the ace and another trump. East would win the second trump, lead a third trump, and leave us with one small trump in the dummy and one in our hand, for a total of three trump tricks. These, added to a spade trick, three diamond tricks, and two club tricks, would total only nine. We would end up with some losers in the black suits because we didn't have enough trumps to trump them with. Now let's take the crossruff view toward the whole business.

We follow suit from the dummy and note that East plays his deuce, showing no interest in the suit. So we let the king hold the first trick. West will probably continue the suit, and we will win that with the ace. Now we do want to pull some of the opponents' trumps, but we want to stay in charge of the hand. So, instead of leading the ace of hearts, we lead a small heart. Whatever they return, we regain the lead and lay down the ace of hearts. Now we will go about our business. Hearts will have broken 3–2, and the only outstanding trump will be the king. We will take three diamonds, two clubs, one spade, the ace of hearts we have already taken, and have four trumps (two in each hand) to take three more tricks. Whoever has the king of hearts can overruff us once, but that will still leave us three tricks with four trumps. And, suppose that when we cash the A K Q of diamonds, the person who holds the trump will trump one of them. Then each of our four remaining small trumps will take tricks, and we will wind up with a total of five trump tricks, one spade, two diamond, and two club tricks, still for a total of ten.

On the next hand (Fig. 6-33), you should not even try to guess which way to finesse for the queen of hearts.

Playing in a contract of six hearts with a lead of the jack of clubs, you should simply bang down the ace and king of hearts and then go about your business. If the queen has not fallen, you still are going to take twelve tricks. You have seven tricks off the top in the side suits, plus the two trump tricks you've already taken. In addition, you now have two trumps left in each hand, plus two spades in the north hand you can trump and two diamonds in the south hand you can trump. Those four remaining trumps are somehow going to bring you three tricks.

Even should the queen of hearts fall doubleton, your best play is still to quit pulling trumps and get your crossruff rolling. You will never take fewer than twelve tricks, and, if the hand breaks right for you, you will take thirteen tricks.

Suppose the hearts, instead of being 3–2, are 4–1? You are probably in trouble no matter which way you go, but your chances of taking twelve tricks are at least as good if you bang down the ace-king of hearts as they are if you take the finesse.

There are hands where the crossruff not only lets you take tricks with each trump separately, but also helps you to establish a long suit. On the next hand, even though there is only one way to take the finesse, the finesse nonetheless should not be taken because you can't afford to lead trumps three times to pull them.

Fig. 6-34

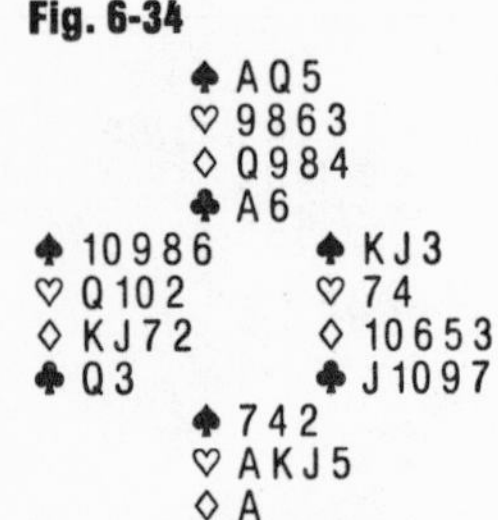

Playing a bid of four hearts, declarer received the ten of spades as the opening lead. Players have been known to lead from the K 10 9, and there was no good reason to defer the finesse. But, the queen lost to the king, and a spade was returned. Counting the ace and king of hearts, declarer had a total of six tricks off the top and needed four more from somewhere else. Depending on how the clubs broke, he could pick up two club tricks, but it was probable that he would gather only one in addition to the ace-king. If that was correct, the four small trumps in the two hands were going to have to bring home three tricks. If trumps broke 3–2, there was an excellent chance they could do exactly that.

So South won the spade return and laid down the ace-king of trumps. Next he won the ace and king of clubs, and, when both followed, he saw the suit was going to break no worse than 4–2. He led a third club. Had West trumped this, South would simply have discarded the five of spades from the north hand and would have been able to take tricks with each of his four remaining small trumps. West saw no reason to be so helpful, so, instead of trumping the club, he discarded a diamond. Declarer trumped the club in the dummy and led a diamond to his ace. He then led his fourth club, and, again, West refused to trump, now discarding a spade. Declarer trumped in the dummy, returned to his hand by trumping a diamond, and laid down the fifth club. This allowed West to choose whether he would let him take the tenth trick or trump it and postpone the inevitable. If he trumped it, he could win a spade trick, as dummy was now out of trumps, but then South's jack of hearts would take the tenth trick.

Fig. 6-35

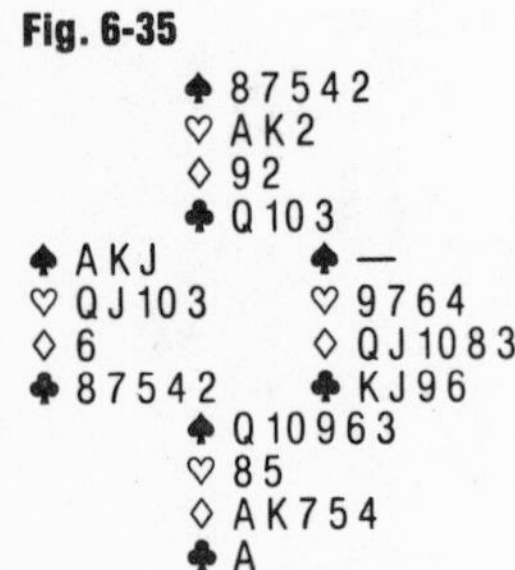

This next hand (Fig. 6-35) must have been played by the beggar who was reduced to that condition because he always pulled trumps.

Playing four spades, my friend got an opening lead of the queen of hearts. The story is that he won that in the dummy and promptly led trumps. That suited West just fine. He was now able to lead three trumps, all of them winners. This left declarer with only two trumps in each hand, and it was impossible to get more than four tricks from four trumps, even with his beautiful crossruff situation. To these four trump tricks he could add the five side suit tricks, but when the diamond suit failed to give him another trick, down he went, and thus ended his career as a bridge player.

He could afford to lose three spade tricks, provided he lost no others. It was hard to see where he could lose any others. Proper play was simply to win the ace and king of hearts and then start his crossruff. Even with West able to trump the king of diamonds when he led it, he still would be in good shape. West, after trumping the king of diamonds, we assume would take the ace and king of trumps, but North would then have three trump tricks left, and South two, in addition to the one he had already taken by trumping a small heart. That would give the declarer a total of six trump tricks, and, although he would have only four tricks in side suits after his king of diamonds got trumped, that would be enough.

RUFFING IN DECLARER'S HAND: THE SCRAMBLE

Fig. 6-36

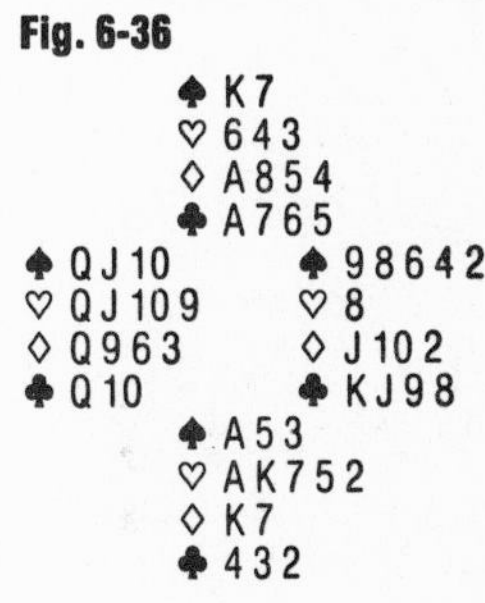

You have seen these north and south hands before. I used them in the section on ruffing tricks in the dummy. There, playing four hearts, South won the queen of spades opening lead with dummy's king and cashed the ace and king of trumps. Everybody nicely followed suit, and now declarer was going to lose only one trump trick and two club tricks. He was going to take the ace of spades and ruff a spade in the dummy. Because of that, he could not afford to lead the third round of trumps.

But trumps don't always break 3–2 like declarer thinks they should. I have changed the hands held by East-West, and now when South leads his two high trumps, he learns that the three small ones in his hand will win only one trick if he goes ahead and leads them. Furthermore, there are two sure trump losers. It's time to stop and reconsider.

Chances are not too good, but all is not yet lost. If declarer cannot take two tricks with small trumps in the south hand by leading them, can he make two tricks by ruffing? He still has his seven tricks in top cards, and, if he can get by with ruffing one spade in the dummy and two diamonds in his hand without being overruffed, he will still have his ten tricks.

All will be well provided West started with as many as three spades and four diamonds. This is far from a sure thing, but it certainly is better than giving up. So, South should go ahead and cash the ace of spades and then trump a spade. A diamond to the king, a diamond back to the ace, and another diamond lets him trump a diamond. A club to the ace and another diamond lets him trump the fourth diamond for his tenth trick. Declarer is sitting there with one trump and two clubs, and West has two trumps and one club. All of West's three cards are good, but not until declarer has taken ten tricks.

So, there are times when you can take extra tricks by ruffing in the long hand. I know of no better name to give this procedure than the scramble.

Declarer is better placed if the four trumps turn up in the East hand. He has his three small trumps back of the opponent's length rather than in front of it as in the previous hand.

Fig. 6-37

Again, on the same contract and opening lead, declarer discovers that he has gotten the 4–1 break in trumps. However, things are considerably better than they were, for it is now East who has the four trumps.

Having won the opening spade lead in the dummy rather than in his hand, and after pulling the ace and king of trumps, declarer goes about getting his trump trick in the dummy by leading the ace of spades and trumping another spade. Now he leads a small diamond to his king, and another to dummy's ace and then leads another one. East is out of diamonds, but if he elects to trump with one of his two remaining hearts, declarer will simply discard a club. He will still lose two trump tricks, but now will lose only one club trick. East might try to wait for something better rather than trumping now, in which event the declarer will simply trump with a small heart, return to dummy with a club, and once more lead a diamond. If East doesn't trump that diamond, it will be declarer's tenth trick. If East does trump it, the declarer will simply throw away a losing club and will get two tricks out of the three small tricks in his hand after all.

Fig. 6-38

My next hand (Fig. 6-38) was played in a match-point duplicate game. Usually, the contract was four hearts, and results ranged anywhere from nine to eleven tricks won.

The opening lead usually chosen was the queen of spades. The lead was won in the dummy, and those who started pulling trumps soon found that they had a sure trump loser. Those who went set decided to gamble either that the club finesse would work or that the clubs would break 3–3. After pulling three trumps, they tried the club finesse. When that lost, there was still another club loser, the trump loser, and the spade loser.

Most of those who made ten tricks also won the opening spade lead and pulled three trumps. Learning that they had a trump loser, they decided to scramble for their tricks by trying to trump diamonds. This way, they could bring in ten tricks, provided West started with as many as three diamonds. By trumping two diamonds with the two remaining small trumps, they would bring in a total of five trump tricks. These, with two spade tricks, the diamond ace, and two club tricks, brought the total up to ten. However, these delcarers could not afford to have one of the high clubs trumped, so they took the king and ace of clubs in that order, foregoing the club finesse altogether.

One wise player, who simply refused to believe the legend that you cannot gain tricks by trumping in the long hand, set out to get a top from the beginning by instigating his scramble play from the start. He won the opening spade in the dummy and promptly laid down the ace of diamonds and then trumped a diamond. Next, he cashed the ace and queen of hearts, and, when East discarded a spade on the second heart, he saw that he was on the right track. He led the king of clubs, went to dummy with the ace of clubs, and trumped a second diamond. Now he was going to take ten tricks, even if the next time he trumped a diamond he got overtrumped. So, he went to the dummy with the high spade and led the last diamond from there and trumped it. When this wasn't overruffed, he had taken ten tricks—five trump tricks plus two spades, two clubs, and one diamond. And, the king of trumps was still in the dummy for his eleventh trick.

Fig. 6-39 Dlr: S Vul: B

North: ♠ A 7 4 3 ♡ 7 6 ◇ A Q 4 ♣ 7 6 5 3

West: ♠ K 10 8 6 ♡ — ◇ K J 10 7 ♣ A K 10 4 2

East: ♠ 9 5 ♡ Q J 10 9 8 ◇ 9 8 ♣ Q J 9 8

South: ♠ Q J 2 ♡ A K 5 4 3 2 ◇ 6 5 3 2 ♣ —

SOUTH	WEST	NORTH	EAST
1♡	Dbl	Rdbl	Pass
Pass	2♣	Pass	3♣
3♡	Pass	4♡	Dbl
Pass	Pass	Pass	

Opening lead: ♣K

With three sure trump tricks and a partner who had made a takeout double, East's penalty double when South reached a four heart contract shook the rafters.

West led the king of clubs, and South trumped it. He then led the ace and king of trumps. That left him with three little trumps, and East with three big trumps. It was a cinch that the trumps in the declarer's hand were not going to take tricks by leading them. If they were going to take any tricks at all, they were going to be ruffing tricks.

South next led the queen of spades which was covered by the king and ace. A little club back let him get in one of those trumps as a ruffing trick. Next, he led a small diamond and finessed dummy's queen. Then he led another club and got in his second little trump as a ruffing trick. A diamond back to dummy's ace let him get in his third little trump as a ruffing trick. He had now taken nine tricks, and when the jack of spades held the trick, he had taken ten. East was left with three trumps, all high. All the cards left in the West hand were high, too. That gave the defenders six tricks. The trouble was, there were only three tricks left.

Winning ruffing tricks with two little trumps in declarer's hand made the difference in the next exhibit (Fig. 6-40).

Fig. 6-40

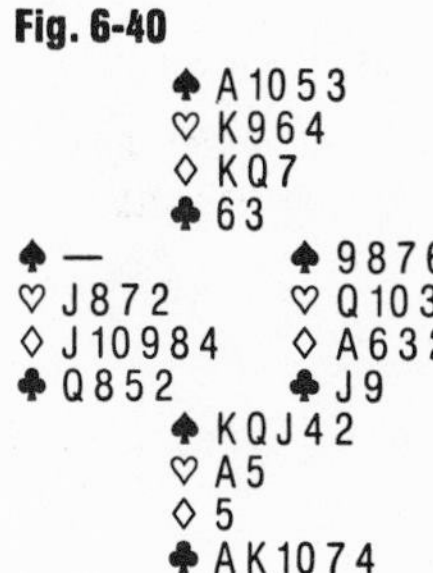

South got into a contract of six spades and got an opening lead of the jack of diamonds. Adding up his tricks and counting on one diamond trick, he saw that off the top he had an additional five trump tricks, plus two hearts and two clubs, for a total of ten. He needed two more.

If the trump suit broke 2-2, he could trump two clubs in the dummy and could win not five trump tricks, but seven, which, added to the others, made twelve tricks total. So, he put up the queen of diamonds to await developments. East won that with the ace and returned a diamond, which was won in the dummy with the king, South discarding a small club. Declarer now led a small trump to the jack in his hand, and West showed out. He was going to have to lead trumps four times to exhaust East, and that would leave him no way to trump two clubs. If clubs broke 3-3, he could lead the ace and king of clubs and trump one in the dummy and would be home free. But with spades breaking 4-0, the declarer was pessimistic about the chances of a 3-3 club break.

Of course, he could lead the ace and king of clubs and trump a club with a high trump in the dummy, but even that would do no good unless clubs broke 3-3, in which event it would not have been necessary to use the high trump.

Declarer found a better chance than finding the clubs 3-3: if he could pick up two ruffing tricks in his hand with the four and two of trumps and then get no worse than a 4-2 break in clubs, he thought he could bring in twelve tricks. That is what he set about doing.

After winning with the jack of spades, he laid down the ace and king of clubs. He abandoned the idea of trumping clubs for the moment, even with the high trump in the dummy, to keep East from taking any discards if he had started with only two. Instead, he led the ace of hearts, led to dummy's king, and then led another heart, trumping it with his small spade. Things were going along just fine. He led a small club and trumped it with dummy's ace. East, sitting there with three spades and two diamonds, threw away one of his diamonds. Declarer then led the seven of diamonds from the dummy and trumped it with his four of spades. Next he led a club and trumped it with dummy's ten-spot. East was sitting there with nothing but three spades and had to underruff. South's queen and jack of spades took the last two tricks.

On the next hand, South felt very confident when he got a look at the dummy.

Fig. 6-41 Dlr: N Vul: B

North: ♠ 9 8 ♡ A 6 4 ◇ A K 5 4 ♣ A K 3 2

West: ♠ — ♡ K J 7 3 2 ◇ J 9 6 3 ♣ Q J 10 9

East: ♠ K Q J 10 ♡ 10 9 8 ◇ Q 10 7 ♣ 8 6 4

South: ♠ A 7 6 5 4 3 2 ♡ Q 5 ◇ 8 2 ♣ 7 5

NORTH	EAST	SOUTH	WEST
1◇	Pass	1♠	Pass
2♣	Pass	2♠	Pass
3 NT	Pass	4♠	All Pass

Opening lead: ♣Q

"We didn't have many tricks at no-trump, partner," said declarer, "but four spades ought to be a cinch." The opening lead of the queen of clubs was won by dummy's king, and declarer promptly led the eight of spades to his ace. South's next comment, when he saw the heart discard from West, was, "Complications have arisen." Now he saw three trump losers and what at first looked like an inevitable loser in hearts. But, the declarer went into a brown study. At least the trumps were in the best place for him; that is, in front of his small trumps rather than behind them. If there was just some way to get four tricks out of those six remaining small trumps, he would still have his ten tricks. Obviously he couldn't do that by leading trumps, as East would immediately cash three trump tricks and leave him only three small ones.

Well, when declarer's trumps cannot take tricks by leading them, the declarer tries to convert them into ruffing tricks. So, that's what he set about trying to do. He led his remaining club to dummy's king and then led a club and trumped it. He led a diamond to the dummy and led the last club. If East trumped that, declarer would simply throw away his losing heart. East would have only two trumps left and could draw only two of South's small trumps. That would leave declarer still in charge. So East gave the best defense possible and discarded a diamond. Declarer trumped the club, and went to the dummy with a high diamond and led another diamond. East still couldn't trump without giving South his contract, so he discarded a heart. Declarer trumped the diamond and had made three of his small trumps. He went to the dummy with the ace of hearts and led dummy's last diamond. East was still in the same bind. If he trumped, he would reduce his trump holding to two trumps and leave South with three and no heart losers, since declarer would discard his losing heart on the club when East trumped. Finally, East threw away his last heart, and declarer trumped for his tenth trick.

Once more, with only three tricks left, each opponent had three winners, and East had the pleasure of winning his partners' high cards with his high trumps.

Fig. 6-42 Dlr: N Vul: B

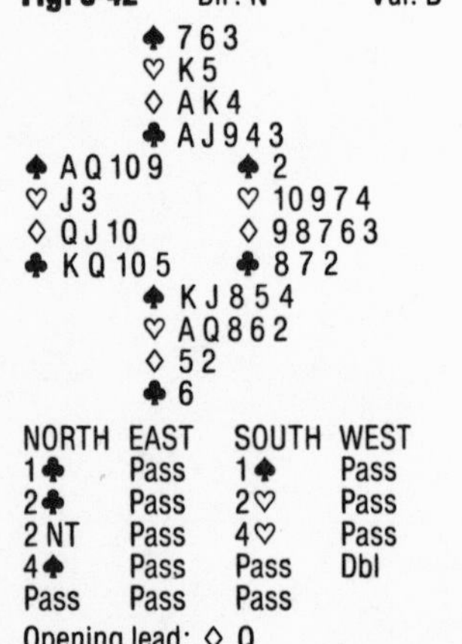

The firmness with which West doubled the four spade contract on the next hand (Fig. 6-42) convinced the declarer that West had quite a few trump tricks.

If West had all the trumps the force of his double indicated, declarer decided it was scramble time. He would just start trumping in his hand with his small trumps, play it by ear, and hope for the best. So, he won with dummy's king of diamonds and promptly led the ace of clubs and then trumped a small club. He went back to the dummy with the ace of diamonds and trumped another small club. He played the ace of hearts and a small heart to dummy's king and trumped still another small club. He had now made three tricks with his own small trumps and five tricks in side suits, giving him a total of eight.

Fig. 6-43 indicates what everybody had left.

South led the queen of hearts, and West had a choice—a choice of two ways to surrender. He could discard his diamond and let the queen of hearts be declarer's ninth trick, in which event South would lead another heart, and West would have to trump and concede a trick to the king of trumps. Or he could trump the queen of hearts and still have two ways to surrender. If he trumped, South would discard dummy's diamond.

Fig. 6-43

♠ 7 6 3
♡ —
◊ 4
♣ J

♠ A Q 10 9 ♡ — ◊ J ♣ —

♠ 2 ♡ 10 ◊ 9 8 7 ♣ —

♠ K J
♡ Q 8 6
◊ —
♣ —

If West then led a diamond, declarer would trump in the dummy and lead the jack of clubs to put West back in the lead, so the king of spades would be the tenth trick.

If, after trumping the queen of hearts, West led the ace and a small spade, declarer would have nothing to lead but hearts, but that would promote dummy's last trump for the tenth winner.

So, I will make my point once more and we will get on with the next subject. Ruffing tricks are tricks made by trumps which could not win tricks if they were led.

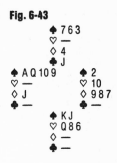

RUFFING IN DECLARER'S HAND: THE DUMMY REVERSAL

There are times when you ruff in declarer's hand with high trumps which are sure to take tricks whether used as ruffing tricks or led. This will occur when the short suit is in your hand and not in dummy and where the dummy has sufficient high trumps to exhaust the opponents' trumps.

Hearts are trump. The opening lead is the queen of diamonds. Counting losers, declarer sees a loser in spades and two in diamonds, but when it comes to counting winners, it doesn't look all that easy. By straightforward play, there are eight tricks off the top.

Fig. 6-44

Four of the winners are in suits other than trumps. If there is any way to increase the number of trump winners from four to six, declarer can take his ten tricks. How about trumping a couple of clubs in his own hand and then using dummy's trumps to pull trumps? That looks like a good idea because it *is* a good idea. However, the cards have to be played in the right order to do this.

The play is to win the first diamond trick with the ace and then take the ace and king of hearts. At this point, hearts must be abandoned, as the two remaining trumps in the South have to be used to trump clubs. Fortunately, there are two entries in the dummy, making this possible, and so, after winning the two heart tricks, the declarer leads the nine of clubs to the dummy and leads a small club to trump with the six of hearts. To be sure that nobody gets a discard, he now cashes his winners in the spade suit, being careful to take the king and then the ace so he will end up in the dummy. From there he will lead his last club, trump it with the queen, and he will have taken eight tricks—four trump tricks, two spade tricks, one diamond, and one club. There in the dummy are the jack and ten of hearts, which, being high, will surely take two more tricks.

Let us see just what characteristics this hand had that made this plan a plausible one. In the first place, notice that the J 10 9 of hearts in the north hand were just as good as the A K Q in the south hand and could be used to pull trumps just as well as declarer's trumps could be used. Then, there were the two black aces in the dummy to give the dummy entry so that two clubs could be led and trumped. All that was necessary was for declarer to imagine that he was playing from the north seat rather than the south seat. I suppose this is where that play got its name, it is called a dummy reversal. It must mean that the declarer, in his mind, reverses himself from his chair to the dummy's chair and plays the hand from that side.

This is not the general sort of hand described as a dummy reversal, as there are four trumps in each hand. However, it does have all of the characteristics of a dummy reversal, and, if you want to challenge my terminology and get technical about it, I will go along and say that it is a half dummy reversal.

Fig. 6-45

♠ A 9 7 5
♡ Q 10 9
◇ 10 8 3
♣ Q 7 6

♠ K Q J 10 ♠ 8 6 4 2
♡ 6 2 ♡ 8 5 3
◇ Q 5 2 ◇ A K 9 7
♣ J 9 4 3 ♣ 10 8

♠ 3
♡ A K J 7 4
◇ J 6 4
♣ A K 5 2

The next hand (Fig. 6-45) is the whole ball of wax.

Again we have South in a four heart contract. This time we get the opening lead of the king of spades. It looks like there are three sure diamond losers whenever the opponents get the lead and bother to take them, and whether there is a club loser or not depends on how the clubs break. If they will break 3–3, there will be no club loser. We don't like to depend on too many 3–3 club breaks to make a living, so we look around to see if there is a better way.

We find one that depends only on the hearts' breaking 3–2. As five outstanding cards are inclined to break 3–2, while six outstanding cards as in the club suit are inclined to break 4–2, let's go for the heart break. But now, dummy is a little short on entries, so we will have to use the trumps themselves for that purpose.

So, we win the opening lead with the ace of spades and lead a low spade, carefully trumping it high. It is essential that we keep those two little hearts to serve as entries back into the north hand. We lead one of them and trump another spade with another trump honor. We now lead our last small trump to dummy, lead dummy's last spade, and trump it with the remaining trump honor. Now we are out of trumps, but the dummy still has the queen of clubs. We go to the dummy with the queen of clubs and finally pull the remaining trump. On this we discard a diamond because now, if clubs do break favorably, we will take eleven tricks. When they do not, and assuming the defenders have defended correctly, we will end up with only ten tricks, but will fulfill our contract.

Now let's look at this dummy reversal from a slightly different angle (Fig. 6-46).

Fig. 6-46

This time we want to take all thirteen tricks with hearts as trumps. We get the lead of the king of spades. Looking at the north and south hands, you are going to ask what in the world we are going to do with that extra diamond. If the trumps would break 2–2, we could lead our clubs and discard a small diamond from the dummy and then have a trump left to trump a diamond, but, don't count on that. We have a better plan. We decide to discard a small diamond from the south hand. *Discard it on what?* Well, believe it or not, we are going to discard it on a trump. And how in the devil are we going to manage to discard a diamond from the south hand on a trump from the north hand? Well, we are going to trump so many spades in the south hand that we will get down to where the north hand has more trumps than the south hand. At the beginning, the south hand had six trumps and the north three. By the time we trump four spades, the north hand will have one more trump than the south hand. By doing this, unless one of our opponents has all four outstanding trumps, we are going to be able to trump all of the spades in the north hand with high trumps, end up with one more trump in north than south, and discard that little diamond on the last trump in the north hand. By this process, we won't be satisfied with taking six trump tricks. Trumping four spades in our hand and leading three trumps from north gives us a total of seven trump tricks. Add these to the two tricks in diamonds and four in clubs, and you have your total of thirteen.

But again, we are a little short on entries in the north hand, and so we have to ruff high. We trump the spade with an honor and then lead a little trump to get back to the north hand. When both opponents follow suit, we are all right unless somebody has a singleton or void in diamonds and has both of the remaining trumps. We lead a second spade and trump it high. Now we lead another small trump to dummy and lead a third spade, trumping it high. Now we have to lead a diamond to get to dummy and lead the fourth spade and ruff it with our last trump. At this point, we have no trumps left, but both dummy and East have a trump. So we lead a small diamond to the dummy again, and finally take East's last trump away from him, at the same time discarding our bad diamond. All we have left in our hand are the four clubs, and they are all going to take a trick.

When dummy's trumps are not all high, you may have to lead a high one from your own hand, while at the same time preparing for the dummy reversal (Fig. 6-47).

Fig. 6-47

This time the contract is six spades, and the opening lead is the king of clubs.

Declarer has more than one way to approach the hand. By straight leads, he can take eleven tricks. If the diamonds will break evenly, he can take another diamond trick. Should the trumps break evenly, he could trump a losing diamond. If the trumps break 3-1, he could still trump a losing diamond, provided the hand that had three trumps also had four diamonds.

But, by the dummy reversal plan, he can take twelve tricks, even if the trumps are 3-1, unless there is terrible distribution in one of the red suits. To make dummy the long hand in trumps, he is going to have to trump four clubs, but this seems to be plausible. So, declarer trumps the opening lead and plays the eight of trumps to dummy's queen to discover that trumps will break no worse than 3-1. He leads another club and trumps it. At this point, he lays down the ace of spades from his hand. Then he goes to the dummy with the king of hearts and trumps a third club. Back to the dummy he goes with the ace of hearts and uses his last trump to trump the fourth club. A diamond to dummy's ace lets him finally lead the king of trumps, extracting the last trump from the opponents; on this he discards a small heart. Had diamonds broken 3-3, he would have taken thirteen tricks; although they failed to do so, he still has his twelve.

Sometimes you can even pull off a dummy reversal when the dummy has only one high trump—by leading two from your hand in the process of reducing your hand to fewer trump than the dummy has.

Fig. 6-48

```
          ♠ Q 5 4
          ♡ 8 6 5 3
          ◇ A K 3
          ♣ A 4 3
♠ 8 3               ♠ 10 9 7
♡ Q J 10 9          ♡ A 7 4 2
◇ 8 6 2             ◇ J 7 5 4
♣ K J 9 7           ♣ Q 10
          ♠ A K J 6 2
          ♡ K
          ◇ Q 10 9
          ♣ 8 6 5 2
```

Against a four spade contract, West led the queen of hearts. Obvious were five spade tricks, three diamonds, and a club, for a total of nine. Also, the hand had the characteristics of a dummy reversal. The shortage was in the south hand. So, declarer set out to take six trump tricks rather than five.

He was helped by East who took the ace of hearts and returned a heart. Declarer trumped this and led the ace and king of spades. He then quit leading spades to save the queen of spades in the dummy to pull the last trump after he had used the two trumps remaining in his hand. Over to the dummy he went with the ace of diamonds and ruffed a heart with his six of spades. Back he went to the dummy with the king of diamonds and trumped another heart with his last spade, the jack. Then he went to the dummy with the ace of clubs, led the queen of spades, and on it discarded a small club. The queen of diamonds in his hand rounded out the tenth trick.

The illustrative hands I have shown you so far each contain just one problem—how to trump in declarer's hand and finally pull trumps with dummy's hand. These are fine for learning the basic principles of the dummy reversal. In real life, the dummy reversal gets mixed up with all sorts of other things. There can be finesses involved, or suit establishment, or whatnot. The next hand is reported to have been taken from a Team of Four contest (Fig. 6-49).

Fig. 6-49

```
          ♠ K 10 8 5
          ♡ K J 9
          ◇ J 10 8
          ♣ A 10 7
♠ J 9 7 2           ♠ —
♡ —                 ♡ 7 6 5 3 2
◇ K 9 6 4 2         ◇ A Q 7 5 3
♣ K Q J 9           ♣ 6 3 2
          ♠ A Q 6 4 3
          ♡ A Q 10 8 4
          ◇ —
          ♣ 8 5 4
```

Both declarers reached a contract of six spades by South, and both received the king of clubs opening lead.

With good breaks, it looked like eleven tricks off the top, with the twelfth one coming by discarding dummy's clubs on declarer's hearts and picking up a ruffing trick in the dummy. The first declarer won the first trick and led a small spade to his ace. When East showed out, declarer decided that complications had arisen.

He decided that his best bet was to go through a dummy reversal procedure. He led a small spade, just covered what West played, and then trumped a diamond. A low trump allowed another spade finesse through West, and the diamond was trumped with declarer's last trump. But when declarer tried to get to the dummy by leading a heart, West trumped that and promptly cashed two club tricks.

In the other room, the declarer also won the king with the ace of clubs and immediately saw that a dummy reversal might be possible; however, the king of clubs had removed one of the entries he needed for that purpose. So, while he was in the dummy, he saw no particular harm in immediately leading a diamond and trumping it. Then he laid down the ace of spades, and it turned out that his immediate trumping of the diamond saved the day for him. When East showed out, he led a small spade through West for the finesse. Another diamond was trumped with the queen of spades. He still had a spade left to lead for the final finesse through West, and then an extra trump left in the dummy to pull West's last trump. On that he discarded a club. By trumping two diamonds in his hand, he had run his winners in trumps up to a total of six and was now able to cash his five hearts without interference. These, added to the ace of clubs, came to twelve tricks. He simply gave up a club at the end.

Fig. 6-50

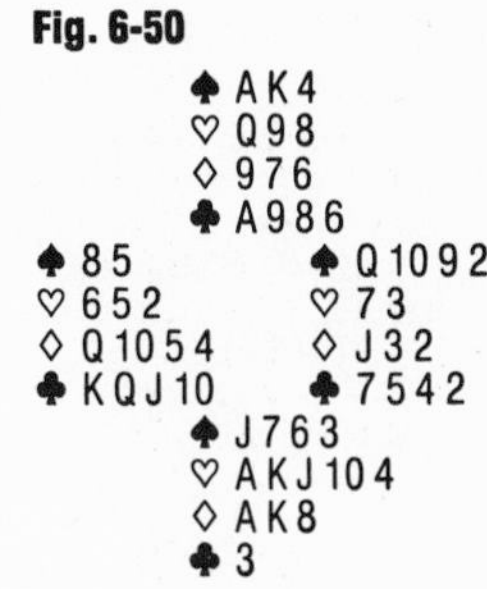

This next hand involved suit establishment, as well as dummy reversal.

Declarer had to be lucky to make his contract of six hearts, but he took about the only play available to him, and it worked. The opening lead of the king of clubs was won by dummy's ace. The declarer could find only ten tricks off the top, leaving him two short. Any one of several favorable breaks in the spade suit would get him another winner in that suit, but he had yet another to find. The symptoms for a dummy reversal were there, with a shortage in declarer's hand and high trumps in the dummy. Having nothing better, declarer set out to see how that would work out.

To preserve entries, he led a second club and trumped it high. A small heart put the lead back in the dummy, and another club was trumped high. The jack of hearts to dummy's queen put dummy on lead to let the declarer trump dummy's last club with declarer's last trump. Now he went to the dummy with the ace of spades and led the nine of trumps, on which he discarded a small diamond. Next he led dummy's high spade and another spade. Lucky fellow. East won that with the queen and had nothing left but spades and diamonds. Declarer was able to take the balance of the tricks. He had won three spade tricks, two diamond tricks, one club trick, and a total of six trump tricks.

Fig. 6-51 is a fancy one mixed up with an unblocking play.

Fig. 6-51

South got up to five clubs and got an opening lead of the king of hearts. When the dummy came down, he could see only ten tricks, and this assumed that he would take five clubs, three diamonds, and then manage to get to the dummy. But declarer saw possible symptoms of a dummy reversal there. Of the four trumps held by North, three were good as gold. The shortage was in the south hand. If he could trump two hearts in his hand, he would raise his trump winners to six tricks, which, added to the five diamond tricks (if he could bring them all home, that is), would bring his contract in.

So, with plenty of high trumps in both hands, declarer took the precaution of trumping the heart lead with the queen of clubs. When he laid down the ace of clubs and East showed out, he still had two entries to the dummy with his two small trumps. He used one of them immediately to go to the dummy and trump dummy's last heart with his high club. Next, he laid down the ace and king of diamonds. When West followed to those two diamonds, he had it made. He didn't dare lead a third diamond for fear West might trump. Instead, he led his small club to the dummy. Then, he led dummy's last club, for the dual purpose of extracting the last trump from West and unblocking diamonds by discarding the queen. That left him with three good diamonds in the dummy, giving him his five diamond tricks to add to his six trump tricks, for a total of eleven.

The last hand in this series is one of the old classics. I have no idea how long it has been around and strongly suspect that whist players gave it to our grandparents to puzzle them. If you have not seen it yet, sooner or later someone is going to give it to you and ask you how South can make seven hearts against an opening lead of the king of clubs. So, I suggest you

Fig. 6-52

```
            ♠ A Q 2
            ♡ A K Q J
            ◇ Q J 10 9 8 7
            ♣ —
♠ K J 10 9 8 7     ♠ 6 5 4 3
♡ 5 4 3 2          ♡ —
◇ —                ◇ 6 5 4 3 2
♣ K Q J            ♣ 5 4 3 2
            ♠ —
            ♡ 10 9 8 7 6
            ◇ A K
            ♣ A 10 9 8 7 6
```

remember this hand well, and, when the hand is finally offered you to perplex you, you can appear to be puzzled for a moment, acting as though you had never seen it before, and then say in a casual way, "Why, it's a very simple dummy reversal." That will put your tormenter in his place.

You must shorten your hand to fewer trumps than held in the dummy, and the only way to do that is to trump two spades. So, you cannot afford to discard a spade on the opening lead. You must discard a diamond. I suggest to carry on the act, you discard the queen of diamonds. After winning with South's club ace, you cross to the dummy with a trump and then trump a small spade. Next you go to the dummy with another trump and trump the queen of spades. Dummy now holds two trumps, and you have only one. You go to the dummy with that one trump and discard the king of diamonds on dummy's ace of trumps. On dummy's ace of spades, discard the ace of diamonds. Now all of dummy's diamonds are good, and you are in the north hand.

It is a fun hand, and I hope you enjoyed it. In addition, it does utilize the basic principles of the dummy reversal.

TRUMPS AS ENTRIES

Fig. 6-53

```
            ♠ A 7 2
            ♡ Q 7
            ◇ 9 5
            ♣ K J 10 7 5 4
♠ 9 5 3            ♠ 10 6
♡ A K J 8 2        ♡ 10 6 5 3
◇ A Q 10           ◇ 8 6 4 2
♣ 8 3              ♣ Q 9 6
            ♠ K Q J 8 4
            ♡ 9 4
            ◇ K J 7 3
            ♣ A 2
```

Another thing those precious trumps can sometimes do for you is get you where you want to be when you want to be there. In other words, they can act as entries. But you can't just push them around and play them anytime you get a notion to. You have to treat them with respect and play them at just the right moment.

In Fig. 6-53, at a four spade contract, West took the first two tricks with the king and ace of hearts and switched to a small trump. South won that with the jack and led the king of trumps, but could not afford to lead a third trump. He didn't know how many diamond losers he had, but if the club suit broke sensibly, he could discard a lot of diamonds on clubs. To do that, he had to have a way to get to the dummy after the clubs were established. So, he took the ace and king of clubs and then a small one which he trumped high. Now that ace of trumps gave him an entry to the three good clubs in the dummy. On these he could discard three diamonds, limiting his losers to two hearts and one diamond.

It isn't always those big trumps that serve as entries. There are times when it pays to be careful about the small ones.

Fig. 6-54

```
            ♠ K 5 4 3
            ♡ 9 6 2
            ◇ 10 6 4
            ♣ 9 7 3
♠ J                ♠ 9 6
♡ 8 7 5 4          ♡ K 10 3
◇ K Q J            ◇ 9 8 7 2
♣ K Q J 8 4        ♣ A 10 6 5
            ♠ A Q 10 8 7 2
            ♡ A Q J
            ◇ A 5 3
            ♣ 2
```

Again South was playing four spades. This time he got the lead of the king of clubs. That won the trick, and West continued with clubs. Be alert, friend South! For you to take ten tricks, you are going to have to take a successful heart finesse not once, but twice. That means you are going to have to get to the dummy twice. I can't find anything to get you into the dummy twice, except trumps, and, to do that, you will have to keep that two of trumps in your hand until the proper moment. So just trump with the seven of trumps, then lay down the ace of spades, and lead the eight of spades to dummy's king. Now lead a small heart and cross your fingers.

When the jack holds the trick, you can lead the two of spades to dummy's three-spot and repeat the finesse to get your ten tricks.

There are times when those little trumps have to have some smaller trumps with them as buddies to do the job for you. On the next hand (Fig. 6-55) you could not afford to spend even one of the buddies.

After East competed in spades, South got to a contract of five clubs. The opening lead was the six of spades. East won that with the queen and, after considerable thought, led a second spade. Now it was South who did some thinking. The diamond suit was blocked, and declarer desperately needed an entry to the dummy after he cashed the ace and king of diamonds. The queen of hearts might conceivably offer the entry, but, in view of the bidding, he considered that somewhat unlikely. A more likely entry was the six of clubs. Of course, that could only occur after he had extracted the opponents' clubs, and the likelihood was that it would take three leads to accomplish that. Declarer finally decided that there was a greater likelihood that the clubs would break no worse than 3–1 than there was that West held the king of hearts, so he did not trump that second spade in the dummy. He just discarded one of dummy's hearts. Now if it took three trump leads to exhaust the opponents' trumps, the six would still be in the dummy as an entry.

Now no matter what East did, the defense was through taking tricks. Whatever he led, declarer would win the next trick, pull trumps in three leads, cash the ace and king of diamonds, and then go to the dummy with the six of clubs where there were plenty of tricks remaining in the diamond suit. Should East continue with a third spade, South had only to be careful to trump with the eight to keep his entry.

It is not only small trumps that sometimes need even smaller trumps to stand as guards so they can become entries; sometimes very big trumps need the same assistance.

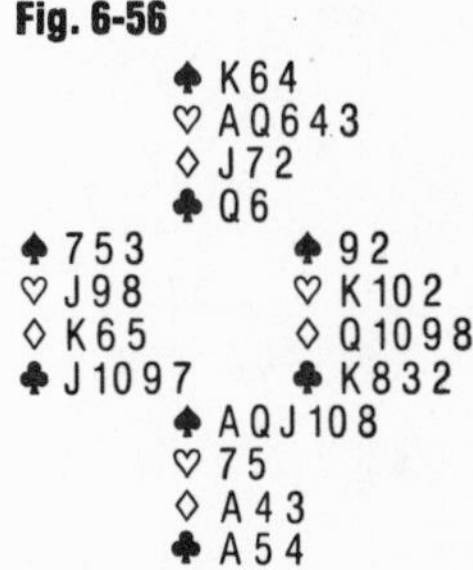

In a contract of four spades, the opening lead was the jack of clubs. Upon examining the dummy, declarer saw that he had eight tricks off the top. He ought to be able to trump a club in the dummy to raise him to nine. There were several other plays for his tenth trick, and he attempted the first one by putting up the queen of clubs, in case West had underled the king. No luck. East played the king, and South had to win with the ace. Now he considered the heart suit. If that finesse worked, that would be his ninth trick, and he could still give up a club and trump a club for his tenth. So he led a small heart and put in his queen. He decided then that it was his unlucky day. All kings seemed to be wrong. Now his only chance seemed to be to establish the heart suit for two discards. Not much of a chance, but apparently all that was left.

East returned the two of clubs to let his partner know that he had started with four of them and that it was time for West to try to size up the situation. He saw that if South held another heart, the suit was going to establish. He also saw that the only entry, once the suit was established, was the king of spades. Well, if he could just get one spade out of the dummy, he would have a spade left when declarer used his entry to get there. So West led another club.

Now it was time for declarer to be awake. He had to refuse to trump the club to preserve the small guards in the dummy so that when he used up his king of spades entry, the opponents would hopefully be out of trumps. So he just discarded a diamond from the dummy.

West switched to a diamond, and South finally got his lucky break. He won that with the ace, cashed two high spades in his hand, and then took his ace of hearts and trumped a heart. Since hearts broke 3–3, he utilized his entry to the dummy and discarded his two losing diamonds on the two good hearts.

If there is a price to pay to make one of dummy's trumps an entry and that entry will enable you to make your contract, pay the price.

Fig. 6-57

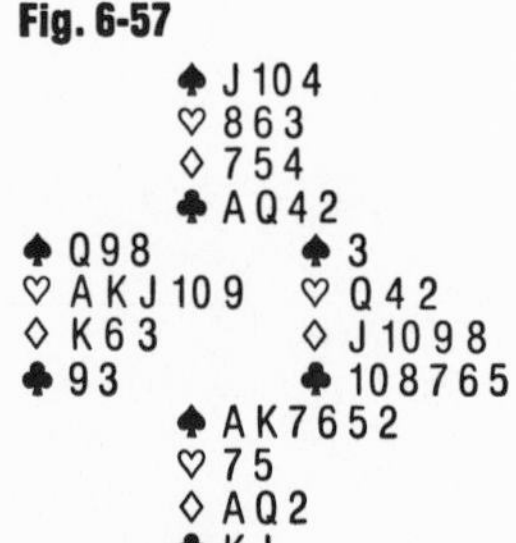

In a contract of four spades, the opening lead was the king of hearts. East signaled, and hearts were continued, but South trumped the third one. He had lost two heart tricks and was looking at two possible diamond losers, in addition to a possible trump loser. Of course, he could discard his two diamonds on dummy's clubs, if he could find a way to get there.

He laid down the ace of trumps, and, when both opponents followed suit, he decided he could find a way to get there. First he cashed his two clubs. Then he led a small spade toward the dummy, giving up all hopes of dropping the queen of spades in the interest of finding that entry. West could win that trick, but declarer could win the next one and go to the dummy with the remaining trump to get rid of those two diamonds on the two top clubs. It would do West no good to refuse to play his queen of spades and then trump the first club led from the dummy. He would have nothing left to lead except red cards, and whatever he led would allow declarer to take the rest of the tricks.

Fig. 6-58

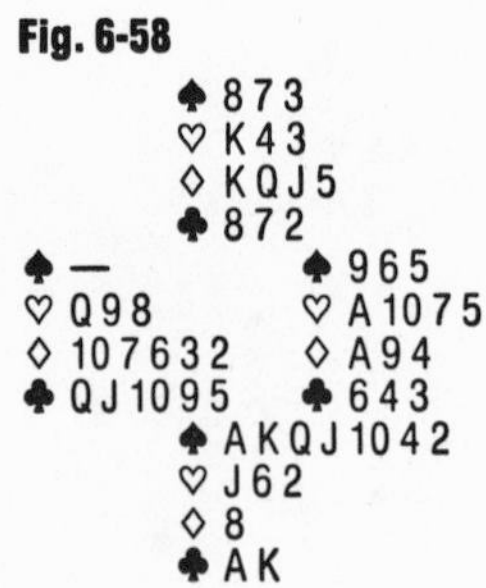

To look at the next hand (Fig. 6-58), you wouldn't think that the declarer would lose a trump trick playing four spades; however, he decided that was what he had to do to make his contract.

West led the queen of clubs, and when the declarer saw the dummy, he thought his chances were pretty good. He won the king and laid down the ace of spades. When West discarded the two of diamonds, declarer decided that his chances were not quite as good as he thought they had been. However, he switched to a diamond to establish that suit. West played the three-spot, and East decided that the manner in which he had played the diamonds indicated an odd number. After some thought, he thought it was probably five rather than three and so when dummy played the jack, he won the ace and returned another club. Now all declarer had to do was find an entry to the dummy. It was there, provided he let East win a trick with the nine of spades, so he led the two-spot and played dummy's seven. It would have done East no good to hold off, so he won that and hopefully led his last club. Declarer was alert and trumped it high and then used his other spade to get to the dummy and discard two hearts on the good diamonds there.

On the next hand, the entry to the dummy was apparent, but declarer found it wise to postpone using it until later so that it could be helpful in establishing clubs.

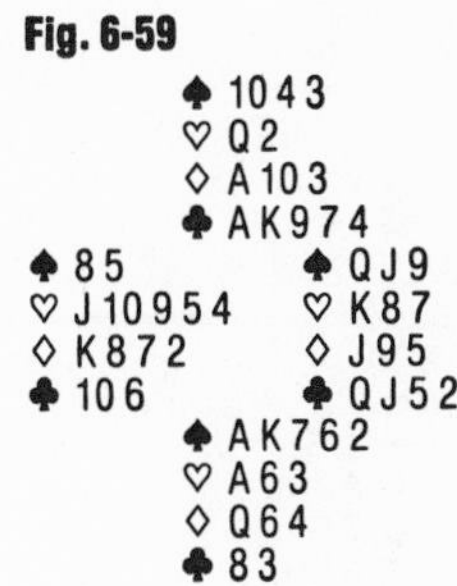

Fig. 6-59

At four spades, West led the jack of hearts. Without too much hope, declarer played the queen from the dummy, and East played the king, as suspected. South saw that with reasonable luck he would lose only one trump trick. Just how many diamond tricks he was going to lose he didn't know. He did intend to limit his losses in hearts to one trick by picking up a ruffing trick in the dummy, but it also is good tactics to let the opponents hold the first trick when you have a doubleton, and that is the action the declarer took on this hand.

East had no doubt about who had the ace of hearts, and rather than help declarer with his timing, he led the queen of trumps. Declarer won the king, led the ace, and saw that he had only one trump loser. He cashed the ace of hearts and now had his ruffing trick established in the dummy. However, that ruffing trick was also one of his entries, and it was too early to win it. To bring in the club suit without loss, he was going to need two entries to the dummy besides the entries in clubs, and he was going to need those after he started working on clubs. Of course, if clubs broke 3–3, one entry would be enough, but declarer knew better than to count on that, when it was likely he could handle the more probable 4–2 split.

So he took the ace and king of clubs and trumped a club. Now was the time to get his ruffing trick and use his entry. He successfully trumped a heart in the dummy. On came the fourth club which declarer trumped. Now he had the ace of diamonds for another entry, and, when he got there, he led his fifth club. East could trump or not, as he liked, but declarer was going to discard a small diamond whichever he did. This left him only one loser in trumps, one in hearts, and one in diamonds and gave him his ten tricks.

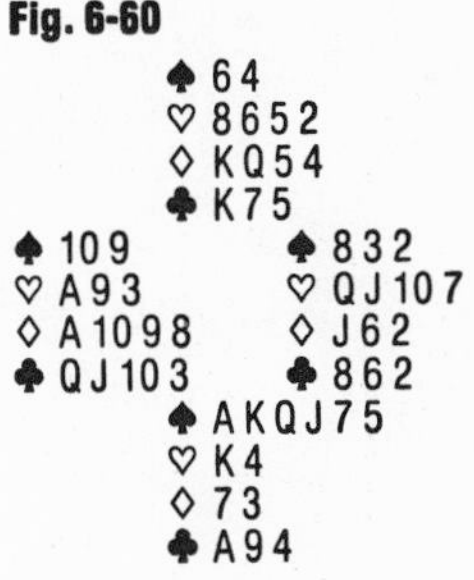

Fig. 6-60

Sometimes the trump entry is needed to get into the declarer's hand rather than the dummy's hand (Fig. 6-60).

When South, in a contract of four spades, got an opening lead of the queen of clubs, it looked like a simple hand. With eight sure tricks in the black suits, all he seemed to need was that the ace of at least one red suit be favorably placed.

To keep his entry in the dummy, declarer won the first club with his ace and quickly led three spades. Then he led a small diamond, and when dummy's queen won the trick, the hand was no longer so simple. Now both red aces had to be favorable for him to bring in ten tricks. A heart back to his king showed that this was not going to work. The defenders were able to knock out dummy's king of clubs while they still retained the ace of diamonds for an entry, and finally they did win a club trick along with the diamond and two hearts.

Declarer should have taken only one trump trick before he led diamonds. If West ducked that, he would have the trump left in the dummy to provide an entry back to his hand and could then go about pulling trumps and leading a second diamond, while the king of clubs was still in the dummy for an entry.

South really meant to only "inkle" one heart after his partner opened the bidding with one club, but North promptly put him in game on hand 6-61.

Fig. 6-61

	North	
	♠ K Q ♡ K Q 9 4 ◇ K 6 4 ♣ A K 4 2	
♠ A 7 5 ♡ 6 5 2 ◇ 10 9 8 3 2 ♣ 9 8		♠ 9 8 6 3 ♡ 7 3 ◇ A Q J ♣ Q J 10 6
	♠ J 10 4 2 ♡ A J 10 8 ◇ 7 5 ♣ 7 5 3	

When declarer got a look at the dummy, he felt a good deal better about the whole business. But now that he had contracted to make game, he would have to be careful to take ten tricks.

Let's say he played carelessly. The opening lead of the ten of diamonds was won by East with the jack. East returned the queen of clubs and declarer had the lead in the dummy. To be sure nobody trumped anything, he led three trumps, noting with satisfaction that they broke favorably. Next he led a spade.

West went up with the ace and led another diamond. East won that with the queen and laid down the ace of diamonds. Whoops! Declarer had to trump that, and there went his last trump. He could then win the king of spades in the dummy, but he did not have the wherewithal to get where he wanted to be when he wanted to be there. In other words, he could not get back to his hand to cash the jack and ten of spades.

That wherewithal could have been provided in the trump suit if declarer had been a bit more careful. After winning the king of clubs, he could afford exactly two trump leads before he led spades. Then, if West went up with the ace and continued with diamonds, declarer would still be able to trump the third diamond and have the high trump in his hand. Over to the dummy he would go with dummy's high spade, and back to his hand he could come with his high trump, at the same time drawing the final trump from the opposition. Now he would be where he wanted to be and could cash those two high spades, discarding on them two losing clubs from the dummy.

Fig. 6-62

	North	
	♠ 8 ♡ A 7 4 2 ◇ A K Q J 7 4 ♣ Q 6	
♠ 7 6 4 2 ♡ 10 8 ◇ 9 ♣ A K J 10 4 2		♠ 9 5 ♡ K Q J 6 ◇ 10 8 5 3 2 ♣ 9 3
	♠ A K Q J 10 3 ♡ 9 5 3 ◇ 6 ♣ 8 7 5	

On the next hand (Fig. 6-62), that singleton trump in the dummy is worth its weight in gold, not because it can take a trick, but because it furnishes an entry.

South is playing four spades, and West leads the king and ace of clubs. East signals vigorously with the nine and three, and so West continues with the third club. Don't trump it in the dummy! East has advertised that he can overruff the dummy. If you trump, East will overtrump, and then he will lead the king of hearts and there will go an important entry to the dummy. Not only that, but when you trump with dummy's eight of spades, you dispense with the best entry into your own hand. An entry by trumping a diamond would be futile, as you need dummy's diamonds for discards. So just play a small heart on the third club, and now it is impossible for them to take out all of the entries you need. If they shift to one of the red suits, you simply win the trick in the dummy and pull trumps. The ace of the other red suit will then provide your entry back to the dummy to throw away the losing hearts from the south hand on dummy's good diamonds.

THE TRUMP POLICEMAN

Let me introduce you to one of the best friends the bridge player has. I refer to the Trump Policeman. That little fellow can save the day for you many times, but you have to treat him right. If you want him to do a job for you, you can't dispose of him until the job is done.

What protection can he give you? He may be needed when you have, in some suit in your hand, a number of small cards with a shortage in the dummy and the possibility that your opponents may gain the lead after you have sent the policeman away. Or he may be needed simply because the opponents are making you trump in your hand too many times and are threatening to take over the trump suit. Let's look at an example in Fig. 6-63.

Fig. 6-63

South naturally was playing a contract of four spades. West, just as naturally led the king of hearts. East, just as naturally as the others, played the two-spot to show he had no interest in that suit. West switched to a club. Declarer played dummy's ace and promptly led a small spade and finessed the nine-spot. The finesse lost, but the eight of spades was still sitting there in the north hand as a policeman to keep West from cashing a lot of hearts.

South thought it would have been nice had the finesse worked, but he also knew that by losing the finesse he had saved the hand. At the worst, he would lose two hearts plus the one trump trick.

The trump policeman helps out where there is some possibility that the opponents might gain the lead after all dummy's trumps are gone when there are losers in your hand which you could have discarded on dummy's long suit if you had timed the hand properly. Declarer knew that 4–1 trump breaks are not all that unusual, and he knew that if he simply laid down the A K Q of trumps and the jack was still outstanding, he was going to lose the lead and there was a good chance he would do so before disposing of his heart losers in his hand.

Fig. 6-64

It does not have to be a finesse that causes you to concede a trump trick to your opponents so that you can keep the policeman on duty. There are times when you just plain give them a trick so you can keep control of the situation.

Again we have South in a contract of four spades with an opening lead of the king of hearts. South trumped in the dummy and decided he didn't like the possibility of his opponents' leading more hearts after he was out of trumps in dummy, especially in view of a possible loser in trumps and two in clubs. So, he simply led a spade from the dummy and played the two-spot from his hand. He felt this left very few opposing distributions which would defeat him, and he was right. The opponents could take their trump trick and two club tricks, but that was all. As soon as declarer regained the lead, he could pull trumps and then have a good time leading diamonds.

On the next hand (Fig. 6-65), declarer knew he had to lose at least one trump trick.

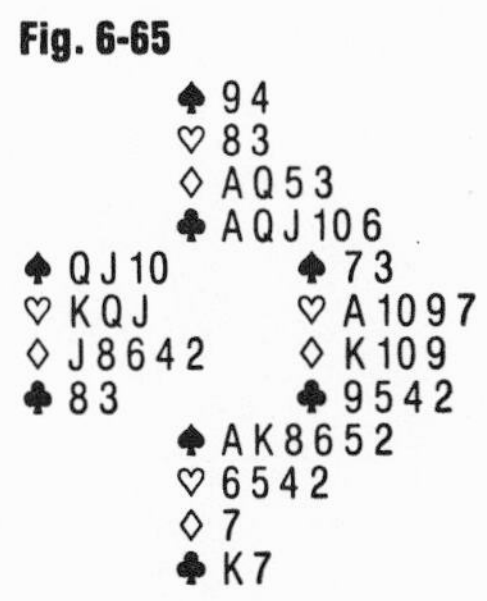

Fig. 6-65

Against the four spade contract, West led the king of hearts. After looking at the dummy, he decided to shift to the queen of spades. There was no way for the Q J 10 of spades to be doubleton, so declarer knew he could not take six spade tricks off the top; the opponents had to win one. A trump policeman was necessary in the dummy until the hand got under control, as declarer had all of those bad hearts in his hand. Had West switched at trick two to a small diamond, declarer would have won with dummy's ace, led a small trump, and conceded a trick. As they had led trumps for him, he decided instead to concede the trick right away and let the queen hold the trick.

After this development, West shrugged his shoulders, took his second heart, and then switched to a diamond. Declarer rose with dummy's ace and led a small diamond and trumped it (just in case the opposing trumps should break badly, making it necessary for him to scramble for all the ruffs he could get). But when he laid down the ace of trumps, he saw this was not necessary, as both opponents followed suit. With everything under control, he led the high spade and could then take all of his club tricks without interference and have a trick left over at the end.

Fig. 6-66

When you get into a contract where you and your partner hold only seven total trumps, you know the chances are that one of your opponents is going to hold four trumps.

Staying with the major suits, South avoided bidding game in either minor and ended up playing four spades. West led the king and ace of hearts, and South trumped the second trick. It looked as though he had plenty of tricks, provided he could bring in all of his club tricks. But, as you see, he could not have brought in all of his club tricks had he tried to pull trumps right away. After the third trump, he would have to stop and leave a trump in the East hand, or the opponents would cash an undue number of hearts. Then, when he tried to cash clubs, East would trump the fourth round with his high trump; South could go ahead and discard a diamond, but he would still have two diamond losers.

So the declarer decided to leave that little trump policeman in the dummy so that he could keep control of the hand while pulling trump. At trick three he led the small spade. Now, if the opponents persisted in heart leads, that little policeman in north would take care of the situation. Actually, East won, and there was no way to keep South from gaining the lead and ending up with four trump tricks, five club tricks, and the ace of diamonds.

Usually, the policeman is needed in the dummy when there is a short suit there. The short suit is not apparent in the next hand (Fig. 6-67), and even though the policeman was not apparent, he was there all the same.

Fig. 6-67

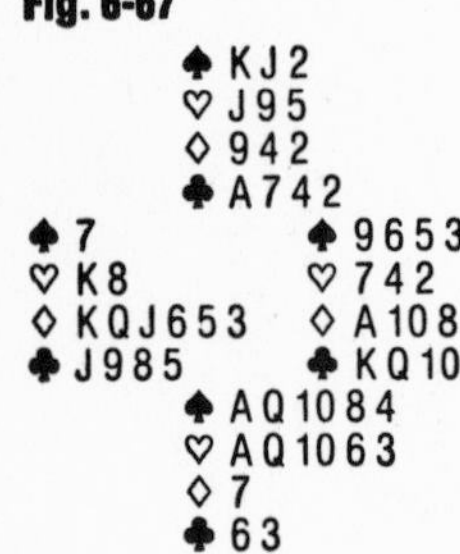

In our favorite contract of four spades, West led the king and then the queen of diamonds. East unblocked by going up with the ace, but declarer trumped that trick. If no complications arose, he now had a total of five trump tricks, plus four heart tricks for sure, and a club trick, totaling ten. So, he laid down the ace and another spade. When West showed out, complications had arisen. East had as many trumps as declarer did. He properly decided that it was necessary to try to establish hearts before leading any more trumps. The heart finesse failed, and, after West won the king, he led a third diamond.

Declarer decided he just couldn't afford to trump that. That would leave him with fewer trumps than East and a club loser as well. He had already lost a diamond and a heart, and if in addition he lost a club and a trump, he was going to go down. But he found a neat solution. He just discarded a small club and let West win that diamond. Now, if West continued diamonds, there was that nice policeman in the north hand to do the trumping so that the South hand could preserve all its trumps, and after dummy trumped a diamond, he would simply come to his hand with a heart and then proceed to finish drawing trumps.

Fig. 6-68

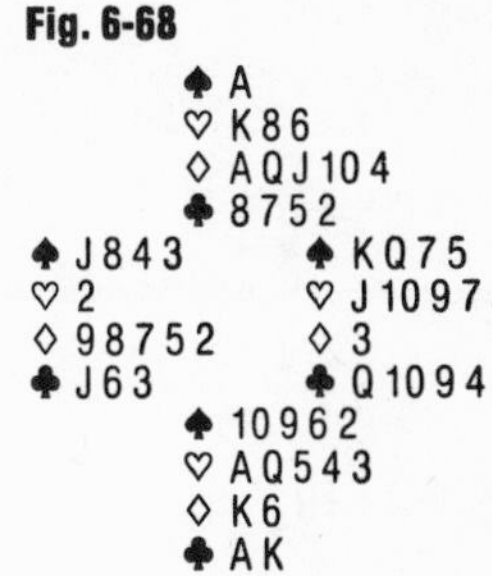

This next hand, Fig. 6-68, was played by Harry Fishbein. Harry was a colorful character. For many years he ran the famous Mayfair Club in New York. He had a collection of berets which made him easy to spot at the many bridge tournaments he attended. He was also a whale of a bridge player.

This hand gives me an opportunity not only to pay a tribute to Harry Fishbein, but also to break the monotony by having hearts trumps rather than spades. Actually, the contract was six hearts, and West got off to a lead of the three of spades which was won in the dummy with the ace. An old-timer like Fishbein knows all about trump policemen. It was only a small slam, not a grand slam, and he decided to leave a worthless trump in the dummy in the event his opponents should persist in spades. At trick two, he led the six of hearts from the dummy and played the three. That did it. If the opponents continued spades, he could trump with dummy's eight-spot, taking the king of hearts, and come back to his hand to finish pulling trumps. If they led anything else, he would simply pull trumps and claim the hand with four trump tricks, a spade trick, five diamond tricks, and two club tricks. If Fishbein had tried to pull trumps, he would have gone set. Had he started off by leading the ace and queen of hearts and switched to diamonds, then East would have trumped the second diamond lead and continued spades so that North would have to trump with the king of hearts and then switched to diamonds, East would trump the second diamond and lead another heart, and the declarer would be in his own hand with the losing spades and no way to reach dummy's good diamonds. And, of course, if he took the three top hearts, then when East got in by trumping the second diamond, the defense could cash three spade tricks.

Fig. 6-69

On the hand in Fig. 6-69, declarer felt he had to keep the policeman on duty until he had taken an important finesse.

With South playing four hearts, West led the king of spades and continued the suit. Declarer had to trump the third spade because he still had a diamond finesse to take and obviously could not afford to lose three spade tricks. However, he didn't want to trump any more spades in his hand and decided it best to leave a policeman in the dummy while he took the diamond finesse. He further decided not to lead the ace of diamonds before going to the dummy for the finesse because that would increase the chances that, should the finesse lose, West might be able to continue diamonds and let East trump one. So, as soon as he trumped a spade, declarer led the ten of trumps to dummy's jack and led a small diamond and finessed it. West won that, but there was nothing he could do with that eight of hearts staring him in the face from the dummy to keep him from leading another spade. If West did not take his queen of diamonds, that would be declarer's tenth trick, and, we hope, he would not have gone to the dummy with a club to try to repeat the finesse, but would have been happy to cash out.

Fig. 6-70

♠ 9
♡ 4 3
◇ K Q 6 5
♣ K Q 8 5 4 2

West	East
♠ 7 6 5 3 2	♠ 8
♡ K Q 10 8 6	♡ A J 9 7 2
◇ 8 7	◇ J 10 9 2
♣ A	♣ 10 9 7

♠ A K Q J 10 4
♡ 5
◇ A 4 3
♣ J 6 3

I don't know who, if anybody, played the next hand. I've seen it around in a number of newspaper columns and think it time to give it a more permanent life than is provided there, as it seems to have been played by a very cautious player. He protected himself against a 5–1 trump break.

We are back to spades. Against a four spade contract, the opening lead was the king of hearts, and the suit was continued. Declarer trumped that, and he must have been reading someone's article on trump policemen. He decided it was essential to establish the club suit while the nine of spades was still in the dummy to stop the run of hearts. And, of course, he was right. Had he started leading trumps, he would have soon found out that West had as many as he had, and that he could not take them away from West without leaving himself wide open in hearts. Then, when he led a club, West could win with the ace and simply retaliate by leading another heart, after which he would have more trumps than declarer. Eventually, the hand would have fallen apart, and declarer would have found himself unable to take ten tricks. By leading a club first, while the nine of spades was still in the dummy, there was not likely to be any problem about taking ten tricks. Even if the opponents could negotiate a club ruff, the declarer would still be in good shape.

Fig. 6-71

♠ 8 6 3
♡ 6 5 3
◇ —
♣ K Q 10 6 5 4 2

West	East
♠ K Q 7 2	♠ A J 10 9 4
♡ K 8 2	♡ 9 7 4
◇ J 9 5 4	◇ K 8 6 3
♣ J 9	♣ 8

♠ 5
♡ A Q J 10
◇ A Q 10 7 2
♣ A 7 3

And now for a really wild one (Fig. 6-71). It was reported as having been played in 1950.

The report states that South got into a contract of four hearts instead of the simple contract of five clubs. West opened the king of spades and, when East signaled with a high one, continued the suit. After North and South exchanged a few words over the bidding sequence that led to the heart contract, South trumped a second spade and led the ace of diamonds to discard the last spade in the dummy. Next he trumped a diamond to reach dummy and led a small heart and finessed it. West must have been some sort of a cruel character. He let the jack hold the trick. South went back to the dummy by leading a club and led dummy's last trump and finessed it. This time, West won with his king and resumed leading spades.

When they counted tricks at the end of the hand, they discovered the declarer had taken exactly six tricks—three in trumps in his hand, one in dummy on a ruff, and the two minor suit aces.

South should have known about his friend the trump policeman. Not only did he have to be lucky to find a 3–3 break in trumps, he also had to leave his policeman in the dummy. How could he do that? He was quite right to lead the ace of diamonds and discard dummy's last spade at trick three, but after that he should simply have led the queen of hearts. Now, if an opponent chose to win that with the king, there were still two trumps left in the dummy to take care of any spade leads. But suppose West refused to take the king? Declarer would lead the jack, and, if West won that, the six of hearts would still be in the dummy to protect declarer against all those spades. If West did not win it, declarer would lay down the ace of hearts and end up taking twelve tricks. Even if West won his king of hearts, South would still end up with eleven tricks.

PROTECTING THE TRUMP SUIT

There are times when you have to protect your trump suit. This can be because you don't have enough of them or because the ones you have are not large enough. One way to give them this protection is the loser-on-loser play, which is often closely related to the trump policeman play. Using this play, you refuse to trump something you could trump when you can afford to lose the trick in question, but fear that if you trump you will lose control of the trump suit.

Fig. 6-72

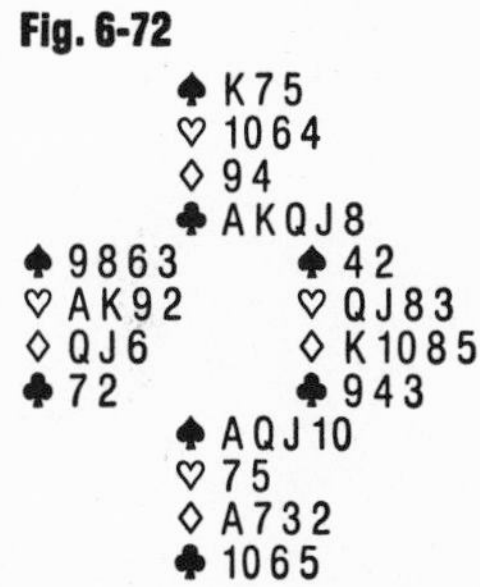

Not knowing that the opposing hearts would break 4–4, North and South avoided bidding three no-trump and ended up playing four spades. The first three leads were hearts. Declarer could have trumped that third heart, but decided not to and discarded a small diamond. Now he was going to make the contract if the trumps broke normally. Whatever the opponents led, he could get the lead, pull trumps, and have his ten tricks. Had he trumped the third heart, he would have been in trouble. Suppose, for example, he had decided to base everything on a 3–3 trump break and, after trumping the first heart, had led three rounds of trump. Now the only trump outstanding would have been in West's hands. Declarer would then have had to go after clubs, and West would have trumped the third club and cashed a heart. After that, diamonds would have been led, and the declarer would have ended up going set three tricks.

While three no-trump was makable on the last hand because the hearts broke 4–4, that is not always the case.

Fig. 6-73

This time in Fig. 6-73, four spades offered the best chance to score a game. After East overcalled in hearts, South duly reached that contract.

West opened his high heart, and East took the queen and king and then led the ace. Declarer decided he could afford to lose that trick, so he simply discarded a club, rather than cut his trump holding down to three cards. East next led the jack of diamonds.

Declarer saw that he was looking at a total of nine tricks: four in spades, three in diamonds, and two in clubs. There were several other chances for additional tricks. One of them was for the diamond suit to break 3-3—not a very good chance. The other was for a club finesse, but declarer thought he saw a better chance than that. He decided if both clubs and spades were no worse than 4–2, he was probably going to make the hand unless West was void in diamonds. So, he won the diamond with his queen and led a small club to dummy's king and another club back to his ace. He led a third club and trumped it with dummy's ace. It was unimportant whether clubs did or didn't break 3-3, as declarer now had ten tricks, provided trumps behaved. When four trump leads pulled all the trumps, declarer cashed his ace and king of diamonds. He made five trump tricks, three diamond tricks, and two club tricks.

If you can afford to lose two tricks to protect your trump suit, lose them.

South opened the bidding with one heart (Fig. 6-74), and West overcalled one spade. South finally ended up playing four hearts and got an opening lead of the king of spades. Declarer saw that once he got the lead,

Fig. 6-74

♠ 987
♡ K43
◇ AK10
♣ Q1042

♠ KQJ104 ♡ 9862 ◇ 53 ♣ 95

♠ A653 ♡ 75 ◇ 762 ♣ KJ87

♠ 2
♡ AQJ10
◇ QJ984
♣ A63

he had ten tricks right off the top, provided nobody had as many as five trumps, but he had no intention of trumping a spade in his hand. So, he let the second spade win a trick, simply discarding a club. On came the third spade, and again he discarded a club. West had had enough of that and switched to a club. There was nothing he could do. South won the ace, pulled trump, and ran off his diamond tricks.

You can see for yourself what a mess the declarer would have gotten into had he trumped the second or third spade.

In the hands I have been showing you, there has been only one problem: that of protecting the trump suit. Studying hands uncomplicated by other problems is the best way to learn the solution to the problem at hand. In real life, there will often be two or more things you will have to accomplish all in one hand. Fig. 6-75 is an example.

I don't know whether you like the bidding or not, but it was effective. It got the declarer into the best contract.

West opened the king of hearts and continued the suit. On the third heart, declarer wisely decided to avoid the complications that might arise from trumping and shortening his trump suit. He saw a way to be assured of his contract if clubs and spades would break normally, So, he simply discarded a small club on the third heart, feeling that the solidity of his trump suit gave him an excellent chance to solve the problem of establishing clubs before pulling trump.

Fig. 6-75 Dlr: N Vul: B

♠ A52
♡ 743
◇ Q7532
♣ AK

♠ 43 ♡ AKJ85 ◇ J94 ♣ Q97

♠ 9876 ♡ 1092 ◇ K1086 ♣ J10

♠ KQJ10
♡ Q6
◇ A
♣ 865432

NORTH	EAST	SOUTH	WEST
1◇	Pass	1♠	Pass
2♠	Pass	4♠	All Pass

Opening lead: ♡K

When South discarded again, West shifted to a small club, and declarer had a few uneasy moments while he cashed both of dummy's clubs. When both followed suit, he felt he was practically home. He came to his hand with a small trump and then trumped a club with dummy's ace of spades. Now, unless somebody had started with five spades, he was home. A spade back to his hand proved that no one started with more than four spades, and all the cards in his hand were now good.

In the cases I have shown you so far, the loser-on-loser play has enabled the declarer to wait until the trump policeman in the dummy came on duty so that the declarer would not have to disastrously shorten an already short suit. The loser-on-loser play can be helpful even with longer trump suits. If you have a loser, or a probable loser, in your hand which you can discard while you wait for the trump policeman to get into position in the dummy, you give up nothing by waiting.

In a contract of four spades, South had eight spades between himself and the dummy, which is usually considered safe. However, it looked as though he had a probable club loser. The chances that the hearts would break 3–3 so a club could be discarded from the south hand were not good. So, to keep the opponents from earning a trump trick, he found he could simply discard a club from his hand until the trump policeman could come on duty in the north hand.

Fig. 6-76

♠ J54
♡ AQ43
◇ Q63
♣ K64

♠ 10976 ♡ 72 ◇ A2 ♣ Q8753

♠ 2 ♡ J1095 ◇ KJ9754 ♣ J10

♠ AKQ83
♡ K86
◇ 108
♣ A92

To get all this straightened out, here is the way it went.

West opened the ace of diamonds against four spades and, when East signaled with the nine-spot, continued the suit. East won with the jack and led the king. It looked as though West had started with only two diamonds and was hoping to trump something. If the spades would break 3–2, declarer could afford to trump with the ace of spades and then pull trumps. Then, if the hearts broke 3–3, he could get rid of a losing club and take eleven tricks.

There were too many "ifs" in this. Declarer decided that by simply discarding that club on the third diamond, the trump policeman in the north hand would come on duty, stopping the run of the diamond suit. Then he could handle even a 4–1 break. The cost of giving up the chance of taking eleven tricks was small, and the reward was great. Had declarer ruffed either high or low, West would have come to a trick, in addition to which South would have found no way to dispose of the club loser.

There are times when there is nothing to lose and everything to gain by discarding a loser, even when you have a total of nine trumps.

Fig. 6-77

East had overcalled in diamonds, and, when South reached a contract of four spades, West led the king of diamonds. East overtook this with the ace, making it clear he had a great many diamonds, continued the queen, and then led a third diamond. It was also clear that West now probably had no diamonds at all, and it looked reasonably safe to trump with a high trump. After all, you don't run into 4–0 breaks very often. But, on the other hand, there was absolutely nothing to gain by doing so. It was clear that there was a club loser no matter how the suit broke, and even if you lost nothing by trumping high, neither could you gain a thing. So why not take the extra precaution of simply discarding a small club? That way the trump policeman would arrive in the north hand, and further leads of diamonds would do the defenders no good. Furthermore, the declarer could be left with the four highest trumps and would be in full command of the hand.

Had he attempted to trump the third diamond either high or low, he would have inevitably lost a trump trick, in addition to the two diamonds and the club loser he still had, and ended up with only nine tricks.

Fig. 6-78

On the next hand (Fig. 6-78), the shoe is on the other foot. In spite of the fact that the declarer had 100 honors in his trump suit and a total of nine between him and the dummy, he found it necessary to take a loser-on-loser play. But, in this case, it was one of those big trumps which had to stand as the policeman in the declarer's own hand, rather than in the dummy.

This time South got into a contract of four hearts. West led the king and ace of spades, and on these East signaled vigorously, playing the nine and five. This made it clear to declarer not only that East was out of spades, but also that he had a higher heart than any in the dummy. When West continued with the jack of spades, the declarer simply discarded one of the small clubs from the dummy, and that was that. Now he could gain the lead no matter what they did, he could pull trumps, and then, since he had discarded a club from the dummy, he could use one of dummy's small trumps to trump a club. In effect, he had transferred the ruff from the spade suit to the club suit.

How about protecting against a 5–1 trump break? Al Moyse, known by all as "Sonny" Moyse, did just that. Moyse was not only one of the great players of the early days, he was one of the great writers on the subject. His famous stories about his wife Jackie and her bridge game became widely known, and his advocacy of playing with a 4–3 trump fit earned that combination of cards the title of "the Moysian fit." But Sonny knew about the loser-on-loser play even when he had better trumps than that 4–3 fit.

Fig. 6-79

North: ♠ 9 5 ♡ 4 3 2 ◇ Q J 8 ♣ A J 10 9 8
West: ♠ 7 ♡ K Q J ◇ 7 5 4 2 ♣ K 7 5 3 2
East: ♠ 8 6 4 3 2 ♡ A 10 8 6 5 ◇ 6 3 ♣ Q
South: ♠ A K Q J 10 ♡ 9 7 ◇ A K 10 9 ♣ 6 4

It was back in 1943 that Sonny got to a contract of four spades with this hand. The trump suit looked sturdy enough to stand almost any sort of an assault. However, Sonny wisely decided not to put it to the test. The opening lead was the king of hearts followed by the queen of hearts which was overtaken by the ace, and East led a third heart. There didn't seem to be any danger, but one of those small clubs in his hand looked like an inevitable loser. Why not just throw it away, now, and, after the third heart was led, the nine of spades in the dummy would rise to the occasion and protect the declarer from any more heart leads. With nothing to lose, that is just what Sonny did. When it turned out, in fact, that East did hold five spades, Sonny's thoughtfulness paid off.

Now let me show you a wild and wooly one where the proper play is to make a loser-on-loser to break communications between the opponents' hands and to keep you from losing two trump tricks, even though you have seven of them in your own hand, with three of the top four honors (Fig. 6-80).

Fig. 6-80 Dlr: E Vul: 0

EAST	SOUTH	WEST	NORTH
1♡	2♡	Pass	3◇
4♡	4♠	All Pass	

Opening lead: ♡5

First let's see what would happen if you did not make the loser-on-loser play. West would open the five of hearts, and you would win with the ace. Unless you had managed to peek into the East hand, you probably would lay down the king of spades. East would win that with the singleton ace and continue the king of hearts. Now, if you trump that, which trump are you going to use? Should you trump with the jack or the queen, West will have two trump tricks, and the defenders will still have the ace of diamonds. So let's say you trump with the seven of spades. West will overtrump with the nine and read his partner's play of the king of hearts as a suit preference signal and lead a diamond to him. Now East will lead yet another heart, and West is bound to get another trump trick. So let's go back and start over.

We are still going to lead the king of spades at trick two, but when East leads the king of hearts, we are going to discard the worthless five of diamonds. This makes it impossible for East to gain the lead later on, and it saves the day. Assuming that East leads a third heart, we now trump with the seven of spades. West can overtrump for his side's third trick, but as far as East and West are concerned, that is the end of the ball game.

FORCING THE DEFENDERS

Sometimes the defenders have a good time forcing declarer, or, if you prefer, "pumping" the declarer. They keep leading a suit he has to trump in the hand that is long in trumps until one of them has more trumps than he has. Then they take over the play of the hand. Well, what is fair for the goose is fair for the gander. This is a game the declarer can also play when he discovers that one of the defenders has too many trumps to suit his convenience. This works out especially well when he has some long solid side suit and can give the defenders the choice of winning their good trumps by trumping his long suit or withholding their trumps and seeing him romp away with enough tricks to make his contract.

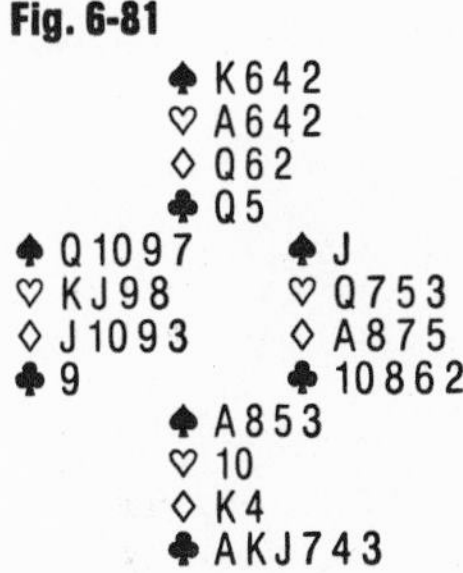

Fig. 6-81

Against a four spade contract, West led the jack of diamonds. Dummy played low, East expressed his approval by playing the eight-spot, and declarer won with the king. Declarer saw that if spades broke 3–2, he was going to lose one diamond and one trump trick and take the balance. So, he led the ace of spades and then the king. When East discarded a club, declarer had to revise his estimate. Both he and dummy had two small spades, but one of his opponents had the high spades. If that opponent could get the lead to take his small spades away from him and then continue leading diamonds, it wouldn't be good.

However, West was in control of the hand only temporarily. That nice club suit furnished the answer. North led the queen of clubs and then a small one to his jack. West puzzled over this one, but could find no play better than trumping with one of his two trumps. Now he had only one trump left which he promptly led. That left one in North's hand and one in South's hand. He continued a diamond, but declarer had a trump left to ruff the third diamond and all of those good looking clubs on which to discard the losing hearts in the dummy. He didn't take eleven tricks, but he lost only two trump tricks and a diamond trick and fulfilled his contract.

The player who impulsively leads trumps once he gets the lead would go set on the next hand. Here it is advisable to shorten any possible trump length in the opponents' hands even before leading trumps (Fig. 6-82).

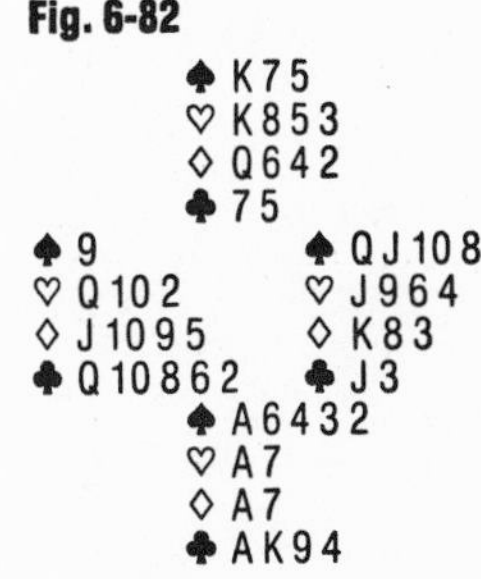

Fig. 6-82

Against four spades, West led the jack of diamonds, and it went Q K A. Trying to get a count of his losers, the declarer saw that he now had a loser in diamonds, hopefully only one loser in trumps, and two club losers, if he led trumps prematurely. He considered the possibility of a crossruff, trying to trump the clubs in the dummy and hearts in his own hand, but decided that he saw a better plan. This simply involved trumping two clubs in the dummy. Obviously, he did not want to trump with dummy's king of spades—that was needed to help pull trumps. He wanted to trump clubs with dummy's small spades.

He was on the verge of starting off by leading a low spade to his king, preserving the small ones there, when it occurred to him that one of the players might have four trumps and might need to be forced. The trouble was that if one player did have four trumps and was able to overruff him when he tried to trump clubs, that player could then lead another trump and there would be only one small trump left to trump two clubs. So declarer decided he'd better leave that big king of spades in the dummy while he trumped clubs, so that the remaining small trump in the dummy could not be blotted out. The only chance he took was that someone would have a singleton club, and he considered that remote.

So, after winning the ace of diamonds, he cashed the ace and king of clubs, led a small club, and trumped it with a small spade. East was able to overtrump, but, as it turned out, he trumped with a natural trump trick anyway, and was only trumping one of declarer's losers. He could cash a diamond and then lead a trump if he wanted to, but declarer could win it with dummy's king, return to his hand with the ace of hearts, and trump his last club. East could overtrump that, but now he was out of business. Declarer would regain the lead no matter what East did, and his trumps would all be good.

Fig. 6-83

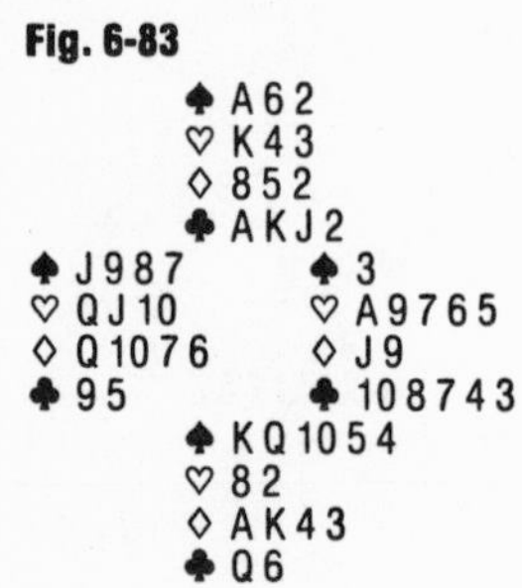

So far as the spade suit in the next hand (Fig. 6-83) is concerned, the safety play is to lead the king of spades first and then a small one to dummy's ace, in the event East should show up with four to the jack (there being no way to protect against West's showing up with four to the jack). That may have been the safe way to play the spade suit, but it was the unsafe way to play the hand.

Against four spades, West led the queen of hearts, and the suit was continued, with South trumping the third round. He had already lost two tricks and could afford to lose only one other. It looked simple enough if he could discard two of his diamonds on dummy's clubs. The only thing he had to fear was the loss of a trump trick, and it occurred to him that should trumps break badly and should one of the defenders trump the third club, he would be able to get rid of only one of his losing diamonds and that would make four losers. He found the solution, provided all five of the trumps were not in one hand and provided nobody had a singleton club. If either of his opponents held four spades to the jack, it didn't make any difference which one of them it was.

This required leaving the ace of spades in the dummy as an entry. So, he took the king and queen of spades in his own hand and was gratified that he had been so careful when East discarded a heart on the second trump lead. West still had two trumps, but declarer could handle that. He led the queen and another club, and, when both followed suit, his problems were over. On one of dummy's high clubs he sluffed a diamond. West trumped this, reducing his trump holding to one card. He led a diamond, but declarer won that in his hand and used his ace of spades as an entry to the dummy, at the same time collecting West's last spade. The losing diamond went off on dummy's high club.

Fig. 6-84

In Fig. 6-84, declarer had to shorten West in trumps so that West had no more than the dummy had.

North opened the bidding with one spade, and East overcalled with two clubs. The final contract was four hearts by South. West opened the three of clubs, and it looked like a picnic for South. There should be five spade tricks, five heart tricks, and a diamond trick—or so it seemed. But, it didn't work out that way. East won the first club trick with the nine-spot, cashed the ace, and made the devilish switch to the nine of spades. At this point, those five spade tricks didn't look so sure. What if one of his opponents had four trumps? Declarer's first inclination was to start cashing spades at once, discarding first the club and then some number of diamonds so that, if anybody wanted to trump a spade, it would hopefully be the player who had length in trumps. But he had a better idea.

He decided he had a way to take his eleven tricks if they broke 3-2, while still being able to make his contract if they broke 4-1. He won the spade lead in his hand with the queen and then led the queen of hearts and a small heart to dummy's ace. When East showed out of hearts, dummy had only one left, while West had two. Well, the only problem was to get West down to only one. A spade was led from the dummy, on which a club was carefully discarded so that any club continuation could be trumped in the south hand. West had to sit there while all those spades took tricks or he had to trump. He did trump, and then he and North had the same number of trumps. No matter whether West led a diamond or a club, that trick could be won in the south hand and the dummy entered with the jack of hearts to let the rest of the spades take tricks.

When it is convenient to do so, offer the defenders a chance to trump one of your losers when you run into a bad trump break.

Fig. 6-85

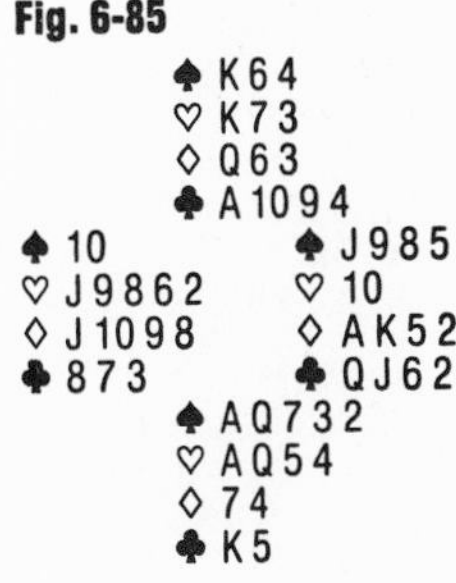

West led the jack of diamonds against a four spade contract, and the suit was continued until South trumped the third round. If trumps broke 3-2, declarer could take ten tricks without any problem, and he might make eleven if hearts broke 3-3 or a squeeze arose. But when declarer took the ace and king of spades, he suddenly saw that even ten tricks were not sure. East now had as many trumps as he did, and it was time to quit leading trumps, leaving one in the dummy, as it might have an important duty to perform. It was time to go to work on hearts, and it was important to take the first heart trick in dummy so that if East was short in hearts, he would be offered the opportunity to trump small cards and not honor cards. Declarer led the king.

On came the second heart, and East had the opportunity to trump, but decided to decline it. He figured if he trumped it, he would be trumping a small heart from each hand. Instead, he discarded a club. Declarer won with the ace of hearts and, before East got to do too much discarding, took the king of clubs and then led to dummy's ace. On came the third heart, and East was again offered the chance to trump a small heart. Again he declined. South won that and led his small heart and trumped it with the trump remaining in the dummy. This just about left East no choice, and it also left all the trumps in the south hand good for tricks.

Now that we have established the basic principles of forcing the defenders, let's look at some hands which have more than just that one problem (Fig. 6-86).

Fig. 6-86

On this hand, declarer made a wise decision not to win the first trick. When West opened the king of hearts against a four spade contract, it didn't look like there were going to be any problems. If South could take five trump tricks, he could add to that five in the side suits, for a total of ten. Nonetheless, he did not win that trick with the ace. Often it is proper to refuse to win the first trick with an ace when you have a doubleton in that suit in either hand, for even if you don't know how it will benefit you in the future, it frequently will. West shrugged his shoulders and led a small heart, which declarer won in dummy with the ace.

Two trump leads showed that East had a sure trump trick. They were definitely entitled to a club trick, as well. At that point, declarer had to either depend on a 3–3 diamond break or offer East the opportunity of trumping a losing diamond.

So declarer cashed the ace and queen of diamonds in the dummy and then led another diamond. East declined the offer of using one of his sure trump tricks on what looked like two small diamonds, and so South won with the king and led his remaining diamond, offering East his trump trick when he trumped low in the dummy. East had to choose whether to trump one of South's losing diamonds or let South make the extra trick with a small trump in the dummy. Either way, South was going to take ten tricks.

Had South not thought to let the king of hearts hold the first trick, it would have been a different story. When the third diamond was led from dummy with East still holding two trumps, East could play a trump and then give the lead to his partner in hearts to get a second diamond ruff. The club trick would still be there for the defenders.

Now let's take another look at the cautious man who guards against 5–0 breaks.

Fig. 6-87

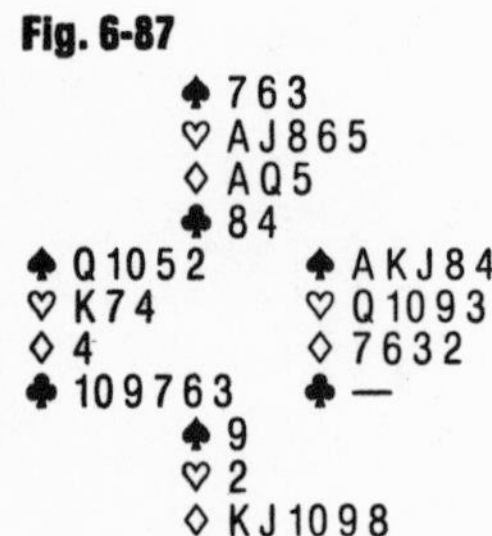

After an opening lead of a spade, South momentarily regretted that he wasn't in six diamonds instead of only five. It looked like he should be able to take five diamond tricks, six club tricks, and a heart trick. However, he was only in five, and he was a cautious man.

He trumped the second spade and then led a diamond to dummy's ace. Then he followed the old-time precept of leading small toward his high cards and led a club. East decided that his trumps might do him more good than using one right here, and he discarded a spade. Declarer won the trick with the jack and laid down the ace of clubs. East, deciding the foolishness had gone on long enough, trumped that one and led another spade to see what problems that could cause South. It couldn't cause him any. He trumped and led a small club toward dummy, trumped it with the queen and used dummy's diamond to return to his hand, and to pull trumps. Then all of his clubs were good, and he still had the ace of hearts in the dummy.

Fig. 6-88

On the next hand (Fig. 6-88), declarer thought he had an easy time of it until he suddenly discovered that one of his defenders had the same number of trumps that were held by both himself and the dummy.

The contract was six diamonds, and West led the king and ace of spades. It looked easy. There ought to be five heart tricks, five diamond tricks, and two club tricks. But when declarer trumped the second spade and laid down the ace of diamonds, West showed out. Now declarer needed to get to the dummy twice. He needed to finesse diamonds to avoid losing a diamond trick, and he needed to get back to the dummy again to take his good heart tricks. There was only one entry to the dummy. West was the only player who had no trumps, and everybody else held three.

Declarer found a way to reduce the trump holding in East's hand so that he would be able to take control. It was only necessary that East have at least a singleton club and as many as two hearts. After getting the bad news about the trump suit, South led the ace and king of hearts. When East followed to both, his troubles were nearly over. A small club to the king settled the matter. Now declarer simply started leading hearts from the north hand. If East refused to trump, declarer would simply throw away losing clubs. If East did trump, declarer would overtrump. Then he and East would have only two trumps left, but the dummy would have three. He could take East's trumps away from him and then lead the ace of clubs, use dummy's diamond to trump a club, and have the second entry he needed to cash the balance of the hearts.

There are times when you might even put a little bait on the hook and give the defenders a chance to make one of their small trumps.

After two passes, South opened the bidding with four spades which concluded the auction. This kept East and West from finding the sacrifice in clubs.

Fig. 6-89

West started the proceedings by leading the jack of clubs, and East won the trick with the king. Either East had never heard the admonition to stay away from dummy's long suit, or else he decided this was a time to ignore it. He led the three of diamonds. It can be presumed that he was hoping to get in a ruff.

South promptly played the king, and West won with the ace. The three could well have been a singleton, and if East wanted to trump diamonds, West was all for it, so he returned the suit. South won that one with the jack and promptly led the queen. This surprise play should have alerted East that something was going on, but he trumped the diamond. He had gotten his ruff, but he had blown the defense.

A little too late it occurred to him that it might be a good idea to shorten the dummy's trumps, so he led the king of clubs. That didn't shorten dummy at all. Declarer ruffed, but being a great showoff, he ruffed with the ace. Next he led the king and queen and the defenders had no trumps left. Declarer stil held the two, and dummy the five, and that was an entry. On two good diamonds, declarer discarded his two losing hearts.

It is not too difficult to follow declarer's thinking in allowing East to ruff a diamond. Once the diamond return was not trumped, the suit had broken 3-2, and all that was needed was an entry to get into the dummy after declarer had led the third diamond. If the trumps would be good enough to break 2-2, the entry would be there, but declarer decided he could afford to spend a trick to bait East into a careless play, in case East had started with three spades. The only real decision declarer had to make was whether East would fall for his ploy if he led the third diamond before touching trumps or if he waited until he cashed two trumps and then led it. Apparently he made the right decision.

THE TRUMP COUP

Usage seems to be making the term "the trump coup" apply only to trump-reducing plays. It seems a pity that the term should be so limited. A coup is better defined as any unexpected and successful stroke. There are trump coups other than trump-reducing plays. In this section, I do intend to discuss trump-reducing plays, but also to add some hands where there are other coups available which apply to the trump suit.

In his great book, *The Play of The Hand,* Louis Watson said of the Grand Coup, "The play has gained the reputation that it does not deserve, for it is far from being a very useful play." Watson is right; it probably will never help you win a tournament or a dime, but it is an interesting play. Let's start off at the top by talking about a double Grand Coup. What makes it so grand is that you are trumping cards which otherwise are winners. In reality, it would work just as well as if you were trumping losers, but it would not be so spectacular. It is called double because you trump not one but two winners.

Fig. 6-90

Against four spades, West opened the king of hearts. When East played the nine, West continued the ace and a small one. When that held the trick, East felt pretty smug about the whole business. Seeing the two trumps in the dummy, he knew there was no way declarer could finesse him out of his king.

East was mistaken. East led a small club to the dummy, and declarer led the jack of spades. East played low, and the jack held, so declarer continued the ten of spades. East again played low, and when West discarded a club, declarer saw he had his work cut out for him.

At this point, he had four spades left in his hand, and East had two. To complete a coup, you have to reduce the number of trumps in your hand to the number held by your right-hand opponent. That meant that South had to get rid of two spades from his hand. The only way to do that was to trump dummy's good clubs. He duly trumped the king of clubs, led the king of diamonds to dummy's ace, and next led the queen of clubs and trumped it. He had now accomplished his purpose of having left the ace-queen of trumps, and that was exactly as many trumps as East had. He led a small diamond back to dummy, and then led his last club. East knew he could not gain by trumping that and threw away a diamond. So, South threw away his diamond. At this point, eleven tricks had been played. South held nothing but the two top spades. East held only the king and a little spade, and North held two diamonds. West might as well have not been there. On the lead of the next diamond, East had the choice of whether to trump with his eight and let South win the last two tricks with the queen and ace in that order, or to trump with the king and let South win with the ace and queen in that order.

In spite of what Watson said about the limited usefulness of the Grand Coup, it is said that he played the next hand (Fig. 6-91), which has an additional twist.

Fig. 6-91

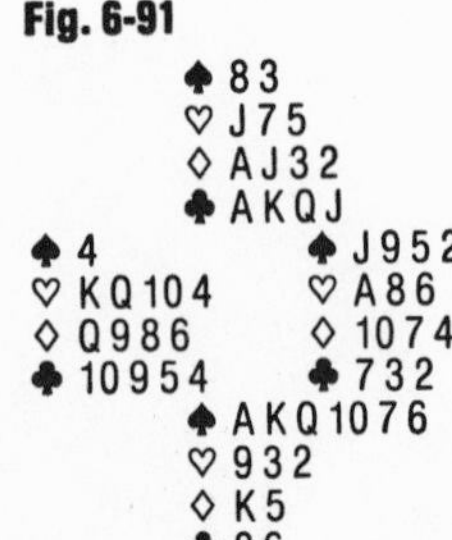

Watson got to four spades, and the defense took three quick heart tricks, with East winning the third one with the ace. He switched to a small spade, and declarer, being unable to see East's hand, made the play of the queen. The ace of spades told him that East still had a guarded jack. The only solution was a coup.

Here is the additional coup. For a coup to be successful, it generally is necessary for dummy to have the lead after the eleventh trick has been played. This makes it necessary for dummy to have one more entry than the number of times declarer has to shorten himself. As the declarer had to shorten himself two times, dummy needed two entries outside of the club suit. But Watson thought he saw a 50–50 chance to get his additional entry if West had the diamond queen and was lacking some sort of special knowledge not available to ordinary mortals. So he led the ace and king of clubs and trumped a club. Next he led a small diamond and, when West played low, he put in dummy's jack. Had West played the queen, that would have spoiled Watson's plans. When the jack held the trick, he had his additional entry. He led dummy's last club and trumped it and now had himself down to the same number of trumps as those held by East. East discarded a diamond which probably didn't worry Watson at all, as West had discarded a heart on the second trump lead, and East's hand could now be counted as four spades and three cards in each of the other suits. The king of diamonds was overtaken by the ace, putting Watson just where he wanted to be after the eleven tricks had been played. The final diamond lead gave the coup de grace to East's hope of getting a trump trick.

On the next hand, the trumps themselves had to provide the entries.

Fig. 6-92

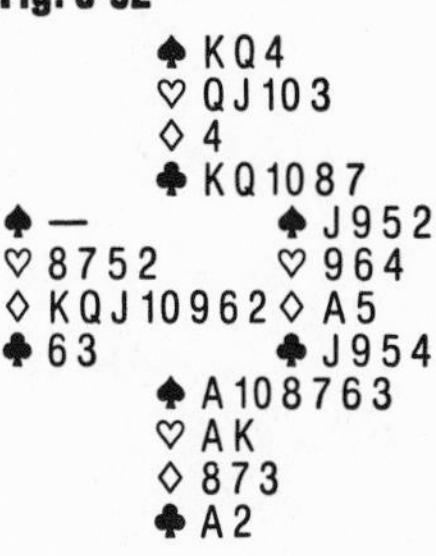

When South bid a small slam in spades, West led the king of diamonds, which East overtook with the ace. East returned a diamond.

South duly trumped that with a small spade in the dummy, and a little reflection told him that the only reason East could have had for wanting declarer to make that small trump in the dummy was his holding in the trump suit. If East indeed had four spades to the jack, getting rid of dummy's small trump well might make his jack a trick. As a matter of fact, it would, unless declarer took precautions. Declarer took those precautions.

If East had four spades to the jack, then he had to have a trump coup. He had to reduce his trumps by two in order to get down to the same number that East had. In order to do this, he had to have three entries into the dummy. Obviously, there was only one entry in clubs, and any additional entries would have to come from the two trumps. Furthermore, declarer would have to get there after eleven tricks had been played. Let's work that one out together.

Two tricks had been played. Now let's take the ace and king of hearts; that comes to four tricks. Now a small spade to dummy's king uses that entry and demonstrates that East was indeed trying to establish a trump trick. This comes to five tricks. Trumping a good heart in his hand makes six; going back to the dummy with the other high trump is seven. Trumping the last heart makes eight tricks. If the A K Q of clubs can be led without being ruffed, that will come to eleven. Fortunately, East started with four clubs, and, although he discarded one on the fourth heart, he still had three left. So, after eleven tricks, declarer was in the dummy with his last two cards being the ace and ten of spades, while East's were the jack and nine of trumps. The lead of one of the remaining clubs in dummy did East in.

Fig. 6-93

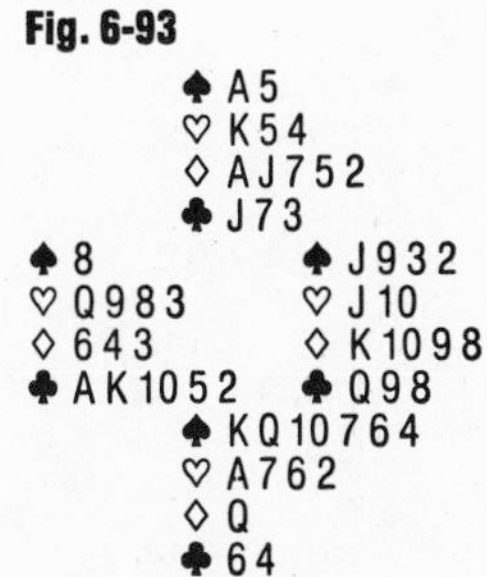

Here's one (Fig. 6-93) where it developed that declarer needed only two entries to the dummy.

Against a four spade contract, the defenders got off to three quick club leads. Declarer trumped the third one and led the queen of diamonds and let it ride, as this established two diamond tricks for him, whether the finesse won or lost. East won and returned a diamond, which was won in the dummy as declarer discarded a heart. There was only one problem left. Unless declarer lost a trump trick, he was going to win six spade tricks, two heart tricks, and two diamond tricks. The only thing that remained to be done was to take every precaution against the loss of a trump trick.

Should West happen to hold four or more spades to the jack, there was nothing declarer could do about it. But if it should happen to be East who held four spades to the jack, there was something to do about it. Had South held only five spades and North three, the safety play would have been to lead first the king of spades and then go over to the ace in the dummy. If East started out with four, West would then show out, and there would be a spade left in the dummy to lead for the natural finesse through East. But with only two spades in the dummy, there would be no spades left to lead after declarer discovered the situation. The alternative play was a trump coup.

But where are those three entries into the dummy for such a coup? There is one in trumps and one in hearts, and that is all. But think about it for a minute. Declarer had already trumped one club, and now, should he need to reduce his trump holding, he would need to reduce it by only one. So—two entries were enough. But declarer had to be careful to use one of the entries when he discovered the trump situation, if indeed it was unfavorable.

Therefore, he won the king of trumps first and then led a small one to dummy's ace. On this, West showed out, and now declarer could set about his trump reducing. He had discarded one heart on the second diamond lead, and now he led the ace of diamonds and discarded a second heart. Next he led a small diamond from the dummy, taking away from East his last diamond, and he trumped it. Then he crossed to the dummy with the king of hearts and led dummy's good diamond. East had two trumps left plus a heart, and South had two trumps plus the ace of hearts. East saw that it would do no good to trump, so he threw away his last heart. With that, South made the spectacular looking, but necessary, play of discarding his ace of hearts. Thus, with eleven tricks played, East held just his two trumps, over which declarer had the queen and ten of trumps. North had two hearts, but it didn't make any difference what he had, just so he had something to lead so that East would not get a trump trick.

The coup does not always have to be against an honor card. Lt. John S. Lynn reports a hand which he played while in China where he had to have the trump-reducing play to capture an opposing nine-spot. It has been quite a few years since American Armed Forces were stationed in China, so obviously this hand was played some time ago.

Lynn got all the way up to six clubs and got an opening lead of the jack of spades. He saw that he had no losers except in the trump suit. He won the spade lead with his ace and laid down the ace of clubs, discarding a small diamond from the dummy. He then led the queen of clubs, and, when West discarded a small diamond, he paused to reflect. He thought he had jobs for dummy's two small diamonds to perform, so he quit discarding from that suit and discarded a heart instead. East won that with the king of clubs, and, had he thought to return his singleton heart, he would have removed from the dummy an important entry. Fortunately

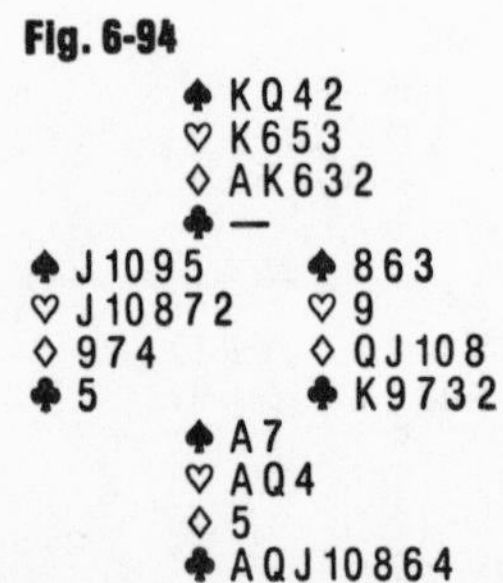

for Lynn and for my story, he led the queen of diamonds. Lynn won that in the dummy and set about his trump-reducing plays by leading a small diamond and trumping it. Next he cashed his jack of clubs, and then he went to the dummy with the queen of spades and led the remaining small diamond and trumped it. He had now accomplished what he wanted to do so far as the trump suit was concerned: East held the nine and seven, while declarer held over him the ten and eight. What was now necessary was to have the lead in the dummy after eleven tricks had been played. He went to the dummy with the king of hearts, and, on the high spade remaining there, he discarded his queen of hearts. On the high diamond, he discarded his ace of hearts. That was eleven tricks, and when he led a small heart from the dummy, his ten and eight of clubs were good for the last two tricks.

The trump reducing coup can be available against two high cards instead of one, as in the example in Fig. 6-95.

Fig. 6-95

Against four spades, West led the king and ace of hearts. South trumped the second heart. West had already reduced South's trumps to the number held by East, which was very nice of him. South led a trump to dummy's ace, and, when West showed out, it looked as though he might have to lose three trump tricks. He would have to lose three trump tricks if he had to lead them from his own hand, but South knew about the trump coup, and one thing he did not plan to do was to lead trumps from his hand. So he continued with the king of trumps, which got East and declarer down to three trumps each. Instead of being in the dummy after eleven tricks, he needed to be there after ten tricks, with East and his hand having left only their three trumps. With those solid suits and those good entries into the dummy, this did not seem too unlikely.

So, he started leading clubs from the dummy. When he led the third club, East thought it over, but he could see no profit from trumping, so he discarded a diamond. Declarer discarded a diamond too, but dummy's diamonds were as good as his, and to be sure to keep his entries into the dummy, he threw away the ace. On came a fourth club. East gave this some thought and finally decided he didn't want that game to continue, so he trumped with the jack of spades. South once more had to reduce his trumps so that he would not have to lead them from his hand, so he just undertrumped. Now he had the two-card holding in trumps which he liked. East saw that it would not do to lead trumps, so he led all he had left, which was a diamond. Declarer won it in the dummy with the ten-spot, and on came that fifth club. There was nothing East could do to get two trump tricks. If he discarded his last diamond, declarer would do the same and then lead the heart from North. If he trumped high, that would obviously give declarer the balance of the tricks. If he trumped with the nine, South would overtrump with the ten and concede one trump trick at the end.

A trump coup similar to the ones we have been looking at because it frequently involves reducing the number of your trump is called the Coup in Passing. If you want to impress someone with your knowledge, you may call this the "Coup en Passant." The name is chosen from chess. The essence of this play is that at the critical moment there is only one trump outstanding against your one trump which is smaller, but your trump is sure to take a trick.

Fig. 6-96

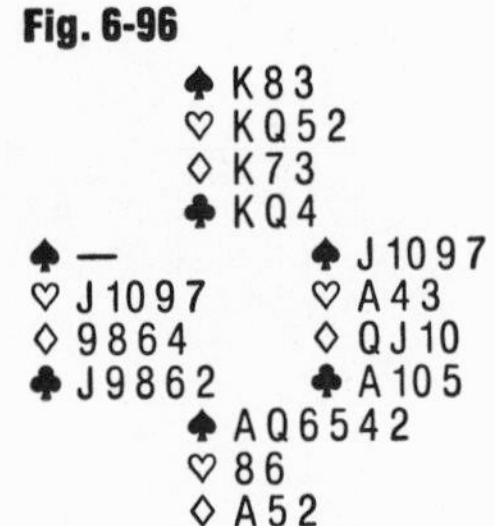

Fig. 6-96 is an example.

The opening lead against the four spade contract was the jack of hearts, duly covered by the queen, and won by East with his ace. East returned the queen of diamonds, won by declarer in his hand. When he laid down the ace of spades and West discarded a club, South had to consider the possibility of losing one trick in each suit. To find out just how the clubs were, he switched to clubs and played dummy's king. East cooperated by winning that trick with his ace and refusing to confuse the matter. As South had so far refused to lead trumps a second time, East decided it might be a good idea for him to do so. The jack of spades was won by South in his hand. The time had come to reduce the number of trumps in South's hand. He went to the dummy with a heart and successfully trumped a heart in his hand. Then he went back with a club and successfully trumped a small club. Now he led a spade to dummy's king and cashed his king of diamonds. Eleven tricks had been played. Dummy held a small heart and a small diamond. East held the jack of spades and a high diamond. South held the six of spades and a small diamond. The heart was led from north, and whatever East did, the six of spades in south was going to take a trick. Should East decide to trump, declarer would simply discard his diamond and let his six of spades take the thirteenth trick. Should East decide to throw away his diamond, declarer would trump with the six of spades for his tenth trick and then let East have the pleasure of trumping his two of diamonds with his high spade.

Even rarer is the trump coup known as the smother play. I show you one, not because I ever expect you to get one, but just to make this section complete. On the other hand, you may have one some day. Who knows?

Fig. 6-97

East opened the bidding with a heart and later bid clubs. South got into a contract of four spades. The first three leads were hearts, and declarer trumped the third one. He was happy when the queen of spades won a trick, and unhappy when the jack won, but East failed to follow suit. If the diamonds would break for him, he would still be all right, so he stopped leading trumps for a moment to lead the ace and king of diamonds. He discovered the diamonds were not going to break, but he still had one chance left.

First he cashed the ace-king of clubs to get them out of his hand and then led a small diamond to dummy's queen. Then, instead of leading a fourth diamond, he led the jack of clubs. East covered with the queen, and declarer discarded his diamond. West had three cards left at this point and obviously could not waste a trump, so he also discarded a diamond, leaving East with the lead. South had two cards—two spades—and West also held two spades. North had the ace of spades and a little diamond. No matter whether East led a heart or a club, declarer was going to trump, and West would never get his trump trick.

The smother play does not have to be against a king. Fig. 6-98 is one which was reported to me where the queen gets smothered.

Against a four spade contract, West led the eight of clubs. Declarer made a good guess and played West for a doubleton rather than a singleton, letting the jack hold the first trick. Clubs were continued, and he won the second one with the ace, leading a small trump then to dummy's king. He tested the heart finesse, and it lost. West shifted to a small diamond. Declarer won that in dummy with the king and then led a heart to his hand to lead the jack of spades. West played low, of course, and the finesse won, but when East showed out, it looked like West had a sure trump trick. He was holding the queen and seven, while dummy held the singleton ace. A club and a heart had been lost, and there was still another club to be lost. The situation looked hopeless. But, it was not as it looked. Declarer cashed the dummy's high diamond and then trumped a diamond. Next he cashed his last heart, and then he led a club.

Fig. 6-98

West couldn't gain by trumping the club, so he discarded a diamond, and East was on lead.

Remaining in the dummy was the ace of spades and a small club. West still had his two spades, and South had the ten and eight of spades. East had nothing left but red cards. Whatever he led, the declarer simply trumped, and, if West overtrumped, dummy's ace would win, as would declarer's last trump. The other choice, undertrumping, was equally hopeless.

To ever make this play, you are going to have to be able to give the lead to the hand which has no trumps at exactly the right moment. It is very rare in actual play.

A play even more rare—one which is practically nonexistent—is known as the devil's coup.

George Coffin, in his book on end plays, reports that the original deal came from a rubber bridge game and caused a lot of excitement when the declarer bid and made a grand slam in hearts on the hand in Fig. 6-99.

Fig. 6-99

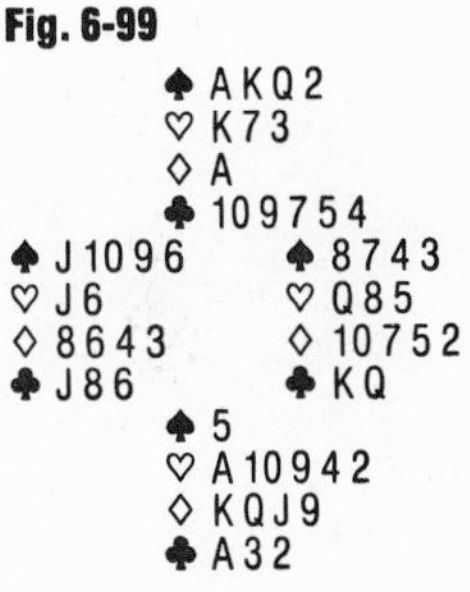

It looks like the defenders are bound to get one trump trick after the opening lead of the jack of spades. However, with the cards distributed exactly as they are, that trick can be denied them. On the A K Q of spades, discard two small clubs. Trump the deuce of spades as a trump-reducing play. Play the ace of clubs and then go to dummy with the ace of diamonds. Trump a club to get to your hand and then cash two diamonds, throwing two clubs away from the dummy. Lead the good diamond, but don't discard dummy's last club; trump the trick. Now you are in the dummy, and Fig. 6-100 is the situation with ten tricks played.

Lead the ten of clubs from the dummy. If East trumps with a small heart, you simply overtrump, and your ace and king will take the last two tricks. If he trumps with the queen, you win that with the ace and then finesse the ten of hearts through West.

Fig. 6-100

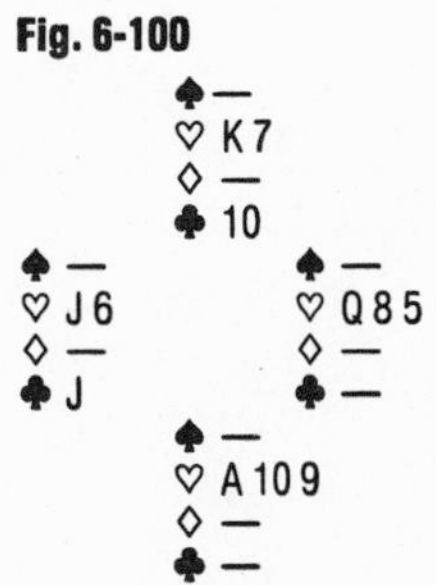

In actual play, this devil's coup must be as rare as being dealt thirteen cards in one suit. Declarer must have just the right spots in trumps. Change the nine of hearts to the four-spot, and the coup doesn't work. In addition, declarer must be able to do all that crossruffing without being overtrumped.

Despite the fact that it is not likely to be useful, I have shown you this hand because it is a delightful and artistic thing to contemplate, whether you are the merest beginner or a real old-timer.

THE most spectacular plays made in bridge are unblocking plays. Instead of following my usual custom of starting off with the simple and then working up to the complex, I am going to start off with about as spectacular an unblocking play as I have ever seen. It has been around for years, and I haven't the least idea who composed it. The problem is to make seven no-trump against an opening lead of a spade.

Fig. 7-1

West	North	East
	♠ K	
	♡ A K	
	◇ A K Q	
	♣ A 10 9 8 7 6 5	
♠ 7 6 5 4		♠ 10 9 8 3 2
♡ 9 7 6		♡ 8 5 4 3 2
◇ 5 4 3 2		◇ —
♣ K J		♣ Q 4 3
	♠ A Q J	
	♡ Q J 10	
	◇ J 10 9 8 7 6	
	♣ 2	

So, here we go. Overtake the king of spades with the ace in the south hand and lead the top two spades, discarding the top two hearts from the north hand. Now lead the three hearts from the south hand, discarding the A K Q of diamonds from the north hand. The six diamonds in the south hand are good, and on those you can discard the six small clubs in the north hand. So North, with 23 high-card points, ends up taking exactly one trick, while you in south take twelve tricks.

George Coffin, in his book, *Bridge Play from A to Z,* promotes the use of the word "jettison" for plays of this kind. When you are throwing away aces and kings, the term is particularly appropriate. But I think it is about time to come down out of the clouds and look at some of those bread-and-butter jettison plays which often make the difference between winning and losing. They don't all involve unblocking great big cards.

In Fig. 7-2, in a contract of three no-trump, South got an opening lead of the jack of spades. Playing low from the dummy, he guaranteed himself two spade tricks. East won with the king and returned the eight-spot. In addition to his two spade tricks, declarer had a sure heart trick and could establish a club trick whenever he wanted to do so. That came to a total of four, and if diamonds would break no worse than 3–1, he would add five diamond tricks to round out the nine he needed. But you will notice there is one little thing he has to be careful about: the first two tricks had taken from the dummy the only entry there except those in the diamond suit. Whenever declarer got around to leading diamonds, he had to be sure that on the A K Q from the north hand he discarded the 9 8 7 from his hand, so he could take five diamond tricks. Had he carelessly played a small diamond on one of dummy's honors, he would have ended up with just four diamond tricks. You may not like so strong a word as jettison to refer to getting rid of those spot cards which may get in your way and trip you up, but whatever you call it, there are times when you had better get rid of them. So, until we reach some of those more exotic situations, we are going to use the old fashioned term of unblocking.

Fig. 7-2

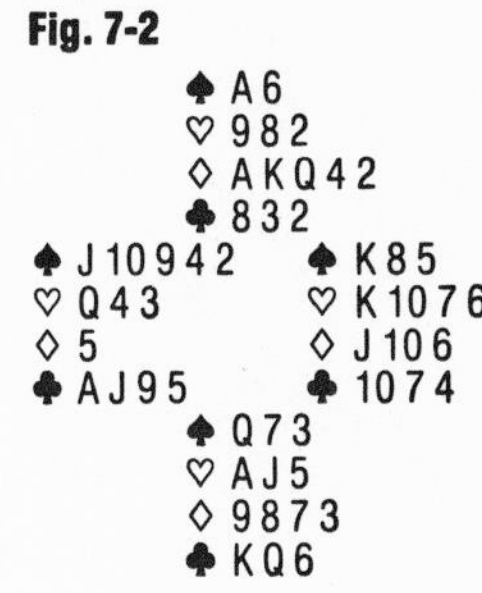

Only a 4–0 break would have defeated that last hand, and the odds were against such a bad break. Sometimes the odds are against getting the good break that you need to make a hand. But, when that's your only chance, you still have to play for it.

We have another three no-trump contract. West was averse to under-leading from queens, so he led the three of spades. Declarer properly played dummy's jack, on the theory that with the holding he had in spades, a doubleton jack in the dummy would win a trick now or never. East covered with the queen, and South saw it was never.

Fig. 7-3

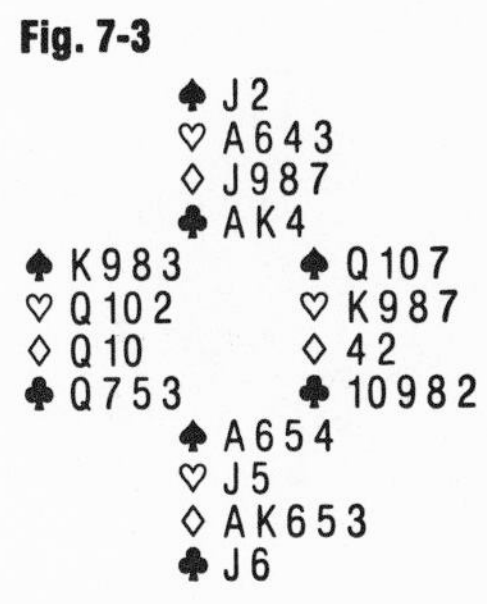

With only four tricks outside of the diamond suit, declarer saw he was going to have to be lucky to bring in the five tricks he needed in that suit. It would be nice if the queen were a singleton, but if it were not, the suit was going to have to break 2–2. Even if it did, how was declarer going to get back to his hand to cash those three small ones? He needed some way to get rid of two diamonds in the north hand.

The defense continued the spade suit, and declarer won the third one with the ace and saw that he had only one more spade loser. At the same time, he got rid of one surplus diamond in the dummy. Now he led the ace of diamonds to see whether the queen would fall singleton. No luck. So, he decided to discard another diamond from dummy, while giving the opponents their spade trick. He led the six of spades and let West win with the king. On that he discarded a second diamond. A switch to a heart let declarer rise with the ace in the dummy, lead the diamond there, and win it with his king. When both opponents followed suit, he had his five diamond tricks.

Some unblocking plays with small cards are pretty subtle (Fig. 7-4).

Fig. 7-4

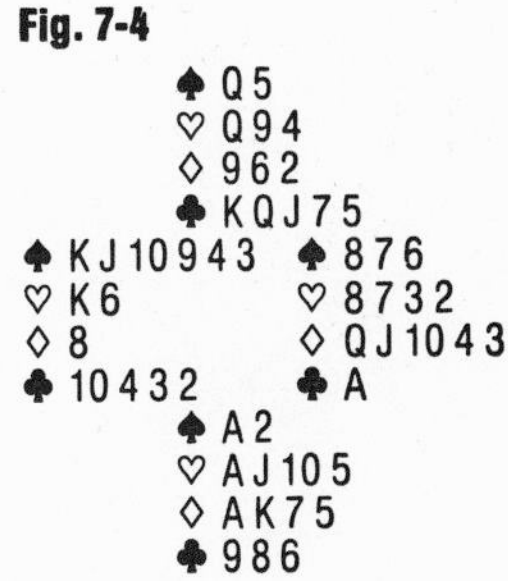

West led the jack of spades against a three no-trump contract, and when dummy's queen held the trick, things were looking up. Those clubs looked pretty good. If four clubs could be brought in, they would bring the total up to nine tricks, without a heart finesse. Declarer decided he could try both plays. So, he came to his hand with a diamond and led a club up to the dummy. Being a very cautious man, he led the nine of clubs. West played low, and I would like to tell you that South had second sight and took the deep finesse. The truth is that he played the jack. East won with the ace and returned a spade to declarer's ace of that suit. Now all declarer had to do was to find a normal break in clubs and his problems were over. But, still exercising caution, for his second lead in clubs he led the eight-spot. If, by any chance, East had started with four clubs including the ten-spot, there was nothing declarer could do about it. But there was something he could do about it if it were West with four to the ten. When he played a high club in the dummy and East discarded a heart, it was proven he had been wise to retain that six of clubs in his hand. He came back with another diamond and led the six of clubs for the finesse of the seven-spot through West. Now he had his nine tricks with no problem, and if West got clever and saved for his last four cards three spades and the singleton king of hearts, declarer would pick up three overtricks.

There are hands where you have to unblock to take a successful finesse and have the lead where you want it. This frequently involves unblocking a jack.

Fig. 7-5

East opened the bidding with one heart, and South went straight to four spades "to keep the ribbon clerks out." He kept the ribbon clerks out, all right, but now was faced with the job of promoting two tricks in the north hand.

The opening lead was the two of hearts. That looked to declarer as though it might be a lead from the king or queen, and he made a wish that it was. Dummy played the seven, East the king, and declarer dropped his jack.

Now the opponents could take two diamond tricks whenever they wanted to, but whenever declarer got the lead, he could pull trumps and then lead the four of hearts to finesse dummy's ten-spot. His losing club would then go off on dummy's ace of hearts.

Fig. 7-6

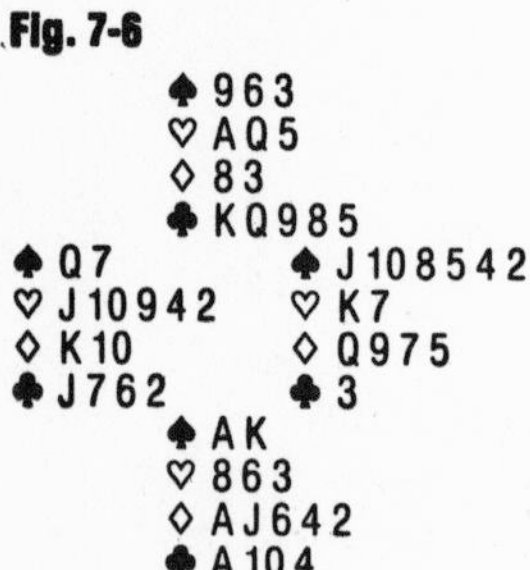

Fig. 7-6 is another situation where the ten should be unblocked that is not quite so easy to see.

West led the jack of hearts against a three no-trump contract. Had declarer been able to see what you and I can see, he would have played the ace from the dummy. Both defenders held their hands close to their chests, so declarer was unable to find that play. He played the queen from the dummy, hoping West might have led from an interior sequence. East won that and returned his seven, knocking out dummy's last entry.

The situation still looked pretty good. If clubs would break as they should, there would be five club tricks, a diamond trick, and two spade tricks, in addition to the heart already won. All declarer had to do was protect himself as far as possible against a bad break in clubs. If there were four clubs in the east hand, declarer was not going to find out about it in time to do anything about it. However, if four to the jack were in the west hand, he could find out about it in time and, by taking proper precautions, do something about it.

The proper play is to win the first club with one of dummy's high honors and the second one with the ace. Where West holds four clubs, East will show out on the second lead, leaving declarer in charge. That is, he will really be in charge provided he has unblocked his ten of clubs when the king was played from the dummy. If he has not done that, West can simply play low on the third club, and that will be the last club the declarer will take. If declarer has played the ten under dummy's king, he will have the four-spot in his hand and the necessary queen-nine in the dummy to let him take a successful finesse against the jack in the West hand. Then he will get his five tricks.

The Fig. 7-7 hand was from the intercollegiate contest of 1953. A group of experts prepared hands to send out to college students over the country and kept records of how many actually found the proper play. The records show that about 10 percent of the players who received this problem solved it.

West was instructed to lead the three of hearts against a three no-trump contract by South. South could see only six tricks off the top and needed three more from somewhere. Spades would seem to offer the best prospect. So, after winning the king of hearts, declarer should lead the four of spades from the dummy. For East to play the jack would make life too simple for the declarer, so East was supposed to go up with the ace of spades and return a second heart.

It was at trick two that South could become a hero. When East played that ace of spades, South was supposed to drop the ten-spot out of his hand, preparing for a possible finesse against West in case East had started with the ace-jack doubleton. When he won the second heart trick in the dummy and led a small spade, East would have to play the jack, and declarer would retain the three-spot in his hand. He would win with the king and take a successful finesse against the nine-spot in the West hand. In this way, he would get his three extra tricks in the spade suit.

I would say that South would have to be paying close attention to make that play, wouldn't you? I salute the 10 percent of the students who made the play in 1953.

Now suppose we play something besides games and slams. Part scores help too.

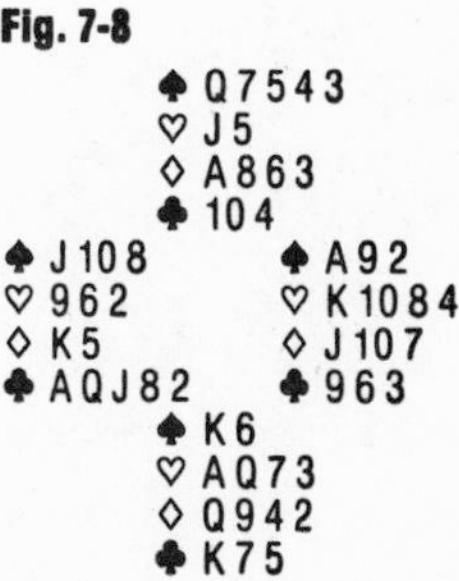

South got into a contract of one no-trump and was faced with the problem of taking seven tricks. West helped a little by leading the queen of clubs, and declarer decided he had better go after diamonds. He won the first trick with the king and led a small diamond to dummy's ace. He led back the six of diamonds, and, when East played the ten, he really had to think. He finally decided to play West for the king doubleton and to duck that trick. That was a good decision, but it was not enough. Holding the Q 9 4 of diamonds, he also decided that he should get that nine out of his hand. To bring in his contract, it looked as though he had to have a successful heart finesse. To have that, he had to have an entry into the dummy. If he left the queen-nine in his hand, he could never find it. But when he got rid of his nine-spot and West had to win the king, the entry was there. After winning another diamond trick with his queen, he could lead to dummy's eight with his four. West won the king of diamonds, cashed his four club tricks (on which three spades were discarded from the dummy and two hearts from the south hand), but then could do no more damage. He switched to the jack of spades which gave South his spade trick. Then South cashed his two diamond tricks, ending in the dummy, and the story had a happy ending when the heart finesse was successful.

Let's go to a slightly higher level and start unblocking some larger cards (Fig. 7-9).

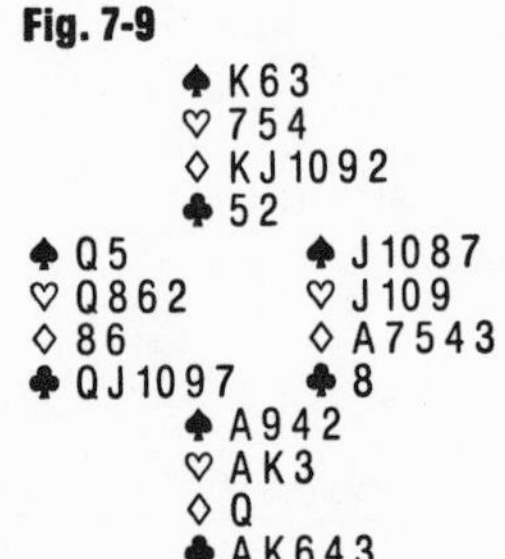

Fig. 7-9

When the queen of clubs was opened against a three no-trump contract, South decided chances were not too good that he would promote any long cards in that suit. Diamonds were sure to promote some extra tricks. It would be nice if, when he led the queen of diamonds, the opponents would be accommodating enough to take their ace. Then he would have the king of spades to go over and cash four good diamonds. But declarer decided they weren't likely to be that accommodating. And, if they didn't take the ace, he could get to the dummy just once with the king of spades. If they figured out just when to take the ace, he would wind up with just one diamond trick. So he stopped and counted his tricks. There were two in each of the other three suits; therefore, he could get by with only three diamond tricks. By overtaking the queen of diamonds with the king, he was assured of getting that many. If the suit broke 4–3, he would still get four diamond tricks.

The suit did not break 4–3, but by overtaking his queen of diamonds, declarer did get the three diamond tricks needed to bring the total up to nine.

It would be nice if the tricks were always as sure as the diamond tricks were in that hand. Sometimes they aren't, and you have to do the best you can.

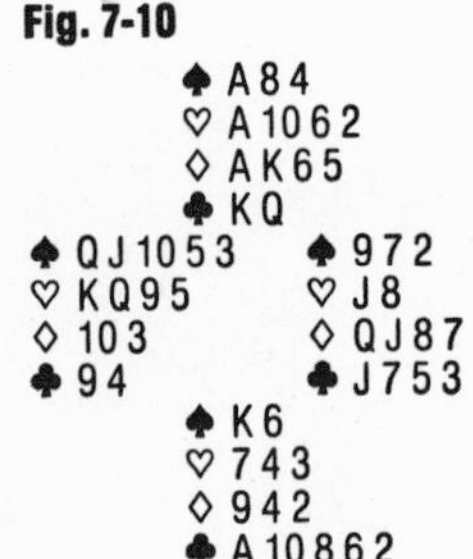

Fig. 7-10

Against three no-trump, West led the queen of spades. Outside the club suit, declarer had five tricks, and chances to develop any additional suit before the defenders took a lot of spades looked mighty distant. Therefore, the tricks had to come from the club suit, if nine tricks were to be brought home. As it was essential to have an entry into the south hand after working on clubs, declarer won the first trick in the dummy with the ace of spades. He led the king of clubs and then the queen. Here it was time to figure what his best chances were. If the clubs would break 3–3, he could let the queen hold the trick, use his only entry into the south hand to lay down the ace, and that way collect five tricks. That 3–3 break was rather on the unlikely side, so declarer had to figure his chances of overtaking the queen with the ace and unblocking. Again, if they were 3–3, he could simply give up a club trick and, with the spade entry still in his hand, bring home four club tricks. But suppose they broke 4–2? Well, even if they did, with his holding the ten and eight, if either the nine-spot or the jack would turn out to be doubleton, he could still bring home four club tricks by overtaking. Obviously, this was the better chance and, added to the possibility of a 3–3 break, made four club tricks likely. So, declarer overtook the queen with the ace to unblock the suit, and the nine fell out of the West hand. Declarer then led the ten of clubs to concede a trick to East, but he still had his four tricks to give him his contract.

Harold Vanderbilt was the inventor of contract bridge and was one of the great players of his time. The next hand (Fig. 7-11) was easy for him, but it does teach us a lesson.

Fig. 7-11

Against a three no-trump contract, the opening lead was the ten of spades. By letting the jack hold the first trick, Vanderbilt could be assured of three spade tricks. The trouble was, if he did that, he would wind up with one diamond trick, where by correct play he could take six diamond tricks. So, he unblocked the hand by overtaking the jack of spades with his king, laying down the ace of diamonds, and going to the dummy with the queen of spades. Not only did he get the six diamonds he wanted, he also got three spade tricks, which gave him three no-trump with something to spare.

A miser would never make the next hand. An experienced bridge player would have no problem.

Fig. 7-12

Against three no-trump, the opening lead was the ten of hearts. You will see that South could win this very cheaply with his jack. You can also see that if he does so, he will have one heck of a time taking a total of nine tricks. East will simply hold off the first diamond and then take the second one, and that's all the diamond tricks declarer will take. By winning the first trick with the ace of hearts, he will have his ninth trick guaranteed. He will start leading with the ten of diamonds and continue them until East wins his ace. The king of hearts will give dummy the needed entry. This way, declarer will be sure to take four diamonds, two spades, two hearts, and the ace of clubs, for a total of nine.

In some cases, the declarer can offer the defenders a chance to hand him his contract. In Fig. 7-13, West took advantage of the opportunity.

Fig. 7-13

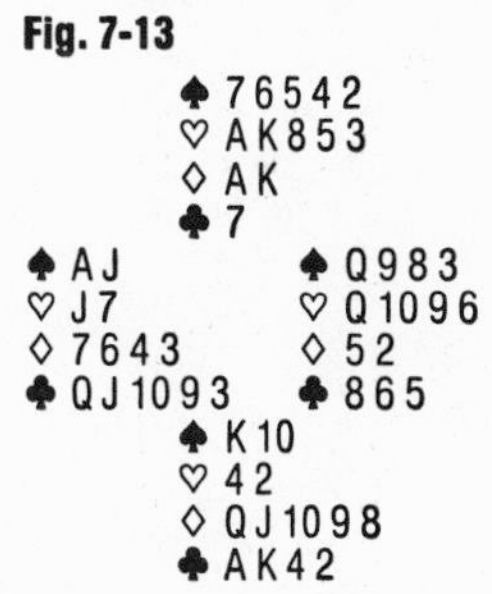

When West opened with the queen of clubs against three no-trump, declarer counted up to nine tricks, including seven in the minor suits and the ace and king of hearts. There was only one problem with his count: the opening lead had taken away the only sure entry to his hand, and the diamond suit was blocked. The king of spades might provide an entry, and then, again, it might not.

So declarer decided it would not be wise to take that trick. Instead, he dropped the four-spot. West looked around for the two and didn't see it. That, coupled with the fact that South had refused to win the first trick, led him to believe he had struck gold with his club lead. On came the jack, and now declarer had an easy road. His ace and king of clubs gave him two discards, and on these he got rid of the ace and king of diamonds in the north hand. The rest was easy.

It is said that we all are offered about the same amount of luck, but that only some of us grasp it, while too many of us let it slip through our fingers.

Fig. 7-14

After declarer opened his hand with a strong two bid, he had no trouble arriving at a contract of six hearts. It was lucky for him that it was East who held the three trumps to the ace. Had those cards been in West's hand, he would not have made his contract. But he had to know how to take advantage of his luck after he got the opening lead of the queen of clubs. He needed very badly to lead trumps twice from the dummy toward his hand, and if he carelessly let that opening club lead come to his king, he would only have one entry. Then East could come to two trump tricks by playing low when trumps were led.

So declarer rose with dummy's ace of clubs, wasting his king of clubs to be sure he had entries where he needed them. On the heart lead, East, of course, played the ten; declarer won with the queen, returned to the dummy with the ace of diamonds, and led a second heart. East now had no better play than the ace of trumps, and, after that, the defenders had no more tricks.

Fig. 7-15

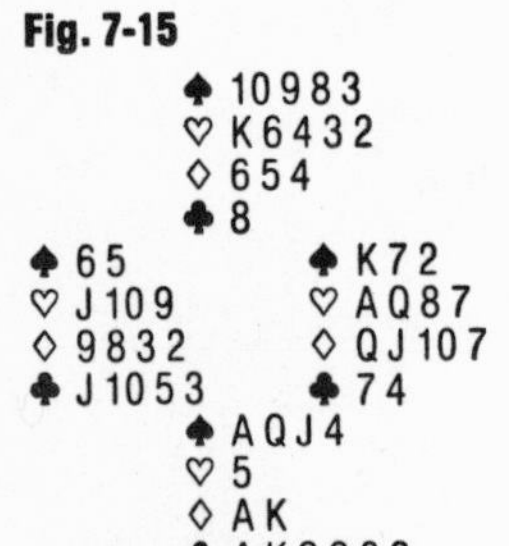

In Fig. 7-15, declarer managed to accomplish two things by an unblocking play in the trump suit. He was able to keep the lead where he wanted it for a finesse, and he was able to establish a side suit.

Whether we bid four spades or six, let's try to make six against a lead of the jack of hearts. Those extra tricks may be important, especially if we are playing match-point duplicate.

When the second heart is led, be sure to trump with the queen or jack of spades and not with the small one. If the spade finesse works, you are going to need to stay in the dummy to repeat the finesse, if East has as many as three to the king. This will still leave you five cards in the broken sequence you have in spades between you and the dummy, and you will have nothing to lose. After that, let's lead the ace of clubs, and then because we don't expect six outstanding cards to break 3–3, let's trump a small club with a small spade. This not only puts the lead in the dummy, it also establishes the club suit. Now we can lead the ten of spades, and, when East plays low, we will have the four to play under it. This way, we will keep the lead in the dummy for a second spade finesse and end up with twelve tricks.

Fig. 7-16

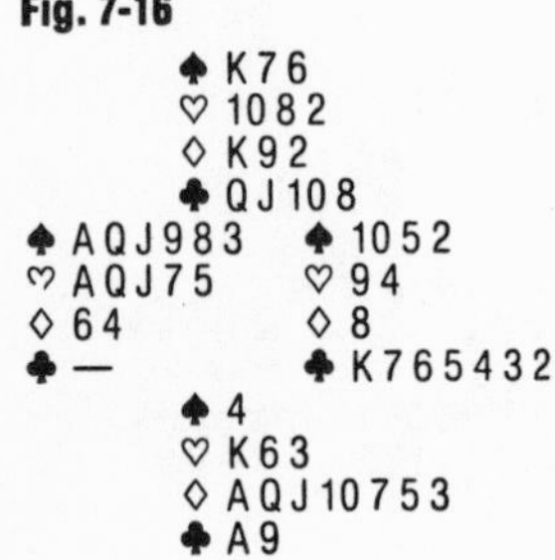

After reaching a contract of five diamonds, declarer had to find a way to avoid losing two heart tricks on the next hand.

On the way up, West had bid both spades and hearts. West started proceedings by cashing the ace of spades. After looking at the dummy, he switched to a small diamond. South could get rid of one of the offending hearts on his king of spades, but that was not good enough. He let the diamond ride to his hand, and then crossed to the dummy with the nine of diamonds. Then he finessed the queen of clubs. Had that lost, West would have had to cash his ace of hearts in a hurry lest South discard his two remaining hearts on a club and the king of spades in the dummy. But when the queen of clubs won the trick and West showed out, declarer saw a way to be sure of his contract. He could not afford to lead a second club yet, as he had that ace of clubs in his hand. Instead, he led the king of spades and discarded the ace of clubs. This not only got the attention of all the players and the assorted kibitzers, it also guaranteed his contract. Now he led the jack of clubs, and East could play his king whenever he wished to do so. When he did, declarer would trump it and then return to the dummy with a diamond. In the process, he would get two heart discards on dummy's clubs. He would end up losing tricks only to the two major suit aces.

On the next hand (Fig. 7-17), declarer had an easy ten tricks, provided he could get to them. To be sure to get to them, he had to take some drastic measures.

Fig. 7-17

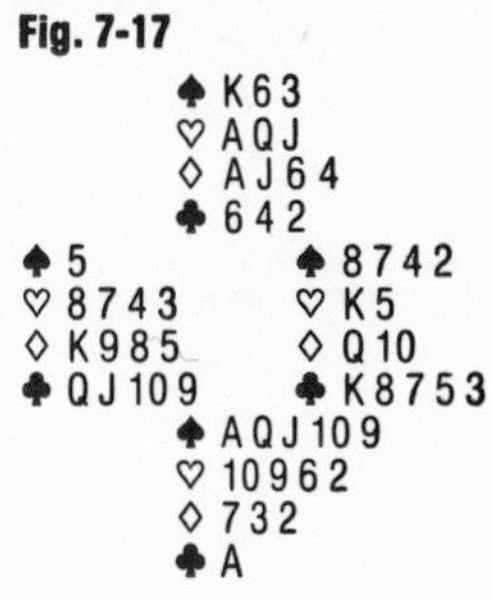

Against the four spade contract, the club queen was led by West. With the ten and nine of hearts in his hand, declarer could count on three heart tricks even if the heart finesse lost. Adding these two, the two minor suit aces, and five sure trump tricks, brought his total up to ten. All he had to do was to be sure he was where he wanted to be when he wanted to be there.

After winning the first trick with the ace of clubs, he won the second with the king of spades and the third with the ace of spades. When West showed out, declarer decided he had to postpone leading any more trumps. He needed to leave that six of trumps in the north hand to be able to get back to his own hand if the heart finesse worked. As a matter of fact, he needed that entry whether the heart finesse worked or not.

So he quit trumps and led a small heart to the jack. East won with the king and returned a club. When declarer trumped this, he had two trumps left, and so did East. He took the queen of hearts in the dummy and used the small trump he had preserved there to return to his hand. He then led his last trump, collecting East's last trump. On that, he discarded dummy's ace of hearts, unblocking the suit so that his ten and nine of hearts could take the two tricks necessary in that suit to bring the total up to ten.

Fig. 7-18

The fact that East had opened the bidding on the next hand helped South decide how to play the hand. East opened the bidding with one heart, but that did not stop North and South from reaching four spades.

West opened the ten of hearts, which was covered by the jack and queen and trumped by South. A lead of a small spade to dummy's ace informed declarer that West now had as many trumps as he had. Declarer had ten tricks if he could figure out a way to take them all. The trouble was that if he pulled trumps and then led a club to establish that suit, the opponents could shift to a diamond and effectively keep him from getting back to his hand to take the fourth club. Having made a profound study of unblocking plays, declarer knew exactly what to do. He overtook dummy's queen of spades and went ahead and pulled all of the spades. That gave him three discards in the dummy, and on these he discarded the clubs. Next he led a club from his hand, and his confidence that East held the ace of clubs was proven to be justified when East had to win that trick. Now East could, if he wished, go ahead and cash the ace of hearts, but declarer would simply discard a diamond on that. If East led another heart, he would allow the declarer to make five-odd, so the best he could do was lead a diamond, which South won with the ace. Now the lead was in the hand where he had his three good clubs. He ended up losing one club trick and two diamond tricks.

Fig. 7-19

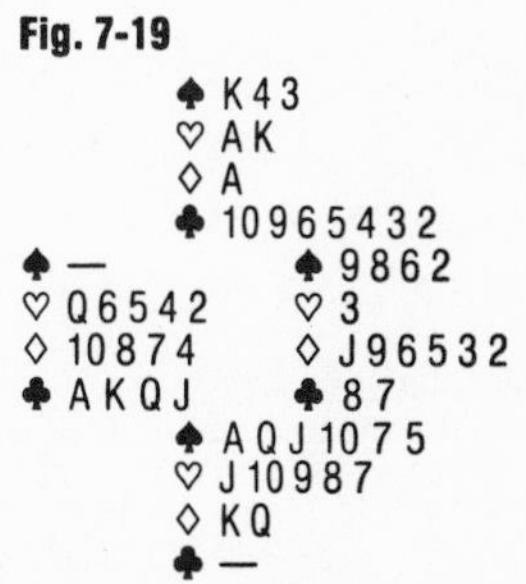

Now let's take one more step in two directions. Let's step up to a small slam contract, and let's discard enough high cards to call this a jettison hand (Fig. 7-19).

We will try this one at six spades. It's obvious we can give up a heart trick and have six spade tricks, two diamond tricks, and four heart tricks.

The problem is how we are going to take them all when the defenders keep leading clubs at us and we finally find that the red suits are blocked.

I think by now you can find the answer. Trump the club lead, and then lead four rounds of trump, discarding the ace of diamonds on the fourth trump. Now lead the king and queen of diamonds and discard dummy's ace and king of hearts. Give them the heart trick they are entitled to, and you still have a trump left to regain the lead to take your four heart tricks.

We have gotten so near to fantasy land that we can go one step further and then move on to the next subject where we will hope to find more practical things.

DUMMY
♠ J 4 3 2
♡ J 5 3
◊ 4
♣ K 5 4 3 2

DECLARER
♠ A Q 10
♡ A Q
◊ A K Q 2
♣ A Q 7 6

We are playing six no-trump and get an opening lead of the jack of diamonds. If that club suit weren't blocked, we would have no problem. With the five club tricks, we could simply give them a spade and have, in addition to three spade tricks, three diamond tricks plus the ace of hearts. But our job is to get that club suit unblocked.

After we win the first trick, we lay down the ace of clubs and find that both opponents follow suit. We now know we will get no worse break than a 3-1 distribution, so the suit will establish, if we can just get rid of one of our small clubs. The line of play that will succeed against any defense and any distribution is to lead the queen of spades. If either opponent takes his king, you can take the next trick, cash your two top spades, cash your high clubs, go to the dummy with its high club, and discard the offending club on the jack of spades. You will now have your twelfth trick.

If your opponents refuse to take the king of spades when you lead your queen, then you lead the other small spade with the same result. If they refuse to take that as well, you lead the queen of hearts. If they don't take that, you don't even need five club tricks anymore. You will have three spade tricks, two heart tricks, three diamond tricks, and four club tricks, and that comes to twelve. So one of your opponents will have to take his king of hearts to keep you from having twelve at once. Then you will cash out and finally discard one of your clubs on dummy's jack of hearts.

THE object of a throw-in play is to force your opponent to give you a trick or, in some instances, several tricks. Sometimes an opponent can be forced to lead into a broken tenace of yours. Or he may be forced to lead a suit where both you and dummy are void and you can trump in one hand while discarding a loser in the other. Or he may even be forced to give an entry into one of your hands which has winning tricks but no entry itself.

For the throw-in play to succeed in its purpose, it is necessary that the lead be given to the opponent at a time when the only cards he has to lead are in the suit or suits where you can gain a trick. Sometimes you have to take away from him all the cards where he might have a safe lead before the throw-in play. Again, when you have plenty of trumps in your hand and the dummy, it is only necessary for both of your hands to be void of a suit which he will have to lead. The preparations necessary for the throw-in play goes under the name of elimination play or strip play. The terms are sometimes used interchangeably, but the tendency today is to use the more violent term—strip play—when you are taking away from the defenders cards they could otherwise successfully lead, and to preserve the gentler name of elimination play for when you are getting rid of all your and dummy's cards in a given suit.

The card which you finally lead to give a trick and, hence, the lead to the opponents is called the exit card. Usually, the exit card is in a suit other than the one the opponents are going to have to lead to give you a trick, but not necessarily.

In the first group of hands, the exit card is in the suit where you expect to gain a trick. Assuming your opponents have no safe lead in any other suit, you yourself can make the first lead in the suit which is going to give you extra tricks.

1. DUMMY	2. DUMMY	3. DUMMY
Q J x	K 10 4	K 9 4
DECLARER	DECLARER	DECLARER
x x x	x x x	J x x
4. DUMMY	5. DUMMY	6. DUMMY
A J 10	A Q 9	A 10 4
DECLARER	DECLARER	DECLARER
x x x	x x x	J 9 7

7. DUMMY
K J 8

DECLARER
A x x x

These are combinations where you expect to get precisely one trick after you have stripped the opponents of any other suits they can safely lead. With number 1, you simply lead low, and, unless West plays the ace or king, you play the jack from the dummy. With number 2, lead toward dummy and put in the ten. If your opponent has to continue this suit, your king is going to make a trick. Neither will it help friend West to put in the jack or queen if he has it. Should he do so, you will simply play your king, and your ten will be bound to make a trick if they have to continue the same suit. Likewise with number 3: West cannot frustrate your plans by playing a ten or queen, as, should he do so, your play of the king will assure you of a trick.

In hands 4–6, the throw-in play will get you a total of two tricks. With all three of these, you simply lead low from your hand and cover as cheaply as possible any card that West plays. No matter how their cards are divided, if they have to continue this suit, you will end up taking two tricks.

There are combinations where proper play will assure you of three tricks, provided you have ample entries in other suits. Hand 7 is one of them. Again, if you lead low from your hand and simply cover any card that West plays, you will be assured of three tricks from the suit.

8. DUMMY	9. DUMMY
J x x	K x x
DECLARER	DECLARER
Q x x	J x x

Hands 8 and 9 show some combinations where you are guaranteed a trick you might not otherwise get, no matter which of your opponents has to lead the suit. With these hands, however, you have no such assurance if you have to lead the suit yourself.

10. DUMMY	11. DUMMY
K 10 x	J x x
DECLARER	DECLARER
Q 9 x	A 10 x

With number 10, you could lead the suit yourself and be sure of getting one trick. If either of your opponents has to lead it, you will be assured of two tricks. With number 11, it looks better if West would have to lead the suit, but if you have enough patience, you will get two tricks out of that suit no matter which of your opponents leads it. Should East lead it, you will simply play low from your hand, and, after West wins, assuming that he does and has to continue the suit, you will have your two tricks.

12. DUMMY
K 10 2

DECLARER
A J x

It is obvious in number 12 that if either of your opponents leads this suit, your guarantee of two tricks increases to a guarantee of three tricks.

Then there is that group of combinations where your extra trick is assured only if a chosen one of your opponents has to lead the suit.

13. DUMMY	14. DUMMY
x x	x x
DECLARER	DECLARER
K x	K J x

In number 13 you can only be guaranteed a trick at all if West leads the suit. With number 14, it is even possible that you may get two tricks, but you are not guaranteed even one unless West leads the suit.

15. DUMMY	16. DUMMY
x x	A x x
DECLARER	DECLARER
A Q	Q x

With both 15 and 16, you can be guaranteed two tricks only if West leads the suit.

17. DUMMY	18. DUMMY
K x x	K x x
DECLARER	DECLARER
Q x x	Q 10 x

Number 17 is a little different. You can get two tricks, if you can make the player who happens to hold the ace lead the suit. You simply play second-hand low, and you will win the trick, whereupon you can lead it through his ace to get your second trick.

In number 18, the addition of that ten-spot assures you of two tricks in the suit, if you can get West to lead the suit.

19. DUMMY
J 10 x

DECLARER
A K x x

20. DUMMY
A K x x

DECLARER
J x x

With both of these holdings, you are assured of three tricks, if you can make West lead the suit.

And then there are some hands where an extra trick is not guaranteed if your chosen opponent leads the suit, but where your chances to get the extra trick are improved.

21. DUMMY
K 9 x

DECLARER
A 10 x

22. DUMMY
A x

DECLARER
Q x

23. DUMMY
A x x

DECLARER
J 9 x

In number 21, if the queen is in one opponent's hand and the jack in the other, you can pick up three tricks when either of your opponents leads the suit. With number 22, you can pick up two tricks provided the player who holds the king leads the suit. The fact that there is not an additional small card in either the north or south hand takes away the guarantee of two tricks which you would have with West on lead if that other small card were there.

In number 23, if the ten-spot is in East and West leads the suit, you are going to get two tricks instead of one if East wins and continues the suit.

These are not all of the combinations where it is to your advantage to have your opponents lead the suit, but they cover most situations. You will see that sometimes you may have to lose as many as two tricks to get one and that quite often you will have to lose one trick to do any gaining. In deciding whether to go for a throw-in play or some other line, you have to judge whether you can afford to lose the requisite number of tricks to gain a trick.

The terminology used for throw-in plays is really not that precise. Usage finally determines the meaning of words, and it has become common practice today to use the terms "throw-in play" and "end play" interchangeably. Neither term accurately describes the situation existing on the next hand. In the vernacular, they would say that West is end-played at trick one. As the term end play means play toward the end of the hand—along about the tenth or eleventh trick—you might wonder how you could be end-played at trick one without ever having been thrown in at all. Well, here is how (Fig. 8-1).

Fig. 8-1

	North	
	♠ J 6 3 ♡ J 4 ◇ 8 5 2 ♣ Q 9 7 4 3	
♠ A 9 4 ♡ A 9 8 3 ◇ Q 10 4 3 ♣ K 8		♠ K 10 8 5 ♡ Q 7 2 ◇ 9 7 ♣ J 10 5 2
	♠ Q 7 2 ♡ K 10 6 5 ◇ A K J 6 ♣ A 6	

The bidding was brief and to the point: South dealt and bid one notrump, and everybody passed. Any card that West led would give declarer a trick he could not get by force. If anybody had thrown West in the lead, it was the dealer. He finally chose the three of diamonds. Declarer won that with the jack, cashed the ace and king of diamonds, and led a fourth diamond. This time West *was* thrown in. Not only that, his hand had been stripped of good exit cards, as he had no diamonds left. So he tried his fourth best heart. Dummy played low, and East's queen was captured by declarer's king. He led back a heart. West won that with his ace and led a third heart. Declarer won that with the ten and led a fourth heart. There was West, thrown in again and stripped of all of his cards in both red suits. Once more, he had to make a lead which gave the declarer a trick. He laid down the ace of spades and led another spade to East's king, but that gave declarer his seventh trick. Declarer won only one club trick, but he added to that a spade trick, two heart tricks, and three diamond tricks.

Let's look at one where West was end-played at trick two—or at least where declarer was able to throw-him-in at trick two (Fig.8-2).

Fig. 8-2 Dlr: S Vul: 0

	North	
	♠ 10 3 ♡ A 10 5 ♢ A 10 6 5 ♣ Q 7 5 2	
West ♠ K Q J 7 ♡ Q 4 3 ♢ K 8 3 ♣ K 9 4		**East** ♠ 9 8 6 5 4 ♡ J 6 ♢ J 7 ♣ 10 8 6 3
	♠ A 2 ♡ K 9 8 7 2 ♢ Q 9 4 2 ♣ A J	

SOUTH	WEST	NORTH	EAST
1♡	Dbl	Rdbl	1♠
Pass	Pass	2♡	Pass
3♡	Pass	4♡	All Pass

Opening lead: ♠K

West led the king of spades. South won that with the ace, and, as West had indicated he had all of the defensive strength in the hand, South thought it a very fine idea to let him lead again. So, South led the two of spades.

West won that, and, if he led any one of the other three suits, South was not going to lose a trick in the suit led. If he led a third spade, declarer would trump in the dummy, discard a club from his hand, and never lose a club trick. So any way that poor West went, South was going to lose one trick in each of three suits, but there was going to be one suit in which he lost no tricks at all.

Before we get serious in our study of this subject, let's look at one more fantastic sort of a hand, and this time let's limit ourselves to what we see in actual play—our own hand and dummy's.

DUMMY
♠ K 6 3
♡ A J 4 3
♢ J 4 3 2
♣ K 2

DECLARER
♠ A J 5
♡ 2
♢ A Q
♣ A J 10 9 8 7 6

We get to a contract of five clubs, and West opens the king of hearts. This indicates he has the queen as well as the king. Looking at the hand, we see possible losers in spades, diamonds, and clubs. But, if we are right that West has the queen of hearts as well as the king, we have a line of play that gives us just about a 99.9-percent chance to make our contract. We just let West hold the trick! He is now end-played. Anything he leads lets us get rid of one of our losers. The worst that could happen would be for him to hold all four clubs to the queen and switch to a club. No problem. We win in our hand, win the king of clubs, and return to our hand by trumping a small heart. We now take the ace of clubs, give West the lead again with the queen of clubs, and he is right back where he started. Anything he leads is going to let us get rid of one of our losers.

Now the fun is over for awhile, and we are going to have to get down to the study of just how to prepare our hand for the throw-in when it is not right there for us in the beginning. First, we are going to talk about those hands where we take from the opponents all of the safe exit cards they have.

STRIP AND THROW-IN

Fig. 8-3

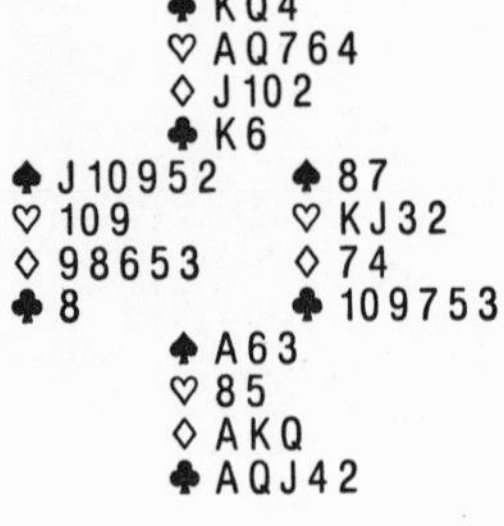

We are going to see whether we can take away from our opponents some cards they would like to have.

North and South had no trouble getting to six no-trump on this hand. West led the jack of spades, and declarer counted his tricks. He saw that if clubs would behave normally, he had twelve top tricks, with a heart finesse for number thirteen. He won the first trick in the dummy with the king and led the king of clubs and then the small club to his jack. When West threw off a small diamond, declarer saw that clubs were not behaving very nicely. Now he had only eleven tricks off the top, and it looked like he would need the heart finesse for his twelfth trick. Or would he? His holding in hearts was one of those where it would be very nice if he could get an opponent to lead the suit for him, provided that opponent was East. Leading hearts was exactly the last thing East wanted to do at this moment. The only way to make him do that would be to leave him nothing else to lead. So, instead of just taking a heart finesse, declarer set out to see whether that would be possible.

After cashing the two club tricks, declarer cashed the remaining two spade tricks. On the third spade, East discarded the deuce of hearts, trying to look like a man who had no interest in that suit at all. Well, at least declarer knew that East didn't have any spades to lead if he should gain the lead. Next he took his diamond tricks. East showed out on the third diamond and demonstrated his contempt for hearts by discarding the three of that suit. Now declarer didn't have to guess. If he took all of the clubs away from East, he would have nothing left to lead but hearts. And he could get all of the clubs out of the East hand while simultaneously throwing East in with the last club. So, he took his two high clubs and led the last one to East, throwing away three hearts from dummy on the three clubs. Poor East was stripped of everything except his two hearts, and a heart lead gave declarer the last two tricks.

Fig. 8-4

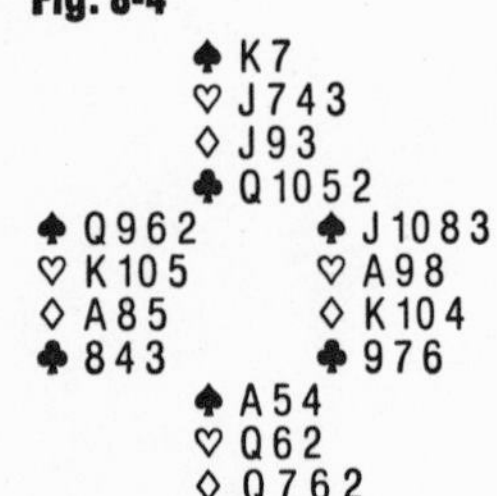

On the next hand (Fig. 8-4), declarer saw that combination in both red suits where you are assured of a trick if the opponents have to lead the suit first.

The opening lead was the two of spades against a one no-trump contract. Declarer decided to trust West for having the four spades which his lead indicated. If so, he was going to give them the privilege of leading red suits for him.

He won the trick with dummy's king and promptly cashed four club tricks, discarding a diamond from his hand. Then he led a small spade to the ace. He had now stripped the opponents of clubs, and he led a spade so they could strip themselves of spades and have nothing left to lead but red-suited cards. As for himself, he would have five cards left after four tricks had been taken in clubs and four in spades, and he would keep two hearts and three diamonds in his own hand and two diamonds and three hearts in the north hand. The defenders could go ahead and cash the ace and king of both red suits, but that last trick was going to be won by either North's jack of hearts or South's queen of diamonds, bringing declarer's total up to seven.

Some version or other of this next hand has appeared in almost every bridge column I ever read and in most of the books which have to do with throw-in plays. It is a good one and illustrates the point beautifully, so here is my version (Fig. 8-5).

Fig. 8-5

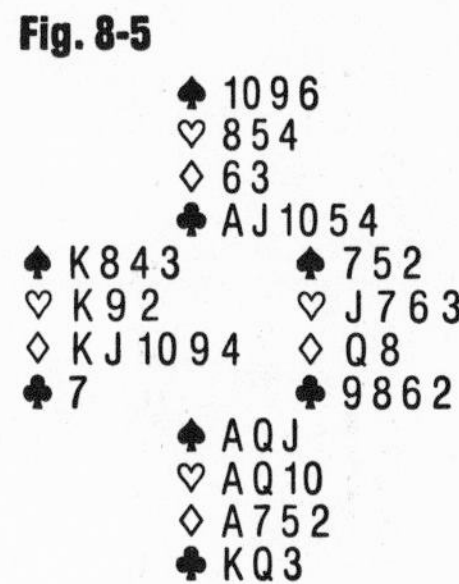

With his 22 high-card points plus the club holding in the north hand, South had no trouble getting to a contract of three no-trump. After the opening lead of the jack of diamonds, he was in danger of going set if he didn't play carefully. East properly played the queen on the opening jack lead and, when South ducked, continued the eight. West won with the king and led a third diamond which declarer won with the ace, as East discarded a spade. Now declarer had five sure club tricks, but the only other sure tricks he had were his aces. If he tried finessing hearts or spades and the finesse lost, he knew that West would then take enough diamond tricks to set him. So, he took his king and queen of clubs, postponing the evil moment when he had to decide which suit to finesse. On the second club trick, West discarded a small spade, and now declarer decided. He decided not to finesse either one. It had been easier than he had expected to strip West of clubs, but that job had been accomplished. He knew that West had two good diamonds left, and so he led a diamond to let West take them, knowing that after he cashed those two diamonds, he would have to lead either a spade or a heart, as he would have nothing else. Whichever one of the major suits he led would give the declarer the two tricks he needed in that suit, and he could proceed with his business of taking his club tricks.

Sometimes the throw-in play is, in some respects, like a finesse—it's not a sure thing, but it gives you a 50–50 chance instead of a chance of practically zero. On the next hand (Fig. 8-6), the declarer opened the bidding three no-trump. Wouldn't you?

Fig. 8-6

West, of course, led the king of clubs. Declarer started with eight sure tricks, and, as he looked at the dummy, he still had eight sure tricks. He let the king of clubs hold the trick to see what might happen, and West continued the suit, with East showing out and discarding a small diamond.

Now let's look at the north and south hands as declarer would, without seeing East's and West's cards. Obviously, an extra trick was not going to be brought in by the club suit. The diamond suit offered one of those possibilities shown in example 22 of our earlier exhibits, where if the opponent who held the king of diamonds could be forced to lead diamonds, declarer would get two tricks. That was his best chance. He knew that West had started with five clubs, and the most frequent holding with a five-card suit is 5-3-3-2. If that was, indeed, the holding in the West hand, then declarer could take away from him all of his spades and hearts and give him the lead in clubs. After winning his club tricks, West would be stripped of all but diamonds and would have to lead a diamond. If he had the king, declarer was going to make the hand. If he did not have the king, declarer was going set. That option was a great improvement over any other that declarer held.

He won the second club, led the A K Q of spades, and noted that West discarded the two of hearts on the third spade. Now he led the A K Q of hearts, and, when West discarded the two of diamonds on the third heart, he knew West's distribution exactly. Now he gave him his club and let him go ahead and win his three club tricks. After doing that, West had to lead a diamond, and, being a firm believer in happy endings, I have carefully put the diamond king in West's hand.

Sometimes a little bit of help from the opponents can guide you to the right line of play (Fig. 8-7).

West led the king of spades against the four-heart contract, and East offered his assist to the declarer when he followed with the eight. Had he not encouraged a spade continuation, West would at least have had a chance to find the diamond shift. But West continued with the ace and a small spade. Declarer trumped the third spade and led the ace of hearts and a small heart to the king. He got the bad news about the heart suit, but went ahead and led a small heart, finessing the jack in the East hand and then taking away from East his last heart. As a matter of fact, nobody had any trumps left. It took all of declarer's trumps to collect East's.

West had to make three discards, and that gave him his chance to make life easy for the declarer. He discarded two spades and a club. The spade discards cleared up any doubt declarer might have had about that suit, and when both opponents followed suit to three leads of clubs, the thirteen cards in that suit were accounted for. When everybody followed suit, that also accounted for all the clubs. Declarer had been watching these goings-on as a good declarer should, and he now knew that East had no more spades, no more hearts, and no more clubs. In other words, he had been stripped of everything but diamonds. Now all he had to do was lead a diamond and cover any card West played. So he led the seven-spot and put in the three from the north hand. That cooked East's goose, as he had to lead a diamond back into the jaws of the diamond holding in the north hand.

If a little help from the opponents is good, a lot of help is even better.

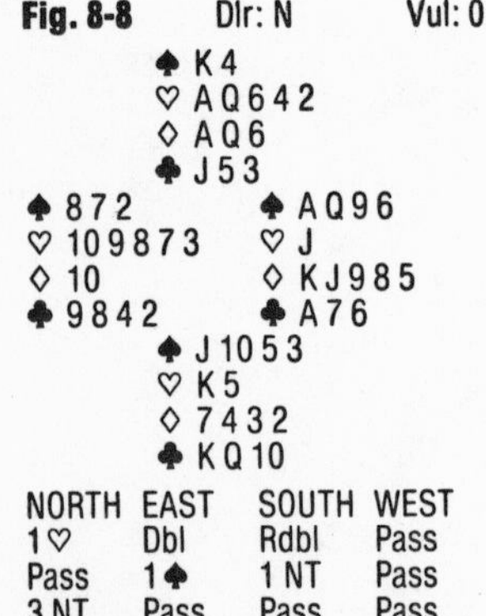

West opened the eight of spades, and, when declarer played low from the dummy, East won with the queen. East decided the time had come to fool the declarer. Acting like a man who was leading the top of a worthless suit, he led his seven of clubs. Declarer was up to some of these "fool-em" tactics himself, so he played the king. Now it was West's turn. Holding four clubs, he decided he had better give his partner a count and played the eight. Declarer found this an interesting trick. He led a small spade to his king, and East won with the ace. Encouraged by his partner's high club, East continued with the six of clubs. He may not have known it, but he was rapidly running out of exit cards. South won that with the queen, and the play of the deuce from West convinced declarer that East now held the singleton ace of clubs in his hand. He cashed his good spade tricks, throwing away a diamond and a heart from the dummy, and then led the king of hearts. The jack from East looked honest to him, as he had not expected East to have many hearts considering his take-out double. To verify that, he led a second heart and won it in the dummy with the ace. When East played the five of diamonds, declarer saw that he had run out of cards in the major suits. Now if he did, in fact, have the singleton ace of clubs left, he was going to be stripped of everything except diamonds when he won the next trick with it. So, declarer led the club, and, when East played the ace had to lead a diamond into the ace-queen, South decided he had enjoyed the hand very much. I don't know whether he said thanks to his opponents or not, but he should have.

In real life, things are not always as clear cut as they have been in the hands we've been looking at. Often, there are possibilities of other techniques which the declarer might use to attain his goal mixed in with the possibilities of a throw-in play. On occasions, the declarer is not able to choose the best procedure until quite late in the play when he has learned more about the distribution of the opposing hands.

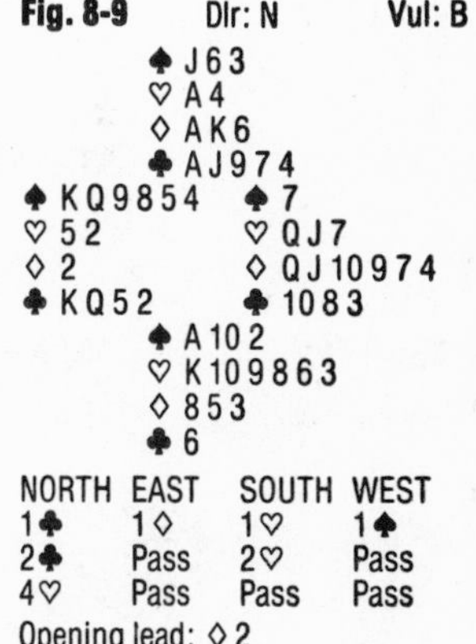

If this were a book on bidding, I would wonder why North hadn't opened with one no-trump instead of one club, and I would have asked where in the world East dug up that vulnerable overcall. But, so far as the bidding is concerned, I am a reporter and not a critic. So, we will forget about the bidding, except as it was useful to the declarer, and concentrate upon the play.

West led the two of diamonds, the dummy came down, and declarer studied his prospects. He could find two losers in spades, one in hearts, and one in diamonds, if the distribution was reasonably favorable. Next, he took a good look at the two of diamonds, and he decided it was almost certainly a singleton. There was, for example, no chance it was small from three to the queen or jack after East had bid the suit. He tucked that bit of information away for future use and thought up procedures which would let him get rid of one of his losers.

One of his opponents might have the queen-jack doubleton of hearts, but that was unlikely.

Could he establish a long club and get back to cash it to discard a diamond or spade from his hand? He could if the clubs would break 4–3, provided dummy had plenty of entries. The diamond lead had taken away one of the entries, and, even if he could get the suit established, he would then have no way to get there to cash it.

Of course, if one of his opponents held the king and queen of clubs with only one small one, then the jack could become established. Not likely—but a possibility. If West had three hearts with one of the honors, he might be stripped of cards in the minor suits and then given the lead with his high heart. Now he would be stripped of everything except spades, and a spade lead from his side would give South two tricks in the suit no matter how the honors were divided.

If West had only two trumps and the high trump remained with East, West might be stripped of all cards but spades, and a small spade toward dummy's jack would bring in the extra trick, provided West had both the king and queen of spades. This was a quite likely possibility in view of the fact that West had bid spades, but one that would not work if East happened to hold either the king or queen.

With these various options available, declarer set out on a process of exploration. He won the diamond in the dummy and then led the ace of clubs and trumped a small club. He went back to the dummy with the ace of trumps and led another club and trumped it. On the third club lead, the queen fell out. Declarer now led his king of trumps, went back to the dummy with the ace of diamonds, and noted that West discarded a spade, confirming declarer's opinion that the opening lead of the deuce was a singleton. On came the fourth club, and this time East showed out!

Now declarer knew how to proceed. West had the king of clubs but no more diamonds. If he had another heart, it was the queen. After this club play, West was going to be stripped of all cards in the minor suits. He would simply have to lead spades (possibly after cashing the queen of hearts) because he would have nothing else to lead. So, instead of trumping the club, declarer simply discarded his losing diamond on it.

West won that, led the king of spades, and you will see that declarer ended up losing one trick in spades, one trump trick, and one club trick.

To complete my record, I had better put in some of those hands where you strip a defender of every card he has except trumps and finally throw him in and make him lead trumps to get extra tricks. I have not found these very useful myself. They require that precise distributions be present in side suits. Every time I think I have one set up, somebody trumps in prematurely and upsets my plans. Maybe you will be luckier.

Fig. 8-10 Dlr: N Vul: N-S

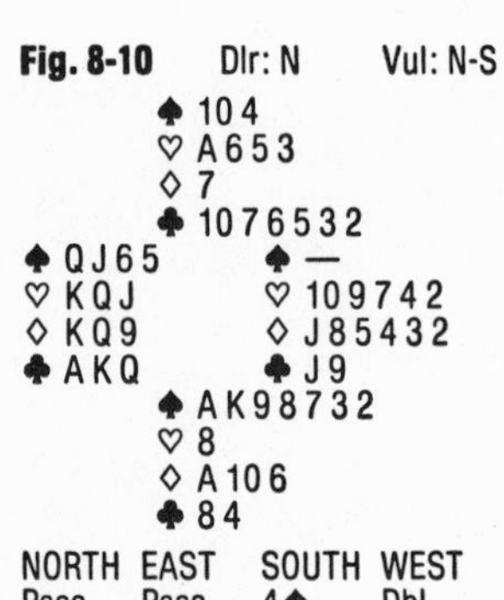

Opening lead: ♣K

When West looked at his hand, he thought utopia had arrived, but he was having trouble counting his points. Everytime he counted them, he got a different answer. He wanted to be sure he was right and could approach his monstrous holding just right, so he ws counting them for the third time when he heard South bid four spades. He dropped a few cards in his lap and simultaneously doubled with such a loud voice that everybody else at the table was completely subdued. In view of what happened, East would have been well advised to bid five diamonds. West was doomed to get a minus score with his big hand, and that contract could have gone set a trick had he been allowed to play it, but that was better than what actually happened.

West led the king of clubs, and South hesitated just long enough to give his partner a reproachful look. North made no apologies, so South proceeded. West cashed two clubs and then switched to the king of hearts. A spade lead by him would have brought about more complications, but that thought never even occurred to West. He had two tricks in and two sure trump tricks. All he had to do was wait for them—or so he thought.

Declarer decided to avail himself of those two ruffing tricks in the dummy, so he took the ace of hearts and promptly trumped a heart. Next came the ace of diamonds, and a diamond was trumped in the dummy. On came a third heart, which also was trumped, and then his last diamond was trumped with dummy's last trump. Next he led a club and trumped it.

Everybody now had four cards left. South had the A K 9 8 of spades, while West was still grimly holding onto his "sure trump tricks." But South decided that the vehemence of West's double justified a lead of the nine of spades.

West now had to decide just which way he wanted to take his one remaining trump trick: If he played low, South would next lead the ace and king of trumps. So, he won the jack, and that was just as bad, as he now had to concede the last three tricks to the declarer.

I don't even think I'll show you the bidding on the next hand (Fig.

8-11); it might distract your attention from the play. Suffice it to say that after South opened one club, North did everything he could to play three no-trump, but South would have none of it and ended up finally in five clubs, doubled by East and redoubled by himself.

Fig. 8-11

♠ K 4 3 2
♡ Q 5 4 2
◊ A Q 2
♣ K 2

West	East
♠ 10 9 8 5	♠ Q J
♡ J 10 9 7	♡ K 8 6 3
◊ 10 9 6 5	◊ J 8 7
♣ 3	♣ A J 10 9

♠ A 7 6
♡ A
◊ K 4 3
♣ Q 8 7 6 5 4

West opened the jack of hearts. South decided this was no time to be leading trump. He won the first trick with the ace, crossed to the dummy with the queen of diamonds, and trumped a second heart. Back to dummy he went with the ace of diamonds to trump a third heart. The king of spades put him back in the dummy, and he trumped a fourth heart. East now had more trumps than the declarer, but the declarer seemed not to mind. He won a trick with the king of diamonds and then with the ace of spades. He had now won nine tricks. East was sitting there with all four of his trumps. Declarer led another spade, and East finally got a trick with one of his trumps, but just when he didn't need it. No matter which club he led next, he was going to get exactly one more trick.

And now for one more of these trump throw-in plays. This one was played by Mr. Pierre Beguin of Switzerland. Mr. Beguin won his share of European championships, and he is considered to be the founder of the Swiss Bridge Federation.

The opening lead was the king of spades, which was won with dummy's ace. The two of hearts was then led for a successful finesse, and West showed out of trumps. I am assured that Mr. Beguin did not bat an eyelash at this point, but that he promptly led his three high clubs, discarding a small spade from the dummy. Next he led the ace of diamonds and then cashed dummy's diamonds, discarding his two remaining spades. East was now stripped of everything except trumps, and when a spade was led from the dummy, he had no choice but to trump it. My reporter says that East made some comment about Beguin's good luck in ridding himself of his spade losers, but that Beguin replied, happily, that he wouldn't dream of taking advantage of his so-called luck but would play the hand as though he had a spade left, and with that, he underruffed. East suddenly realized that the ball game was over. He was left with the K 9 8 of hearts. Whichever one of those he led, Beguin was going to take the balance of the tricks.

I have saved a tricky one to complete this section (Fig. 8-13).

Some people might say that South's rebid of four hearts was an overbid, especially after taking a look at his hand with the dummy where there seemed to be four losers in the minor suits. But if you have that opinion, don't express it until you see how the hand came out. South made his bid.

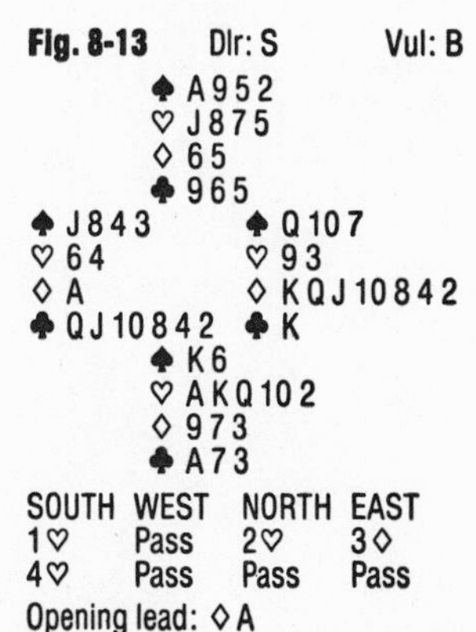

West led the ace of diamonds and, in spite of his partner's vigorous signal with the ten-spot, switched to the queen of clubs. At this point, declarer made a mental note that East had started with seven diamonds and West had no more. East played the king of clubs, and declarer won with the ace. Two leads of trumps took all of the trumps away from the opponents, and declarer then led the king of spades, followed by a spade to dummy's ace, then declarer trumped a spade.

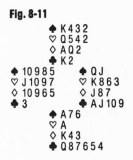

South now knew that East had been stripped of everything except diamonds, and so he led a diamond. East won that and continued another diamond. Declarer could have trumped that one in the dummy. Instead, he threw away a club. For lack of any other cards, East had to lead yet another diamond, and this one declarer trumped in his own hand, while throwing away the last club from the dummy. South now had two trumps in the dummy to take care of his two losing clubs and a trump in his own hand to take care of dummy's losing spade.

How did declarer know after trumping a spade that he had stripped East of all cards except diamonds? Couldn't East have held the long spade? Well, let's go back to trick one.

When West did not continue diamonds, declarer decided that East had started with seven diamonds. In the course of the play, he had shown up with one club, three spades, and two hearts. That totaled six more cards. If the first idea that East started with seven diamonds was correct, he could not still have another spade unless the hand was a misdeal.

Now I seem to have moved over into that area called elimination plays where the declarer can discard a loser in one hand while he trumps an opponent's lead in the other. That is where I wanted to be right now, as that is my next subject.

ELIMINATION AND THROW-IN

The elimination play has a variety of names. The *Official Encyclopedia of Bridge* calls it, "a trump throw-in." That does not necessarily mean that you throw your opponents in with trumps. You throw them in with whatever you have that is handy at a time when you and the dummy are void in a suit they would have to lead and you both have trumps. If you can do this, you can discard a loser from one hand, while you trump with the other, and that is just about as good as leading a trump, not having to follow suit, and throwing away a loser. I think George Coffin has a better name when he suggests this be called a "cross-ruff elimination" or "ruffing elimination." Whatever you choose to call the play, it is one of declarer's best friends. Let's illustrate (Fig. 8-14).

Fig. 8-14

The bidding was short and to the point. South opened one heart, and North went to four, with South then jumping to six. West led the king of spades, and when the ace held that trick, the declarer knew he had the contract made because he held the nine of clubs.

Because he had the nine of clubs? Yes, his club holding is one of those I showed you at the beginning of this chapter where the declarer himself can lead the suit which has the throw-in card. All he had to do, at the proper moment, was to lead a small club from the dummy and cover whatever East played. West could not return a club without losing a trick. But, before declarer did that, he had something else to do.

Obviously, at this point, if West got in, he could lead a card from any suit except clubs with impunity. So declarer had to correct that situation. He led the queen of hearts, and, when both followed, he knew they'd been stripped of hearts. He had plenty of trumps and could have led them a second time if it had been necessary, but it was not. He led a spade and trumped it. Then he led the ace of diamonds and trumped a diamond in the dummy. On came another spade which he trumped, and the last diamond was trumped in the dummy. Now he had eliminated all spades and diamonds from his hand and the dummy. This process was the prerequisite for throwing West in with the club. He led a small club, and, when East played low, he played the nine. Had East chosen to play the ten, he could have played the queen with equal effectiveness. Either way, when West won the trick, he could not return a club without giving declarer the extra trick he needed. Neither could he lead a spade or a heart. Had he led either, declarer could have trumped either in the dummy, while throwing away the queen of clubs from his hand, and the balance would have been his.

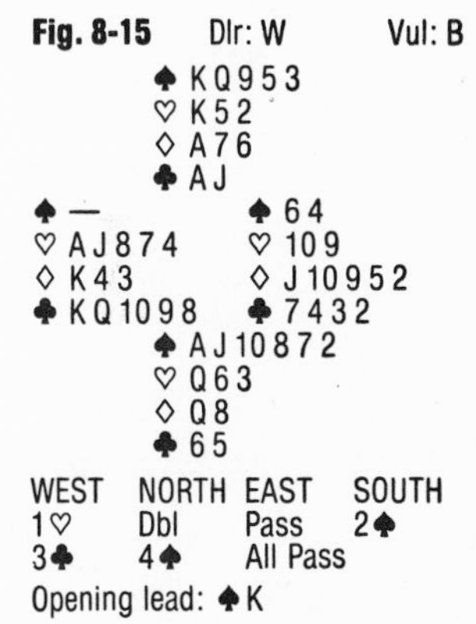

Fig. 8-15

When you hold those split honors where you would welcome a lead, an elimination in only one suit may be all that is necessary.

Declarer won the opening lead with dummy's ace, and found he had to lead trumps twice to take the enemy's trumps away from him, but that caused him no pain. He was confident that by leading a club he could throw West in the lead and, at the same time, eliminate clubs from his combined holding. When West won the queen, he had no lead that would not cost him a trick. If he led a small heart, declarer would let that ride to his queen and then lead a second heart toward his king. A small diamond would ride to declarer's queen. If West persisted in clubs, declarer would trump the third club in the dummy, while he discarded a diamond from his hand. Of course, if West decided to lay down the ace of hearts, that would limit the losers in that suit to one trick.

Knowledge of the card combinations that yield themselves to throw-in plays makes the next hand a cinch (Fig. 8-16).

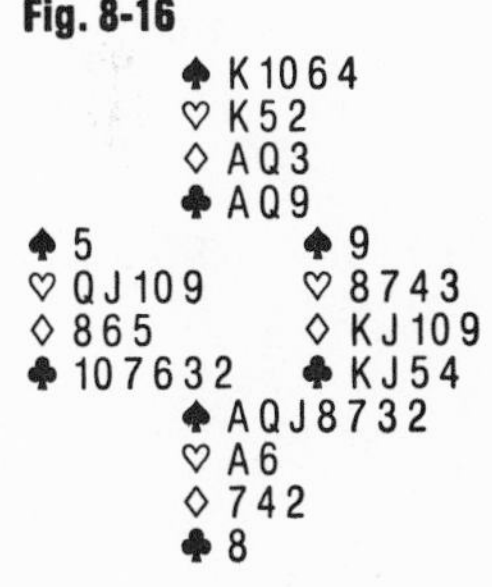

Fig. 8-16

Against a contract of six spades, West led the queen of hearts, and South won with the ace. At first glance, it looked like there might be two diamond losers. Not a chance.

With eleven trumps between North and South, there was going to be no question about having adequate trumps in each hand for an elimination play to work after the opponents' trumps had been drawn. Eliminating hearts was not going to prove to be any problem—all that had to be done was to, at the proper moment, cash the king of hearts and then trump one. Then declarer would reach the point of his throw-in play in the minor suits.

There is all the difference in the world between the club suit and the diamond suit. That nine of clubs makes the difference. This is one of those combinations listed where you can use the very suit itself for a throw-in. After you have pulled trumps and then eliminated hearts, simply lead your club and cover any card West plays to be sure he doesn't win the trick. No matter how the clubs are divided, you are going to lose that trick and no more. Assuming East wins the trick, he obviously cannot lead another heart. If he does, you will discard a diamond from the south hand, while trumping in dummy, and the two minor suit aces will cover the two remaining diamonds. If East chooses to return a diamond, obviously the ace and queen of diamonds in the north hand plus the ace of clubs will take care of all of South's losers. If East returns a club, the ace and queen of clubs and ace of diamonds will take care of all the losers.

On the next hand, the throw-in combination is not so obvious, but it is there.

Yes, it is the spades. Assuming you do not get the unlikely opening lead of a spade before you have gone through the elimination process, you are going to take ten tricks at a four heart contract. Let's say you get the likely lead of the jack of clubs and a club return. You have now eliminated clubs. Two leads of trumps take care of the opponents' trumps, and now you take all three diamond tricks, ending in your own hand. You have now eliminated diamonds. Lead a small spade, and, again, no matter what West plays and no matter how the spades are divided, you are going to hold your spade losers to two tricks. Just cover whatever card West plays. If East wins and continues spades, you will have a spade trick. If he leads anything else, you will get that old ruff-and-sluff, getting rid of a spade in one hand, while you trump in the other.

The bidding on the hand in Fig. 8-18 went on for some time before anybody passed.

West led the king of hearts, took a look at the dummy, and switched to the nine of spades.

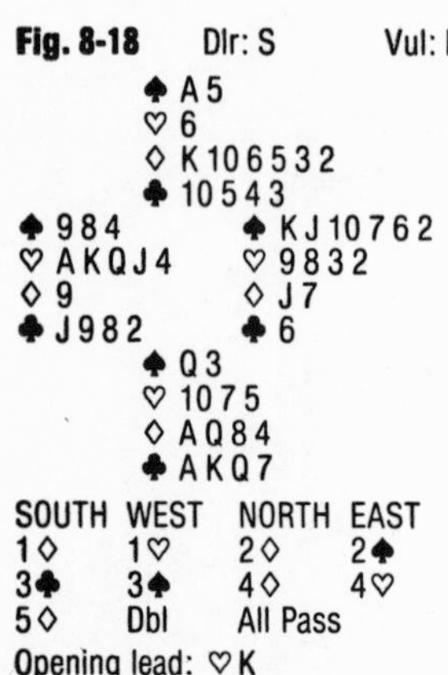

Declarer felt pretty good about the whole thing. His side held only slightly more than half of the high cards, but they had a lot of distribution. He saw one heart loser and one spade loser, and, if the minor suits broke normally, that was all. However, he saw no advantage to ducking the spade, so he played dummy's ace.

Just in case something bad should happen, he led a small diamond to his ace and started eliminating hearts from his hand. He led a second heart, trumped it, and came back to his hand with the queen of diamonds to trump his last heart. Then he won the ace of clubs and then the king of clubs, intending, if both players followed suit, to spread his hand and claim his doubled contract, East didn't follow suit, so he spread his hand and claimed it anyway. He knew that East was now out of diamonds and clubs and had nothing left except major suit cards. He wasn't going to lose a club trick after all. He just led the queen of spades and let East win that trick. Whatever East led back, he was going to discard a club from his hand while trumping in the dummy.

Suppose West had had the king of spades after all? That would have been all right, too, for while West did hold some clubs, he obviously could not win a trick by leading them.

On the next hand, declarer had a choice between a finesse and a guess or a throw-in play which was a sure thing.

Fig. 8-19

♠ Q J 8 5 2
♡ A Q 4
◊ A 10 6
♣ 7 5

♠ 10
♡ J 10 9 7
◊ 7 5 3
♣ K J 9 8 2

♠ 7 4
♡ 6 5 3
◊ Q 9 8 2
♣ 10 6 4 3

♠ A K 9 6 3
♡ K 8 2
◊ K J 4
♣ A Q

South quickly got to a six spade contract, and West led the jack of hearts. There were two possible losers: one in diamonds and one in clubs. The clubs offered a finesse, and the diamonds offered not only a finesse, but also one of those combinations where, if you can make either opponent lead diamonds, you will be sure of losing no tricks in the suit. Declarer decided to forgo the club finesse and make sure of his contract.

First he had to pull trumps (which he did in two leads) and eliminate the hearts from his hands, which was no problem. He could not eliminate clubs by finessing them, for after the finesse, he would still have a club (the ace) in his hand if the finesse lost. So, after clearing hearts, he took the ace of clubs and led the queen. Whoever won that had to give him a sluff-and-ruff or lead diamonds, which was just as bad.

Actually, the play would have been easier to see if he had not had the queen of clubs. In this case, the ace and deuce of clubs would have done just as well.

Fig. 8-20

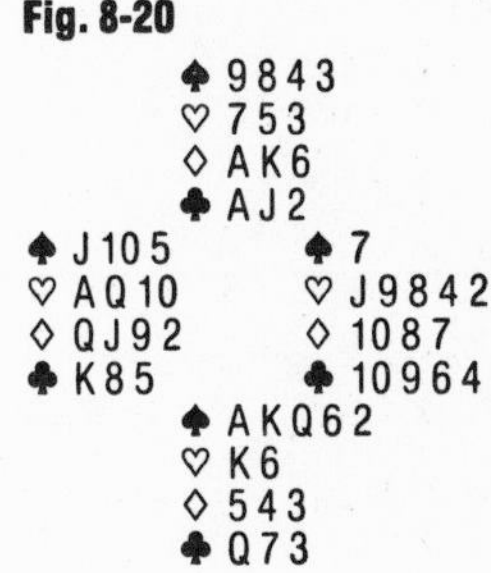

I especially like the next hand (Fig. 8-20) because it was played by the late Ewart Kempson of England. That gallant gentleman was one of the bright stars of bridge.

After West opened the bidding with one diamond, Kempson got to a contract of four spades with the South hand. The opening lead was the queen of diamonds. When the dummy came down, Kempson was looking at 26 high-card points, and it was easy to see that the chance of finding the ace of hearts in the east hand was virtually nil in view of West's opening bid. Unless West had been dealt the doubleton king of clubs, it looked as though there was a club loser. Adding all this together, there were two heart losers, one diamond loser, and one club loser. Something had to be done about that.

Preparing for an elimination play, Kempson let the queen of diamonds hold the first trick. West continued with the deuce of diamonds, and dummy's king won. Kempson cashed two trump tricks, noting that East showed out, and felt safe at this point leading a third diamond to take dummy's ace. He now led the third spade, leaving one spade in the dummy and two in his hand. He led a small club and put in dummy's jack. It held the trick, and he laid down the ace. As you see, the king did not fall. That was quite all right. Kempson now had his sure throw-in card. He led a third club to his queen and West's king. A diamond lead would obviously give Kempson a ruff-and-sluff, so West had no better play than to lead his ace of hearts, which gave Kempson his king for his tenth trick.

Fig. 8-21

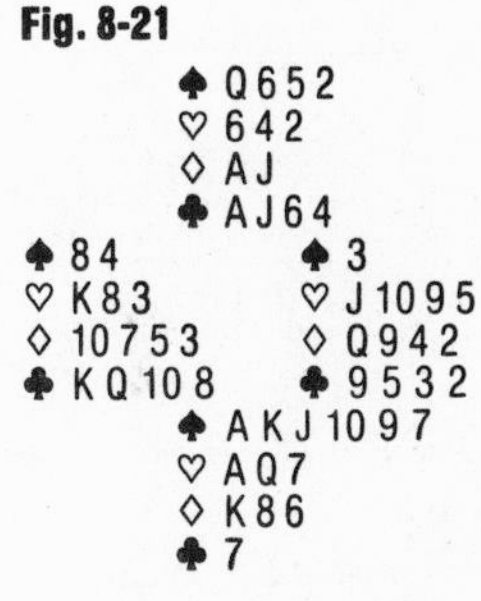

One of the prettier throw-in plays occurs when on your exit card you discard another loser, getting rid of two losers at the same time you throw-in an opponent. That happened on the hand in Fig. 8-21.

Against a contract of six spades, West led the king of clubs. Declarer won that with dummy's ace and set about eliminating the suits. He led a second club and trumped it. Next he went to dummy with the queen of spades, led a third club, and trumped it. At this point, he pulled the last trump and then cashed the ace of diamonds and the king of diamonds and trumped a diamond in the dummy. Feeling sure from the opening lead that West had the queen of clubs, but not knowing who had the king of hearts, declarer simply led the jack of clubs from dummy and instead of trumping it, discarded his seven of hearts.

Fig. 8-22 is a variation on the same theme.

Fig. 8-22

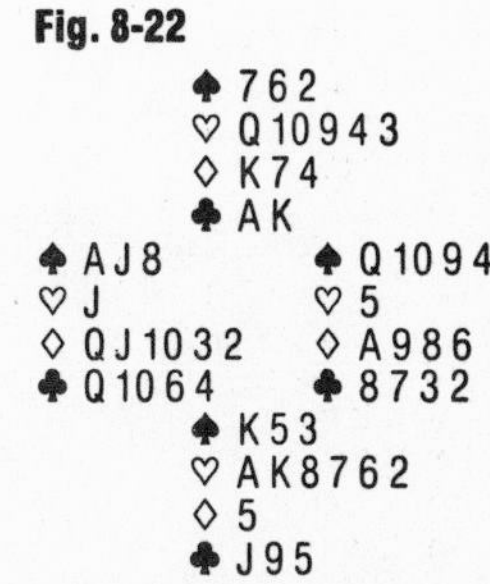

This time declarer got to a contract of only four hearts. The opening lead was the queen of diamonds, and when dummy came down, declarer envisioned the possibility of losing one diamond trick and three spade tricks. He decided to give the opponents a chance to help him eliminate diamonds and played small from the dummy. Not having looked into the opponents' hands, East missed an opportunity for the brilliant play of the year. Had he played the ace of diamonds and returned the queen of spades, the defense would have taken the first four tricks. But East was mortal and simply signaled with the nine-spot. The diamond continuation was trumped by declarer who then laid down one trump to exhaust all of the opposing trumps. Next he cashed the ace and king of clubs and trumped dummy's last diamond. Then he led the jack of clubs to see just what would happen. West covered with his queen, with the remark, "Not through the Iron Duke." In some quarters, a heavy fine is assessed for making that remark. West would have done better to play the ten-spot. The declarer wouldn't have known what to do and doubtless would have trumped the trick and tried to locate the ace of spades. But when West played his queen, declarer simply discarded a spade from dummy. That left West on lead in a hopeless situation. Obviously, leading a spade would enable South to make his king, while leading anything else would let South take another discard from the dummy, while trumping in his hand.

You may have noticed that elimination plays and strip plays are often together in the same deal. It is nice when you can be sure you have stripped one opponent of all cards in a suit, but when you can't know whether you did or not, you just proceed as if you had.

Fig. 8-23

This time declarer got himself into a contract of six diamonds, and West opened the seven of hearts. Declarer won that and, when he led the ace and king of diamonds, saw he had a trump loser. Eliminating spades and hearts was not going to be any problem, and the trump was there for a throw-in, but how about that club situation? Well, the only chance was that after the ace and king of clubs were led, West would be out. You'll see that a very kind dealer has arranged it that way. After cashing two trumps, declarer won tricks with his two remaining hearts, with dummy's two spades, and with his ace and king of clubs. Then he led a diamond, and West won that with nothing left to lead but spades. Isn't it awful that you and I are never that lucky?

Fig. 8-24

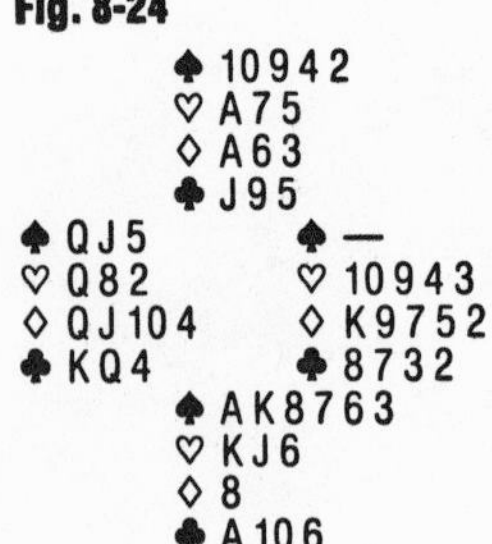

Let's take a look at a hand (Fig. 8-24) which has many of the symptoms which call for a throw-in play.

The queen of diamonds was led against four spades, and the declarer examined the dummy to judge his prospects. Unless he got a very bad break in spades, he had six tricks there, and in the side suits he had four tricks off the top. No problem about making game unless there was a terrible spade break.

It never hurts to prepare for an elimination should it become necessary, so declarer took the first diamond with dummy's ace and instead of leading trump at trick two, led a diamond and ruffed it. Then he laid down the ace of spades and got the news that the terrible trump break had materialized.

While ten tricks were no longer assured, prospects were still excellent. The trump winner was in the West hand and not with East, so that when declarer decided to exit with a trump after cashing the king of trumps, it would be West's lead. After leading three trumps, South would have trumps in both hands—a requisite for an elimination play. There was only one diamond to be eliminated in the dummy, and a lead to the ace of hearts would enable declarer to accomplish that before exiting with a trump. That would leave him with the king-jack of hearts, and, if West had to lead hearts, that would give him the extra trick he needed. Should West lead clubs, East would have to hold both the king and the queen in order to gain the lead. Even if that happened, West would have to have the queen of hearts, or the heart finesse would work.

Declarer cashed the second trump trick, went to the dummy with the ace of hearts, and trumped dummy's last diamond. Having eliminated diamonds, it was time to give the lead to West, and a trump was led. West could see that a club lead would be fatal, as the bidding indicated that South had the ace of clubs. He also knew that a diamond lead would allow a ruff-and-sluff, so he led a heart, hoping East would have at least the jack of that suit. Of course, East did not, and South cashed his king and jack. He was now assured of ten tricks, but saw nothing to lose by trying for an eleventh, so he led a small club. Now it was curtains, as West had to let the jack win or else win with the queen of clubs. With all of the red cards gone from both declarer and dummy, he had no choice but to lead a small club, just in case his partner had the ten and declarer had guessed wrong. So the use of the throw-in play turned up eleven tricks after all, losing only one trump trick and one club trick.

Among those hands where a throw-in is available, provided the distribution of the opponents' hands is favorable to the declarer, there are those which will only work where one of the opponents has an honor in a doubleton.

Fig. 8-25

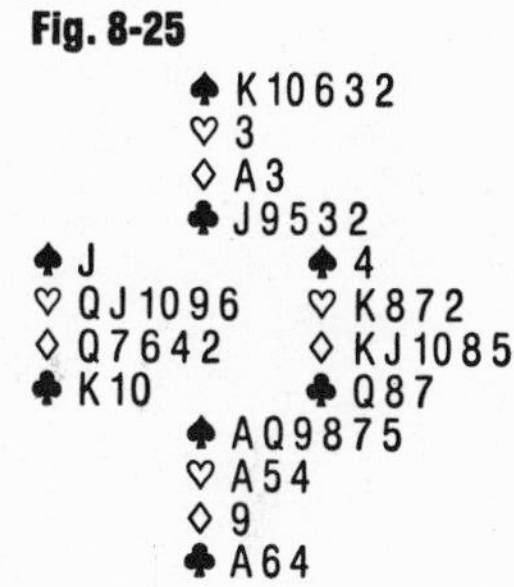

The six spade contract reached by South needed a bit of luck in the club suit. The elements for the elimation were easy. Declarer simply won the opening heart lead with the ace, laid down one trump, and then trumped a heart. Next he led the ace of diamonds and trumped a diamond; then he led the last heart and trumped it. He led a small club to his ace. West saw what was about to happen to him, but the spot cards in his hand and the dummy were such that he could do nothing about it. He played his ten-spot, and, when declarer continued with a small club, he had nothing to lead but red cards. Declarer simply trumped that lead in the dummy and discarded his losing club.

Sometimes these hands are more "iffy" than the one we just looked at.

Fig. 8-26

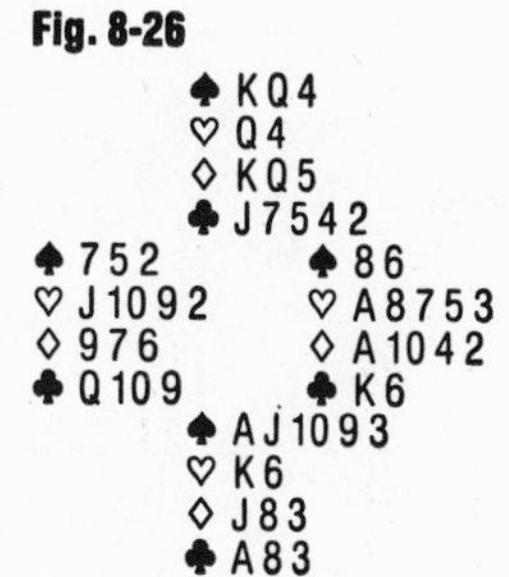

Let's watch declarer work this one out to a happy ending with quite a bit of luck. Against a four spade contract, West led the jack of hearts. East won with the ace and continued the suit. Declarer had a bit of duplication with the heart suit, but at least that suit was eliminated. Now he had a diamond loser for sure and could not stand two club losers in addition. He had to go for the throw-in play, which meant he had to eliminate diamonds and then find a favorable distribution in the club suit while he still had trumps in both hands. This meant that he could not afford to pull trumps before attacking diamonds, lest the player with the ace of diamonds have a third trump to lead which would destroy his chances for an elimination play. So, he laid down the ace of trumps and then led the small diamond to dummy's king. East saw no reason for not taking that trick and did indeed lead back a trump. Now declarer took his two remaining diamond tricks, leaving a trump outstanding, and then cashed his ace of clubs and led a small club. Poor East had to win that trick, and he did not have the remaining trump to exit with. Either red suit he led would allow declarer a ruff in the dummy while discarding a club from his hand, and the rest would be good.

Declarer was lucky in more ways than one. He was lucky that the player with the doubleton club did not have the third trump. He was also lucky that East did not have three clubs instead of two, including not only an honor, but also the ten-spot. Had East had this holding, a clever West, who would have only the queen and one club, could drop his queen under declarer's ace to keep from being thrown-in, and, when declarer led a club East would take two club tricks.

Yes, declarer was lucky. But, as I mentioned before, a lot of luck passes by all of us, and it's the players who reach out to grab that luck who are called the "lucky" players.

Five of a major is an awkward spot to get to, but when you get there, you might as well try to make it (Fig. 8-27).

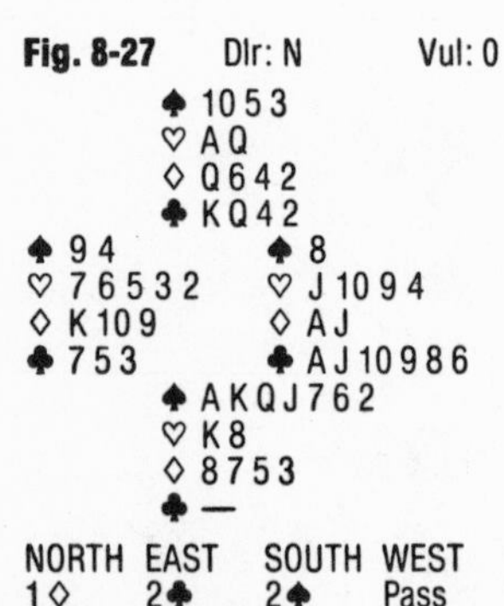

After North opened the bidding, you can understand South's enthusiasm and North's reluctance. North got out as soon as he could, and South had to have some luck to take eleven tricks. As a matter of fact, the lead of a small diamond by West could have settled his hash at once, but naturally West couldn't know that and led his partner's suit.

Declarer played the king from the dummy and trumped the ace. Looking the hand over, he got to wondering what he was going to do about those bad diamonds. East must have had some of the diamond honors for his overcall. Declarer made a wish: He wished that East had exactly two of the diamond honors and that he had one or two trumps. He laid down the ace and king of trumps and quit that suit because he was planning a sort of elimination play and needed trumps in both hands. Next he led the eight of hearts to dummy's queen and cashed the queen of clubs, on which he discarded one of his diamonds. Then he trumped the third club, after which he led his king of hearts, overtook it with dummy's ace, and trumped dummy's last club. He had eliminated clubs and hearts from his hand. He led a diamond, and, when West played low, declarer played low from the dummy. Poor East! He had to win with the jack, cash the ace, and then lead either a club or a heart. On either, declarer could discard his last diamond, while trumping with dummy's last trump.

The late John Crawford earned a reputation for getting his opponents to help him out by leading what he wanted led when he was in trouble. The hand in Fig. 8-28 is an example of Crawford's artistry. He played this against two of the world's finest players, who came in second in a Master's Pair Championship some years ago. Crawford and his partner were first.

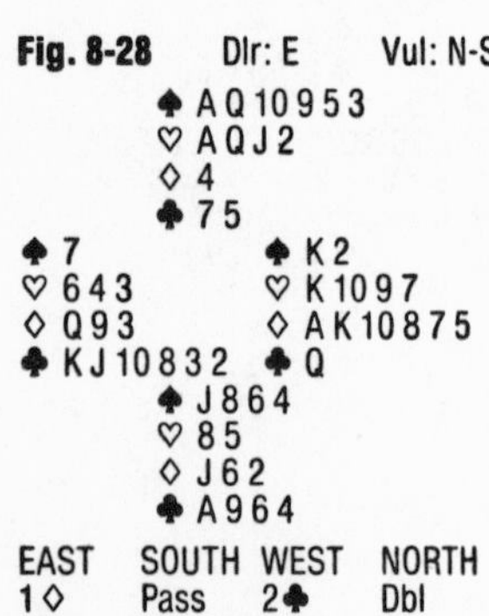

The opening lead was the three of diamonds, won by East. East switched to the queen of clubs. East had bid that hand like the player who had most of the high cards, so Crawford credited East with both of the major suit kings. What, then, did West have to justify his response of two clubs? He must have six clubs and some sort of diamond suit support. So Crawford decided the queen of clubs return was probably a singleton.

With both major suit finesses wrong and a loser in each of the minor suits, Crawford could count four losers. He had to bring off some sort of throw-in play against East to have a chance for his contract. The technical requirements for a throw-in were not there. First, he would have to give up the lead once in clubs and that would be an invitation for West to switch to a heart. Furthermore, he simply didn't have enough entries to do all of the ruffing necessary to eliminate any suit from his hand. But he decided he knew a way to bring it off, if he got a bit of help from East.

He won the ace of clubs and, doing the best he could to promote the elimination of diamonds, led a diamond and trumped it. Next he cashed the ace of spades and led a small spade, giving the lead to East. At this point, East had been stripped of spades and clubs, and the only chance for survival was to get off lead with a small diamond. But we surely cannot fault East for leading the king of diamonds. If East assumed that Crawford was going to trump that, East was wrong. Declarer simply discarded dummy's losing club and left East on lead. Now East had to choose between leading a third diamond, which would allow Crawford to sluff a heart while he trumped in the dummy and would set up the heart ruffing finesse for him, or leading a heart right into the ace-queen and letting him accomplish the same thing.

One of the aspects of a really great player is that he not only knows the technical aspects of the game, but that he takes every opportunity to put his opponents on the spot. Let's see how it might go on another hand.

It looks to me like a lot of useless bidding went on, but it is recorded as I have shown it. West led the ten of hearts, which declarer won. South then laid down the ace and king of spades and saw he had a trump loser. He had two or three ways to go about trying to get his twelfth trick. He could eliminate hearts and then take the ace and king of clubs and lead a small trump, hoping West started with only two clubs. With the ten of diamonds in his hand, he could simply go for an extra diamond trick. He decided to see, first, if his opponents would solve his problems for him. He cashed his other heart, eliminating that suit, and threw West in with a spade.

We might say that West was not ready for that play. Who would be? The way heart honors had tumbled convinced him that to lead another heart would give declarer a sluff-and-ruff, so he was left with trying to decide which minor suit to lead. He reviewed all the bidding he'd heard, trying to decide whether declarer was more likely to have a tenace position in the club suit or the diamond suit. He couldn't find a clue. Maybe you can play detective and tell West he should have exited with a club, and, furthermore, that he should have unblocked his queen, but West was not up to it. In real life, he led a small diamond, that enabled declarer to win a trick with his ten-spot and discard a losing club on the long diamond in the dummy.

In my next hand, Figure 8-30, from the 1970 World Championship, Bobby Wolff managed to endplay *both* his opponents. To be more precise, he endplayed whichever one chose to win the lead when he surrendered it.

Against Wolff's four spade contract, the West defender started proceedings by leading his singleton heart. East won that with the ace and returned the nine spot. The defense was off to a splendid start, having won the first two tricks. They didn't know it, but that was about all the fun they were going to have on this hand.

West switched to a club and Wolff won East's king with his ace. He won a trump trick and then laid down the ace of diamonds and then won two more trump tricks, ending in his hand. Now he led the jack of diamonds. West covered with the queen so dummy won with the king, and then Wolff took the ten of diamonds. Now he led his remaining club, in effect inviting his opponents to help themselves. If West won that trick, he

Fig. 8-30

♠ K 10 5 3
♡ J 8 6 3
◇ A K 5
♣ 10 3
♠ 7 6 ♠ 9 8 2
♡ 7 ♡ A Q 10 9
◇ Q 9 6 4 3 2 ◇ 7
♣ Q 9 7 2 ♣ K J 6 5 4
♠ A Q J 4
♡ K 5 4 2
◇ J 10 8
♣ A 8

would have to give the balance of the tricks to Wolff. He had nothing left in his hand but minor suit cards and on the lead of either of those, Wolff could discard a losing heart from one hand while trumping in the other. Should East elect to win the club trick, he was in no better shape. He had nothing left but clubs and hearts. A club lead would give Wolff that sluff and ruff and a heart lead would guarantee him two heart tricks.

1970 was the first time the United States had won the World Championship since 1954. Ira Corn, an industrialist from Dallas, Texas, had brought together a group of bright young players named the Aces and deliberately set out with the purpose of winning back the World Championship. The hand above played by Wolff showed the style played by the Americans and contributed toward that victory.

In the 1970's, Wolff and Bob Hamman, another member of the Aces, formed a regular partnership. They won the World Championship in the Olympiad games of 1974, and then the World Championship in the Team Game in the Bermuda Bowl of 1977, making them the only pair to ever hold both titles at the same time.

ENTRY THROW-IN PLAYS

Throw-in plays for the purpose of gaining entry to an otherwise entryless hand can be pretty spectacular. So that I can finish my chapter on throw-in plays on the upbeat, let's look at a few of them.

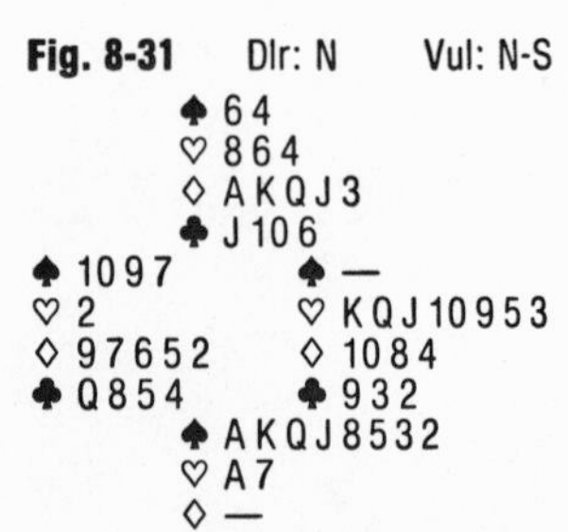

NORTH	EAST	SOUTH	WEST
1◇	4♡	6♠	All Pass

Opening lead: ♡2

Let's describe the bidding as "brisk" and let it go at that. West led the two of hearts, and declarer, holding two losers in his hand, surveyed that entryless dummy which North put on the table and with which he had opened the bidding. Well, maybe the queen of clubs would fall singleton or doubleton or something good would happen. Declarer won the heart lead with the ace and laid down the ace of spades. When East discarded, declarer thought it over again. He decided that something good had happened.

The lead of the two of hearts plus East's jump to four hearts indicated that West had started with a singleton heart. In effect, his hand had been stripped of hearts. He had a total of three spades, and, if they were led three times, he would have no spades either. Furthermore, declarer was blessed with the smallest spade in the deck, and, instead of leading three big spades, he could lead two big spades and one little spade, throwing West in the lead at the same time that he eliminated spades from his hand. Now West had the choice of leading a diamond to provide an immediate entry into the dummy or doing the same thing with a small club. The effect would have been the same if East had led a club, as one way or the other, the entry would have been there.

The next hand (Fig. 8-32) is more realistic. It's more than that. It's really a hand from play. It was played by the late Harry Fishbein.

After North opened the bidding with one heart, Harry got into a contract of six spades. West led the queen of clubs, and Fishbein won that with dummy's ace. Now Fishbein was a spectacular player, but he was also a very cautious player. If there was any chance that an end play might come up, he would always eliminate whatever suits he could safely eliminate early in the hand. So, it was pure Fishbein to win the opening lead with the ace of clubs and promptly trump a club in his hand, eliminating that suit. Next he laid down the ace of trumps and, when West discarded, saw that he had a trump loser. He also had a couple of diamonds he wasn't too sure about. Taking another look, he was a wee bit short on entries into the dummy. But he found the solution to these several problems.

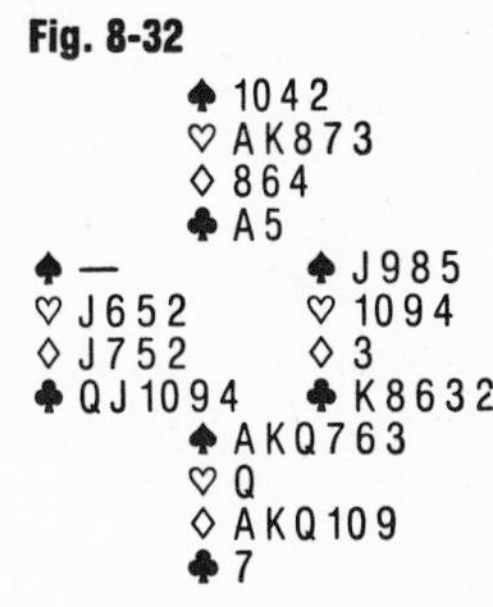

Fig. 8-32

He quit leading trumps and led the queen of hearts. Then he started leading diamonds. Anytime East wanted to trump a diamond, he could do so, but when he did so, he would not only shorten his trumps, he would be faced with the necessity of giving the dummy the lead. Once dummy had the lead, the two losing diamonds could be discarded on dummy's two good hearts. Neither would it do East any good to start discarding hearts on diamonds. If he kept that up and refused to ruff at all, Fishbein would finally trump the ten of diamonds with one of the trumps in the dummy, and, if East overtrumped, he would again shorten his trump holding, and that would be his one and only trick.

East saw his problem and discarded one heart on the second diamond, but when the third diamond came along, he trumped it and led his now singleton heart. That was won in the dummy, and the king of hearts was led, which East trumped. But now he had only one trump left, and Fishbein was able to overtrump him, pull his trump, and leave one trump in the dummy for trumping a diamond.

I shall finish up with one I particularly like.

Fig. 8-33

North opened the bidding with one diamond, and declarer reached a contract of four spades. West opened the king of diamonds to see just what that opening diamond bit meant and, when the dummy came down, he saw there were indeed five of them. He also saw his partner play the ten-spot, so he cashed a second diamond trick on which his partner dropped the nine of hearts. West thought that over a few minutes and then decided to play a forcing game. He continued with a small diamond which East trumped, and when South overtrumped, West had as many trumps as declarer had.

But declarer had been noticing what had been going on, too. He led the ace of spades, and East completed his heart echo by playing the two-spot. He saw that East had been stripped of both diamonds and spades and that he was enthusiastic about having hearts led. Declarer decided to grant him his request. But first he pulled trump. On the fourth one, he had a discard coming, and he discarded a heart from the north hand. He didn't just discard a heart—he discarded the ace of hearts. Otherwise he was going to have no way to get back to his hand. Having done this, he cashed the A K Q of clubs and then led the ten of hearts from the dummy. East won that with the king, but declarer was sitting there with a good heart and a good club, and East had to lead one or the other because that is all he had left.

THE SIMPLE SQUEEZE

IN olden times, programs in New York theatres included a bridge problem to keep their patrons entertained during intermission and sometimes for hours after the show was over. These did not consist of the showing of fifty-two cards, but would have four, five, or six cards remaining in each hand, and you were supposed to figure out how to take four tricks out of the last five, or four of the six, or something like that. These problems were generally composed and are not likely to appear in real life.

If you wanted to compose one that would give even the experts a headache, chances are that it would include some sort of a squeeze play. Those are not the kind of squeeze plays we are going to talk about here. We are going to study those bread and butter squeeze plays which will help you win points.

Don't let the terminology frighten you. Frankly, it is terrible. We talk about a "menace" and a "threat." Who likes to be menaced or threatened? Or, more to the point, not too many people like to be a menace or a threat. In spite of the vocabulary, the squeeze play is not the sole possession of some secret fraternity which uses words like this to keep their secrets from all except the initiated. It is just that nobody has been able, yet, to think of any good words to substitute. Ely Culbertson, that master of public relations, substituted the words "establishable suit." Using five syllables where one would do the job never took hold, and today we read about "threats" and not "establishable suits."

Really, the squeeze in its useful form is merely an extension of the suit establishment principles we have previously studied. With a squeeze play, you simply try to force discards from an opponent to gain yourself an extra trick. You can't do this unless he holds cards which need guarding in more than one suit or winners in one suit and cards needing guarding in another.

Deciding how many cards he needs to hold in these suits is itself merely a different version of the Rule of Fourteen, our old friend. It is a simpler version, at that. It takes a little arithmetic to say that the eight-spot is the sixth highest card in the suit because eight from fourteen leaves six. You don't even have to think hard to know that the ace is the highest card in the suit, the king the second highest, the queen the third highest, the jack the fourth highest, etc. Generally, your squeeze plays will not be concerned with cards much lower than that. With the jack being the fourth highest card in a suit, the defender must keep four cards in that suit to keep the jack from falling if you lead the three higher cards. Likewise, if the king is the second highest, he needs two cards in that suit, while with the ace he needs only the ace itself. Of course, at times, the king will be promoted to the highest card because the ace has been played, or the jack might even be the highest, if the three higher cards have all been played.

What you are trying to do with a squeeze play is find one of your opponents with these guards in two suits and make him discard one of those cards. To illustrate, in the ending shown here when South leads the ace of clubs, West has to keep six cards, but can't because he is required to play and will have only five left in his hand.

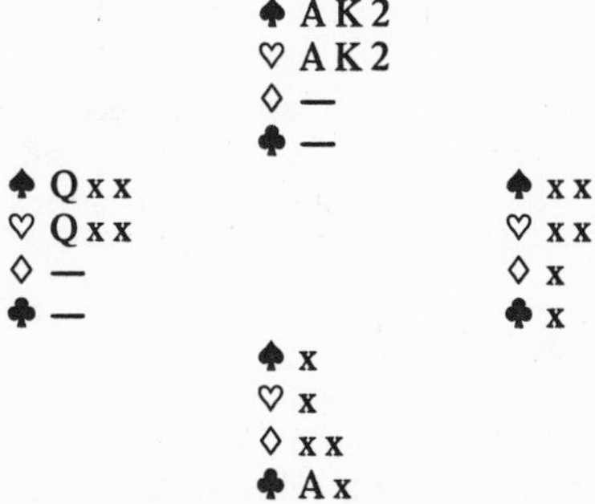

For a squeeze to be effective, it is necessary for the leader to have more cards in the critical suits than the defender holds. Until South leads the ace of clubs, West and North have the same number of cards in each of the major suits. But West must get down to five cards before North does and the squeeze is on. Place the cards so that North has to get down to five cards before the defender does and there is no squeeze.

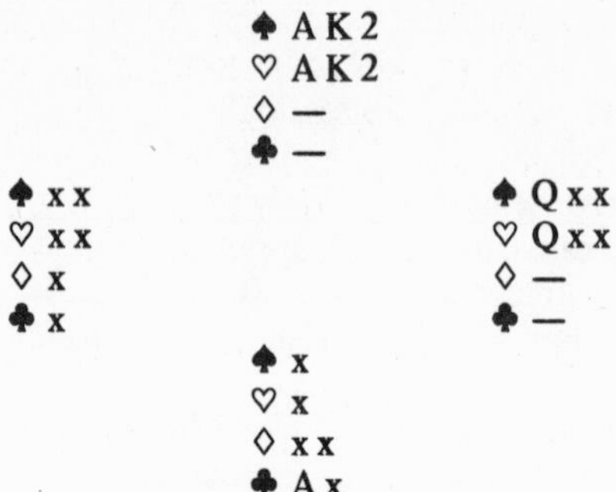

You might say that North got squeezed before East did. Because the squeeze can be effective only if the position of the cards is advantageous to the squeezer, this squeeze is called a Simple Distributional Squeeze.

However, when the declarer's critical suits are one in each of his two hands, it is a different story. No matter which of the defenders holds both suits, he can be squeezed provided entry cards are available.

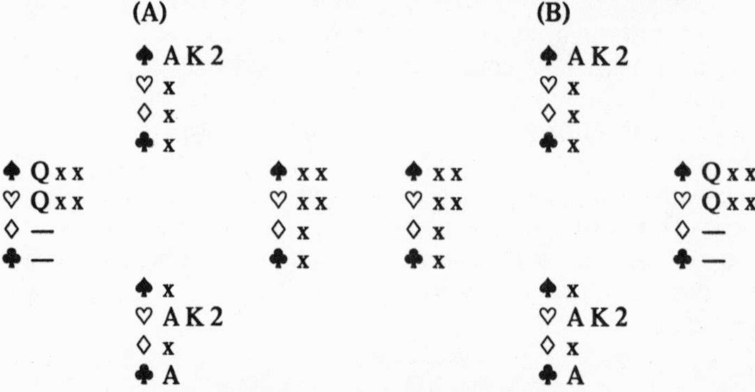

When the ace of clubs is led, the declarer can keep all six of his major suit cards because they are divided between his two hands, each of which will have a total of five cards left after South wins the trick with the ace of clubs. Among these ten cards he can keep six in the major suits with no anguish. Either defender who holds all the guards in the two major suits is in a mess, because he needs to hold six cards and can keep only five.

Notice that in all of these illustrations, the leader holds five winners among the six tricks left and is just one trick short of taking all the remaining tricks. This is an important element in many squeezes and we will discuss it in more detail later.

About the surest early symptom that a squeeze play might be available is the absence of any other play to develop the tricks you happen to need. Let's look at an example (Fig. 9-1).

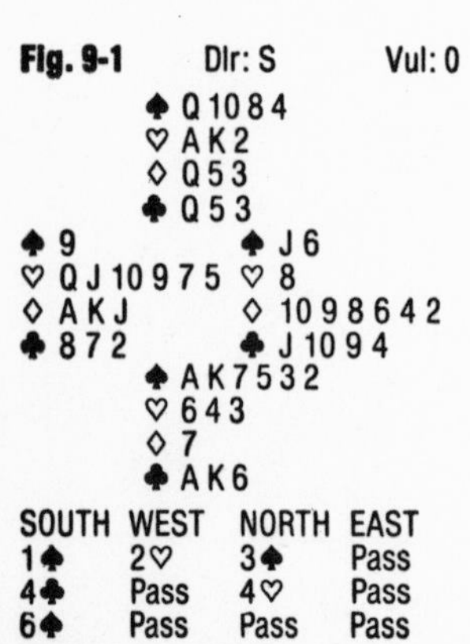

The opening lead was the king of diamonds. At trick two, West led the queen of hearts. Counting his tricks, declarer saw that he had six trump tricks plus two in hearts and three in clubs. That came to only eleven, and he needed an additional one. He surely had that first requirement for a squeeze: there seemed to be no other way to get the extra trick. Certainly, it could not come from hearts or clubs, and an attempt at a dummy reversal by trumping two diamonds in the south hand was doomed to failure, as that would not reduce the south hand to fewer trumps than those held by North and would not increase the number of tricks taken at all. So, how about a squeeze?

The lead of the king of diamonds by West strongly indicated that he held the ace, as well, and he was going to have to hang onto that ace to keep dummy's queen from becoming good. The fact that he bid hearts strongly suggested that he had at least five of them, which would have left East with not more than two. As dummy had the ace and king, East had no way to keep the dummy's two-spot from winning; only West could accomplish that. Using our simple rule to determine how many cards West would have to keep in each of the red suits to keep dummy's cards from becoming high, we see that he has the highest card in diamonds and has to keep one there. After the king of hearts wins a heart trick, West's queen of hearts will be the second highest card, and he will have to keep two cards in that suit. So declarer can win the queen of hearts with the king of hearts and then take nine more tricks in the black suits without interruption. That would make a total of eleven tricks played, leaving everybody with two cards.

But we have just seen that West has to hold a total of three cards to guard the red suits. Playing before the dummy at the eleventh trick, West doesn't have a chance. To hang onto two hearts he will have to throw away the ace of diamonds, and dummy's queen of diamonds will be good. To hang onto the ace of diamonds, he can keep only one heart, and dummy's ace of hearts will take the twelfth trick, and the neat little two-spot will take the thirteenth.

This play is called "the simple squeeze." To add further confusion to the terminology, the word "simple" simply does not mean simple. There are some simple simple squeezes and there are complicated simple squeezes. The term simply implies that it is a squeeze that acts against one opponent in two suits, and however complicated that may be makes no difference at all. So, we had better get away from that and see just what we can learn from this one hand.

Here is a little terminology that makes more sense. All of the cards that West has to hold onto to keep one of dummy's cards from becoming established are called "busy cards." All of the cards he can throw away are called "idle cards." For instance, those three little clubs he has are all idle. The purpose of a squeeze play is to make him use up all of his idle cards and finally force him to discard one of his busy cards.

At the point where declarer led to the eleventh trick, leaving himself only two cards and everybody else three, both West and the dummy had no idle cards left. However, the dummy could play after West, and after West played, dummy would have an idle card. Had West thrown away his last heart, North's queen of diamonds would have become idle. Had West thrown away the ace of diamonds, North's deuce of hearts would have become idle. This hand illustrates not only that fact, but several other facts about the so-called simple squeeze. Let's outline these facts, and then we will proceed with our study to determine just how we can bring about the situation where these various factors are in our favor.

1. The deuce of hearts and the queen of diamonds in the north hand are those cards which are called threats. Where declarer's threats are both in one hand, that hand must play after the squeeze victim, or the threats won't be effective. For instance, swap the east and west hands so that the busy cards are behind the threats, and the squeeze would not operate because North would have to throw away a busy card first.

2. The card that is finally led to force an opponent to throw away a busy card is called the "squeeze card." Where both of the threats are in one hand, as in our first example, the squeeze card must be in the hand which is opposite the two threats. In other words, South should not by some sort of awkward maneuver end up winning trick eleven with the dummy's queen of clubs. The eleventh trick must be won by the south hand. And so, as soon as he could safely do so, the declarer got those clubs out of the way by taking his three tricks. That way he would be sure that the squeeze card was led from the south hand.

3. In a squeeze, there will usually be a one-card threat like the queen of diamonds in our illustrative hand, and there will always be a longer threat. Frequently, this long threat is two cards, but it can be more. That long threat will always have the highest card outstanding in the suit.

4. After the squeeze card has been played, there must be a "get there" card. In other words, there must be an entry. The entry must be in the suit which has the long threat. That suit can be called the "entry threat."

Usually, cards must be played in the right sequence so that the various factors above will still be available at the proper moment. For instance, in the hand above, should declarer cash his ace and king of hearts before leading all of his other cards, there would not be a semblance of a squeeze. There would not be any sort of long threat, nor would there be an entry into the dummy when the squeeze card was played.

This seems like several things to remember, but there are many varieties of useful squeezes, and as all of them are variations based on these principles, it pays to learn them all now; then, as we go on to look at other varieties, we will only have to look for variations on these four themes.

For practice, let's do another where there aren't any variations. Instead of starting off by showing the end position as many textbooks do, let's start off by showing the entire hand first. That's the way the thing comes up in real life. We will then end up in the end position.

West led the king of hearts and, after East played the two, switched to the queen of diamonds which you won with dummy's king. Now let's try some questions and answers.

Q. We have lost one trick—do we have another loser?

A. We surely do. There is a small diamond to dispose of somehow or another.

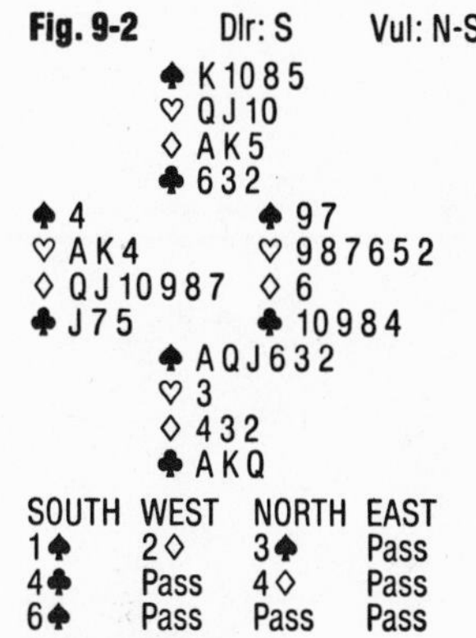

Q. Are there any of the standard procedures we can use to get rid of that losing diamond? Is there a finesse to take or a suit to establish without losing a trick, or even some sort of manipulation with the trump suit?

A. I've looked as hard as I can and I can't find any way to get rid of the diamond loser while losing no additional tricks by any of these procedures.

Q. There is frequently the situation which calls for an attempted squeeze play. Dummy seems to hold threats in the red suits; how many hearts does West have to hold to keep one of dummy's hearts from becoming a winner?

A. It's obvious that he will need to have only one heart to prevent that, as he has the highest heart.

Q. How many diamonds will he have to keep to stop dummy's small diamond from becoming a winner?

A. Now that one of dummy's high diamonds has gone, West holds the second highest diamond and, therefore, would have to keep two diamonds.

Q. Does it seem likely that East could protect either hearts or diamonds?

A. No. Since West overcalled in diamonds, you certainly would not expect East to hold as many as the three diamonds he would need to hold to protect the suit. The bidding plus the lead of the king of hearts indicate that West is the only player who can protect these two suits.

Q. Two tricks have been taken; how many more tricks can you win right now?

A. Right now I can win six spade tricks and three club tricks, for a total of nine. These added to the two already played make a total of eleven tricks played.

Q. Both of your threats are in the north hand, so it is necessary that the squeeze cards be led from the south hand. Is there any way to manage this?

A. It would be practically impossible to manage it any other way. Obviously, the lead is going to be with South at the eleventh trick.

Q. Will you then have an entry into the hand with the threats?

A. Yes, unless I turn silly and somehow in the process have cashed dummy's high diamonds, the diamonds will furnish the entry.

Q. So, when you lead the eleventh card, which will probably be a small spade, West will have no idle cards and will have to discard either his high heart or the guard for his diamond. Now how about dummy—will dummy have an idle card to discard?

Q. Not until West plays. But West has to play before the dummy does, and, after West plays, dummy will have an idle card. If West discards the ace of hearts, the small diamond will be idle and can be thrown away. If West discards the jack of diamonds, the queen of hearts will be idle and can be thrown away.

This form of squeeze is called a simple positional squeeze because it is the position of the cards that makes the squeeze work. Where both of the

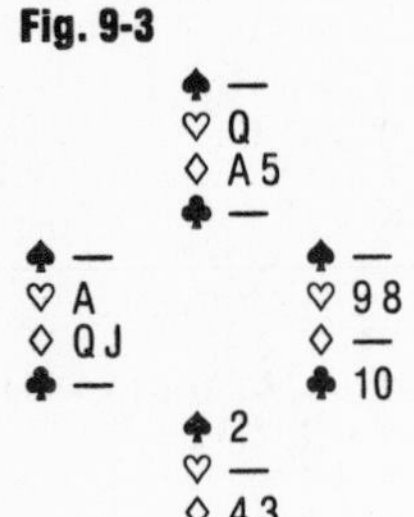

Fig. 9-3

establishable suits or threats are in one hand, that hand must play after the player who has control in those suits.

Here is the way it looked just before South led the two of spades to the eleventh trick (Fig. 9-3).

Poor West!

It is not so easy to see when the squeeze card comes from the dummy while the two establishable suits are in your own hand. You have to look at it as a sort of a dummy-reversal squeeze play. I believe the technical term is a "backward squeeze."

After North responded one diamond to the opening one club bid (Fig. 9-4), South went straight to three no-trump with his 20 high-card points. West struck gold when he opened his five of hearts. The defenders won the first four tricks. South discarded a small club. East sluffed the eight and three of diamonds, in that order. The way it turned out, that was not too smart. When West, after cashing his fourth heart, led the ten of diamonds, South was convinced that he had another loser which he simply could not afford. If he won the ace of diamonds, he could only count eight winners no matter how he twisted and turned. With the opponents holding seven clubs between them, one or the other was sure to hold as many as four clubs. So, when everything else you look for is not there, it is time to look for a squeeze.

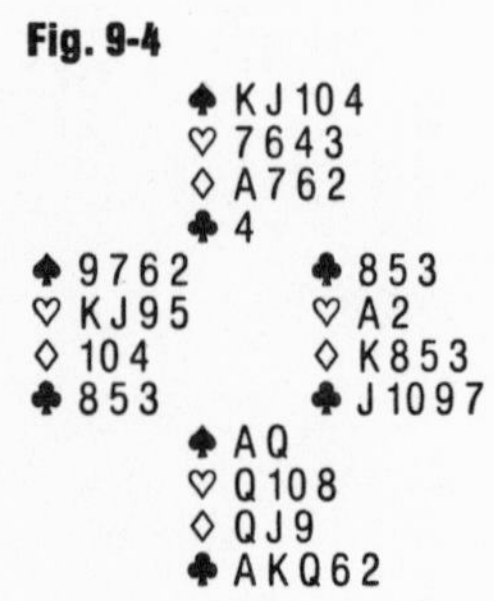

Fig. 9-4

By taking that trick with the ace of diamonds, the menace of the queen of diamonds would be established against the presumed king in the East hand. And, what if in addition to his king of diamonds, East should be the player with a long club? Then the six of clubs in the south hand would be a threat against East. So, there would be two threats behind East, and a squeeze card in the form of the long spade could come from North. Provided declarer did not touch clubs, the entry back into the south hand would be there in the form of the singleton club. East would have to hold only one diamond, as he held the highest diamond outstanding, but he would have to hold four clubs, as he could not have anything higher than the fourth highest club. That was a total of five cards. Counting the play of the ace of diamonds, five tricks had been taken, and declarer could now take four more in the spade suit, coming to a total of nine. There was no way for East to hang onto five cards after the spades had been led. On the third spade, South could discard another diamond, and, when the fourth spade was led, East, if he did hold long clubs, would have no idle cards. After winning with the ace of diamonds, declarer won the ace of spades, overtook the queen with the king, and took two more spades. Here is the way it looked when he led the last spade (Fig. 9-5).

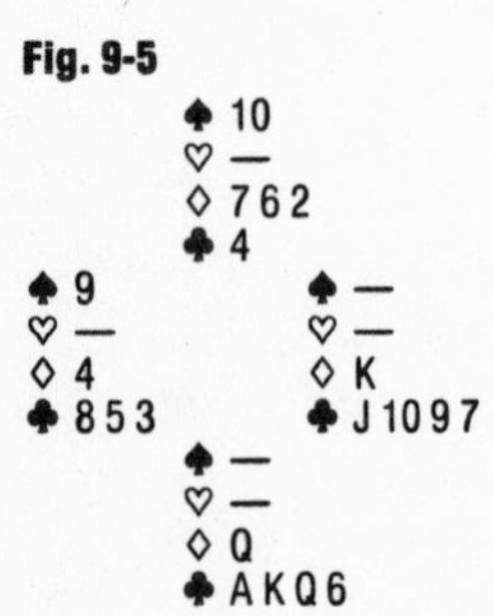

Fig. 9-5

Of course, had it been West with the long club, the contract could not have been made, but after the vigorous diamond signaling by East, declarer properly decided that he had no chance to take nine tricks if he did not win the ace of diamonds, and it must be 50–50 if he did, as East was just about as likely to hold long clubs as West was to hold them.

THE SPLIT MENACE

For a squeeze to operate, there must be at least one long menace, as the master card in the menace provides the entry. But, provided the master card is in the hand opposite the hand with the squeeze card, a long menace may be divided between the two hands. Such a menace is called a "split menace" (Fig. 9-6).

It took West some time to pass the six spade bid. When declarer proceeded to take all of the tricks, West was happy he had not pushed him into a seven spade contract. What looked like a club loser in the north-south hands actually turned out to be a split menace with the ace of clubs as winner in the north hand and the queen of clubs as the threat in the south hand, along with the squeeze card.

West's opening lead of the king of hearts went to declarer's ace. Declarer studied his assets. If West had the queen and jack, the ten of hearts in the dummy was a threat against it. Should he also hold the king of clubs, then the queen of clubs in the south hand was also a threat. Holding the highest heart and the second highest club, West had three busy cards which he had to hang onto to avoid disaster. Declarer saw that he could take seven trump tricks plus three diamond tricks, which, with the heart trick he had already won, came to a total of eleven tricks. When he led the final trump for the eleventh trick, West would have to get down to two cards.

But just as a matter of good technique, declarer won the ace and king of spades and then led a heart and trumped it. When East had to play the jack on that trick, the ten of hearts looked like a sure menace.

Declarer cashed his three diamond tricks to be sure to have the lead in his hand at the crucial moment and then ran all the spades. Fig. 9-7 is the way it looked before he led the spade to the eleventh trick.

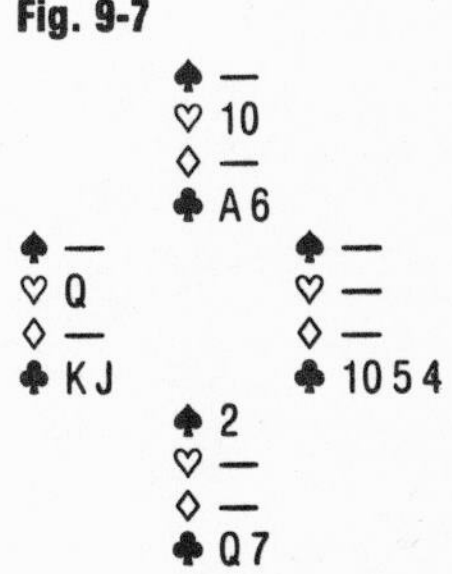

East had done the best he could with his miserable hand. Noticing after diamonds had been led three times that nobody had any left, he not only hung onto his clubs like he had something important to keep, but even went so far as to signal with the eight and three of clubs. Whether he had done this or not, when South led the deuce of spades, West saw it would be fatal to discard his heart and discarded the jack of clubs, which would have saved the extra trick if East had held the queen. Declarer now threw off the useless ten of hearts in the north hand, and his two clubs took the last two tricks.

But there is yet another lesson we have learned about squeezes with this hand. I am sure you spotted it. If declarer had not trumped that heart, East could have hung onto the jack of hearts, and, if West read the situation correctly, he could have thrown away his queen of hearts at the end and hung onto his clubs. There is available a sort of a strip play preparing for a squeeze. By trumping that heart, declarer had fixed it so that only West could control the heart situation. This is not an unusual play, and when you are preparing for a squeeze and have an opportunity to ruff some cards in the dummy which otherwise you could dispose of by simply discarding them, it is a matter of good technique to ruff them when you can safely do so. You may be able to take all the cards that one of the players holds in that suit away from him and leave the entire burden of guarding that suit on his partner. So here we meet again an old friend—this time the strip play from our studies of end plays.

While it is frequently true that when you go for a squeeze play there is no other play available, it is not always so. Sometimes you have a choice, and there are also times when you can try the other play first and only fall back on the squeeze play if the first play fails.

After West led the king of spades, South took a good look at the dummy and added up his losers. He saw two in spades, one probable in hearts, and one in clubs. Of course, East could have the king of hearts, but as West had made both a takeout double and a bid, declarer was inclined to place all of the high cards with West. So, assuming the heart finesse was going to lose, declarer also saw the possibility of establishing the diamonds on which he could discard his club. If that failed, there was also the possibility of a squeeze with a split menace in the club suit, with a long diamond in north being the menace there. To try out these different possibilities, declarer won the spade lead with the ace and led a small heart, losing the king finesse. West cashed his two good spade tricks and, after some thought, decided the long diamond suit in the dummy was something to be concerned with. So he led a second heart to take one of the dummy's entries which might be helpful in establishing the diamond suit and getting back to it after it was established.

Declarer decided to try for the diamond play anyway. If the suit broke 3–3, the suit would be established and the two entries in the dummy represented by the ace of clubs and the high heart were adequate. Failing that, the diamond might become established as a menace against West. So, declarer led two diamonds and then went to the dummy with a good heart to lead the third diamond. When East showed out, the possibility of discarding on the fifth diamond was gone, but the squeeze possibility still remained. It was necessary for West to have the king of clubs, as well as the diamond he was known to hold, but in view of his bidding, that seemed most likely. Having the highest diamond, he would have to hold only one diamond, and having the second highest club, he would have to hold two clubs. In his hand, declarer had two trumps and two clubs, so nine tricks had been played. If he led his two trumps, that would make eleven tricks, and it would be impossible for West to keep his assumed king, one club, and the high diamond. Fig. 9-9 is the way it looked just before declarer led his final heart.

Now here are some things to know about the split threat where the winner is in one hand of the partnership and the threat is in the other. In this hand, the ace in the north hand was the winner and the queen in the south hand was the threat. In the hand with the winner, there must be an additional single threat, but the squeeze card, as usual, must be in the hand opposite the single threat, which means it is in the hand with the threat and the split menace. The squeeze is positional in that it will operate only against the hand which plays before the hand with the winner and the single threat. For that reason it is called a simple squeeze and not an automatic squeeze.

Is the so-called "simple" squeeze really simple in the normal meaning of the word? My answer is sometimes it is, but sometimes it's pretty darned complicated. If you don't understand why they call it a simple squeeze, see if you can figure out what they mean by a play they call the "automatic" squeeze.

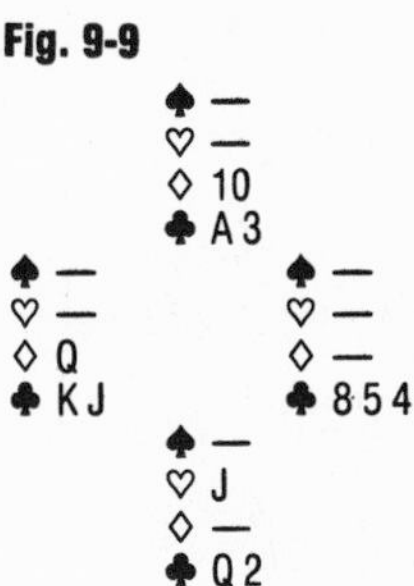

Fig. 9-9

THE AUTOMATIC SQUEEZE

There is nothing automatic about the so-called "automatic" squeeze except its name. You can't just wind it up and go off and leave it. It is simply a squeeze where there is one menace in each hand instead of two in one hand. You still have to preserve your entry card, and the master card of the long sequence must still be in the hand opposite the squeeze card when you get around to playing the squeeze card. The word "automatic" simply means that when these conditions prevail, the squeeze will be effective against either of your opponents who happens to have to guard two suits.

Let's look at a hand which is an old friend. You saw this hand (Fig. 9-10) in our section on suit establishment.

Fig. 9-10

Of course, if either minor suit breaks 3–3, thirteen tricks are there for the taking. Even if the suits do not break 3–3, a good player can still make thirteen tricks, provided one opponent holds length in both the minor suits. Whoever holds length in the minor suits is going to have to hold four cards to keep the deuce of diamonds or the deuce of clubs from becoming established. So, we can say those two deuces are the threats, or we can call those suits the "establishable" suits. If the same player holds length in both suits, he is going to have to keep eight cards in his hand to keep one of those two-spots from becoming established. When declarer cashes three spades and three heart tricks, each will have only seven cards left, and it will be impossible for anyone to guard both suits. Because one threat is in north and one in south, the squeeze can be effective against either.

Now let's play around with this hand a little bit. The way to maintain entries is to keep at least one small card in the hand opposite the hand that holds the master card of each suit. Should a careless declarer start off by cashing three clubs and then three diamonds, he would have destroyed all of his entries, and the squeeze would not come off. By judicious discarding, East could keep declarer from getting the thirteenth trick. However, if declarer wished to cash a couple of cards in each of the minor suits, no harm would be done, as he would still retain entries back and forth.

Actually, if he wished to cash the three high cards in one of the minor suits, he could even do that, provided he cashed not more than two in the other minor suit. In that event, he would have to be careful where the lead ended up when the squeeze card was played. Suppose, for instance, he won the opening lead of the jack of hearts and promptly cashed his three clubs? When that suit failed to break, he could go ahead and cash two

Fig. 9-11 Dlr: N Vul: B

♠ Q J 9
♡ Q 9 4 2
◇ A Q 4
♣ K 10 4

West	East
♠ 6 2	♠ 4 3
♡ 8 7 6 5	♡ A K J 10
◇ 10 6 3	◇ 9 8 5 2
♣ 8 5 3 2	♣ Q J 7

♠ A K 10 8 7 5
♡ 3
◇ K J 7
♣ A 9 6

NORTH	EAST	SOUTH	WEST
1♣	Pass	2♠	Pass
3♠	Pass	4♣	Pass
4◇	Pass	6♠	All Pass

Opening lead: ♡8

diamonds if he wanted to. Now he would have a single threat in the south hand in the deuce of clubs, and what amounted to an entry threat in the north hand with the queen and deuce of diamonds. He would have an entry to the long threat because he still retained a diamond. The high cards in the major suits would provide the squeeze card. He would have to be sure to take spades last, so that when the squeeze card was finally played, the lead would be in the hand opposite the long threat.

On hand 9-11, East got squeezed. It was not because he had length in one of the suits, but because he had the outstanding high cards in that suit.

West didn't have much to go on for his opening lead, but the bidding seemed to call for a heart. The dummy came down, and the declarer started looking for twelve tricks, but found them hard to find. If the dummy had had one more diamond, or if he himself had held one more diamond, twelve tricks would have been available. However, South was plagued with a problem that often afflicts bridge players: there was a duplication of values in the diamond suit. The 10 high-card points there would take only three tricks.

Well, what were the other chances? One was that the queen and jack of clubs might fall doubleton. Another was the squeeze play. He now had one of the requirements for a squeeze. After East won the first trick with the ten of hearts, South had only one loser left. The queen of hearts looked like it would be a threat against East. Should East have five clubs in his hand, West could have only two, and only East could protect clubs. This meant that the nine of clubs might become a threat against East also. And, one more option was available. If the queen and jack of clubs were in the hand with the high hearts, then West would be unable to protect clubs, and the long club in the south hand would still become a threat card against East. As this would place menaces with both North and South, the squeeze would work against either opponent, provided declarer simply took good care of his get-there cards—his entries back and forth.

So declarer trumped the king of hearts return and cashed two high trumps in the dummy. Then, just in case West did have an honor left in hearts, he led the nine of hearts and trumped it. He then cashed the three diamonds. He now had two trumps left, and he proceeded to cash those. On the last trump, he discarded the four of clubs from the dummy. This was the position when South led the last trump (Fig. 9-12).

Fig. 9-12

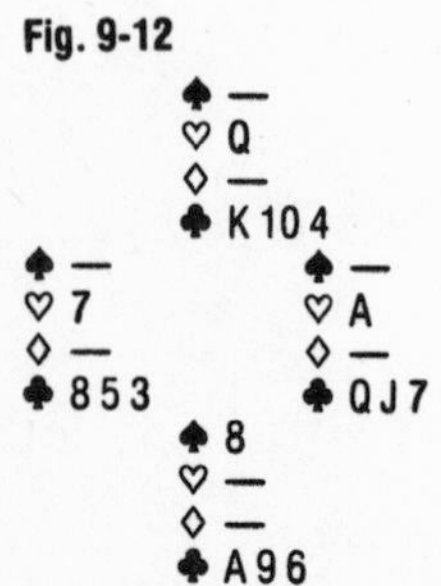

East obviously couldn't throw away his ace of hearts, so he had to discard one of his clubs. Declarer then cashed the king of clubs and took the last two tricks with his ace and nine. With a menace in each hand, the squeeze was automatic and would have worked against either opponent who held guards in hearts and clubs.

For a squeeze to operate, the lead must be in the hand with the single threat and opposite the hand with the double threat *after* the squeeze card is played and not necessarily before it is led.

The nine of diamonds was led and covered by the jack and the king. East switched to the jack of hearts, and declarer played his queen with

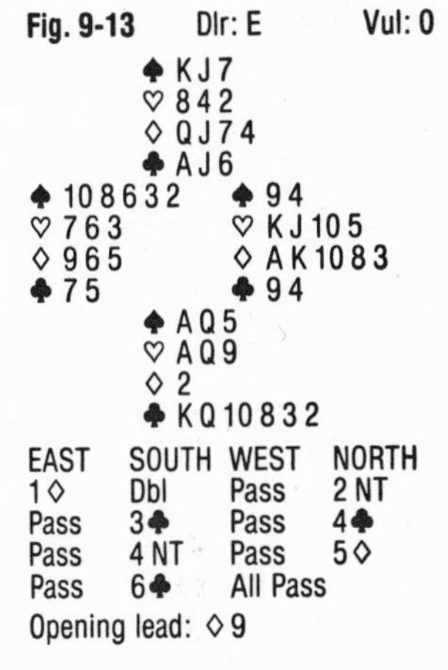

every expectation that this would win the trick. East had to have all of the outstanding high cards to justify his opening bid. However, South still had a losing heart unless he could do something about it.

It looked like everything needed for a squeeze against East was present. East's lead of the jack of hearts marked him with the ten as well as the king, so only he could guard hearts. East had the highest diamond and the second highest heart and would have to hold three cards. Two tricks had been played, and declarer could cash the next nine with clubs and spades, making a total of eleven tricks. He would leave, in the dummy, a one-card threat in the form of the queen of diamonds, while in the South he would leave a two-card threat in the form of the two hearts. In the dummy, he would have an entry. However, he would have to be careful which of his black suits he ran first. The eleventh card played would be the squeeze card, and, after that was played, the lead had to be in the hand with the one-card threat and opposite the hand with the two-card threat. In other words, at the eleventh trick, he had to be in dummy.

That could be easily arranged, provided declarer did not carelessly cash all of his spade tricks after he cashed his club tricks. So he cashed his six clubs, throwing away from the dummy two diamonds and one heart. Then he took the ace and queen of spades and led the five of spades to dummy's king. East was holding the ace of diamonds and the king and ten of hearts. He had to get down to two cards, so he threw away the ten of hearts. Now declarer's ace and nine of hearts were good for the last two tricks.

Before the days when the World Bridge Federation sponsored official world championship matches, certain events, because of the high caliber of the players, were considered unofficial world championship events. The next hand is from such an event which pitted the American ladies champions against the champions of Europe. That particular year, the lady champions of Europe were the British.

When the British ladies had hand 9-14, they bid six hearts, tried for a finesse in both hearts and spades, lost them both, and went set. When the hand came to the American ladies, South was Helen Sobel. The American ladies also bid six hearts. Helen got an opening lead of the five of diamonds, which she won in the dummy.

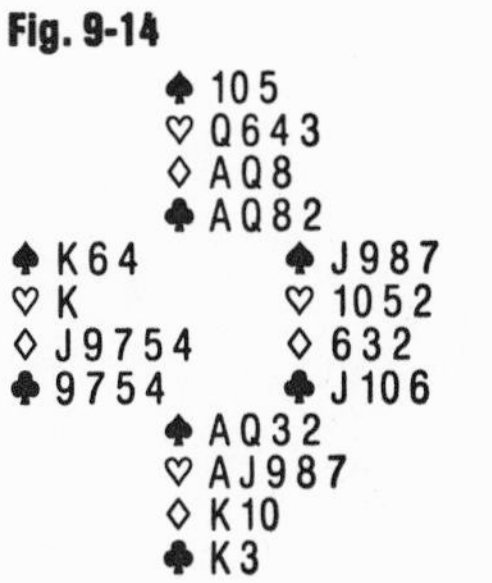

She too, then, finessed trumps and lost a trick to the singleton king of hearts. Another diamond was led, and this time Helen won in her own hand with the king. She took two more rounds of trumps, ending in the dummy, and then discarded a small spade on the ace of diamonds. She then led the rest of her trumps.

Whoever had the long clubs was going to have to hold four of them to keep dummy's clubs from becoming good, and whoever had the king of spades had to hold two cards in that suit. If it turned out to be the same player, then that player would have to hold a total of six cards. The play of the last heart would make a total of eight tricks (five hearts plus three diamonds) and would make it impossible for either opponent to hold six cards. Dummy could get down to five cards without any trouble, holding one spade and all four clubs. Declarer would have no problems, either, holding two clubs and three spades. So that is the play Helen made.

The trouble was that, technically, declarer had no way of knowing at the end whether West had kept for her last five cards two spades and three clubs or one spade and all four clubs. I said "technically she had no way of knowing." In real life, it doesn't always work out that way.

The official report of this hand states, "West did not like the situation. When the last trump was played, she was forced to either blank the king of spades or discard a small club. After some hesitation, she let go of a club, and the need for a successful spade finesse was eliminated. Dummy's four clubs were now good."

Now go back to where the last trump was led and West had to get down to five cards. Place yourself in West's position where you can see only your hand, the dummy, and the cards already played. Would you have known to drop that six of spades as though you had not a care in the world? Whether you and I would have known or not, the fact is that a player on a team that has been good enough to win the European championship did not put Helen to the guess by blanking the king of spades. "Technically," there would be no way to avoid the guess, but in real life you are not going to find it necessary to guess in a situation like this.

Now let's take the first hand we used to illustrate the automatic squeeze and make one substantial change in it.

RECTIFYING THE COUNT

Fig. 9-15

All I have done is take the queen of spades away from South and give it to West. Again we have West leading the jack of hearts and South with no apparent resources, should the minor suits fail to break favorably. So, of course, South looks for a squeeze. But now he can only take five tricks in the two majors, and that will leave each of his opponents with eight cards. Unless one of the minor suits does break favorably, he is going to be limited to eleven tricks. When he had the queen of spades, he could take thirteen tricks, but by giving up this one card, he only comes to eleven tricks. It is most annoying to find that giving up one trick would cost two. Is there a way out?

There is. What is needed to have the squeeze work is to have six tricks *played,* not necessarily to have six tricks won. If you can't win six outside of the threat suits, how about losing one and winning five? That will make six played. So at trick two, declarer should just play a small spade from both hands. A miracle has occurred. By giving up one trick, declarer has gained one. He is back up to twelve if either opponent holds length in both minors. He just needs to win the return and cash the major suit cards. Everybody will be down to seven cards, and neither opponent can hold all eight cards in both minor suits.

So here we have learned one more important principle of the squeeze play. When the time comes to play the squeeze card, in all hands where an opponent is being squeezed in two suits, it is necessary that you have precisely one loser. This can occur at the beginning of the hand, or, by losing a couple of tricks, you can arrive at that stage later on. South started off with eleven taking tricks and two losing tricks. That meant no squeeze was going to operate. By giving up the spade trick, he had left only one loser, and now the squeeze would be on if either opponent held length in both minor suits.

This play has also been given a fancy name. They call it "rectifying the count."

On hand 9-16, declarer accomplished a double purpose when he rectified the count.

Fig. 9-16 Dlr: S Vul: B

North: ♠ A 8 6 4 ♡ 10 3 ◇ 10 7 5 3 ♣ A 10 4

West: ♠ K Q 10 9 5 3 ♡ 5 ◇ K 9 ♣ Q J 7 2

East: ♠ J 2 ♡ 8 7 2 ◇ Q J 8 6 2 ♣ 8 6 5

South: ♠ 7 ♡ A K Q J 9 6 4 ◇ A 4 ♣ K 9 3

SOUTH	WEST	NORTH	EAST
2♡	2♠	2 NT	Pass
3♡	Pass	4♡	Pass
4 NT	Pass	5♡	Pass
5 NT	Pass	6♣	Pass
6♡	Pass	Pass	Pass

Opening lead: ♠K

When South learned through the Blackwood convention that North had no kings at all, he put on the brakes at six hearts. When the dummy came down, he saw a loser in each of the minor suits, and it looked as though unless a miracle occurred, he would lose two tricks. It didn't take a miracle; it took a knowledge of squeeze plays.

West led the king of spades which was won by dummy's ace. Declarer could count up to eleven tricks right off the top, but any way he counted it, it looked like two losers unless somebody had the doubleton queen-jack of clubs. When nothing else looks like it will work, you look for a squeeze play. With the two losers, a squeeze play couldn't work, and to get the hand down to one loser, declarer had to lose a trick. As clubs might be involved in the squeeze play, he didn't want to lose the trick there—he wanted to lose it in diamonds.

He was on the verge of leading a small diamond from dummy when he had a better thought. In view of the bidding and the opening lead, it was quite likely that West had all of the high spades, but it was not necessary. If East had just one spade higher than the eight-spot left, he could protect spades. That would take the burden off West and might foil any plan for a squeeze.

So instead of leading a diamond to lose the trick immediately, declarer led a small spade from north and, when East played the jack, he discarded his diamond rather than trumping it. East was a bit surprised to win that trick, but decided to lead the queen of diamonds. Declarer won that with his ace. Just to be sure that East was not fooling anybody about his spade holding, declarer led a small trump to dummy's ten-spot and trumped his third spade, as East discarded a diamond. Now it was West who would have to guard spades, and the eight of spades remaining in the north hand had become a threat against West.

It turned out that it was West alone who could guard clubs. West had the highest outstanding spade and had to keep one spade. He had the third highest outstanding club, so he had to keep three clubs, or a total of four cards. After declarer had won tricks with the aces of spades and diamonds, lost one trick, and then run all his trumps, he had only his three clubs left in his hand while the dummy had the eight of spades and two clubs. When the last heart was led, West also had to get down to three cards and was unable to guard both clubs and spades. He knew he could not throw away the queen of spades, so he kept it and two clubs. On the lead of the last heart, declarer threw away dummy's now worthless eight of spades and took the last three tricks with the A K 9 of clubs.

There is another technical name for the play declarer used when he led a spade at trick two in an attempt to take away from East any cards he might have which would guard the spade suit. It is called "isolating the menace." We have been flirting with it for some time now. Let's take a good look at it.

ISOLATING THE MENACE

If both of your opponents can control a suit, the squeeze will not work. What they call "isolating the menace" means that you strip from one opponent all of the cards he holds in a given suit so that only his partner can guard that particular suit. So, we have run up against another friend whom we have met earlier—the strip play. I suppose the term means that you don't want your menace to have a guard both to his right and his left and that by stripping one of your opponents, you leave your menace with a guard on one side only. Should you tell me that the term "isolating the menace" is a strange term for what you actually do, I am afraid I will have to agree with you. But that is what they call it, and you can't fight city hall. Let's forget about the confusion which can be caused by the terminology and see how it works.

Fig. 9-17

Against a seven spade contract, West led the king of hearts. When the dummy came down, declarer could count twelve tricks right off the top—six in spades, one in hearts, three in diamonds, and two in clubs. How about the thirteenth trick?

If the diamond suit broke, there would be four diamond tricks instead of three, and that would make the thirteenth trick. If the diamond suit was not going to break, then there might be a squeeze play, and the candidates were the diamond suit and the club suit. Assuming the diamond suit would not break, declarer would have only one loser, and that is the first requirement for a two-suit squeeze. How about the club suit? Since declarer and dummy together held six of them, if declarer would take the ace and king and then trump one, one opponent or the other would be sure to be out of clubs. If the only player who had a club left was also the player who had length in diamonds, he was going to be hard pressed to hold onto enough cards to protect both suits.

Declarer couldn't afford to test diamonds first because that would spoil the entries he needed for his squeeze play the way he had it planned. So he planned to first pull trumps and then to take his two top clubs and trump a club. Now there would be one club left in the dummy and one club left in the hand of one of his opponents. That opponent would have to hold onto a club to keep the little club in the dummy from winning a trick, assuming the declarer was going to be able to reach the dummy. That he planned to be able to do.

If the same player who held the one outstanding club was also long in diamonds, then he would have the fourth highest diamond and would have to hold on to four diamonds, for a total of five cards. Could South make it? He would take six spade tricks (including the one he would use to trump a club). He would also win a trick with the ace of hearts and would lead the ace and king of clubs, making a total of nine tricks. This would leave four cards in everyone's hand. The four in his hand would be the four diamonds, while the four in dummy would be three diamonds and the club. Any player who held length in both minor suits would just be out of luck. In this case, it was East.

So declarer won the ace of hearts and found it took three leads to pull trumps. Next he led the ace of clubs and a small club to the king; then he trumped a club. He then led the rest of his spades, discarding a heart and one diamond from the dummy. East had counted clubs and knew he could not throw away his queen of clubs without making dummy's six-spot good, so he had to throw away one of his diamonds. Declarer then took the king and queen of diamonds in the dummy and came back to his hand to win the last two tricks with two good diamonds.

Let's look at Fig. 9-18 where the need for the squeeze play does not develop until several tricks have been played and see how it works.

Fig. 9-18

The ideal holding for isolating the menace is showing in the heart suit in this hand. Where your opponents hold exactly seven cards in a suit, it is impossible that both of them will have cards in the suit after it has been led three times. So, if you can lead it three times, only one of your opponents will be able to guard it. It's most convenient when you can manage not to lose a trick one of the three times you lead it because you can trump the third one. Let's see how this play helped declarer overcome a lot of misfortune on this hand.

Against a four spade contract, West opened the jack of clubs, and the opponents took two club tricks and led a third one, which declarer trumped with his nine of spades. He then crossed over to the dummy with the king of hearts to try a spade finesse. He led the queen of spades, but that went to West with his king, and West led back a spade.

Poor declarer. So far he had found two cards wrong. Had the ace of clubs been with West or the king of spades with East, he would have had an easy ten tricks. Now, he has already played six tricks, and here is what he is looking at (Fig. 9-19).

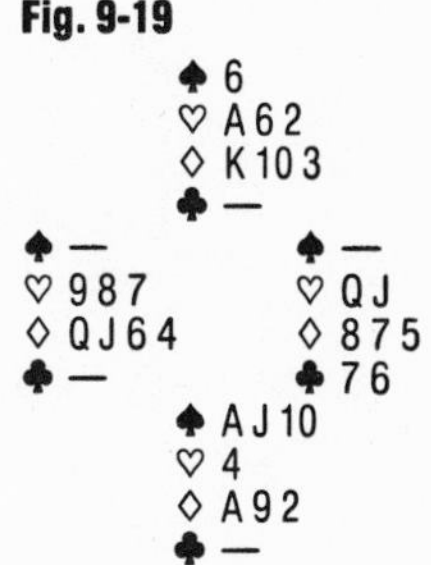

Fig. 9-19

Of course, declarer didn't look at all of it; he could see only his hand and the dummy's. If all else fails, you look around to see if a squeeze is possible. Looking it over, he saw that with seven cards left, he had only one loser. That is the first requirement for a two-suit squeeze. If there was a squeeze, it obviously had to be in the red suits. But, instead of just leading a trump, declarer decided to fix it so that only one of his opponents could guard hearts, so he led a small heart to the ace and then trumped dummy's two of hearts. Now, only one opponent had hearts left, and in view of the play of the Q J 10 by East, declarer thought that it was probably West. Of course, if West had started with five diamonds, then he and he only could guard diamonds. But now there were only five cards left. And if West did indeed have the heart, he couldn't have started with five diamonds, as he had not thrown a diamond. However, there was still one chance left. In view of the spots, should West happen to hold both the queen and the jack of diamonds, then only he could guard that suit. So declarer played the ace of spades and had a spade in the dummy to follow suit with. At this point, West felt no pain. He simply discarded a small diamond. But when declarer led his last spade, West had to surrender. Obviously, he couldn't discard a heart and make dummy's remaining heart good, so he discarded a diamond. Declarer took the last three tricks with his diamonds.

Playing no-trump, you aren't able to trump off an extra trick. But sometimes you need to give up a trick to get down to one loser anyway, so that is not such a great loss.

Fig. 9-20

Let's say that with your combined 33 high-card points, you did what the book said you should do and got to a contract of six no-trump. West led the queen of spades.

Right off the top, you can count only eleven tricks. It's too bad that one or the other of your two hands doesn't hold a fifth diamond so that the 10 high-card points in that suit would provide a total of five tricks rather than four. The thought might go through your mind that you might be better off with a slam in diamonds, but it's too late for that now. The problem is where you are going to get that twelfth trick at no-trump.

Apparently your only chances are that hearts will break 3–3 or that you will have a squeeze.

If hearts don't break 3–3, you have two losers, and as long as you have two losers, a two-suit squeeze cannot materialize. You can rectify that by giving them a trick. How about giving them a club trick?

Looking at all four hands, you can easily see that that won't work. You would be going for a spade-heart squeeze, and East could hang onto three spades and West four hearts, and nothing good would happen.

Without looking at the east and west hands, but just remembering that 4–2 in spades holding that suggests you might try to isolate the menace in that suit, you can decide that the place to give up a trick is in the spade suit. When should you do it? How about right now?

That is the answer. Let them win the first spade trick. They will have no better lead than to come off with a second spade. You can now cash two spade tricks, two club tricks, and four diamond tricks, ending in the dummy where the single threat is. Added to the trick you have conceded, this totals nine tricks. Somebody or the other will have one spade which he will have to hang onto, or the small spade in the north hand will be good. If that same person has four or more hearts, he will have the fourth highest heart and will have to hang onto four of them. Both of those things he cannot do when he has only four cards left.

So by knowing how to operate a squeeze play, you have improved the chances from very slim to quite good indeed. This way you will take your twelve tricks if the hearts break 3–3, as well as when the player with heart length has spade length also.

It is not just with a 4–2 holding that you try to isolate the menace. You try to strip one hand of holdings in a suit whenever you think there is a chance for a squeeze and hope or have reason to believe that the hand with cards left in that suit will have to guard an additional suit as well.

Fig. 9-21 Dlr: S Vul: 0

North: ♠ Q986 ♡ 93 ◊ A432 ♣ AJ9

West: ♠ 5 ♡ J10 ◊ KQJ95 ♣ KQ432

East: ♠ 7 ♡ Q87542 ◊ 1086 ♣ 1086

South: ♠ AKJ10432 ♡ AK6 ◊ 7 ♣ 75

SOUTH	WEST	NORTH	EAST
2♠	2 NT*	4 NT	Pass
5♡	Pass	7♠	All Pass

Opening lead: ◊ K

*The unusual no-trump.

I am not sure I want to comment on the bidding. Let's let that pass by saying that North had complete confidence in his partner's ability when he took him to a grand slam. And then let's shed a tear for poor West. He led the wrong king. Had he led the king of clubs, he would have taken an entry out of the north hand, and a squeeze could not have materialized, but he led the king of diamonds instead.

When declarer looked at the dummy, it looked like a sure club loser, but if West had both the king and queen of clubs for his unusual two no-trump bid and East could not trump the first diamond lead, it looked like chances were good that West was going to rue the time he annoyed North into trying for a grand slam. After winning the ace of diamonds, declarer could pull trumps, take the ace and king of hearts, and trump a heart. Then he could lead all of his trumps. If, in the meantime, he could exhaust East of diamonds and leave the burden of guarding both suits on West, things were going to turn out just fine. In the course of the play, South could lead hearts three times, trumping the third one, and spades seven times. In addition to that, one trick had been played in diamonds, so the total was eleven. If he could manage it so that only West could guard both minor suits, West would have the highest diamond and would have to keep one of them. He would have the second highest club and would have to keep two of them. So that is what declarer set out to do. He won the ace of diamonds, led a small diamond and trumped it. He returned to the dummy with a trump, noting that both of his opponents were now out of trump, and led a second small diamond and trumped it. Next he took the ace and king of hearts and trumped a heart. He had a trump left in the dummy to get back to his hand. The three diamond leads had indeed stripped East of diamonds, and when declarer led his last trump, he had left in his hand only two clubs. West had two clubs and a diamond and had to discard one of those three cards. Dummy had two clubs and a diamond and was discarding after West. Whichever way West went, declarer was going to take the balance of the tricks.

Not all squeeze plays are slam hands. Fig. 9-22 is one where the opponents took the first three tricks.

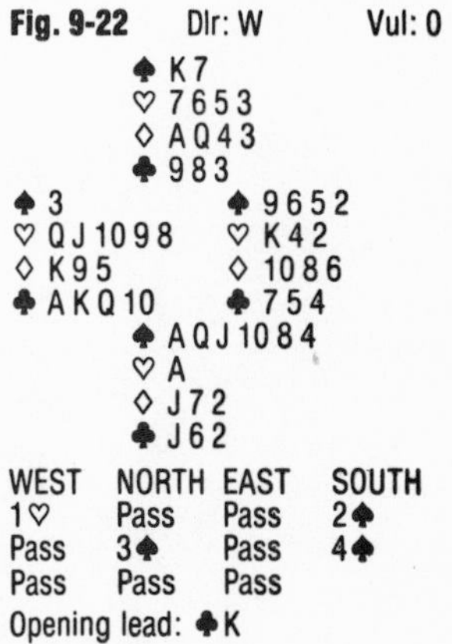

The defense started off by cashing three club tricks. They didn't know it, but they were saving the declarer the trouble of rectifying the count by doing it for him. After taking his three club tricks, West switched to the queen of hearts.

Strangely enough, the play of the queen of hearts convinced the declarer that West had the king of diamonds. When West led the queen of hearts, he indicated that he didn't have the king. If he didn't, East did. But East was not likely to hold two kings because he had passed the opening bid. So declarer, looking over the ten cards he had left, decided he only had one loser; he was confident the diamond finesse would work. So, of course, he got to thinking about a squeeze to get rid of the only loser. If three leads of hearts would strip East of that suit, West would be the only player left to guard the heart suit. So, after winning the ace of hearts, declarer went to the dummy with the king of trumps to trump a second heart. Now he made one more trip to the dummy by finessing the queen of diamonds and trumped another heart, leaving a single heart in the dummy. The lead of another trump left everybody with four cards. South still had two diamonds and two trumps. West was able to throw away his ten of clubs and keep two diamonds and two hearts. North had three diamonds and one heart. East had two trumps and two diamonds, but no hearts at all, which was what declarer had been trying to accomplish. Declarer's jack and one diamond in his hand plus his ace and a small one in the north hand gave him the split menace, with the single menace of the seven of hearts in north and the squeeze card in south—just the setup required for a squeeze against West. On came another trump, and West got down to a single heart and two diamonds, while dummy kept the ace and a small diamond and one heart. The last trump lead did West in. He couldn't throw away his heart, as it was a certain winner, so he blanked his king of diamonds, hoping his partner might hold the jack. Declarer won the last two tricks with the ace and jack of diamonds.

Fig. 9-23

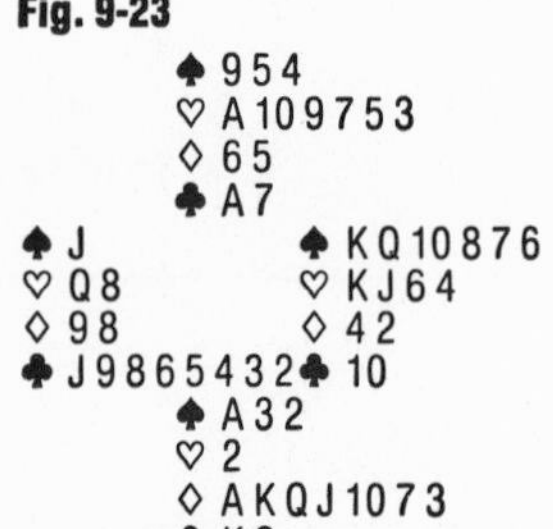

A slight chance is better than no chance at all. In Fig. 9-23, South got to a contract of six diamonds, after East had competed in spades. West led the jack of spades.

A quick survey of dummy showed declarer that he had only eleven tricks off the top because of the lack of a small club. That old devil, the duplication of values, had gotten him. Chances looked pretty bleak. East signaled with the eight-spot. That wasn't nearly high enough. Had East been thinking, he would have overtaken the jack of spades with the queen, and South would have had to win his ace or gone set at trick two. Declarer decided to rectify the count and let the jack hold the trick.

West went into deep thought and finally led a trump. Declarer saw that he was still alive. He now had one of the requirements for a squeeze—he had only one loser. What sort of a squeeze could he bring about? West obviously had no more spades, so East was the only player who could protect that suit. It was a lot to hope that East would also be the only player who could protect hearts, but that was the only chance. Should that turn out to be the case, declarer could turn up with a spade threat in his hand, since East who held only the second highest spade would have to keep two cards in that suit. There would also be a single threat in a heart in the north hand, and by deferring the lead of clubs until the proper moment, the lead could be placed in the north hand with the squeeze card, giving the declarer a backwards squeeze. That would fulfill the requirement that the trick on which the squeeze card was played was played by the hand with the single threat and opposite the hand with the double threat.

Declarer first thought that he would give his opponents every possible opportunity to discard a heart, should they wish to do so, and so, without touching clubs, he promptly led six of his seven trumps. That plus the opening spade lead made a total of seven tricks and left everybody with six cards. Declarer had to take four discards in the dummy. He discarded three small hearts like a man who had no interest in that suit and finally discarded one of dummy's spades. East wasn't born yesterday. He hung onto two spades and four hearts for his last six cards. Declarer finally quit leading trumps, led a small heart to dummy's ace, and then led a heart back and trumped it. That left East with two spades and two hearts. On the king of clubs lead, East was still able to discard one of his hearts, but when the queen of clubs was led to dummy's ace, he was in the vise. He could keep only two cards and had to either blank his king of spades or throw away his king of hearts.

DEMOTING THE OPPONENTS' HONOR CARDS

What a delightful idea! It's nice to promote our own cards and must be simply beautiful to demote those held by the opponents. But it can be done. Notice this hand played by Harold Ogust against some world champions (Fig. 9-24).

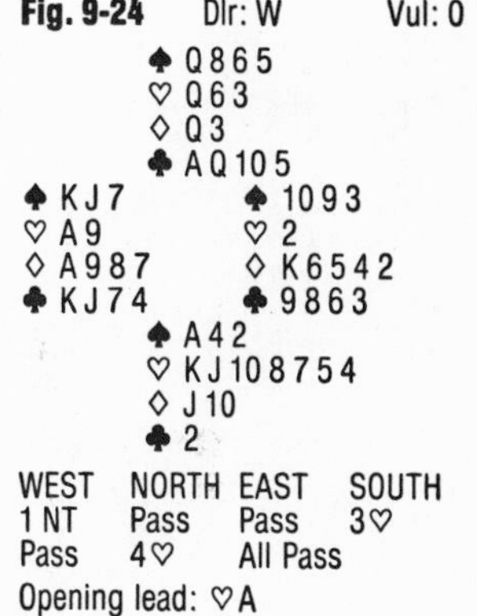

The defenders started the proceedings by taking the first three tricks with the ace of hearts, the ace of diamonds, and the king of diamonds. They had taken their book. They also had saved Ogust the trouble of trying to rectify the count.

At trick four East switched to the ten of spades. Ogust was under no illusions about who held the king. Between his hand and the dummy's, there were 21 high-card points, and when East showed up with the king of diamonds, that totaled 24. If West had 16 high-card points for his one no-trump bid, he had not only the king of spades but the king of clubs also. If he also had the jack, only he could guard clubs.

That being true, Ogust could count on two club winners. He also had six trump winners left in his hand, and the ace of spades brought the total up to nine, leaving him only one loser. That part looked all right for a squeeze. If he played the ace of spades, West would have to have the high spade and would hold that one spade to avoid being squeezed. With the king of clubs in his hand, he would have to hold two clubs, or so it appeared until you took another look.

While kings ordinarily are the second highest card in a suit, when they are finessable, they are reduced to at best third highest. A small club could be led and the queen finessed. Then the ace could be played, and only then would the king be good. So, let's change it a little bit and demote the king to the third highest club and say that West would have to hold three clubs and one spade to avoid the squeeze. Could he do that? When Ogust took the ace of spades, that was the fourth trick, and he had a straight run of six trump tricks, bringing the total up to ten. No, West could not hold three clubs and one spade.

So, Ogust went up with his ace of spades and led all of his hearts. When he led his last heart, he was leading to the tenth trick. West was holding one spade and three clubs and had to get down to three cards. Dummy had saved three clubs and the queen of spades and was going to play after West. West had no least intention of throwing away the king of spades, so he discarded a small club, leaving himself only two of them. Ogust now discarded the queen of spades from the dummy, and dummy's three clubs took the last three tricks.

Take another look at the lead of the ten of spades from the East hand. He had a lead which could have defeated the hand. Had he led a club, Ogust could have taken only two club tricks and inevitably would have had to finally lose a spade. That club lead would have taken out of the north hand the entry which was essential for a squeeze.

So here is a particular advantage in knowing about squeeze plays. Defense against them is not easy. Even some of the best players in the world will overlook the necessity of removing a card which might serve as an entry for a squeeze.

Too often, you have no way of guessing whether a squeeze will or will not work. But when it is the play of last resort, it has to be tried.

Fig. 9-25

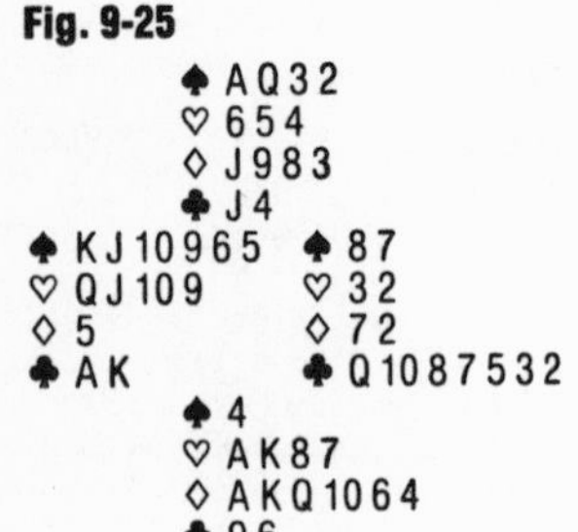

After West opened the bidding with one spade, South got to a contract of five diamonds. West cashed the ace and king of clubs in that order and switched to the queen of hearts. With an obvious heart loser and nothing else to do about it, declarer considered the possibilities of a squeeze play. The spade finesse was an overwhelming favorite to win, which would demote the king to the third highest, making it necessary for West to hold onto three spades to guard the suit. If West had six, East would have only two and could not guard the suit. Or, if East could be induced to discard one of three, he would still be unable to guard the suit. Two tricks had been played, and declarer could win two hearts and then six more diamond tricks, making a total of ten tricks played. In addition to having to guard spades, West might be the only player who could guard hearts. That would be true if he started with four or more of them, or, again, if East could be induced to discard a few. That was the only chance declarer had, so that is the play he made. After declarer took his two hearts and ran his six diamonds, West had to get down to three cards. He decided that South must have a spade to have played the hand the way he did, so he hung onto the spades and discarded all of his hearts, hoping East would be able to guard that suit. So South then took two tricks with his two good hearts and finally won a trick with the ace of spades—not having to finesse spades at all.

Fig. 9-26 Dlr: S Vul: B

North: ♠ A 7 6 ♡ K 10 8 ◇ A Q J 2 ♣ 8 6 2

West: ♠ Q J 10 9 8 2 ♡ 4 ◇ K 10 8 7 ♣ K 4

East: ♠ K 4 3 ♡ 9 3 ◇ 9 6 5 ♣ 10 9 7 5 3

South: ♠ 5 ♡ A Q J 7 6 5 2 ◇ 4 3 ♣ A Q J

SOUTH	WEST	NORTH	EAST
1♡	1♠	2◇	Pass
2♡	Pass	2♠	Pass
3♣	Pass	4♡	Pass
4 NT	Pass	5♡	Pass
5 NT	Pass	6◇	Pass
6♡	Pass	Pass	Pass

Opening lead: ♠Q

Now let's look at one where the king gets demoted twice and becomes the fourth best card in a suit (Fig. 9-26).

South was playing before a large gallery of kibitzers and gave some thought to giving them a good show by bidding a grand slam, but when his partner turned up with only one king and he found the opponents had three kings, he gave up that idea. After the queen of spades was led and the dummy came down, he assumed that East had the king of spades or West would have led that card. Unless West was also playing to the gallery, it seemed that he had to have both of the minor suit kings to justify a vulnerable overcall in a suit headed by the queen. Assuming the diamond finesse was right, he had twelve tricks by taking the diamond finesse twice. But he also saw prospects of a squeeze for the thirteenth trick. If he hadn't been able to excite his kibitzers by bidding to take thirteen tricks, maybe he could earn their applause by taking them with a squeeze.

This might require, among other things, that only West be able to guard the spade suit. This meant that West would have to hold six of them, unless East got careless discarding them. If East had only three spades, there would be no problem stripping him of these and leaving West in charge of that suit. But dummy would be left with no spades also. A squeeze involving spades was unlikely. So declarer looked for a squeeze in the two minor suits. The king was obviously the second highest card in a suit, and if West held it in clubs, he would have to hold onto two clubs, assuming South could hold onto two clubs. In the diamond suit, the king had actually been demoted to the fourth highest card in the suit. This hand differed from the ones we have been looking at in that South had two diamonds opposite the ace, queen, and jack over the king, making it possible for him to finesse twice and then lay down the ace. So, if everything laid right for a squeeze, West would have to hold four diamonds and two clubs, for a total of six cards. In addition to the spade trick declarer took, he could take seven trump tricks one way or another, making a total of eight cards, and leaving everybody with five. It was a reasonable chance, so declarer went after it.

Winning the first spade trick in the dummy, he promptly led a spade and trumped it. He went back to dummy with a high trump and led dummy's last spade, trumped it, and was gratified to see the king fall out of the East hand. That confirmed his opinion that East did not have the king of clubs. Now he led a diamond and finessed it, thereby graciously promoting the king to the third highest card. He led dummy's last trump and then led all of his trumps. When he led his last trump, he had one diamond and his three clubs left in his hand. West was holding three diamonds and two clubs and had to discard one of them. He didn't have much difficulty deciding that it would be fatal to discard a diamond, so, with an air of great innocence, he played his four of clubs. Declarer finessed diamonds again and then cashed the ace of diamonds on which he discarded the jack of clubs. Now he led a club, but being determined not to miss the squeeze, played his ace of clubs, dropping the king from the West hand. His queen of clubs took the thirteenth trick.

He listened for applause, but heard nothing but silence. Then he heard one of his kibitzers say to her lady friend, "You see, Elsie, it's like I told you—not even the experts bid all of them right."

We will leave that declarer with his wounded pride and look for a hand where the king of a suit is demoted to the fifth best.

West competed in spades, but declarer had no problem arriving at a four heart contract. West won the first trick with the king of spades. Already he was squeezed because the peculiar distribution of the diamond suit demoted his king to the fifth best diamond. Of course, nobody knew that until several plays later.

Declarer was feeling pretty good about the whole affair. It looked as though he had six sure tricks in hearts plus the ace of clubs, and it seemed there would be no problem developing three tricks in the diamond suit.

Fig. 9-27

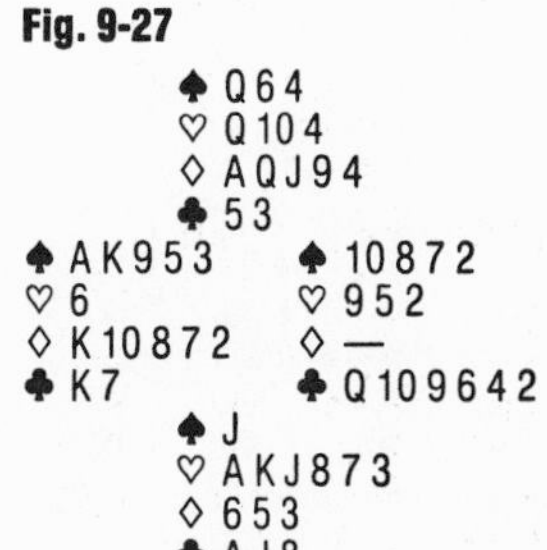

Developments soon made him reconsider. West switched to a small diamond. Declarer put in dummy's jack, but East trumped with the five of hearts and returned a small club. Declarer had to win that with the ace to avoid going set before he got started. If he let West win that trick, East could trump another diamond, and that would be the fourth trick for the defense.

But declarer thought he saw a way that he could dispose of two club losers in his hand and actually end up winning eleven tricks. The king of diamonds had had a promotion, but that didn't do it much good. It now was the fourth best diamond instead of the fifth, but that meant that West would have to keep four diamonds to keep all of dummy's diamonds from being good. In addition, he had to hold onto one spade to keep dummy's spade from being a winner. That was a total of five cards. When South won the third trick with the ace of clubs, he still had six good heart tricks, and that would be a total of nine tricks played, cutting everybody down to four cards. If West could keep only four cards, he would find it impossible to hang onto four diamonds and also a spade. So declarer won the queen of hearts and then the ace. Now that everybody was out of trumps, he led another diamond and finessed dummy's nine. It would have done West no good to play the ten or king. Then he led the ten of hearts back to his hand and continued leading hearts. The king of diamonds had had another promotion to number three, but he was doomed. When declarer led his last heart, Fig. 9-28 shows what everybody had left.

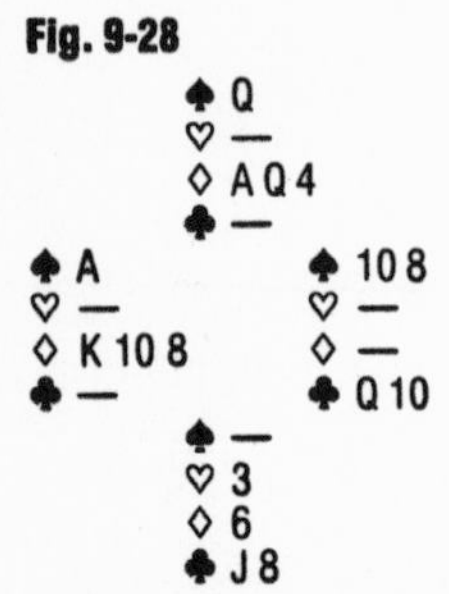

West knew he couldn't throw away the ace of spades, so he played his eight of diamonds. With that, South discarded the queen of spades from the dummy, and that enabled all three diamonds to take tricks.

It is not only kings that can be demoted—lower honors can also suffer that fate (Fig. 9-29).

Against the six diamond contract, West led the king of hearts. After this won the trick, only a spade lead would break all contact declarer had with the dummy, but how could West tell that? If South happened to be void in spades instead of having a singleton, that play would allow South three discards. So West continued with the second heart.

Declarer trumped that, and it looked as though he had a sure loser left in clubs. That was assuming he could finesse the jack of spades so he could discard two clubs. But when he made that assumption, he also made an assumption which caused him to be on the lookout for a squeeze play. So, he led all of his diamonds and followed these by the ace and king of clubs. West's spade was the fourth highest because the dummy could win three tricks—first with the jack and then with the ace and king. To be sure the dummy did not take four spade tricks, West had to hold onto four cards in that suit. In addition, he had to hold onto a high heart to be sure dummy's jack of hearts didn't win a trick. When declarer led the king of clubs, that was the ninth trick, and West found it impossible to hold onto a total of five cards. He discarded a spade and held onto his high heart, so the heart was discarded from the dummy and the spade finesse taken. The little two-spot in the suit bid by the opponents took the last trick.

THE VIENNA COUP

We have been having a lot of fun demoting honor cards in the opponents' hands. Now let's be versatile and see whether we can gain by *promoting* cards in their hands. Believe it or not, it can be done!

DUMMY
♠ Q 6 4
♡ A 9
♢ K J 6 4
♣ A K Q 6

DECLARER
♠ A K J
♡ Q 6 2
♢ A Q 10 5 3
♣ 3 2

In a six no-trump contract, you get the opening lead of a spade. Twelve tricks are no problem. You can count them off the top. How about going for the thirteenth trick? If you are playing matchpoint duplicate bridge and can pick up an extra trick by a squeeze play, you probably are going to get a whale of a score on the hand. This looks like a hand where a trick can be developed by a squeeze or not at all. Even if you are only playing for fun, many people think the most fun of all is to pull off a squeeze. So, let's see what our prospects are. The holding in the heart suit looks like a split menace squeeze. We remember that such a squeeze is a directional squeeze which can operate against one opponent only and that that is the opponent who has to discard before the player with the winner in the split menace plays—in this case, it is West. If we cash five diamond tricks and three spade tricks, West will have five cards left. But, if he has length in clubs and also has the king of hearts, he is going to have to hold onto six cards. His king of hearts being second highest, he would have to keep two cards there; he would also have to keep four clubs. So, if that is his holding, the situation should be like this when we lead the last diamond.

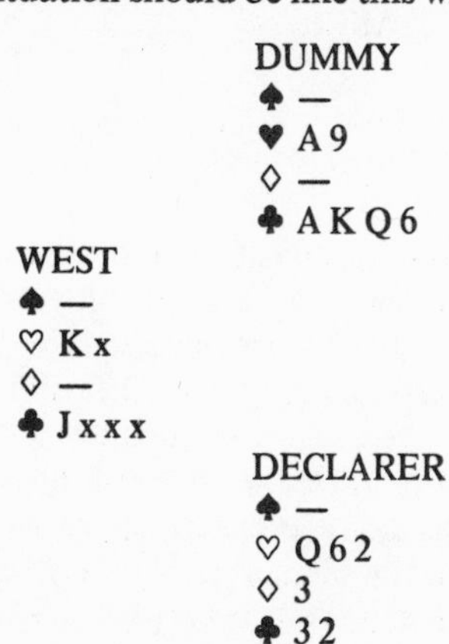

That looks very pretty, but there seems to be a fly in the ointment. Just because West discards a small heart, for example, how are we going to know if he has kept one heart and four clubs or two hearts and three clubs? And, unless we can be sure, we don't know what to discard from the dummy. Maybe we could have worked it all out if we watched carefully what was discarded in both suits as we went along.

The truth of the matter is that there are times when it is completely impossible to do this, and even when it can be done, it is one heck of a strain. Surely there should be a better way.

There is.

Let's think back a minute to the requirements for a so-called automatic squeeze which works against both opponents. To have that, we need a single threat in the hand which is leading the squeeze card, an entry threat in the opposing hand, and a card in the suit of the entry threat so we can reach that hand. Is there some way we can reach that set up on this hand? There is. But, strangely enough, to do that we have to do our opponents a temporary favor. We have to promote their king of hearts from the number two card to the number one card. Of course, we are going to chop him down in a moment, but right now we are going to make him feel awfully good.

Somewhere along the route, you simply cash the ace of hearts; then, when you get around to leading the squeeze card, the layout will be like this:

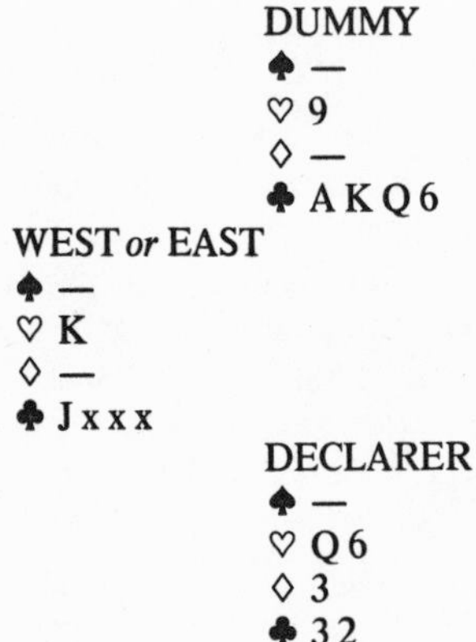

Now the squeeze card will be the ninth card played and not the eighth. We have the queen of hearts in south as a single threat and the club holding in north as a long threat. Further, we have an idle card—the nine of hearts—in the north hand to throw away on the three of diamonds. And now, wonder of wonders, instead of being able to squeeze only West, we will squeeze either opponent who started with the king of hearts plus length in clubs. The squeeze has become exactly twice as good and, in addition, we don't have to do a lot of counting. The only card we have to watch for is the king of hearts. If it has not been played after we lead the three of diamonds, we simply lead clubs. If the long clubs were with the king of hearts, the squeeze is going to work. If the long clubs were not with the king of hearts, the squeeze is not going to work, and there was nothing we could have done about it.

Take another look at my last illustration: when we led the three of diamonds, the south hand, which held the squeeze card, had no winners at all—it only had a threat. That is typical of the end situation in Vienna Coups. One of the problems has been the lack of entries. Give yourself plenty of entries in both hands, and the Vienna may not even be necessary. It might be wise, and it simplifies the play of the hand, but technically it would not be necessary, if you would change North's ace of clubs with South's deuce of clubs. Go back to my first illustration for this hand and, in your imagination, make that change. Now lead the three of diamonds and throw away the nine of hearts. Cash dummy's ace of hearts, return to your hand with the ace of clubs, and the automatic squeeze against both opponents would have been effective. The matter of entries plays an especially important part in squeeze plays. Observe the next hand:

DUMMY
♠ A J
♡ A
♢ 6 5 4 3 2
♣ K J 6 3 2

DECLARER
♠ 2
♡ Q 3
♢ A K Q 8 7
♣ A Q 7 5 4

Don't you wish you had gone for a grand slam in one of the minor suits instead of being so determined to play no-trump that you put this hand in six no-trump? Well, there you are, and if you can figure out a way to take all thirteen tricks, you at least will beat those people who also tried for no-trump and managed to take only twelve.

You can run ten tricks in the minor suits. To protect both hearts and spades in the suits where your opponents hold the second highest card in both, they are going to have to hold four cards. Obviously, they can't hold four cards if you leave them only three. And, if the same opponent holds the king and queen of spades as well as the king of hearts so that he alone is able to guard those two suits, you may pull it off. Not very good prospects, but the best you have. Having received an opening lead of the jack of diamonds, you haven't been hurt yet. You blithely cash all of your clubs and then start leading diamonds. You have one diamond left and are about to lead it. STOP! Something has gone wrong. You are on the verge of committing suicide. If anybody gets squeezed on the lead of that last diamond, it is going to be you in your dummy. All your opponent holding those key cards has to do is to throw away a heart, and, while his king is now singleton, you have no way to get back to your hand to cash the queen of hearts after you take the spade. Fortunately, you stop in time. Get that ace of hearts out of North's hand while you still have an entry back into your hand. In other words, don't cash that last diamond right now: cash the ace of hearts and then return to your hand with the seven of diamonds. The results will be devastating to the player who happens to hold the three key cards. That probably is East if it's anybody, for had West held all three, he probably would have led the king of hearts. But it doesn't really matter which it is. Here is where you are now:

DUMMY
♠ A J
♡ —
♢ 2
♣ —

DECLARER
♠ 2
♡ Q
♢ 7
♣ —

True, they have to hold only one heart, but they also have to hold two spades, and they are going to have only two cards left. Whew! That was a close one. We just cashed that ace of hearts in time. From now on, let's resolve when we have this situation to cash it earlier. It will be easier on our nerves.

Now, before we get involved in other matters, let's give ourselves the final test and figure in advance what our chances are. This time let's have the hand upside down. Let's have the squeeze card in the dummy hand instead of in our own hand.

DUMMY
♠ Q 6 5
♡ 4 2
♢ A K
♣ A K Q J 10 8

DECLARER
♠ A 4
♡ A K 6 5 3
♢ Q 6 4
♣ 9 7 4

Our enthusiastic partner fell madly in love with his solid club suit and, after you opened the bidding, put us in a contract of seven no-trump. West has led the jack of diamonds, and we have counted our tricks three times and can find only twelve. If he loved that club suit so, why didn't he bid his grand slam in clubs! At least then we might have had a chance of establishing the heart suit without loss. But, here we are. Obviously, our only chance is a squeeze. The spade suit makes it pretty obvious that it must be a Vienna. Let's see how it is going to work out.

If we cash three diamond tricks and six club tricks, everybody will have only four cards left. Somebody will have to hang onto three hearts and two spades, and if one person is burdened with all of the guards in those two suits, we may get him into trouble. How about the heart suit? Well, if it breaks 3–3, no squeeze play is going to work. This is one time when we feel fortunate that an even break in six outstanding cards is rather unlikely. We want somebody to have length in hearts. If that same person has the king of spades, a squeeze will materialize, provided we handle the entry properly.

We are going to have to cross from the north hand to the south hand once to cash the queen of diamonds. Then we are going back to north and run all of those club tricks. However, after we do this, there will be no winners in the north hand, so the Vienna coup becomes not a luxury, but a must. So, after we cash the ace of diamonds (just to be sure we unblock the spade suit), we are going to use the ace of spades as a way to reach the south hand. On the queen of diamonds, we are going to discard one of dummy's small spades. While we are at it, we can cash exactly one heart and no more. That second little heart in the north hand is worth its weight in gold. It is the key to the entry back to the south hand. Getting back to the north hand is no problem at all, as we have three clubs. Now we have led not only three diamonds and six clubs, but also one spade and one heart. In the dummy, we have left the lone queen of spades and the heart. In our own hand, we have the king and another heart, having thrown away a small spade and two hearts on dummy's clubs. If anyone has the king of spades and all the remaining hearts, he is now handsomely squeezed.

It isn't only kings you can promote to your advantage. Sometimes you can promote smaller cards.

Some of the bidding on some of these hands I merely report and do not necessarily recommend. The four club bid by West was intended to be the Landy convention, asking his partner to bid his longer major suit. It turned out to be a disastrous bid. It not only made South mad enough to bid a grand slam, it also told him how to play the hand.

South had twelve tricks off the top. Left to his own devices, he doubtless would have tried the heart finesse for the thirteenth trick. South saw only six high-card points missing from his hand and the dummy. The bid by West convinced him that West must have the high cards in both hearts and spades. Had South not known this and decided to go for the squeeze play, he would eventually have gotten down to a two-card ending with only the ace and queen of hearts in his own hand, and West could have blanked his king of hearts to protect his queen of spades. South would still have had to guess whether to play for the finesse or the squeeze. That happens when the king and the other threatened suit are both positioned behind your ace-queen doubleton. But with knowledge that West almost certainly had both of these cards, South had no problem.

This time he had to promote the queen in the West hand all the way from the third highest card to the very highest so that his menace in north would be operative. The opening lead was the four of diamonds, and declarer promptly cashed his three top diamonds, discarding one of dummy's hearts, and then cashed his ace and king of spades. He started leading clubs and just kept on leading clubs. When he led the last club he had, it was the eleventh trick. Declarer had thrown away one of the diamonds and two of the hearts, and his two remaining cards were the ace and queen of hearts. North still had the jack of spades and the jack of hearts. West couldn't afford to throw away the queen of spades, so he dropped the ten of hearts like a person who couldn't care less. Declarer was not to be deceived. He led the jack of hearts and went up with his ace, felling the lone king, and his queen took the thirteenth trick.

The bidding often guides you to the right line of play. Here is another example (Fig. 9-31).

WEST	NORTH	EAST	SOUTH
2♠*	Dbl	Pass	4♡
Pass	Pass	Pass	

Opening lead: ♠K

*Weak two bid.

The defense took the first three tricks in a hurry. West cashed the king and ace of spades and then led the eight-spot for East to trump. East returned a heart. Declarer saw that a finesse in either minor suit would give him his tenth trick, but he had no faith in either finesse. A nonvulnerable West had made a weak two bid with eight high-card points in spades. With either minor suit king, West would probably have opened the bidding with one spade. So, declarer set about looking for a way to make the hand with East holding both kings.

He had only one loser, and that situation was correct for a squeeze. However, the hand to be squeezed was behind the hand with the threats, so an ordinary squeeze wouldn't work. How about a Vienna?

The squeeze card would have to be in hearts, and, when it finally was led, South would surely have no more winners in his hand. That was ample evidence that it had to be a Vienna or nothing. Clubs had to be intact, as that was the only entry. How about a Vienna in diamonds?

Well, there would be no trouble promoting East's king to the highest diamond, the trouble was that the single menace in the south hand had to be number two. Was it possible for declarer to not only promote East's assumed king to number one, but also to promote his own ten to number two? After thinking that over, declarer decided it was indeed possible. He won the fourth trick with the king of hearts. Trumps were all out, so he cashed dummy's ace of diamonds, preparing to put the hammerlock on East. Next he ran all of his hearts. This gave him four discards from the north hand; he discarded his five of clubs and those three diamonds. When he led his last heart, his ten had been promoted all the way from fifth highest to second highest, and East was through. In addition to the ten of diamonds, declarer had the six of clubs. Dummy had nothing but the ace and queen of clubs. East had to get down to two cards and was obviously unable to hold both two clubs and the king of diamonds. East knew that to discard a club would be fatal, but he didn't know who held the ten of diamonds, so he discarded that red king. Declarer won the twelfth trick with his ten of diamonds, throwing away dummy's queen of clubs, and the last trick with dummy's ace of clubs.

Now let's watch an eight-spot grow up (Fig. 9-32).

North must have been a bit startled to hear his partner open the bidding. He took it easy the first round, but really stepped on the gas for his rebid. West's opening lead was a card declarer wished he had. West led a small spade. Declarer saw he had twelve tricks off the top and that, if he had a small spade in either hand, he could spread the hand for thirteen tricks. However, the spade suit was going to bring only two tricks, so he looked to see what his other chances were.

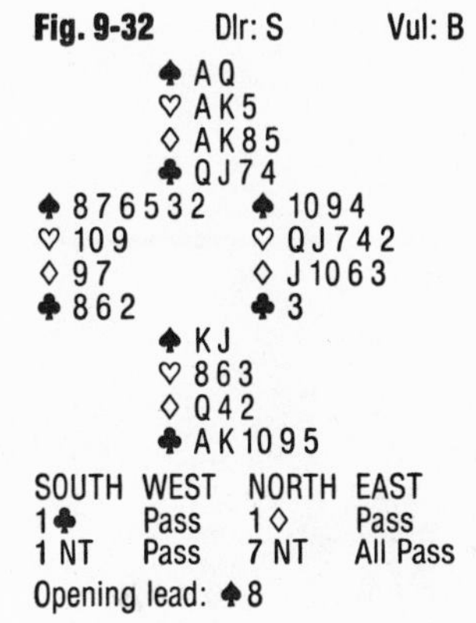

Of course, the diamonds might break 3–3, and that would give him the extra trick. How about a squeeze in the red suits? Suppose one player had all of the guards in those two suits? Not very likely, but always possible. That does add another possibility to the possibility of diamonds' breaking, so there was no reason why he shouldn't try it. It does involve cashing the ace and king of hearts somewhere along the line so that the eight of hearts in the south hand will become the single threat there. With that, the small diamond is the threat in the north hand.

So the technicians are going to say to promptly take two spade tricks; then to take the ace and king of hearts; then to take the ace and queen of diamonds, leaving the deuce in the south hand for an entry; and then to start leading clubs until this three-card ending (Fig. 9-33).

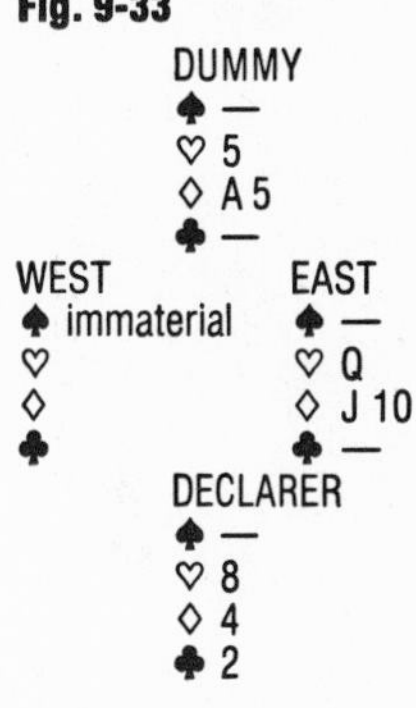

Now when declarer leads the last club and throws away the five of hearts from the north hand, East will be handsomely squeezed because West held the doubleton ten-nine of hearts.

The authorities seem to adore those three-card endings, and sometimes even show them before they show the whole hand.

I am going to tell you no such thing. Let's see whether we can find a more confusing way to arrive at that three-card ending. There is no reason to let the opponents know what declarer is up to, if he can avoid doing so. After all, the distribution is not always so convenient as in the hands we writers show you, and it is rather unusual that the nine and ten of hearts are doubleton so the eight can be promoted so quickly.

We see that declarer can take twelve tricks and that the possibility of a squeeze does exist. If the same player guards both of the red suits, he will have to hold three hearts (having the third highest) and four diamonds (having the fourth highest), making a total of seven cards. South could, right now, take the first seven tricks in the black suits and get his opponents down to six cards. But one should always stop and look over the entry situation. The heart holding does suggest the possibility of a Vienna Coup, but the numerous entries in the south hand take away any urgency about cashing them too soon. Declarer does want to end up leading a squeeze card from the south hand, with the eight of hearts as a single menace there and a long diamond as a menace in the north hand. But, let's have declarer do it our way.

He wins the first spade with the ace and immediately cashes five clubs, throwing away a small heart from the dummy, just as though he weren't a bit interested in that suit. Next he cashes the king of spades, and then he goes to the dummy with the ace of diamonds. Now he cashes the ace and king of hearts. A small diamond puts him back into his hand, and he has exactly the ending that the technicians arrived at, holding in his hand the eight of hearts and the four of diamonds and in the north hand the king and one diamond. Not only has he put the vise on any hand unfortunate enough to hold all of the cards in the two red suits, but he hopes that his opponents had one heck of a time discarding and in the confusion they may have allowed him to win what he could not have won by straightforward play.

To conclude this section on the Vienna Coup, let me show you a curiosity—a double Vienna Coup.

Fig. 9-34

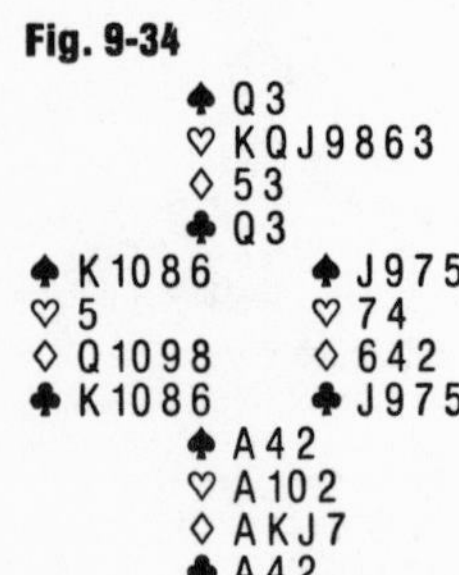

With a heart lead, the problem is the same whether the hand is being played in no-trump or in hearts: to take all thirteen tricks, declarer has to promote both of West's kings! If he takes the two black aces and runs the seven heart tricks, nine cards will have been played. South can keep all four of his diamonds, and North will have his two black queens and two diamonds. West, holding the third best diamond, would have to hold onto three of them, and holding the best spade and club, would have to keep one each of these. No can do. The technical way to look at it is to say that North is holding two one-card threats and has no other winners, while South holds the long entry threat in the diamond suit with the two high cards.

Did you notice that although declarer has only eleven winners at the beginning, and therefore two losers, his squeeze is still operative? I was afraid you would. That is because while you can have only one loser in a two-suit squeeze, a squeeze will be effective if you have a squeeze in three suits even though you have two losers. That subject comes up more in detail later on, but it is worthwhile noticing now.

THE TRANSFER SQUEEZE

For a squeeze to be successful, it is sometimes necessary for the person making the squeeze to have establishable suits in two hands, while the defenders have all of their guards in those suits in one hand. Obviously, two hands can have more cards than one hand, and the squeezee has to discard a card in one of the suits, allowing the squeezor to establish or win tricks with it. If one of your opponents guards one of the suits and the other guards the remaining, the squeeze will not come off. There are times, though, when this unhappy situation can be corrected by eliminating the guard in one of the hands and throwing the full responsibility for the two suits on the other. These situations are extremely rare, but they are lovely to look at. Such a play is called a transfer squeeze. Who can say that you won't have an opportunity to use one someday?

Fig. 9-35

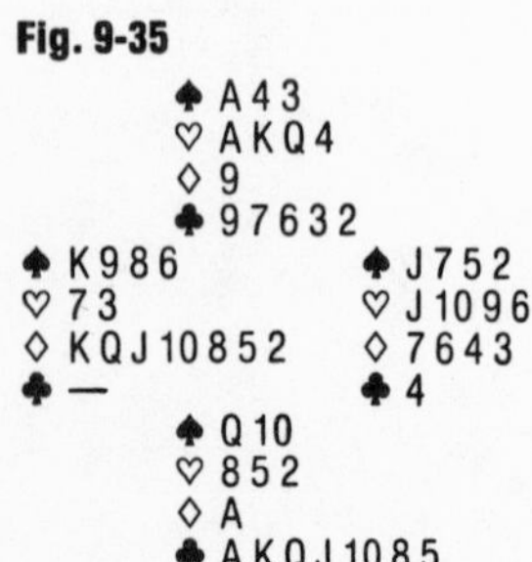

Here is one played by Oswald Jacoby (Fig. 9-35).

The detailed bidding is not given, but the report does state that Jacoby played seven clubs after some vigorous bidding by West in diamonds. The opening lead was the king of diamonds. Jacoby could count up to twelve tricks, and the thirteenth was available if the heart suit would break 3–3. The vigorous bidding by West suggested that the hearts were not going to break, so Jacoby checked on squeeze possibilities.

A simple Vienna coup was available if the same player held the king of spades and length in hearts. It would only be necessary to take away from the opponents the one trump, cash the ace of spades, and then run the clubs. The trouble with this thought was that the strong bidding by West suggested that it was he who had the king of spades. If it was East who held the length in hearts, then no squeeze would operate.

But, the ten of spades in Jacoby's hand gave him an additional chance. After winning the ace of diamonds, he took four clubs to see what sort of discards he got. He had to leave one club in the dummy as the reentry into his hand. Nobody sluffed any hearts or spades, so those four tricks told him nothing. Jacoby decided that while West probably had the king of spades, it was not necessary for him to have the jack. He led the queen. West covered, and dummy won with the ace. Now the protection of the spade suit had been transferred to East who did, in fact, hold the jack. If he did hold long hearts as well, he was a dead duck. Jacoby returned to his hand with a club and cashed his last two trumps, throwing away the two small spades in the dummy. That made nine tricks played altogether, and Jacoby had left his ten of spades and three hearts. Dummy had four hearts. East saw it would be suicide to throw away a heart, so he threw away his jack of spades, making Jacoby's ten-spot good.

One reason the transfer squeeze is rare is because it often is difficult and sometimes impossible to tell that it is called for rather than a straightforward squeeze. However, sometimes the bidding and play will give you clues which may help you find one if you watch carefully.

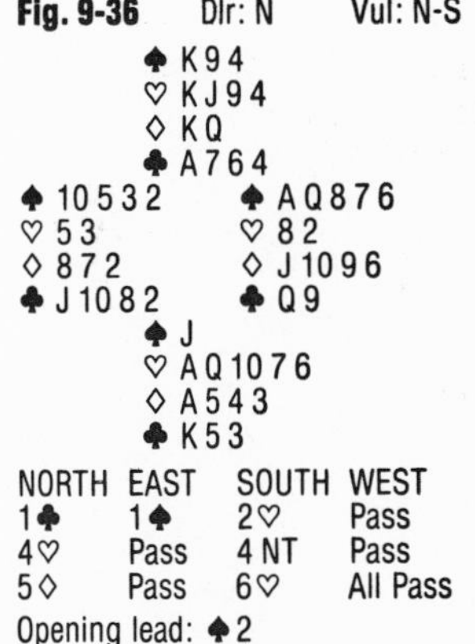

West led the two of spades, dummy played low, and East won with the queen and switched to the jack of diamonds. Declarer counted up three diamond tricks, a diamond ruff in the dummy, and five heart tricks, for a total of nine, which, when added to the spade trick already played, made ten tricks played. Declarer was sure he knew who had the ace of spades. If East also held four clubs, he alone could not guard both black suits and would be squeezed. When declarer led the last trump from his hand, he would have three clubs left, while the dummy would have the king of spades and two clubs. So, declarer set out to find out what he could discover about the opposing hands.

Two leads of trumps took care of that situation. South next cashed dummy's king of diamonds and returned to his hand with a trump. He played the ace of diamonds discarding a club from dummy, and then led his last diamond and trumped it with a high heart so that suit could not become blocked. Now he stopped to reconnoiter. East had followed suit to four diamonds and two hearts, giving him six red cards. Reasonably, he had five spades for his overcall. He couldn't have four clubs unless he had started with fifteen cards. Considering that unlikely, declarer decided there was no club-spade squeeze for him. But suppose West held the four clubs, which now seemed much more than likely. Could he be squeezed? The problem was that he was protecting clubs, while East was protecting spades, and unless West could somehow be made to have to guard both suits, he couldn't be squeezed. There was a chance for that. If West had started with the ten of spades, he would have to guard both suits. Declarer led the king of spades from dummy. East had to cover with the ace or give up, so declarer trumped it. That left West responsible for guarding both clubs and spades. Nine tricks had been played. South still had one trump and three clubs. Dummy had the nine of spades and three clubs. West was holding the ten of spades and three clubs. Declarer led his last trump and discarded one of dummy's clubs. West couldn't play his ten of spades, so for his last three cards he held only two clubs. That was not enough. South won the ace of clubs and had one club left to get back to his hand for the king and five which were both good.

Fig. 9-37

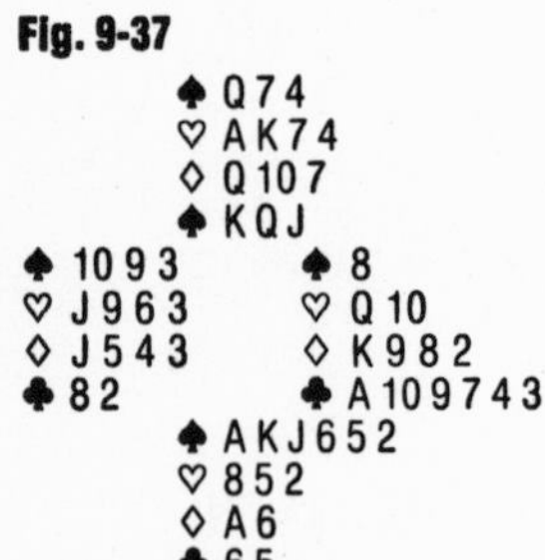

I've always been fond of this next hand (Fig. 9-37) because two of my favorite people played it. North was Ewart Kempson of England and South was Al Morehead of New York City.

Without giving all of the bidding, Kempson said he put Morehead in a contract of six spades, doubled and redoubled, after East had overcalled in clubs. One reason I've always liked this hand is because of the way Kempson reported the play. Let me quote him.

"West led the eight of clubs. East won and returned the suit. West played the two. At this stage, Mr. Morehead placed his head in his hand and appeared to be in prayer.

"South seemed to think that the hearts would not break, for after pulling West's three trumps, he discarded a heart on the winning club and then led dummy's queen of diamonds.

"Up to this moment, I had always thought Mr. Morehead was a good player, but how could he hope to get away with this sort of play in this sort of company? Unless fast asleep, East was bound to cover if he held the diamond king, and I concluded that South's prayer (referred to above) was a request that East should not cover. But the prayer went unanswered. East did cover.

"South played his last three trumps, on the last of which West, who had already discarded one heart, held hearts J 9 6 and diamond J. The poor fellow had to keep the diamond, so dummy took three heart tricks and the slam was delivered.

"'I think,' said Mr. Morehead, 'the best chance was a transfer squeeze.'"

THE THREE-SUIT SQUEEZE

It is not too often that one opponent can be squeezed because he holds guards in three separate suits. Neither is it rare enough for us to ignore that situation here. Such a squeeze has acquired the title of "A Triple Squeeze."

First, let's look at the technical aspects of the triple squeeze, and then let's look at some of the more practical aspects.

The three-suit squeeze will do its stuff when you have two losers. At times, after the squeeze has taken effect, you then cash the winning card or cards produced by the squeeze and there will be a second squeeze. When this happens, the three-suit squeeze is called a "progressive squeeze" or "repeating squeeze." It's just like having two squeezes in succession. The first one will gain you one trick and the second, if it comes off, will gain a second trick. So, a triple squeeze can not only be made when you have two losers, but, if you can promote the second squeeze, you can actually gain two tricks with it.

Let's look at an example (Fig. 9-38).

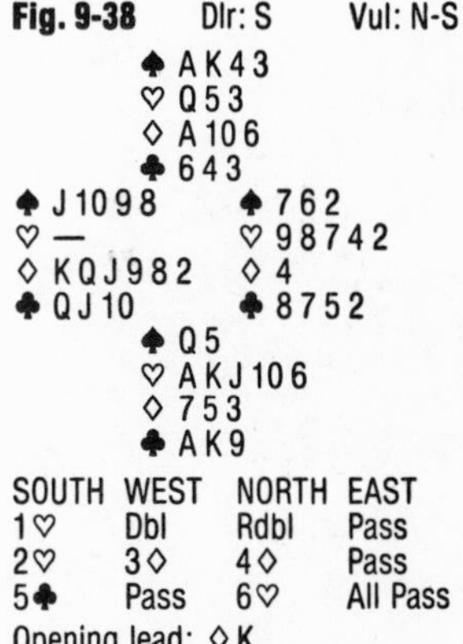

Fig. 9-38 Dlr: S Vul: N-S

North: ♠ A K 4 3 ♡ Q 5 3 ◇ A 10 6 ♣ 6 4 3

West: ♠ J 10 9 8 ♡ — ◇ K Q J 9 8 2 ♣ Q J 10

East: ♠ 7 6 2 ♡ 9 8 7 4 2 ◇ 4 ♣ 8 7 5 2

South: ♠ Q 5 ♡ A K J 10 6 ◇ 7 5 3 ♣ A K 9

SOUTH	WEST	NORTH	EAST
1♡	Dbl	Rdbl	Pass
2♡	3◇	4◇	Pass
5♣	Pass	6♡	All Pass

Opening lead: ◇ K

After the opening lead of the king of diamonds, declarer could count only eleven winners; therefore, he had two losers. He would like to have conceded a diamond trick to try to rectify the count, but, in view of the bidding, he was afraid that if he did do so, the second diamond would get trumped, and he would lose the first two tricks. So, he played the ace of diamonds, not feeling too secure about that trick. However, East followed suit, and there he was.

He couldn't see any way to pick up extra tricks except by a squeeze. As he had two losers, this would require a triple squeeze. With all of the bidding West had done, this was possible if West had just the right distribution. One lead of trump told him he was going to have to lead all five trumps to exhaust his opponents' trumps. He also knew that West was going to have to take five discards. That prospect pleased him. When he led his last heart, that was the sixth trick played, and West had to get down to seven cards. The dummy had discarded a club on one of the trumps and was prepared to let go of a diamond or a club on the other. Those were idle cards for him. West sought in vain for an idle card. With the fourth best spade, he had to hold four spades, with the third best club, he had to hold three clubs. If those were the seven cards he held onto, he would have to throw away his last diamond, and dummy's ten-spot would be good. Finally he threw away a club.

The first squeeze had succeeded, and declarer had picked up his twelfth trick. But he still had another squeeze left. He cashed the ace and king of clubs and then led the nine of clubs. That was the ninth trick, leaving West with only four cards. He had in his hand the four spades necessary to protect that suit and the one diamond necessary to keep the ten-spot in the dummy from taking a trick. The discard of a diamond was hopeless, so he discarded a spade, hoping against hope that his partner might have the queen of that suit. But it was no go. Remaining in the dummy were four spades and the ten of diamonds. The declarer simply discarded the now worthless ten of diamonds, and his spades took the last four tricks.

Let's see what makes these things work.

It is all a matter of having the threats in the right place at the right time and the entries in the right place at the right time. At times, you will have what are called "Extended Threats," and then you will just have to be reasonably careful about your entries, etc. Let's see just what extended threats are.

An extended threat is one of three cards or more which threatens to win more than one trick. Let's look at some examples:

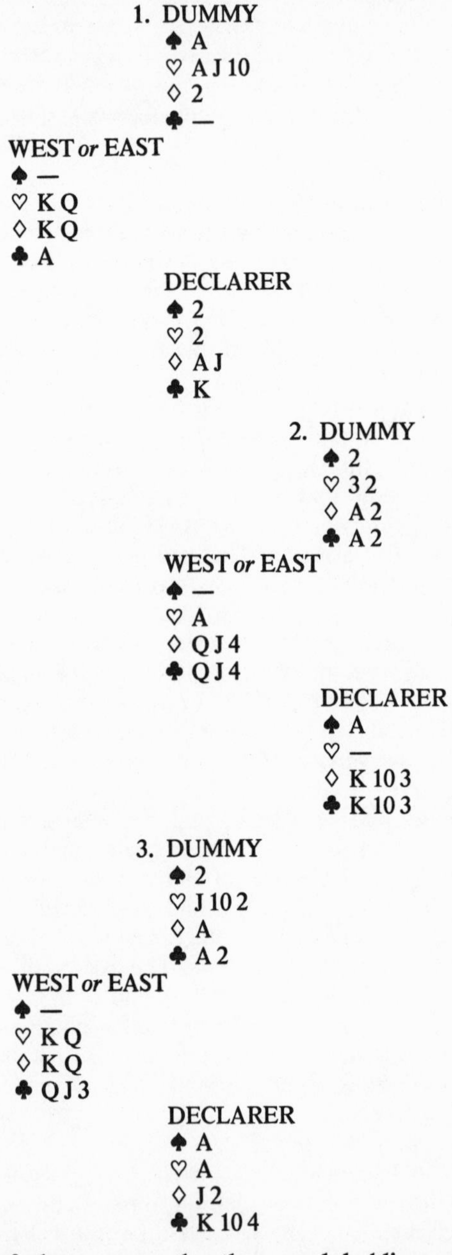

In each of these cases, the three-card holdings are the extended threats. In each case, the lead of the spade wins a trick by a squeeze and establishes a second squeeze to win a second trick. Hands 2 and 3 have what is called Twin-Entry Threats. These are especially helpful. But in the examples shown, they are all good and doubly automatic. By that I mean that they would win two tricks against either opponent who happens to hold all of the guards in all three suits as illustrated here.

But, alas, all too often you don't have those extended threats and have to make do with what you have. When this occurs, just think of the hand as having two separate squeezes, each of which follows the normal rules for squeeze plays except that the first one may be effective when you have two losers. Each requires an entry threat opposite the squeeze card, and the hand with the squeeze card must have a card in the double threat for an entry. Whether they are directional, operating against only one of the opponents, or automatic, operating against either of them, depends on the placement of the threats.

When all three threats are opposite the hand with the squeeze card, the first squeeze is directional and will operate only against the player who has to play ahead of the hand with the threat. That first squeeze will gain one trick, but in the absence of extended threats, the second squeeze cannot come off.

When the threats are divided between the two hands with one or two of them in the hand with the squeeze card, the first squeeze is automatic and will operate against the opponent who holds guards in all three suits, always assuming the entry situation is satisfactory. A second squeeze will operate against a defender who has to play ahead of the hand which has two threats, provided the entry situation is right. For the entry situation to be right, lacking an extended threat, it is necessary that North have an entry in his own suit and that South have an entry in one of his. This second squeeze is directional and will not operate against the player who maintains his guard in back of the hand which has two threats.

Let's see how that works.

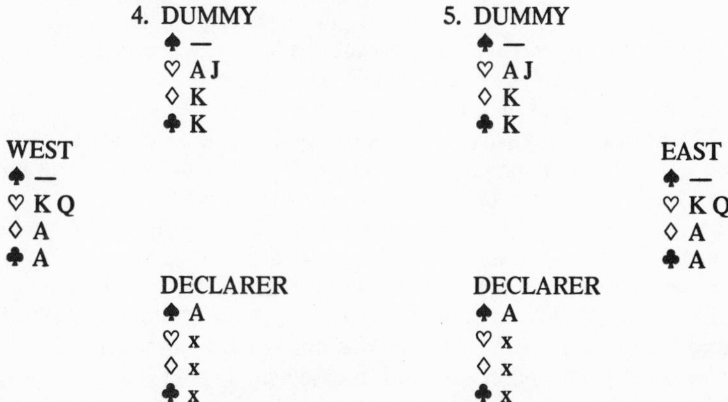

Here South has the squeeze card and North has the threat in all three suits. Declarer has two winners of the four tricks left. But when he leads the ace of spades, he is going to get a third trick in hand 4, as it is West who is under the gun with guards in all three suits. However, there will never be a second squeeze. Not only is West going to have to discard on that ace of spades, so is North. Let's say West discards the queen of hearts. North then has to discard one or the other of his kings. He can now take two heart tricks, but West can hold onto the ace of whichever king declarer has retained in the north seat.

With illustration 5, even the first squeeze will not operate. Whatever declarer discards from the north hand, East will simply discard a card in the same suit, and declarer will end up with only his two tricks.

Now let's look at the situation where South has one of the threats in addition to his squeeze cards.

6\. DUMMY
♠ x
♡ x
♢ K
♣ A J

WEST
♠ —
♡ K Q
♢ A
♣ K Q

DECLARER
♠ A
♡ A J
♢ x
♣ x

7\. DUMMY
♠ x
♡ x
♢ K
♣ A J

EAST
♠ —
♡ K Q
♢ A
♣ K Q

DECLARER
♠ A
♡ A J
♢ x
♣ x

South leads his ace of spades, and the first squeeze is automatic. No matter whether all the cards are in East or West, the squeeze is going to work, and declarer is going to gain a trick. How about the second squeeze? The entry situation is just right for the repeating squeeze. There is an entry into the north hand for the club suit and an entry into the south hand in the heart suit. If it is West who has to guard all three suits, the second squeeze is going to operate, and declarer is going to gain two tricks. Should West discard one of his queens on the ace of spades, declarer would cash his ace and jack in that suit, and the squeeze would repeat. Should West discard his ace of diamonds, South would lead the dummy's king of diamonds, and, again, West would have to discard from one of his two-card holdings, giving declarer the balance of the tricks.

However, the second squeeze will not operate in illustration 7, as in that illustration the three suits which the defenders will have to guard are behind the hand which has two threats and not in front of it. All the defender has to do is to be careful not to discard in one of those suits where the hand has two threats. His first discard must be from that suit which is in the hand with only one threat—in this case hearts. That is almost automatic here, as East is looking at the club and diamond holding in the dummy and can see that a discard of either minor suit is fatal. However, he cannot see the south hand and has some hopes that discarding a heart will not be fatal. After he has discarded a heart, South can cash two heart tricks, but on the second one, he will have to discard a diamond or club, and he is discarding ahead of East. Whichever suit South discards from, East will discard from also, and the second squeeze will not come off.

Let's keep the same favorable entry situation and see the situation where South has two threats along with his squeeze card, leaving only one threat in the dummy.

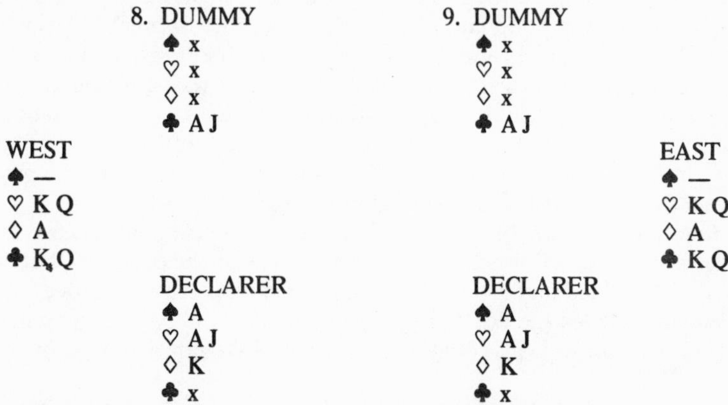

Once more, South has three out of the last five tricks and, therefore, two losers. However, if either opponent has to guard all three suits, the first squeeze is going to be automatic when South leads the ace of spades, and he is sure to gain one trick. This time, I want you to examine illustration 9 before number 8 in looking for the second squeeze. In 9, all of the guards are in front of the hand which has two threats, and there is a directional squeeze for squeeze number two. Declarer is going to gain two tricks.

Now take a look at number 8. Here the three guards are back of the hand which has the two threats, and, if West knows how to discard, the second squeeze is not going to come off. If he will just discard a club, he will have averted the second squeeze because he discarded in front of the hand which has a single squeeze. Now the declarer can cash two club tricks, but on the second one he is going to have to discard ahead of West, and West can simply discard from whatever suit declarer discards.

Now I promised you some practical aspects of the triple squeeze, as well as some technical aspects. Don't let what I have said convince you the second squeeze is not going to work very often. In real life it is going to work much more often than it sounds as though it will. Not only are you going to have extended squeezes which will help you work out the second squeeze, but also, as in situation 8 above, it is difficult, if not impossible, to know how to defend. Remember the defender is looking at the ace and jack of clubs in the dummy, cannot see the south hand, and is called upon to discard a club. How many players will do that? It practically comes down to the fact that only those who have had a peek in your hand will be able to do it. In other words, if you just hold your hand up you are probably going to bring home the second squeeze. West is probably going to discard the queen of hearts, hoping his partner has at least the jack. Now

when you lead the ace and jack of hearts, you will have him in a simple squeeze. Should he discard the ace of diamonds on the ace of spades, you will then lead the king of diamonds and let him choose whether to give you the extra trick in hearts or in clubs.

Fig. 9-39 Dlr: S Vul: 0
♠ 4 3
♡ A J 6 4
◇ 6 5 3 2
♣ A K 9
♠ K Q 10 9 7 5 ♠ 8 6 2
♡ — ♡ 7 5 3 2
◇ J 10 9 7 ◇ 4
♣ Q J 10 ♣ 8 7 5 4 2
♠ A J
♡ K Q 10 9 8
◇ A K Q 8
♣ 6 3
SOUTH WEST NORTH EAST
1♡ 2♠* 4♡ Pass
4♠ Pass 5♣ Pass
6♡ Pass Pass Pass
Opening lead: ♠K
*Preemptive jump overcall.

Let's look at an entire hand and see how some of this works out.

When West led the king of spades, declarer might have given some thought to ducking it. Should diamonds happen not to break, he would have only eleven winners and, hence, only two losers in his hand, and he well might need to rectify the count in case there was a diamond-club squeeze against East. But it looked to the declarer like diamonds ought to break, and, in that event, he could peel twelve tricks off the top, and he wasn't in the mood to do any heavy thinking at this moment. Lucky guy. His carelessness contributed toward getting him an extra trick.

He won with his ace of spades and started leading trumps. When West showed out, he started wondering about how freakish the hand was, but he went ahead and led four rounds of hearts, noting that West discarded four spades. Next he led the ace and king of diamonds and got the news that the diamond suit was not going to break. Fig. 9-40 indicates what everybody had left.

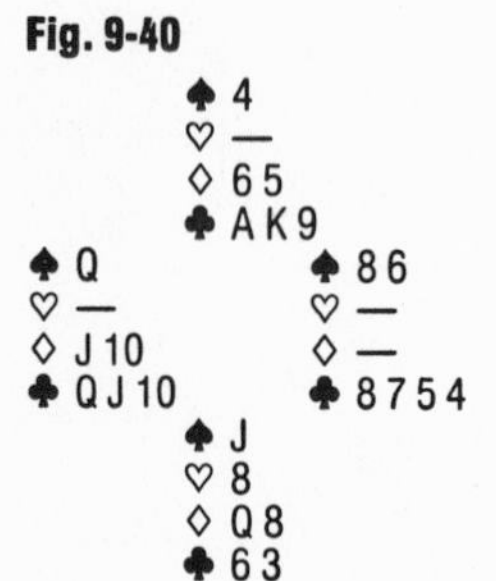

Some might think it a little late for heavy thinking, but late is better than never. It looked like a squeeze or nothing, so declarer led his eight of hearts. Now let's transfer our attention to West. He had been paying attention enough to know that the diamond discard would be disastrous, and all he had to do was look at the dummy to see that a club discard would be disastrous. So, he discarded his queen of spades. With that, the declarer led the jack of spades, and West was again victimized. He had to choose whether to let declarer take the balance of the tricks by discarding a diamond or by discarding a club. What he did was fold up his hand and say, "I give."

Of course, had West known about the jack of spades, he could have saved one trick by discarding the ten of clubs on the eight of hearts. This would give declarer one extra trick, but not two.

Of course, West had to give up that extra 30 points to retain the possibility of defeating the slam hand. The 30 points in this case were not important, but let's look at a hand where the extra trick was very important. It was played by Mike Cappelletti of Alexandria, Virginia, one of the bright stars from the Washington, D.C. area. It also involved getting two tricks out of a triple squeeze where technically only one was available.

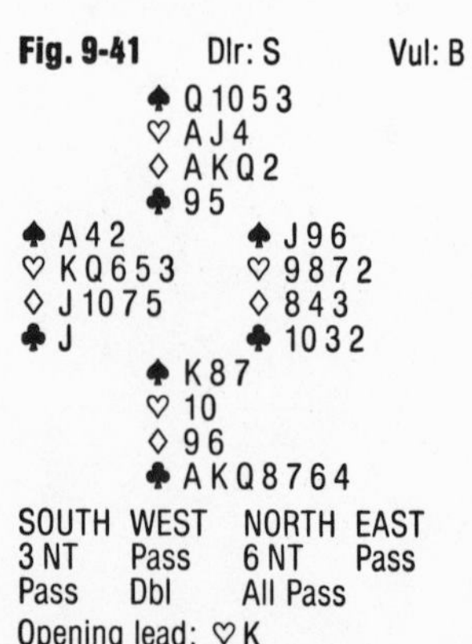

The three no-trump bid by Mike was the "gambling three no-trump" which is made by a player with a long solid minor suit. Some players limit its use to those times when there is a king on the side. I presume that is the understanding Mike and his partner had because his partner went straight to six no-trump, obviously hoping that the side king was in spades and not hearts. West had an immediately establishable heart trick and the ace of spades, and he gave his expression to these proceedings by doubling the six no-trump bid. The king of hearts was duly led and won in the dummy. Now south started the run of clubs. When he led his last club, it was the eighth trick, and everybody had to get down to five cards. Dummy was going to discard, holding four diamonds, the jack of hearts, and the queen of spades. West had to discard first. He also was holding four diamonds, in addition to the queen of hearts and the ace of spades. West was hurting. He knew he couldn't discard his queen of hearts without surrendering a trick, and, as East had discarded three diamonds on the run of clubs, "to give you a count, partner," he knew he couldn't spare a diamond either. Well, at least he couldn't see the king of spades, so he made the only play that gave him a chance to set the hand: He discarded his ace of spades. That was also the discard that gave Mike an extra trick. The queen of spades was discarded from the dummy, and then South led the king of spades, putting West under the hammer again. That extra trick vulnerable was worth 200 points.

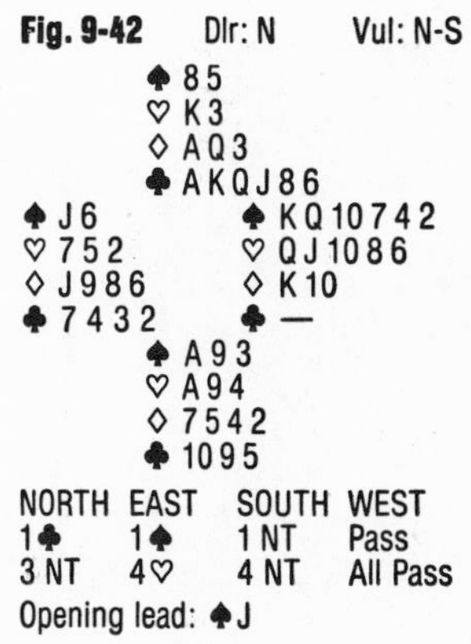

Fig. 9-42 Dlr: N Vul: N-S

Two extra tricks are profitable and enjoyable even though you are not doubled.

West led the jack of spades, and East put up his queen. Declarer saw that taking ten tricks was not going to be any problem. Ten tricks were there for the taking. It was only a matter of extra tricks.

If East had all the high cards his bidding indicated, he might be subject to a repeating squeeze. The squeeze card this time would be in the north hand in the club suit, and the single menaces in the south hand would be in the suits which East had bid, with a single menace in the north hand in the diamond suit. However, holding only ten tricks, he had three losers, and not even a double squeeze was likely to work out when you have three losers. As East obviously intended to continue spades, South just let him hold the trick. Yes, you can rectify the count in triple squeezes, too.

East continued the spade suit, and this time South won the trick. He then cashed dummy's king of hearts and started leading clubs. As two spades and one heart had been played, when he led his last club, it was the ninth trick, and everybody had to get down to four cards. North had his three diamonds and his small heart. East had to get down to four cards from a holding of the high spade, two hearts, and two diamonds. South was in back of him with the nine of spades, two diamonds, and the ace-nine of hearts. There was no escape for East. Although South held only three winners in the last five tricks, he was able to take all five of them because East was subjected to two squeezes in a row.

Now let me show you an amusing one, reported from England, where the defense failed to beat six no-trump although they held two aces:

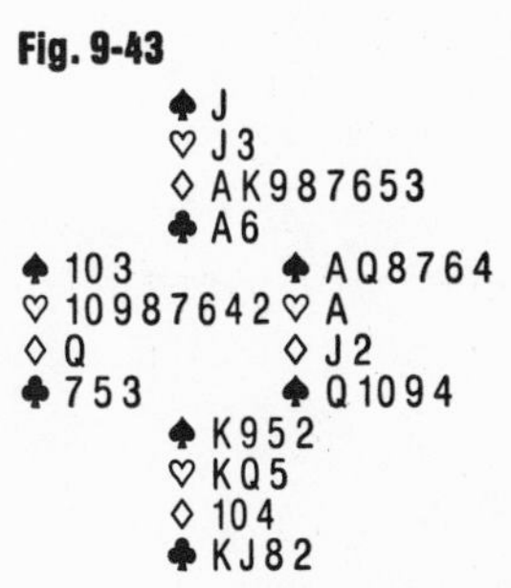

Fig. 9-43

Hand 9-43 is reported by H. G. Freehill in his excellent book, *The Squeeze at Bridge.* He does not give the entire bidding, but states that South played in six no-trump, doubled by East who had overcalled in spades. The hand demonstrates, among other things, that sometimes a little knowledge is worse than no knowledge at all. West had heard something about a double of no-trump asking for a lead through the first suit bid by dummy, but apparently had not heard that when your partner has bid a suit, a double of no-trump demands the lead of that suit. So, West led the queen of diamonds. That suited declarer just fine. At least his opponents weren't going to take the first two tricks. If among his other goodies, East had the queen of clubs, declarer had eleven winners, hence two losers, and a triple squeeze might come off. The first seven diamond tricks left everybody with six cards. East hung onto one spade, one heart, and four clubs. South had exactly the same distribution. When north led the eighth diamond, East decided not to throw away either of his two aces and instead discarded a club. This was a case where he had guards in all three suits, and while the first squeeze would succeed in these conditions if South held threats in all the suits, the second squeeze could never succeed anyway. All South needed now was one trick, so he threw away the king of spades. Then he led the ace of clubs, and when the jack of clubs held the second trick, he had a total of four club tricks, bringing his total up to twelve. He graciously gave East the last trick with the ace of hearts.

Now let's look at one where extended threats took care of the situation, although the position of the menaces didn't follow the classic mold.

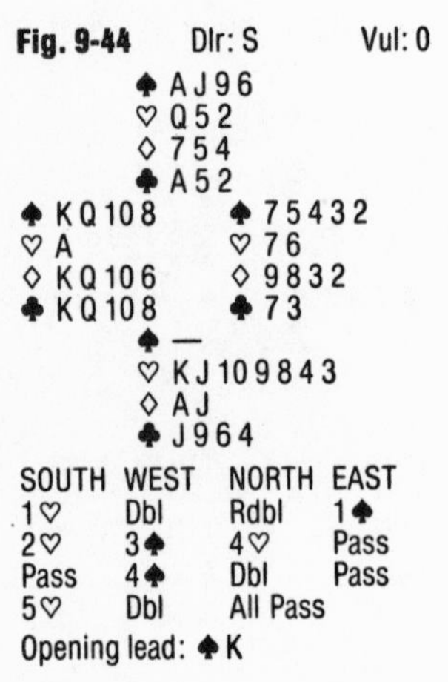
Fig. 9-44 Dlr: S Vul: 0

North: ♠ A J 9 6 / ♡ Q 5 2 / ◊ 7 5 4 / ♣ A 5 2
West: ♠ K Q 10 8 / ♡ A / ◊ K Q 10 6 / ♣ K Q 10 8
East: ♠ 7 5 4 3 2 / ♡ 7 6 / ◊ 9 8 3 2 / ♣ 7 3
South: ♠ — / ♡ K J 10 9 8 4 3 / ◊ A J / ♣ J 9 6 4

SOUTH	WEST	NORTH	EAST
1♡	Dbl	Rdbl	1♠
2♡	3♠	4♡	Pass
Pass	4♠	Dbl	Pass
5♡	Dbl	All Pass	

Opening lead: ♠K

West led the king of spades, and declarer considered his prospects. He had six heart winners and three side aces, making a total of nine. If there was any squeeze to bring home his contract, it had to be a three-suit squeeze, as two additional winners were needed. The possession of nine winners indicated four losers, and somehow that had to be brought down to two losers to rectify the count and make a three-suit squeeze effective.

The bidding indicated that all of the high cards were in West's hand, so declarer went looking for the position of his threats. The spade threat was properly positioned behind the victim, but in diamonds that did not seem to be true. If the squeeze was going to come off, the jack of diamonds was going to have to be a threat, and the long club was going to have to be a threat. Presumably, these were both in front of the intended victim. However, there might be extended threats in both black suits which conceivably could offer a remedy for the misplacement of the threats in the minor suits.

Declarer let the spade run to his hand, trumped it, and then led a trump to see what developed. West won that and switched to the king of clubs. That ace of clubs in the dummy was vital to the declarer, and, besides, letting West win that trick offered him the option of a Bath Coup if he chose to continue clubs. West didn't want any part of a Bath Coup in either black suit, so he tried the king of diamonds.

Declarer won that with the ace and started leading trumps. When he led his last trump, here is the way it looked:

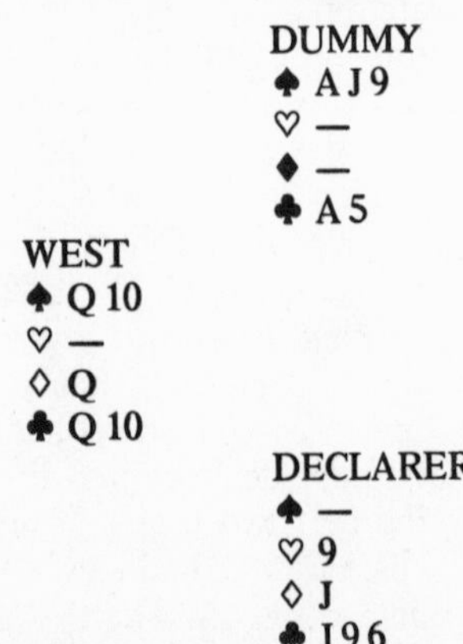
DUMMY: ♠ A J 9 / ♡ — / ♦ — / ♣ A 5
WEST: ♠ Q 10 / ♡ — / ◊ Q / ♣ Q 10
DECLARER: ♠ — / ♡ 9 / ◊ J / ♣ J 9 6

Declarer's nine of trumps was going to take a trick, and that would leave four to be taken. One way or the other, he was going to win all four of them.

If West discarded a spade, the small club would be discarded from the dummy, and all four cards in the dummy would be good. If West discarded a club, then a spade would be discarded from the dummy. Then the dummy would be entered with the ace of clubs and the ace of spades would be cashed, on which the diamond would be discarded and the two clubs in the south hand would be good. If West discarded the queen of diamonds, dummy would discard the nine of spades, and then the lead of the jack of diamonds would be a simple directional split squeeze against West.

As the second squeeze was directional, that squeeze would not have come off had the east and west hands been reversed. The nine of trumps would have squeezed East out of one trick, but he could have discarded a spade and let declarer go ahead and taken his three spade tricks. However, the extra trick would not come in because the entry into South's hand was lacking.

THE DOUBLE SQUEEZE

You might think that, if a triple squeeze refers to a squeeze in three suits, a double squeeze must refer to a squeeze in two suits, but that is not the way it is. The phrase "double squeeze" refers to a squeeze against two *people.* Why the number "three" should refer to suits and the number "two" refer to opponents is not clear, but the expressions are imbedded deep into bridge vocabulary, and it is too late to do anything about it now. Actually, a double squeeze itself is also a squeeze in three suits, except at this time the three suits are not all in one of your opponents' hands. When you have a double squeeze, you have one suit which your left-hand opponent has to guard, another which your right-hand opponent has to guard, and a third which they both have to guard.

The double squeeze resembles the two-suit squeeze more closely than it does the three-suit squeeze. The double squeeze will gain only one trick, not two, and it will only operate when you have one loser. And, like other forms of the squeeze play, it may be necessary to rectify the count. Let's look at an example in Fig. 9-45.

Fig. 9-45

This hand was played by Mr. Edward Hymes, Jr., back in the early days when bidding was bolder, if less scientific, than it is today. Mr. Hymes got to a contract of seven diamonds.

Mr. Hymes was Life Master No. 14 in the American Contract Bridge League, and he made his bold bids pay off by playing them beautifully.

The opening lead was the ten of spades. History does not record the exact order in which he played his cards, but as we do know the ending position, we can pretty well guess how he played. So, let's put ourselves in his place and see how we might go about trying to locate that thirteenth trick.

A quick count shows twelve tricks, leaving us short just one, and the best prospect seems to be a squeeze play for number thirteen. Of course, if the dealer was kind enough to put the queen of spades doubleton in either hand, that problem could be solved but if the dealer didn't do that, maybe we could make the person who has the queen of spades discard it. That would be just as good.

So, we win the first spade trick in the dummy, lead the queen of diamonds, and cash a total of four diamond tricks. On the fourth diamond, we discard the small spade in the dummy. Now we win with dummy's remaining spade and decide that this would be a good time to isolate the menace in the club suit. So, we cash the ace and king of clubs and trump one. This leaves one of the other players with the lone outstanding club and the job of protecting that suit. Next we lead the ace of hearts to get the ending as simple as possible. We have now taken ten tricks, and Fig. 9-46 is the way the remaining cards are divided among the four hands.

Fig. 9-46

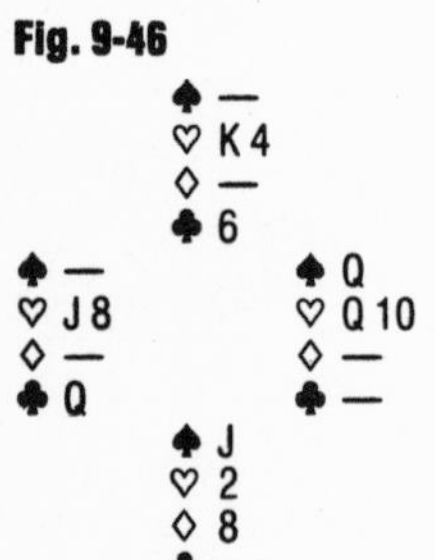

On comes the eight of trumps. West has bothered to count clubs and knows he can't throw away that queen, so he discards the eight of hearts, hoping his partner can protect hearts. His partner does have the queen and ten of hearts and can protect them, but he has an additional burden to bear. He also has the queen of spades. After dummy throws away the six of clubs, which is now useless, East has to decide which way to hand South his contract with the last two tricks. He knows that South holds the jack of spades because West's opening lead had been the ten-spot of that suit, so he throws away a heart. Now dummy's two hearts take the last two tricks, with East discarding the queen of spades at trick thirteen.

Now let's look at that end position a little bit more. It is one of the classic end positions in the double squeeze. The heart suit was the one which threatened both opponents, so let's call it a double threat, not because of the number of cards it holds, but because of the number of opponents it threatens. Likewise, let's call the jack of spades and six of clubs each a single threat, again not because of the cards they hold, but because of the number of people they threaten. The eight of diamonds, of course, was the squeeze card.

For the squeeze to operate, the squeeze card must be opposite the double threat, as it is in this example. In addition, the hand with the squeeze card must have a card in the double threat suit to serve as an entry to it in the opposing hand.

You will have noticed that, as there are three suits which the opponents have to guard, there are also three threats which the declarer must have. Two of these are single threats in that they threaten one opponent only, while the third one is a double threat. No squeeze can work if all three of these threats are in the same hand; there must be two in one hand and one in the other. Whether the hand that has only one threat has one of the single threats or the double threat has a great deal of bearing on the nature of the squeeze. In this hand, South had the single threat in spades, while North had the other single threat in clubs and the double threat in hearts. In those cases where the single threat is in one hand, it must lie behind and not in front of the card which is being threatened, or there will be no squeeze. The hand which has only one single threat is the south hand.

That card is the jack of spades. It does lie behind East. Were it in front of East, there could be no squeeze. Let us reverse the holdings of East and West and see how it would look.

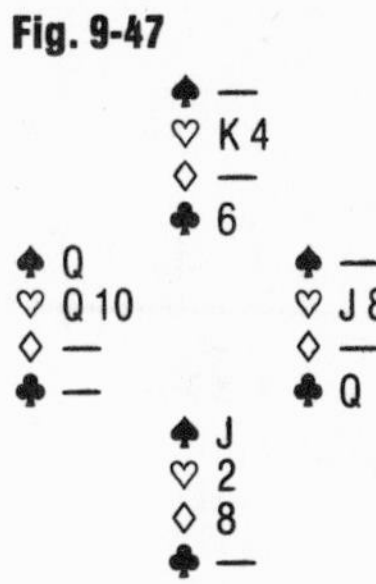

Fig. 9-47

Now when the eight of diamonds was led, West could freely discard his ten of hearts, trusting his partner to protect the suit. North would have to discard before East, and whichever suit he discarded, East would discard from the same suit, and there would be no squeeze.

You will recall that in the simple two-suit squeeze when the two threats are opposite the squeeze card, the squeeze is directional and will work against one player only. There is a similar situation with the double squeeze in that when two different kinds of threats (a double threat and a single threat) are opposite the squeeze card, the squeeze is also directional and will only work when every winner the opponents have is, in effect, 'covered' by a threat. By that it is meant that the threat in each suit must be behind the winner.

When the squeeze card is in the hand with the double threat and the single threat, and the other single threat is out there all by itself, complications arise. However, with the right setup, these complications can be solved. There must be an extended threat consisting of three or more cards, and there must be entries into both hands. If the extended threat has entry cards in both hands, that will suffice. Lacking that, where all of the winners and the extended threat are in one hand, there must be some sort of a "get there" card in the form of another entry back to the opposing hand. Knowledge of this fact saved the declarer from a horrible fate on the next hand (Fig. 9-48).

Fig. 9-48

South opened the bidding with one no-trump. North checked on aces and, with an obvious five diamond tricks, put the hand in a grand slam. West led the ten of diamonds, and the dummy came down. Declarer counted his tricks. There were four in spades, three in hearts, five in diamonds, and the ace of clubs, for a total of thirteen. "Thank you, partner," he said, as he played the ace of diamonds. East decided to throw the jack of hearts to show that he could protect that suit, and suddenly declarer's assumed thirteen tricks had shrunk to twelve. With the misery showing plainly on his face, he went into the library. That cheered his opponents no end.

It was obvious nothing was going to bring home the extra trick unless it was a squeeze, and declarer was studying his prospects on that. Obviously, West could protect diamonds, and East had indicated he could protect hearts. If the entry situation and the position of the menaces were satisfactory, declarer started wondering who then could protect clubs? He finally decided that clubs would have to be protected by the little man who wasn't there.

The heart menace was properly positioned in back of East, and the diamond menace was properly positioned in back of West. After cashing two diamonds, there would be an extended diamond threat left in the north hand. Declarer could then cash three tricks in hearts and four in spades. He did so, and when he cashed the last spade, the situation looked like the example in Fig. 9-49.

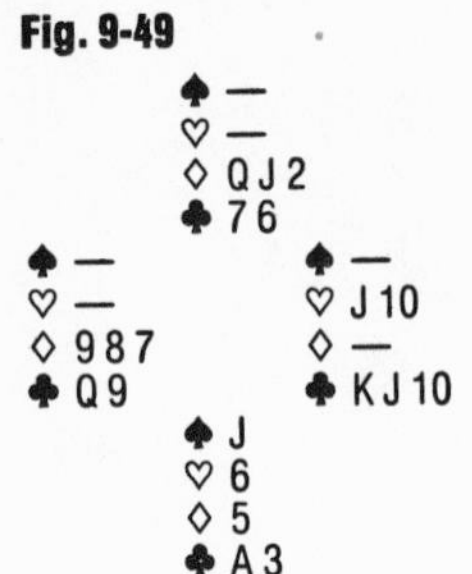

The lead of the jack of spades didn't seem to pain anybody too much. West discarded a club, confident that his partner could handle that situation. Clubs were also discarded by both North and East. Now declarer led a diamond to dummy's jack, and this time East still had no problem; he discarded a heart. But on the lead of the second diamond, the cheerfulness East had displayed over South's indecision disappeared. He was now the one who showed complete misery. He could discard a club and let South's hand win the last two tricks with his two clubs, or he could discard a heart and let South win the last two tricks with the ace of clubs and the six of hearts.

There is another thing we should notice on this hand: West had the third best diamond and had to hold three diamonds, and he had the second best club and had to hold two clubs; he had to hold five cards to avoid being squeezed. East had the highest heart and had to hold only one card there; he had the second best club and had to hold two cards there. So, West had to hold five cards, while East had to hold only three. You have also noticed that West got squeezed before East did. Actually, the lead of the jack of spades squeezed West, and it was two tricks later that East was squeezed. This was because West had to hold two cards more to guard his suits than East had to hold. It is not necessary that both players are squeezed at the same time. It is sometimes called "an interrupted squeeze" when one opponent is squeezed before the other. With such a squeeze, however, it is necessary that there be a threat of more than two cards or that there be entries in each hand.

Successful squeeze plays where the suit which threatens both opponents is in one hand opposite two suits, each of which threatens one opponent, do not occur too often. For such a squeeze to be successful, it is necessary that there be entries into both hands when the squeeze card is played, or that the double threat suit has more than one winner.

Let's follow the play on one where we find a double threat in hearts which has more than one winner, but where the winners are in different hands.

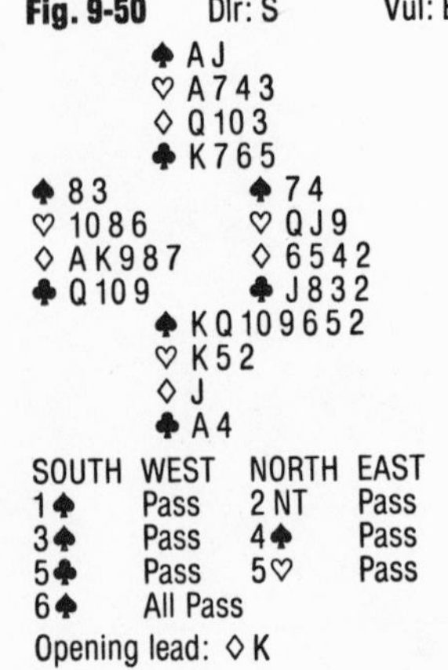

West opened the king of diamonds. When South played the jack, West carefully went over the bidding and decided the chances were that South was not fooling and that he played the jack because he didn't have anymore. West switched to a trump.

Declarer had lost one trick, and it looked like there was another loser in hearts unless some sort of a squeeze could be developed. He knew about one threat already. The queen of diamonds was almost certainly a threat against West. What other threats could be developed? Declarer cashed the two trumps and then thought it might be a good idea to isolate the threat in clubs, so he cashed the ace and king of clubs, in that order, and then trumped a club. It looked very much like the small club was now a threat against East. No threat in two suits against one opponent had appeared, but there seemed to be threats against each opponent in separate suits. How about a threat against both of them in the remaining suit—hearts? That looked possible. If East had to hang onto a club and West had to hang onto a diamond, was it possible nobody could hang onto hearts?

Trumps had been led twice, and declarer had trumped one club, so he now had four trumps left. Prior to leading the squeeze card, he would have to lead three trumps. Did he have three idle cards in the north hand which he could discard? He could spare one diamond and two hearts, making the small heart in his own hand the threat against both opponents. When he finally led his last spade, he would have only three cards in his own hand—his three hearts. Everybody else would have to get down to three cards also. The dummy would be sitting there with two hearts, a diamond, and a club, but would not have to discard until West did. To avoid being squeezed, West would have to hang onto three hearts and one diamond. Obviously he couldn't do that, and, to postpone the inevitable, he would discard a heart, leaving it up to his partner to protect that suit. Now the diamond in the north hand would be worthless, and he could throw that away. Then it would be up to East. East would have to hold a club to keep dummy's clubs from being good, so he also would have to throw a heart and trust his partner to protect the suit. Each opponent would find his partner untrustworthy, as neither would keep the required three hearts. Declarer would now have three hearts in his hand and the ace and a little heart in the north hand to provide the entry back to his hand. A small heart to dummy's ace and the heart back to his king would allow him to take the last three tricks in hearts.

Now let's examine one where the fact that the double threat held two winners made the double squeeze effective (Fig. 9-51).

Fig. 9-51

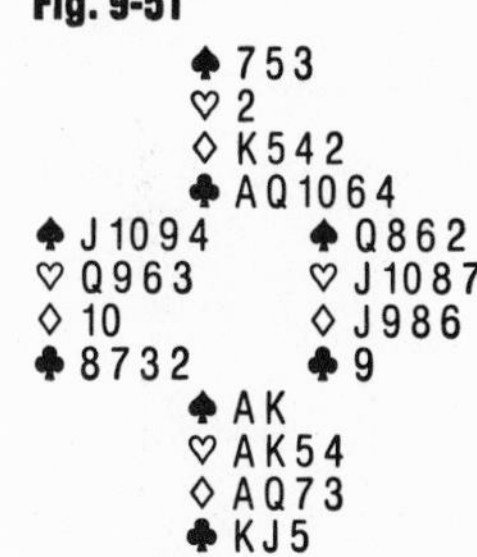

With the diamond suit breaking badly, only twelve tricks are in evidence. The thirteenth, if available, obviously will have to come from a squeeze.

Let's say the contract was seven no-trump and that West led the jack of spades. Declarer sees an easy thirteen tricks if the diamonds break, so he wins the ace of spades, tests diamonds, and finds that they are foul. That was a bad break, but he did have a good break to compensate. Had the opponents led hearts, an important entry to the south hand would have been taken out of the south hand.

So, declarer cashed his other good spade and his three top diamonds and started leading clubs. The fourth club led was the ninth card, and Fig. 9-52 is the way it looked.

Fig. 9-52

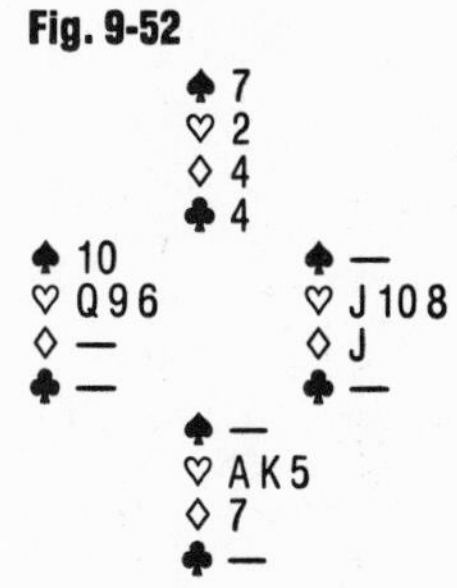

This time the squeeze card is in the north hand. The heart suit is a threat against both opponents, with the seven of spades a threat against West and the four of diamonds a threat against East. This left South with an idle seven of diamonds to discard on the four of clubs. East was not so fortunate. He couldn't let his jack of diamonds go without making the four-spot good in the north hand, and the alternative was to discard a heart. South discarded the seven of diamonds, and West had to either discard his ten of spades and let North's seven of spades be good or discard a heart. With both opponents discarding hearts, all three hearts in the south hand became winners.

Sometimes you will read in the bridge columns or in a bridge book where Mr. Smart Aleck after about three tricks had been played, spread his hand and said, "I claim the balance—East has to guard spades, West has to guard hearts, you both have to guard diamonds, and you can't do it. So on the double squeeze, the rest are mine."

What really happened is that he started an argument. Of course, there are times when you get an early count on the hand and could do this. You can even make up a hand where you could claim all the tricks on a double squeeze at trick one. Suppose you are dealt the following hand and received the lead of any card except a club:

DUMMY
♠ A K Q
♡ 5 4 3 2
◊ 6 5 4 3 2
♣ 3

DECLARER
♠ 3 2
♡ A K Q 6
◊ A K Q
♣ A K Q 2

You could, if you wished, spread the hand and say, "The rest are mine." If one of your opponents challenged this, telling you that you had only twelve tricks, you could give him the appropriate contemptuous look and proceed to explain.

In both of the red suits, you and dummy together have eight cards. If either of those suits breaks 3–2, the small card in that suit will provide the thirteenth trick. If neither breaks 3–2, you can win the balance on an automatic squeeze against one player or a double squeeze against both, depending on whether one player has to guard both suits, or whether the length in the suits is divided between your opponents. You can determine whether the two suits are or are not breaking by leading at the most two cards in each suit.

Let us say that neither suit breaks 3–2 and that the same opponent who holds length in hearts also holds length in diamonds. Now you will plan to keep one diamond in the north hand as a menace, along with a heart to act as an entry to the doubleton heart in the south hand. To be more explicit, you will cash three diamonds and then three clubs. On the clubs, discard a diamond and a heart from the north hand. Then cash exactly two hearts, leaving one in north and two in south. Now lead the A K Q of spades from the dummy. At this point, after you have cashed three diamonds, three clubs, two hearts, and three spades, you will have taken eleven tricks, and here's what is left:

DUMMY
♠ —
♡ 5
◊ 6
♣ --

DECLARER
♠ —
♡ A 6
◊ —
♣ —

That fellow who had length in both of the red suits has not been able to keep two hearts and one diamond, and the rest of the tricks are yours.

But suppose one of your opponents has length in hearts and the other has length in diamonds? Now you intend to keep clubs in your hand as an extended threat against both, while in the north hand you will have your queen of spades as the final squeeze card, a club as an entry to the south hand, a heart, and two diamonds. So you cash three diamonds and three hearts and then go to the dummy and cash three spades, discarding a heart from south on the third spade. You've now cashed nine tricks, and here is what you have left:

DUMMY
♠ —
♡ 5
◇ 6 5
♣ 3

DECLARER
♠ —
♡ —
◇ —
♣ A K Q 2

Neither of your opponents has been able to hold onto four clubs plus a card in the red suit which he has guarded, and the balance of the tricks are yours.

When you do get this hand, I recommend that you go ahead and play it out, instead of claiming at trick one. Taking time out to explain all of this and win any possible argument in addition would certainly take a great deal more time than to simply play the hand out and get on with the game.

I have already come awfully close to presenting material which isn't likely ever to win you any money or points, so I had best just leave further discussion of the double squeezes to some of the fine books which are available on the subject. There are a number of complete volumes on the subject of squeeze plays, and, if you find them fascinating, I recommend you get one of them.

OTHER FORMS OF A SQUEEZE PLAY

On second thought, I probably have gone too far already in giving you material that is not going to be extremely helpful in winning. However, I hope that you, like I, play bridge for pleasure, and I believe you will agree with me that there is no greater thrill in bridge than seeing and bringing off a successful squeeze play. And so that you will be acquainted with some other forms of squeezes and be on the lookout for them should they arise, let me give you some samples.

In my first exhibit, the fourth suit for the squeeze card is nonexistent, and the squeeze card is in one of the hands which has one of the menaces.

Fig. 9-53

South opened the bidding with one diamond, and North, with his 21 high-card points, immediately had visions of grandeur. He contented himself with a response of one heart, and South's rebid of one no-trump cooled his ardor to the extent that he jumped only to six no-trump. It was a good thing he did because when the dummy came down and declarer counted his tricks, he saw that if he took only three club tricks, he had only eleven tricks total. Extra chances were a 3-3 club break and, of course, where nothing else exists, the possibility of a squeeze.

However, it was time to rectify the count. On the assumption that clubs were not going to break, there were two losers, and that had to be reduced to one to make any kind of a squeeze operate. So to West's surprise, he won the first trick with his queen of hearts. Declarer won the second heart lead and cashed four diamonds, throwing away dummy's four of clubs on the last one. You can see what he was up to. He was saving both of dummy's hearts for a possible squeeze, along with all three of dummy's spades. Next he cashed the ace and king of clubs in the dummy, and he had arrived at the position in Fig. 9-54.

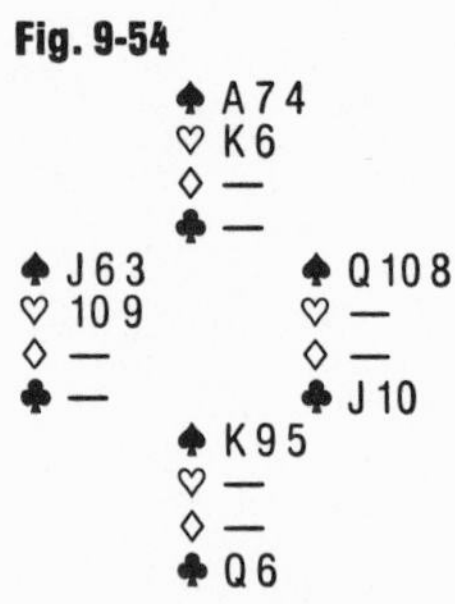

Fig. 9-54

The lead of the king of hearts from the north hand started all the trouble. East could not discard a club, so he discarded a spade. West, of course, followed suit. Now the lead of the four of spades put South on lead, and the lead of the queen of clubs from South put the bind on West. He couldn't discard a heart, so he too had to discard a spade. This made the three remaining spades good for the last three tricks.

Now let's look at one called a "trump squeeze" where the final trump is not led but is reserved to serve the vital function of providing an entry.

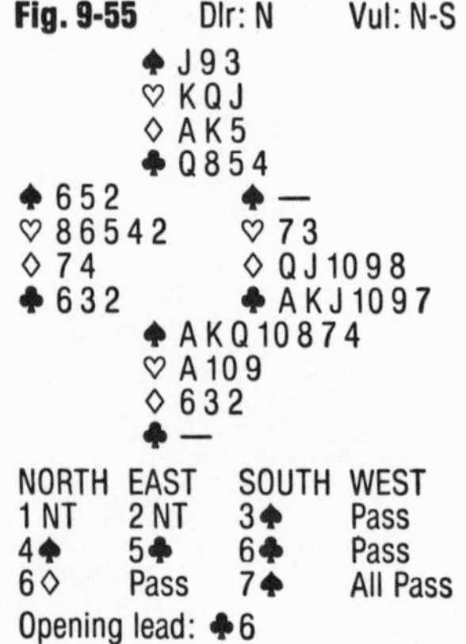

Fig. 9-55 Dlr: N Vul: N-S

After a lot of exciting bidding, South made the final exciting bid of a grand slam. The first trick was in clubs and went six, eight, nine, with South playing the four of spades. Assuming East had all the cards in the minor suits which he had advertised, declarer looked for a way to manage it so that his wealth would embarrass him. Holding the highest club, he would have to hang onto one club at the end, and, with the third highest diamond, he would have to hold onto three of those, making a total of four cards. Declarer could cash seven spade tricks and three heart tricks and make that impossible, but it could not be done in a straightforward manner, as the setup would be a positional squeeze, and the position was wrong. Dummy would have to discard before East.

Due to the power of a trump, it would be possible to discard one of the diamonds from the north hand and make the long diamond in the south hand the menace. Here is how it worked.

After trumping the opening lead, declarer first pulled trumps and then cashed his three hearts, ending in the south hand. When he still had two trumps left, it looked like the example in Fig. 9-56.

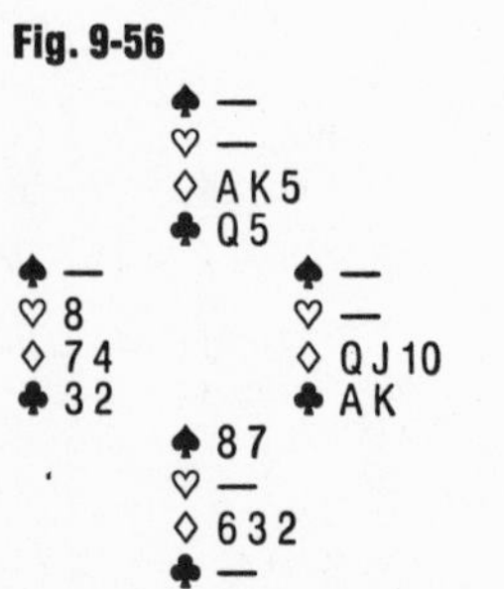

Fig. 9-56

On the lead of the next spade, declarer discarded the five of diamonds from the dummy and not the five of clubs. That made the six of diamonds in his hand the threat, and he had another spade for an entry back if and when needed. If East discarded a diamond, he would simply cash dummy's ace and king of diamonds, making his six good, and return to his hand by trumping the club. On the other hand, if East discarded a club, he would go to the dummy with a diamond, lead the small club, and trump it, making his queen of clubs good. There would be a diamond entry left to return to the dummy to cash the good queen of clubs.

One little tip which is obvious from this hand: for a trump squeeze to work, there must be two entries in the hand opposite the trump suit, so that if it is the long card in the dummy which is to be established by ruffing, you will have one entry to get there and another to get back after that card has been established.

The strip-squeeze is just what it sounds like. First, you strip an opponent of all of his exit cards. At the same time, you make him throw away winners or potential winners to guard another suit. When you get him down to the number of winners you like, you give him the lead, but after cashing his winners, his lead will give you an extra trick. Let's look at one.

Fig. 9-57 Dlr: N Vul: B

North: ♠ K 7 ♡ 6 5 2 ◊ A J 10 4 ♣ K Q 5 4

West: ♠ 10 8 6 5 2 ♡ K ◊ 7 ♣ J 9 7 6 3 2

East: ♠ J 9 ♡ Q J 10 9 7 4 ◊ K Q 9 6 ♣ 8

South: ♠ A Q 4 3 ♡ A 8 3 ◊ 8 5 3 2 ♣ A 10

NORTH	EAST	SOUTH	WEST
1◊	1♡	1♠	Pass
2♣	Pass	3 NT	All Pass

Opening lead: ♡K

West led the king of hearts, and South counted up his tricks. He could find only eight, unless the jack of clubs was singleton or unless he could manufacture another one. He let the king of hearts hold the trick to see what would happen next. He was pleased with what happened next. West couldn't lead another heart because he didn't have another one, so he led a the seven of diamonds. Declarer put in dummy's ten, and the trick was won by East with the queen. East led the queen of hearts. The big question for South was, "Who has the king of diamonds?" If West had that card, there was a natural finesse for the ninth trick, but if West had the king of diamonds, East had made a vulnerable overcall without an ace or a king in his hand. Declarer decided it was more likely that East had the king of diamonds. How nice it would be if East would lead diamonds for him.

To try to accomplish that, he won the heart lead with the ace, leaving a heart in his hand to serve an important purpose later on. Then he cashed the three club tricks and noted with some interest that East discarded one heart and one diamond on these tricks. Next, he took the king of spades, followed by the ace and queen. On the queen of spades, East discarded yet another heart. This left everybody with four cards each. Declarer knew that East didn't have anymore spades or clubs, as he had shown out. East had started with six hearts, and he had played two and discarded two, so he had two hearts left. His other two cards must be diamonds. This meant that East had started with six hearts and four diamonds, so, when West led the seven-spot, he was leading the only one he had. That made it positive that East had the king of diamonds, but by now it didn't make any difference who had it. Declarer led a heart to let East take his two heart tricks, leaving him with nothing to lead but diamonds.

The guard squeeze is where you make one opponent give up a card that is keeping you from finessing his partner, unless he opts to give you a trick by surrendering another card in his hand.

Fig. 9-58

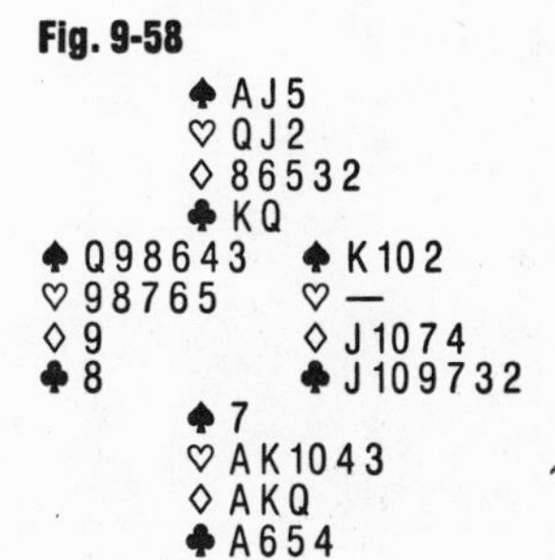

Looking at Fig. 9-58, you see that there are twelve tricks off the top; however, the guard squeeze will give you the thirteenth trick at no-trump, provided West doesn't get off to the opening lead of a spade.

Let's say against a slam contract in no-trump he makes the more likely lead of the nine of hearts.

Win that in the dummy and notice that East discarded a club. Wow! West started with five hearts.

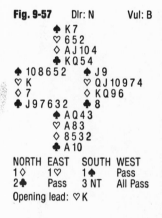

Cash the king and queen of clubs and *wow* again! West shows out of that suit.

Come to your hand with the ace of diamonds, cash the king of diamonds, and now observe your third and last "wow"—West started with a singleton diamond. At least I've made it easy for you to count this hand. West, having started with five hearts, one diamond, and one club, must also have started with six spades. This means that East started with three spades, four diamonds, and six clubs.

There should be a squeeze against East in diamonds and clubs, but where is the entry necessary for that to succeed? How about a three-suit squeeze against East? Yes, that would work, if in addition to his length in diamonds and clubs East has both the king and queen of spades. That does not seem too likely, as he started with only three spades, while West started with six. However, it is likely that East holds either the king or queen, for if West had both of them, he would have been likely to choose the king for his opening lead. So, maybe you can squeeze East between his length in diamonds and clubs and the one high spade he has. If you do that and East has to discard the one high spade he has, obviously you can finesse against West.

So you cash the queen of hearts, cash your other high diamonds, and then start running your hearts. Just before you lead your last heart (you will have played four cards in that suit, three in diamonds, and two in clubs), you hope things are looking something like Fig. 9-59.

Fig. 9-59

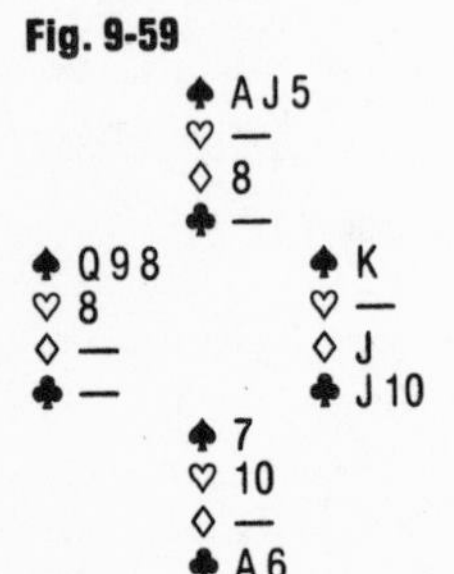

You lead the ten of hearts and discard dummy's five of spades. If East discards a club, you have two club tricks and a spade trick for the last three. If East discards a diamond, you have a club trick, a spade trick, and a diamond trick for the last three. So, let's say he discards his king of spades.

Now you cash your ace of clubs and discard dummy's diamond, and you are able to lead a spade and finesse West out of his queen for the last three tricks.

For my last hand in this chapter on squeeze plays, let me show you one played by Omar Sharif, where he combined a squeeze play with the establishment of a side suit. Doubtless many people think of Sharif as a cinema star, but we bridge players think of him as a bridge player.

Fig. 9-60 Dlr: W Vul: N-S

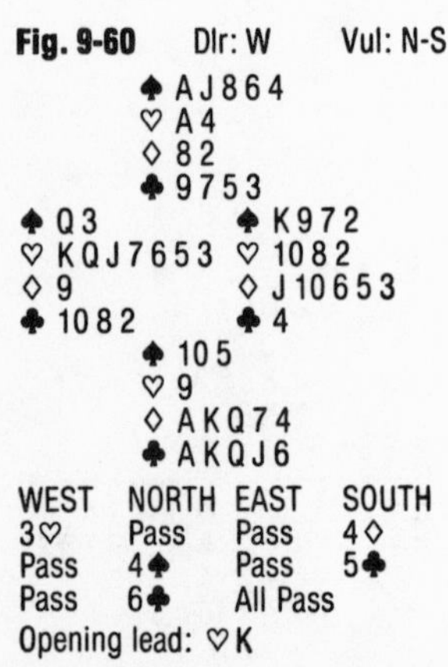

Against the six club contract, the opening lead was the king of hearts. Sharif won this with dummy's ace and promptly led a small heart and trumped it. This turned out to be a very wise move, as we shall soon see.

Sharif then pulled trumps and noted with interest that West was able to follow suit three times. With his opening three heart bid, West had announced great length in that suit, and when he showed up with three clubs as well, it was quite obvious he didn't have many cards in spades and diamonds. Sharif knew now that East had a lot of cards in those two suits.

In the meantime, East had already been squeezed. He followed suit to the first club lead and discarded his last heart on the second one, but on the third one he didn't feel like playing a diamond, after South had announced great length in that suit, so he discarded a spade.

This left Sharif one trump in his hand and one in the dummy.

Now let's put ourselves in his place in the south seat. It looked like West didn't have over about three cards in spades and diamonds combined, and this made it unlikely that the diamond suit would run. It even raised the question of whether it would become established after he had used up dummy's trump to trump one of the diamonds. An alternative play would be to try to establish the spade suit on which one of the diamonds could be discarded. If anybody had length in spades, it just about had to be East and not West. If East still had four spades, spades would have to be led a total of five times to make the fifth one good. By giving up a spade, cashing the ace, trumping a spade, and then reentering the dummy by trumping a diamond, spades could be led a fourth time. But that was not enough if East held four spades. However, East had discarded a spade. It was entirely likely that the lead of the third club had already put the pressure on East.

If East held five or more diamonds, he had to hold onto at least five of them, for if he held only four, Sharif would cash his high diamonds and then establish a fifth diamond by ruffing. In addition to his five diamonds, East had to hold onto four spades to keep that suit from being established by ruffing. That was a total of nine cards. As the third club led by Sharif was the fifth trick played, East cold not hold onto nine cards. Now you see the wisdom of trumping that four of hearts at trick two. This made it possible to take a total of five tricks and still leave a trump in the dummy. That trump was vital if the spade suit was to be established. If he had simply won the ace of hearts, he would have had to lead trump four times to take five tricks, and would have lacked the vital entry into the dummy to get the spade suit established and still have an entry for cashing the good spade.

It was pretty much a cinch that one suit or the other was going to bring in the extra trick. Sharif quit leading trumps. He led a small spade and played small from the dummy. East won that and returned a diamond. Sharif won that with a high diamond and led a second spade to the ace. Now he led a small spade, trumped it, and found that the spades in the dummy were established. He then cashed his two good diamonds and then trumped a diamond with dummy's last trump and threw away the last diamond on what was now dummy's good spade.

I have been talking about squeeze plays, and my next subject is counting, so I have prepared a nice transition hand for you.

Fig. 10-1

	♠ A Q 10 3 ♡ K Q 4 ◇ K Q 5 ♣ 7 4 3	
♠ J 8 7 5 ♡ J 8 6 5 3 ◇ 10 9 ♣ Q 2		♠ 9 2 ♡ 10 ◇ 8 6 4 3 2 ♣ J 10 9 8 6
	♠ K 6 4 ♡ A 9 7 2 ◇ A J 7 ♣ A K 5	

In a contract of six no-trump, West avoided underleading any honor card and led the ten of diamonds. When South took a count of his tricks off the top, he found only eleven. The twelfth trick could come from one of the major suits if either broke 3–3; if the jack of spades would fall after two leads; or if the jack and ten of hearts would be doubleton. Another alternative was a squeeze in those two suits. If either player held length in both, he would have to keep a total of eight cards in those two suits to protect the fourth best card in each. However, it was necessary to rectify the count for such a squeeze to operate because there were two losers. This could be done by conceding a trick in clubs—the suit which was not to be used for the squeeze. So, declarer won the opening diamond lead in the dummy and led a little club and ducked it. East was somewhat surprised to win it with the six-spot, but saw no reason why he should not continue the suit by leading his jack. South won that with the king, while West dropped his queen, so declarer led a third club. West was looking at the dummy and decided it would not be good to discard a spade, so he discarded a heart.

South cashed his other two diamonds, and West again discarded a heart. East, in the meantime, had had no problem following suit. West's two heart discards had become very interesting, and South now led a small heart to dummy's king and followed it with the queen of hearts. Finally, East had to discard, and he threw away a diamond.

Suddenly declarer realized that he had not one way to win the balance of the tricks, but two ways—how nice. Since East had shown up with only one heart, it was a sure thing that West had started with five of them. As he had discarded two and followed suit twice, he had only one left. Therefore, the ace and nine in South's hand were both good for tricks. In addition, West was known to have started with two diamonds and two clubs. When you add these to the five hearts, he was sure to have four spades. So, for a change of pace, instead of winning the last tricks with hearts, declarer took the ace and king of spades and then led a small spade and finessed dummy's ten-spot. On the queen of spades, he discarded his own good nine of hearts, and his ace of hearts won the last trick.

So, we see that in addition to helping with a squeeze play, giving up a trick can sometimes help count the hand. Let's see how declarer improved his odds all the way up to 100 percent by doing that (Fig. 10-2).

The bidding was short and sweet, and West led the king of spades. South saw that his only job was to locate the queen of diamonds. If he could take five diamond tricks, he could take twelve tricks without worrying about it. Also, he could afford to lose one trick, and he could lose it now rather than later, so he let West hold the king of spades. On came the queen of spades; this time East discarded a club, and South won with the ace. So, here was one suit already counted: West had started with seven spades and East with only one. That meant that West started with six unknown cards, and East with twelve. If declarer had gone no further than this, he would have made up his mind that the odds were 12 to 6 or 2 to 1 that East had any specific card, and that this included the queen of diamonds. So, he would first have taken the ace of diamonds and then led a small diamond and finessed against East. South would have been correct. The odds would be 2 to 1. But when there are solid suits around where you can cash a few tricks, it pays to do that first and see what you can learn.

So declarer cashed three club tricks and noted that West discarded a spade on the third one. Next he cashed three heart tricks and noticed that West followed two times and then discarded a spade on the third heart. So, in addition to his seven-card spade suit, West had two hearts and two clubs, and that left him exactly two diamonds. And, if West started with two diamonds, so did East! So, there was not going to be a finesse at all. Instead of the odds being 2 to 1 in favor of the finesse, they had risen to 100 to nothing in favor of playing the ace and then the king.

Here we have learned another thing about counting. Very often the easy way to count is to start counting the cards in the hand of the defender who has the long suit. At trick two, declarer found out that East had only one spade and West had seven. From then on, it was likely to be easier to keep up the side cards in the west hand than in the east. After all, East had twelve cards to count, while West had only six.

I am not by any means suggesting that you count out the distribution in all the hands you play. If you have one which you will make if the finesse works and you will not make if the finesse fails and if there is no other possible play for the hand, just go ahead and take the finesse and forget it. Counting out a hand is arduous and can be tedious and is only to be done when a diagnosis tells you that the information you need is the distribution in the opposing hands. That will not occur too often.

When it does occur, it is more likely to be because you are trying to locate a minor honor, such as a queen or a jack. That is not its exclusive purpose, but it is its most frequent. Even there, it may not be necessary to count out all the suits.

On the next hand, you would want to make mental notes of the distribution as it went along, in case you needed to go back and pick up that information, but when the last few cards came down, that information became absolutely useless when it came to determining who did or did not have the queen of clubs, which was the key card. Let me show you how in Fig. 10-3.

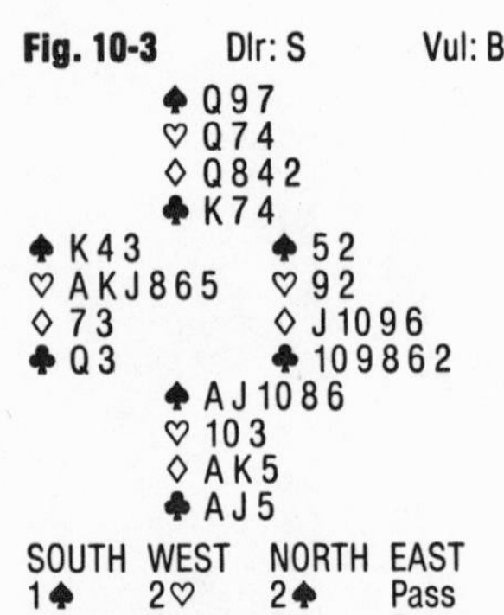

Opening lead: ♡K

West led the king of hearts and, in response to his partner's play of the nine-spot, continued with the ace and a third heart which was ruffed by East and overruffed by South. South made a mental note that the distribution of the heart suit was six in the West hand and two in the East hand. He led a small club to enter the dummy and take the trump finesse. West won with the king of spades and got off lead with a second spade. Declarer was not gathering much information, except that he could not afford to lose a club trick. On the face of it, it looked like the play was to finesse for the queen, but he started to play out the balance of the hand before coming to that decision.

So, he cashed his other two trumps, discarding a small club from the dummy, and again referred to his memory cell, in case it should be needed, the fact that West started with three spades and East with only two. He was now down to five cards, but East was not naive and had not discarded a diamond. He was holding four diamonds and the ten of clubs.

Declarer cashed the ace and king of diamonds, and then went to the dummy with the queen. When West showed out, declarer knew that East had a diamond left. Now he could forget about the distribution of spades and hearts. The fact that East had a diamond left was all that he needed to know.

When he won the queen of diamonds in the dummy there were only two cards left in each hand. Dummy had a diamond and a club, and declarer had in his hand the ace and jack of clubs. When he led a club toward his hand and East followed suit, East had only one card left, and that was a diamond. East could not have the queen of clubs.

Declarer didn't even have to count how many spades, hearts, and diamonds West had started with to know that now he had to play the ace of clubs. Either West was going to play the queen on it, or South was going to go set.

On those hands where you have a two-way finesse for a queen, counting may be the only solution. Sometimes you will have a more difficult task, as you have to count as many suits as you can. In those cases, lead out just as many cards in each of the side suits as you possibly can to find out what is going on.

The defenders won the first two tricks with the ace and jack of spades, and East switched to the queen of hearts. It was easy for the declarer to diagnose his problem. If he could find out who held the queen of clubs, he could bring in the rest of the tricks without loss. He was already guessing that of the eight spades the opponents had, East had started with either five or six, but there was more work to be done.

Declarer won the heart trick in the dummy and promptly led a small heart and trumped it. Next he led the ace of diamonds, then a small diamond to dummy's king. When both opponents followed suit, the diamond suit was counted. East had started with length in spades and two diamonds. Declarer cashed the ace of hearts, discarding a club, and then led dummy's last heart and trumped it. West discarded a small club. As declarer had between his hand and dummy five hearts, the opponents had started with eight, and it was now known that West had had only three of those. That made a second suit counted. In addition to his spade length, East had started with five hearts. Declarer led his last spade and trumped it and noted that West followed suit.

Declarer was now sure about the red suits. How about the spade suit? Could East have overcalled with a four-card suit?

That was possible, but certainly unlikely. Good players do not usually overcall with four-card suits and weak hands, especially when they have five cards in a major suit bid ahead of them. Declarer decided that the odds were overwhelming that East had started with a five-card spade suit, which left him ten cards in the major suits, plus two diamonds, and, as such, he could not hold more than one club. So declarer led a small club to his king and then led toward the ace, putting in dummy's jack for his eleventh trick.

What if all the counting discloses that the queen you are looking for is in the wrong hand when you have only one way to finesse for it? Often there is nothing you can do about it, but, on the other hand, sometimes there is (Fig. 10-5).

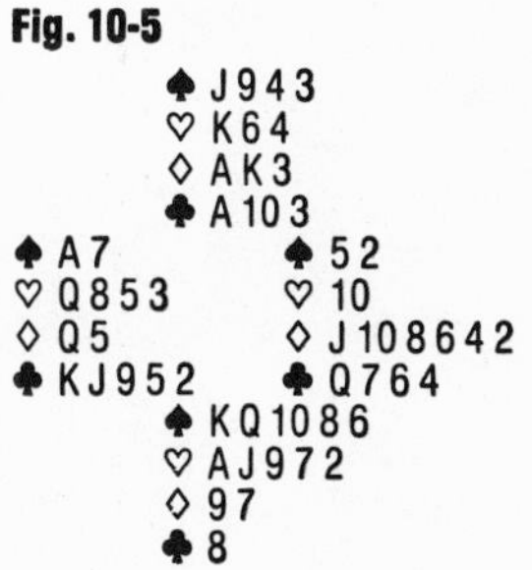

With no adverse bidding, South got to the ambitious contract of six spades. For his opening lead, West chose the five of clubs.

There is more to this counting business than just *how many* cards each of your opponents has. Sometimes there is also the question of *which* cards they have. This lead convinced South that West did not have both the king and queen of clubs, for had he held these two cards against a slam contract, he surely would have led the king. So, he mentally placed at least one of those honors in the east hand. Declarer won that trick with the ace of clubs and led a spade to his king; West won the trick with the ace. West laid down the king of clubs, and South trumped that. One more trump lead revealed the fact that each opponent had started with two spades.

Declarer wanted to see what else he could find out about the club suit, so he led to dummy's ace of diamonds and then led a small club and trumped it. It didn't occur to East to play the queen and muddy the waters, and when he followed suit with the seven-spot, declarer was convinced that he had at least one club left, as he had started with either the king or the queen.

Was there anything to be learned about the diamond suit? He led another diamond to dummy, led dummy's last diamond, trumped it, and noticed that West had started with only two diamonds. He was rather startled to see that East started with six of them, but he started putting together the bits of information he had secured.

East was known to have started with two spades and six diamonds exactly, and was presumed to have started with at least four clubs. That made twelve cards, and he could not have more than one heart. And, unless that was the queen, declarer was doomed.

Or was he? Taking a little deeper look, declarer decided that he had two chances instead of one. If East had the singleton ten of hearts, the rest of the tricks could be brought in without loss because of the holding of the jack and nine in the south hand. So, instead of taking what would be a normal finesse in hearts, declarer played the ace.

My story has a happy ending, as many of my stories do. After the play of the ten-spot from East, declarer was convinced that East had no more hearts, so he led the jack through West for a successful finesse.

Sometimes you have to base your action on inferences rather than known facts. When this occurs, just piece together all of the clues available and you stand a good chance of coming up with the right answer.

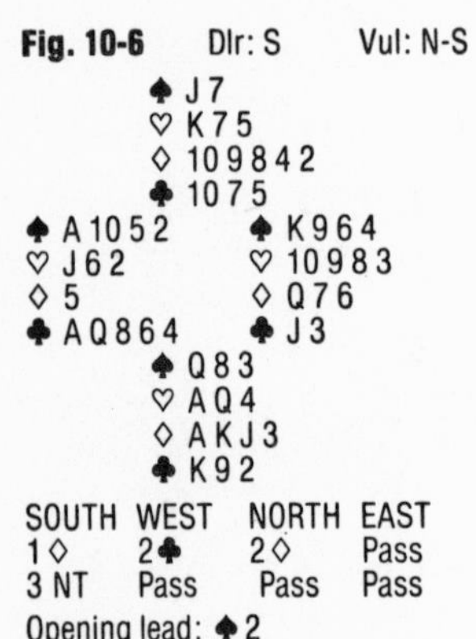

After North gave a single raise in diamonds, South went straight to three no-trump, expecting more in the dummy than appeared.

West led the two of spades, which East won with the king. In spite of the dummy's holding, declarer saw that he had a good chance to bring in nine tricks, provided he could bring in five diamond tricks. So, he decided to exert all of his attention on trying to discover the situation in diamonds.

East gave his return a little thought and finally led the jack of clubs. South played the king, and the trick was won by West with the ace. West then led the queen of clubs and then the eight-spot, letting dummy's ten win. On this last club, East discarded a spade. At this point, declarer had a count on the club suit, but on no others.

He turned his attention to the only suit where any cards had been played—the spade suit. The lead of the two of spades seemed to indicate precisely a four-card suit. Could it have been otherwise? Almost certainly it was not a five-card suit—not only would the lead have been something other than the two-spot, but also West would have overcalled in spades rather than clubs had he held five spades. Could his lead be from a holding less than four cards long? If so, East would have had five or more and would have been likely to continue the suit rather than to switch to clubs.

South decided that all of the evidence pointed to the holding of four spades by West. With the five clubs he was known to hold, that would leave him four cards in the red suits. Declarer led the ten of diamonds, but when East played low, he went up with the king. East had played the six, and West the five, and he'd learned exactly nothing. However, if he could not learn about diamonds, maybe he could learn about hearts. So, he took three heart tricks, ending in the dummy. West followed to all three. Now, if declarer's assumption that West had started with only four red cards was correct, he had played them all, and the queen of diamonds was going to be with East. Having the courage of his convictions, declarer led dummy's two and put in his jack. When that won the trick, he had his five diamond tricks to add to the club and three heart tricks he had already won.

Odds are not much to go on when you are in a grand slam, but if that is all you have, it is at least better than nothing.

Fig. 10-7

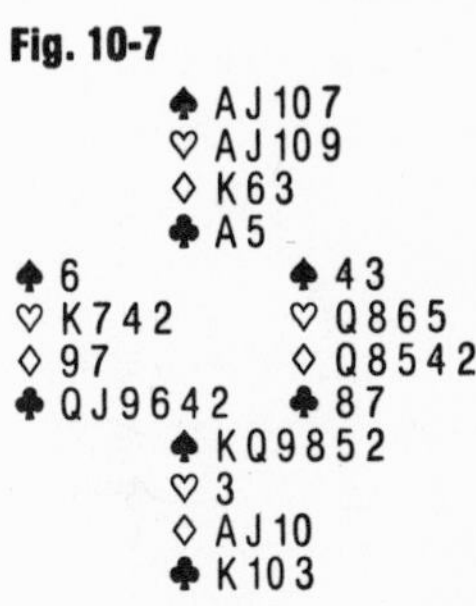

After North opened the bidding with one no-trump, South bid the hand up to seven spades. After the opening lead, he saw he was in a grand slam which probably depended on a finesse in the diamond suit. He decided to find out all he could about the hand before he took that finesse.

The opening lead was the queen of clubs. With the opponents holding eight hearts between them, declarer could find out all about the heart suit by leading the ace and then trumping three of them. To do that, he might need extra entries into the dummy, and so he won the first club trick with his king. The lead of two spades told him the distribution of the trump suit, so he got busy on the hearts. He led the ace of hearts and trumped one. Next he went back to the dummy with the ace of clubs and trumped a second heart. Then he trumped a club into the dummy and discovered that he had the club suit counted. His side started with five clubs, leaving eight for the opponents, and East had shown up with only two. That meant that West had started with six clubs. When declarer led the last heart, he was fascinated to see if West could follow suit. When he trumped this and West did follow suit, he knew that West had started with exactly one spade, four hearts, and six clubs. That left him exactly two diamonds. As his side had started with six diamonds, the opponents had started with seven.

With West starting with two, East had five. This made it 5 to 2 that East had started with the queen of diamonds. Those are scary odds when you have bid a grand slam, but at least it is better than 50–50, and so declarer played the king of diamonds and then took a successful diamond finesse.

It would have served South right for overbidding if West had started with the doubleton queen of diamonds. However, I wouldn't dare have it that way in my demonstration hand because, if I did things like that, not too many people would buy my books. So, at least South lived happily ever after, or at least for a short period of time. As for the defenders, we'd better not talk about how they felt about the whole business.

Fig. 10-8

It is not always the queen that you are trying to locate by counting. In a holding like the spade holding on the next hand (Fig. 10-8), the distribution of the spade suit can become vitally important to a declarer.

South got to a contract of three no-trump, and West opened the queen of clubs. South could count eight tricks off the top, and there were chances for an additional trick in diamonds or spades. However, to get the additional trick in spades, it was vital to declarer to determine the spade distribution. By being an exceedingly patient man, he managed to do it. Getting the information involved giving up the four tricks he could afford to lose at a time convenient to him, so he could get a count on the hands.

East overtook the lead of the queen of clubs with the king, and declarer let him hold the trick. East returned the nine of clubs and again declarer let it go. West overtook with the ten. West then led his jack of clubs, and East discarded a heart. South now had one suit counted. West had started with five clubs; East with two.

Declarer won with his ace, led a small diamond, and put in dummy's ten-spot. East won with the jack and led the queen of hearts. South had lost three tricks and could afford to lose one more, so he let the queen of hearts hold a trick. East persisted in hearts, but now declarer won with dummy's ace. Then he tested diamonds. He led the king and then a small one. When West discarded a club, declarer had a second suit counted. In addition to five clubs, West had started with two diamonds. Next he cashed dummy's ace of hearts and then the king of hearts. Again West discarded a club, this time his last one. Now declarer had all the information he wanted. West had also started with two hearts. It had now been demonstrated that West had started with precisely two hearts, two diamonds, and five clubs. That meant that he had exactly four spades, leaving two in the East hand. So declarer cashed the ace of spades and came back to his hand with the king (in case East had held the jack doubleton). When East did not play the jack, declarer knew he was out of spades, and he also knew exactly where the jack was. He led the four and put in dummy's ten-spot, and his queen of spades took the ninth trick.

When it becomes necessary to count the invisible cards held by the opponents, it sometimes can be done. While these occasions do not occur too often, counting can be a great trick-earner when the do occur. So let's go on another expedition, this time one involving both a king and a ten-spot (Fig. 10-9).

West cashed the two top hearts and then led the queen of clubs. Declarer won in the dummy and took a losing spade finesse. West won this and led his jack of clubs. Declarer won in the dummy and discarded a diamond from his hand instead of his last heart. He saved that heart. He had a job for it to do.

He led dummy's small diamond and finessed the jack. When that held the trick, he was still alive. Then he took two trump tricks and noted that West had started with three trumps. He then led his carefully preserved deuce of hearts and trumped it in the dummy.

The time had come to decide how to play the balance of the diamonds.

There was little doubt that East held the king after the finesse of the jack had succeeded. Declarer had no way of knowing who held the ten-spot. If East had the ten as well as the king, declarer was going to lose a diamond trick. Assuming that West had the ten-spot, there was still a big question to be answered. The opponents now had three diamonds between them. If East's king was now singleton, the proper play was to lead a small diamond from dummy. If West's ten-spot was now singleton, it was necessary to lead the queen of diamonds from the dummy. East would have to cover that to keep it from winning, and West would have to play the ten-spot, making dummy's nine-spot good. So declarer went back over the hand to count.

He had learned quite early that West started with three spades. When he led that carefully preserved small heart to trump and East showed out, he knew that West started with six of the eight outstanding hearts. That came to nine cards, and West had also shown up with two clubs, totaling eleven. West simply could not have started with more than two diamonds, and as one had already been played, he could not have more than one left. So declarer made the only play that would win and led the queen of diamonds from dummy, successfully smothering the ten-spot.

Counting can, at times, be an aid to the other devices which develop tricks: the finesse; suit establishment; squeeze plays; throw-in plays. For my final hand on this subject, I have one that involves a throw-in play and is pretty far out, but I think you will find it fun.

Fig. 10-10

South got to a contract of six spades after East had overcalled in clubs. West led the two of clubs, and that was so obviously a singleton, that South gave no thought to holding up. Furthermore, if spades and hearts both broke normally, it looked like he had thirteen tricks. So he won the ace of clubs and started cashing spades. West discarded a diamond on the second spade, and it was obvious that suit was not going to break normally. Declarer went ahead and cashed dummy's three spades, came to his hand with a heart, and led the jack of spades, discarding a club from the dummy. On the trumps, West discarded three diamonds. Declarer now led a top heart, and, when East discarded a club, he saw that hearts weren't going to break either. Complications had arisen. How was he going to get rid of those two losing clubs in his hand? It was time to do a little counting.

It was East who had four spades, and, therefore, West had started with one. The opening lead indicated West had started with only one club. It was East who showed out on the second heart, so West had started with four hearts. Any way you added it up, that came to a total of seven diamonds that West had been dealt. He had hung onto those four hearts to the jack through thick and thin. How was South going to get rid of those two bad clubs? He could get to the dummy with a diamond to trump a heart and ruff out the last heart West had, but then how could he get back to cash one?

He found a way to let West give him the lead to cash the good hearts in the dummy. He led his last heart and then went over to the dummy by leading a small diamond. He led the ten of hearts, and what did he throw away on it? He threw away his good ace of diamonds. He knew that after West won with the jack of hearts he would have nothing left but diamonds, and that would leave the dummy with a good diamond and a good heart on which to discard those two bad clubs.

11
The Loser-on-Loser Play: The Faithful Servant

WE have been studying those plays which a declarer uses to develop tricks. In addition to those attacking plays, a declarer must have plays which ward off attacks made by the opposition. Loser-on-loser plays make a good transition from one subject to the other because these plays are useful for both.

We have already had a glimpse of some of these loser-on-loser plays, but the subject is worthy of study on its own. The loser-on-loser play is a good servant, because it really does not gain tricks itself. It only serves as an aid to other plays which gain tricks and other techniques which defend declarer against attack. But it can do both jobs, and it frequently can do them well.

LOSER-ON-LOSER PLAYS AND TRUMP CONTROL

Loser-on-loser plays enable the declarer to get the most out of his trumps and thwart the opposition in their attempt to capitalize on their trumps. A loser-on-loser play can keep the opponents from shortening the declarer's trump suit. It can enable the declarer to get in his ruffs. It can prevent the opponents from getting in their ruffs. Let's see some examples.

South got to a contract of four hearts, after West had overcalled in spades. Dummy came down after the opening lead of the king of spades and declarer saw a loser in clubs, another in diamonds, and as many as two in spades, unless he could do something about it. Just to check up on himself, he counted his probable winners. If hearts would behave to suit him, there would be five heart winners, plus one in spades, two in diamonds, and one in clubs, for a total of nine. The obvious way to get rid of one of the losers was to trump a spade in the north hand, and, if he could still take five trump tricks in his hand, that would give him a total of six trump tricks and bring his total up to ten.

Fig. 11-1

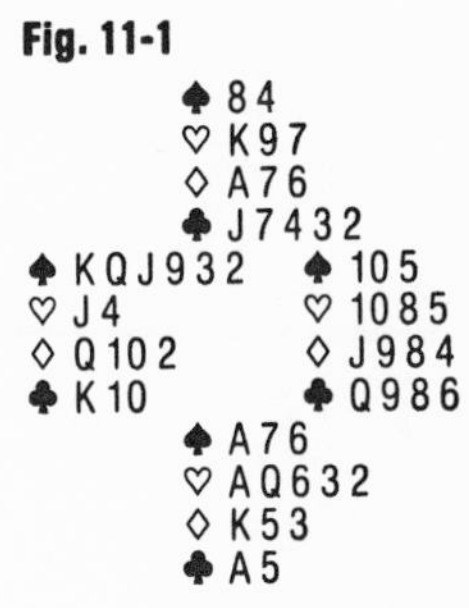

So he won the opening lead with the ace of spades and then promptly led a spade back. East showed his enthusiasm for the whole business by signaling with the ten and then the five-spot. Now when West led the third spade, getting that ruff in the dummy seemed a doubtful proposition. East acted like a man who had trump higher than the nine-spot, and the only ruff that would work would be the king. If declarer ruffed with dummy's king of hearts, then it was likely he would not be able to take five trumps in his hand. The opponents would still have five hearts between them, and, with the king gone, they would have the third and fourth highest trumps. After South won tricks with the ace and queen one of them would be likely to hold a high trump.

So declarer called in his faithful servant—the loser on loser play. If he couldn't trump a spade in the dummy, he probably could transfer that ruff to the diamond suit. He had a sure loser in diamonds anyway, so instead of trumping spades, he discarded one of dummy's diamonds and let the defenders have their second spade trick. Now if they continued the suit, he could ruff in the dummy with the nine spot, and, if East could overtrump the dummy, declarer could overtrump East, and, in addition to declarer's having his trump suit shortened, East would have his shortened. The ace and king of trumps would probably exhaust the trumps from the opponent's hands. West switched to a diamond, but that caused declarer no pain. He won with dummy's ace and cashed the king and ace of hearts, leaving one heart in the dummy. Next he cashed the king of diamonds and trumped a diamond. He came back to his hand with the ace of clubs, extracted the last trump from East, and had his ten tricks. He ended up losing two spades and a club trick, but no diamond tricks.

When it is obvious that the opponents are trying to get a ruff and you have what looks like a probable loser, often the best thing to do is to go ahead and throw away that loser (Fig. 11-2).

Fig. 11-2

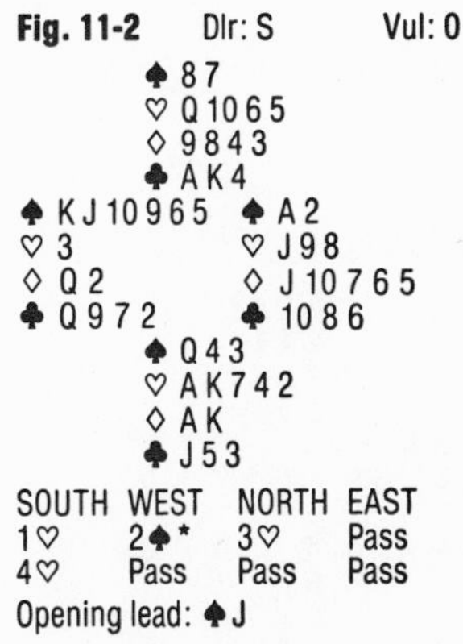

*Preemptive jump overcall.

The opening lead was the jack of spades. East won with the ace and returned a spade, won by West with the nine-spot. The way East had played the spades indicated that South had the queen, so West continued with the king to see what damage he could do.

There were various possibilities for declarer on the hand. He might ruff with dummy's ten of hearts, and, if East overruffed, he still could take ten tricks if he found the queen of clubs doubleton. The simplest chance of all seemed to be not to ruff the third spade, but just to throw away the four of clubs from the north hand. It looked like a probable loser anyway. So declarer wisely decided to "keep it simple" and discarded a small club. After that he had no problems.

See how neatly declarer kept West from getting in his ruff on the next hand.

West led the king of clubs, and East signaled with the nine. West thought he saw a better way to defeat the hand than continuing clubs, so he switched to the two of diamonds. When the jack in the dummy held the trick, it turned out that East did not have the ace of that suit, but West still felt very good about the whole thing. Trumps could not be drawn without giving him the lead, and then a small club to East's ace ought to get by without South's trumping it. Then West could trump a diamond. There might even be a heart trick for a bonus.

South had other ideas. He saw through the plot. Winning the second trick with dummy's jack of diamonds, he led dummy's king of hearts and, instead of trumping it, discarded his club. Now there was no way West could reach his partner's hand for a ruff, and South ended up losing only a trump trick, a heart trick which he did not have to lose, and a club trick. He didn't lose two trump tricks and go set.

The faithful servant can protect you against a bad trump break—and at no cost at all (Fig. 11-4).

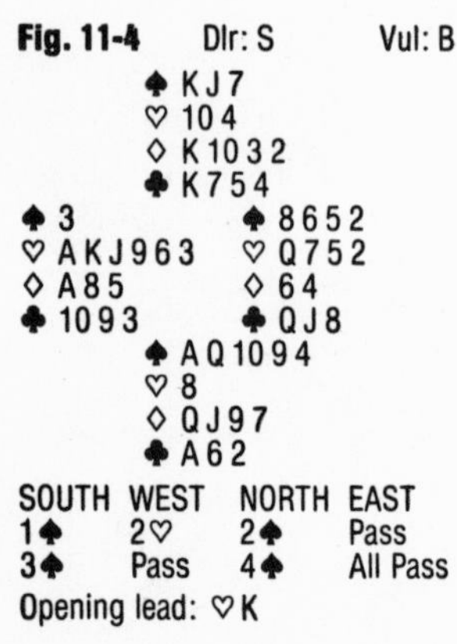

Fig. 11-4 Dlr: S Vul: B
♠ K J 7
♡ 10 4
◇ K 10 3 2
♣ K 7 5 4
♠ 3
♡ A K J 9 6 3
◇ A 8 5
♣ 10 9 3
♠ 8 6 5 2
♡ Q 7 5 2
◇ 6 4
♣ Q J 8
♠ A Q 10 9 4
♡ 8
◇ Q J 9 7
♣ A 6 2
SOUTH WEST NORTH EAST
1♠ 2♡ 2♠ Pass
3♠ Pass 4♠ All Pass
Opening lead: ♡K

West led the king and then the ace of hearts. It looked so easy to trump that, but declarer thought better of it. He still had the ace of diamonds to knock out to bring home his contract, and he well might have to trump again when he gave up a trick to that ace. A 4–1 trump break is not all that rare, and if he had to trump twice with his five-card holding, complications might arise.

That extra club was a sure loser anyway. So, declarer simply decided that he would discard the deuce of clubs on the second heart lead. Now, if West persisted in hearts, the next heart could be trumped in the dummy, and declarer could preserve his five-card length. Now when he got the lead and pulled trumps, he would still have one left to keep the heart suit under control after he surrendered the diamond.

When you get into one of the 4–3 trump fits, you must try very hard to avoid trumping in the hand with the four-card trump holding.

South got to a contract of four spades (Fig. 11-5). There is no doubt that this was his best game contract. West started leading clubs. Declarer saw that he had four good spade tricks plus five good diamond tricks and the ace of hearts, if he could just take them all without being bothered. That meant he could give the defenders there tricks if he wanted to. He wanted to. He didn't care about trumping the third club and shortening his trump. To avoid complications, he just threw away a small heart on the lead of the third club. Once he avoided shortening his trump suit, his ten tricks were there no matter what West led at trick four.

Let's go all the way and see how the declarer can protect himself against a 5–1 trump break, free of charge, with the help of the loser-on-loser play (Fig. 11-6).

South could have loused up my story and made life simple if after his partner's bid of one no-trump he had jumped at once to three no-trump. But that way he would not have scored his 150 honors, and I would not have had my story to tell.

West duly led a heart. When declarer looked at dummy, counted up the points there, and added them to those in his hand, he saw that together with the dummy he held 28 of the 40 high-card points. Unless East was only kidding, he had the rest. So that looked like three diamond losers for sure. Was there any other danger?

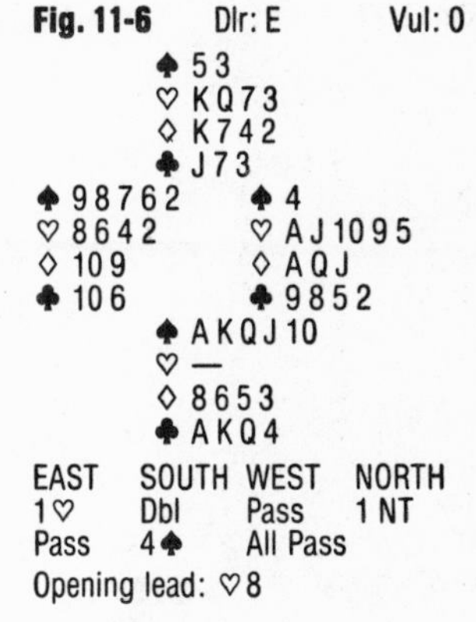

Not much really, but if there was a horrible trump break, declarer knew what to do about it. He put up dummy's queen of hearts, and, when East won the ace, he didn't trump, but just threw away a diamond. Now whatever East led, declarer could pull trumps and get to the dummy with the jack of clubs, discard another diamond on the high heart, and end up losing two diamonds and a heart.

Now let's look at some situations where declarer calls upon his faithful servant to make it possible for him to get his ruffing tricks.

On hand 11-7 the contract was six spades. You don't get hands like the south hand very often, and declarer thought he was entitled to at least the small slam bonus for having been dealt such a hand. West led the king of clubs, feeling he had a reasonable chance to take more than one trick. This was won by the ace, and declarer saw he had some losers in the red suits to dispose of. At tricks two and three, he took the ace and king of hearts and then led a small heart and carefully trumped it with dummy's ten so it could not be overtrumped. East discarded a diamond. Declarer still had a losing heart and a losing diamond, but thought he might see a way to play both of them at the same time.

He returned to his hand with the ace of diamonds and led a fourth heart. West had to play the queen on that one, but declarer did not trump. He discarded the diamond loser from the dummy and managed to get both of his losing cards on one trick. West continued clubs, but South trumped that and then led his remaining diamond and trumped it in the dummy. Then he led a spade to his hand and claimed the balance of the tricks.

On the next hand, declarer decided it was better to trust a normal break than to try for lucky breaks (Fig. 11-8).

If diamonds would break 3–3 and clubs would break 2–2, twelve tricks would be there for the taking. But declarer had bid only to take eleven tricks, and he considered whether he could make the hand with the more normal breaks of diamonds' being 4–2 and clubs' being 3–1. To get diamonds established with that distribution, he would have to trump two diamonds. And if he was going to trump two diamonds, he couldn't pull three rounds of trumps.

If he tried to trump diamonds without pulling trumps, he could trump one of them with a big trump so he couldn't be overruffed, but the three remaining trumps were small, and somebody was almost sure to be able to overruff that and cash a heart.

So declarer decided to call upon the bridge player's faithful servant and see whether he might combine two losers on one trick as a solution for his dilemma. He decided that was a better plan than trying for a diamond finesse of the jack.

So he won the opening lead of the king of hearts with dummy's ace and led the king of diamonds and then a small one. He went straight up with the ace on that, led back a third diamond, and noted that West played the ten. Declarer didn't trump at all, but just played the four of hearts from the dummy. Now he was going to be able to trump one of his diamonds with the king of clubs, getting that suit established, and trump one of his hearts with a small club.

So he ended up losing one trick in spades and another to West's ten of diamonds, but the other eleven were his.

Fig. 11-9

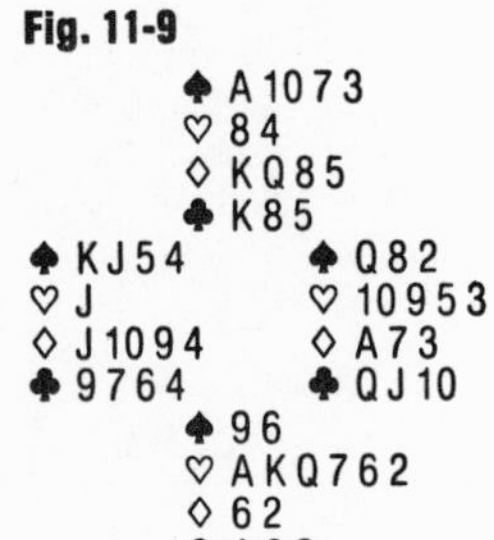

On the next hand (Fig. 11-9), when the declarer discovered he had a trump loser, he also noticed that he had a total of four losers. He had to call for help.

South reached a contract of four hearts and got the opening lead of the jack of diamonds. Dummy's queen lost to the ace, and East returned the queen of clubs. South won this in his own hand with the ace and laid down the ace and king of hearts. South gave the situation a bit of thought. He planned to duck a spade, but decided it would be premature to do that because whoever won the spade would almost certainly take the club entry out of the dummy. So first he cashed dummy's king of diamonds and trumped a diamond. Then he led a small spade and, when West played low, put in his ten-spot. East won with the queen and continued with a second club. This was won in the dummy, and declarer led the fourth diamond.

East was quite uncomfortable about that. He knew that trumping it would get him nowhere—south would simply discard a loser. So he discarded a spade. Declarer trumped that diamond and then laid down the queen of hearts, discarding the seven of spades from the dummy. He went to the dummy with the ace of spades. Here is what everybody had left (Fig. 11-10).

Fig. 11-10

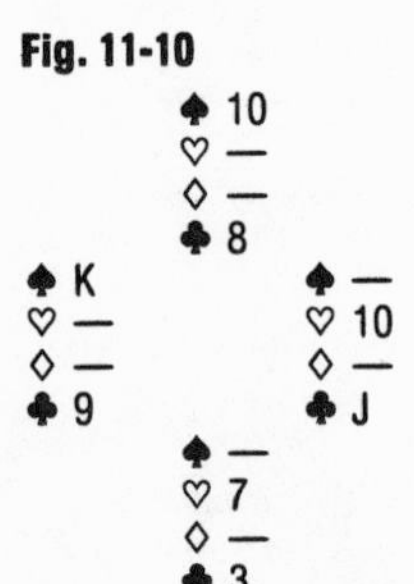

At this point, the defenders had the highest cards remaining in all three suits (there were no diamonds left). They had the highest spade, the highest heart, and the highest club. However, when North led the ten of spades, he was going to get one trick, and that trick would be his tenth. If East trumped it, he would throw away his losing club, and his seven of hearts would take the last trick. So East discarded the jack of clubs instead. South trumped the ten of spades and then let East have the pleasure of trumping his partner's high club on the thirteenth trick.

LOSER-ON-LOSER PLAYS AND SUIT ESTABLISHMENT

Establishing a long suit is another area where the loser-on-loser play can show its worth.

On hand 11-1, when West led the king of spades, declarer saw a loser in spades and one in diamonds, and he didn't feel too good about the king of clubs, in view of West's overcall. Two losers in clubs he could not afford.

He let the king of spades hold the trick and was interested in seeing that West persisted with the queen, although East had played the two on trick one. Winning that trick with the ace, declarer now led a heart to the dummy to be sure that suit was not going to break 4–0. Next, he led the ten of spades from the dummy, and, when East confirmed his opinion that West held the jack by playing his seven-spot, declarer discarded the two of diamonds. West won that with the jack and at this point could have saved one trick by cashing the ace of clubs, but he couldn't bring himself to do that. Instead he led another trump. When both followed suit to that, declarer felt pretty good about the whole thing.

He cashed the ace and king of diamonds, and, when both followed suit, he led a small diamond and trumped it, getting the suit established. He had a trump to go back to the dummy where there were two good diamonds to take care of both of his clubs. West had the dubious pleasure of going to bed with the ace of clubs.

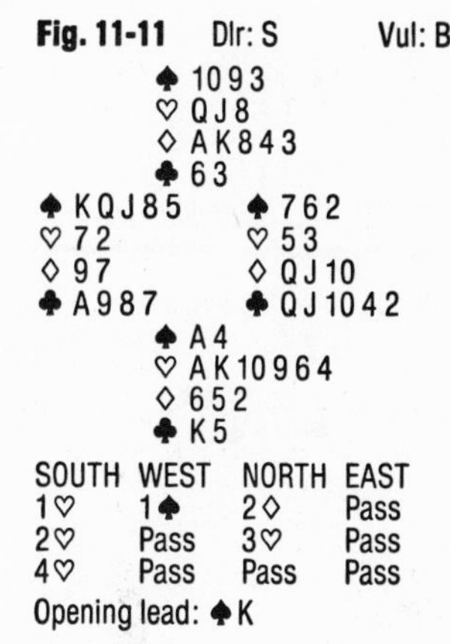

On the next hand (Fig. 11-12), East opened the bidding with one no-trump, but that didn't keep North and South from reaching a contract of four spades.

West led the ten of diamonds, and East cashed two tricks in that suit. He decided there was no future in continuing diamonds and switched to a trump. South cashed two trumps and discovered that East was one of those players who have no reluctance to open one no-trump with a worthless doubleton. He also sensed that East had the king of hearts and that the heart finesse was doomed to failure. He called for help, and here came the ever-ready servant, the loser-on-loser. He led the king of clubs, a small club to the ace, and a third club back toward his hand. When East played the jack, he decided that East still had the queen of clubs left. He had seen 11 high-card points in his hand, and 13 in the dummy, for a total of 24; that left only 16 between both of his opponents. East could not possibly have a one no-trump opening bid unless he held the queen of clubs. So instead of trumping the third club, declarer discarded one of his hearts. The loser-on-loser had now demonstrated how versatile it could be. East had no fewer than three ways to let declarer take the balance of the tricks. It is obvious that the lead of hearts would be a give-up play. The lead of another diamond would allow declarer to discard a heart in his hand while trumping in the dummy. The fifth club could then be established. The lead of a club would allow South to trump, establishing the long club in the dummy for a heart discard, and the dummy was not lacking in entries.

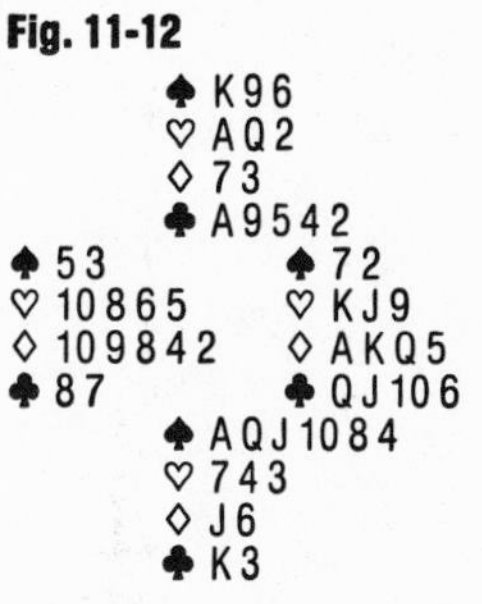

LOSER-ON-LOSER PLAYS AND THROW-INS

It is quite nice to put two losers on one trick at the same time that you give the lead to the opponent who is going to have to concede you an additional trick.

South reached a contract of five diamonds, after West had overcalled in spades. In addition to the sure spade loser, there were a couple of hearts to worry about. It would be most convenient if West would lead hearts—could that be arranged?

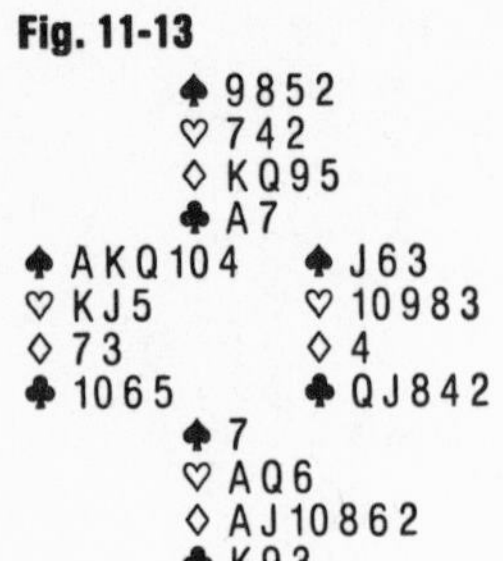

West started off leading two high spades, and South trumped the second one. He then went to the dummy with a diamond to trump a third spade so that, when he got ready to yield the lead, it could not be East who won it. He then cashed one more trump and led the ace and king of clubs. He led a third club and trumped it in the dummy. Then he led dummy's remaining spade, on which East had to discard. South did the same thing. He discarded the six of hearts.

West had had to follow suit all along. He saw for sure that if he led his last spade, dummy would trump, while declarer discarded a second heart, so his only chance was that East held the queen of hearts. His heart lead was as fatal as the spade lead would have been, and South duly racked up eleven tricks, losing only two spades.

On the next hand (Fig. 11-14), things looked simple at first, but when events took a nasty turn, declarer had to call in his faithful servant to extricate him.

When West led the king of spades and South got his look at the dummy, prospects were good. He had one spade loser, and all he had to do to hold his club losers down to two was to trump a club in the dummy. This meant he had to lead clubs before he pulled trump, but that didn't seem to be a problem.

At trick two he changed his mind. After winning the first trick with the king of spades, West switched to a heart! Declarer didn't want trumps pulled, but he guessed that every time the opponents got the lead in clubs, they would lead another trump to keep him from trumping a club.

Well, decided the declarer, there are more ways to kill a cat than choking him on butter. He won the trump lead and then pulled trumps in three leads. Next he laid down the ace and king of diamonds and then, to make things look more spectacular than they were, led the jack of diamonds and overtook it with dummy's queen. Then he led the queen of spades from the dummy, right into the jaws of the ace-jack held by West, but instead of trumping it, he discarded a club. West won with the ace and was left with nothing but black cards. If he led a club, declarer's losses would be limited to one club trick, as his deuce of clubs had been discarded. So West led the jack of spades. South trumped that, led his two of diamonds to dummy's ten-spot, and then led the ten of spades. The nine fell out of the east hand. Declarer was able to discard both the king and jack of clubs and ended up losing only two tricks.

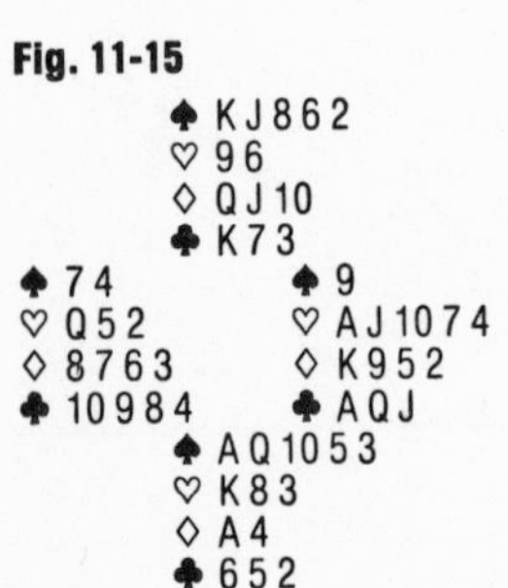

Bidding done by the opponents can be helpful to a declarer. It can alert him not to be careless, if nothing else.

After East opened the bidding at one heart, South arrived at a contract of four spades. West led the two of hearts, which was won by East with the ace. East continued with the jack of hearts, and declarer won with the king. At this time, he had lost one trick and had another possible loser in diamonds and no fewer than three in clubs. However, the fact that East had bid increased the chances that it was he who held the king of diamonds and, if he would play it when declarer led the queen of diamonds for a finesse, declarer could discard one of his clubs on a good diamond in dummy and hold his losses to three tricks. So he set about seeing how that would work out. He cashed the two high trumps and then led his last heart, which he trumped in the dummy. Next he led his queen of diamonds. East knew better than to cover that, and so the dummy won the trick. South then led the jack of diamonds and did everything but push it over toward East, but East wasn't buying. He played low, and declarer's ace won the trick.

At this point, South was overwhelmingly convinced that East held the ace of clubs. Between his hand and the dummy, he could see 23 high-card points, leaving 17 for the opponents. West had played the queen of hearts and should he hold the ace of clubs as well, he would have had 6 of the 17 points, and East would have opened the bidding with 11 high-card points, and nothing to brag about in distribution. Still, declarer thought he saw a way to limit his losses to two more tricks, no matter who had the ace of clubs. He went to the dummy with a trump and led the ten of diamonds. East knew he had to cover that, or else, but South didn't trump it. He merely discarded a club, putting his loser on a loser. Now if East led a red card, declarer was going to discard a second club from his hand, while dummy trumped. Of course, if East led a club instead, that would limit South's losses to one trick in that suit.

LOSER-ON-LOSER PLAY FOR A SQUEEZE

The loser-on-loser has a special affinity for squeeze plays. It is sometimes necessary in squeeze plays to lose a trick or two to "rectify the count," and this makes plays which lose tricks valuable. Bridge is a strange game!

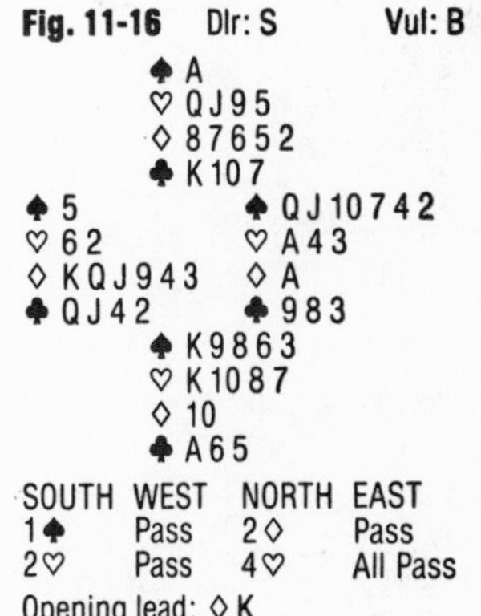

My next hand (Fig. 11-16) was reported by M. Harrison-Gray, who was one of the early stars of Britain both in play and in writing on the game. It was played by a young Polish player by the name of Marius Wlodarczyk who seems to have been living in London at the time. I understand the bridge players of London quickly got on a first name basis with him, and I hope he does not mind if I do the same.

Marius and his partner were playing the Acol system. My son learned to play bridge while a student in Europe, and I played Acol with him for several years. I will say this about the Acol system—if you are going to bid according to their methods, you have to play awfully well. You can see there was nothing timid about the way Marius and his partner arrived at a contract of four hearts.

After the opening lead of the king of diamonds, Marius took a good look at the dummy. There were four quick tricks in the black suits. If he could take all of those and manage to pick up six trump tricks in addition on a crossruff, everything would be fine. East soon blasted that dream. He won the first trick with the ace of diamonds and promptly led back the ace of hearts and a small heart. Now Marius had taken one trump trick, and there is no way known to man to take five trump tricks when only four trumps are left. So his maximum number of trump tricks was five.

He set about taking as many tricks as he could and seeing what he could find out. He won the second trump lead in the dummy and promptly ruffed a diamond. He then went to the dummy with the ace of spades and trumped another diamond with his last trump. Next he led the king of spades, and, when West discarded yet another diamond, he seemed to have the whole story. West would have trumped had he had the trump to keep Marius from taking the discard in the dummy, so it looked like East had the remaining trump.

Marius threw away a diamond on the spade king and considered the situation.

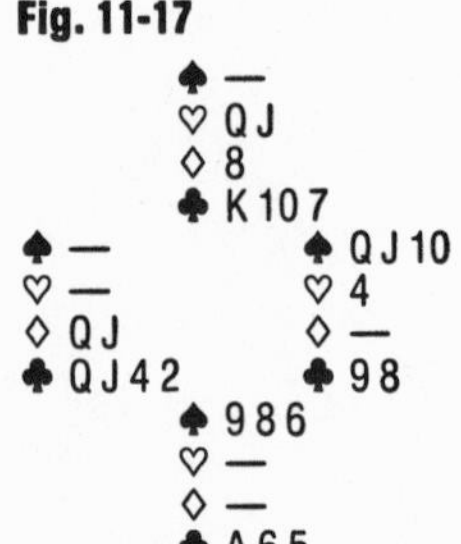

Seven tricks had been played and Fig. 11-17 is what was left. Marius had already lost two tricks to the aces in the red suits. There were six tricks remaining, and, with only four winners, he had two losers. Nevertheless, he could have claimed his contract at this point. Instead he played it out.

He led the six of spades and instead of trumping it, threw off the club from the dummy. With the loser-on-loser play, he got down to where he had only one loser left. That's what you need for a squeeze play. No matter what East played, Marius could now cash one trump and the king of clubs and get everybody down to three cards. When he led the last trump in the north hand, East would have to hang onto a spade to keep the nine of spades from being good and couldn't hold two clubs. West would have to hang onto a diamond and couldn't hold onto two clubs. Fig. 11-18 is the way it looked.

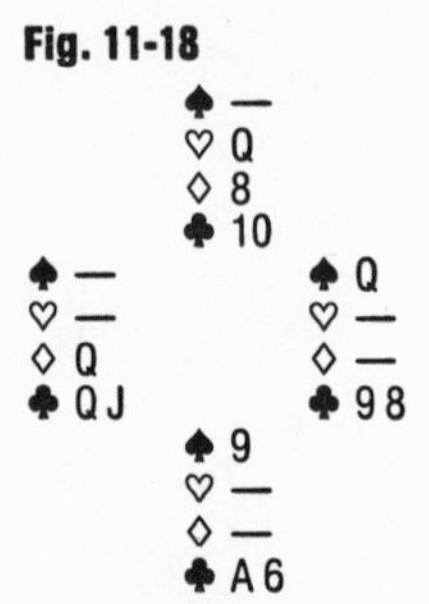

On the lead of the queen of hearts, East couldn't spare the queen of spades, so he threw a club, trusting his partner to protect that suit. Marius now threw away his nine of spades, and it was up to West. He couldn't throw away his diamond and let North's eight take the last trick, so he too had to throw away a club. Marius took the last two tricks with the ace and six of clubs.

LOSER-ON-LOSER PLAYS AND AVOIDANCE

There are times when the declarer is resigned to losing a trick, but when it makes a great deal of difference to him which opponent wins a trick, our friend the loser-on-loser can sometimes help to resolve the problem.

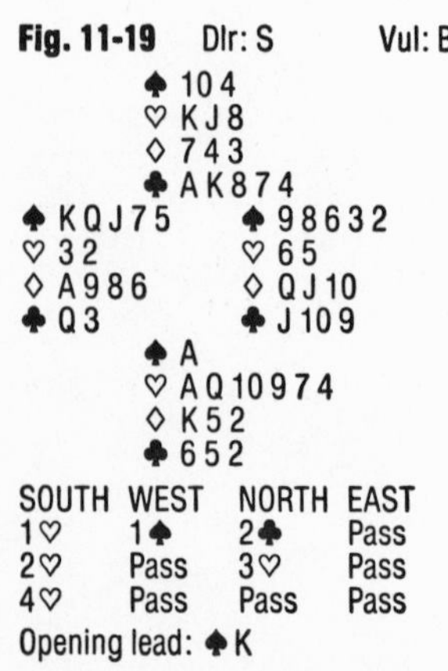

West led the king of spades to the ace in the south hand, and declarer saw what looked like one sure club loser. In view of the vulnerable overcall by West, it seemed likely there would be three diamond losers unless something could be done about it. Well, maybe something could.

Declarer crossed to the dummy with a trump and led the ten of spades. When East could produce nothing better than the three-spot, declarer discarded a club and let West win the trick. He had lost a spade trick which he didn't have to lose, but he wasn't going to lose a club trick. West could see what was about to happen to him, but there wasn't much he could do about it. His actual feeble gesture was to lead a second trump. When East followed to that, it all depended on a normal 3–2 break in the club suit. South cashed the ace and king of clubs and trumped one, and there were two good clubs in the dummy. The heart provided an entry for those, and, on the two clubs, South discarded the two diamonds, taking eleven tricks in all.

Another defensive maneuver where the loser-on-loser play can sometimes save the day is in frustrating the efforts of one opponent to give his partner the lead so that he, himself, can take a trick with a small trump (Fig. 11-20).

Fig. 11-20

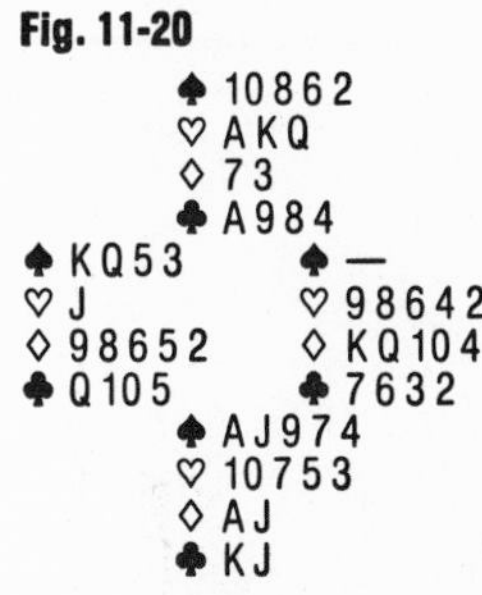

South got into a contract of four spades. When the jack of hearts was led, he gave some thought to the "O" of the C.O.B. procedure. He had the ten of hearts in his own hand, so the jack obviously was not from a sequence. He won that trick in the dummy, and, when he led a spade and East showed out, he was even more convinced that the jack of hearts lead was a singleton and that West, who was holding two sure trump tricks, was trying to get in another trick with one of his small trumps. So a grim struggle ensued between South trying to keep East from getting the lead and West trying to give the lead to East.

Declarer played the nine-spot and let West win with the queen of trumps. A look at the dummy and his hand convinced West that he could not give his partner the lead in clubs, and he decided that East was going to get the lead in diamonds or in nothing. So, at trick three, he led a diamond. East put up the queen, and South won with the ace and had no trouble seeing what was about to happen to him. He didn't know whether the loser-on-loser play was available or not, but he felt that if that servant did not come to his aid, he was doomed. So he led the king of clubs from his hand and then the jack. West covered with the queen, and declarer played the ace and led back the eight of clubs. When East did not cover that, declarer discarded his jack of diamonds. Dummy's eight was now high.

West, on lead, continued with another diamond, anyway, and declarer trumped it. From his hand he led a small spade, offering West his spade now. Whether West took his jack now or later, he could get only one club trick plus his two high spades, but nothing with his small spades.

The next hand was played in a team of four contest. In both rooms, the final contract was four spades by South, but in one room the contract was set three tricks, while in the other room, it was made.

Fig. 11-21

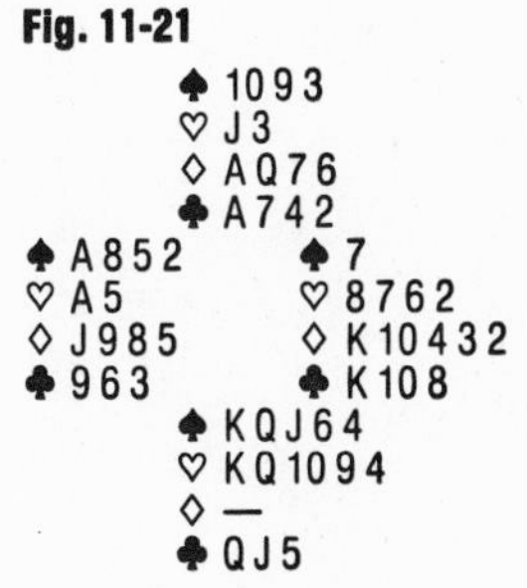

In both rooms, the opening lead was the five of diamonds. The declarer who had the disaster did not see danger and took a "free finesse" of the queen of diamonds, hoping that, should it work, he would be able to discard a small club. It looked as though he might take as many as eleven tricks, provided the club finesse worked, losing only to the two major suit aces. Declarer trumped East's king and did not get his discard. He led a small spade, which was won by dummy's ten-spot, and then returned a spade. East discarded a heart, and West won that and led the jack of diamonds. Probably at about this time, declarer started worrying. It was too late. He won that with the ace and discarded a small club. Then he led spades twice more, at which point nobody had any spades left. On these, East discarded another heart and the eight of clubs.

Now declarer led small to dummy's jack of hearts, which held the trick, but when he returned the heart to his hand, West won with the ace and led a diamond. East overtook that with the ten-spot and led back another diamond. For his last three cards, declarer had held onto two clubs and the king of hearts. East had two clubs and a diamond. West had left his three original clubs. He led a club, and, desperately trying to save something out of the wreckage, declarer played low from the dummy. East won with the king and cashed yet another diamond. The thirteenth trick went to declarer with the ace of clubs.

He had lost the two major suit aces and the club trick, all right, but had not achieved his hopes of losing no tricks in diamonds. Actually, he lost three diamond tricks.

The declarer in the other room decided to protect himself against the not unlikely 4–1 trump break. This is a good thing to do when you have eight trumps and will have to lose the lead several times to get your hand established. To achieve his purpose, he called in the faithful servant, the loser-on-loser play. Instead of playing the queen of diamonds at trick one, he played the six of diamonds, planning to discard two clubs on diamonds —one of them a losing diamond and the other the ace. East won that trick with the ten-spot as South discarded a club, but already the declarer had performed an avoidance play so far as the minor suits were concerned. East could not lead either clubs or diamonds without giving up a trick. At this point, it made no difference which of the major suits he led, as declarer was in full control. Actually, he led a small heart. West won that with the ace and continued diamonds. This time declarer rose with dummy's ace of diamonds and discarded the second club. Now he started leading trumps. West won a trump and continued diamonds, but declarer had no further problems. His heart suit was established for him, and he could trump a diamond and claim the rest of the tricks.

SAFETY plays are made not specifically to gain a particular trick, but rather to try to make sure that the contract will be made, or at least to increase the chances. Frequently their purpose is to limit the loss of tricks when the distribution turns out to be unfavorable. These plays show up in a great many of the techniques of play of the hand. In our section on finessing, we covered quite a few of them. We have also seen them in the use of the trump policeman, in the suit establishment, in throw-in plays, and in loser-on-loser plays. Later on we are going to look at plays called "hold-up plays" and "avoidance plays" which have many of the characteristics of safety plays. While I'm going to show you a few hands where the entire twenty-six cards on your side have to be considered to play the hand with maximum safety, the term "safety play" usually applies to the method of playing the cards in a specific suit.

Usually the play of the cards from a specific suit with the greatest safety depends on four factors:

1. How many of the cards in the particular suit do the opponents have? Of course, the declarer can determine this by seeing how many his hand and dummy have together.
2. Which of the high cards do the opponents have?
3. How are the high cards for declarer's side divided between his hand and the dummy?

4. How many of the cards his side holds in a suit are held in his hand and how many in the dummy?

Within this framework, there are three basic types of safety plays:

Type A. With type A, you are trying to determine which card to lead first from a given suit to have the best chance of having no losers at all in the suit.

Type B. With type B, you have a sure loser in the suit, but you are trying to play the card from the suit in a manner which increases the likelihood that you will lose no more than one trick in the suit. Sometimes you can play the cards in a fashion that will *guarantee* you will lose no more than one trick in the suit.

Type C. With type C, you are buying insurance. You are giving up a trick or tricks, which, with favorable distribution, you might win, to increase the chances that you can limit your losses in that suit to no more tricks than you can afford to lose and still make your contract.

HOW GOOD ARE SAFETY PLAYS?

Type A and B safety plays should be made no matter whether you are in a part-score contract, game, or slam, and regardless of whether you are playing match-point duplicate, international match points, or some form of rubber bridge. With these safety plays, you are simply trying to limit your losses to the inevitable.

Type C is something else again. The literature gives insufficient attention to the use of type C safety plays in part-score situations. You can look in a great many textbooks on the subject before you find even any mention of the part-score situations. Actually, between 35 percent and 40 percent of all hands are played at below game level, and the basic knowledge of bridge would involve knowing just when type C safety plays are appropriate for part-score contracts.

Let me show you an example that will illustrate my point. Let us say that the illustration below is a suit holding in which you have to take four tricks to make your contract.

1. DUMMY
654

DECLARER
A Q J 3 2

If you find this one in your textbook, you will probably see that the recommended play is to play the ace first in case West has the singleton king. Now there is no question but what you will take only three tricks in the suit if you lead small from the dummy and finesse the jack, losing to the singleton king. And, it is also true that if you lay down the ace first and have plenty of entries to the dummy to lead back toward your queen-jack, you will win four tricks in those cases where West started with the singleton king. So this is a true type C safety play—or is it?

You have to measure what you give up against what you gain. West will hold that singleton king less than 3 times out of 100. It is true that you will gain on those three occasions. It is also true that you could have taken five tricks every time East held the king either doubleton or tripleton. That happens nearly 34 times out of 100. With any other distribution of the opposing cards, it makes no difference whether you first take a finesse or whether you first lay down an ace, that is, always assuming that you have all of the entries you need to go about your business. That is quite an assumption, by the way.

But there are still other questions to be answered. In measuring what you give up, it differs depending on whether you are in a part score and international match points, a part-score contract at Chicago, a part-score contract at rubber bridge, a game contract or a slam contract, not to mention the different values of games or slams depending upon vulnerability. So, let's say that we are playing international match points because here we know what a part score is worth. And, say that the contract is one no-trump. If we make an extra trick, we get 120 points; if we make our contract exactly, we get 90 points; if we go set one trick (not vulnerable), we lose 50 points. So, if we go set one trick on a hand we could have made, we have lost the 90 we could have made plus the 50 we lost, for a total of 140.

To get the figures as accurately as possible, let's use a lot of decimal places and see what the net result will be on 100 hands. Here we see the amount you give up when you take the safety play, as compared to the amount you gain by taking the safety play in those 100 hands:

Loss 100 x 30 x .339131 =	1017.39
Gain 100 x 140 x .028261 =	395.64
Net loss from safety play	621.75

Those little 30-point items you give up by failing to get that extra trick will cost you over a thousand points, and the gain you have made by picking up those extra successful tricks in your contracts have given you something less than 400 points. Actually you have lost a little over 6 points per hand by taking this so-called "safety play."

We are talking about international match points, and, of course, these total points should be translated into IMPS. That is not so easy. Plus 120 instead of plus 90 is not always 1 IMP. Neither is plus 90 instead of minus 50 always 4 IMPS. It depends on what happens at the other tables. If somebody goes set 800, it is going to work out differently. But, as a basis of comparison, let us make the assumption that one team always takes the safety play and that the other team does not; that the final contract is always one no-trump, and that the play at both tables is impeccable. This is a lot to assume, but it will give us an indication of the value of the safety play.

So that we can get in a lot of those decimal places, let's figure the gain and loss on the safety play on the basis of 1,000 hands. We will see that in 1,000 hands we give up 1 IMP on 339 hands, for a total of 339 IMPS. We gain 140 points on 28 hands, giving us a gain of 113 IMPS. So, translating this into IMPS, we lose 226 IMPS in 1,000 deals by going for the safety play. Twenty-three IMPS per 100 hand may not be a massive loss, but many a long match has been decided by a smaller margin.

Now let's look at a different situation.

2. DUMMY
♠ A 7 6 5 4
♡ A K
◇ 6 5 4
♣ Q J 5

DECLARER
♠ 3 2
♡ 4 3 2
◇ A K Q 3 2
♣ 4 3 2

Again you are in a contract of one no-trump, and this time you have received the opening lead of the queen of hearts. You have six tricks in aces, kings, and queens and need one more. It seems unlikely you are going to be able to scramble any more tricks out of spades, hearts, or clubs before the defenders can take enough tricks to set you. By all odds your best chance is to get an extra diamond trick. This will materialize unless the diamonds are 5–0. You win the ace of hearts and then lay down the ace of diamonds to test them. When both opponents follow suit, they are going to break no worse than 4–1. If you wish to take the safety play, you must now lead a small diamond so that you will have one left in the dummy for an entry back into your hand. Nearly 68 percent of the time the diamonds will break 3–2, and the safety play will be unnecessary. Again you are playing IMPS. Do you take the safety play?

This time the odds favor the safety play decisively. The 4–1 break occurs 28.26 percent of the time—just exactly ten times as often as those occasions on which you will find the singleton king in a specific hand when your opponents hold five cards of the suit.

Let's assume in a team of four contest that one team takes all of these safety plays and the other team takes none. The player who takes the safety play will gain 4 IMPS every time the suit breaks 4–1. He will give up 1 IMP every time the suit breaks 3–2. here is how he does it.

Gain 1000 x .2826 x 4 =	1130
Loss 1000 x .6783 x 1 =	678
Net IMP gain from safety play	452

In 1,000 deals, he will pick up 452 IMPS, or better than 45 IMPS in 100 chances.

Obviously, when you get up to game contracts and even slam contracts, the amount you gain by safety precaution becomes greater, and the need for them increases. But when you are protecting yourself against a distribution which is extremely infrequent, you probably should not take the safety play; as long as you are in a part score and even at game contracts, the safety play becomes of little value. This, of course, is assuming that you have the requisite entries so that you can take the safety play.*

I am not making an attempt to give an example of every possible holding which might call for a safety play. To do so, even if it could be accomplished, would be to take up many more pages than that subject deserves. I will try to give examples of the most frequent ones. I find that by studying the reason for each of these, I find it easier to remember when I meet them in actual play. I have arranged them according to the number of cards held by your opponents in the suit in question and have indicated in each case whether it is a Type A safety play (where you are trying to avoid the loss of any tricks), a Type B (where you must lose one or more tricks, but are trying to limit your losses), or Type C (where you are giving up tricks to attempt to avoid losing a larger number of tricks).

YOUR SIDE HOLDS 7; THEY HOLD 6

1. DUMMY	2. DUMMY
5 4 3	Q 4 3
DECLARER	DECLARER
A K J 2	A J 10 2

1. (Type C.) In these illustrations we are going to assume that you have adequate side suit entries to lead toward whichever hand pleases you and that you have adequate stoppers in other suits so that you can afford to give up a trick without losing control. Where these conditions do not exist, it may be that you cannot afford the safety play.

In many, if not most, of these type C safety plays, the procedures you adopt will depend on the number of tricks you have to have. If you simply must have four tricks from this suit, you are going to have to find the queen three long in the east hand. I hate to tell you, but on eleven tries for this, you should succeed only two times. If you are in your hand, you might lay down the ace first (in case the queen falls singleton). This will not get you a fourth trick, but it will enable you to keep control of the hand and possibly limit your losses. However, if you are in the dummy and entries are a problem, you might as well go ahead and take a first-round finesse of the jack.

If three tricks will satisfy your needs and you can afford to lose one, your best play is to lay down the ace and king in your hand, then go to the dummy and lead up toward the jack. This will give you the third trick whenever East has the queen, no matter how many he has; whenever the suit breaks 3–3, no matter where the queen is, and whenever West has the queen singleton or doubleton. It is obvious that this safety play should be taken in all forms of bridge, with the possible exception of match-point duplicate.

How about it when you are playing match-point duplicate? I don't think you would want to take the safety play. The safety play will bring you

*For a detailed discussion of the mathematics of safety plays, see Appendix B.

in three tricks or more 77 percent of the time. Leading a top one and then going to the dummy and taking the finesse will bring you in three or more tricks every time East has the queen, regardless of the number he has, plus those times when West has a singleton queen, and that comes to a bit more than 51 percent of the time. The field is almost surely going to go for the finesse. Unless you are in an exceptionally fine contract, which you do not expect the field to reach, or unless the safety play offers twice as good a chance for the contract to succeed as would the normal finesse, it is best to go along with the field.

2. (Type A) With the nine-spot in either hand, you would have that broken sequence that justifies leading high from the dummy. You don't have the nine-spot. The proper play is to lead low from the dummy and take the finesse. If it succeeds, return to the dummy and again lead low to finesse. This will bring in four tricks whenever East started with the king and not more than three cards in the suit. Generally, these type A safety plays should be taken no matter what kind of bridge you are playing—even at match-point duplicate.

3. DUMMY	4. DUMMY
3 2	5 4
DECLARER	DECLARER
A K J 10 9	A K Q 3 2

3. (Type A) Here, the fact that you have only two cards in the dummy determines the safest way to play the suit for all tricks. When there are three in the dummy, the safety play is to lay down the ace, and there will still be two cards left in the dummy for finessing, if necessary. With only two cards in the dummy, if you take the ace first, there will be only one finesse. Laying down the ace first wins when West has the singleton queen and loses when East has Q x x x. Taking a first-round finesse wins when East has Q x x x, but loses when West has the singleton queen. Four to the queen in East will occur more frequently than the singleton queen with West.

4. (Type C) Giving up a trick to increase your chances of taking four is essential when you have no extra entries into your own hand. This is an exceptional case where the safety play should be made even if you are playing match-point duplicate.

5. DUMMY	6. DUMMY
9 3	K 10
DECLARER	DECLARER
A K Q 10 2	A 9 7 6 5

5. (Type C) The nine and ten are the key cards here. If you can settle for only four tricks, lead the nine from the dummy and let it ride if it isn't covered. You still may take five tricks. If you are in your hand and short of entries to dummy, you still can make sure of four tricks by leading low toward the nine-spot.

6. (Type B) With the eight-spot in the south hand instead of the seven, you could bring in all five tricks if the queen-jack were doubleton in either hand. As it is, proper defense will keep you from bringing in five tricks. To increase your chances to take four tricks, lead small from your hand and put in dummy's ten-spot. You will then take four tricks whenever West started with four to the queen-jack, a doubleton honor, or any 3–3 split. On those days when West has the Q J x and fails to split his honors, you will do even better.

7. DUMMY	8. DUMMY
none	A
DECLARER	DECLARER
K Q 8 5 4 3 2	J 10 5 4 3 2

7. (Type B) When you lead this suit yourself, the most favorable distribution will give your opponents two tricks and you five. With bad distribution, you could get as few as three tricks, conceivably only two. The best chance to get four tricks is to make your initial lead a small one and not a high one, catering to the singleton ace. When you recover the lead, lead a high one. On those occasions where the opponents' cards are split 3–3, this will bring you five tricks. It will bring you four tricks when the opposing cards split 4–2.

8. (Type B) After taking dummy's ace and returning to your hand, lead a small one in case there is a doubleton honor.

YOUR SIDE HOLDS 8; THEY HOLD 5

1. DUMMY	2. DUMMY
7 6	10 5
DECLARER	DECLARER
A K Q 4 3 2	A K Q 8 4 3

1. (Type C) If you just bang down the A K Q, you will take six tricks about 68 percent of the time. This is exactly what you should do when playing match-point duplicate. Let us assume you have no other entries into your hand and you would like to increase your chances of taking five tricks in the suit up to better than 90 percent. With the dummy's having two cards, you have no time to explore without using up entries back into your hand. The play is to play small from both hands, that will allow you to take your five tricks whenever you have a 4–1 break.

2. (Type C) The ten-spot in the dummy and the eight in your hand are key cards here. By leading low toward the dummy, you can be assured of five tricks if either of your opponents has all five of the outstanding cards. This assumes you will have an entry into the dummy so you can finesse the nine-spot in the east hand, if it should be East who has all five outstanding cards.

3. DUMMY	4. DUMMY
J 4 3	J 4 3
DECLARER	DECLARER
A K Q 9 2	A K Q 8 2

3. (Type A) The nine-spot in your hand is the key card. Lead low toward dummy's jack, and, even on those rare occasions where East holds all five of the outstanding cards, you will have a natural finesse against him to take all five tricks. You won't run into this wild distribution very often, but as the insurance against it is free, why not take it?

4. (Type A) Here the eight-spot in your hand is the key card. By leading low toward the jack, you can still take all five tricks if East holds all five outstanding cards, assuming dummy has another entry. Three cards in the dummy give you more flexibility than when there are only two. Because you are in a position to win one trick and still have two cards left for the double finesse against the ten-nine in the east hand, it works.

5. DUMMY	6. DUMMY
K 6 5	A Q 6
DECLARER	DECLARER
A 10 4 3 2	10 5 4 3 2

5. (Type B) This safety play arises in this classic situation after you have won a trick in the short hand with the king, have led back toward the long hand (the ace and ten), and East has followed suit with a small card. To be sure you lose only one trick and take four, put in the ten-spot. Should that lose to an honor with West, there will be only one card outstanding, and your ace will pick it up.

6. (Type C) This is the first of several examples where you have the A Q 10 divided between the two hands and wish to make sure you lose no more than two tricks in the suit. This safety play is recommended only for pessimists. Optimists will try to take five tricks in the suit, hoping the king-jack is doubleton in the west hand. The play to limit your losses to two tricks is always to cash the ace and lead toward the remaining honor in the short hand. This obviously implies sufficient entries. The play is not recommended for match-point duplicate.

7. DUMMY	8. DUMMY
A Q 6 5 4	A 10 6
DECLARER	DECLARER
10 3 2	Q 5 4 3 2

7, 8. (Type C) These are both variations of illustration 6. In 7, you first cash the ace and lead low toward the ten. With 8, you cash the ace in the dummy, come back to your own hand, and again lead toward the ten.

9. DUMMY	10. DUMMY
A 10 6 5	A Q 6 5
DECLARER	DECLARER
Q 4 3 2	10 4 3 2

9, 10. (Type C) These are both examples of where there is no short hand and you want to be sure to take at least two tricks. You can achieve this by leading the ace; if both opponents follow with small cards, you can, at the next trick, lead from either hand.

11. DUMMY	12. DUMMY
J 5 4	J 10 5
DECLARER	DECLARER
A K 9 3 2	A K 4 3 2

11. (Type C) Those three cards in the dummy make it possible again to lay down the ace first in case someone has a singleton queen. If both follow suit, you can then make sure of taking four tricks by leading low toward the jack. The nine-spot in the south hand is the key card, making it possible to finesse in those cases where East holds any four.

12. (Type C) Here we have removed that key card of the nine-spot from the south hand, but we have buttressed the north hand with the ten-spot. Now with two key cards in the three-card holding, you can't afford the luxury of laying down the ace. Lead low toward the jack, and you will take four tricks if West has all of the five outstanding cards.

13. DUMMY	14. DUMMY
K 9 5	K J 5
DECLARER	DECLARER
A J 4 3 2	A 9 4 3 2

13. (Type C) Many years ago I had a mentor who thought I could learn better if I had little verses to aid my memory. It must have worked, because I still remember that one of them ended "it is safe to bare the knave." This brings back mental pictures of the jack of spades streaking and always alerts me when the bare-the-knave safety play comes up. This applies when your side holds the ace-king of a suit, split between the two hands, and the jack-nine, split between the two hands, and the eight cards held are divided 5–3 or 4–4. The play for four tricks which protects you against any 4–1 split is first to cash the high cards in the hand which has the jack (leaving him "bare"). Then, you lead toward the short hand. In 13, if both follow suit when you cash the ace, lead low and, if West plays low, put in the nine-spot.

14. (Type C) Here the play is to first cash the king and then come back to your hand in some other suit and lead toward the jack.

15. DUMMY	16. DUMMY
K J 5 4	7 6 5 4
DECLARER	DECLARER
A 9 3 2	A Q 3 2

15. (Type C) Where there are four cards in each hand, first cash the high card with the jack and then lead low toward the other high card and the nine. If East follows low, put in the nine-spot. Of course, if East follows

with the queen or ten, you can play the ace and be assured of another trick.

16. (Type B) Here you have eight cards, but, in addition to missing the king, you lack all the cards between the seven and queen. No matter how the opponents' cards are divided, you are going to lose at least one trick. The best way to try to lose no more is to first play the ace and then go to the dummy and lead up toward the queen. Should East play low on this, play low. If West started with the king doubleton, he will have to play it. If East started with four and has ducked with the king, you can get your queen later on by going back to the dummy and leading up to it again.

17. DUMMY	18. DUMMY
J 6 5 4	Q 8 4
DECLARER	DECLARER
A 10 3 2	A K 9 3 2

17. (Type B) If you need three tricks from this holding, your best bet is to lead low from the dummy. If East does not play an honor, put in the ten-spot, hoping that East started with the doubleton king or queen. However, should it turn out that West has the singleton king or queen, you will end up taking exactly one trick. To be sure of two tricks, play the ace first, then lead low. No matter how the opposing cards are divided, you will always get two tricks, assuming you have plenty of entries to lead from the hand of your choice.

18. (Type C) the key cards here are the eight and nine. You can always get four tricks with this combination by leading small from either hand, planning to play the eight or nine if second hand plays low. If the second hand shows out, go up with an honor and then lead toward the eight or nine in the other hand.

19. DUMMY	20. DUMMY
A 5 4	A 5 4
DECLARER	DECLARER
K Q 10 3 2	K Q 9 3 2

19. (Type A) We have seen hands similar to these two in our study of finesses. In 19, the key card is the ten-spot. It enables you to protect yourself against four to the jack in the east hand. Just be sure you don't leave it "bare" by cashing the king and queen of the suit first. You must cash the king and ace, leaving the queen-ten over the possible jack. If you have plenty of entries, it doesn't make any difference which you cash first, but the neat way and proper way when you don't have a surplus of entries is to first cash the card in the hand with two honors and next take the trick in the hand with one honor. The ace, king, and queen all being equal, you could put any one of the three in the north hand, leaving the other in the south hand, and still make the safety play effectively.

20. (Type A) Here the key card is the nine-spot. This illustration is generally shown with a holding of nine cards, as the idea is to protect yourself against a void in the west hand. A void in west is much more

frequent when the opponents have only four cards than when they have five. However, there is no law against a void in west when the opponents have five cards, so even when you have only eight, you still should make the safety play. As you are missing two cards in sequence (jack and ten), it is essential to keep two cards over any potential villain who happens to hold both of these and who will be exposed at trick one when one shows out. So here you do exactly the opposite of what you did with 19—you cash the ace first. Should West show out, you can lead twice through the jack-ten held by East and can pick up the two cards with the K Q 9.

YOUR SIDE HOLDS 9; THEY HOLD 4

1. DUMMY	2. DUMMY
J	Q 8
DECLARER	DECLARER
A K 10 6 5 4 3 2	J 7 6 5 4 3 2

1. (Type C) I know that you don't get dealt an eight-card suit very often, but I wanted to use this example because it clearly illustrates a common feature of safety plays. In the heat of battle, it is going to be extremely difficult, if not impossible, to dig up from your memory cells all of these various combinations of cards. A thing that has helped me most has been to try to translate my thinking from thinking in terms of how many cards my side has in a suit to how many cards the opponents hold in a suit. This sounds simple enough, but it takes a bit of training to do it automatically. Once that first step has been taken, it becomes relatively easy to go a step further and see how many cards they will have left after the suit has been played one time. On this illustration, the first thought should be, "They have four cards." The second thought should be, "After they have been led one round, even if the suit breaks 4–0, they will have only three cards left." A 4–0 split occurs frequently enough to warrant paying a small insurance premium to protect against it at game and slam contracts in other than match-point duplicate. Assuming that you have another entry into the south hand and assuming you are willing to give up the probability of winning eight tricks to make it 100-percent sure that you win seven tricks in this suit, just lead a small card toward the jack. If it loses to a queen which is in a 4–0 split, that opponent will have only three cards left in that suit, and your A K 10 will take care of them.

2. (Type B) It is obvious you always have two losers in this suit, no matter how you play it. If the opponents' cards are split 2–2, that's all you are going to lose. What, then, is your best chance to lose no more than two tricks after you have led small from your hand and West did not play the ace or king? Your best play is to play the eight from the dummy. If the suit breaks 2–2, you have lost nothing; but if East has a singleton ace or king, you have limited your losses to two tricks. Occasionally you will pay a pretty high price for this semi-safety play, as you will lose four tricks on

those occasions when West happens to hold all four of the outstanding cards. Of course, it is much more likely that East started with a singleton ace or king than that West started with all four of them.

3. DUMMY	4. DUMMY
7 6	7 6
DECLARER	DECLARER
A K Q 5 4 3 2	A K J 5 4 3 2

3. (Type C) Here again, the problem arises when you have no further entries into your own hand. Note, also, the different treatment that would be given if dummy had three small opposite your six, rather than two small opposite your seven. With three small in the dummy, you could afford to lay down the ace, and still be assured of losing only one trick against a 4–0 split. If either hand shows out, you could then lead low and concede a trick, having one left in the dummy for your own safety. With only two cards in the dummy, you cannot afford that luxury. When you have no entry and wish to be assured that you can run the suit with a loss of not more than one trick, just play low from both hands. After that, nobody can have more than three cards left, and your A K Q will take care of those.

4. (Type C) Here you can protect yourself against all four in the east hand, but not against all four in the west hand. You play low from both hands, and, if West shows out, you will know that East has three to the queen left. If both hands follow the first time, there will be only two remaining in their hands, and, obviously, you will bang down the ace and king.

5. DUMMY	6. DUMMY
Q 6 5 4	Q 6 5 4
DECLARER	DECLARER
A K 9 3 2	K J 8 3 2

5. (Type A) Here we meet a general principle we have met before: the nine in the south hand is the key card in connection with the three top cards. Always play the queen first, not the ace or king. When you have a potential finesse against two cards touching in rank, you must keep behind those two cards two cards of your own of a higher rank. If East turns out to have the four missing cards, playing the queen first allows you to finesse him twice to bring in the entire suit. If West has all four of them, you are bound to lose a trick. Unless all four of them are in one hand, you are going to bring in the entire suit anyway.

6. (Type B) With the ace missing in this combination, the eight-spot has taken the position of the nine-spot from number five. Should East hold all four of the outstanding cards, he will have the ten-nine, and, after the ace is gone, you will want to have the K J 8 behind the ten-nine. For this reason, the neat way to play seems to be to lead small from your hand toward dummy's queen. However, if you are in the dummy and somewhat short of entries, you can just as well lead the queen from the dummy. If

West has all four of the outstanding cards, you are going to lose two tricks no matter what way you play it.

7. DUMMY	8. DUMMY
J 6	J 6 5
DECLARER	DECLARER
A K 9 5 4 3 2	A 9 7 4 3 2

7. (Type C) The jack and nine are the key cards. Leading low toward the jack gives you protection against all four outstanding cards in either hand. You cannot afford the luxury of laying down the ace first to see whether the queen will fall, as that will leave the jack without a guard.

8. (Type B) Lead low toward the jack to be sure you take four tricks.

9. DUMMY	10. DUMMY
A K 9	A K 4
DECLARER	DECLARER
8 7 6 5 4 2	9 8 7 6 5 2

9, 10. (Type C) In 9, after you lead the two-spot toward dummy and West has played low, you can protect yourself against all four being with West and guarantee you will lose not more than one trick, if you will put in dummy's nine-spot. If East follows suit, there will be only two cards left, and the ace-king will take care of those. In 10, the situation is identical, but here the play is more spectacular. Actually, all cards from the four through the nine are equals in both hands, but let us hope that when you get the combination shown in 10 and do find all four of them in the West hand, you have a large gallery of kibitzers when you lead the two-spot and cover his three spot with the four-spot. This play should occasion an enthusiastic round of applause.

11. DUMMY	12. DUMMY
A 9 6 4	J 8 5 4
DECLARER	DECLARER
K J 8 3 2	K Q 9 3 2

11. (Type C) In addition to the honor cards, the key cards are the nine and eight. The safety play is to lead the king first, so that you will retain a tenace position against the ten-spot, should either of your opponents have all four of the missing cards.

12. (Type B) Again, the key cards are the nine-eight, but with the ace missing. Either lead toward the hand with the two honors or, if leading from your own hand, lead one of the high honors, so that a tenace position remains over the ten on either opponent who happens to hold all four of the missing cards.

13. DUMMY	14. DUMMY
K J 8 2	Q 6 5
DECLARER	DECLARER
Q 6 5 4 3	A J 8 4 3 2

13. (Type B) Here we have the honor cards along with the eight-spot, but the nine-spot is missing. As usual, when you have two touching cards against which you may have to finesse, you will need two higher cards back of them to accomplish that. This means that the K J 8 must be preserved in north in the event West happens to have all four of the outstanding cards. You go from dummy toward your queen or, if you happen to prefer to lead from your hand, lead the queen. There is no way to protect yourself against the loss of two tricks when it is East who has all of the outstanding cards.

14. (Type B) Of course, you might get by with no losers by leading small from the dummy when East has the singleton king, or by leading anything from the dummy when he has the doubleton king. But when you want to play the hand as safely as possible for five tricks, lead the queen from the dummy to protect yourself when East has all four of the missing cards. Again, you are missing both the ten and the nine, and to keep a finessing situation behind them, you must maintain the two high honors in your own hand.

15. DUMMY	16. DUMMY
A 9 6 5	A 10 6 5
DECLARER	DECLARER
Q J 4 3 2	K 9 4 3 2

15. (Type C) You can handle any adverse distribution for four tricks by giving up the chance of taking five and leading low from the dummy toward your queen. That nine-spot in the dummy is the key card, enabling you to finesse the ten-spot with West when he happens to hold all of them.

16. (Type C) Here you have the nine in one hand and the ten in the other. With these key cards, you can be assured that you will lose no more than one trick, no matter how the cards are distributed. Lead low from either hand and, if the next hand plays small, insert the ten or nine. Of course, if second hand shows out, you can achieve the same end by going up with the ace or king and then leading the suit back.

17. DUMMY	18. DUMMY
7 6 5	J 7 5 4
DECLARER	DECLARER
A Q 10 4 3 2	Q 10 8 3 2

17. (Type C) Your best chance to try for five tricks is to plank down the ace. It might even bring in six tricks, when West has the singleton king. Of course, if West holds three including the king-jack, there isn't anything you can do about it, and it is still worse if he holds all four of the missing cards. However, you can still limit your losses to one trick when it is East who holds both the king and jack with one or two more.

18. (Type B) Looking at the intermediate cards, you see both the seven and eight, so the nine is the only card against which there is a potential finesse. When there is a potential finesse against one card only, try to

maintain a finessing position in both hands. That means the first high card should be played from your hand and not the dummy. This can be accomplished either by leading low from the dummy toward your hand or, if it is more convenient, by just leading the queen. Now, if either opponent shows up with all four cards, you will have a natural finesse remaining in both hands against the nine-spot.

YOUR SIDE HOLDS 10; THEY HOLD 3

Under the heading of finesses, we discussed those hands where the opponents hold three cards consisting precisely of the second highest, fifth highest, and a smaller card. We have reserved those cases where the missing cards are the second and fourth highest and a smaller card for our discussion on safety plays.

1. DUMMY	2. DUMMY
A 10 8 7 6	A 7 6 5 4
DECLARER	DECLARER
Q 5 4 3 2	Q 10 9 3 2

1. (Type C) You can bring in this entire suit without a loss by laying down the ace, if either opponent has the singleton king, or by leading the queen, if East has the singleton jack. As a singleton king in either hand is twice as likely as a singleton jack in a specific hand, the best play to win all of the tricks is to lay down the ace. However, if you wish to guarantee losing only one trick in that suit, lead neither. Leading the ace will lose when all three are in the west hand; while leading the queen will lose when all three are in the east hand.

The play is to lead small toward the dummy, planning to play the ten if West plays low. If East wins that trick, there will be only one card in the suit outstanding, and the ace will take care of that. This is a better play than leading low from the dummy toward the queen, as it will give you all of the tricks in the suit when the singleton king is with West. However, if you are stuck in the dummy, you can still guarantee that you will lose not more than one trick by leading low toward the queen. The trouble is that that play also guarantees that you *will* lose one trick.

This safety play occurs when the ace and queen are in opposite hands and the ten is with the ace. You will notice that the king and jack, the two missing cards, are the second and fourth-highest cards.

2. (Type B) If the ten is in the hand with the queen instead of in the hand with the ace, you can be sure of losing not more than one trick by leading low toward the queen and ten. However, to have the additional chance of losing no tricks at all and leading toward the ace, it is necessary to buttress the ten with the nine-spot as shown in this example. Here you lead the ten or the nine toward the dummy and play low from the dummy if West plays small. This makes it possible for you to bring in the entire suit without loss on the occasions when West has the singleton king.

3. DUMMY	4. DUMMY
K 9 5 4	K 4 3 2
DECLARER	DECLARER
A J 3 2	A J 9 8

3. (Type C) Because it is the number of cards your opponents hold which is important rather than the number of cards you hold, you can arrive at exactly the same situation represented by exhibit 1 with this holding. If you are willing to sacrifice one trick to be sure you win three, you lay down the ace. Assuming both of your opponents follow, they now have three cards left. Included in those three cards are the number two and four cards; the queen has become number two, and the ten has become number four, since the ace has been led. The jack has taken the place of the queen in hand 1, and the nine has taken the place of the ten-spot. Now you lead low toward the king-nine, intending to put in the nine if West plays a small card. When West started with the doubleton queen, you still may take all four cards but with this line of play you will always be able to take at least three tricks in the suit.

4. (Type C) Notice that you could put the ace in north and the king in south and have the same situation as when you and dummy hold both of these cards; their trick taking value is equal. So often, when you have the jack with either the ace or king, the safety play turns out to be to lead first the honor which accompanies the jack. It is true in both 3 and 4. With 4, after you lead the ace and both opponents play low, you have a situation equivalent to 2. There are now three cards outstanding, and they include the second and fourth highest. The queen has become number two, and the ten number four. The nine is no longer in north, but in south, and must be buttressed by the next lower card (in this case, the eight-spot). After the ace wins the trick, lead the eight and plan to play low from the dummy unless West plays a high card or shows out. If he does either, win the next trick with the king in dummy, and now you can always win one more trick.

PLAYING THE ENTIRE HAND WITH SAFETY

It is nice when you have plenty of entries in both hands and can proceed with your safety play, knowing that you are going to finally end up where the tricks are. When you don't have that many entries, special precautions may have to be taken (Fig. 12-1).

Fig. 12-1

	North	
	♠ A 5 ♡ 6 5 3 ◊ 9 4 3 ♣ A Q J 7 5	
West		**East**
♠ J 8 2 ♡ J 10 7 2 ◊ 10 8 6 5 ♣ 3 2		♠ Q 10 9 6 ♡ K 8 4 ◊ Q J ♣ K 10 9 8
	South	
	♠ K 7 4 3 ♡ A Q 9 ◊ A K 7 2 ♣ 6 4	

South got into a contract of three no-trump and got an opening lead of the two of hearts. This gave him, for sure, two heart tricks, and he had two additional tricks in spades and two in diamonds. He needed three club tricks to bring home his contract. If the lead of the two of hearts was from only a four-card suit, he did not anticipate the opponents' getting that suit established and winning a lot of tricks in it, as it looked like any club losers could be given to East who would run out of hearts in three rounds. In this, declarer was correct. However, I hope it didn't look to him as though he had a lot of entries in the north hand so that he became careless, for bad things could happen.

Let us suppose he would win the king of hearts with the ace and lead a small club, putting in dummy's jack. Assuming East hadn't just taken up the game yesterday, he would surely let the jack hold the trick. Now declarer would return to his hand, probably with a diamond, and lead another club and put in dummy's queen. This time East would win with the king. It made a whale of a difference whether he won the first club or the second. Had he won the first one, South would still have had a club to lead. After he won the second one, South was out of clubs. Declarer could now hold up the second round of hearts and take the third one, but now to get to the ace of clubs in the dummy, he had to use up dummy's only entry. After he led the ace, East still had a high club, and, while declarer could go ahead and lead another club to establish the suit, he would have no way of getting back there. It is a pretty bad situation when you have winning tricks in one hand and no way to reach them. But there was a cure. Declarer should simply lead a small club from his hand and play the five from the dummy. After all, he needed only three tricks, not five, or even four. He would hold up one round of hearts (assuming that suit was continued) and then lead a small club and finesse the jack. East could win that and lead whatever he pleased, but after South gave the lead to the dummy with the ace of spades, there would be three good clubs waiting for the taking.

Whether you do or do not take a safety play in a suit will often depend on the number of tricks you have to take in that suit to fulfill your contract.

DUMMY
♠ A Q 5
♡ A Q 6
♢ A 9 6 3
♣ A K J

DECLARER
♠ K 9 3
♡ K J 7
♢ K J 7 4
♣ 6 5 2

The diamond suit is offering the classic safety play situation. To be sure to lose no more than one trick in the suit, the proper play is to lead the king and, if everyone plays small, lead low toward the dummy, intending to put in the nine if West plays small or the ace if West does anything else. However, just examining the hand, you have no idea of whether you want to take the safety play in diamonds or not. It well may be that you will need four tricks in diamonds to fulfill the contract.

Let us assume that you are playing six no-trump and get a lead of one of the major suits. You now have three tricks in each of the major suits, and the big question is, "How many tricks do you have in clubs?" First, try the club finesse. If the jack holds the trick, you are going to take three club tricks and need only three diamond tricks. And, by all means, take the safety play. However, if the club jack loses to the queen, you are going to need four diamond tricks. If you are in a big hurry to find out your fate, you might, upon regaining the lead, lay down the ace of diamonds and then lead small and finesse the jack. If you are not in such a great rush, it might be wise to cash all of your tricks in the side suits to see what you can learn about the opposing distribution before you try to guess the diamond suit.

Knowing the combinations which call for safety plays is good. Knowing when to and when not to use safety plays is even better. There are times when you have to go on an exploration trip before you arrive at that decision.

The more you have to lose if unexpected unfavorable distribution turns up, the more important safety plays are. Where only an extremely unlikely distribution will cause you to lose an overtrick, safety plays seldom should be made at match-point duplicate and are frequently bad plays in part-score situations and not worth too much in some game situations, but they are always to be used in slam situations. The loss on those rare occasions when things go wrong is simply too great.

DUMMY
♠ A 9 6 4
♡ Q J 3
◊ 7 5
♣ A 7 5 2

DECLARER
♠ 5
♡ A K 10 9 8 4
◊ A K 9 4 2
♣ 8

Terence Reese reports that this hand was played in a rubber bridge game in London and that the declarer reached what appeared to be a conservative contract of six hearts and went set. The opening lead was a spade, won in the dummy with the ace. At trick two, a diamond was led to the king. Declarer then entered the dummy with the ace of clubs to lead a second diamond, so that, if East should happen to trump it, declarer would still have the king. East followed suit all right, but when declarer played the king, West trumped it and then led another trump. This left only two trumps in the dummy to take care of three diamonds, so declarer finally had to lose another diamond trick.

Of course the chances that East would hold five diamonds and West only one were quite small, but after the ace of diamonds held the trick, fulfillment of the contract became almost a certainty. Instead of trying to take a trick with the king of diamonds at trick two, declarer could simply lead a small diamond. Now whoever won that couldn't even hurt him by leading trumps. He would still have two good trumps in the dummy to take care of his two losing diamonds, and the chances that anybody could trump the ace of clubs were really remote.

It can be the opening lead which gives you a chance to make a safety play.

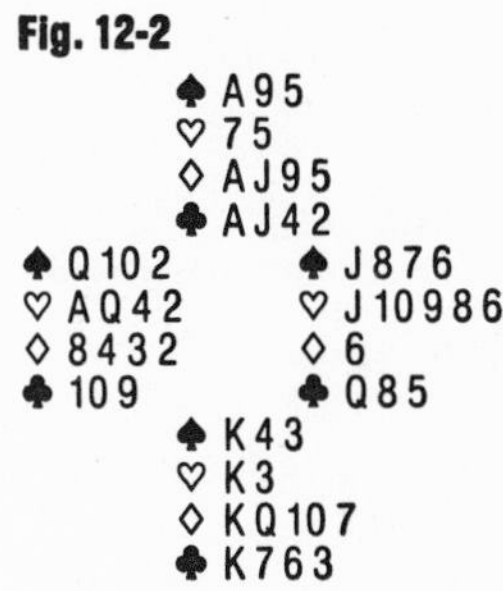

West didn't care to lead from his four-card heart holding against the three no-trump contract, and the way the cards were, he would have presented declarer with his ninth trick had he done so. Instead, he selected the ten of clubs.

When the dummy came down, declarer saw that he had off the top two spade tricks, four diamond tricks, and two club tricks, and was left looking for the ninth trick. That lead of the ten of clubs could have meant any of several things. For instance, had West held the Q 10 9 8, that would have been his opening lead. On the other hand, it might have been exactly what it was. Thinking about the safety of the hand, declarer decided that it would be decidedly unsafe to let East get the lead in view of his own heart holding. He needed only three club tricks to bring home his contract and decided to delay taking any club tricks until he found out what was going on. So, he played low from the dummy, and, when East played the five-spot, he played the seven to encourage West to continue the suit. West did continue the suit, and, when East followed again with the eight-spot, declarer saw he would have no problem taking his three club tricks without having to let East have the lead. The ball game was over after the second inning.

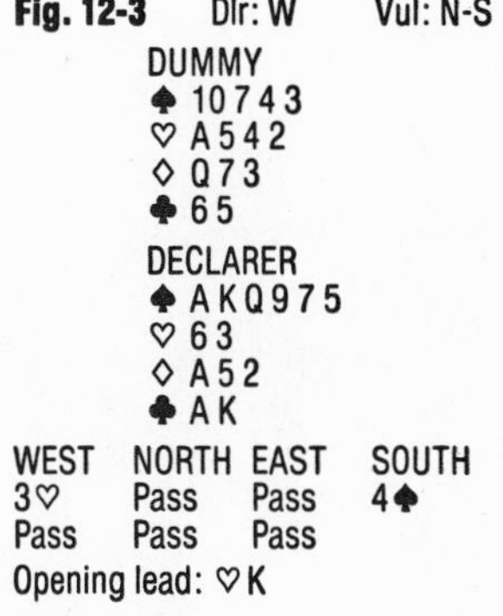

On the next hand (Fig. 12-3), a preemptive bid alerted declarer to a safety play he might have overlooked, had he been careless.

West led the king of hearts, and declarer counted his winning tricks: six in spades, plus one in hearts, one in diamonds, and two in clubs, came to ten—provided he took them all. But the opening bid of three hearts by West suggested that declarer might not take that ace of hearts if he played it now. If West had indeed started with a seven-card suit, East could trump the ace. Declarer had a solution—he just didn't play the ace. Sure enough, East showed out, but from this point on, declarer had no problem. West won the second heart and led a third heart. Declarer trumped the third heart, and now the ace was standing in the dummy healthy and strong, and the trump suit guaranteed an entry so it could be cashed.

I hope someday you and I can get a hand like my last one. Hands like this are so spectacular and so much fun.

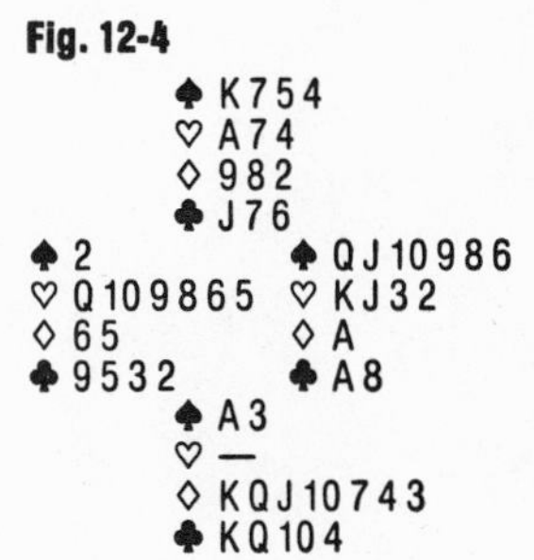

On hand 12-4, the bid was five diamonds, and West led the two of spades, which was almost certainly a singleton. South didn't see how he could pull trumps without letting someone win the ace, and it looked entirely possible that West might get to trump a spade. With the defenders' having two winners in the minor suit aces, declarer simply couldn't allow West to trump a spade. The solution was spectacular, but obvious. The first trick was won in the north hand by the king. Before he pulled trumps, declarer led the ace of hearts, and on it he discarded the ace of spades! Now West was not going to make any small trump he had—declarer lost tricks only to the two minor suit aces.

SAFETY plays are an attempt to defend yourself against adverse distribution. Hold-up plays are intended to help you defend yourself against an attack being launched by your opponents. The general purpose of hold-up plays is to wait and take your tricks in a suit led by the opponents until further leads in that suit will do you no more harm. More often, that is when one of your opponents is out of cards in the suit being led. Sometimes it is until you yourself are out of cards in their suit so that you can trump and keep your two opponents from having communication between their hands.

Hold-up plays are sometimes helpful when you are playing in a trump contract, but they are used to advantage most frequently when your contract is in no-trump.

First, let's look at some basic examples.

Fig. 13-1

West	North / South	East
	♠ 9 7 2 ♡ A 8 4 ♢ 8 4 ♣ A J 9 3 2	
♠ K 10 6 ♡ 10 7 5 ♢ K Q J 9 6 ♣ 6 4		♠ J 5 4 3 ♡ J 9 6 2 ♢ 7 5 3 ♣ K 5
	♠ A Q 8 ♡ K Q 3 ♢ A 10 2 ♣ Q 10 8 7	

West led the king of diamonds against a three no-trump contract. Declarer counted his winners and saw that he had six right off the top, so he needed three more. A successful club finesse would bring four more tricks. Even if the finesse failed, he would gain three more tricks, provided he could get his tricks before the opponents got theirs. It looked as though West had length in diamonds. To be as sure as possible that the opponents didn't get four diamonds plus one club trick, declarer decided to wait to take his ace of diamonds until East was out of diamonds. He let West have the first two diamonds, and, when West persisted, he had to take the ace.

At this time, the hand was just about as near a sure thing as you can find. It would only fail if East started with five diamonds and the king of clubs, and that did not seem likely. If East still had one diamond left, then West would have started with only four. Then, even if the club finesse failed, the defenders could take only three diamonds and one club trick. Of course, when declarer took the finesse and East won with the king, he had no diamonds left to return. He led back a small spade. Declarer would have no part of that finesse. With his four club tricks assured, he now had a diamond trick, plus three heart tricks, and needed only one spade trick to be sure of his contract.

Just swap one card and instead of being almost a cinch, the hold-up play becomes about the only chance.

Fig. 13-2

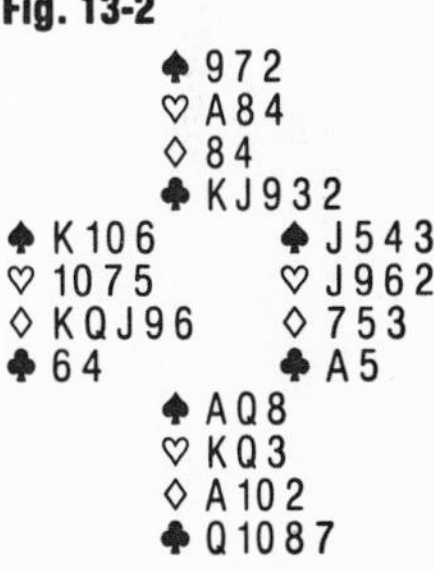

On the first hand, declarer knew that the only player to whom he could lose the lead in clubs was East. On this hand, he knows no such thing. He is going to lose a club trick to whomever happens to hold the ace. If West has five or more diamonds plus the ace of clubs, well—declarer is just going set. But he is going set, too, if he takes either the first or second diamond, no matter who has the ace of clubs. So, he can increase his chances of winning by the hold-up play. Of course, in this chapter on the virtues of hold-up plays, I simply have to put the ace in the east hand rather than with West to make my point. But my real point is that while declarer did not give himself a 100-percent sure thing from his hold-up play, he certainly increased his chances mightily.

The hold-up play, when there are trumps, is usually made so that you can wait until you or your dummy or both are out of cards in the suit, so that you can keep a dangerous opponent from regaining the lead. These plays are frequently a sort of combination of safety play, avoidance play, and hold-up play all rolled into one.

Fig. 13-3

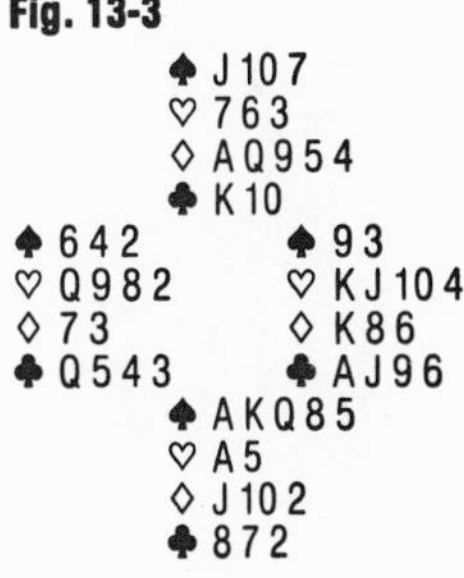

Against a four spade contract, West got off to the lead of the two of hearts. On examining the dummy, declarer saw one loser in hearts, a potential loser in diamonds, and two potential losers in clubs. East played the king of hearts, and that made it appear that West started with the queen. Declarer was pleased that West hadn't led a club and decided his best bet was to prevent West from ever leading clubs. The way to do that was to keep West from getting the lead again, so that declarer would have time to get his diamonds established without West's ever having a chance to lead clubs. To accomplish this, declarer simply played the five of hearts and conceded the first trick to East. East continued the suit, but declarer won that with the ace. He then pulled trumps and led the jack of diamonds for a finesse. The finesse failed, but declarer still had two discards coming on dummy's diamonds. He ended up losing one trick in hearts, one in diamonds, and, by discarding two of his own clubs, only one in clubs.

WHEN NOT TO HOLD UP

If I go ahead with my dissertation on hold-up plays, it will seem that hold-up plays should always be made when available. Actually, there are many reasons why they should not. To keep the record straight, I am going to interrupt my discussion of these plays right here and show you when and why the hold-up play should *not* be made.

When the opening lead has guaranteed you two tricks not otherwise available, it is time to take a good look before you decide whether or not to hold up. While there are some exceptions, generally, the hold-up play should not be taken under these circumstances.

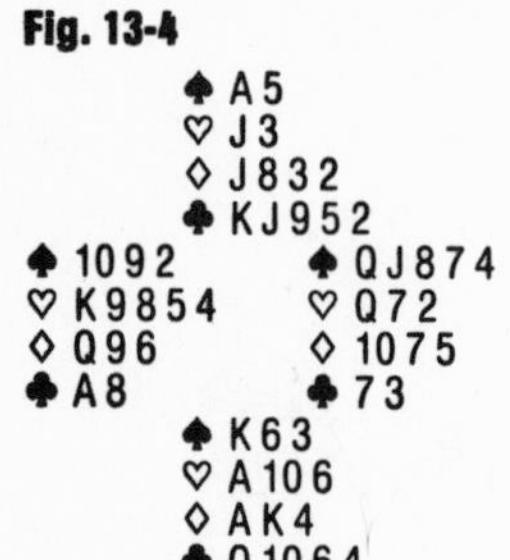

Against three no-trump, West led the five of hearts. The holding in the dummy and south was of the sort where two tricks are guaranteed, provided the opponents lead the suit and provided you play second-hand-low. So the three went on from the dummy, and East played the queen.

Declarer saw that he had a total of five tricks without giving up the lead, but that by giving the opponents a club trick, he could take an additional four tricks in that suit. If his knowledge of hold-up plays did not include knowing when *not* to take them and he played low, he would give up one of his heart tricks. If the player with length in hearts happened to have the ace of clubs, he would also have given up his contract. However, the declarer knew better than that and won the queen with his ace. He promptly led clubs, and, with a second heart trick available whether the suit was led by his opponents or himself, he had no trouble sailing home with ten tricks.

South missed a couple of chances to make his contract on the next hand (Fig. 13-5) with his excessive use of the hold-up play.

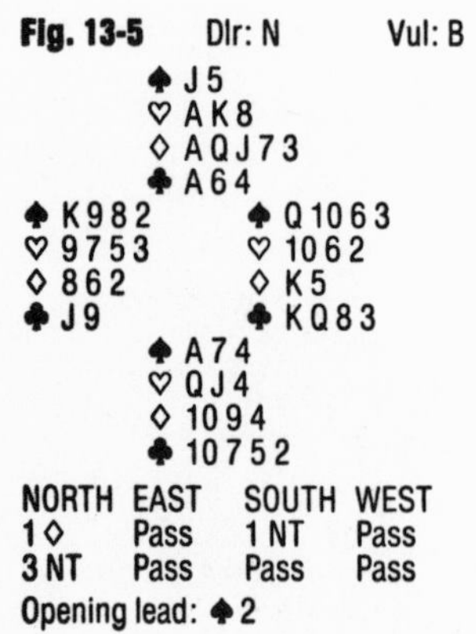

West led the two of spades. On the theory that a doubleton jack of spades in the dummy with no supporting cards in the other hand will win a first trick led in the suit or none at all, declarer played the jack. East put on the queen, and declarer came to the conclusion that he should hold up. East studied the formidable dummy and the opening lead and decided it was time to switch suits. His partner's lead of the two-spot indicated he had started with only four spades. There was a vicious looking diamond suit in the dummy, which, sooner or later, would furnish declarer with four tricks, and hearts and clubs would bring the total up to seven. East decided that the best he could do if he returned a spade was to win three spade tricks and one diamond trick, and that would not be enough to satisfy him. So, he decided to experiment in clubs and led back the three.

South should have noticed the lead of the two of spades and come to the same conclusion East had—that West had started with only four spades. If so, they could win only three tricks in that suit, and South should have taken the ace and finessed the diamond. Even if he had lost three spades and a diamond, he would have taken nine tricks—four diamond tricks, three heart tricks, and one in each of the black suits. He looked like he had been double-crossed when East failed to continue the suit. He played the two-spot, and, when East played the nine, decided he had better hold up in that suit. He still had a chance to make his contract by winning the ace and coming to his hand with a heart to take the diamond finesse, as the club suit would block, but he had no way of knowing that. West continued with the jack of clubs, and, again, South held up.

Now West switched back to spades, and it began to appear that South might even go set before he got the lead if he didn't take a trick somewhere along the line. So having lost the first three tricks, he won the ace of spades and finessed the diamond. When that lost to the king, the defenders had two spade tricks to add to their total, and declarer was set two tricks on a hand he could have made, had he given thought to the proposition that it is sometimes wise not to hold up when the opponents have other suits to which they can switch and with which they can cause you difficulty.

On the next hand (Fig. 13-6), the hold-up play was not only unnecessary, it was dangerous.

Fig. 13-6

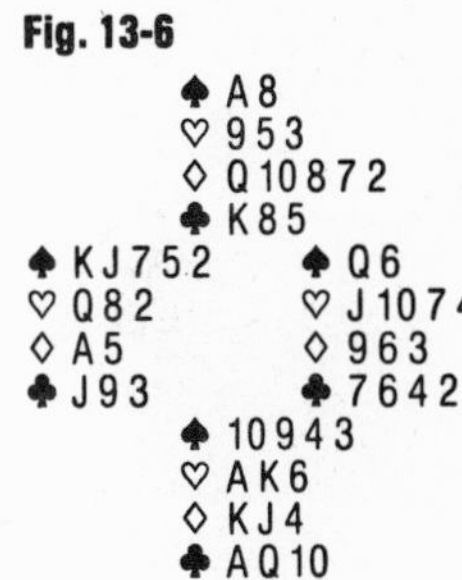

Against three no-trump, West led the five of spades. South counted ten tricks for himself, once he forced out the ace of diamonds. The only question was how many tricks the opponents could take when he did force out that ace of diamonds. Between them they had seven spades. If they broke 4–3, declarer had nothing to fear, as he would lose only three spades and one diamond. It was a 5–2 or 6–1 break he had to worry about. The missing top honors were the K Q J. It occurred to South that if West had those three cards, he probably would have led the king instead of a small spade. So he came to the conclusion that East had one of the three. In that event, even with a 5–2 break, they could not run the spade suit, as it would be sure to block. When you can tell from the spots in your hand and the opening lead that the opponents are not likely to take enough tricks to set you, go ahead and take your ace. South did so, and when West got the lead, there was no way for him to take more than two spade tricks. If he let East win with the queen, East would have none to return. If he laid down the king and jack, South's ten would be good. Of course, if South had ducked, East would have won with the queen. Then with the ace singleton in the dummy, it would have been unnecessary for West to waste a high one on the return, and he would be left with the king-jack and a small one to win tricks when he got in with the ace of diamonds.

There are times when whether or not you should hold up is determined by which of your opponents may gain the lead.

Fig. 13-7

West led the five of spades against three no-trump. East played his queen. South saw that even if he lost a club finesse, he could take four club tricks, four diamond tricks, and a heart trick. The question was how many tricks the opponents could take if the club finesse lost.

Had it been necessary to take a club finesse into East's hand, declarer would have had to decide whether to try to hold up until East ran out of spades or to take the risk that he might switch to a heart. But as it was West who was going to gain the lead if the club finesse lost, the proper play was to take the king of spades at once. Then, even if the club finesse lost, West could not do declarer any harm by continuing spades, as the jack of spades would be a stopper. So, the declarer won the king of spades, went to the dummy with a diamond, and led the queen of clubs for a finesse. He was going to make game no matter how the clubs were divided. If East had all five of them, he could still take three club tricks, four diamond tricks, and one trick in each of the major suits.

In actual play, West won the club finesse with his king and, desperately trying to give his partner the lead, led the five of hearts. But it was no-go, as declarer now had his ten tricks.

On my next hand, declarer could determine whether or not to hold up after he saw what happened to the first trick.

DUMMY
♠ Q 5
♡ A J 7
◇ A Q 9 6 3
♣ J 10 5

DECLARER
♠ K 6 4
♡ K Q
◇ J 10 5
♣ A Q 9 6 3

The opening lead of the jack of spades against the three no-trump contract was going to establish a spade trick right away. To these, declarer could add three heart tricks. In the minor suits, he could add four in either suit, even if the finesse lost. This, with the ace of the other suit, would give him a total of nine. You can see, by examining the hand, that unless West has led from a short suit, declarer is going to make his contract. At the first trick, he should play the queen of spades from the dummy. If East wins that and returns a spade, declarer should hold up until the third lead, if there is such a lead. Now, he should finesse diamonds and not clubs, allowing East to get the lead, if either of them does. If East has a spade left, the suit will have broken 4–4, and you will lose only three spades and the club. If West started with five spades, East had only three, and now has no more spades to lead. Whatever he returns, declarer wins the trick and is now in a position to cash his nine tricks.

If, however, the queen of spades holds the first trick, the declarer should immediately finesse clubs. He doesn't mind losing a trick to West who can only concede a trick by further spade leads. Again, whether the finesse wins or loses, declarer is going to take at least his nine tricks.

WHEN YOU HAVE TO SURRENDER THE LEAD ONE TIME

Fig. 13-8

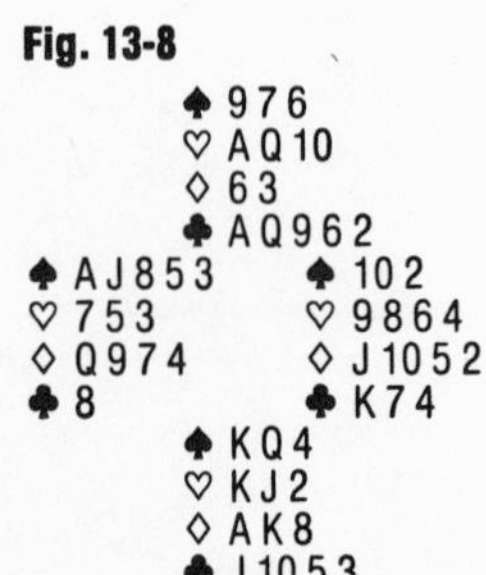

Whether you need to invoke the hold-up play will also depend on the number of tricks you can take in the suit they are trying to establish and the number of times you may have to surrender the lead to get your suit established.

For a moment, let's imagine that you are playing three no-trump and that the opening lead has been a diamond. In the red suits, you have five tricks, and you can always take at least four in clubs, even if the finesse fails. At the worst, you are going to have to give up the lead one time in clubs to get your hand established. As you have more tricks in that suit than the number of times you might have to give up the lead, the hold-up play is not called for, and you simply win the ace of diamonds and go about your business with clubs. But now let us suppose the lead has been the five of spades, and East has played the ten. The question is, "How many tricks do you have in spades?" With both the king and queen, it looks like you might have two, and, indeed, you would if East had the ace. But if you win that trick, it seems likely that it will be your first and only trick in the suit, unless West leads it again. If you have to lose the lead in clubs, you will have to lose it to East, and I would say, without seeing the east-west hands, that that would make it extremely likely that you have one trick in spades and not two. You can always get your trick in spades if you don't take it now, and the best procedure is to let the ten win the trick. If East started with the singleton ten, he already is going to have to lead something else. If he started with a doubleton, you will want to win your one spade trick when he is out of spades. If he started with three spades, leaving only four with West, the worst thing that can happen to you is to lose three spades and one club trick.

The point is that you only make a hold-up play when you do not have more tricks in the suit they led than the number of times you are likely to give up the lead. Some holdings look deceptive, and it may look like you have two tricks in their suit, when in fact you have only one.

Let us say that you are in a contract of three no-trump, get an opening lead of the six of hearts, and East plays the queen. You have every reason to be happy, because you now have one sure trick in a suit where you might have had no tricks at all if you had had to lead it yourself. But don't get too happy. It might just be that you have only that one trick.

Fig. 13-9

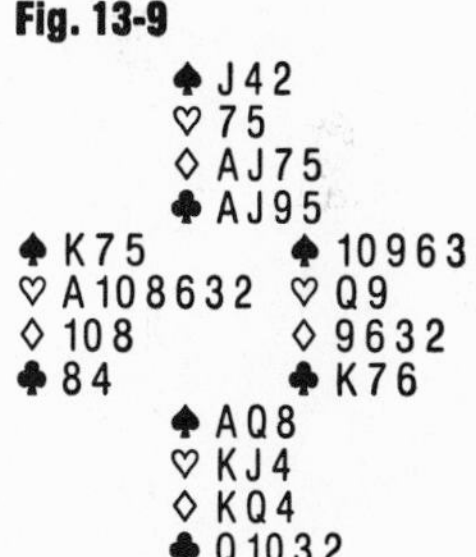

In spades you have one trick for sure. In diamonds you have four, and in clubs you have only one. That comes to seven tricks altogether, and certainly makes it appear that the best way to pick up two extra ones is to get the clubs established by finessing. But if the club finesse fails and East has a heart left, you don't know how many heart tricks West will be able to take. So, let's look around and see if there is any shift that East can make which might hurt us if we let him win with the queen. If he leads a spade, we can simply play low from our hand and will have developed one of the extra tricks (even if West wins with the king). And, if West continues leading hearts, we can still get our one heart trick and, hopefully, East will be out of hearts by the time we finesse clubs. Obviously, a lead from East of clubs or diamonds is not going to hurt us at all. And, when we play low, if East persists in leading hearts, we will still always get our one trick, hopefully when East has run out of hearts.

All the evidence says we must let the queen win the trick. To take nine tricks we need the club finesse, and that may mean we will have to lose the lead one time. If we do, we probably will have only one heart trick, and we need more tricks in their suit than the number of times we have to lose the lead. We just defer taking our heart trick, we don't lose it. So we let the queen win the trick, hoping that if East wins the club finesse, he will not be able to do us harm.

Fig. 13-10

```
          ♠ K 6 4
          ♡ Q 6
          ◇ K 10 7
          ♣ A J 9 5 3
♠ Q 8             ♠ J 10 9 3 2
♡ A J 8 7 4 2     ♡ 10 5
◇ J 8 5           ◇ 9 6 4 2
♣ 7 4             ♣ K 8
          ♠ A 7 5
          ♡ K 9 3
          ◇ A Q 3
          ♣ Q 10 6 2
```

The next hand (Fig. 13-10) looks different, but the principle is the same.

Against three no-trump, West led the seven of hearts. Now, if West started with five hearts and East has the king of clubs, you may go set if the opponents defend properly, in spite of your 28 high-card points. But don't be a pessimist: hope that either the king of clubs is right, or that West has started with six hearts, leaving only two in the east hand.

Often when your heart holding is as it is in this hand, it is proper to play the queen at trick one, trying to win two tricks when West has led from the ace. That would hold true this time if it were West to whom you had to surrender the lead to get your hand established. But it is East who is going to win a trick in clubs, if either of your opponents does, and so the hold-up play becomes your best chance. It seems strange to play the six from north and let East have the trick with the ten-spot, but it is the proper play. You still have the heart trick coming at some future time, and, if East is going to gain the lead in clubs, you want it to be some future time when East is out of hearts.

If you have enough small cards, it might pay just to keep on holding up for a while (Fig. 13-11).

Fig. 13-11

```
          ♠ K 6 4
          ♡ K 8 6 4
          ◇ 6
          ♣ A J 10 7 2
♠ J 8 5 2         ♠ 10 7 3
♡ Q 5             ♡ J 10 7 3
◇ A 10 8 7 3      ◇ J 9 4
♣ 5 3             ♣ K 8 4
          ♠ A Q 9
          ♡ A 9 2
          ◇ K Q 5 2
          ♣ Q 9 6
```

Against three no-trump, West led the seven of diamonds, and East played the jack. The minute declarer got in, he could get clubs established, losing one if necessary, and have plenty of tricks to fulfill his contract. However, if East had the king of clubs, declarer wanted to be as sure as possible that East was out of diamonds before he made that club play. As he could afford to lose a total of four tricks, he could afford to lose three of them in diamonds. So, when East played the jack, he just played the two-spot. East came on with the nine, and South played the five-spot. Actually, a third diamond was led, covered by the queen, and won by the ace. West could think of nothing better to do than lead another diamond. Now declarer had his one and only diamond trick, which he'd had from the beginning, but when he lost to the king of clubs in East, East had no more diamonds to lead, and declarer romped home with nine tricks.

I have mentioned before that I started getting my bridge lessons when I was 11 years old from my parents and our neighbors. There was one elderly lady in our neighborhood who frequently followed suit with her highest card, even when it was not a winning card, and carefully explained to all who cared to listen that she did this to "force the ace." Or, maybe it was to force the king or queen. I noticed that she was a consistent loser. Once, when she was not around, I asked one of my other neighbors about playing second-hand high to force something, and she patiently explained to me that the score was determined not by what you forced but by how many tricks you took. She made it obvious that forcing an opponent to play something was only the proper thing to do when it was used as a means to an end, rather than as the end itself. Of course, the end should always be to take more tricks. My "force the ace" lady would have surely come a cropper with this next hand (Fig. 13-12).

Against three no-trump, West would open the five of hearts, and East would win with the king and lead the nine-spot. My eccentric neighbor would certainly play the jack to force the ace. My other mentor, who had explained the folly of the procedure, would certainly have refused to have her ace forced. She would just have played the three-spot. Eventually, East would have gotten the lead with the king of diamonds and would still have had a heart left, at which time West would have taken three more heart tricks to add to the one heart and diamond East had taken, to bring the total up to five tricks for defense.

Fig. 13-12

West	North	East
	♠ K 5 3 ♡ 6 ◇ A J 9 7 4 2 ♣ K 10 5	
♠ Q 9 7 6 ♡ A 10 8 5 3 ◇ 8 ♣ 9 6 4		♠ J 8 2 ♡ K 9 4 ◇ K 5 3 ♣ 8 7 3 2
	♠ A 10 4 ♡ Q J 7 2 ◇ Q 10 6 ♣ A Q J	

Of course, when the nine of hearts was led, we should have held up. After the king was played, the queen and jack became the second- and third-highest cards, and we were in the same situation we were in when we held up with the king and queen. There seems to be no way to bring in nine tricks without bringing in lots of diamond tricks. If a diamond finesse loses, it must be East who will gain the lead. Therefore, we want to be as sure as we can be that East is out of hearts when and if he gains the lead with the king of diamonds. So, when he leads back the nine, we just play the seven-spot. That makes only the second trick for the defenders. If East comes on with a third heart, West can win the defenders' third trick with the ace, but we now are in control. They will get their fourth trick with the king of diamonds, but East will have no more hearts to lead.

WHEN YOU MAY HAVE TO SURRENDER THE LEAD TWO TIMES

When you must lose the lead more than once to get your hand established, the situation is similar to those just discussed.

Fig. 13-13

Against South's three no-trump, West led the six of clubs. Declarer counted up to seven tricks off the top, and two more were readily available in diamonds after the ace and king were knocked out. He could have sat there for some time figuring out that, if East had either the ace or king of diamonds with two clubs, it would be better not to win the first trick. Instead of having to figure it out every time it comes up, it is simpler to remember the formula. Unless there is something unusual about the hand, in a situation like this, it is better to hold up unless you have more tricks in the suit they've led than the number of times you have to lose the lead. You want to do all you can to tackle the diamond suit after East has run out of clubs. By letting him hold the first trick, you will accomplish that.

South saw nothing exceptional about the hand and didn't see any suit East could switch to that would cause him problems, so he let the ten of clubs hold the first trick. Now he was going to be able to establish his two diamond tricks before West could get his clubs established and run them, unless West had started off with five clubs and both the ace and king of diamonds. East could go ahead and return the jack of clubs, but whenever he got in with the ace of diamonds, he would have no more clubs to lead.

Good guessers would do as well as a good player on the next hand (Fig. 13-14).

This time, declarer is going to have to give up the lead in two separate suits instead of twice in one suit to get his hand established.

Fig. 13-14

After West led the queen of clubs against a three no-trump contract, a good guesser would win with the king and then guess to get diamonds established before hearts. By doing that, he would hit the suit where West had the entry first, and, when West led a second club to establish the suit, he would at the same time get rid of all the clubs in East's hand. East would then have no clubs to lead when he got in with the ace of hearts.

A good player wouldn't have to guess. He would just remember the formula and see that he would have to give up the lead twice to get his hand established and let the queen of clubs hold the trick. Then, no matter whether he guessed to lead hearts or diamonds first, when East got the lead, he would have no clubs left and declarer could establish both of his red suits, while limiting West to only one club trick.

On the next hand (Fig. 13-15), the declarer was elated when the opening lead solved one of his problems. However, other problems existed, and he had to proceed with care.

Against three no-trump, the opening lead was the jack of spades, and East played the king. It's a good feeling to get an opening lead into your ace-queen, but the truth of the business is, on this hand, that it was not particularly good luck. Even with two spade tricks, declarer could find only eight quick tricks in the two hands. One more had to be developed somewhere, and it looked like it just about had to be in diamonds. How many times was he going to have to give up the lead to establish a diamond trick? Two times. How many tricks does he have in spades after the king is played? Only two. And what does our formula say when you don't have more tricks in the suit led than the number of times you have to relinquish the lead to establish your hand? "Stay cool and hold up."

Fig. 13-15

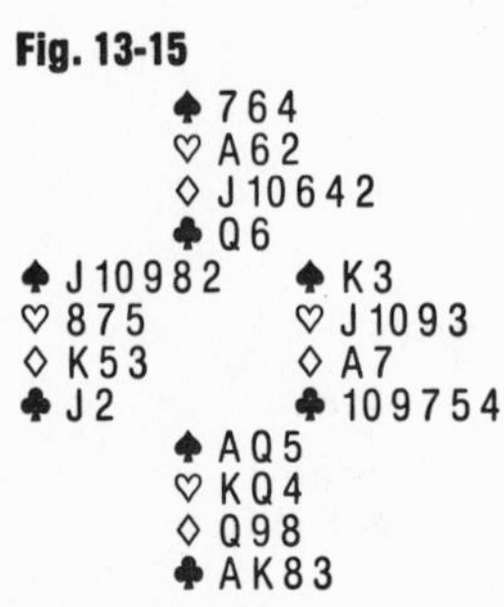

Had declarer received a club lead, he would not have held up, since he had three tricks there. And, of course, had he received a heart lead where he had three tricks, holding up would have been foolish, in view of the fact that he had only three cards in each hand. But what he got was a spade lead where he had only two tricks, and so he let East have that trick with his king. Now all he had to hope for was that West did not have both the ace and king of diamonds. East persisted in spades, but when he won the ace of diamonds, whether he took it before West took the king or after, he had no spades left to lead. Had South won the opening lead with the ace of spades, East could have won the ace of diamonds and had a spade left to clear the suit, while West still had his king of diamonds for an entry.

There is an old saying that you can't solve a problem unless you know what the problem is. Well, you might luck into a solution without knowing the problem, but I think your chances are much better when you do know what the problem is.

Fig. 13-16

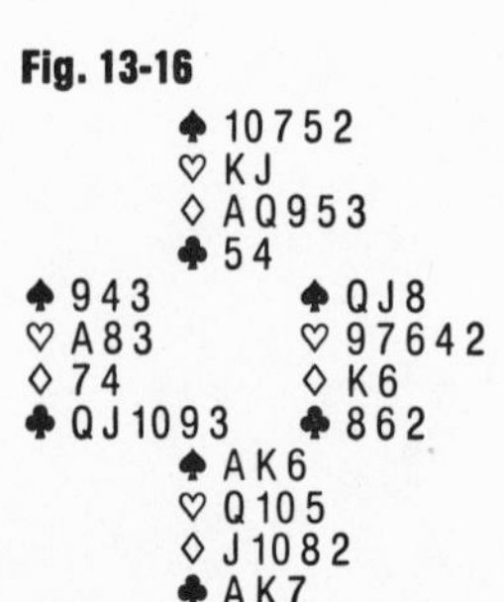

Against three no-trump, the opening lead was the queen of clubs. The situation here is a little different from any we've seen. Instead of having a couple of sure losers to establish his suit, declarer finds he has one trick he has to lose and another he may or may not lose. So, it's best to play for the worst to happen, and then you will be happily surprised if the best happens. The thought went through declarer's mind that he'd better hold up on the opening club lead, in the event he was going to have to lose the lead two times.

In the black suits, he had four tricks. If the diamond finesse failed, he would have only an additional four there and was going to have to get a heart trick as well. So he had to take every precaution to prevent West from getting his clubs established while he had an entry or while East still had a club. His first step was to play the seven of clubs, letting West's queen win the trick. West continued clubs, and South won with the king. Now, while declarer might have two losers, there was only one of them that could give the lead to West. Therefore, he should try to remove that possible winner from West before taking the chance of giving East the lead. If West got the lead and continued clubs, then West would be seeing to it that East ran out of clubs and couldn't lead them if he won the king of diamonds. If declarer took the diamond finesse first, East could win that while he still had a club and while West had an entry.

So, after winning the king of clubs, declarer simply led a small heart toward the dummy. West decided not to take that, and the king won the trick. It was now time to abandon hearts, for if they were led again, somebody might have the notion of taking the ace, continuing hearts, and getting that suit established instead of clubs. So, now that he had everything under control, declarer returned to his hand with a spade, led the jack of diamonds, and finessed it. East won with the king, but declarer still had a club stopper and was now assured of four tricks in the black suits, the one trick in hearts he had already taken, and four diamond tricks.

Fig. 13-17

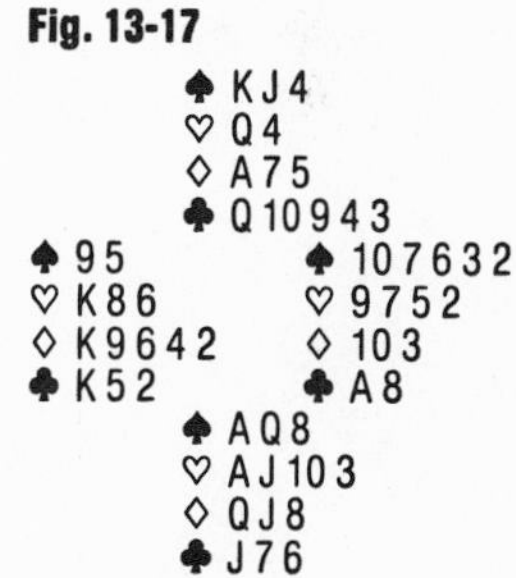

On the next hand (Fig. 13-17), the need for the hold-up play may not have been too apparent, but it was there.

Against three no-trump, West led the four of diamonds, dummy played low, and East played the ten-spot. Declarer could win that with the jack and be assured of two diamond tricks. But even that left him way short of the nine required, and it was obvious that the club suit was going to have to produce some tricks. It was also obvious that he was going to have to give up the lead two times to develop the club suit. But what wasn't so obvious, but nonetheless true, was that he had two diamonds whether he played the jack or the eight at trick one. Surely, if East had the king of diamonds, he would have played it. To try to get East out of diamonds before winning his tricks, declarer decided to postpone winning his diamond tricks, and he simply played the eight-spot. Whether West continued diamonds or not, declarer's two diamond tricks were going to be there waiting for him whenever he wanted them. Actually, East did continue diamonds, and the jack was covered by the king and ace. Declarer now led a small club toward his jack, and whether East won that immediately or waited and won the second club trick, he was not going to have any diamonds to lead to his partner. The best he could do would be to hop up with the ace of clubs and lead a heart. South wanted to be sure he had the club suit cleared before West got the diamond suit cleared, so he immediately took the ace of hearts and continued clubs. He could end up losing one trick to the ten of diamonds, two in clubs, and one in hearts, but he would always limit his losses to those four tricks.

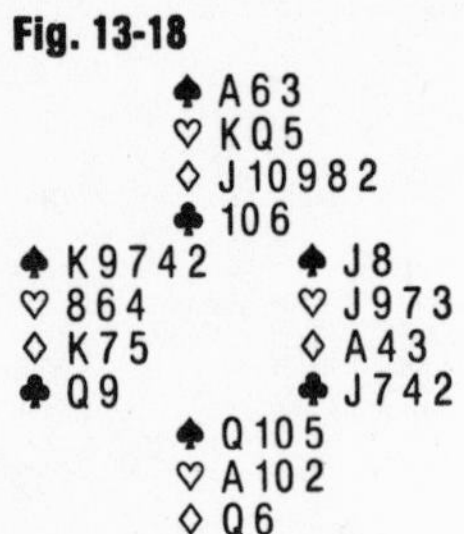

Those tenace positions we saw when you held ace-queen or king-jack can be treacherous at the lower level also.

At three no-trump, West led the four of spades, dummy played low, and East played the jack. How nice. What could have been only one trick in spades was now guaranteed to be two tricks. All declarer had to do was win the queen, and the ace would certainly be a second trick. That's exactly what he should not do. He will still have two tricks in the suit if he doesn't win this with the queen. Surely, had East held the king, he would have played it. So the king is marked in the west hand. This means that declarer can get his two tricks at a time of his choosing. And he does well to choose a time for winning the first of his two tricks when East is exhausted of the suit. There is no chance of bringing in nine tricks off the top, but the solid diamond suit, missing the ace and king, will certainly guarantee three tricks, provided the declarer can take them before the defenders take some large number of spade tricks. And, the declarer is going to have to give up the lead twice to establish the diamonds. Where you have to give up the lead two times, you need two tricks in their suit, plus a spare tire in the form of a third trick in their suit. Here you have the two tricks, but no spare tire. There doesn't seem to be any switch which East can make to cause declarer problems, so he just lets East keep that trick with the jack of spades. The chances are good that East will continue the suit. In the process of getting the diamonds established, East is going to win the trick one time, but when he does, he is not going to have any more spades to lead to his partner, and declarer is going to make his contract probably with an overtrick.

Once when I was explaining an exception to one of my pupils, he said, "Easley, don't tell me the exceptions, I haven't got the rules yet." Well, how about an exception to an exception? It is a basic part of bridge, and so I'm afraid I'm going to have to put it in (Fig. 13-19).

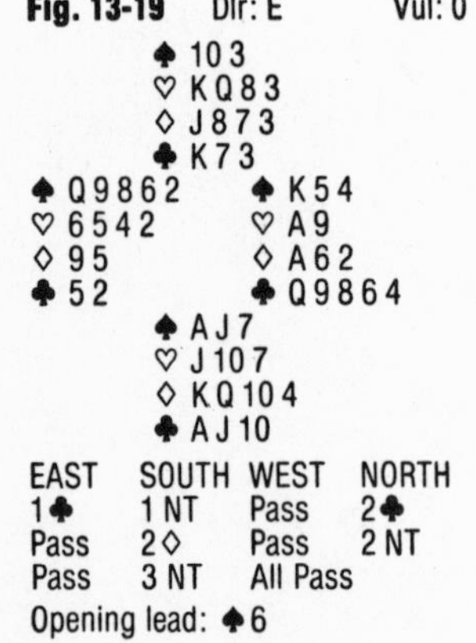

Not too long ago, I said that as an exception you should not hold up when the opening lead had given you an extra trick you probably could not have gotten under your own power. Let's see what we can decide about this hand.

West led the six of spades, declarer played dummy's three, and East played the king. Declarer can take the ace and another spade trick will develop where only one was likely if declarer had to lead the suit himself. It looked like South had to develop both of the red suits to bring his total up to nine, so that meant he had to lose tricks to two aces. If the spades were 4–4 in the defender's hands, he would lose two spades if he took the ace, and that would give the opponents only a total of four. If he held up the ace, they would take *three* spades and two aces.

But, let's look a little deeper. Suppose West led from a five card spade suit? When East played the king at trick one, it looked like West had the queen. Between his hand and dummy, declarer saw 25 high-card points leaving only 15 for his two combined opponents. East had opened the bidding, and if West had those two points represented by the queen, East had to have every other missing high card to have had 13 for his opening bid. This meant East had both red aces. When East gained the lead with one of these aces he would return a spade, and West could hold up and leave a spade in his partner's hand to lead when he got the lead with his other ace. The defenders would end up taking *three* spades and their two aces.

So, if the spades were 5–3 instead of 4–4, declarer wanted to hold up to cut communications between the two hands. Were the spades 4–4, or 5–3, the two critical distributions declarer had to consider? On a purely mathematical basis eight outstanding cards will divide 5–3 144 times every time they will divide 4–4 100 times. Mathematics is fascinating to mathematicians, but to bridge players it should run a poor second to other forms of evidence. Was other evidence available?

Declarer decided that West would not have been anxious to lead a suit of only four cards headed by only a queen in preference to the suit his partner had bid. The mathematical probabilities strengthened this evidence. All turned out well for declarer when he let the defenders win the first two spade tricks. There was no way East could reach his partner's hand when he won his two aces. Declarer had found an exception to an exception.

On my next hand, East found a switch to a different suit after holding the first trick. As my story is about those times when the hold up succeeds and not when it fails, I had to let the declarer find a way out.

Fig. 13-20 Dlr: S Vul: B

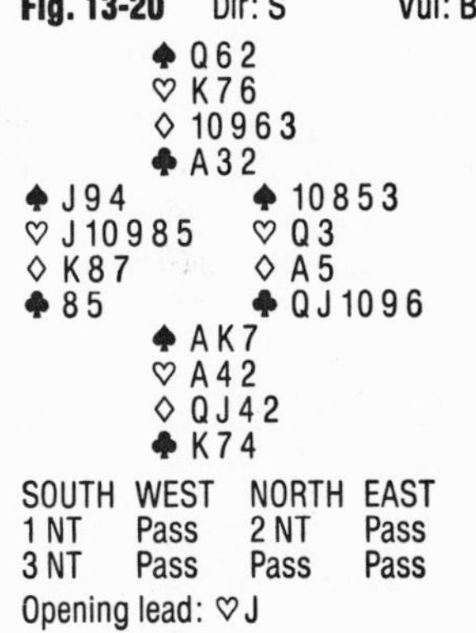

Of course, we can't be sure of what other people are thinking, but I do know what happened on this hand, so let's pretend that we can read the minds of the participants. Probably we are not going to be too far wrong.

At trick one, West led the jack of hearts, dummy played small, and East played the queen. South found seven tricks off the top and needed two diamond tricks to bring home his contract. He had the two tricks in hearts, all right, but he didn't have the spare tire, and, as he had to lose the lead two times, it seemed wise for him to let East win the trick. Conceivably, East might be out of hearts already and have to switch. If he were not, the play of the queen looked like it would be from a doubleton. In that event, when he led a second heart, he would be exhausted, and declarer would have a good chance to go about his business, unless West held both missing high cards in the diamond suit.

Now let's put ourselves in the position of East, when declarer let him hold the trick. What were the chances that West had the ace of hearts? As East had seen the jack, queen,and king, if West had the ace also, then South had bid one no-trump and gone on to three no-trump with no stoppers in hearts. It was possible for South to hold 17 high-card points with nothing in hearts (spades—8; diamonds—6; clubs—3), but if that were the case, a heart return was not going to beat the hand. Whether West took his ace or not, he would have no entry to cash his hearts, and declarer would roll happily home with three spades, a heart, three diamonds, and two clubs. East decided his best chance was that South did have the ace of hearts, and, in that event, his play indicated he was going to have to lose the lead twice to get his hand established for nine tricks. A little simple arithmetic told East that his partner had about 5 high-card points somewhere in his hand and that South thought an entry was included in those points. So East decided to switch to clubs, hoping his partner's entry could be utilized while he had a club left. In that event, clubs might get rolling before declarer could establish his hand.

This switch was a rude shock to South, but if his first hold up had been intended to get East out of hearts, then he had to do the same thing to exhaust West of clubs. So, declarer held up in a second suit. That took care of the situation for him. West needed an extra heart in the East hand, and East needed an extra club in the West hand, and neither was there. Declarer was able to get his two diamond tricks established without losing control and bring in his nine tricks.

Good spot cards can play their part in hold-up plays as they can, at times, in most of the plays available to declarer (Fig. 13-21).

SOUTH	WEST	NORTH	EAST
1♣	Pass	1◇	Pass
2 NT	Pass	3 NT	All Pass

Opening lead: ♡4

After North made a one diamond response to South's opening bid of one club, South decided to show his strength rather than his heart suit, and North made the bold bid of three no-trump, hoping the diamond suit might come home. West led the four of hearts, and when declarer got a look at the dummy, he saw that he was going to have his hands full taking nine tricks. With only four off the top, he had to develop an additional five somewhere. He couldn't think of any way to develop the diamond suit without losing at least one trick there, so he had to get an additional trick from spades. In the meantime, he had to ward off the attack which the opponents were making in hearts. He played the seven-spot from dummy, and, when East played the jack, he played the three. Not only was it right to hold up on general principles when he had to give up two tricks to establish his hand, but also, if West started with both the king and queen of hearts, the ten-spot in dummy and the nine-spot in his hand became key cards. If East continued with a small heart and West won with the queen, he then could not continue the suit without promoting declarer's nine-spot. When East continued with the queen of hearts, South had to reconsider.

The ten-spot was going to be smothered, and the time had come to take the ace. It was possible that West had started with five hearts and East had no more left. If East had one left, declarer still would be all right if the player to whom he gave up the lead was West.

So, he led the queen of diamonds. West properly played his king, and declarer decided that the time had come for a second hold up. He played low from the dummy. That increased his chances of bringing in the diamond suit from slight to considerable and also left his favorite player on lead. If West had gone ahead and continued with the king of hearts, the nine would have become the game-going trick, if the diamond suit came in. But West was having none of this and switched to a small club.

From here on, it was easy sledding. All South had to do was to give up a spade trick, and, with the diamonds breaking 3–2, he was home free. Had declarer taken the first heart trick with his ace, then when West gained the lead, he would have been able to lead a small heart to East's queen, and the deuce of hearts back from East would have given the defenders a total of three hearts, in addition to their inevitable spade trick and diamond trick.

Suppose you are going to have to give up the lead three times to get your hand established? Should you then hold up unless you have four tricks in the suit which they are attacking? Well, it might be a good idea, if you can do so.

South opened the bidding with two no-trump, and North went on to three no-trump. West didn't see where he was going to have any entries to his long suit, even if he got it established, and so he led the nine of hearts, trying to hit his partner's long suit. He was successful in this, and just to be sure the suit was continued, East overtook with his ten-spot.

Fig. 13-22

Had South won that first trick, West's opening lead would have turned out to be a winner. South was going to have to try to establish clubs, and West could win the first club lead and have a heart to continue that suit. That would use up declarer's second stopper, and when East gained the lead with another club, he could get rid of the last stopper South had. Then the defenders would finally come to their three club tricks plus two heart tricks.

But South knew better than to take that first trick. Count as he could, he could find only eight tricks without bringing in a trick in clubs. Of course, he might have a chance to bring in a ninth trick in diamonds if the opponents would be good enough to lead the suit, but if he had to lead it himself, chances for the ninth trick there were slim indeed. So, it looked like he was going to have to establish a club trick for a ninth trick or do without a ninth trick. With the opponents' holding three high cards in that suit, he needed four heart tricks to start off taking them right away. So he just played the three of hearts and let East hold the trick. He hoped that East, who held the length in hearts, would not have all three of the club entries.

East continued hearts, and South won the second heart trick, but that exhausted West of hearts. South now led a club which West duly won with the queen. West did the best he could and led a spade, but declarer won that in his own hand, preserving entries into the dummy, and led another club. East won that, and could choose between knocking out a second heart stopper or trying to kill both of dummy's entries. Actually, he continued hearts, but when he got in with the last club lead from South, declarer still had a stopper in the heart suit.

The last hand in this series is from my favorite composer of fanciful bridge hands, the late Robert Darvas. I give the hand and the bidding just as he reported it in 1951 (Fig. 13-23).

According to Mr. Darvas, when he was visiting in Italy he met two beautiful girls who wanted to spend their time playing bridge instead of going to a dance next door. One of them had a gentleman friend who agreed to join the game, and, on this hand, the girls were East and South. West got off to a lead of the ten of spades, and East, either because she was a fine bridge player or because she had her mind on something else, played the six-spot. You can see that had she played the king, when she returned the suit, West could win the ace, but the jack in South would stop the suit, and declarer would have time to knock out the two minor suit aces and take the balance of the tricks without even bothering about the heart finesse.

Fig. 13-23 Dlr: N Vul: E-W

North: ♠ Q 4 ♡ K 6 4 ◇ J 7 ♣ Q J 9 7 5 2

West: ♠ A 10 9 7 5 3 ♡ 8 3 2 ◇ 4 3 ♣ 6 3

East: ♠ K 6 ♡ Q 9 5 ◇ A 10 8 5 2 ♣ A 8 4

South: ♠ J 8 2 ♡ A J 10 7 ◇ K Q 9 6 ♣ K 10

NORTH	EAST	SOUTH	WEST
Pass	1◇	Dbl	1♠
2♣	Pass	2 NT	Pass
3 NT	Pass	Pass	Pass

Opening lead: ♠10

As for the young lady in south, she was even a greater genius, or else she also had her mind on something else. She played the two-spot and let the ten win the trick. This probably belongs in the *Guinness Book of World Records* as the finest hold-up play ever made. Had she won the trick with the jack, when East led the king, West could simply overtake it with the ace and bring in a lot of spade tricks. However, after South made that sensational play, there was no way for the defenders to take more than one additional spade trick, and the hold-up play scored another triumph.

THE HOLD-UP PLAY WITH TRUMPS

When there are trumps, the hold-up play can be used to break the communications between the defenders' two hands. You can wait until one of your hands is out of their suit so you can trump or until one of them is out of cards in their suit and has none left to reach his partner. Fig. 13-24 is another example where declarer waited until he was out of cards in their suit.

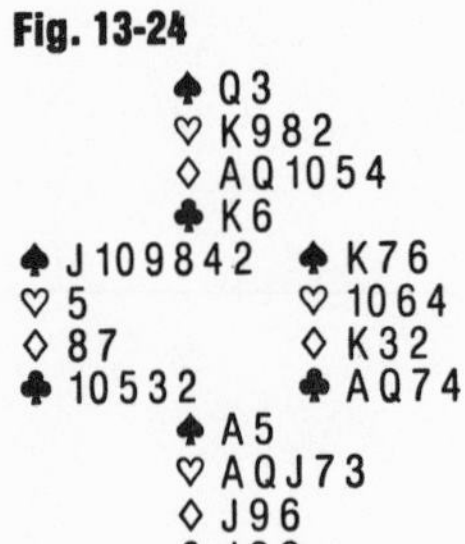

Fig. 13-24

In a four heart contract, West led the jack of spades. So far as declarer was concerned, West could have had the king, so he hopefully played the queen from the dummy. But when East turned up with the king, declarer decided he was in no hurry to win his ace. He had a spade loser, a possible diamond loser, and possibly two losers in clubs. He could get rid of his losing clubs on dummy's diamonds, but to do so, he had to finesse diamonds. Should East happen to have the king of diamonds, declarer wanted to be sure there was no way he could put West in the lead to lead clubs. So, he let East hold the king of spades, not particularly caring what he led. East continued spades; South won the ace; and no longer could West get the lead. Declarer pulled trumps in three leads, ending in his own hand, and then led the jack of diamonds for a finesse. East won with the king, but had no effective card to return. If he led a club, he would only get one club trick. He would get the same thing if he led a diamond, for two of South's clubs could be discarded on the diamonds. The lead of a spade would let declarer discard a club in his hand, while trumping in the dummy, and make an extra trick.

On the next hand, declarer was not trying to get himself or his dummy out of cards in a suit, he was trying to get East void in their suit.

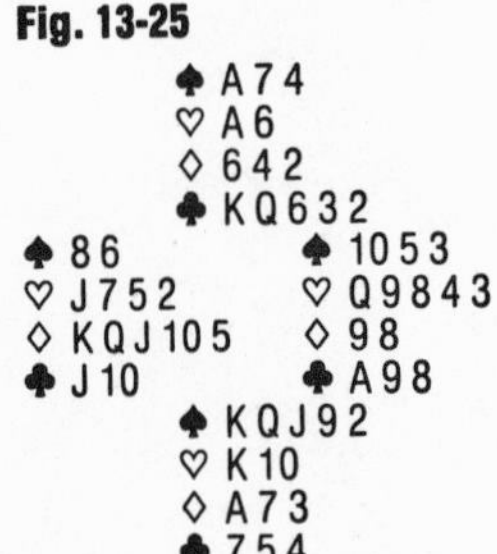

Fig. 13-25

Against a four spade contract, West led the king of diamonds. Declarer saw two diamond losers, and, if East happened to hold the ace of clubs, it looked like there were two club losers as well. One nice solution would be for West to hold the ace of clubs, but declarer saw he had better prepare for the worst. If West had started with five diamonds, then East had only two, and holding up one round could easily disrupt communications between their hands. There was no absolutely safe way to play the hand, as East might have held a singleton diamond and West the ace of clubs, but declarer thought the best of several probabilities was to let the king of diamonds win the trick. East led a second diamond, and this time South won. He led the ace and king of spades, and then led a small club toward the king. East wasn't going to make life easy for him, and he held up too. The declarer returned to his hand with another trump and led another club. This time East did win the ace and led back the heart, trying to take the entry out of the dummy. Declarer won that in his own hand and then led a third club. Fortunately, East had to win that, and declarer now had the club suit established and was able to reach the dummy with the ace of hearts to discard the losing diamond on the last club.

On the next hand, declarer gained time by letting East hold the first trick because he thought East had no lead that could do him damage.

Fig. 13-26

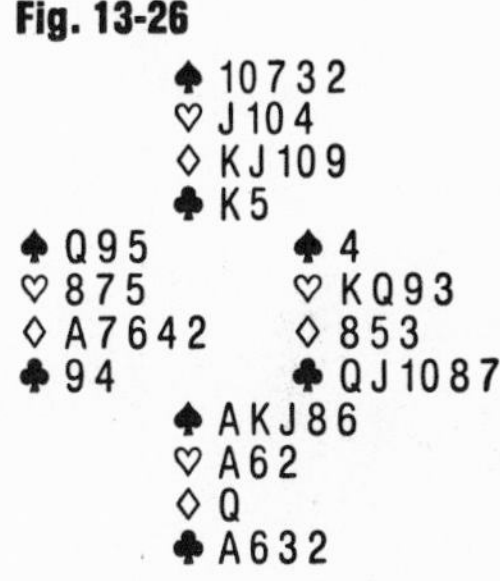

Against four spades, West got off to a lead of the eight of hearts: the ten was played from the dummy; and East covered with the queen. Declarer thought he might be on the verge of losing two heart tricks if he let West gain the lead before he had his diamonds established. But the lead of the eight of hearts convinced declarer that East had both the king and queen. In that event, East could not pursue the suit. So, declarer put off taking his ace of hearts and let East do his best to do something about it. East had no trouble figuring out the real situation in hearts and led the queen of clubs won by South with the ace. South had no idea of taking any finesse in spades, so he won that in his hand and laid down the ace and king of spades. This left West with a winning spade, but it left South in full control. He led the queen of diamonds, planning to play dummy's king, but West was impatient to lead another heart and won the diamond lead with the ace. On came a second heart, but this time declarer won his ace. He went to the dummy with the king of clubs and started leading diamonds, on the first of which he discarded his remaining heart. So, declarer lost only one heart trick—not two—and only three tricks in all: a heart, a diamond, and a spade.

It is almost axiomatic that when you are playing trumps and have in the suit led by the opponents a doubleton in one hand and the ace in either hand you should hold up unless you can see some good reason why you should not. Of course, when you have reason to believe that a second lead of the suit will be trumped, or when you have some way to take a quick discard of the second card in the hand with a doubleton, or when there is some switch which the defenders might take which would prove embarrassing, you may have a good reason for not holding up. Usually, you don't have such a reason, as is shown in the next hand (Fig. 13-27).

Fig. 13-27

Against a four spade contract, West led the king of clubs. A look at the dummy told declarer he was in a very aggressive contract, as he had at least one loser in trumps, probably two in hearts, and one in clubs. The heart suit offered one possibility of salvation, and the diamond suit another. To take advantage of which of these might work the best, declarer, unable to see any reason for not holding up, let the king hold the first trick. On came the queen of clubs, which he won with his ace. Now he led the ace and king of trumps and was gratified to see that he had only one trump loser. Next he tested the diamonds, taking the ace and king, and, when both opponents followed suit, he saw that he would get no break worse than 4–2. He came on with a third diamond, which he trumped. It would have done West no good to trump with his high trump, so he discarded a club. Now declarer led his small club toward dummy, trumped it, and led the fourth diamond, which he also trumped. Again, West felt very frustrated. If he let the declarer win this, it was his eighth trick. If he trumped, he was wasting his high trump on thin air. Finally, he discarded a heart. Now the declarer went to the dummy with the ace of hearts and led the fifth diamond, on which he discarded a small heart. These made his ninth and tenth tricks. Altogether, he lost one trump trick, one heart trick, and one club trick.

Had declarer taken the first lead with the ace of clubs, he could have gone set. If he led a club back, West could win that and then lead a third club to make dummy trump, and one of those precious entries used to develop the diamond suit would be gone.

THE BATH COUP

A simple hold-up play where the king is led and you hold both the ace and jack seems to have been discovered during the days of whist at Bath, England.

43
KQ1095 76
AJ82

The idea was that when West led the king, South would trick him into continuing the suit if he didn't win the ace. I suppose South would play his eight-spot to try to create the impression that East had signaled. This trickery must have been considered extremely smart back in those days, for the play was dubbed the "Bath Coup." It still works occasionally in these more sophisticated days.

However, today it is simply considered a hold-up play and is generally used to keep control of the suit while you go about establishing your own tricks.

Fig. 13-28

Against three no-trump, West led the king of diamonds, and declarer had a cinch, provided he did not win with the ace. He had four sure heart tricks and four club tricks, even if the club finesse failed. However, if he won the first trick with the ace of diamonds, he would have no more stoppers in that suit, and, when East got in with the king of clubs, he could continue diamonds, and West could win four tricks in that suit. But when South declined to take the first trick, had West continued the suit, South could have won the second lead. Then, if East got the lead with the king of clubs, declarer would still have a stopper in diamonds and would be able to bring in his nine tricks. If after winning the king of diamonds West switched to a spade, hoping that East could win the ace and return a diamond, East could do that, all right, but, in the process, they would develop three spade tricks for South. This added to his four heart tricks and two minor suit aces would certainly give him nine tricks. No other lead could prevent declarer from establishing his four club tricks while he had everything under control.

It is not necessary that the ace and jack be in the same hand (Fig. 13-29).

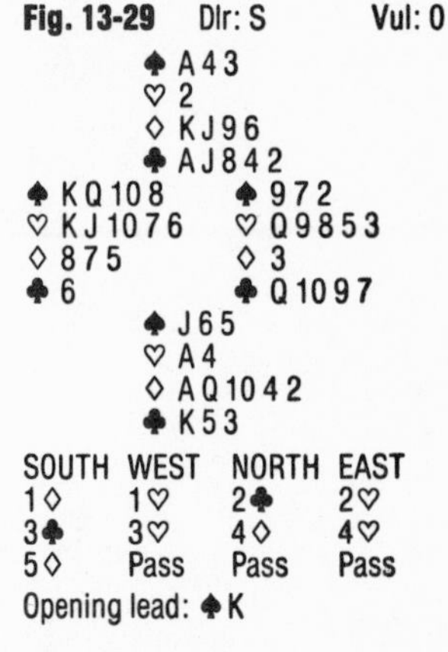

After nine consecutive bids without a pass, everybody ran out of gas at once, and declarer had overshot the three no-trump mark and ended up playing five diamonds. West launched a surprise attack by leading the king of spades. Declarer saw a sort of split "Bath Coup" and played small from the dummy. East expressed his opinion of the surprise attack by playing the two-spot. As we will see, declarer's refusal to take the first trick gave him time to develop the club suit while he still had everything under control.

West became a little worried about all of those clubs in the dummy and led a heart to get that trick in now, if it was available. It was not available. Declarer won with the ace and led three trumps, while East was discarding two hearts. South then led the king of clubs and a small one. When West showed out, declarer played small from the dummy to keep communications there. East won and came back with a spade, but declarer won that in the dummy and then led the ace of clubs and another club, which he trumped. That got the long club in the dummy established, and, by trumping a small heart, the dummy could be reached so that the losing spade could be discarded on the club.

At times, when it is not there at first, it can be developed.

Against three no-trump, West led the ten of spades. Declarer covered with dummy's jack, and East put on the queen. At this point, declarer examined the dummy, and something familiar seemed to be there, but it seemed a little strange. On a closer look, he saw what it was. There was the Bath Coup, upside down, on its head, so to speak, but there, nonetheless. True, the jack of spades was no longer in the dummy, but with both it and the ten gone, the nine had replaced it. Declarer just let the queen win the trick. Now East could not continue the suit without giving the declarer both an additional trick and plenty of time to do whatever he wanted to do with his two tricks in spades, thus warding off an attack from that source. So, East switched to the queen of hearts, but that didn't do any good either. As soon as declarer knocked out the ace of diamonds, he had plenty of tricks. There would be waiting for him one spade trick, two heart tricks, three diamond tricks, and three club tricks. So, having to lose the lead only one time and having two stoppers in the suit they were now attacking, no further hold up was necessary. Declarer simply won with the dummy's heart, led diamonds until the ace was played, and had his nine tricks.

Before I go on to my final example, let's stop and take a good look to see what makes the thing tick.

1.	2.	3.
DUMMY	DUMMY	DUMMY
3 2	Q 3	A 3
DECLARER	DECLARER	DECLARER
A Q	A 2	Q 2

In each of these illustrations, the ace represents the highest card in the suit, and the queen represents the third highest. The opponents have the king, which is the second highest. In each case, if the opponent who holds the king has to lead the suit, you can get two tricks.

Now let's look at another illustration where the jack has replaced the queen:

4. DUMMY	5. DUMMY	6. DUMMY
3 2	J 3	A 3
DECLARER	DECLARER	DECLARER
A J	A 2	J 2

Let us assume that the king has been played. Now the situation in 4, 5, and 6 is identical with that in 1, 2, and 3. With the king gone, we will have the first and third highest cards in the suit, and the opponents have the second highest card. If the player who holds the queen has to lead the suit, you can always get two tricks. Of course, in 1 and 4, you can get two tricks if the second highest card is in East by simply leading from the dummy and taking a finesse, but you cannot do so on the other illustrations.

In hand 13-30, we had a situation where after the first trick the nine-spot in north became the third highest card, which made it impossible for East to lead the second highest card without giving you an extra trick. When the ten, jack, and queen all went on the first trick, three cards higher than the nine-spot had been played, and the nine had been promoted from sixth highest all the way up to third highest in one fell swoop. And here we have met another old friend—the matter of the promotion of intermediate cards.

Fig. 13-31

Sometimes other forms of promotion can be arranged.

Against three no-trump, West opened the eight of spades. Counting one spade trick for sure after the first trick, declarer could see seven tricks; he needed to develop two more. Obviously, they could come from clubs, but that involved the possibility of losing the lead if West had the king of clubs.

Having done his counting, declarer asked the next question about the opening lead: "What is it?" Could it be a fourth best? If so, West had three cards higher than the eight-spot and they must be the A J 9 because declarer was looking at the other three. If that's what West had, declarer could make sure of two spade tricks by putting in dummy's ten-spot and, after finessing clubs, establishing a spade. But declarer considered it more likely that West had led a short suit and that the eight-spot was the highest spade West had. In that event, East had the A J 9. How about it now? If the ten were played, East would simply cover with the jack, and then, if West got in with the king of clubs and had a spade left to lead, South would be in serious trouble. If the three were played, East could simply play the nine, and the same situation would arise. How about playing the king at trick one? That ignored the old rule of "second-hand low," but it might conform with the new thinking rule. East would have to win that with the ace. Or, if he didn't win with the ace, concede two spade tricks to South. After winning it with the ace, what would the situation be? There would be promotion all over the lot. With the two highest cards gone, South's queen would rise to the number one spot, and North's ten would rise to the number three spot. East would have the jack which was the second highest card and would find he could not continue the suit without giving declarer two tricks in it. So, if declarer had analyzed the opening lead correctly and played the king of spades, this would guarantee his contract, no matter whether West had led the top of nothing or fourth best. With the club finesse going into the West hand, if he had started with the ace of spades, after he won the king of clubs, he could not continue that suit. So here we have a third-generation Bath Coup. When those people at Bath, England, first hit upon this in the days of whist, I doubt that they fully realized what they had discovered.

You have noticed, of course, in our various illustrations, that when the player who has the lead does not have the second highest card, it doesn't always turn out so well. This brings us right up to our next subject, which involves the attempt to avoid giving the lead to that player who can do you harm, offering it instead to the fellow who is harmless. Of course, this play has acquired the name "the avoidance play."

THE avoidance play is another important defensive device. It is supposed to keep you from being defeated at your contract, rather than help you fulfill it. There is a difference. You avoid defeat by trying to arrange to lose whatever tricks you have to lose to the opponent who can't harm you.

We have seen avoidance plays in connection with finesses, suit establishment, some loser-on-loser plays, and hold-up plays, most of which are a special form of avoidance. While we may see a few more hands which have some of those elements, our emphasis is going to be on pure and simple avoidance. Before we get out and see some more complicated situations, let's lay a solid groundwork and look at the play in its simplest form.

DUMMY
♠ K J 9 2
♡ 7 5 4
◇ K 2
♣ K J 4 2

DECLARER
♠ A 10 8 4 3
♡ K 6 2
◇ A 4
♣ A Q 6

Against a four spade contract, West led the eight of diamonds. Counting your losers, you see that you may lose a trick in spades and that you could lose three tricks in hearts. Of course, you can always discard one of your hearts on the long club in the dummy, but you had better wait until trumps have been pulled before you do that. If, while you are accomplishing these things you can be sure that East never gets the lead, you can also be sure that the opponents will never take three heart tricks.

It doesn't make any difference which hand wins the opening lead, so you win it with the ace. You then lead a small spade to the king in the dummy, with both opponents following suit. Now you are going to make your contract, no matter what happens. You are going to lead back the jack, and, if East follows with a small card, you have no intention of playing your ace. The books tell you that the odds favor going up with the ace 52 to 48 percent, but forget it. You are 100-percent sure to make your contract if you take the finesse. If West is able to win that with the queen, everybody will be out of trumps, and you can soon regain the lead and go about your business, discarding one of your hearts on dummy's clubs. You can then try for an overtrick by leading toward the king of hearts. If West shows out and the queen is still in East's hand, all you have to do is lead a second high trump and still go about your business. All you have done is make sure that East does not gain the lead.

Unfortunately, you cannot always be positive that the bad guy won't get the lead. When that happens, you just have to do the best you can and make every effort to avoid letting him do so.

DUMMY
♠ Q 10 4
♡ Q 10 5
♢ 8 5
♣ A K 10 5 3

DECLARER
♠ A K J 6
♡ A 9 7
♢ K J 3
♣ J 6 2

Against three no-trump, the opening lead was the six of diamonds, and East played the ten. Had East played the queen, declarer would not have taken the trick because it looked like he might have to lose a club to East and he would have wanted to wait until East was out of diamonds, if possible. However, when East played the ten, he felt he had little choice, for it looked like West was sitting with both the ace and the queen. So he won the jack and, with a little counting, saw that he had only seven more tricks off the top and had to gain another. Apparently, his best chance for doing this was in the club suit, but one thing he was not going to do was take the club finesse. He led a small club and went right up with the ace. If everybody followed suit, he planned to play the king of clubs next. Should East happen to show out, he would lead a small club toward his jack to establish dummy's clubs, while giving West the lead. He was going to

Fig. 14-1

West	North	East
	♠ K Q 5 ♡ 8 6 ◇ K 8 4 ♣ A 10 8 4 3	
♠ 10 7 ♡ A 10 7 5 2 ◇ Q 7 6 2 ♣ Q 5		♠ J 9 8 3 ♡ Q 9 3 ◇ J 10 9 ♣ J 7 6
	♠ A 6 4 2 ♡ K J 4 ◇ A 5 3 ♣ K 9 2	

make his contract if West had the queen of clubs with any number at all and also if East had it either singleton or doubleton. That was far from a sure thing, but it is the best declarer could do.

The hold-up play itself may be dangerous, and when you have a better alternative, it should be taken.

Against three no-trump, West led the five of hearts, and East played the queen.

Counting the one heart trick of which he was assured, declarer still could come to only eight tricks off the top. He had to get another trick out of the black suits, and clubs obviously offered the best chance.

Had declarer felt that to establish his hand he might have to lose the lead to East, he would have played small on that trick. That would save the day if East had started with only two hearts. That play would not work if East started with three hearts. Then, after declarer held up, East would lead a second heart, declarer would have to play his jack, and West could hold up and let declarer win. Then, if either opponent got the lead, West could cash more heart tricks.

If, however, declarer could manipulate things so that West got the lead while he was getting his suit established, West was the good fellow who could not hurt him with further heart leads. So, the declarer won the first heart trick with the king of hearts and crossed to the dummy with the king of spades to lead a club. When East played low, he put in his nine of clubs. West won with the queen, and, when the suit broke 3–2, declarer had established his hand without letting East get the lead.

Fig. 14-2

West	North	East
	♠ Q 2 ♡ 9 5 3 ◇ A 7 ♣ A K 10 8 7 2	
♠ A 10 8 5 3 ♡ K 10 7 ◇ J 6 5 3 ♣ 4		♠ J 9 7 ♡ J 8 2 ◇ Q 10 4 ♣ J 6 5 3
	♠ K 6 4 ♡ A Q 6 4 ◇ K 9 8 2 ♣ Q 9	

On the next hand (Fig. 14-2), declarer took what looked like a sensational first-round finesse, but what on closer inspection turned out to be entirely sensible.

West led the five of spades against three no-trump, and the queen in the dummy held the first trick. At trick two, declarer led the deuce of clubs and, when East played low, played his nine-spot. When West was able to follow suit, declarer had six club tricks, two diamond tricks, a heart trick, a spade trick he had already won, and everybody was going to have a lot of difficulty discarding on that run of clubs.

It is unusual to take a deep first-round finesse against a jack, but, in this case, it was so right. If the finesse lost, declarer would still have a guarantee of nine tricks unless East had all five of the outstanding clubs. As the cards were, with East holding four to the jack, South was going to be a busy boy trying to scramble for nine tricks if he did not take the finesse. And, of course, if he surrendered the lead to East, disaster was going to overtake him.

Avoidance will sometimes be the very good reason you finesse for a queen when you are missing only four cards in the suit.

On hand 14-3, in response to his partner's overcall, West opened the three of clubs. Declarer trumped the second club and saw that he would have no difficulties, provided he got his diamond suit established before West had a chance to switch to hearts. He laid down the king of trumps and then led a small one and finessed the jack. That won the trick, so he led the ace of trumps and then led the diamonds. West took the first diamond, but it was too late for him to do any damage by leading hearts. Although he switched, declarer rose with dummy's ace and then was able to discard the two hearts in his hand on dummy's diamonds.

Fig. 14-3 Dlr: N Vul: B

♠ A J 4
♡ A Q 3
◇ J 10 9 7 3
♣ J 8

West	East
♠ Q 8 3	♠ 7
♡ 10 8 5	♡ K 9 6 2
◇ A 6 2	◇ 8 5
♣ 9 5 4 3	♣ A K Q 10 6 2

♠ K 10 9 6 5 2
♡ J 7 4
◇ K Q 4
♣ 7

NORTH	EAST	SOUTH	WEST
1◇	2♣	2♠	Pass
3♠	Pass	4♠	All Pass

Opening lead: ♣3

Declarer took eleven tricks. He would have taken ten, even if the trump finesse had lost to the queen in the east hand. That would have been all of the trumps, and East could have had no way to reach his partners' hand except with the ace of diamonds. If he'd led that, he would have established the diamond suit for South.

However, if declarer had just laid down the ace and king of trumps, then, when West got in, he could lead hearts while he still had another entry, and the defense would have taken one trick in each suit.

So instead of taking the play which gave him an almost 52-percent chance to lose no spade tricks, declarer took the play which gave him an almost 100-percent chance to take a total of ten tricks.

When you have to take two finesses, it might make a big difference which one you take first (Fig. 14-4).

Against three no-trump, West opened the queen of spades. Declarer counted six tricks off the top and knew he had to develop three more. He could get all three of them out of diamonds if the diamond finesse worked. If the diamond finesse failed, he would get only two additional tricks and would still have to take the heart finesse. When he looked at it this way, the question almost answered itself. If he won the first trick with the ace of spades, West would not be able to continue spades without giving him both an extra trick and an extra stopper. However, he wouldn't want East in the lead before all of the tricks he wanted were established. Obviously, he had to take first the finesse which would give the lead to West.

Fig. 14-4

So he led the queen of hearts. If West refused to take his king, declarer would, with two heart tricks in hand, abandon the suit and come to his hand with the ace of clubs to tackle diamonds. However, West did take his king of hearts and shifted to a club. Declarer won that in his hand and then led his queen of diamonds.

Both finesses failed, but the contract succeeded, and that was the big thing. Had he taken his finesses in the wrong order, the contract would have gone down with the finesses.

While it is not nearly so good as a sure thing, a probable thing is the next best bet (Fig. 14-5).

Fig. 14-5

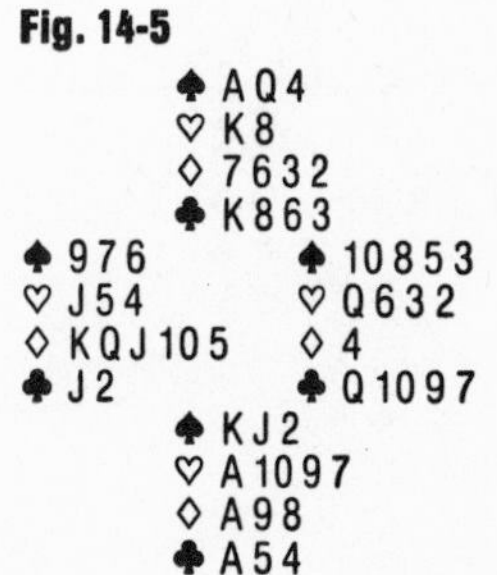

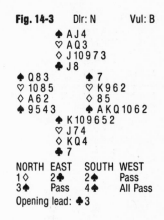

West led the king of diamonds against three no-trump, and, when the dummy came down, declarer was looking at a total of eight tricks. He and dummy had seven clubs and only six hearts, but hearts looked like the best bet because of the good intermediate cards. Declarer let the king hold the first trick to see what he could learn, and on came the queen. This time East discarded a small spade. There was no longer any reason to hold up, as East was already out of diamonds, so South took the ace. Having read this book, declarer knew better than those who read other books that East was much more likely to have length in hearts than was West because South knew that West started with five diamonds and East with only one. This left West only eight unknown cards, compared to twelve with East. This suited declarer fine. When you are missing both the queen and jack and plan to finesse in a hand to lose one of these and hope you can drop the other, naturally you always take the finesse into the hand which you think is long. If you have judged right and the honors are split, then when you lay down the top one, you will drop the honor in the hand which was short. So, all declarer had to do was hope not only that West had only two or three hearts, but that one was either the queen or jack. If his wishing would come true, he would lose the lead to East, who could do him no further harm by leading diamonds, and drop the other honor in the west hand.

Of course, his wish did come true. He led the seven-spot and put in the eight from the dummy. East won with the queen and, having no diamonds left, shifted to a club. Declarer won that in the dummy and laid down the king of hearts. He returned to his hand with a spade, and, when West's jack fell under the ace, the ten of hearts gave him his ninth trick.

Even if you can't keep a dangerous opponent out of the lead forever, you may be able to keep him out of the lead until such time as he can do you no damage.

Fig. 14-6

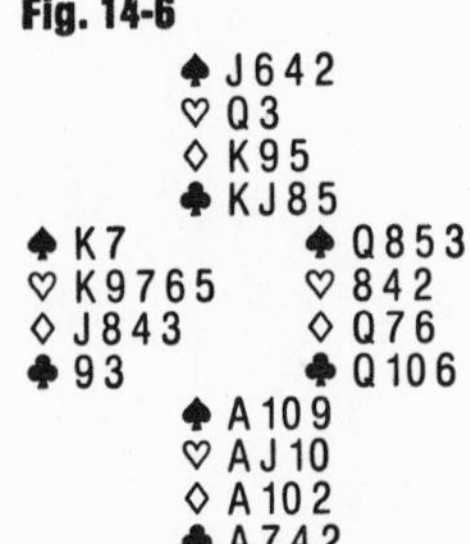

Against three no-trump, West led the six of hearts. Declarer put up the queen from the dummy, and it held the trick. He now had six additional tricks, making a total of seven, and, if there would be two or three clubs to the queen in the west hand, he could pick up an extra two there. But the declarer wasn't ready for that play. Suppose the finesse failed and East got the lead with the queen and continued hearts? It might prove embarrassing. So, declarer set out to develop a spade trick first. He led the two of spades and put in the nine. West won with the king and refused to continue hearts, leading instead the nine of clubs. Declarer still hadn't developed his extra spade trick and still wasn't ready to try clubs, so he won with dummy's king and led a second spade. This time when he put in the ten-spot, it held the trick. Now he was ready to see what he could do about getting an additional club trick.

He went to the dummy with the king of diamonds and led a small club toward his hand. When East put in the ten, he went up with the ace, and when West followed suit, all he had to do was concede a club trick to East. Having developed an extra trick in each of the black suits, he had his nine tricks.

Those of you who play match-point duplicate know how important the extra trick can be (Fig. 14-7).

Fig. 14-7

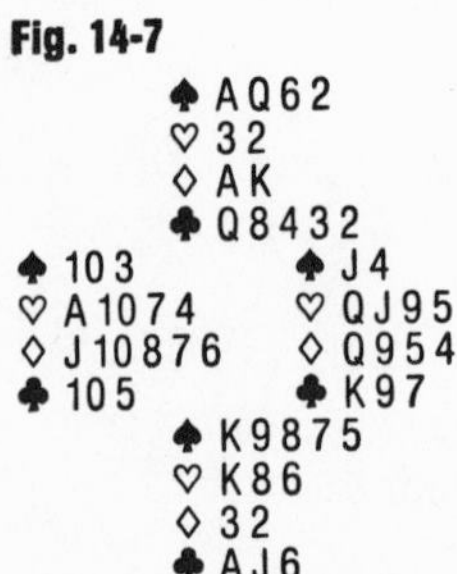

Each year there is an intercollegiate match, the winners of which get master points from the ACBL. Prior to 1969, the hands in the finals were called "par" hands, prepared by various experts to test the mettle of the collegiate contenders. It was expected that each hand played would have some rather tricky play in it. Back in 1955, Eddie Kantar of Los Angeles, one of the great player-writers, reported from the University of Minnesota a hand dealt in the qualifying round which he said might just as well have been set up by the experts. It is Fig. 14-7, and the whole problem involved a mere extra trick. The hand was played in a match-point duplicate contest, and Kantar reports that in almost every case, North and South got to a contract of four spades, and West led the jack of diamonds. After winning that, declarer had no problem pulling trumps in two leads, ending in the dummy. He then led a small club and finessed the jack. In every case but one, says Kantar, the declarer then banged down the ace and a small club and ended up losing one club trick and two heart tricks, just making the contract. The one exception came home with eleven tricks. After he successfully finessed the jack of clubs, he crossed back to the dummy with a diamond and led a second club. When East played the nine, he just played his small one. Now West had the lead, and he had no way to garner two heart tricks. Whatever he led, declarer cashed the ace of clubs and then crossed to the dummy with a trump and discarded two of his hearts on dummy's established clubs for a "cold top." Of course, if West had dropped the ten of clubs under the jack when the suit was first led, declarer could not have pulled off this coup. But as Kantar asks, "Would you have dropped the ten?"

When West got a look at the dummy on the next hand (Fig. 14-8), he thought he might have done well to lead a trump to keep declarer from trumping clubs in the dummy. It never occurred to him that the declarer would end up trumping diamonds in the dummy.

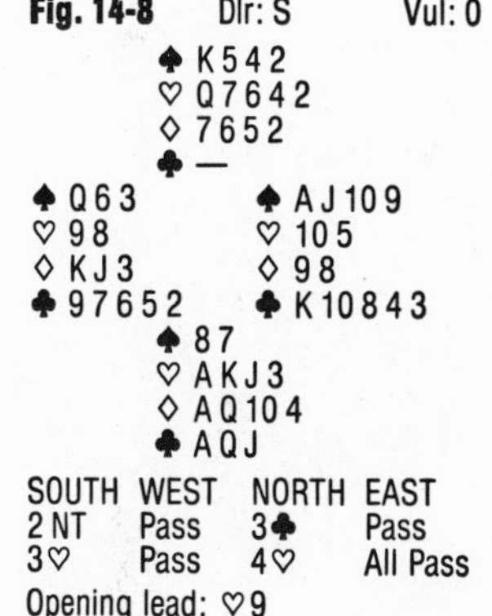

This is not a treatise on bidding, and I am not going to tell you whether or not I approve of South's opening bid of two no-trump with the spade suit wide open. Instead, I am going to tell you how he gave the lead to East only when a diamond lead could do him no harm.

Had West led a spade, my story might not have had a happy ending, but West was not about to underlead any honor into the two no-trump opening bid and decided, instead, on the nine of hearts. When declarer got a look at the dummy, it occurred to him that if West had the ace of spades and East had the king and jack of diamonds, he could take twelve tricks. But then it occurred to him that East might have the ace of spades and West the king-jack of diamonds. In that event, he might have trouble taking ten tricks.

He won the trick with the ace of hearts and led the king, noting that both opponents followed suit. He decided that instead of trying to finesse diamonds, he would see if he could discard three diamonds in the dummy and never take a finesse in that suit. That way he could not lose more than one club trick and two spade tricks. So, he laid down the ace of clubs and discarded a diamond on it. He then led the queen of clubs and discarded another diamond. East won with the king and switched to the nine of diamonds. Declarer simply played his ace; that left one diamond in the dummy which he discarded on the jack of clubs. Next he led a spade to the king and found out that the ace of spades was wrong. When he discovered that both of the diamonds were also wrong, he saw how right he had been not to lead spades before clubs. Had he done so, East, when he won the spade, almost certainly would have switched to the nine of diamonds. But declarer didn't give East the chance to lead diamonds until it was too late for the lead to do him any harm.

Fig. 14-9 is another one where declarer threw away quite a number of diamonds.

Against a four spade contract, West led the jack of hearts. When the dummy came down, declarer saw what looked like a loser in clubs and possibly as many as three in diamonds. So far, he had been lucky. They

had not taken their club trick, and that gave him a chance to discard his king of clubs. But that would still leave him a lot of diamonds to cope with, if they were divided unfavorably.

Declarer decided there was a good chance the hearts were either 4–4 or 5–3 and that he could take his club discard before touching trumps. He might need those trumps in the dummy for entries. He took the king of hearts and then the ace and queen, throwing away the king of clubs. Next he led the jack of clubs, planning to discard a diamond if East played low. East played the ace, and declarer was not ready for a diamond lead yet, so he trumped it. Then he returned to the dummy with a trump and led the ten of clubs. This time he did discard a diamond. West was on lead with the queen, but obviously couldn't hurt declarer with diamonds. Actually, there was nothing he could do to hurt declarer who could now pull trumps and discard two more diamonds on dummy's clubs, ending up with eleven tricks.

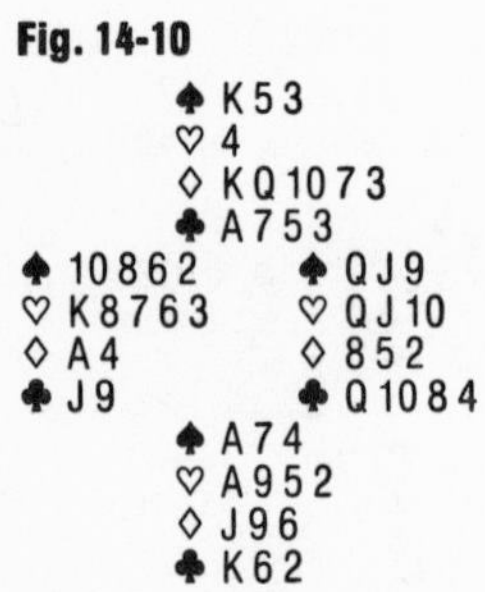

On the next hand (Fig. 14-10), declarer changed his mind in the middle of the play.

South got to the ambitious contract of three no-trump, and West led the six of hearts. South could find only five tricks without developing the diamond suit. But once the ace of that suit was gone, there would be four more tricks waiting for him. His first appraisal was that his best chance was to wait and take the third lead of hearts, hoping that East would have the ace of diamonds, and, in case West had opened with a five-card suit, communications would be destroyed. So he let the ten hold the first trick. East continued with the queen, and declarer took a second look. It looked as though East had started with the Q J 10. If he had a small heart with them, West had started with only four hearts and there was nothing to fear. If West started with five hearts, East had the singleton jack left, and suddenly that nine of hearts began to take on a magic color. Declarer decided that his chances to take nine tricks were good no matter who had the ace of diamonds. He rose with the ace of hearts and led diamonds. It turned out to be West who had the ace, but if he led a small heart to the jack in the East hand, that would be the end of the heart tricks for his side. If he led his king, that would establish the nine for declarer. In view of the fact that he could tell the diamonds were going to run, he cashed the king of hearts and switched to a spade as his only hope. There was no hope left, and declarer ended up taking ten tricks.

The next hand is a sort of optical illusion:

DUMMY
♠ K 7 2
♡ A J 9 3
◊ 7 5 3 2
♣ A Q

DECLARER
♠ A Q 6
♡ Q 6 5
◊ K 4
♣ K J 10 6 4

Against three no-trump, West leads the four of hearts. How do you play? Of course, the problem is to avoid letting East get the lead because he might switch to diamonds. It looks like you are going to take a lot of heart tricks, as West has probably underled the king and conceivably the ten, as well. And, you might even turn up with a total of twelve tricks.

Don't try for it! At least, don't try for it unless you are playing match-point duplicate. You can play the ace of hearts and take nine tricks before you give up the lead; then you might be able to get another one or two by leading the queen of hearts. On the other hand, you can play low from the dummy, and, if it does happen that East has that king instead of West, and East chooses to switch to diamonds at trick two, you could go set before you even get started.

This next hand is a cousin to the last one:

DUMMY
♠ A 5
♡ 7 6 5 4
◇ Q 7 3 2
♣ K J 8

DECLARER
♠ Q 3 2
♡ A 2
◇ A K 4
♣ A 10 9 6 2

Again you are in three no-trump, and this time you get a lead of the four of spades. Don't become too intrigued by trying to figure out which way to finesse the clubs. If you take the king of clubs first, you are going to take nine tricks no matter who has the queen of clubs.

But I forgot something. I forgot the first play. If you play the five of spades from dummy and East happens to turn up with the king and then switches to a heart, you are really going to have to guess right on the club suit, or you are probably going set. So, before we deal with clubs, let's deal with spades. Don't play the five-spot. Play the ace. Now when you lead the king of clubs and then lead the jack for a finesse, you are assured of four club tricks no matter what happens. In addition, you will have three diamond tricks, a spade trick, and also a heart trick. So avoid giving East a chance to win at trick one and switch to hearts.

We all feel badly that the right play is not always the winning play—a fact of life that we teachers and writers try to overlook. To avoid such a sour note in my last hand in this series, let me show you one where the right play brought unexpected good results (Fig. 14-11).

South had opened one club, and North had responded one diamond, so when the opponents reached three no-trump, West decided against leading either of their suits. He led, instead, the eight of hearts, hoping that might turn out to be his partner's suit. South looked at that and decided it was not a fourth best. If it had been, West would have started with the K J 10 8 and surely would have led the jack from the combination. Therefore, he played small from the dummy and decided to

Fig. 14-11

do all he could to keep West from getting the lead again to come through those hearts.

East put up the ten, and South won with the ace. If South could bring in five diamond tricks, he would have no problem at all, but four diamond tricks would give him all he really needed. He decided to play as safely as possible to be sure to take four diamond tricks. He went after diamonds rather than clubs because giving up a club trick would put West in the lead, and declarer didn't care for any part of that. He led the nine of diamonds, intending to play low from the dummy and concede the trick to East if he could get by with it. He couldn't get by with it. West wasn't going to have any of that, so he played the ten-spot. Declarer won with dummy's queen and duly noted the fall of the seven from East. He led a spade back to his hand and led the six of diamonds, intending to let *that* ride if it wasn't covered. It was covered with West's eight, so he won with dummy's king. East discarded a spade. Now declarer came back to his hand with the king of clubs and led the two of diamonds. At this spot, West had the jack and four left, and dummy had the A 5 3. So, when West played the four, declarer just put in the 5 for a marked finesse. As a reward for playing so carefully, he ended up taking not four diamond tricks, but five diamond tricks, in spite of the 4-1 break. That's only a little reward of 20 points for his virtuous action, but 20 points are better than none at all.

IT has been aptly said that the art of deception in bridge is the art of creating illusions. You set out to make the opponents believe that what is fact is not true. You try to appear to be weak where you are strong or strong where you are weak. You act like you are trying to accomplish one thing when it is really an entirely different goal you have in mind. I believe all of that, but I have been wondering for many years just how it applies to a hand which has been in my files for a long, long time.

DUMMY
♠ K J 3
♡ K 8 2
◊ K Q 7 2
♣ 9 7 4

DECLARER
♠ Q 8 2
♡ A 5 4
◊ A J 9 3
♣ A 6 3

A few years after the introduction of contract bridge, I found myself living in Chicago, and I made my first visit to what was then called the Auction Bridge Club, where they played nothing but contract bridge. A man whom I later found out was the house man helped us form a table, and on my first hand, I was East, as he played three no-trump with the above hand.

I was determined to count every card played on this, my first visit to this emporium, and, of course, saw the south cards one at a time, but I want to show you just how they were played.

My partner got off to a lead of the six of spades. After some thought, the jack was played from the dummy and the eight from the south hand. The jack held the trick. Declarer then carefully picked the eight of hearts from the dummy, on which he played the ace. Next he led the two of spades, and, when my partner played low, he played the king. His next play was the king of diamonds, and the nine from his hand, followed by the two of diamonds to his ace. Now he led the ace of clubs and, after some thought, carefully took the seven from the dummy and played it on the trick. Next came the diamond queen, on which the three was played, and then the heart king, on which the five was played. Finally he led the diamond seven to the jack. The four remaining tricks belonged to our side.

It then appeared to me, and still appears to me, that after he didn't get a club lead, he had exactly nine tricks, no more and no less, without all of those dramatics. Figure as hard as I could, I couldn't see how a player good enough to be the house man for a club could have either gained a trick or lost a trick. I was so intrigued by the whole matter, that on the following hand I misdefended and let him make his contract.

After a number of visits to this club, I found that, after he was my opponent, I was mentally fatigued. The trouble was, you never knew when some of this falsecarding meant something and when it didn't. At times, he would not falsecard at all—he would simply play in a straightforward manner. But you always felt that he was on the verge of getting by with something, and you often discovered that all too often he did exactly that. I am now convinced that all that tomfoolery was not as foolish as it seemed to me at the time.

I have yet to discover any good reason why the declarer should not falsecard as much as he pleases, just so long as he doesn't do himself any harm by so doing. I am also firmly convinced that if he falsecards both when it will and will not help him, he will be a hard man to play against. He will keep up that pressure on his opponents that makes it hard for them to avoid mistakes. So I am starting off my subject of deception by recommending that you deceive when you can and that you frequently appear to be trying to deceive when you know you can't.

While deception is more of an art than a science, there are certain plays which become almost standard, and I would like to start by showing some of them to you.

DECEPTION WHEN YOU ARE WINNING THE TRICK

When you, as declarer, have more than one card which will win the opening lead, you may have sufficient reason to want to deceive your opponents about your holding in the suit led. Sometimes you can, sometimes you can't. Let's look at some examples:

	1.			2.	
	932			92	
6 led		J	6 led		10
	AK8			AQJ	

1. First, assume you are playing no-trump. Your best play is the king and not the ace. The Rule of Eleven tells you that the jack which East has played is the only card in the suit which he has higher than the six-spot; therefore you know West started with the queen. If you play the ace, West will know you have the king because East would have played the king at trick one if he had had the king and jack both. Neither are you likely to fool East—he also knows about the Rule of Eleven and knows that you have three cards in the suit led higher than the six-spot. If you had only the ace higher than the jack, you still would have been likely to hold up for a round or two to exhaust East of the suit before you won the ace. So, playing the ace will fool no one, but playing the king, strangely enough, might. After all, it is not unusual for a player to underlead the ace-queen against a no-trump contract, and, if you play the king, East may well figure that his partner started with the ace and queen.

It is not so easy to deceive them when they are playing with trumps and you hold the ace. If you don't play it, West will figure that East does not have it, and East will figure that West surely would not have underled it against a trump contract. The best play you can make when they do have trumps is to play the card that both opponents are supposed to know you have—in this case, the ace. East should not be fooled, as that would place his partner with the king and queen, but at least it is the best you have.

2. When you have two cards immediately above the one which East has played, as are the queen and jack, it is virtually a no-lose play to win the trick with the higher of the two. When you cover the ten with the queen, West will have no way of knowing who has the jack. If East held both of them, he still would have played the ten. You are simply making life easy for your opponents if you win that trick with the jack.

	3.			4.	
	43			43	
5 led		10	5 led		J
	KQJ			AKQ	

3. Likewise here, when East plays the ten, you could play the king or queen, but never the jack. Probably the play of the queen will work out more often, for West is more likely to believe his partner has the jack and ten than he is to believe that he has the Q J 10.

4. Here again, against no-trump, the preferred play is the king, with the ace being the second choice; against a suit contract, the ace should be played.

	5.			6.	
	643			64	
J led		5	5 led		Q
	AKQ			AK10	

5. Here is a different situation. The jack has come from the west. East knows that you have the queen, and, if you wish to keep him from knowing who has the ace and king, don't play either of them; just play the card East already knows about. If, on the other hand, you wish to deceive West, don't play the queen. East might easily have the queen and not play it, or by some distribution might have the king and queen and play neither. To leave doubt in West's mind rather than East's, play the king or ace as seems best.

6. Here you have the ace and king topping the queen, and if you want to do all you can to get West to lead the suit again when next he gains the lead, play the ace. He will have no way of knowing who has the king unless you play it at trick one. In that event, he will know you started with both the ace and king.

	7.			8.	
	653			73	
4 led		10	4 led		9
	AKJ			AQ10	

7. Here, playing the jack assures you three tricks in the suit. However, if you figure you can throw the lead to West rather than East and there is some other suit you wish to avoid having led at all costs, take the chance of giving up the trick by playing the king. This will convince West that his partner surely has the jack, and, when you do give him the lead, he will no doubt continue the suit, and you will get your jack for a trick after all. Old-time players are wise in this strategem, so don't do it just for the fun of fooling them. Do it only when the situation is desperate.

8. Here you have a similar situation. Playing the queen on the nine-spot will probably cause West to continue the suit with a small one when he gains the lead. If you've a suit where they could run away with you if you let them in, this well may be worth the slight risk involved.

	9.			10.	
	72			43	
6 led		J	5 led		10
	AQ5			KJ72	

9. This is another example of the principle shown in 7 and 8. Play the ace on the jack to encourage West to lead a second low one when he regains the lead. Of course, he will have no way of knowing who has the queen.

10. This is an extreme case of the same sort, but you might save the day by playing the king on the ten-spot to encourage West to continue leading the suit he started out with.

Now let's take some of these combinations and, instead of looking at them in the abstract, place them in their proper framework with the 52 cards in the deck and see what makes them necessary or useful. Also, we will see how—hopefully—they will work out.

Freewheeling bidding methods got South into three no-trump, and West led the seven of spades. Declarer properly did his thinking before he played a card from the dummy, so that when East played the jack, he was able to play the ace without flinching. Declarer had seen that he needed a lot of diamond tricks to fulfill his contract, and he wished with all his might that the spade overcall made by West included the ace of diamonds. At trick two, he led the ten of daimonds, and West won with his ace. Had he thought to lead the ace of hearts at this point, it would have been the defenders who ended up with ten tricks, but he was in a hurry to lead to the queen of spades which he assumed to be in the east hand. It turned out that the queen of spades won the trick but was in the South hand. Now it was the declarer who ended up with ten tricks. If I have added that up right, it comes to a 20-trick swing.

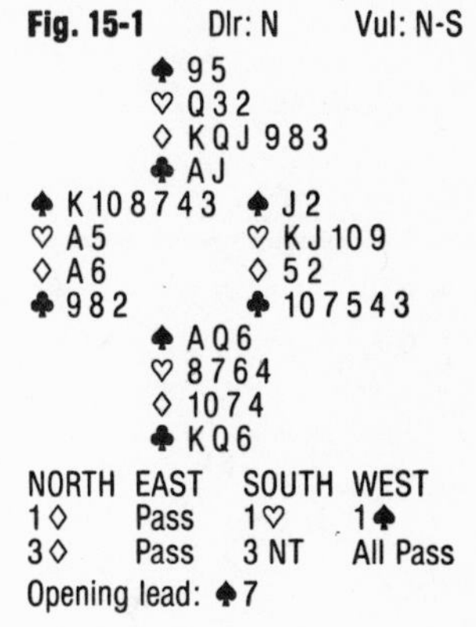
Fig. 15-1 Dlr: N Vul: N-S

North: ♠ 9 5 ♡ Q 3 2 ◇ K Q J 9 8 3 ♣ A J
West: ♠ K 10 8 7 4 3 ♡ A 5 ◇ A 6 ♣ 9 8 2
East: ♠ J 2 ♡ K J 10 9 ◇ 5 2 ♣ 10 7 5 4 3
South: ♠ A Q 6 ♡ 8 7 6 4 ◇ 10 7 4 ♣ K Q 6

NORTH	EAST	SOUTH	WEST
1◇	Pass	1♡	1♠
3◇	Pass	3 NT	All Pass

Opening lead: ♠7

On the next hand (Fig. 15-2), declarer was convinced that he could take three tricks in his opponents' suit, but he wisely decided to settle for two.

It took West a little time to decide upon his opening lead, but finally he came out with the seven of diamonds. The Rule of Eleven told declarer that East probably had no diamonds higher than the seven-spot, and declarer saw he could probably win that trick with the nine in the dummy or the ten in his hand, as he saw fit. He saw fit to win in the dummy with the ace. While he thought he could win three diamond tricks if he wanted to, he didn't want West to know that he could do that. Furthermore, in view of the heart situation, he wanted to stop West from doing any further thinking if it was possible to do so. At trick two, he led the queen of clubs and played the nine on it. West won with the ace and noted that declarer didn't seem to have too many club tricks. He took a little time to think, but what he was thinking about was which diamond to lead. Finally he decided to lead the queen, in case his partner was left with the singleton ten-spot. South won that with the king and, needless to say, started cashing tricks. Skillful signaling and discarding on the part of East and West held him to ten tricks. But he was quite happy to get that many.

Fig. 15-2 Dlr: S Vul: 0

North: ♠ K Q 7 4 3 ♡ 9 8 3 ◇ A 9 3 ♣ Q 6
West: ♠ J 8 5 2 ♡ A 4 2 ◇ Q J 8 7 5 ♣ A
East: ♠ 10 9 ♡ K J 10 7 6 ◇ 6 4 ♣ 8 7 5 2
South: ♠ A 6 ♡ Q 5 ◇ K 10 2 ♣ K J 10 9 4 3

SOUTH	WEST	NORTH	EAST
1♣	1◇	1♠	Pass
1 NT	Pass	2 NT	Pass
3 NT	Pass	Pass	Pass

Opening lead: ◇7

Variations on the next hand have appeared in numerous books and newspaper columns. Here, I think, is the original (Fig. 15-3). It is reported from the 1954 Summer Nationals in Washington, D.C., as played by Sam Fry, Jr., long time secretary of the Regency Bridge Club in New York.

Fry got into a contract of six clubs, and, after considerable thought, West led the deuce of diamonds. The story says that without apparent thought, Fry called for the queen from the dummy, which was duly covered by the king and then the ace. Fry's next move was to lead the ten of clubs to the jack in the dummy and then lead a small heart before anybody got any chance to do any signaling with discards. He finessed the jack, and West won the king. Triumphantly, he continued with the jack of diamonds. To his consternation, Fry trumped that, finished pulling trumps, and discarded dummy's three spades on his hearts.

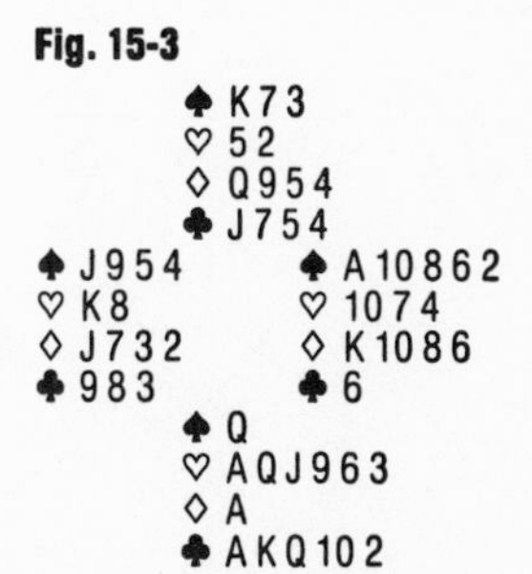
Fig. 15-3

North: ♠ K 7 3 ♡ 5 2 ◇ Q 9 5 4 ♣ J 7 5 4
West: ♠ J 9 5 4 ♡ K 8 ◇ J 7 3 2 ♣ 9 8 3
East: ♠ A 10 8 6 2 ♡ 10 7 4 ◇ K 10 8 6 ♣ 6
South: ♠ Q ♡ A Q J 9 6 3 ◇ A ♣ A K Q 10 2

If you have an early discard coming, you might try discarding from the suit you want led rather than from the one you don't want led. No guarantee goes with this, but it frequently works (Fig. 15-4).

Fig. 15-4

West	North	East
	♠ J 10 6 2	
	♡ 7 5 4	
	◇ A K	
	♣ K J 4 2	
♠ K 9		♠ 5 3
♡ A 6 3		♡ K Q 9
◇ Q J 10 7 4		◇ 9 8 6 5 3
♣ 10 9 8		♣ 7 6 3
	♠ A Q 8 7 4	
	♡ J 10 8 2	
	◇ 2	
	♣ A Q 5	

Against four spades, West led the queen of diamonds. Declarer saw no problem if the spade finesse would work. If it didn't work, there were three heart losers lying there exposed if the opponents took a notion to bring them in. So declarer thought he might discourage that attempt before he took the spade finesse, and, after winning the first trick with the king of diamonds, he led the ace and discarded a club from the south hand. Next, he took the spade finesse, and, I am pleased to report, when West won his king, he duly shifted to a club. Declarer was able, after pulling trumps, to cash the other club in his hand and reach the dummy to throw away two of his hearts on the good clubs in the dummy.

When Ewart Kempson first published a hand like the next one, in the American magazine *Bridge World*, the magazine labeled it, the "Kempson Coup." The name does not seem to have taken hold, but I would like to do my best to revive it out of respect for the many courtesies Mr. Kempson showed to my wife and me and for his many contributions to the game of bridge.

Fig. 15-5

West	North	East
	♠ 10 4	
	♡ 6 5	
	◇ Q 10 9 8	
	♣ A K 7 5 4	
♠ Q 8 7 5 3		♠ J 6
♡ K Q 4		♡ J 10 9 8 3
◇ K 2		◇ 7 6 5
♣ 9 8 2		♣ Q 10 3
	♠ A K 9 2	
	♡ A 7 2	
	◇ A J 4 3	
	♣ J 6	

I don't remember the exact cards in the original presentation, but the above is a reasonable replica of it. Against three no-trump, West opened the five of spades. A review of his assets told South that if the diamond finesse worked, he was going to take nine tricks without any complications. On the other hand, if the diamond finesse failed, complications might arise. He was going to have to bring in, somehow or the other, either an extra spade trick or a club trick; in the meantime, he had to keep his opponents from getting the bright idea of leading hearts. Chances for bringing in the extra spade trick were dim unless West had both the queen and jack. If he did, the extra trick could be achieved either by playing the ten-spot from the dummy or by letting the trick ride to the nine in his hand. On the other hand, if the ten did not bring in the desired trick, that play might serve as a smokescreen to keep the opponents from finding the killing shift. So, the ten was duly played, but East put up the jack. South won with the king and led a small club to the dummy to test the diamond situation. To preserve entries into the dummy, he led the queen, on which he dropped the jack, but West won that with the king. Surely, no good declarer with the nine-spot in his hand would have played the ten at trick one, so West continued with a small spade, and South's nine took a trick after all. That gave him his ninth trick. However, since he still had everything under control, he led a small club and ducked it in the dummy. When the club suit broke for him, he came home with eleven tricks.

DECEPTION WHEN YOU ARE FOLLOWING SUIT

After your left-hand opponent has made an opening lead, his partner is going to attempt to tell him whether he does or does not want that suit continued, by using the standard signaling procedure. It may be that you, as declarer, wish to attempt to interfere with these signals and try to convince the opening leader that his partner means the opposite of what he intended. Let's look at some example situations.

	1.			2.	
	Q853			QJ6	
AK104		76	AK942		1085
	J92			73	

1. In a trump contract, the opening lead is the king of the side suit, as indicated in 1. You, as declarer, are looking at seven cards in this suit and have every reason to fear that East can trump the third round and that he is going to signal his desire to do so. You play the three from the dummy, and East plays the seven-spot. Strangely enough, if West is paying attention and is up to it, your best way to discourage him from leading the second card in this suit is to play the two-spot. Usually the same signal you would give your partner to discontinue the suit is most likely to inhibit the opposition, while the same signal you would use to encourage him to continue a suit is most likely to encourage the opponents. Let us say you play the jack. If West has never played bridge before in his life, that may scare him to death, and he will be afraid that after he plays the ace, you will trump it, and your queen will be good. But I presume you wouldn't be playing against anybody who hasn't played before, so let's see what your competent West is going to think of the play of the jack. He's going to think that you're trying to fool him because, if the jack is indeed a singleton, then his partner started with 9 7 6 2 and certainly would never have played the seven.

Now let's say that you credit West with knowing more about bridge than that and you still play the nine to try to frighten him. Well, if that nine is a singleton, West won't believe his partner started with the J 7 6 2. If the nine is doubleton with the jack, then East holds the 7 6 2 and would have played the two. As a matter of fact, West would probably know that you don't even hold the nine-two doubleton. Because in that case, East would have held the J 7 6 and, again, would have played the six-spot.

But suppose you play the two-spot. Now West must be in doubt. It is possible that East started with the J 9 7 and, in that event, West should shift suits and look for other ways to conquer the world.

2. Again, we are playing with trumps, and West has led the king of a side suit. This time, we have only five cards between us and the dummy and we would like very much for West to continue. I don't know whether we can talk him into it or not, but the best chance is to play the seven-spot, the same card we would play to ask our partner to continue if we were defending. East has played the five, and West will notice that the three is missing. We are trying to talk him into believing that East started with the doubleton 5-3 and is asking West to continue the suit. If it works, fine, if it doesn't, it hasn't cost anything.

3.			4.	
	63			A8
QJ108		94	J765		109
	AK752			KQ432

3. We are playing a no-trump contract, and West has led the queen of a minor suit which we have not bid in the auction. East plays the four-spot, and we would very much like to have West continue the suit. Should we play the five-spot, or the seven?

Here is a little rule which turns out pretty well. If we play the five-spot, we are hiding one card from West, while if we play the seven-spot, we are hiding two cards. If we are trying to get him to continue the suit so a high card of ours, such as a queen, or a tenace position becomes a winner, it usually is better to conceal only one card and play the smallest one you have which is higher than the one played to your right. Among other things, it makes it impossible for the right-hand player to use the odd-even signal successfully, as you have made what he intended to show as an odd number into an even number and what he intended to show as an even number into an odd number. However, when it is length you are trying to conceal, as in this example, try to conceal two cards, unless the one you will play is so flamboyant as to be ridiculous. In this case, I would recommend the play of the seven-spot. Now West can work out that both the five and two are missing, and where the nine and king are he doesn't know. So, he is likely to continue the suit.

4. Again you have a concealed five-card minor suit, and West has led it against a no-trump contract. You play the eight from the dummy, and East plays the nine. East is likely to continue the suit if he has another card in that suit. The Rule of Eleven tells you East has one left. The best chance to get him to continue the suit is to play the four-spot.

5.
J32
K led
Q4

6.
QJ2
5 led
K64

5. Here the old-fashioned way to get West to shift after he has led the king from a side suit is to drop the queen. Even in these sophisticated days, that will sometimes work.

Fig. 15-6 Dlr: S Vul: B

North: ♠ 7642 ♡ 109 ◇ A74 ♣ 9765
West: ♠ J5 ♡ AKJ63 ◇ KJ85 ♣ J8
East: ♠ 108 ♡ 874 ◇ Q106 ♣ Q10432
South: ♠ AKQ93 ♡ Q52 ◇ 932 ♣ AK

SOUTH	WEST	NORTH	EAST
1♠	2♡	2♠	Pass
4♠	Pass	Pass	Pass

Opening lead: ♡K

6. This one is a bit more subtle. If you play the jack from the dummy, East will come up with the idea that his partner has the king. If and when he gains the lead in another suit, he may continue it to your advantage.

A picture always looks better in a proper frame. Let's put some of these situations in their proper frame—an entire deal—and see how they look.

On hand 15-6, West led the heart king, and the dummy came down. Declarer somehow managed to avoid saying, "I thought you might have a little bit more partner," and acted like a man who had not a problem in the world. The nine went on from the dummy, the four from East, and the five from South.

Looking at all four hands it looks easy. It wasn't that easy for West. The two-spot was missing. East would be disappointed if he had two hearts and was able to overruff the dummy. Probably West should not have done it. And almost certainly you and I would not. But the story insists that West did, in fact, lead the ace of hearts. I am not sure just what he said when East duly played the seven and South the deuce, but from here on it didn't make much difference what he did. One of dummy's losing diamonds was going to go off on the queen of hearts, and declarer was going to lose two heart tricks and one diamond trick and score game and rubber with his 22 high-card points.

Even with his 28 high-card points, declarer could see only eight tricks in the next hand (Fig. 15-7). He decided to let his opponents help him develop the ninth trick.

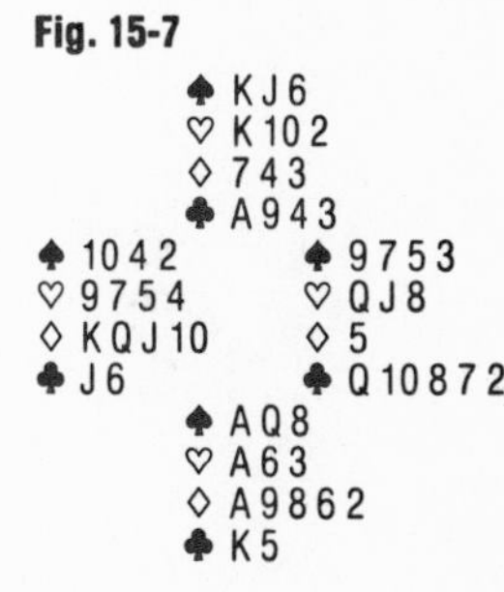

Fig. 15-7

South opened the bidding with one no-trump, and North went straight to three no-trump, so West knew nothing about the distribution of the hand. He made his normal lead of the king of diamonds. When the five went on from East, declarer decided to conceal the six and two and played the eight. It wasn't hard for declarer to tell that, if West had indeed opened a four-card suit, East had none left, and the suit could be established. West naturally continued with the queen, and, with all suits doubly stopped, declarer had time to win the ace and give West two more diamond tricks while establishing one for himself. That one would be the precious ninth trick.

My next hand was very much in the literature back in the 1940's. I haven't seen it in anybody's newspaper column for quite a long time. It is worth reviving, as it clearly illustrates a point.

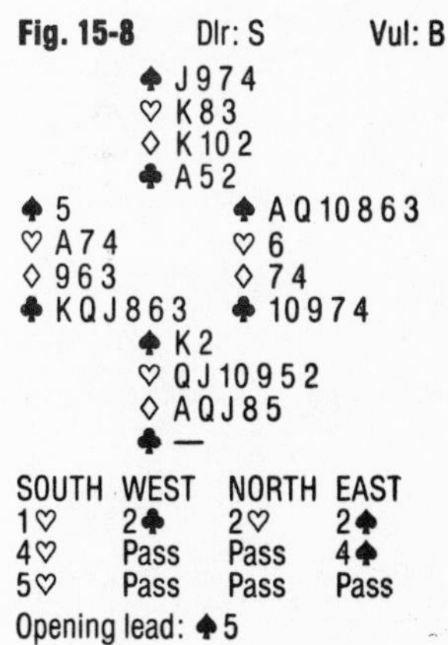

Fig. 15-8

The story is that West led the five of spades, East put up the ace, and South, having no trouble sizing up the opening lead as a singleton, dropped the king. From here on, it depends upon whose account you read to determine what happened next. Some said that while it may have been obvious to South that the lead of the five was singleton, it was not so obvious to East who feared to lay down the queen and establish the jack in the dummy and so switched suits. This allowed declarer to go to the dummy with the king of diamonds and discard the two of spades on the ace of clubs before he led trumps.

Another version is that East worked it all out that South was only kidding and went ahead and cashed the queen of spades. The various explanations of how East arrived at this conclusion are a little lengthy for here, so I'll leave them to you. The hands where the player drops the queen from the queen-doubleton to try to convince his opponents he is void in the suit are rather commonplace, but I thought you might like to look at one where he is supposed to have dropped a king from the king doubleton to achieve the same purpose.

To get back from what may or may not be a flight of the imagination to the real world, my next hand (Fig. 15-9) was played in a contest between two British teams to decide which should represent their country in the European Championships. One was captained by Maurice Harrison-Gray, the other by Dr. Sidney Lee.

Both teams reached a contract of four spades played by South. In one room, Boris Shapiro led a club, and the defenders had no trouble taking

Fig. 15-9

	♠ 10 8 ♡ Q J 3 ◇ A K 7 4 2 ♣ K 7 4	
♠ K 2 ♡ 10 9 6 5 4 ◇ J 8 ♣ 10 8 3 2		♠ Q J 4 ♡ A 8 7 ◇ 10 6 3 ♣ A Q 9 5
	♠ A 9 7 6 5 3 ♡ K 2 ◇ Q 9 5 ♣ J 6	

two club tricks, the ace of hearts, and two trump tricks for down two. In the other room, Harrison-Gray received a lead of a heart and, with a bit of hocus-pocus, actually made the contract. The first play was the jack of hearts from the dummy. This suggested to East that West had the king of hearts, so he won with the ace and led back a heart, hoping West would win that and shift to a club. But, to his surprise, Gray won with the king. He could have saved one trick here by going to the dummy with the ace of diamonds and discarding a club on the queen of hearts, but he was after bigger game. He led a small spade from his hand. West won that and decided his partner's decision to return a heart had indicated a doubleton and that he was now prepared to trump a heart. So West led the heart. Dummy's queen won that, and the six of clubs was discarded from the south hand. Gray now led a trump to his ace, and, then, leaving the good queen of spades outstanding, started leading diamonds, beginning with the queen. Poor East had to follow three times, and, when he finally trumped the fourth diamond, Gray discarded his other losing club. He lost a heart trick and two trump tricks, but no club tricks at all.

DECEPTION WHEN YOU ARE LEADING

When you, as declarer, are leading to the trick, you are in charge, and it is here that your chances to deceive about the strength of the suit occur more frequently than anywhere else. Let me show you some typical situations:

1. DUMMY	2. DUMMY
A Q 5 4	A Q 9 4 3
DECLARER	DECLARER
K 3 2	J 10 2

1. Unless you particularly want them to know you have the king, lead low from your hand and put up the queen. When East does not take the trick, West will have a pretty good idea you have the king, but East will have no way of knowing.

2. When you don't want your opponents to know how strong this suit is and you have plenty of entries, lead the two from your hand and put in the queen. If you lead the jack and it loses to the king, East will have a pretty good idea that you can run away with this suit and he had better cash out, but when you lead the two and he wins your queen, he will not know this.

3. DUMMY
4 3 2

DECLARER
K Q J 10 9

3. There are all sorts of situations where either you or you and dummy combined will have cards which are in a sequence and are equal but for one reason or another you don't want the opponents to take the first trick.

The best bet is to lead some card other than the highest. With the holding in 3, if the suit is trumps and you have bid it vigorously, your best chance to get by with leading without having them take the trick is the queen. Should it be a side suit and should there be a singleton in the dummy instead of three cards, the best chance would be to lead the nine-spot. You lead the one which you think most likely to deceive under the situation which exists when the time comes to lead the suit.

	4.	
	K Q J 8	
10 6 4		A 7 3
	9 5 2	

4. In leading toward the dummy, lead the five-spot and not the deuce. When you play the jack from the dummy, East will see that the deuce is missing and will not know whether his partner has started a signal or not. When you are convinced that it is East who holds the ace and not West, continue by leading another high one from the dummy. East will still have to decide whether to play his ace or not before seeing his partner's signal. He may well decide that after the second trick you will be void in the suit because East has started a signal with a four-card holding, and he may play his ace, leaving you with an entry back into the dummy in the suit.

5. DUMMY	6. DUMMY
A 3 2	K 6 5 4 3
DECLARER	DECLARER
Q 5 4	Q 2

5. West would not expect you to lead the queen with this holding. If you are convinced that he has the king, you might put him to the test. Of course, if he has the jack as well as the king, he will have no problem, but I have seen a couple of mighty good players fail to cover holding the king, but not the jack. Somewhere along the line, this play became known as the Chinese finesse.

6. After you have led low from the dummy and your queen has held the trick, instead of leading back the two-spot and ducking, hoping that East started with the ace doubleton, how about going to the dummy in a side suit and leading a small one. East may become frightened that you have the jack as well as the queen and may play his ace even though he has small cards with it.

7. DUMMY	8. DUMMY
J 5 4 3	7 6 5 4 3
DECLARER	DECLARER
A K 10 9 2	A K 2

7. With this holding, lead the jack from the dummy. Of course, you intend to play the king if East doesn't cover, but give an eager beaver East

an opportunity to cover if he is willing to do so. You may just catch a queen which you otherwise would not catch.

8. Here, if you want to conceal your intentions and you need to establish this suit in a no-trump contract, first lead a small one from your hand and not the ace or king. You will not only need a 3–2 break, you will also need entries into the dummy after you have cashed your ace and king. Your opponents are not accustomed to having anyone underlead both the ace and king.

	9.		10.
	A Q 7 3		A J 4 3
J 10 5 4		K 9	
	8 6 2		K Q 2

9. The safety play with this combination is first to play small from both hands, then to lay down the ace, and then, if the king has not been played, to go to the dummy and lead up toward the queen. That gives you the best chance to take two tricks, but it also involves a very high probability of losing two. If you want to increase your chances of bringing in two tricks while losing only one, try leading low from north. East may have the king doubleton and may play the king, thinking you are leading up to the jack. If the king does not appear, then instead of playing the ace the next time around, you can lead low and finesse the queen.

10. There are times when you will need to get three tricks out of this suit when there are still some trumps outstanding. The best chance is to lead the king from your hand, lead the two to the dummy, and then lead low from the dummy toward your hand. You may have persuaded East who held a small doubleton in the suit and who has a trump that his partner has the queen. And, he may not trump.

11. DUMMY	12. DUMMY
J x x x	Q x x x
DECLARER	DECLARER
10 x x x x	10 x x x x

11. Sometimes you can have a lot of excitement when you and dummy have between you nine cards in a suit which is missing the top cards. With 11, suppose poor East started with the king, queen, and a small one, and you lead the jack from the dummy and he covers. What do you think his partner would say to him? On the other hand, you'd better be pretty sure that West doesn't have all four of them, in which event it may be your partner who has something to say about the situation.

12. Again, you had better think you know something about the distribution before attempting to be a gay deceiver on this one. If, however, you have reason to believe that East does not hold a singleton, try leading the queen from the dummy. If East has the king, jack, and a small one, or even the ace, jack, and a small one and decides to go up, there'll be a hot time in the old town tonight.

13. DUMMY	14. DUMMY
♠ K 6 4	♠ A Q 10
♡ A 5	♡ K 6 5
◇ 7 5 3 2	◇ Q J 5 3
♣ A 8 5 4	♣ 7 6 3
DECLARER	DECLARER
♠ A J 10 9 8	♠ K J 4
♡ 7 3	♡ Q J 10 3
◇ A K 4	◇ K 10 6 4
♣ K 3 2	♣ A Q

13. In a four spade contract, you get an opening lead of a heart. What you would like best of all would be to have your opponents lead trump. Win with the ace and promptly lead back a heart. They may decide it best to accommodate you. With this particular holding, you are not likely to lose by making this play. In the unlikely event that they continue hearts, they probably have given you a sluff-and-ruff. If they lead one of the minor suits, you still may guess the trump situation, and your best bet is probably to guess that the person who led the minor suit is the one who has the queen. If you misguess it, you still have a chance that the suit they led will break 3–3 and that you will find your tenth trick there.

14. Here you are playing three no-trump and—lucky player that you are—get the lead of a club. Even with that favorable lead, you can see that you have only five tricks in the black suits and are going to need four from the red suits, neither of which can give you more than three. So, you have to get tricks from both suits. Here the lead of the jack of hearts at trick two is your best bet. Should West have the ace, you might convince him that you are going to play low from the dummy, and he might duck, hoping his partner's queen will win the trick. If your jack wins, you've already had enough fun—don't do it again. You have one trick in hearts now, so switch back to diamonds very quickly and get your three diamonds established; that will bring your total up to nine tricks.

Now let's put some of these jewels into their proper setting.

In spite of the enthusiasm South had shown for no-trump, West could think of no better lead than the seven of hearts. The nine was played from the dummy, and, even though it would have held the trick, declarer overtook with the jack and led the six of diamonds. West was not ready for that play, and he ducked it, waiting for a signal from East. Declarer put up dummy's ten-spot, and East duly signaled with his nine to show an even number of cards. The information was a little bit late. Declarer switched to clubs and got his four club tricks established. He was able to establish the second heart trick at his leisure and the four club tricks plus the hearts, the diamond, and the two spades gave him a total of nine.

The next hand (Fig. 15-11) was played by Dr. Lajos Widder of Budapest, Hungary, a many-time Hungarian champion.

History records the bidding, but not the vulnerability. Everybody was pretty frisky. Be that as it may, West led the nine of hearts. Dr. Widder saw that if diamonds would break 2–2, he could quickly run nine tricks, and he saw no reason for holding up with his ace of hearts. So, he won the

Fig. 15-11 Dlr: S Vul: Unknow

♠ A 8 7 4
♡ 6
◇ 10 7 5
♣ A 10 8 7 4

West	East
♠ K 6 2	♠ J 10 5 3
♡ 9 5 4	♡ K Q J 8 7 3
◇ J 6 3	◇ Q
♣ J 9 5 3	♣ K 2

♠ Q 9
♡ A 10 2
◇ A K 9 8 4 2
♣ Q 6

SOUTH	WEST	NORTH	EAST
1◇	Pass	2♣	2♡
2 NT	Pass	3◇	3♡
3 NT	Pass	Pass	Pass

Opening lead: ♡9

first trick with the ace of hearts and laid down the ace of diamonds. When East played the queen, he followed smoothly with the two-spot. West thought that over. Since the doctor had never rebid his diamonds, he didn't much think he had six of them. He decided he would look a little foolish putting up his jack and having his partner win with the king. So, he played the six. As you can see, the good doctor had his six diamond tricks, in spite of the fact that the suit did not break 2–2.

My next hand is from a team of four contest. One of the teams got into a contract of four spades and duly took eleven tricks. The other team got into the more ambitious contract of six spades and had to find an additional trick:

♠ A J 10
♡ K Q 2
◇ A 10 7 4 2
♣ 6 5

♠ K Q 9 7 6 5
♡ A 6 5 3
◇ 5
♣ A 8

Against the small slam contract, the opening lead was the ten of hearts. Upon examining the dummy, declarer saw that he had a problem of somehow disposing of a club, and also had to do something about the fourth heart in his hand. If the seven outstanding diamonds would break normally, declarer could get them established and discard a club, and then, even if he lost a heart trick, he would be all right. There was always the chance, also, that the spades would break 2–2 so that long heart could be trumped, and the additional chance the hearts themselves would break 3–3, letting the long heart take a trick. He put up the king, and, when East played the jack, he felt inclined to abandon the hope that the hearts would break 3–3—it looked more like East had started with a singleton.

He went after the diamonds, leading the ace and a small one, which he trumped. Then he led a spade to the dummy, and, when West played the eight-spot, he noted that all of his trumps were now high and he didn't have to take any precautions about trumping diamonds high. He led a third diamond and trumped it, and this time West showed out, playing the seven of clubs. There went the hope for getting a diamond trick established. Back went a spade to the dummy, and West showed out of spades, as well, dropping the two of clubs. It now looked like West had started with five hearts, two diamonds, one spade, and five clubs. If that were the case, all attempts at good technique had failed, and only guile was left. Declarer did not pull the last trump from East, but instead led the two of hearts from the dummy.

East should have thought a few moments about Greeks and others bearing gifts. He gleefully made his small trump, while declarer followed suit with a small heart. He was now in charge. East duly led a club, but declarer went up with the ace. He then took dummy's king of hearts and regained the lead by trumping a diamond. On the ace of hearts, he discarded a losing club from the dummy and ended up losing only one trick, to East's small trump.

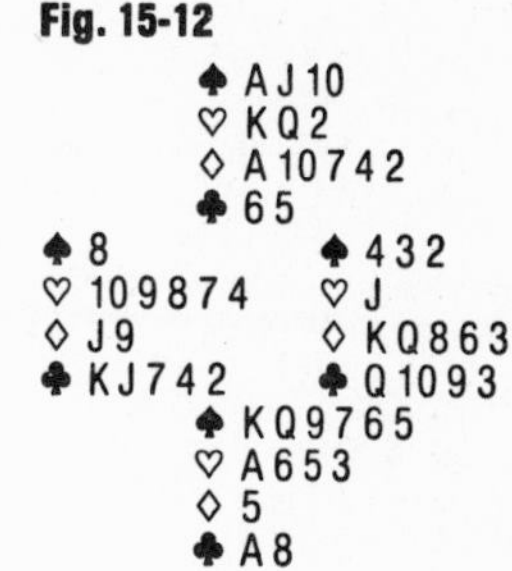

Fig. 15-12

Fig. 15-12 is the entire hand.

You will see that East succeeded in trumping only declarer's losing heart. Had he somehow managed to control himself and not trump that heart, declarer would have had to win with the ace and would have been unable to maneuver twelve tricks.

Declarer had some exceedingly bad luck on the next hand, but he made the best of it.

Against four spades, West led the jack of clubs on hand 15-13. Well, players have been known to lead from interior sequences, so the declarer, without much hope that it would win, put in dummy's queen. Sure enough, East won with the king and led back the eight-spot. Maybe the trumps would break. Declarer played the ace and king of trumps, but when East discarded a heart on the second one, declarer began to wonder if this was his unlucky day. He just felt in his bones that the ace of diamonds was in back of the king and that none of the three chances to make the hand was going to materialize.

Fig. 15-13

Well, he had a couple of hearts to trump, so he laid down the ace and king of that suit. Fortunately, his sense of gloom did not keep him from noticing that the nine and seven were now high. But, he didn't lead the nine; he led the seven. He knew that it was higher than any heart East had, but he also knew that West didn't know that. Sure enough, West threw away a diamond, and South proved to be a copycat. He threw away a diamond from the dummy. After the seven won the trick, he led the nine of hearts. Like a man in a great big hurry, West trumped that with the queen and, before the trick was finished, had a diamond on the table. He couldn't go quite fast enough. The declarer threw away the second diamond from the table. He was right about the ace of diamonds' being in back of the king, but he'd limited his losers to one diamond, one club, and one spade.

Declarer didn't have any nice high sequence like the K Q J 10 to lead his opponents astray, but a good nine-seven served him well.

On my next hand (Fig. 15-14), declarer decided that what is the normal way to play a suit was not on this occasion the best way to play this suit.

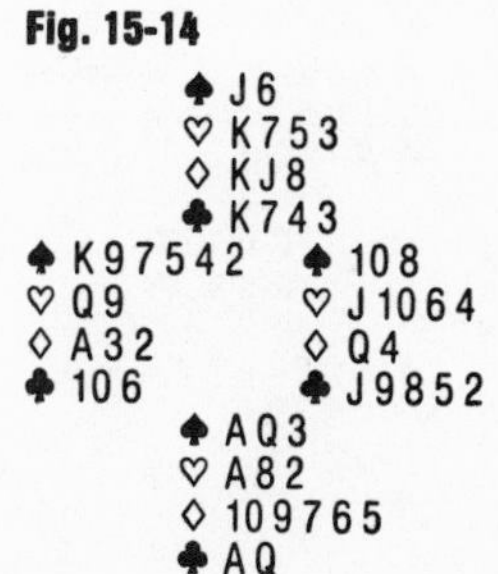

Fig. 15-14

Against three no-trump, West opened the five of spades, and dummy's jack held the trick. Declarer's next play was the eight of diamonds from the dummy. Let's see why he played the diamond suit that way. It looked in the other three suits as though there were only seven tricks, and there was probably no way to get West to lead spades again. That meant that somehow two tricks had to be secured from the diamond suit. Declarer could afford to give the opponents two tricks. If West had both the ace and queen of diamonds, South would be perfectly content to let him take tricks with both of them. If East happened to have both the ace and queen, declarer would probably still be all right, for either East would run out of spades to lead or the suit would break 4–4 if he did not, limiting the defense to two spades and two diamonds. Declarer did not want to let East gain the lead while West still had a card with which he could gain the lead. Suppose East had the ace of diamonds and played it? In that event, South would have good reason to believe that West had started with the queen, and he would win in his hand and finesse diamonds. On the other hand, if East had the queen but not the ace, it was most unlikely that he would play second-hand high. So, South led the eight, and, when East played the four, he overtook with the nine just in case. West won with the ace and shifted to the ten of clubs, but that got him nowhere. Declarer was now perfectly convinced that West did not have the queen of diamonds (or else he would have won the first diamond trick with it), so he led small, played dummy's king, and dropped the queen from East. This way he ended up taking a total of eleven tricks.

My next hand was played by Lee Hazen, a member of the U.S. World Championship Teams of 1956 and 1959, nonplaying captain of the American Team in 1971, winner of about every championship there is, member of the National Laws Commission, a founder of the Greater New York Bridge Association, and, for many years, attorney for the ACBL. When it comes to doing things that have advanced bridge, you name it, and Hazen has done it.

Fig. 15-15

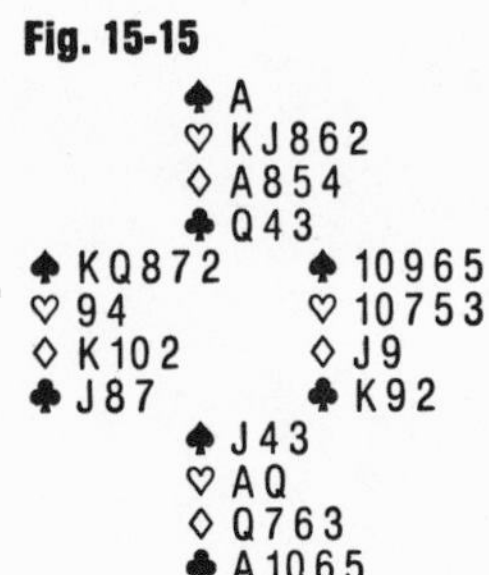

Against a three no-trump contract, West led the seven of spades, and Hazen was left no option about his play at trick one. He noted, however, that he had only eight tricks and that spades were now pretty wide open. He won the next two tricks in his own hand with the ace and queen of hearts and then led, of all things, the jack of spades. Of course, West won that one. East must have been sound asleep, for he certainly offered West no assistance. West must have known of the old adage, "If two sides lead the same suit, one of them is crazy." He didn't want to be considered crazy. Surely Hazen must have the ten and nine to back up his play, and West decided he had to look elsewhere for tricks. He chose clubs as the most likely spot. This still gave Hazen the guess, but the declarer reached a happy ending. He guessed right and played low from the dummy, and the queen of clubs became his ninth trick.

DECEPTION AS TO YOUR INTENTIONS

In war and in many sports, you try to make it look as though you are aiming at the right flank, when your intentions are really to attack the left flank or the center. I am told that this sometimes even happens in romance. It is also a good policy in bridge.

Fig. 15-16

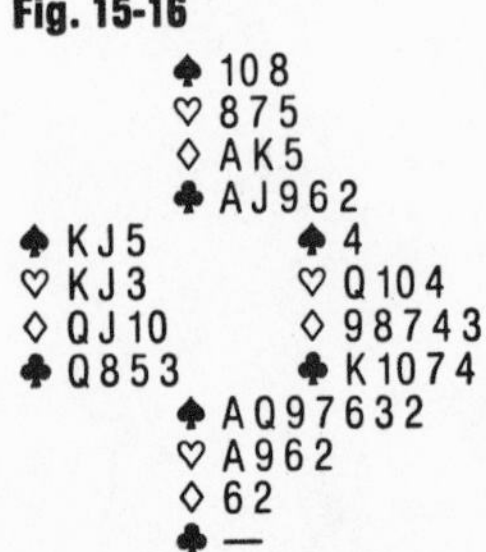

Let's presume you are playing in four spades and the opening lead is the queen of diamonds. You see some number of trump losers, depending on the location of the opponents' trumps, and a collection of heart losers. Of course, you could discard one of your hearts on dummy's ace of clubs, but that wouldn't go very far toward solving your problems. You win with the king and lead the ten of spades for a finesse, and it loses. On comes the second diamond. You win it in the dummy and then abandon the ace of clubs to lead a second spade. East discards a diamond, and you now know that you have two trump losers. You go ahead and let West win that. He leads the third diamond, which you trump. You now lead all of your trumps except one. That will leave everybody with five cards. What you hope is that they have been eyeing those clubs, thinking that you plan to strike there, and that each of them has held onto three clubs and, hence, only two hearts. As they examine the dummy, the heart suit looks so innocent and the club suit so dangerous, I would say you have a pretty good chance that they would do exactly what you want them to do. Of course, you will reserve that one trump to keep control. You lead a small heart. Now you trump whatever they lead back and bang down the ace of hearts. If things have worked out as you want them to, you will have two more winners in the heart suit in your hand.

This next hand (Fig. 15-17)—or reasonable facsimiles of it—has been in the literature for a great many years, and you will still see it from time to time. The principle is right. Let them keep their eyes on one suit, while you are planning to slug them with another.

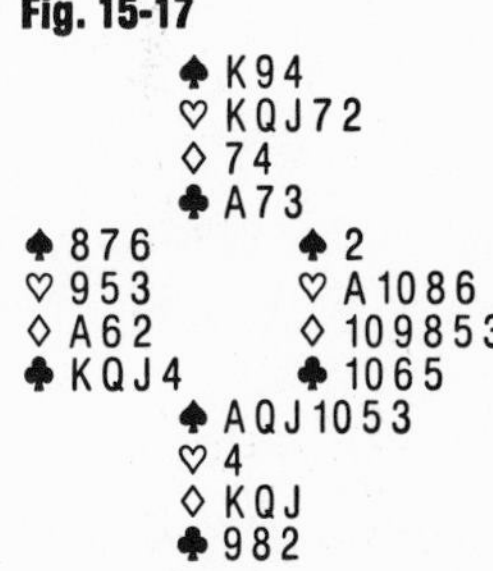

Fig. 15-17

This hand was played in a team of four game, and both teams reached a contract of four spades with the south hand. In each room, the opening lead was the king of clubs. In the first room, the declarer ducked the first club and took the second. Then he led two spades, leaving the king in the dummy as an entry, and led a heart. East had no trouble at all taking the first heart trick, and the defenders ended up with two clubs, a diamond, and a heart.

In the other room, the south player took a different tactic. He won with the ace of clubs at trick one like he didn't have a worry in the world, and, when it took three trump leads to exhaust the opponents, he took three trumps ending in the dummy, and led the king of hearts. East just knew that the declarer would not take all of the entries out of the dummy if he had a singleton heart so he let the king hold the trick. My report on this hand does not go so far as to tell me what comments West had to make when he and his partner held their after-game conference.

I am sure you have sometimes tried leading out a long suit, hoping your opponents will make bad discards. Sometimes it works and sometimes it doesn't. In the right circumstances, the chances are greatly improved.

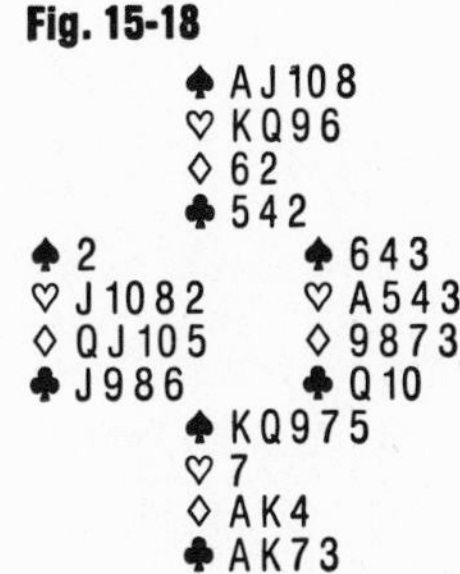

Fig. 15-18

South got into a six spade contract, and West led the queen of diamonds. Declarer won that and saw that he would have no problems if West had the ace of hearts. So, at trick two, he led toward dummy and put up the queen. East won the ace and returned another diamond. Declarer took that and trumped his last diamond in the dummy. He could have gone quietly for down one by leading the queen of hearts to discard a small club, but somehow that did not seem to be a very satisfactory result. So, he decided to lead all of his trumps and abandon the good-looking hearts "on the other side of the river," as they say. On the run of trumps, he discarded two of dummy's clubs. As everybody got down to four cards, West was sitting there staring at those hearts in the dummy and simply could not imagine that the declarer had gone off and left them. The idea was that some victim who held both good hearts and four cards in the club suit would discard a couple of clubs. The story is that that was exactly what West did, and declarer was finally able to throw away dummy's hearts on his good clubs.

Fig. 15-19

On the next hand (Fig. 15-19), declarer called his opponents' attention to one suit and then socked it to 'em in another.

The bidding was short and sweet: South dealt and bid four spades. West led the king of diamonds, and declarer saw four losers staring him in the face just as plain as anything. A little hocus-pocus was called for.

Declarer won the dummy's ace and led a small heart toward his hand. East naturally went up with the king, so declarer tried that old stunt of dropping the queen under it. East couldn't see establishing dummy's jack of hearts, but apparently thought he might stop a diamond ruff by leading trumps. At least, that's what he did. Declarer won that with the ace and led a small club toward the dummy and put up the queen. East won that and decided to continue with his lead of trumps. Declarer just let that one ride around to the dummy and then led the queen of clubs and discarded his three of hearts. Now he had no trouble giving up a diamond trick and trumping his losing diamond with dummy's ten of trumps.

Fig. 15-20

When you wish to go in for a bit of chicanery, do it as early as possible, before the opponents have a chance to size up the situation (Fig. 15-20).

North and South bid smartly up to six spades, and West led the queen of clubs. Declarer found the diamond situation distressing. He could sluff one diamond from his hand on the king of clubs and another from the dummy on a heart, but that would still leave him with two diamond losers. He recognized a classic situation where you have to find one of the opponents with a doubleton honor. Furthermore, you might have to find that before that opponent has a chance to discard that doubleton honor. So, declarer won with the ace and, at trick two, led a small diamond and played dummy's ace. When West failed to play his queen, he was doomed. Declarer next pulled trumps in three leads, ending in the dummy, took the king of clubs, and trumped a club in his hand. Then he took the Q A K of hearts, discarding a diamond, and West had to follow suit to all of these plays. Then came the diamond, and East had to either overtake West's queen with his king and set up dummy's jack or let West hold the queen and be end-played. East let West suffer, and, on his lead, declarer had the pleasure of discarding a diamond in the dummy while trumping in his hand.

You should be warned, however, that this is a sword that cuts two ways.

This hand was played by Claggett Bowie of Virginia. Some people credit Mr. Bowie for having originated the idea that the queen lies over the jack. Let's overlook that and see how he hornswoggled his opponents into letting him make seven spades when everybody else who played the hand in a match-point duplicate made only six.

At six spades, the opening lead was the three of trumps. Bowie won that, as East discarded a heart. He found that heart discard interesting. It suggested to him that East did not have the king. However, he decided that it didn't make any difference. If East did have the king, declarer still would have a heart loser after the finesse succeeded, and, if East didn't have it, declarer still could make six by giving a heart trick to West. But then the thought occurred to him—what would West do when he laid down the ace? He decided to set the stage properly before making that play. West was a worthy opponent, and South was going to give him a chance to show his mettle. So he pulled three rounds of trumps, took two rounds of diamonds, and then took three rounds of clubs, ending in his hand. With nothing to lose, he laid down the ace of hearts. West had seen that play before and he didn't have the least idea of being thrown in with his king to give brother Bowie a sluff-and-ruff. Hoping that his partner held the queen and ten, he dropped the king under the ace!

In my next hand (Fig. 15-22), declarer found himself in a terrible predicament, so he looked for a way to flimflam himself out of it.

After he got a look at the dummy, declarer saw that he had gotten into a contract of six hearts missing the ace and king of clubs. However, he was lucky in that his left-hand opponent was not one of those who followed Blackwood's advice to lead aces against slam contracts. Instead, West had led the queen of diamonds.

Declarer decided to make his move as quickly as possible. He won that with dummy's ace and led the club suit which West had refused to lead. East naturally played low, and declarer played the queen. West had no way to know what was happening to him when he took the ace, so he continued with a diamond. South won that in his hand and then led out all of his hearts. This put East in an impossible position. After six heart tricks, two diamond tricks, and a club trick, there were only four cards in everybody's hand. North had nothing left but his four spades. South had two spades and two clubs. East had no way to hold onto all four of his spades and the king of clubs, but he guessed that playing a spade would be fatal (as it would have been), so he played the king of clubs, not knowing whether that was fatal or not. It was. On the jack of clubs, declarer was able to discard dummy's five of spades; and he then took the last three tricks in the dummy with the top spades.

For my last hand, I give you a demonstration of the magic of that old master, Howard Schenken.

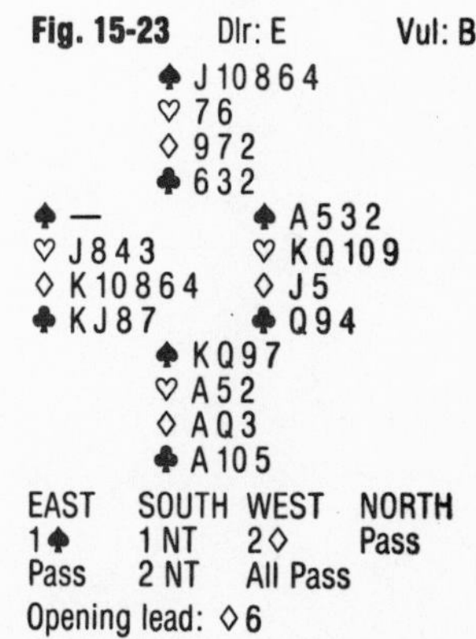

It is obvious that East was not an advocate of bidding only five-card major suits. Our problem here is how in the world did Schenken manage to take eight tricks? Well, here is how it went.

West led the six of diamonds, and Schenken captured East's jack with his queen. At trick two, to the surprise of West, Schenken led the three of diamonds. West looked that over, decided he must have pulled the wrong card, won with the ten, and continued the suit.

Had Schenken played the hand in a straightforward manner and led the king of spades after winning the queen of diamonds, West would have shown out if East had the four spades he had advertised with his opening bid. East would then be alerted to duck spades three times, and, if he did that, Schenken could find only seven tricks. So why did Schenken lead a small diamond at trick two? He wanted to give East a chance to discard. On the third diamond lead, East did just that. Naturally, he discarded what appeared to be the most worthless card in his hand—a small spade. Now it was time for Schenken to start leading spades because East was going to have to play his ace while Schenken still had a spade left to reach the dummy.

WHEN I was learning to play auction bridge at the age of 11, my mentors taught me a lot of "rules" which were supposed to save me the trouble of thinking. One of these was represented by the maxim, "eight ever; nine never." I was told that when I held eight cards including all the high ones but the queen, I should always finesse; though, as my instruction became more sophisticated, I was told that I should lay down an ace or king first to protect against a singleton queen. On the other hand, if the dummy and I held nine cards, I should never finesse for the missing queen, but should bang down the ace and king. I was told not to worry if that went wrong because in the long run the averages would take care of me.

The number of bridge hands I played increased into tens, then hundreds, and then thousands, and I had an uneasy sense that things were not working out as they should. In 1952, a number of consecutively dealt hands became available for a statistical study, and I made such a study. I decided that there *were* times when the mathematical probabilities did not work out—times when I should finesse with nine cards—and there was internal evidence in the cards which told me when those times had occurred. I attributed this to the imperfect shuffle because there was no mathematical basis to justify my findings. In May 1952, the *Bridge World* published an article on my statistical studies. Those findings have been verified again and again in hands that are people-dealt, but are not valid in hands that are dealt by a computer, provided the computer has been properly programed. From all internal evidence, the hands issued by the ACBL are properly programed—they do conform with mathematical probabilities. All of that is another story. Further study of these hands shows that with the computer-dealt hands, the probabilities offered in most of the textbooks are all right as far as they go, but that they don't go far enough. First, let's take a good look at the probabilities as they are shown in all of the books I have ever read covering the subject of probabilities in bridge, and then let's take the next step together.

To set the stage for our discussion, let us say that in spades we have the following holding:

DUMMY
K 4 2

DECLARER
A J 7 6 5 3

We lead the three-spot from our hand to dummy's king, and both opponents follow suit. The queen does not appear. We then lead the two-spot toward our hand, and East follows suit with a small card. What should we do now? Here is a table of the significant distributions as it might be furnished us by the mathematicians. The mathematicians call it an *a priori* table.

TABLE 1. A Priori Distributional Probabilities of a Suit in Which Your Opponents Hold Four Cards

	West	East	Probability (percent)
A	none	Qxxx	4.78
B	Q	xxx	6.22
C	x	Qxx	18.65
D	Qx	xx	20.35
E	xx	Qx	20.35
F	Qxx	x	18.65
G	xxx	Q	6.22
H	Qxxx	none	4.78

We know that distribution A did not occur because West was not void; we know that distribution B did not occur because West did not play the queen. As a matter of fact, distributions E, F, G, and H have also been ruled out, and the only distributions which remain possible are C and D. D occurs 20.35 percent of the time, and C occurs only 18.65 percent of the time. Therefore, D is more frequent than C, and we should play the ace. If you want to translate the relative frequencies of C and D into percentages, you find that distribution D occurs 52.18 percent of the time when only distributions C and D are left.

If I were taking a public opinion poll, I would say that this one is too close to call. Mathematical probabilities don't really become significant until they reach the neighborhood of 60 percent. I don't mean that you should ignore them when they are less. I only mean that when they are less, you should count on them only when you can find nothing else to guide you. These occasions should not be too frequent.

Here we see the solution of another seeming paradox which has bothered me for years. I was told that when four cards of a suit are outstanding, the distribution of 3-1 occurs more frequently than 2-2. At the same time, I was told that if the queen was among the four cards missing, I should play for the drop and not the finesse. Here we see the answer. Distributions B, C, F, and G are all 3-1 distributions. Added together, they come to 49.7 percent. Distributions D and E are 2-2 distributions; added together they come to only 40.70 percent. In spite of that, when you arrive at the point where you have to decide whether to finesse or play for the drop, only distributions C and D are possible, and, of these, D occurs more frequently than C.

Now we are not going to argue with the a priori probabilities—nobody can. But the term a priori seems to mean, "before you know anything else," and you just about never have to make this play before you know anything else about the opposing hands. If you do know anything at all about them, the a priori table becomes worthless. What you need is an a posteriori table of probabilities. That is, a table built on whatever you know about the distribution of the opposing hands in any particular suit or suits.

Players who have played many thousands of hands do not need these tables; through their great experience, they have come to learn that these things are true. However, the construction of some of these a posteriori tables cut years off the learning process for players who simply have not had that much experience. Throughout this appendix, I have included some samples of probability tables based on your knowledge of the distribution of one or more suits in the opponents' hands. These will serve as a pretty good sample for other situations which are too numerous to list in detail.

What you have found out about the distribution in your opponents' hands in one or more suits affects your probability in three different areas:

1. The probability that a finesse will succeed or fail.
2. The chances that a long suit can be established.
3. The determination of whether you should finesse or play for the drop when you are missing four cards including the queen. The a priori odds are so close that the odds are affected by almost anything you know about the distribution of the other hands.

To correct the long-standing misconception that you just play the ace and king, I am going to look at number three above in close detail.

But first, let's take up the matter of the finesse. I can best illustrate this by an example:

DUMMY
♠ K J 10 7 4 2
♡ A 6
◇ 7 3
♣ A Q J

DECLARER
♠ A Q 9 8 6 5
♡ 4 2
◇ A Q J
♣ 5 4

Let us assume that a nonvulnerable West opened the bidding with three hearts; that your partner made a takeout double; and that after you jumped to four spades, you ended up in a contract of six spades. Let us further say that the opening lead from West was the king of hearts.

You see that unless West started with nine hearts, in which event he would have opened with a bid of four, the ace of hearts is going to hold the first trick. You further see that you only have to lead trumps once to exhaust the opponents of trumps. Now you can either finesse diamonds and, if that works, return to the dummy to finesse diamonds a second time, discarding a heart on the ace of diamonds to guarantee your twelve tricks, or you can go through the same procedure with the club suit. The question is, should you go after diamonds or should you go after clubs?

If you think West's nonvulnerable opening bid of three hearts told you anything about the likelihood of his holding minor suit kings, you know West better than I do. So, after worrying a bit, trying to decide whether we can identify either king with West from his bid, we give up and see what we can determine about distribution from his opening bid.

Obviously, West has a whole lot more hearts than East. The most likely distribution is 7–2, although it could be anywhere from 6–3 to 8–1. Let us settle on 7–2 and see what that tells us about the probabilities that East will hold the king of diamonds.

The probability that East will hold the king of diamonds is exactly the same as the probability that East will hold any other specific card in spades, diamonds, or clubs.

With West holding seven hearts, he holds six cards in the other three suits. We will refer to these as "other cards." With East holding two cards in hearts, he holds eleven other cards. Therefore, the chances are eleven-seventeenths that East holds any one of these other cards. That figures out to 64.71 percent that East holds any of these other cards. With the diamond finesse nearly a 65-percent favorite and the club finesse not much better than 35 percent, I think you had better go for the diamond finesse.

Of course, you will pull the one trump first and learn who happened to have the thirteenth spade. This will make a slight change in the odds, but it is too small to be significant.

Now, had the bidding gone somewhat differently, you would play differently. Let us suppose that it is East who opened with three hearts, that you, nevertheless, were successful in bidding six spades from your side of the table, and that West leads the jack of hearts. The lead of the jack of hearts looks like a singleton or doubleton, and you have the same situation you had with West's bidding three hearts, except it is now in reverse. Now, any specific card in the other suits is more likely to be with West than with East, and the club finesse should be tried.

You can easily figure out for yourself that had the heart suit broken 6–3, the percentages would have come to not quite 59 percent; had the suit broken 8–1, the odds would have been almost 71 percent. These odds do not change as play progresses. The odds were established with the deal. What does change as you learn about the distribution of the opponent's hands is your knowledge of the deal. So, you are able to substitute a posteriori probability for a priori probability. Whenever you discover an adverse distribution, you can refigure the odds which are exactly what they were when the hand was originally dealt.

How much does the discovery of the distribution of the deal change your odds in calculating a finesse? I leave you with Table 2 which you could easily work out yourself; I have just saved you the trouble. The first column shows the chances of a successful finesse taken through the hand which is shorter in the discovered suit, when the difference between the length of the hand with the longer suit and that with the shorter suit is two cards. The second column gives these same figures when the difference is three cards, and the third column gives the figures when the difference is four cards. When there is a difference of five cards or more, the probabilities are automatically 60 percent or more, and, according to my definition, this makes them significant, and they should be given the full weight

TABLE 2. Probabilities that a specific card will be in the hand which is short in a suit where distribution is known, based on the opposing distribution of the known suit.

Two-Card Difference		Three-Card Difference		Four-Card Difference	
Distribution	*Probability (percent)*	*Distribution*	*Probability (percent)*	*Distribution*	*Probability (percent)*
2–0	54.17	3–0	56.52	4–0	59.09
3–1	54.55	4–1	57.14	5–1	60.00
4–2	55.00	5–2	57.89	6–2	61.11
5–3	55.56	6–3	58.82	7–3	62.50
6–4	56.25	7–4	60.00	8–4	64.29
7–5	57.14	8–5	61.54		
Five-Card Difference		**Six-Card Difference**		**Seven-Card Difference**	
Distribution	*Probability (percent)*	*Distribution*	*Probability (percent)*	*Distribution*	*Probability (percent)*
5–0	61.90	6–0	65.00	7–0	68.42
6–1	63.16	7–1	66.67	8–1	70.50
7–2	64.71	8–2	68.75		
8–3	66.67				

due them in deciding how to proceed. When the percentages are down around 55 percent to 56 percent, I recommend that you pay no attention to them except in those cases where you can find absolutely nothing else to go on. They are better than nothing at all, but that is about it.

You are not going to have too many hands where you have to choose between taking equal finesses into the dummy or into your hand. However, this table will become more significant when you get to the next subject of distribution and weighing the chances of a finesse against the chances of establishing a suit.

There are times when you have to compare the chances that a finesse will succeed with those that a suit will break favorably (Fig. A-1).

Fig. A-1 Dlr: S Vul: 0

DUMMY
♠ A 6 4 3 2
♡ 5 3
◇ Q J 6 4
♣ 4 3

DECLARER
♠ 8
♡ 7 4 2
◇ A K 10 9 8 7 5
♣ A Q

SOUTH	WEST	NORTH	EAST
1◇	2♡*	2♠	3♡
4◇	Pass	5◇	All Pass

Opening lead: ♡K

*Preemptive jump overcall.

You get the opening lead of the king of hearts and are not displeased when you see the dummy. It looks like you are going to lose two heart tricks and then have a chance either to establish the spade for a discard of the queen of clubs or take the club finesse. If all goes well, you will be able to test out both plays by trying for the spade establishment first.

But all does not go well. West holds the first heart trick with his king, and East overtakes the second heart trick with his ace and leads back a club. Now you have to decide at once. You no longer have time to try both plays.

A priori, the chances that a seven-card suit would break 4–3 were 62 percent, compared with only 50 percent for a finesse. But, if you will look at Tables 2 and 3 you will see that these chances have become reversed.

TABLE 3. Probabilities that five outstanding cards will break 3–2 when the distribution of another suit is known.

A priori probability = 67.83 percent

Distribution	Probability (percent)	Distribution	Probability (percent)	Distribution	Probability (percent)	Distribution	Probability (percent)
1–0	67.83	1–1	68.32				
2–0	67.29	2–1	68.32	2–2	68.92		
3–0	66.06	3–1	67.67	3–2	68.92	3–3	69.66
4–0	63.98	4–1	66.16	4–2	68.11	4–3	69.66
5–0	60.82	5–1	63.57	5–2	66.22	5–3	68.63
6–0	56.35	6–1	59.60	6–2	62.91	6–3	66.16
7–0	50.31	7–1	53.92	7–2	57.77	7–3	61.81
8–0	42.48	8–1	46.22	8–2	50.37	8–3	54.95

Probabilities that seven outstanding cards will break 4–3 when the distribution of another suit is known.

A priori probability = 62.17 percent

Distribution	Probability (percent)	Distribution	Probability (percent)	Distribution	Probability (percent)	Distribution	Probability (percent)
1–0	62.17	1–1	62.93				
2–0	61.36	2–1	62.93	2–2	63.85		
3–0	59.50	3–1	61.92	3–2	63.85	3–3	65.02
4–0	56.35	4–1	59.60	4–2	62.58	4–3	65.02
5–0	51.65	5–1	55.63	5–2	59.60	5–3	63.35
6–0	45.19	6–1	49.66	6–2	54.44	6–3	59.39
7–0	36.89	7–1	41.48	7–2	46.66	7–3	52.45
8–0	26.96	8–1	31.11	8–2	36.06	8–3	41.96

Your opponents and the cards you hold have advertised the fact that West was dealt six hearts and East only two. Looking at Table 2, under the column Four-Card Difference, you see that the chances are now 61 percent that East, who is short in hearts, holds the king of clubs. Now take a look at Table 3. Under the section for seven-card suits, you can discover the chances that the suit will break 4–3 when you know that one of your opponents was dealt six cards in a suit and the other only two. Finding in the table the distribution 6–2, you see that now the 4–3 break will materialize only a little more than 54 percent of the time. Probabilities of from 61 to 54 percent must be judged too close to call. What other factors are there to consider? Does the so-called weak jump overcall give any indication at all as to whether or not West holds the king of clubs? How about that raise by East with only a doubleton ace of hearts? What sort of a player is East? Is he an old timer who recognizes the danger of the five spades in the dummy and is putting you under pressure right now? Or, is he putting you under pressure because he knows the spade suit is not going to break? Do you think he would or would not underlead the king of clubs under these circumstances?

To me, all of the evidence looks pretty nebulous, and I would just about say that you would have to be at the table to make the decision. I hate to leave you that way, but I'm afraid that's the way it is sometimes. However, sometimes things are a little more conclusive. Let's look at another example in Fig. A-2.

Fig. A-2 Dlr: S Vul: 0

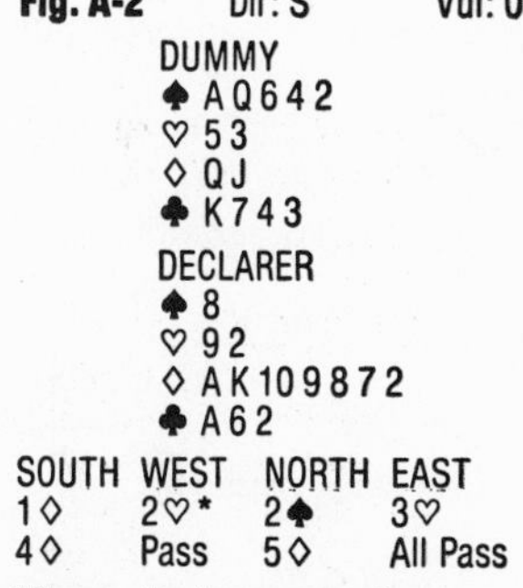

DUMMY
♠ A Q 6 4 2
♡ 5 3
◇ Q J
♣ K 7 4 3
DECLARER
♠ 8
♡ 9 2
◇ A K 10 9 8 7 2
♣ A 6 2
SOUTH WEST NORTH EAST
1◇ 2♡* 2♠ 3♡
4◇ Pass 5◇ All Pass

*Preemptive jump overcall.

Here we have the same bidding, but a different problem because we are going to have to decide whether to finesse against West or not. This time, West held the first two tricks with the king and queen of hearts and then led a small spade. I am going to assume the hearts have broken 6–3. East must have the ace of hearts. Had West had six of them headed by the A K Q, I don't think he would have made a preemptive jump overcall.

I still have a club loser to get rid of and a choice of procedures to get this done. I can either take the spade finesse right now, or I can take the ace and try to establish the fifth spade. I have just enough entries in the dummy to do this and get back to cash the fifth spade, provided the suit breaks 4–3.

Looking at Table 3, I see that the chances the suit will break 4–3 are slightly better than 59 percent (remember, we are assuming hearts have broken 6–3). This alone is in the area of significance. What about the chances of the finesse? Looking at Table 2, I see that the chance that the king of spades is in the east hand is almost 59 percent. This means that the chance that West has the king of spades and that the finesse will succeed is just slightly over 41 percent. The difference between 59 and 41 percent is significant. To the 59-percent chance that the spade suit will break 4–3, I can add a small percent because West may just be the sort of fellow who would underlead the king doubleton in this situation. Due to the bidding, I do not expect to find the king singleton or doubleton in the east hand.

The arithmetic of the situation seems to confirm rather than contradict the evidence from the bidding and play, and the proper play must be up with the ace and a small spade right back to start the establishment. The two diamonds and the king of clubs in the dummy are entries for the establishment and cashing of the long spade.

Now let's look at a different problem:

DUMMY
♠ K Q 10 7
♡ K Q 4
◇ 8 6 4
♣ A 4 3

DECLARER
♠ A 9 8 6
♡ A 3 2
◇ 7 5 3
♣ K Q 2

Now you are playing four spades, and West has cashed three top diamond tricks on the third of which, East has discarded a small heart. West now switched to a club, and you have the lead. It looks like you don't have too many problems left. With a 3–2 spade break, you have ten tricks looking you in the face. A look at Table 3 tells you that the chances of this, now that you know the diamond suit broke 5–2, are almost, but not quite as good as they were a priori. The chances are 66 percent that you will get this favorable break, but that still means that 34 percent of the time they will not break 3–2, and you'd better pause a moment and think that one over. Fortunately, your spade holding is such that you could take care of

TABLE 4. A priori probabilities of distribution of 4, 5, 6, or 7 cards in a suit held by opponents and a posteriori probabilities of distribution in short hand in a suit where distribution is known.

Four Cards Outstanding				Five Cards Outstanding			
Cards Held	*A Priori Probability (percent)*	*Probability With Known Suit 5–2 (percent)*	*Probability With Known Suit 7–2 (percent)*	*Cards Held*	*A Priori Probability (percent)*	*Probability With Known Suit 5–2 (percent)*	*Probability With Known Suit 7–2 (percent)*
0	4.78	1.81	0.63	0	1.96	0.48	0.01
1	24.87	15.89	9.24	1	14.13	6.62	2.76
2	40.70	39.73	34.66	2	33.91	26.49	17.78
3	24.87	34.06	41.60	3	33.91	39.73	40.00
4	4.78	8.51	13.87	4	14.13	22.70	32.00
5				5	1.96	3.97	7.47

Six Cards Outstanding				Seven Cards Outstanding			
Cards Held	*A Priori Probability (percent)*	*Probability With Known Suit 5–2 (percent)*	*Probability With Known Suit 7–2 (percent)*	*Cards Held*	*A Priori Probability (percent)*	*Probability With Known Suit 5–2 (percent)*	*Probability With Known Suit 7–2 (percent)*
0	0.75	0.10	0.01	0	0.26	0.02	Impossible
1	7.27	2.27	0.53	1	3.39	0.61	0.06
2	24.22	14.19	6.67	2	15.26	6.11	1.70
3	35.53	34.06	26.66	3	31.09	22.92	12.73
4	24.22	34.06	40.00	4	31.09	36.68	33.94
5	7.27	13.62	22.40	5	15.26	25.67	35.63
6	0.75	1.70	3.73	6	3.39	7.34	14.25
7				7	0.26	0.65	1.70

four spades to the jack in either hand. The only problem is that you don't know which hand. Should East have four to the jack, you want to take the king and queen of spades first. West would duly show out on the second spade lead, and you could finesse East on the jack. On the other hand, should West have four to the jack, you would need to take the king and then the ace. East would show out, and you could finesse against West.

Let's look at Table 4 and see if we can find anything there to guide us. We are especially interested in the chances of a 4–1 break with five cards outstanding. In the a priori column with five cards outstanding, we see that 14.13 percent of the time East will hold a singleton and that he will hold four cards with the same frequency. This comes to a total of 28.26 percent of the time that a 4–1 break will be expected. The subsequent columns are samples telling you just what the probabilities are after you have discovered a 5–2 or 7–2 break in some other suit. These tables are not complete, but do show pretty well what has happened. Under each column are the probabilities that the player with the short number of cards in the known suit will hold the number of cards you are inquiring about in the five or seven-card suit. So, under 5–2, we find that the chances that East will hold a singleton are 6.62 percent. That, of course, is the same as the chances that West will hold four of them. The chances that East will hold four is 22.70 percent. Adding all these together, we get 29.32 percent, which represents the probability that the spade suit will break 4–1 after we learn that the diamond suit is breaking 5–2. This is not much different from the 28.26 percent we had estimated before we knew anything about the diamond suit, but wait a minute. There is a tremendous difference when we think about the chances of whether it will be East or West who holds the four-card suit. East will have the four-card holding nearly 23 percent of the time, while West will have the four-card holding something less than 7 percent of the time. Translate this into percentages, and it means that when the spade suit *does* break 4–1, more than 77 percent of the time it will be East who will hold the four bagger. These indeed are substantial odds, and probably rather unexpected just because you found a not unusual distribution of 5–2 in the diamond suit. By all odds, you should start spades by taking the king and the queen, in that order. Of course, had it been East who had five diamonds and West having only two, you would have taken the first spade trick in the north hand and the second trick to your ace.

Now let's take a look at that "eight ever, nine never" theory, again when West is known to have five diamonds and East only two.

DUMMY
♠ K 10 9 7
♡ K Q 4
♢ 8 6 4
♣ A 4 3

DECLARER
♠ A J 8 6 4
♡ A 2
♢ 7 4 3
♣ K Q 2

You are playing in four spades. West cashes the first three diamond tricks, East showing out on the third one, and switches to a small club. All you have to do is avoid losing a trump trick. You are fortunate that the cards are so divided that you can finesse against West or against East or play for the drop.

Earlier I showed you the a priori distributional probabilities of a suit in which your opponents held four cards, including the queen (see Table 1). Now I am showing you the probabilities after you know the distribution of the diamond suit to be five with West and two with East.

TABLE 5. Distributional Probabilities of a Suit in Which Your Opponents Hold Four Cards, When the Distribution of Another Suit is Known to be East two, West, five.

	West	East	Probability (percent)
A	none	Qxxx	8.51
B	Q	xxx	8.52
C	x	Qxx	25.55
D	Qx	xx	19.86
E	xx	Qx	19.86
F	Qxx	x	11.92
G	xxx	A	3.97
H	Qxxx	none	1.81

Obviously, you win the first trick in north with the king and then lead toward your hand. If everybody has followed suit with small cards, the only possible distributions remaining are either C or D. In this case, it is C which is the greater probability and not D. Translating these figures to a percentage basis, the finesse is now a better than 56-percent chance compared to less than 44 percent for the drop.

When the hands are more distributional, the odds become even greater.

DUMMY
♠ 8 7 3
♡ 5
♢ K J 4
♣ K J 10 6 4 3

DECLARER
♠ A K J 10 9 5
♡ 6 2
♢ A Q
♣ A Q 5

Let us say that West has opened the bidding with three hearts, and you have reached a contract of six spades, or, whether you bid six or not, you would like to make six if you are playing match-point duplicate. West starts proceedings by cashing the king of hearts and then shifts to a small diamond. That should be won with the ace in case entries to the dummy are needed.

Obviously, your only problem is to avoid the loss of a trump trick. What is going to be your guess about the distribution of the heart suit? There are ten of them outstanding. My guess is that they are 7–3. I plan to lay down the ace of trump and, if both players follow suit with small cards, go to the dummy by trumping a heart and lead dummy's last trump. If East follows with a small card, I plan to take the finesse. The odds in favor of the finesse as compared with the drop are almost 62 percent for the finesse, assuming I have judged the heart distribution correctly. Nearly 12 percent of the time, West will show out on the lead of the top spade. This pretty well solves all problems: overtake the queen of diamonds with dummy's king to take the finesse; go to the dummy once more with a club for the other finesse; pull trumps; and, finally, discard your heart on a long club or diamond in the dummy.

But suppose it was East who opened the bidding with three hearts? To better illustrate my point, let me change the hand a bit:

DUMMY
♠ K 4 3
♡ 5
♢ K J 4
♣ K J 10 6 4 3

DECLARER
♠ A J 7 6 5 2
♡ 6 2
♢ A Q
♣ A Q 5

This time West leads the ace of hearts, looks the dummy over, and switches to a diamond which you win with the ace. I hope you didn't bid six spades this time—the odds are against taking twelve tricks. But, you do the best you can and win this trick and then lead a small spade to dummy's king. Both opponents follow with low spades, and you are mildly encouraged. At least West did not hold all four of the outstanding trumps, which he well might have done. You now lead a small spade from the dummy, and, wonder of wonders, East again follows suit with a small spade. You now have to decide whether to finesse or play for the drop. You have learned quite a bit about the spade suit: neither player was void; neither player had a singleton queen; East was not dealt a doubleton queen. Indeed, the only chances left are either that East was dealt three to the queen, in which event you should finesse, or he was dealt a small doubleton, in which event West is sitting there with the singleton queen. Any way you figure it, you play the ace and play for the drop. Assuming your estimate that East started with seven hearts and West with three, the doubleton queen in West's hand is more than twice as likely as three to the queen with East. The actual percentage is something more than 69 percent that the proper play will be the ace.

An old schoolteacher once told me that if I would learn more about a subject than I could really use, it would help me utilize to better advantage that part which I could find useful. Based on that theory, I have prepared for you some rather exhaustive tables concerning the break of four outstanding cards in one suit when you know the exact distribution in another suit, and I refer to my Table 6. Let me tell you a little about this table.

The left-hand column indicates the distribution in the discovered suit. The percentages are always those for the hand which is short in the discovered suit. Of course, from these you can always determine the probabilities in the hand which the suit is long in the discovered suit by simply turning the table upside-down. In the 1-0 line, the 27.13 percent chances that East will hold three cards also represents the chances that West will hold one.

Let's look for a moment at the A Priori line. East will hold three of the four outstanding cards 24.87 percent of the time. One time out of 4 he will

TABLE 6. Probable Distribution of Four Cards in the Short Hand in a Suit or Suits Where Distribution is Known.

	Probability Of Having 0 Cards (percent)	Probability Of Having 1 Card (percent)	Probability Of Having 2 Cards (percent)	Probability Of Having 3 Cards (percent)	Probability Of Having 4 Cards (percent)
A priori	4.78	24.87	40.70	24.87	4.78
Distribution of known suit(s)	2	3	4	5	6
1-0	3.91	22.61	40.70	27.13	5.65
2-0	3.11	20.19	40.37	29.61	6.73
3-0	2.37	17.62	39.64	32.30	8.07
4-0	1.72	14.93	38.39	35.19	9.77
5-0	1.17	12.16	36.49	38.23	11.95
6-0	0.72	9.39	33.81	41.32	14.76
7-0	0.39	6.71	30.19	44.27	18.45
8-0	0.16	4.25	25.49	46.73	23.37
1-1	4.66	24.84	40.99	24.84	4.66
2-1	3.73	22.36	40.99	27.32	5.59
3-1	2.87	19.69	40.60	30.08	6.77
4-1	2.11	16.84	39.70	33.08	8.27
5-1	1.44	13.87	38.14	36.33	10.22
6-1	0.90	10.84	35.76	39.73	12.77
7-1	0.49	7.84	32.35	43.14	16.18
8-1	0.21	5.04	27.73	46.22	20.80
2-2	4.51	24.81	41.35	24.81	4.51
3-2	3.51	22.06	41.35	27.57	5.51
4-2	2.60	19.07	40.87	30.65	6.81
5-2	1.81	15.89	39.73	34.06	8.51
6-2	1.14	12.58	37.75	37.75	10.78
7-2	0.63	9.24	34.66	41.60	13.87
8-2	0.27	6.04	30.22	45.33	18.13
3-3	4.33	24.77	41.80	24.77	4.33
4-3	3.25	21.67	41.80	27.86	5.42
5-3	2.29	18.30	41.18	31.37	6.86
6-3	1.47	14.71	39.71	35.29	8.82
7-3	0.82	10.99	37.09	39.56	11.54
8-3	0.37	7.33	32.97	43.96	15.38

hold the three small cards without the queen, and 3 times out of 4 he will hold the queen and two small cards. Three-fourths of 24.87 percent is 18.65 percent, and so we could say that East will hold the queen three long 18.65 percent of the time. East will hold two cards 40.7 percent of the time. One-half of these times he will not hold the queen and one-half of the time he will. One half of 40.7 percent is 20.35 percent. Now we have hit those a priori figures which tell us why a priori we should play for the drop rather than for the finesse. Obviously, 20.35 percent is more than 18.65 percent, and, converting these two distributions, you should have your old figures of 52 to 48.

An arithmetical shortcut for comparing these figures would be to add 50 percent to East's chances of holding three cards. When this figure exceeds East's chances of holding two cards, the finesse becomes the mathematical favorite. When the two-card holding is more than 150 percent of the three-card holding, playing for the drop is the mathematical favorite. For instance, in the a priori problem, if you add 12.44 percent to 24.87 percent, you get 37.32 percent. That is not as large as 40.70 percent for a holding of two cards, and, therefore, the drop is the favorite.

Jump down to the 7–1 distribution where a three-card holding is 43.14 percent and you will see what an overwhelming favorite the finesse has become. One half of 43.14 percent is 21.57; add that to 43.14 percent, and you come up with 64.71 percent, which is almost exactly twice as large as the 32.35 percent of the time East will hold two cards. This means that the finesse is twice as good a chance as playing for the drop.

When you have to finesse through the hand long in the known suit or not at all, these chances become exactly reversed. Let's go back to the last hand where we decided East probably had seven hearts. There is only one way to finesse. The moment of decision comes after you have cashed the king of spades and led a small one and East has followed small. It must have been your lucky day. But let's see whether this is a "nine never" situation.

East held either two small cards or three to the queen. All other possibilities have been proved nonexistent. Look at Table 6 on the 7–3 line. The chances that West, who is short in hearts, started with one spade are 10.99 percent. Those are the chances that East started with three. Those three will include the queen three-fourths of the time. Three-fourths of 10.99 percent is 8.24 percent. East started with two spades 37.09 percent of the time. Half the time the queen will be one of those two. Half of 37.09 percent is 18.55 percent. So, the odds are 18.55 to 8.24 in favor of the drop as compared to the finesse. Run that up to a percentage basis, and you will get the 69 percent in favor of the drop. We finally found that "nine ever" situation.

Further examination of Table 6 will show you that, if West has just one more card in a suit than East has, it is a draw; you are on your own; it is 50–50.

Whenever one of your opponents holds two or more cards in a known distribution than his partner, the odds favor the finesse through the hand with a short holding to an increasing degree as the long suit gets longer and the short suit gets shorter.

Let me show you a hand which was played by Sam Stayman some years ago.

DUMMY
♠ A 7
♡ Q 8 4
◇ A Q 2
♣ A Q 10 9 3

DECLARER
♠ K Q 5
♡ A K 10 2
◇ K 10 4
♣ K 6 4

Sam got into a contract of seven no-trump with twelve tricks off the top and chances in both hearts and clubs for the thirteenth. In the course of the play, Sam discovered that East had started with four clubs to the jack and, by leading the ten of clubs from the north hand, was able to bring his thirteenth trick in.

I'm sure Sam did not stop along the way to calculate the odds as he discovered more about the hand as I am going to do, but that he took the direct route to getting the information that he wanted. History does not record the order in which he played his cards, but let's you and I play them in such a manner that the solution becomes visible to us in steps rather than all at once as it must have to Sam. For those of you who find the arithmetic fascinating, here we go.

The opening lead was the jack of spades. In trying to get a count on the hand, take the A K Q of spades in that order and discard a club on the third spade. East will show out on the third spade, and we will then know that West was dealt six of them and East two. This makes it more likely that East will have length in hearts or clubs or both than West, and so we become interested in the probabilities of the distribution in the east hand. Let's focus our attention on the club suit where the defenders between themselves have five cards.

In Table 7, below, I show in the first column the a priori probabilities that East will hold from zero to five clubs. In the second column, I show

TABLE 7. Distributional Odds of Clubs Held by East (the Short Hand).

	A Priori Probability (percent)	Probability With 6–2 Distribution Discovered (percent)	Probability With 10–4 Distribution Discovered (percent)
5	1.96	5.39	15.91
4	14.13	26.96	47.73
3	33.91	40.44	31.82
2	33.91	22.47	4.55
1	14.13	4.49	impossible
0	1.96	0.25	impossible

these probabilities after we have discovered that the spade suit is divided 6–2. Some changes have occurred. The chances that East has four clubs have almost doubled.

Reserving the club suit, let's sample hearts. First take the ace and then go to the dummy with the queen so, if by any chance West has the singleton heart, we will know about it after we win with dummy's queen and will be able to take a finesse against the jack in the east hand for our thirteenth trick. Surprise! Both follow to the ace and queen, but when we lead a third heart back, East shows out. We had thought it likely that East held more hearts than West, but we now discover that West was dealt four and East only two.

Now we know the exact distribution of both major suits. In these two suits, West was dealt ten cards and East only four. Take another look at our revised estimate of the probabilities shown in column 3 in our table. Now the most likely distribution is for East to hold four clubs. Actually, the chance that he holds all five of them has jumped from less than 2 percent to almost 16 percent.

At this point, someone may ask, "Should we go to the dummy with a diamond and take a first-round finesse against the jack?" The answer is no. There is still a 25-percent chance that West holds the jack of clubs.

Now how do we know this? Well, there is a hard way and an easy way to calculate it. Let's do both. If the clubs are 4–1 there is a 20-percent chance that the one he holds is the jack. If he has only two, there is a 40-percent chance that one of them is the jack. So, we can add 20 percent of 47.73 percent plus 40 percent of 31.82 percent plus 60 percent of 4.55 percent and—presto—we have 25 percent. We really went around the barn to get that one. Here is the easy way. Knowing that West was dealt six spades and four hearts, we know that in the major suits which we have counted exactly there are fourteen cards in the two hands divided ten in west and four in east. That leaves twelve cards in the two minor suits where we do not know the distribution. Of those twelve cards, three are in West and nine are in East. This makes it three divided by twelve or exactly 25 percent that West will have any one of these nine cards you name.

But, it is now a simple matter to learn exactly how many clubs West has. First, let's lead a small diamond to dummy's ace and notice that West follows suit. Then let's lead a small diamond back to our king, preserving our queen in the dummy. Notice that West again follows suit. Now we are about to catch up with Sam Stayman. With ten major suit cards, and as many as two diamonds, we know that West started at the most with one club. So let's lead a small club toward dummy's ace. When West follows to that, we know all thirteen of the cards he started with. As West started with exactly one club, East started with four to the jack, and we have found our thirteenth trick. We just lead the ten of clubs, and, if East doesn't cover, we let it ride; if he does cover, then our king and nine will both take tricks.

Of course, no one can remember all of the figures in these various tables, but a study of them can give you, in a few weeks' time, knowledge of distribution which it would take years to acquire by experience. It should be some useful knowledge. It has been the style in American bridge for some years now to advertise to all of those interested the holding of long suits with weak hands. This has been especially true with a weak jump overcall and, to a lesser degree, of the so-called weak opening two-bid. The weaker your opponents are in high cards when they make these revealing bids, the more likely it is that you are going to wind up playing the hand. The information they have given you about both their weakness and their distribution can sometimes be the equivalent of a good road map in guiding your play.

This does raise some serious questions about the preemptive attitude itself. Preemptive jump overcalls and opening weak two-bids will show some sensational results when they hustle the opposition into the wrong contract or when they lay the groundwork for a beautiful sacrifice bid. I wonder how many times they lose hands in a way less easily discernible. I am talking about those times when the opposing declarer plays the hand like a magician because of the information concerning weakness and distribution which was given to him. A look at the record for the last several years will show that these preemptive tactics have not been paying off as well as they used to. As a matter of fact, a great many of our players are dropping them. They are using two diamonds and two hearts to show two-suited and three-suited hands, and about the only weak two bid left to some players is an opening bid of two spades.

Has the time come to use jump overcalls and opening two bids to show certain types of distribution in hands which are strong where you hope your side will be playing the hand, rather than using them trying to disrupt the opponents? There are a lot of interesting ideas in this area. The old Marmic system used jump overcalls to show strong, two-suited hands in the unbid suits. If the opening bid were one heart, a jump overcall of three diamonds would show a hand strong in spades and clubs, etc. The Roman system jump overcalls showed strong two-suited hands in the suit bid and the next higher ranking suit, excluding the openers' suit. I think it is time for our younger players to get busy experimenting and trying to come up with something more useful than the apparently faltering preemptive bids which were promoted by the older generation.

WHEN you make a Type C safety play, you deliberately give up an overtrick you might otherwise make to guarantee or to improve your chances for making your contract. It would seem that simple arithmetic ought to be able to tell you when you should or should not make this sort of safety play. Unfortunately, it does not. Nonetheless, imprecise as it is, we should have some knowledge of whatever information is available about the arithmetic so that when we ignore it, we will at least know what we are doing.

There are imponderables other than those of simple arithmetic. How important is it to us to make the contract we have bid for? Are we in a rubber bridge game where we will change partners once this rubber is completed, and, if so, are we anxious to get rid of the partner we have at the moment or are we anxious to hold onto him. Or, could it be that it is time to go home and we are anxious to get the rubber over with?

Some of these holdings which call for safety plays are so infrequent that, should we wait for the law of averages to take care of us, we might have to wait a long time.

We know that when we give up an extra trick we might have made, we are giving up 30 points if it is in no-trump or a major suit and 20 points if it is a minor suit. The laws of probabilities will tell us how often giving up a chance for the extra trick will assure our contract, and, if only we knew exactly what that contract is worth, we could easily arrive at the mathematics of the situation. The trouble here is that no one knows how much a game is worth, let alone how much a part score is worth. Imponderables enter the picture here as well. A precise mathematical answer is unavailable, and, even if there were one, we would still have to weigh the consequences of making a fine safety play as a result of which we scored our contract against failing to make the safety play and going set. Is the fact that we went set on a hand we could have made going to affect our partner? How about ourselves? Not to forget the opponents.

Let's make the not unreasonable assumption that the first game is worth 300 points plus the trick score; the second game is worth 400 points plus the trick score; and the third game is worth 500 points plus the trick score. When we go set on a hand we could have made, we lose the hidden value of game, the trick score, and the penalty paid for going set. As we never overbid all that much, let's say that we only go set one trick, so the penalty is 50 points when we are not vulnerable and 100 points when we are. To further simplify matters, let's say that our game contract is always four hearts or four spades. Then our loss, when we fail to make a contract we could have made, would look like the following:

1. 470 points when neither side is vulnerable
2. 570 points when we are not vulnerable and the opponents are
3. 620 points when we are vulnerable and they are not
4. 720 points when both sides are vulnerable.

The situation with part scores is even more difficult—different people react differently to part scores, both when they have them themselves and when the opponents have them. In some games, they have a value considerably beyond their mathematical value, whatever that might happen to be. Another imponderable is the fact that nonvulnerable opponents can compete against part scores more easily than can vulnerable opponents. Jean Besse of Switzerland took the only sensible approach to this problem—he took the statistical approach. Having kept a record of over a thousand part-score situations, he arrived at the following value of part scores:

1. The value over and above the trick score of a nonvulnerable partial of 40 or more is 90 points.

2. The value of a vulnerable part score of 40 or more when the opponents are not vulnerable is 110 points.

3. The value of a part score of 40 or more when both sides are vulnerable is 220 points.

If you happen to play in the same game in which Jean Besse played, this will be what those part scores are worth, provided the players in that game have not changed their style since Besse kept his statistics. In any event, the statistical approach taken by Besse is by far the most sensible approach available, so let us accept it. So that we can come up with some sort of a figure, let's see how much we lose when we go set in a part score we could have made when we are in a contract of two in a major suit. Failure to make a possible part score results in the loss of the trick value of 60, plus the hidden value of the part score, plus the penalty paid for undertricks. Let us again assume that when we go set, we go set only one trick.

1. 200 points when we are not vulnerable.
2. 270 points when we are vulnerable and the opponents are not.
3. 380 points when both sides are vulnerable.

So far as I know, no one has bothered to keep statistics on the value of part scores at the Chicago version of the game. Of course, on the fourth deal, a bonus of 100 points is given for a part score, and, as everyone is vulnerable, you would lose 200 points plus the trick score of 60 points if you failed to make a major-suit part-score contract of two-odd which you could have made. The situation must change on each deal prior to that last one, and part scores must be worth more to players who are going to be vulnerable on the succeeding deal than otherwise. In the absence of any statistics on the subject, let us go along with the figure of about 260 points for all hands, with the possible exception of the third deal, where a part score would seem to be worth about 100 extra points, or a total of 360.

Now let's take a couple of examples: First, let's give you and your dummy the following holding:

1. DUMMY
54

DECLARER
A K Q J 3 2

You have no side entries at all into your hand, and, to fulfill your contract, you must take five tricks in this suit. By simply leading out the top ones, you will take six tricks unless all five are in one hand. The way to be sure of taking five tricks is to lead a small one at trick one. Because dummy has only two cards, you can't afford to lay down the ace to test.

Now the book on statistics tells us that all five of the cards will be in one hand 3.9 percent of the time, while you will not meet such disasters 96.1 percent of the time. So in 100 tries, you would give up 30 points 96 times by conceding a trick. That comes to 2,883 points. However, you could gain nearly 4 times—3.9, to be more precise—by giving up this trick. To determine just how much you would have to gain each time to come out even, just divide the 3.9 into 2,883, and you come up with the answer to 739. Unless each time you take the safety play you are going to save a possible 739 points, you had better not take it, if you are measuring the thing mathematically. This means you should only take the safety play when the loss by not doing so exceeds 739 points. If you will look back at our calculations on this, you will see that at rubber bridge, the safety play is a losing proposition unless you are in a slam contract.

However, you are not going to find too often that you have this exact holding with no entries into your hand and with these precise requirements. If you find making the particular game which you have bid extremely important, you might go ahead and take the safety play, figuring that during the balance of your life you are not going to get that holding enough to even out the averages, you should run into that 5-0 split this one time. Whether you do or not, I leave it up to you and your conscience.

Now let's look at one you should take:

2. DUMMY
65

DECLARER
A K Q 4 3 2

Again you have no entries into your own hand and must take five tricks in this suit to fulfill your contract. If one of your opponents has all five of the outstanding cards, you can't do it. If they split 4–1, you have to lead low from both hands so that you will have the entry into your hand to cash the tricks after the opponents have both followed suit. However, by laying down the A K Q, you would take six tricks whenever the suit broke 3–2. By taking the safety play, you are deliberately giving up the value of an over-trick to increase your chances of making your contract.

The textbooks all tell us that five outstanding cards will break 3–2 67.8 percent of the time. If you are in a major suit, you would give up 2,034 points in 100 deals as an insurance premium against that 4–1 break. That 4–1 break will occur 28.3 percent of the time. Dividing 28.3 into 2,034, we find that whenever the totaling loss for failing to make a contract that could otherwise have been made exceeds 72 points, you should make the safety play. So here is one you should make any time you are playing any form of bridge, with the exception of match-point duplicate.

Of course, when the contract is in a minor suit, the potential extra trick you are surrendering to try to improve the chances of your contract is worth only 20 points, and the price you pay for the safety play is only two-thirds as great.

Of course, all of the odds quoted on probable distribution are a priori probabilities, assuming you know nothing about the distribution of the opposing hands. These odds would be different if you knew something about the opposing hands. Let us say, for example, that before you decide whether to take a safety play, you have discovered in some suit that the cards in the opponents' hands are divided 7–2. Now, instead of the chance that you will get a 4–1 break of five outstanding cards being a little over 28 percent, it is almost 35 percent, making the safety play even more attractive than it otherwise would have been. Just for completeness, here is a little table showing the theoretical distribution when you know nothing about the opponents' hands, compared to when you do know that they have the 7–2 holding. For more details on this, I refer you to Appendix A.

Probable Distribution of Five Outstanding Cards

When nothing is known of outstanding distributions		When it is known that another suit is 7–2	
3–2	67.8%	3–2	57.8%
4–1	28.3%	4–1	34.7%
5–0	3.9%	5–0	7.6%

In spite of the fact that none of these figures can be too precise, a general knowledge of the basic principles should give you guidance in selecting the play of your choice when deciding whether or not to make a safety play.